ITALIAN
DAYS

ITALIAN DAYS

Barbara Grizzuti Harrison

TICKNOR & FIELDS

NEW YORK

For information about permission to reproduce selections
from this book, write to Permissions, Ticknor & Fields,
215 Park Avenue South, New York, New York 10003.

Reprinted by permission of Grove Weidenfeld.

Library of Congress Cataloging-in-Publication Data

Harrison, Barbara Grizzuti.
Italian days / Barbara Grizzuti Harrison.
p.   cm.
Includes bibliographical references.
ISBN 0-395-55131-5
1. Italy — Description and travel — 1975–   2. Harrison, Barbara
Grizzuti — Journeys — Italy.   3. Authors, American — 20th century —
Journeys — Italy.   I. Title.
DG430.2.H37   1990   90-4845
914.504 — dc20   CIP

Printed in the United States of America

VB 10 9 8 7 6 5 4 3 2 1

Portions of this book have appeared, in slightly different form,
in *Church, European Travel and Life, Harper's Magazine, Lear's,
Mademoiselle,* and the *New York Times,* and in *The Iowa Review*
and the 1989 edition of the *O. Henry Prize Stories Collection.*

Additional acknowledgments and permissions appear on page 479.

For my mother,
CARMELA DINARDO GRIZZUTI,
in memory and in expectation

ACKNOWLEDGMENTS

I owe a great debt of gratitude to writers who have loved Italy, and written about Italy, before me: to Stendhal, of course, and Goethe and Henry James and Dickens and Montaigne and Hawthorne, and to Italo Calvino, but especially to the indefatigable travelers and scholars H. V. Morton and Georgina Masson. I owe at least as much to Georges Duby, and to Gaston Bachelard, traveler to the interior of the human heart and mind.

My friends—among whom I count my son, Joshua Harrison, and my daughter and frequent traveling companion, Anna Harrison—have been good to me during the long period of gestation a book requires; I especially wish to thank, for their several and varied and invaluable contributions, Bethany and Giancarlo Alhadeff, Joseph Caldwell, Ewart Cousins, Mimi and Nello D'Aponte, Mary DiNardo and Pasquale DiNardo, Franca Gavinelli, Alice Hagan, Richard Heitzman, Amerigo Iannacone, Armando Iannotti, Philip Murnion, Judita Natalucci, Nura Osman, Susan Pierres, and Mary Margaret Schroeder.

Ente Turismo, the Italian government tourist board, extended every courtesy to me, as did Angelo Manzi of the Cicerone Hotel in Rome and Benito Menucci of the Hotel Atlante in Rome. I thank them very much, and I thank Mario Claudio DiMaio of the Hotel President in Sorrento; Pino Caprio; and Dottore Nino Del Papa of the wonderful Grand Hotel Cocumella in Sant'Agnello, Sorrento. Mary Ann and Amedeo Pinto, who make the Hotel Pitti Palace in Florence such a delight, have all my gratitude.

John Herman has given me what every writer needs—a fair measure of love and keen intelligence; I am immensely grateful to him.

Laura Polla Scanlon and Elizabeth Scanlon were all one could wish for as traveling companions; I thank them both.

Once again, I acknowledge my indebtedness to the MacDowell Colony and the Corporation of Yaddo for long and happy weeks of silence and beauty in which to write.

CONTENTS

Chapter I
MILAN:
"THE ASTONISHED AND DISTURBED CITY"
BERGAMO: COMMEDIA DELL'ARTE
STRESA: HÔTEL DU LAC

3

Chapter II
VENICE:
"MIRROR OF WATER"

89

Chapter III
"LOVELY FLORENCE"
SAN GIMIGNANO:
"CITY OF FINE TOWERS"

119

Chapter IV
ROME:
THE ART OF LIVING

191

Contents

Chapter V

TO THE MEZZOGIORNO:

NAPLES, THE SORRENTINE
PENINSULA, THE AMALFI COAST . . .
"BRIGHTNESS FALLS FROM THE AIR"

343

Chapter VI

MOLISE AND ABRUZZO:

THE MOTHER COUNTRY . . . BLESSING AND BONDAGE

387

Chapter VII

PUGLIA:

FAIRYLAND

435

Chapter VIII

CALABRIA:

BETWEEN TWO SEAS

451

Selected Bibliography

475

I did not know, when I went to Italy, the nature of my undertaking, nor did I anticipate the meaning of my journey. I lived every day as I found it. I know now—writing this book has taught me this—that it was a journey of reconciliation. I understood this more more clearly as I traveled south, to the sun . . . and to my family. I discovered everything I feared and everything I loved. There was more to love than to fear; it was a lovely journey.

ITALIAN DAYS

Chapter I

MILAN:
"THE ASTONISHED
AND DISTURBED CITY"

BERGAMO: COMMEDIA DELL'ARTE
STRESA: HÔTEL DU LAC

1985. The Alps make you feel all starched and clean as you fly into Milan—they punctuate the long transatlantic sleep of a nighttime flight; groaning bodies stir and strengthen and come to morning life as the mountains exert a rosy magnetic pull that won't allow you not to pay them the compliment of being crisply awake.

But we don't land in Milan; we land in Genoa. Milan is smoky with fog. The pilot announces that those whose final destiny is Genoa may disembark, and several Americans do so—never minding that they will in any case have to return to Milan (ninety minutes by plane) to retrieve their luggage. It is a futile disembarkation—what can have prepared them to believe that they and their luggage will ever be reunited? They have allowed the urge to touch land to overwhelm them. Everything about flying is absurd, anyway; all rules of logic are suspended; to make a decision affecting one's own welfare seems like an act of temerity; passengers who file out seem as much the playthings of inertia as those, grumbling, who remain inside.

The pilot announces that we may, depending on weather conditions, all have to disembark, in which case those of us bound for Milan will be bused into that city.

I like the idea of being bused to my destination; can anyone like airports? There ought to be some way of being gracefully eased into a foreign city; this business of gray ramp connecting to gray tube connecting to gray ramp, the knots and snarls of modern airports at either end, destroys the sense of travel (one doesn't travel, one is dumped), and travel—the means of getting to a place—used to figure just as pleasantly, certainly just as largely, in a traveler's plan as did his final destination. Travel used to be a matter of the means not only justifying the end but being indistinguishable from it; the slow and grand progression that took you places knit those places into the fabric of your being. Places weren't isolated spots on a map, they were part of an unfolding continuum. All travelers were pilgrims, once; jet planes changed that.

To traverse vast distances by ship and train permitted one to see the world as the Psalmist did and to put aside the notion of the world as global village—which notion, on the high seas, appears, paradoxically, to stem from a parochial urban sensibility. To change one's space or place is to change one's nature—"Space, vast space," Bachelard wrote, "is the friend of being"—and air travel, the friend of time, is the enemy of being. When you've been obliged to sail through the Suez Canal you certainly know you've been somewhere; I'm glad I'm old enough to have enjoyed sea travel and train travel in the days when sea and train travel were both affordable and plausible. (I am the only person I know who has taken a train from New York City to Quezaltenango, Guatemala.) Now no place that any but the most intrepid explorer is likely to find his way to is more than a phone call away or a twenty-four-hour flight away from home, as a result of which all of literature and all of human relations have changed, all of life has changed . . . and I don't like it. To say that a sea lay between you and your beloved used to mean something, everything; now it means you are a beverage, a snack, a bad movie (and a travel agent) away from him, and absence has lost its poetry. When absence loses its poetry, presence—being there—does, too.

The captain is exercising his prerogative to change his mind. First-class passengers are given a second breakfast while the captain and the weather determine our fate. Flight attendants—stewards—fuss. Americans on board

4

deal with this uncertainty querulously or with quiet resignation, according to their natures. Italians use it as an occasion for an impromptu town hall meeting (grouped, gesticulating, at exit doors) or to demonstrate rugged disdain (eloquent shrugs: *Que será, será*).

At last the weather clears—in fact we have been on the ground for only a little over an hour, but even caviar doesn't quite make up for a gratuitous landing and takeoff; the plane having been refueled, we take off for Milan, the luggage of the Genoa-bound Americans with us.

I am irritably southern in my affections, but even a lover of northern Italy would not have been cheered by what greeted us as we taxied into Milan: fog; the dirty March remains of three feet of late-winter snow (Milanese officials had to go back into the archives 387 years to find an equivalent snowfall); an impression of ashes.

Except for a flight that landed at the airport that serves Venice—and to arrive in a city by water taxi is, while ever so improbably, to arrive indeed and in state—all my previous trips to Italy have taken me through Rome's Fiumicino Airport. Fiumicino is at best and even in sunny times a disorderly place. I have never but once had occasion to threaten to knock someone's pearls down her throat. That once was in Fiumicino, and the person I threatened was a duchess with whom I was engaged in hand-to-hand combat for a luggage cart; when I asked her whatever happened to noblesse oblige she told me where I could accommodate the concept of noblesse oblige; and while luggage went unweighed and computers blinked unwatched (spectacle takes precedence over order in Rome), the duchess's pearls became everybody's business. The only time I have ever seen Fiumicino's overworked ground attendants positively happy was when they were obliged to tell check-in passengers that England's air-traffic controllers were on strike: While southern Italians themselves take what might be called an inordinate or perverse pleasure in their own unruliness, viewing it as a vital sign of life, they are bound to notice that not all visitors to their shores are charmed by chaos. So for them to be able to say that the English—the English!—were causing chaos in the skies was bliss.

I'd been warned that Milan's newly renovated airport, Malpensa, was often "quite up to Fiumicino's standards"—that is, demonically chaotic. I was also told to be on the lookout for a certain countess who keeps peacocks (except, poor thing, she got confused, and they're drab pea*hens*) in her conservatory. The peacocks were to have been her answer to a neighboring contessa who keeps flamingos in her garden, which is next to a butcher shop that sells cockscombs, snipes, bullfinches, larks, figpeckers, and doves. As part of her endless and apparently doomed search for color, the peahen countess once arrived at Malpensa dressed as a miniskirted maid (her elderly thighs looking, as someone remarked, very well scrubbed but not beautifully ironed), driving a golf cart equipped with all the makings for tea, which the countess wished to serve to a young man of her acquaintance whom the rigors of travel evidently reduced to a vapor. The young man called himself Hyacinth. The carabinieri arrested the contessa. The flamingo countess gave a party to celebrate her neighbor's arrest.

In the event, perhaps because our flight was an early-morning one, all went unremarkably, except, alas!, for one poor young man whom the German shepherds had sniffed and the customs officials had chosen as a target. Customs officials, up to their wrists in pink and white goo as a result, felt their way through the acned young man's many skin creams and remedies for all the world to see. His acne married itself to a dull red painful blush that looked as if it, too, would leave a permanent mark. His companion, a pretty young woman (skin of peaches and cream), stared off stolidly in the direction of Switzerland. He cast pleading looks in her direction while she occasionally wriggled a shoulder in mute acknowledgment of the flashing appreciation she was receiving from the customs officials. Their first night in Milan would not be a happy one.

The road signs are Italian. Otherwise, no clues, no idiosyncrasy of landscape, to tell you where you are. I have never experienced this phenomenon before. Two minutes out of Heathrow and you know that you are approaching London (although the attached houses are ugly, they are ugly in a singularly English way). And one could never mistake England for (say) India or India for New York. . . . But if one were dropped from another planet, one might, on the *superstrada* to Milan, be anywhere—Austria, for example. The approach to Milan has a Teutonic feel, as does Milan itself, which was in fact occupied not once but twice by Austria. Montaigne thought Milan looked like a French city and found little more to say about it than that in size "it beats them"—Naples, Genoa, and Florence—"all."

A half hour from the center of Milan I see two joggers. They are the last joggers I will see in all of Italy.

From the air, I am told, Milan looks green—though you couldn't prove it in this fog. Built on a lost imperial Roman city, Milan was greatly expanded in the late nineteenth and early twentieth centuries; blocks of flats were built around courtyards. Whatever wealth of green there is in Milan is said to be in those courtyards, which are, however, not inviting. Unlike the courtyards of Florence or Rome, which practically suck you into them, so declamatory is their invitation (which is sometimes embodied in the form of a building caretaker), the courtyards of Milan, gated against view, repel entrance. The doorways of Milan look most inviting when they are draped with the purple that signifies that someone has died. The great snows of 1985 killed off much that was green in Milan, and diesel fumes have blighted much else, so one must take the green of oaks and horse-chestnut trees, cedars of Lebanon and flowering magnolias largely on faith.

Milan is not a sunny city, nor is it a city that declares itself brazenly. It is withdrawn, though—it is, after all, an industrial city—it is also aggressive. All cities have a gender as well as a personality. London is a male city; Hyderabad, my favorite city in India, is a city of slender minarets in which water can almost always be heard lapping, slipping, and sliding over boulders; it is a quintessentially feminine city. Venice is disturbing, after three days of magic, precisely because its "sexuality" is ambivalent. Male? Female? It is a city of masks, and one doesn't know. This uncertainty leads to uneasiness, which translates into claustrophobia. To overstay a visit to Venice is like staying too long at the ball in the company of someone of whose sexual identity you are not sure. Milan, aggressive and withdrawn, is male.

I was in Milan for one month. For four of those days it did not rain. It did not rain so much as it misted—making an umbrella both too much and too little protection.

One feels a quickening of the pulse when one crosses a border. It is strange: What difference is there (for example) between the landscape of Canada and that of the northern United States; or, in North Africa, what difference exists between the stretch of land on the coastal road of Tunisia and that of Libya? None, one would say; and yet one knows—I have always known—when one crosses these or any other borders. Are the trees different? the sky? It is mysterious; but one senses subliminally on these long and lonely stretches of road that one is in another country, and it is only after the subliminal awareness reaches one's consciousness that one looks for tangible proofs (in Canada, a maple leaf on a mailbox; in Tunisia, a road sign in French). This phenomenon stems from a change in character so subtle it is indescribable. Milan's physical character lies, at first acquaintance, in its not having a character.

Though its partisans, envious, perhaps, of the ocher and sienna of Tuscany and Rome, claim there is a Milan *giallo,* to an unprejudiced eye the pervasive color of Milan is not yellow, but gray.

From the terrace of my apartment hotel, its marble greasy from diesel fumes and dirty March rain, I am able to see the Duomo—Milan's great cathedral—or so I am told. I never go out on the terrace. No one uses his terrace, it seems architecturally to serve the function of a moat; and even if I did use my terrace, I couldn't see the Duomo because it is always raining.

I chose to live in a "residence" rather than a *pensione* or a hotel because, I told myself, I wanted to "plunge into" Italian life—though what exactly I meant by that I don't think I knew, and why I thought this ill-defined urge could be satisfied among people who were for the most part transients I cannot now remember.

The residence—Residenza Missori—was a ten-minute walk from the Duomo and the Galleria (Milan's conservatorylike arcade that encloses shops and cafés), on a broad street lined with airline offices guarded by bored-looking carabinieri, a bar, a stationery shop, a restaurant, a scrap of Roman wall. I never felt precisely "placed." Unlike Rome or London, each of which is a collection of distinct villages, Milan has neither the sense of a hub or heart from which spokes or arteries extend nor that of a patchwork quilt. This is so in spite of the fact that Milan consists of a series of concentric circles, which may conform to the lost imperial city. Concentric circles, like whirling rose windows of cathedrals, reflect the idea that the universe moves and is moved by God, and that the movement is circular and cyclical: "Day turns into night and season into season," Georges Duby writes, "and all types of biological growth followed cyclical patterns, and their periodic repetitions had to be taken as signs of eternity." For the walker in Milan, however, it seems merely perversity that one may get to one's destination by walking either to one's left or to one's right. No set of directions is ever issued the same way twice. No one, except for those who live in a vaguely bohemian quarter, the Brera, which looks quite French, ever says I live in such and such a neighborhood. People live in the vicinity of museums or in the vicinity of publishing houses or near the fashionable shopping streets, but one hears little of neighborhoods. . . . What happens to the concept of neighborliness when the concept of neighborhoods is eroded is an interesting question.

The upholstered furniture in my two-room apartment is unyieldingly square, hard, and complacent, the kind of furniture that comes in "suites," made not for comfort but for show. It is "company" or Sunday furniture; only here there is no inner sanctum—that is, no proper kitchen to retreat to. It reminds me of the ugly furniture I saw in the houses of Libya's Italian colonists, furniture that looked always "on parade." (Where are those colonists now? I wonder; in what part of Italy do they live? And do they now dream of Libya; of oases and of the Mediterranean, which, once a year, tasted of the tomatoes dumped into its coastal waters when the lovely supply exceeded the demand? First the Libyans evict the Italians and then Fiat makes brothers of old enemies and Libyans come to live in Italy, and then Italy, because of Qaddafi's terrorism, evicts Libyans; and Libya, making a vast profit, sells its stake in Fiat for three billion dollars—one turn of the wheel and we are all nomads or millionaires.) In my residence only the honey-brown wood of doors and closets and the beautiful streamlined hardware, a pleasure to touch, remind me that I am living in what many consider the style as well as the fashion capital of the world—a reminder that is reinforced when I make a purchase at the office supply shop next door to the Missori. Nothing in it—not a staple machine or a pencil sharpener or a notebook—doesn't please the eye and the hand; everything is inexpensive, though nothing is cheap.

My efficient pullman kitchen, tucked neatly behind doors of honey-brown wood, is minimally equipped; but there are colanders of two sizes, there is a spare bottle opener, there is a cruet for olive oil, and there is a cheese grater. This is proof to me that Milan is part of Italy, and that Italians have a sure instinct for life's necessities.

In Milan the Sunday-morning equivalent of "Agronsky and Company" is a learned oenophile lecturing on what wines to drink with truffles.

Italy's legislature has today—my first full day in Milan—outlawed artificial insemination by an unknown donor. Why it has chosen to cleave to tradition in this regard when it permits abortion and divorce is a mystery. Italian law is mystical, severely poetical.

I am dining with Bethany and Giancarlo, friends of an American friend, at a Tuscan trattoria; Giancarlo is beaming with gastronomic pride. The simplicity and the obscure location of the trattoria do not prepare me for what is to come. It is: crostini, thin slices of bread brushed with olive oil and toasted over charcoal, one slice covered with fresh tomato pulp and basil, one with milled chicken liver (mixed here—every restaurant has its own recipe—with sage and a bit of anchovy, enough to make it piquant); this chicken liver makes New York chopped liver seem gross. Then a pasta with a peppery tomato sauce (puttanesca; *puttana* = "whore"); this does not call for a cheese, nor in fact do many pasta dishes, though most Americans, determined to gild the lily, insist otherwise. Bethany is meanwhile happily eating slices of Parmesan and raw artichoke dressed in olive oil; the leaves of the artichoke are so thin and entirely digestible one needn't scrape them with one's teeth, an unlovely and unrewarding exercise (artichokes—*carciofi*—are one of the joys of Italy in the spring). Then we each have a simple veal cutlet Milanese (breaded; lemon slices); purists insist that a tiny bit of the bone, like a button-sized handle, be left on the flattened cut of meat, and it is. And finally a sweet in which a fantastic amount is going on, taste yielding to new taste and texture, all harmoniously: a heart of cream; a shell of chocolate gelato dusted with dark chocolate and ground hazelnuts. Giancarlo has knowledgeably ordered two bottles of wine; and this repast has cost us fifty-four dollars. Our plates go back to the kitchen clean, and a good thing, too, because one doesn't take food home from Italian restaurants; there is always a happy culinary tomorrow (and besides, one's stomach should have been smart enough to know what it could accommodate; in Italy it is common and pragmatic practice to order one course, not a whole meal, at a time). To the rule that you don't take uneaten food home there is an exception—radish stems, which you may want to fry with garlic for your breakfast tomorrow morning.

Eggs are invisible in Milan. They hide at the fruiterer's behind pyramid-shaped bunches of grapes or apples or they are taken from a dark recess by the proprietor; they must always be asked for. This minor inconvenience (combined with problems arising from the use of the metric system) may not seem too much to ask a grown woman with all her faculties intact to suffer; but it is compounded by other problems—and I am overwhelmed.

Milan is the most polluted city in Europe. "You will love living in Italy," a representative of the Italian government tourist board said to me in New York; "the air is different there." Milan made her point, but not in the way she'd intended: You can't breathe in Milan. There are throat lozenges at the cashier's stand of every café and bar; the characteristic Milanese voice is gritty and gravelly. A journalist from the *Corriere della Sera* says that for children Milan is like living in a gas chamber: If you are under twelve, you are just tall enough to get the worst of the fumes. And one is always aware of the danger of slipping and sliding on greasy marble and winding up in the Fracture Hospital.

There are no liquor stores. One buys one's liquor at a coffee bar or at a *drogheria* (which is different from a *farmacia*) or from a supermarket, of which there are few, and those few not in the center; one buys one's wine at a wine merchant's. One buys salt at a *tabacchi* (a tobacco store), salt being a government monopoly.

None of these minor difficulties would amount to difficulties if one were in a city one loved—or if one were in a city that didn't pretend to be the most efficient in Italy. "Abroad is closed all the time," moaned Nancy Mitford's insular Englishwoman; and the poor thing had a point: How can a city that closes from 12:30 to 3:00 or 4:00 in the afternoon vie with Tokyo or New York? Of course, not all business establishments close down. Milanesi, perhaps recognizing the silliness of having a siesta in a city where mink is worn through March, are engaged in an ongoing debate about business hours, a political issue. Milan is a city of banners, so the dialogue is a public one. Gay banners strung across streets demand shorter working hours, longer working hours, different working hours (8:00 A.M. to 2:00 P.M.). Meanwhile, shops are closed from 12:00 to 4:00, as are *tabacchi* (where one also buys bus and tram tickets), and in the city where St. Augustine was converted and the Arian heresy was defeated, mink-clad matrons jostle and shove in shops, their manners worse than I have seen exhibited by barefooted South American campesinos standing in mud and haggling over three pathetic eggplants, though the whole point of their dress is to appear well bred. Milanesi do not saunter; they are always purposeful, though to what purpose it is not always clear. Their voices are staccato, like their heels clicking on the slick marble floors.

Nothing to get petulant about, you may say. But I had set, as my first order of business, becoming self-sufficient in Milan . . . and that meant not being defeated by ordinary shopping, an activity every Milanese housewife engages in at least three times a week—it's enough to justify a life. (From a taxi I see a banner that proclaims HOUSEWIFE—THE HONORABLE PROFESSION.) Feminism is not exactly in the air here. . . . In other Italian cities, certainly in Rome and south of Rome, shopping is a garrulous, convivial, and happy activity. Here it appears to be simply a duty.

Custom and delicacy require that you point to certain items, rather than name them; if you don't, you may wind up with baby diapers instead of sanitary napkins, both of which are named Lines. Double D batteries are to be found where cameras are sold and apparently nowhere else. I discovered this by accident after I'd had a forty-minute-long conversation with workers for the Italian government tourist board, one of whom involved four of her colleagues in a discussion of my typewriter and its innards; at first I thought the apparent content of the conversation—my batteries—was the real content of the conversation; it was not. Even in so small a matter as batteries, form (the opportunity to exercise operatic differences) is likely to take precedence over substance (the actual purchase of batteries).

It is impossible for anyone to be as fastidiously dressed as a Milanese matron with the means to regard convention (shoving toward the *prosciutto crudo,* never a hair out of place). It is possible to tell how old the average Milanese woman is from her back: By the time she is of a certain age, she is doomed to silk foulard and pearls forever; you cannot have your hair dyed aubergine unless you are under thirty—no respectable hairdresser would abet you in this folly. When you shop, the impeccability of Milanese ladies makes you feel—until you've learned the lessons, the measurements, the anomalies, the protocol—like a gawky American behemoth steering through an unmarked obstacle course. You can also—and sometimes simultaneously—feel invisible, as failure to observe protocol leads to your being completely disregarded. You learn that there is a gratuitous step in the purchase of almost anything. For example, if, in an *alimentari,* you wish to buy two *etti* of *provolone dolce,* you tell the man behind the cheese counter, who gives you not the provolone but a slip of paper on which hieroglyphics are scrawled. You present this to the cashier, along with your payment. You then take the cashier's receipt to the cheese counter, where you recover your cheese. This is true except when it is not true, and nothing seems to govern the exceptions but caprice.

A similar system prevails at coffee bars, where you first tell the cashier what you are going to have and pay for it before you are given it. This is true except when it is not true. It costs more to have coffee sitting down than it does to have coffee standing up . . . in some coffee bars, some of the time.

In order to send a money order to Rome, it is necessary to go first to a bank, then to the Ufficio di Vaglia, then to a post office, where, in order to send mail registered, one must stand on two different lines. The bank, the Ufficio di Vaglia, and the registry post office are in different parts of the city. Henry James said that Europe was "the American sedative." Milan has no soporific qualities.

Women learn to cope by the exercise of charm. It is very hard to be charming in a foreign language. If I were much younger or much older, my lack of competence would work for me. I am both too old and too young to use helplessness as a crutch.

Historically, Milan was a stopover, a way place to and from the Alps. Now people come for the fashion and design shows. Nobody ever claimed to love Milan for itself alone—except for Stendhal, who was viewed with suspicion and finally cast out of Milan by the Austrian police. Stendhal said he adored post-Napoleonic Milan; but Stendhal was, as even his editor admits, not only guilty of "larcenies" or plagiarism (as are all travel writers) but a gorgeous liar. Stendhal, who groused about Milan, also said he wished to be buried as a citizen of Milan; he was suicidal at the time.

It is the season for blood-red oranges.

Unlike Henry James, who was cosseted by a great hotel, where "servants, frescoes, tapestries, antiquities [offer] the thorough make-believe of a settlement," searching for eggs, batteries, language, and that which a woman, in particular, feels most deprived of without full command of language and customs—anonymity—I thought of Montaigne, cheerfully visiting the sights, the pain of his gallstones notwithstanding. Inspired by his happy example, I bought great bunches of yellow freesias (late, this year, because of the snows in Lombardy) in the sooty rain.

Disposable syringes litter the streets. They are bought over the counter. In full daylight a beautiful young woman with a face like that of a predatory cat (great green-yellow eyes) and a casually elegant young man inject each other with heroin.

I have been here eight days. I feel cranky and parochial. What's the point of traveling if one isn't changed—I don't say uplifted—by the experience? (I would be lying, and my response to Milan would not bode well for an extended stay in Italy, if I did not say that for me Italy begins with Rome; that which lies north of Rome is, no matter in what part magnificent and beautiful, incidental to the heart.) I long for Rome. In some ways it was easier to live in India than in Milan. In India I suffered no illusion that life would be easy; here I expected to be able to cope, and when I can't, I am embarrassed (though I am accountable to no one but myself). Of course in India I was young. . . . My parents were Italian immigrants, poor. At one point in my life I almost came to Italy—to dole out CARE parcels. Perhaps unconsciously I think of Italy as a Third World country still. Does this account for my confusion? . . . It occurs to me that the reason I was unselfconscious in India had nothing to do with my youth. Perhaps I was guilty of harboring a corrupting sense of racial superiority (how can one know for certain these things about oneself?); after all, when things went wrong in India, I seldom blamed or bludgeoned myself. I want to love Milan—or at least to like it—and I cannot; and sometimes I blame myself. At other times I remember Stendhal: "The important thing is to admire only what really gives pleasure, and always to believe that the man next to you who is admiring is being paid to deceive you."

What am I doing here?

Food, in my first days in Milan, seemed a sufficient and sufficiently serious answer to that question:

Turkey, not the whole boring bird but the upper part of the drumstick, cooked as osso buco is cooked—in a sauce of white wine, tomatoes, carrots, parsley, garlic, lemon peel.

Slivers of *gianchetti,* a delicate white fish, served with silken skeins of golden olive oil and lemon juice.

Osso buco (veal shanks) and saffron risotto (rice cooked in butter and chicken broth), served with six lemon halves and a silver implement for extracting the marrow from the bone; a salad with as many shades of green as a Persian garden.

Lunch with Bethany at a discreetly elegant popular restaurant: butterfly macaroni in a light cream sauce with a hint of smoked salmon; grilled lettuce. Bethany has a Gorgonzola pizza; this, with a bottle of wine, costs us thirteen dollars.

(Elegant ladies press their napkins to their bosoms throughout a pasta course; talcum powder is provided in every ladies' room to remove whatever spots get past their guard.)

Antipasti symphonic in color: *carciofi crudi* (raw artichoke) and slices of Parmesan cheese, squid, a cold zucchini frittata (squash omelet); yellow, red, green roast peppers, shrimp, clams, mussels, cut lemons in crystal or pottery bowls.

Spaghetti with a simple sauce of fresh tomatoes, fresh basil, olive oil, and garlic; succulent grilled chicken.

Green noodles light as air with a butter–cream–tomato–bacon sauce; giant crayfish; a salad of red and green leaves; profiteroles . . .

Home-cooked food is never wasted in Italy. Leftover saffron rice finds its way into minestrone; leftover spaghetti finds its way into frittate, making lovely whorls in the pancakelike omelet; a smidgen of ricotta cheese is saved to whip with fresh blueberries, a homely delight.

Milan's is a butter-based cuisine; but olive oil—smoky, lapidary, green, yellow—is honored all over Italy; it is not merely a cooking element but a food in and of itself. Thirteenth-century Florence produced a riddle about the olive ("*L'Oliva*"):

> I am the fair one of the palace field;
> I fall to earth, and yet I am not killed;
> For that High Lord I go to make a light,
> And I am served with love, both day and night.
>
> —*translated by Grace Warrack**

In the wonderful folktales collected by Italo Calvino, a man sees his beloved in a splash of blood on white ricotta; a queen is delivered not of a baby but of a rosemary bush, from which—years later and awakened by love—a comely maiden springs; a beautiful young girl hides herself in a rosy apple. Metamorphoses and transformations. Italians use food as metaphor (a slowpoke is called a polenta—cornmeal mush) and moral:

> What thinks the goose
> on the canal bank croaking with all her might?
> She . . . surely doesn't dream of Christmas night
> Or of the cook's bright weapons and their use.
>
> O gosling, my sister . . .
> Death does not exist, you teach us all:
> Only as he thought did man begin to die . . .
> . . . Since to be fried is not sad at all,
> What's sad is the thought that we must fry.
>
> —*Guido Gozzano,*
> *translated by Carlo L. Golino*

> Human beings in this world are the same
> As coffee-beans before the espresso machine:
> First one, and then another . . .
> All of 'em going alike to one sure fate . . .
> Down to the bottom through the throat of death.
>
> —*Giuseppe Giochino Belli,*
> *translated by Harold Norse*

*This and the Belli selection are from *Poems from Italy,* edited by William Jay Smith. The Gozzano is from *Contemporary Poetry: An Anthology,* edited by Carlo L. Golino.

(Through the throat of death . . . It is no wonder critics speak of the gloom underlying the exuberance of Italians. After eight days in Milan, though, I am not prepared to make grand judgments about the national character—especially as there is so little exuberance in Milan.)

There are miles of rice fields and lagoons around Milan. The Milanesi have a passion for rice, which was brought to Italy not, as is commonly supposed, by Marco Polo, but in all probability by the Arabs, by way of Sicily. Pasta, as that indefatigable traveler H. V. Morton points out, is a more ancient food than rice, which, in medieval Italy, was handled by the doctor and the chemist, not by the cook. In cosmopolitan Milan, pasta and gnocchi (the dumplings made of semolina or of potatoes that the Romans serve always on Thursdays) are held in almost as high esteem as rice. Milan is too much of a crossroads to have kept its regional cooking "pure"—a fact that only the most insular could bemoan. There is so much variety in Milanese cooking it is not possible to weary of it.

The story that pasta was brought to Italy by Marco Polo from China is so romantic and charming that it is almost churlish to refute it. Its charm derives partly from its being one of those Facts we learn in the nursery—proof that Daddy is full of delicious surprises—and so adhere to forever. But food historians tell us that fifty years before Marco Polo left Venice, Indians and Arabs were already eating noodles; they suggest that pasta reached the trading cities of Venice, Florence, and Genoa in the Middle Ages, by way of Arab lands. Food historian Reay Tannahill says that at a 1972 trade fair in Peking, the Italians tried—one hopes by way of a joke—to sell the Chinese a spaghetti-making machine in which "you put flour, water, and tomato sauce in at one end of the machine and five minutes later hot spaghetti, already prepared and with cheese sauce on top, comes out at the other end." There could not possibly have been a domestic market for this contraption. (If it wasn't a joke, it was proof of the cynicism we are also told—and I am not yet prepared to say—also underlies Italian exuberance.)

Tannahill says that the most common name for pasta in the Middle Ages appears to have been *maccheroni,* which ought to silence food snobs, and which is the generic name by which all forms of pasta, flat and tubular, were called by earlier generations of Italian immigrants. *Pasta* was not a word we ever heard in Italian Bensonhurst; my brother calls it a designer name for "macaronies," and he has a point.

Italians—unlike urban Americans we read about who have all the right kinds of mustard and then go out to eat in the trendiest new restaurant every night—do not, even in fashionable Milan, regard food as a status symbol.

This does not mean they will not go to any length to get exactly the taste sensation they crave. Giancarlo's Tuscan mother will drive into the country-side to buy ricotta directly from the shepherd only on the day it is made. Bethany says the difference between America and Italy is the difference between a "consumer culture" and a "food culture." Italians do not regard food merely as fuel. They regard it as medicine for the soul, one of life's abiding pleasures. "We have had forty-seven changes of government since the end of the war," a waiter said to me, "but pasta never changes."

One of the most enduring friendships I made in Italy began in the dining car of a train from Milan to Venice when two American tourists demanded rather wearily—they had apparently been disappointed in their hopes before—low-fat cottage cheese, absurd in a country where the variety and goodness of cheese could make you weep for joy. The very pretty young Italian woman seated across the table from me began to giggle uncontrolla-bly, and so did I, and so our friendship began.

Italians do diet—but not quite as we do. For almost any ailment, one is told to go on a "white diet"—veal, chicken, rice (and, depending on your physician, white wine)—a low-cholesterol diet; but just as Italians don't have the same relationship to food that we have, they appear not to have the same diseases. Just as gout is an English ailment—everything is in the terminol-ogy—Italians (like the French, I am told) are forever having *crisi di fegato* (crisis of the liver). We say we have stomachaches or stomach problems—and if TV commercials are any guide, American stomachs extend from their throats to their pelvic areas; Italians, for medical purposes, don't have stom-achs, they have *fegati*. (We say a brave man has guts; Italians say he has *fegato*.) Even before they achieve middle age, Italian men swaddle themselves around their middles in the privacy of their homes, after cheese and before coffee, to avoid something called kidney colitis. What Americans are apt to call anxiety attacks, Italians call gastritis. Gas is a frequent subject of conver-sation. As American sophisticates discuss sexual mores at a dinner party, Italians discuss gas. An irascible man is *fegatoso*. Giambattista Vico tells us that the Romans—"who regarded the blood as the juice of the fibers of which the flesh is composed"—located concupiscence in the liver, which they defined as "the blood factory."

If a German child in lederhosen gets wet in the park, he is rushed home by his Italian nanny so as not to get a draft on his *fegato*. The only children one sees in the park in March are the children of foreigners with their foreign mothers; cold winds are said to affect the liver adversely. Milan's dreary zoo is empty of children in March; its most famous animal, an elephant called

Bombay, performs for foreigners: With a snort Bombay's trunk inhales candied popcorn along with coins for his keeper; with an exhalation he empties the coins into his keeper's hand. This is as good as seeing a dog walk on two legs.

The tender livers of children must be protected at all cost: Shopkeepers will tell you what brand of *acqua minerale* to give your baby, depending on its symptoms. (And once, years ago in Genoa, when my own children were small and we all fell sick of what turned out to be German measles, the hotel physician seemed ready to hand me over to the authorities because it had "become known" to him that I had permitted them to sip my espresso. Toddlers may drink wine, but not coffee. . . . In fact, I had ordered three espressi because the children admired the pretty porcelain cups; I drank them all. When I managed to explain this to the glowering *medico,* he pronounced me a most un-American—which is to say admirable—mother.)

The sense of Milan as an old European city often gets misplaced as one suffers an indigestion of impressions. The medieval character of the city declared itself in the narrow winding streets between my residence and the great cathedral square, the Piazza del Duomo, in spite of the industrial overlay, the huge signs advertising the twin giants of industry, Fiat and Olivetti. On one of these streets—Via Spadari ("street of the swordmakers")—is a shop that has seen several waves of conquerors and more than one war: Pecks Casa di Formaggio (House of Cheese), founded by a Czech in 1892. Pecks is an establishment so wonderful that for days I forbade myself the pleasure of entering, content to peer into the plate-glass windows . . . cheeses heaped upon cheeses. I used to fancy I could see them ripen from one day to the next, hundreds and hundreds of cheeses, a world of cheese; it seemed impossible to go in and say, "This one," when so many tantalized, a confusion of delight.

From my residence on the Piazza di Missori to the Duomo was a brisk ten-minute walk—twenty minutes as I walk. Another five minutes brought me to La Scala. Even omitting the Galleria, Milan's great glass-domed, Greek-cross–shaped, mosaic-floored meeting place with its shops, its bars, and its restaurants (the Galleria being to a suburban shopping mall what Pecks' cheese is to Velveeta), in this very circumscribed area one can find every possible kind of café, some of which double as *gelaterie,* all of which offer caffelatte, cappuccino, espresso (and all of these in decaffeinated versions), and—solace on a rainy day—caffè corretto, espresso with a few drops (which the French call "tears") of one's preferred liqueur; and croissants and sweet rolls and sometimes more substantial fare, like sandwiches; and mid-morning gathering places for small pizzas or finger sandwiches or aperitifs; and numberless *rosticcerie,* which are a cross between delicatessens and cafe-terias and which serve as Italy's fast-food restaurants, the fast food being whole roast chickens stuffed with lemon and thyme, peasant soups, grilled sandwiches; and *salumerie,* food shops that are the Italian equivalent of our take-out shops (salmon mousse; tomatoes stuffed with saffron rice and pine nuts; squash flowers dipped in flour and fried, an anchovy in each gold-green center; vitello tonnato, cold veal with a puree of tuna; chicken in aspic adorned with prosciutto and tomato; thick salmon steak in pastry crust stuffed with egg yolk and parsley). In my first days in Milan the thought of disciplined sightseeing did not, given my ineptitude and my lack of love for the unsunny city, appeal to me; I used instead to find my pleasures in the cafés that lined my path to the Piazza del Duomo. (My ineptitude was such that I once, because it was there, pulled an innocent-looking cord in my bathtub, which, insofar as I thought at all, I thought must do something exotic to the shower curtain; it triggered an alarm, and the hall porter and the reception clerk and various unknown persons flew into my flat, where, hastily clad in towels, I had to explain that I had *not* slipped in the tub, I was *not* having a heart attack . . . or a baby. . . . Why Italians put these alarm systems only in bathrooms continues to be a mystery to me. Don't accidents of a reparable nature ever occur in kitchens? or in bedrooms?)

Caffè corretto saw me through many a gloomy day; and it was easy to while away time watching beautiful young men lovingly shine the beautiful brass of the café and scrubbing the marble floors with sawdust; this manual labor was considered dignified and decent. A rejuvenating consciousness was applied to these activities. Bachelard says: "I once read an Italian novel in which there was a street sweeper who swung his broom with the majestic gesture of a reaper. In his daydream he was reaping an imaginary field on the asphalt, a wide field in real nature in which he recaptured his youth and the noble calling of reaper under the rising sun." I do not know what memories or dreams these young men brought to their labors; I know there was nothing hostile in their relationship to inanimate things.

I was almost always the only woman eating alone in Milan in a *ristorante* or trattoria. I was never looked upon askance—except by my own country-men—although Bethany saw fit, for propriety's sake, to introduce me to the headwaiter of the restaurant across the street from my residence and to explain my presence in Milan. I was thereafter treated like a quasi celebrity, which is to say, with as much care and deference as any *Italian* diner, and with an invisible mantle of protection. Almost always the only other woman dining alone would be Japanese. And just as inevitably, she would order two or three kinds of pasta, the torrent of advice from waiters and their capitulating shrugs notwithstanding, eschewing fish, meat, and vegetables, for what reason I do not know. I watched the hands of these Japanese women flutter becomingly over their remarkable dinners with particular pleasure; their manners were so pretty, the waiters, after briefly condescending to them, would watch them, too, as if trying to unravel a mystery.

The sun is shining. It is my tenth day in Milan. Weather creates character. As heat is the central fact of India, sun is the central fact of Italy; this is something Marx did not take into account. Today no skies of zinc. I am thwarted in my desire to have my hair tinted aubergine (Milan, like Venice, was famous during the Renaissance for its hair dyes, used by women and men alike); but I am otherwise happy. I have seen sixteen Corinthian pillars near a tram stop on the Corso di Porta Ticinese, and today I am enamored of the scrap of Roman wall outside my residence.

In Milan, when you see something, anything, suggesting antiquity, you feel as if you have done something clever, particularly if the old stones are graced with wisteria. In the Italy I have known till now, especially in Rome, one's subjectivity is not in question—the world is beautiful, and one is grateful to it, not self-congratulatory. Here—because, as to beauty, it's catch-as-catch-can—the difference between subjectivity and objectivity is extreme; there is no question of drowning in beauty; there isn't enough to wade in. . . . I have never felt my cleverness or lack of it to be at issue in Rome.

Bethany has made me a dinner of fettuccine Bolognese (she makes her own egg noodles, though she could buy fresh egg noodles across the street from her house, which is a remodeled railroad worker's house, with the charm of a New York mews dwelling); a pot roast in its own juices; a mixed salad; and Gorgonzola, the acknowledged king of cheeses, with a creamy, silky sheen, nothing at all like blue cheese or Roquefort, much more delicate, though it, too, is threaded with blue-green veins; and a smoky fontina. Afterward we go to the theater to see a carnival version of Dostoyevsky's *The Possessed,* directed by the Soviet Yuri Lyubimov in English; and Bethany, Giancarlo, and I all fall asleep, as do most of the few Italians who are present. (There have been more banners heralding than people attending the play, giving rise to a visiting Roman's comment that Milan is all hype, to which the Milanesi smilingly agree.) Then we go to a popular *gelateria,* Mangi e Bevi, where Giancarlo and I have hazelnut ice cream with mixed liqueurs and chocolate syrup, and Bethany, wise girl, has champagne and strawberries, which is just as good as it sounds.

A public relations genius could lure tourists to Milan simply by reeling off the names of tram and bus stops: Gioia, Passione, Magenta, Botticelli. The tourists who come to Milan stop here principally to see the cathedral and *The Last Supper—Il Cenacolo.* Leonardo da Vinci's masterpiece is to the left of a Renaissance church, Santa Maria delle Grazie, in what used to be the Dominican friars' refectory—and very austere, not to say bleak, the refectory must have been. I went back several times and never found the church—which is said to have a lovely Baroque chapel—open; "abroad is always closed," even its churches.

Il Cenacolo has been restored so many times (and it is again being restored); the building that houses it was bombed on August 16, 1943; protected by sandbags, the end wall on which *The Last Supper* is painted remained standing; the walls on which Leonardo painted in oils were always damp. . . . How faded it is! Scaffolding obscures much of it. By craning your neck, you can see the Son of God in prescient isolation, betrayed so that, according to solemn doctrine, we might live. Judas is more clearly present, in the dim fresco, than is Christ. The great work seems to be vaporizing before our eyes, its mortal music thinning. But to stand in its presence is unutterably moving. "Behold the hand that betrayeth me," Jesus said; Leonardo didn't use an arrangement of hands simply as a means to solve a technical problem. One is conscious of that hand, it is like a blow to the heart; it is also a glory; Judas's betrayal set in motion the wheels of salvation. And the photographs of the bombed refectory (the roof and one wall were destroyed) are a kind of counterpoint to Leonardo's work: They tell us that the Prince of Peace is betrayed daily.

If we are to believe Giorgio Vasari's lovely account, Leonardo was humble in the face of his great task, his task being by means of his art to make the sacrificial death of Christ and the Eucharistic Sacrament the focal point of all human history, of life and of light. The artist was "convinced he would fail to give [*The Last Supper*] the divine spirituality it demands . . . he was unwilling to look for any human model [for Jesus], nor did he dare suppose that his imagination could conceive the beauty and divine grace that properly belonged to the incarnate Deity. . . . Judas . . . troubled him since he did not think he could imagine the features that would form the countenance of a man who, despite all the blessings he had been given, could so cruelly steel his will to betray his own master and the creator of the world." I choose to believe Vasari's account because, I suppose, Leonardo's combined profound humility and certain faith is so appealing—and (talk about God twice at a dinner party, and you're never invited back) would be so much out of place in modern Milan. Or in New York.

"Let us sit upon the ground and tell sad stories of the death of Kings." The music of that line is perfect.

Do we love or venerate works of art only because (a deconstructionist propounded this theory to me) we succumb to propaganda subtly inculcated? My son, when he was five years old and for the first time saw the Pantheon, cried. He said he was crying "because it is perfect." (If emotions have a geometry, happiness is round; and he was crying for happiness in the beautiful round Pantheon.) *The Last Supper* is not perfect—time has seen to that; but the impulse that guided the hand—this fresco has nothing at all to do with those reproductions on velvet, horrible, anathema—is visible still. It still sings.

St. Augustine—who has endeared himself to generations of believers by praying for "continence and chastity . . . but not yet"—lived in Milan (in a house with a small garden, he tells us), with his beloved mother, Monica, who never ceased praying for his happiness and salvation. Benito Mussolini lived here, too, with his common-law wife, Rachele; it was in Milan, in 1919, that he founded the organization called Il Fascio, whose members were the disenchanted of the left and of the right. It was also in Milan that he met his final end. He had always believed in the loyalty of the Milanesi; even his death did not satisfy the hunger of the Milanesi for his humiliation.

I had passed the Piazzale Loreto several times in my wanderings and had seen no reason to pause. The *piazzale* is undistinguished and commonplace: banks, a cinema, an underground garage for garbage trucks.

This is the piazza where Benito Mussolini and his mistress, Claretta Petacci, were hung, like sides of beef, head down from the roof beams of a gas station, after having been shot by partisans on the western shore of Lake Como. He had never liked lakes, pronouncing them "compromises between seas and rivers." (Still today most of my Italian friends invariably call lakes *triste,* perhaps because their surface gives no clue to their depth. Thoreau called a lake "the landscape's most beautiful and expressive feature. It is earth's eye," he said, "looking into which the beholder measures the depth of his own nature." Mussolini would not have wished to measure the depth of his true nature.)

Where Fascism had been born, Fascism died. *"Duce, Duce,"* Italian children sang in the brief moment of Fascist glory, *"chi non saprà morir?* [who among us will not know how to die?]" But they didn't know how to die: In death Mussolini was spat upon, stoned, and reviled. Claretta, whose death, prompted and determined by her love for Mussolini, has endeared her to more people than her life ever did, was dressed for death and hanging in blue high-heeled shoes, a lacy blouse, and a respectable gray suit. Some biographers say that for propriety's sake her skirt was held in place by a rope between her legs; others that a British officer fastened her skirt around her legs with his belt so as not to reveal her underwear, and that the crowd as a consequence was maddened.

Mussolini had, according to a sympathetic biographer, Laura Fermi, in the last months of his life "collapsed into a state of pain, depression, and apathy" . . . proving the truth of St. Augustine's axiom that a disordered mind is its own punishment.

What is spooky about the Piazzale Loreto is that it's *not* spooky. No hint of that carnage remains. The Italians, whose love for commemorative plaques is legendary, have not chosen to memorialize that fall from power. The Piazzale Loreto appears in *Tutta Milano,* the official guidebook of the Milan tourist organization, only as a stop on the *metropolitana,* the underground train system.

Twenty years ago H. V. Morton wrote that "Italy is a country where women allow men to believe themselves to be strong and masterful." That is as may be. But "it is part of the pretense . . . that women's shops should be hidden away; . . . there is scarcely a hint in Milan"—which has for centuries been famous for its silks—"that women need clothes at all." That could not now be further from the truth. All the "small, select shops leading to the Cathedral" were men's shops, twenty years ago, "all aids to that Italian state of male well-being, *far figura*"; now it is hard to find a shop catering to men on those streets; they are given over to women, as are the shops on the fashionable Via Montenapoleone. Twenty years ago Paris was the undisputed fashion capital of the world. Today many would accord that honor, if honor it is, to Milan.

In 1827 Stendhal wrote of "a Milanese burgher, a dandy by profession [who] used to carry one shoulder a little higher than the other because the last print in the Paris fashion journal had this fault in drawing." The gods of fashion are still appeased and aped in Milan, where, one often feels, everything is scorned which is not fashionable, brilliant, and brittle.

This is the week the great fashion houses are exhibiting their wares. I go to a fashion brunch hosted by designer Laura Biagiotti. I am sitting with the American ambassador and his wife and the American consul general in Milan. The American ambassador and his wife speak of America as if it were a beloved foreign country held in very capable hands. The consul general is friendly and helpful. He tells me that I must go to the *questura,* the Ufficio degli Stranieri, to apply for a visa if I wish to stay in Italy for more than three months. This is a fact of life the Italian tourist board has advised me to disregard. This is an Italian fact of life that every au pair girl working for Americans in Milan disregards. The consul general is bound to support Italian law, even though I can hear weariness entering his voice as he describes the procedure. "In Italy, under the law everything is permitted, especially that which is prohibited"—as opposed to France, where "everything is permitted except that which is prohibited," and Germany, where "everything is prohibited except that which is permitted," and the Soviet Union, where "everything is prohibited, including that which is permitted." That's what Newton Minow, who used to be chairman of the Federal Communications Commission, says. Giambattista Vico said (in 1744): "Men of limited ideas take for law what the words expressly say. Intelligent men take for law whatever impartial utility dictates in each case." While I am prepared to believe that in Italy under the law everything is permitted, especially that which is prohibited, I am terrified that some concierge someday in Rome will realize my time has run out and will report me to the officials. I am equally unhappy about spending a daunting day at the Ufficio degli Stranieri with bureaucrats, and for months—until it no longer matters—I will vacillate between doing that which is legal and doing that which everyone else does.

The consul general has heard a bird sing this morning and can hardly believe it; Milan's wintery spring has not prepared him for small miracles. The consul general aside, I feel that glib, impersonal friendliness I remember so well from years of living abroad, the wife, then, of a CARE official—effusive offers of help and friendship from people who don't get your name right and thereafter neglect to return your phone calls. Except that the cast of characters is different, the conversation I hear might be held in New York ("Sergio is sick—we know with *what*—so Giorgio is *very* difficult"). The talk turns, as it would in New York, to real estate: real estate in Rome, Milan, Florence, Georgetown . . . and New York. (In my wildest dreams, when I tried to imagine what living in Italy would be like, did I think I'd be eating salmon with expatriates and discussing condos? At this brunch I'm afraid to admit I rent; it seems like proof of a bad character.) The wife of the ambassador has arranged to establish a branch of New York's Fashion Institute of Technology in Florence.

"Why not in Milan?" someone asks, innocently and reasonably.

"Because I prefer Florence," she says.

A few words about Nicaragua—where my daughter is visiting as I speak with my countrymen—serve to convince me, to remind me, that politics are absolutely to be avoided when one is with political expatriates. I am sure that the Foreign Service officer who called me a traitor almost twenty years ago when, at a cocktail party in Guatemala, I expressed agreement with Senator J. William Fulbright ("also a traitor," according to the Foreign Service officer) has by this time taken to denying that he ever supported the war in Vietnam; it is hard to find anyone who claims he did support the war. But one can't anticipate, and at brunch, as at dinner, and as at cocktail parties of this sort, one's only obligation is to be pleasant, more's the pity.

The ambassador's wife introduces me to someone named Mr. Traub. "Be sure to see the Italian exhibit at Bloomingdale's in the fall," she says.

"Are you with Bloomingdale's?" I ask Mr. Traub.

"He *is* Bloomingdale's," she says.

"I'd like to talk to you about your third floor," I say, to laugh away my gaffe. This, however, is an invitation he takes seriously.

Laura Biagiotti's face is innocent of makeup; she is wearing a breezy oversized blouse of creamy cotton, white cotton oversized pants, strings of coral beads of varying sizes and colors, several unimportant rings. She is not at all "done"—and she achieves a look of casual simplicity and stylishness that would be the envy of any fashion slave, precisely because it looks, to the untutored eye, as if it cost her nothing at all in money or time to achieve it. I have a snapshot of Biagiotti with Lidya Gromyko. Both are dressed informally; Biagiotti, her artifice so perfected as to look like naturalness, looks like a million dollars. Even a million dollars would not transform the stolid, ample wife of the Soviet foreign minister into a treat for the clothes-conscious eye. The snapshot is an eloquent essay on the difference between clothes as covering and dressing as art. All the same, I love clothes and I don't love fashion. I like to play with clothes, and fashion codifies. It even codifies playfulness.

To get to Modit, the exhibition hall on the outskirts of Milan, which is today a temple of fashion, we drive down an avenue called Naviglio Grande, a reminder that Milan once had a series of canals that linked it to the Adriatic—to Venice.

The handouts at Modit are masterpieces of obfuscation (or bad translation), silly attempts to elevate fashion to ideology (it's like reading rubbishy jargon about modern art; the one word that is forbidden is *beautiful*): "A determinedly stylistic philosophy emerges on the lines of an austere and clear essentiality. . . ." I have met some of the young girls from rich families who write this copy; dilettantes in designer clothes, they cherish their connection to "literature" and drop Umberto Eco's name.

Everybody is fond of saying that fashion makes "a statement," but I can't read the language of fashion, I don't know what is being stated. "These are *clothes,*" B. says, "not fashion." This is not haute couture. Exhibiting here are not the great houses, only the second-string names (names, nevertheless, that one has seen in *Vogue*); these clothes are last year's great collections vitiated and diffused, modified to suit more popular taste, less extreme. The finlike appendages one saw on Krizia's dresses last year appear here in a less exaggerated form, as massive sleeves; one could actually imagine getting into a taxi unaided with these clothes, as opposed to last year's Krizia's, which called for a limo and a chauffeur with a helping hand.

The clothes I am drawn to—soft cashmeres, simple silk sheaths—do not draw the attention of the buyers (these clothes will go on year after year and sell themselves). The buyers are flocking to exhibitors with tarty beaded confections, aggressive, armorlike clothes (Milan used to make the best armor in the world; in a sense, it still does); beaded, encrusted excretions repel touch, offer no tactile pleasure. Each of these dresses says: I can have it all—leather, velvet, wired flowers, sequins, brass—all in one piece of apparel. "Ah, they're thinking of India this year," someone remarks. Not of the starving millions, they're not.

This is what I think these clothes say: "This is a suffering world. So what. Fuck it. I'm-nouveau-riche-and-fuck-you-I-don't-care-if-you-know-it." Even the floors of the exhibition halls are aggressive—black, mirrorlike vinyl.

One could touch the models, the mannequins, and they wouldn't flinch, stick pins in them and they wouldn't bleed. Their faces are vacant, their lips painted a mortuary purple-blue; that strange walk, that unnatural pelvic thrust (how unlike the Madonnas of art; and how will these animated dress hangers ever bear children?). They flirt with empty eyes, their unnatural lips in little moues; or they present faces of icy disdain.

Everyone is on parade, buyers and viewers as well as models (everyone but the German buyers, who clump along mannishly in tweed). "Oooooh," says a friend, "I'm all wrong." She feels despised—an acquaintance has snubbed her—in her simple five-hundred-dollar dress, which she wears with grace and éclat, trailing her mink behind her. "But you look beautiful!" I say. "My scarf," she says forlornly, "my scarf is wrong."

And this is the International Day of Woman, an event that has no observable political overtones in Milan. International Woman's Day appears to consist of mothers and daughters exchanging mimosa plants. (If there were political activities—which I am assured there are not—how would one know of them? The newspaper distributors are—as they were for two days last week—on strike.)

On the way back to the center of town, we see two young women, one black, one white, each with mimosa in her hair, holding hands in that unselfconscious European way. How nice! Neither of them is "done." They make me happy—until B. tells me that they are standing on the exact spot where a man was killed by an orange tram that morning.

The next day. For the great collections of the great houses, Modit is transformed; the Italian genius for design is evident in small things—great banks of white lilacs exude their heady fragrance, and everywhere there is forsythia for the spring that has not yet arrived.

Young women who represent the great houses manage to contain hyper-activity under a pose of languor—which is to say, their hauteur would be difficult to equal. ("This is not just any little fashion show to which you can bring a friend," says an attenuated designer in black to a young woman who, insufficiently haughty, is reduced to angry tears.) Everyone wears self-importance demonstrably. In Krizia's runway arena, it is hot and crowded and strobe lights pierce the din and people fight for seating. Deneuve has been flown in, and God knows who else. One hears photographers speak of their "girls," so proprietary, so objectifying (my prejudice against photographers is confirmed); one would think the "girls" had no function but to be mute and draped. The "girls" twirl, dance, stride down the runway (pelvic interplay with male photographers), demonstrating the truth of Oscar

Wilde's dictum that "the most difficult pose is naturalness." Clusters of black models appear in electric red, electric green, electric blue. They look like gumdrops on the darkened runway.

Bronzed leather and lamé for evening wear. We are meant to glitter asexually in our armor. Flashy—the flash not of fire but of ice. It would take a very determined man to undo these artfully wrapped evening clothes; they are not an invitation to touch. They may bewitch, but they won't—it's fair to assume—deliver. Fox furs worn bandolier style, dyed tangerine, lavender, fuchsia, slate blue. "Rigged out and malicious," Krizia's fashion copy calls the fox, and it is. Mixed messages—over come-hither unstructured, soft jackets and coats, those mean little eyes, vulpine, predatory, say (just as they used to say when they hung so scarily in Grandma's closet), "Go away or I'll bite." Fashion's mixed messages exist to keep us in a permanent state of imbalance.

Well, if we are all flesh and a wind that goes and does not return, why *not* go in frippery? But shouldn't clothes be fun? Nobody's smiling. Jodhpur-type trousers; Nehru-type jackets: "Treasures from the Indies on the shoulders of the brocade tunic-jacket, which could compete with a maharajah!" Bronze and gold and faux jewels: Bhopal. Fendi's furs: sable pullovers, "the ultimate in throwaway luxury elegance"; clothes that are "reminiscent of what the Russians wore while riding in their troikas." How earnest I feel. "Put it in another place," my companion says, "don't try to make connections between the real world and this world. Have fun. . . . Are you viscerally offended or intellectually offended? Do you only *think* you should be offended?"

"I'm hot." The truth is, I am thinking of Bhopal.

Why does English fashion—which the Milanesi have little use for—rise from the bottom up? Why does it start out—playful and rebellious—with kids in Camden Town and end up, modified, in Oxford Street, the reverse of Milan, where it is dictated from the top down? A friend suggests that it is because where institutions are stable (as in Italy they are not), where the queen and her heirs will be God-saved presumably forever, kids are "allowed" the luxury of playing and arbitrating fashion. It's as good an explanation as I'm likely to get.

For dinner I have antipasto: squid with lemon, roast peppers, grilled eggplant, fried and grilled zucchini, mushroom frittata; and bollito misto—chicken with skin and sausage and veal and tongue boiled with carrots and potatoes, served with a green sauce made of parsley, garlic and oil and a mostarda, a relish made of cooked unripe fruit marinated in a mustard-flavored syrup (not unlike, but more refined than, a New England boiled dinner); very soothing.

This is the day of Russian General Secretary Chernenko's death.

Sitting in one of the cafés of the Galleria has become an almost daily occupation, a refuge from the rain, a way to be absorbed into the city, its ebb and flow; Milanesi of all classes use the Galleria almost as a living room. Here footsteps lose their staccato emphasis. Sauntering does not seem like an act of civil disobedience. The shops—bookshops, boutiques, jewelers—in the cruciform arcade don't observe the afternoon siesta; and cigarettes and shampoo as exquisitely wrapped as a bridal present and valeriana—the vegetable soporific Byron used, hence irresistible—can be found here, as can Vecchia Romagna brandy and scotch and chocolates at Motta (one of a chain of confectionery shops). Part of the glass-and-iron dome of the arcade is being renovated, and tight green mesh netting is stretched across it to prevent debris from falling upon pedestrians' heads. This net is a common sight in Milan, one only wishes one could stretch it across the sky to hold back the rain.

Mussolini used to have long political discussions with a journalist at the Café Campari in the Galleria in the shadow of the cathedral, which granted him neither help nor sanctuary on the eve of his fatal trip to Como.

Sometimes I have a light meal in the Galleria's Downtown Café, the music of Ethel Merman and Mario Lanza in the background. On this day of pouring rain a British couple—he with an upper-class accent, she with a lower, and neither wearing a wedding band—whisper furtively at the table next to mine. It is the waitress's first day on the job and she is harried and the bill is slow in coming. Which is nice because it is raining. "That bitch," the Englishman says, "that bitch," and he goes to the proprietor to complain and soon the waitress is crying and so is the Englishman's mistress, who says, "I'm a waitress, too, I'm a waitress, too." He says: "Bitch."

Reading the *Herald Tribune,* I am amused to see that Raisa Gorbachev has "won over Britain with smiles and fashionable clothes"; that which just yesterday I regarded as frippery and Bedlam I am today obliged to consider a weapon in the foreign policy arsenal. I am bemused by Gorbachev's decision to see the crown jewels rather than to lay flowers on Karl Marx's grave. While there is hardly an uglier monument and bust in all of Highgate Cemetery than that of Karl Marx, there is hardly a more romantic and jungly cemetery than Highgate, in which the corpses of dogs as well as of persons are interred . . . and in which my favorite epitaph reads, "To My Husband

and Drinking Pal, Sam," the equivalent of which would be unthinkable on an Italian tombstone, sacrilege. The *Corriere,* no longer on strike, proclaims, ALLARME, QUASI PANICO; the dollar has risen to over two thousand against the lira. I think of my tidy hoard of traveler's checks and begin to understand (a chastening experience) bloated men in three-piece suits who spend their days anxiously watching the ticker tape; there is nothing like having money to make you think of money.

A woman sitting next to me reading *Newsweek* smiles tentatively, and we exchange newspapers. She is a runway model, and I am hard pressed to say whether she is homely or beautiful; she is certainly not pretty, and no one would call her insipid, though some might judge her plain. She is skinny, of course; wide-spaced dark eyes, a large, beaked nose, a thin, wide mouth, and cheekbones that seem to start at the corners of her mouth and extend to the edges of her eyes. (When I speak of her to Giancarlo—she is famous for her runway magic in Milan, where all models have their fans—he says, *"Uffa!"* that wonderful Italian expletive, which in this case means he thinks she is ugly.) She likes her job. "I have no talent," she says, "and I'm tall and funny-looking. It's a good job. Shorter on glamour than people think. Fendi nearly yanked my arm off the other day. . . ." What job is glamorous to the one who has it? Her choice, she says, is to protest that it is not glamorous and be perceived as spoiled, or to yield and say it is glamorous and be envied. She is a white South African living in Canadian exile, and she won't speak to a Colored South African model, who, having achieved success, insists that all is well in South Africa: "She talks so brightly to her black friends—and she knows it's coming, the bloodbath, the horror, and it won't make any difference then, our gay talk." She is able to buy some dresses cheap "because you have to weigh three pounds and be seven feet tall to wear them," and then she dresses up for dinner parties in her small town, "and we all have a good laugh. It looks so silly, you see, off the runway, and I can't have them thinking I'm glamorous, can I?" She misses her husband.

There is scaffolding and netting on my residence, too, and scaffolding and netting on the Duomo.

I miss my children.

After my first dogged days in Milan, when I had gone about like a drudge, small pleasures began to insinuate themselves into my daily rounds. Milan is not an outdoor museum as Venice and Florence and Rome are outdoor museums; one walks to get from Point A to Point B. But once the miasmal mist recedes, even the shortest walk yields pleasures: shops with the most beautiful babies' clothes in the world (do all Italian newborns look like baby infantas?); dresses smocked and ribboned and embroidered and laced. Artisans: custom-made tiles of surpassing beauty and incomparable variety. (I knew an Italian tilemaker in Tripoli whose work reflected years spent admiring the tiles of Isfahan; I thought his tiled fountain a perfect thing, but the Libyans had no use for his work. I thought of him in Milan; in the black-and-white, cool but welcoming reception room of Krizia's palazzo showplace a tiled serpent weaves its sinuous way around an eighteenth-century column, illustrating the Italian genius for felicitously combining the old with the new, a remarkable ability to worship at two shrines.) A young girl repairs a muted Persian rug behind the plate-glass window of a shop; in the antique shops on the Via Solferino, stylized briarwood acorns for holding thread and a "pinecone" needle holder also of briar speak of a leisured way of life in which everything one took to hand satisfied the necessity for beauty, a principle Milan's designers have tried to honor (stepladders—what could be more homely?—of yellow laminated wood, for example, that make you long for cupboards and kitchen chores). A shoemaker who is a maestro will extend the same courtesy to you if you are buying shoes for six hundred thousand lire or having a sole repaired; and there are shops for repairing purses, dolls, old lace; and bookbinders, practitioners of what Henry James called "the most elegant of the mechanical arts"; dry cleaners who will not despise you for bringing in one cherished handkerchief and who will do it exquisitely. (Teddy bears and Raggedy Ann dolls are dry-cleaned as well. Italian middle-class children are kept so clean even their toys are spotless; imagine an American child's teddy bear dry-cleaned, all its history washed away!) There are shops given over entirely to marzipan: green bursting figs, ripe and red at the marzipan core; black bursting figs; greengages; cherries; purple plums; peaches; and—where else but in Italy?—marzipan garlic; marzipan chestnuts wrapped in chocolate; and—where else but in Italy, where people still know they can't jog or diet death away?—marzipan bones in marzipan caskets. Pastry shops *(pasticcerie),* sweets to take away the taste of diesel fumes—burled wood and fin-de-siècle mirrors, Old World and dignified or pink and pretty, all very Viennese.

One day I went with Bethany to Taveggio in Porta Vittoria for tea and petits fours, and Bethany's small Fiat—her good gray horse—was parked by a grizzled old man, thin as a dime, carrying a huge red-and-white umbrella, issuing rapid-fire instructions; I thought he was like the 1950s civic-minded gentleman of my acquaintance who, inebriated at the time, single-handedly diverted traffic from the great Montgomery Ward fire on the Lower East Side until the police and firemen arrived; in fact, the old man was a municipal employee, a human parking meter. Parking is a terrible problem in Milan; people park on sidewalks when they think they can get away with it, which is often, or they say, "I've brought my car," by which they mean their car is a mile away, and your final destination two miles away. The medieval streets that wind around Via Spadari were not made for cars.

Italians call Art Nouveau "Liberty," according to some because Liberty of London was the first prestigious shop to make Nouveau objects popular, according to others because of a political impulse that is now lost to memory. One sunny day, when the golden Madonnina that crowns the Duomo shines as if lit from within, I pause on my way to Pecks—where today the window displays six kinds of Parmesan cheese—and crane my neck to see a small gray Art Nouveau building with wrought-iron lace more fanciful than any in New Orleans, wrapped around balconies that seem made of Plasticine by Gaudí ("the sublime grace of created things": Vasari), and the night reception clerk at my residence sees me and stops in alarm: Is there something wrong with me? Why am I standing still? (Even when two trams going in opposite directions find themselves on the same track and on a collision course and the conductors noisily sort matters out, Milanesi do not long pause for what in Rome would be an afternoon's sport and spectacle, a matter of orchestrated conjecture and contention.) As I cannot convince the friendly clerk that there is nothing amiss, she takes me firmly by the elbow—who would gaze at a small gray house wedged between a shoe shop and an airline building?—and deposits me at a taxi rank, and I feel obliged to place myself in a taxi, though in fact I have little more than Parmesan on my mind, and little more than six blocks to go. For reasons I cannot determine (maybe the sunshine is intoxicating), the taxi driver tells me how his mother prepares sardines; he loves fish; he recites a litany of fish and fish dishes—*acciughe, antipasto di mare, astice, baccalà, calamari, carpa, cozze, dentice*—he clogs traffic as he works his way through the alphabet. He must recognize a kindred soul: In my living room I have made a centerpiece of artichokes and dried red peppers, which Mima, the maid, regards quizzically for several moments every day. She doesn't know whether to dust it or not. Mima has worked up the courage to ask me a question that has been vexing her for some time: "Why," she asks, "do you shower every day but not wash your dishes every day?" This is not meant to be impertinent; it is a question of an anthropological nature; Mima, who cheerfully washes my dishes, thinks my priorities are cockeyed: Bodies may go unwashed, in Mima's world; kitchens must be spotless, a clean kitchen being proof of moral character. How well I know this thinking; I learned it as a child. My Aunt Lee cleaned the oven every night in case she should die in her sleep; I used to dream of lines of mourners poking their heads in our stove.

On another day—a day in which soft, runny cheeses (Gorgonzola, with almost as many patterns as snowflakes; ricotta) have replaced the Parmesan at Pecks (even food shops are design-conscious)—I stop to have coffee and Sambuca at a café I have not frequented before, though I have walked down this street countless times. On the wall of an unremarkable church I see a primitive painting of the Virgin and Child. Mary Queen of Heaven sits Egyptian fashion, legs squared and apart; and she holds out her hand in a gesture that, together with the singular mixture of surprise and resignation on her face, says (I am familiar with this gesture, it was worn by the women of my childhood): "Well, what am *I* supposed to do about this, eh?" And the Child looks no less puzzled. I like a puzzled Jesus. His bewilderment is so human; His bewilderment reminds us that God became man (and must occasionally have astonished even Himself).

Wedged among these snarled and tangled streets is the Piazza dei Mercanti, a happy medieval space doubly blessed—a haven of openness after crooked, winding streets that is also a warm, womblike enclosure. The space was created during the late Middle Ages, and from this period only a well exists; the black-and-white Loggia degli Osii, with its balcony from which penal sentences were pronounced, is no longer black and white, as the white marble has suffered the fate of white marble all over Milan—it is soot-encrusted, black. The Court of Justice is being repaired,* but one can still take pleasure in this enclosure, which I remember less for its statues of Augustine and Ambrose than for the beauty of the men in the Ristorante Mercanti. There are days in Italy when human flesh seems victorious over all remorse. There was scarcely a man in that restaurant I would not, at that moment, have happily made love to. I applied myself instead to the serious business of eating: beautiful fresh slices of meaty tomato mated with slices of fresh sweet mozzarella, olive oil, and *basilico* ("Basil is the plant that flourishes from a murdered man's head," I heard someone, not an Italian, say—a line from a poem by Keats and not a

---

*The Court of Justice, or Palazzo della Ragione, has been fancifully and controversially restored and is now a museum.

malediction); spaghetti with garlic and oil and tiny clams the size of a baby's fingernail in their shells; strawberries—spring must have arrived somewhere—and cream.

One late afternoon, on my way to the Piazza del Duomo, I stopped in a small, undistinguished church, San Giuseppe, for refuge from the rain. The purple, red, and white candles of the Lenten season were burning, and six men and two women—one of the women in blue fox, the other in a blue smock and floppy, backless felt slippers with a dustcloth in her hand—were praying, chanting, contrapuntally; I let the lovely sounds, half song, half speech, wash over me. I thought idly: How much I love to see men in church, how touched I always am to see men bow the knee in an attitude of submission. There is no cheap victory in this, I do not rejoice in seeing a man brought low; for men to be humble in the house of God, for them to declare that their need is equal to my need to be healed, releases some wellspring of tenderness in me. . . . I thought of my father, and a wave of longing for his touch—which I will never again experience on this earth— suffused me. God's peace protects the frailest; that is perhaps why I like to see men pray: They assume a frailty and a vulnerability they are elsewhere at pains to deny. In church, in the attitude of prayer, we are all God's vassals, and the only lord is the Lord.

An old man asks me to join my voice to theirs in prayer. Painfully aware of the deficiencies of my Italian, I decline, and he, as courtly as he is threadbare, says, "God understands English." The elegant woman in the blue fox coat edges over to me and says, "I work all day, but this is peace." *Pace.* A girl with a glory of uncovered red hair comes in to light a candle. The wonderful words break over me: *Misericordia,* a word that has always delighted me because it sounds like *misery* and means "mercy." *Luce a luce*—"light unto light"; now and in the hour of our death. With the beaming approval of the old man I renounce—for the first time in Italian— Satan, his seductions, his works. And I wonder: What will Heaven be like? Will I feel my father's hand? Where Heaven is concerned, I have faith, but no imagination. The saints of Italy, plaster and stone, ridiculous and sublime, are aids not to faith but to imagination. The Jesus of the Gospels called to Himself those judged foolish by the world—no god in mythology was ever as patient as He; He loved and chose them for their faith . . . whereas it was Pontius Pilate who asked the imaginative question.

* * *

The Piazza del Duomo—the huge paved esplanade onto which the huge doors of Milan's white marble Gothic cathedral open—looks like a board game the rules of which have not yet been invented: There are squares within squares, and white marble squares which, if they were of malleable material, would suggest that giant fingers had made symmetrical indentations on two ends of them—or bitten off two identical, tidy mouthfuls. In the Middle Ages the square symbolized the earth (as the circle symbolized Heaven); one can imagine the great bronze doors of the cathedral swinging open and the bishops and prelates instructing the faithful: Heaven speaking to earth. The faithful now have their own sermons to offer, discourses on the nature of God delivered in colored chalks on white squares.

On Palm Sunday there is a large drawing of Mary with seven arrows piercing her breast; a smaller drawing of Christ crucified with a legend the artist attributes to Simone Weil—"Unless it is possible to believe in God it is impossible to climb the cross and enter into or imitate imaginatively the suffering of the world"—and another painting, still smaller, of Mary, its legend exhorting us to think gentle thoughts as light calls unto light and a time of "pensive joy" begins.

From the twelfth century on—building of Milan's cathedral began in 1386—theologians equated God with light (hence the stained-glass windows of the Duomo, the colors of which are echoed in the fat chalks of latter-day mendicants). In the twelfth and thirteenth centuries it was believed that sin made the body opaque; were it not for sin, the soul would perceive the blaze of divine love directly. Church teaching evolves, but it is always prompted by the same irresistible urges, one of which is the desire to bathe in the light of God, another of which is to return an answering spark to the heart of God, to ignite His warmth and love.

Near to the artists who remind us that we are entering the final stages of the season of pensive joy is another man, working in a more conventional mode on a drawing of Mary; and next to his Mary there is a chalked plea, in English and in French, for money—and indeed his cap is filled with coins, while that of the artist given to metaphysical musing is not. What a practical city Milan is. It has always understood trade.

Inside the cathedral—it is impossible to believe that one could ever be warm in this severe immensity of space—blue incense rises and thins, curling around a great cross bearing the crucified Christ. The Eucharist is celebrated at a makeshift altar. The organ, too, is being restored. The high sweet voices of boys sing the Gloria. Soon hosannas will yield to mourning; Passion Sunday is a bittersweet feast day—bittersweet because of the beautiful yet remorseless progression of the liturgical year. He who entered Jerusalem a king will, within a week's short time, be mocked and will suffer the anointing of vinegar and gall, and wear a crown of thorns.

As we exchange the greeting of peace, an old woman embraces me. *"Congratulationi!"* she says, as if we were all jointly responsible for the music, the celebration of the Mass, the day itself; and, anticipating, *"Buon Pasqua,"* she says. I kiss her cheek, so old it feels spongy. Although the church is overflowing, so few people receive Communion that by the time I make my way to the altar rail, it is over; the chalice and the Host have been removed. I must look stricken, because a young boy shyly offers me laurel (Milan's fragrant substitute for palms). His gift reminds me that no Italian man—ever, in any church—leaves without genuflection, even if he leaves, as many men who are not communicants do, before the elevation of the Host . . . to talk outside, it is presumed, about politics. The act of genuflection might be—and has been—called habit or reflex; it might also be called a noncommunicant's offering to God, to Whom no gift is unacceptable.

The massive doors swing open. Before they exit, many worshipers make private devotions at the Mary altar. I do. Now Mary is present in our imagination not as the Queen of Heaven, not even as the Mother of God, to whom the cathedral is dedicated, but as a grieving human mother whose human son will soon be dead. The great doors swing open, and the secular world proclaims itself: blinking in the mist across the piazza an electric sign, TOSHIBA.

On the roof of the Duomo a young boy in a red jacket carries a yellow balloon.

White and orange Day-Glo plastic arcades, junky but amusing echoes of the porticoes that extend on either side of the Galleria, are set up in the piazza for today's *festa*—candies and toys, fake Guccis and silks from India, "antiqued" copper, shoes and umbrellas and fuzzy yellow Easter bunnies and flowering cacti and prints. . . . I want to buy Art Deco magazine covers, but I am stupidly put off by the stallkeeper, who has told the man next to me, "I charge Americans much more, of course." The odd thing is that I feel not angry with her but lowered in my self-esteem. I buy a marzipan strawberry the size of a heart instead.

Upon this rag fair the saints that sprout from the roof of the cathedral look with perfect indifference.

"Credo quia absurdum," St. Augustine said. "I believe because it is absurd." If absurdity is grounds for belief, and if Gothic architecture is the Incarnation made visible, why are we not all believers? The Duomo is at first sight absurd. It took me almost a month before I could form any affection for it. It seemed at first both bleak (Michelin says "colossal") and silly (Michelin says "ethereal"). It is certainly colossal, second in size only to St. Peter's, which, however, is its direct antithesis; St. Peter's provides ample and dazzling visual nourishment, whereas the interior of the Duomo, almost completely devoid of adornment—St. Charles Borromeo, who was adamant that nothing secular or pagan intrude on ecclesiastical splendor, swept it bare of relics and most statuary in the seventeenth century in a fervor of Counter Reformation zeal—is an agoraphobic's nightmare, 485 feet long, and every foot dizzyingly uncluttered.

Morton, who was himself overpowered by the "mysterious gloom" of the cathedral, tells us that Shelley was able to find one place behind the altar where there was enough light to read Dante (though he cannot tell us why Shelley would want to engage in such self-conscious romanticism). Now, however, you can read small print, so well has the cathedral been illuminated by overhead lamps; and the glaring light serves only to give it the feel of a vast surgical theater.

Inside the cathedral my heart palpitated; viewing it from the outside, I was often moved to laughter—so many belfries and gables, and so many marble saints on needlelike marble pinnacles that a kind of madness takes over when people try to count them. One edition of Michelin says there are over two hundred; one edition of Baedeker says there are over three thousand. From the ground they look like ivory miniatures pricked with a crochet needle—as improbable as ships in bottles. D. H. Lawrence, in a letter to Lady Cynthia Asquith, called the cathedral an "imitation hedgehog of a cathedral"—it bristles. (And he called Milan "beastly . . . with its hateful city Italians, all socks and purple cravats and hats over the ear.")

If the Gothic cathedral is indeed the visual equivalent of the Incarnation, there can hardly be a cathedral in Christendom that better illustrates the point that God was made man (embodied); yet one feels, at first, that half as many saints would make the point twice as well.

On my first visit to the Duomo passersby were more interested in a Shiseido makeup simulator in the window of La Rinascente, Milan's impressive department store on the Galleria side of the square, than in the cathedral. I saw a priest looking out of a confessional unashamedly at a group of Japanese tourists, cameras around their necks like leis; meanwhile, a woman could be heard (disregarded by the priest) making her confession. I suppressed a giggle; the confessional has always been an object of intense interest—which is to say, revulsion as well as fascination—to non-Catholics . . . and here the need of the woman making her confession was so unmatched by her confessor's interest that the Sacrament of Confession (a Sacrament wisely attuned to human nature) was rendered absurd.

I stopped at an anonymous painting of a Madonna and Child, she holding out a firm, perfect breast, the size of an apple, to the sulking child; Mary seems to be saying—as well she might—"What have I wrought?" and the Child looks not at her (as suckling babies always do, their eyes locked in perfect trust with those of their mother . . . every mother knows she will never receive that intensity of love and trust again) but outwardly. He gazes serenely and with adult self-possession, as if in anticipation of the day He will say, "Woman, what have I to do with you?"

I joined a wheezy nun with a mustache at a bank of blazing candles and added to my more conventional prayers the fervent wish that the look on the waiter's face at Savini's had not meant I didn't tip him enough (fat, pulpy sausagelike spinach pasta with butter and sage and cheese; beef in crust with *carciofi;* a tingly lemon sherbet and a double coffee; also Campari, *acqua minerale,* a Lombardy rosé: seventeen dollars).

A truck rolled out from behind an improvised partition and made its way down one of the four aisles. It took almost five centuries to build the Duomo (and manual labor—paid—was rehabilitated in the process: "Each workman was a conqueror, and the Cathedral itself meted out praise to him," Duby says; the workmen who built the great cathedrals were not peasants but professionals). The pious were not disturbed by the truck. What is one vehicle, one load of sand and stone, one restoration, more or less?

After a while I began to regard the cathedral not as bleak and silly but as lacy and monumental. To the inside I never warmed; the great and true joy of the Duomo is its roof, on which, one rainy day, I walked, magnificently alone. God seemed both whimsical and magisterial to me that vertiginous and thrilling day, as I wandered among pinnacles and saints (so varied, so elegant), up and down worn gray-pink marble stairs, over scary catwalks (what Hitchcock could have done with this!), where one clutches rails and dares to regard only one's feet (to look up or down is to invite a sinking, a fall as if from grace), through and under narrow, low arches, where I paused, feeling safely sheltered, to view the piazza and the dwarfed throngs with their gay umbrellas below, Chesterton's "topsy-turveydom of stone in midair . . . a glimpse of great things made small and small things great."

One takes an elevator to the roof—and is beamed upon by the elevator operator, who anticipates one's astonishment and joy.

The roof of the Duomo has often been called a forest of saints; and this is appropriate, because the universe was regarded, during the time of its construction, as a forest no human could measure.

The final ascent, to the golden Madonna, Milan's beloved Madonnina, can be reached only by foot—a steep and airy climb, in equal parts daunting and exhilarating—and to the faint of heart the Madonnina extends a graceful hand.

Galeazzo Visconti III, the first Duke of Milan, began the cathedral as a gift to the Virgin, hoping for a male child in return. He married his cousin, who presented him with two sons. The first, Giovanni Maria, Galeazzo's heir, was murdered by Milanese noblemen when he was twenty-four, perhaps because he liked to amuse himself by watching criminals being torn apart by wolfhounds. His body was thrown into the cathedral. Galeazzo's second son fared somewhat better but was repulsed by his own gross flesh, had an unhappy domestic life, and was riddled with fears. . . . All of which goes to show that one invites trouble when one bargains with God.

There are V-shaped prongs wrapped around electrical wires to keep pigeons off the roof. St. Francis of Assisi would not have approved. But the electrical shocks must be very mild; I saw no dead pigeons.

It is tempting to believe that writers like Henry James and George Eliot took their characters inside the great Italian cathedrals as a device to enable them to give utterance to a much-vexed question: Do the monumental cathedrals inspire and uplift and exalt the soul and bring it closer to God, or does their size reduce man to the size of an atom, and if so, is it not after all appropriate to feel like an atom in the presence of God? (In some cathedrals the question is now mooted: The last time I was in Notre-Dame, women in purdah pushed strollers and drank orange soda, English boys played transistor radios, a man in white socks could be seen by hundreds behind a Plexiglas wall making his confession, and, taken all in all, beautiful Notre-Dame presented the face of a squalid carnival.)

The twelfth-century Basilica of St. Ambrose is a Lombard Romanesque church, one that does not occasion such vexing questions. On this spot St. Ambrose converted St. Augustine; and in this basilica rest the mortal remains of St. Ambrose. One day, when the sun was a white disk in a pewter sky, I made my way to it.

Fuzzy-minded and misled by a statue of St. Ambrose outside, I entered first a cryptlike war memorial adjacent to the basilica. Outside the memorial an eternal flame discreetly blazed; inside, the marble steps had just been washed, making descent perilous. The place was clammy cold. Row upon row of bronze plaques commemorated the dead of the First and Second World Wars. I descended till I reached a platform beneath which there was a large and deep well-like space, down into which I peered to see more plaques. Heavy dampness rose from the brightly lit enclosure. One doesn't walk familiarly among these dead; that is a shame, because one doesn't wish to feel like a voyeur in the company of the dead, the braided pain and pleasure of cemeteries being that one feels a tender and necessary connection between oneself and the dead. This sense of continuity, without which it is impossible to feel vivaciously alive and to comprehend and recognize one's mortality, is present in graveyards but not in such memorials. The restful dead comfort me; not here. But in this damp and dismal place I did believe that it didn't matter that the Italians were once our enemies. The dead are never our enemies; they are harmless as children.

From the war memorial I turned to the basilica, walking through a lovely atrium with arches opening onto arches, an infinity bounded by massive bronze doors and a wooden doorway with fourth-century bas-reliefs consecrated by St. Ambrose. My main purpose in coming to the basilica—which has been called the queen and mother of Lombard churches—was to see the remains of St. Ambrose, which have been called one of the world's most awesome survivals.

Behind the high altar is a flight of steps descending to the crypt housing the bones of the saint, as well as those of the martyrs St. Gervasius and St. Protasius; about these Roman soldiers, said to have died for their faith even before the death of St. Ambrose in 397, little is known. The bones of Bishop Ambrose were, just a little over twenty years ago, held to be too sacred to be made available to the common view. (Even today Milan's official tourist guidebook does not mention them; visitors to the basilica are not directed to them by arrow or printed word.) One had—twenty years ago—to come to the basilica very early in the morning to watch the verger unlock four steel panels, which were then cranked down into four slots or grooves to reveal a sheet of glass, behind which lay the relics. Today Ambrose and the Roman martyrs are not hidden behind steel doors; they lie in the crypt in a rectangular crystal box, surrounded by a silver Virgin and a chorus of silver angels. The effect is that of an ornate four-poster bed in which three good men are enjoying their final rest. The effect is mesmerizing. The bishop, who is elevated on a thin, faded mauve satin cushion between the martyrs, who flank him, wears—or his bones do wear—dull purple faded to lavender; he carries a silver staff; his naked skull is crowned with a miter. Jeweled white gloves cover the thin bones of his hands; white slippers and stockings, his feet. The Romans, resting on red velvet plush, wear red vestments and carry the graceful silver palm branches of martyrdom; they wear silver crowns. On the very tips of their feet—hundreds of amber bones are visible—they wear red slippers embroidered in gold.

Augustine relates that when the bodies of Gervasius and Protasius were brought forth uncorrupted, those tormented with unclean spirits were healed, and the eyes of a blind man were opened. For centuries Christendom's faith was sustained by just such relics; in the darkness of the crypt reposed the heart of faith, all the riches of the world surrounding it. These bones embodied divine mystery in the midst of the physical world.

A group of giggly Italian schoolchildren pass the relics, pausing no longer than a minute—it is as difficult for the young to believe that they will someday be old as it is for them to believe that we were one day young.

St. Ambrose is credited with being preeminently responsible for the ascension of Western Christianity in the twilight of the Roman Empire. He was thought by his contemporaries to embody all the traits a bishop must own: He was holy, erudite and wise, brave, long-suffering, and steadfast for the faith. He has been called the first statesman of the Church, which may be another way of saying that he was instrumental in the persecution of heretics and of pagans, whose temples he closed, disbanding the Vestal Virgins. Ambrose held fast against secular authorities and against the anti-Trinitarian Arian heresy.

St. Augustine (directing his words to God, his beloved and his familiar) says that Ambrose, slave to crowds of busy men, "zealously provided your people with the fat of your wheat, the gladness of your oil, and the sobering intoxication of your wine. All unknowing, I was led to him by you. . . . I began to love him." And indeed it was Ambrose whose teachings weaned Augustine both from flirtation with the Manichaean heresy—which holds matter to be evil—and from the fleshpots of the world. Augustine's mother also loved Ambrose: "she loved him greatly because of my salvation, while he loved her because of her most devout life. . . . But he did not know what sort of son she had, for I doubted all things."

Augustine's doubts, uniquely and beautifully expressed in his *Confessions,* have been not the undoing but the making of the faith of multitudes of others. Theologian, philosopher, poet, and—so deep was his knowledge of human nature, which started with his knowledge of his own—psychologist, Augustine was baptized by St. Ambrose during the night of Holy Saturday and Easter Sunday, April 24 and 25, 387. (On these facts I prefer to dwell rather than on Ambrose's persecution of heretics.)

Ambrose was a musician as well as a lawyer; it was through his offices that hymns were for the first time heard in a Western church as Ambrose and the congregation kept watch against the Empress Justine, who adhered to the Arian heresy. (Homer wrote about ambrosia a thousand years before Ambrose gave his honeyed sermons, however; it is not to him that we owe the use of that word.) St. Augustine and his mother sang with him; and in his *Confessions* Augustine says: "How greatly did I weep during hymns and canticles, keenly affected by the voices of your sweet-smelling Church! Those voices flowed into my ears, and your truth was distilled into my heart, and from that truth holy emotions overflowed, and the tears ran down, and amid those tears all was well with me. . . . At that time," Augustine writes, "it was established that, after the custom of the Eastern lands, hymns and canticles should be sung, so that the people would not become weak through . . . tedium and sorrow. . . . I wept . . . at the singing of your hymns, for long had I sighed after you, and at length I breathed you in, as far as breath may enter into this house of grass."

It is said that Augustine left Milan—"the astonished and disturbed city"— with the words of Ambrose on his lips: *"Deus, Creator OMNIUM."*

St. Benedict, echoing the Psalmist, said: "Before the gods will I sing praise unto Thee." He believed that choirs of monks placed man before the God-head; and monks believed that nothing enabled man to communicate more directly with the invisible than choral liturgy. Why is the music one hears in Catholic churches so often listless and pallid? If one were to choose a religion on the basis of its music, one would surely choose the Church of England or a black Baptist or Pentecostal church (that is what Simone Weil did when she was in New York; she went to Harlem storefront churches to refresh her soul with that consoling and exciting music).

In 1562 the Council of Trent excluded from churches all music that introduced anything impure or lascivious. According to Luigi Barzini, "Most of the choirs sang holy words to ribald tunes. . . . Masses bore the titles of popular melodies on which they were founded, names . . . suited for contemporary perfumes. . . . The very explicit words of love ditties and obscene ballads rang out often during religious services. . . ." Barzini's cynicism—a trait he attributes to all Italians—may have led him to hyperbole. But it is a fact that Pope Pius IV directed a congregation of eight cardinals to determine whether music could suggest anything *but* the impure or lascivious. The cardinals determined that it could. But the dampening effect of this procedure remains with us to this day . . . at least in cold climates.

I bought two postcards depicting the venerated bones of Ambrose, Protasius, and Gervasius, wondering, even as I bought them, who would want to receive bones in the mail. Two of the giggly schoolgirls were chanting, sotto voce, "Gervasio/Protaso, Gervasio/Protaso," delighting in the deliciousness of the rhyme—not at all put off by bones, as Americans might be.

When I left the basilica, which is below street level, I sat on a bench, turned my back to the dead, took pleasure in the sight and sound of trams and buses, took comfort in chocolate, and made my way to the nearby Bramante cloisters of the Catholic University of the Sacred Heart, to stroll among the living: bright voices saluting one another; posters proclaiming the goodness of Mother Teresa next to posters soliciting money for Amnesty International; tennis tournaments announced on billboards heralding the word loved and proclaimed by John Paul II: *Reconciliation.*

In 1982 the Milan-based Banco Ambrosiano, rocked by scandal that spanned three continents, collapsed. The Milanesi simply changed the signs on the banks to read *Nuovo* Banco Ambrosiano—an efficient, restrained, economical response . . . a Milanese response.

Everyone's mind is on money; mine, too. The dollar has never been stronger. To dine extravagantly costs fifteen dollars in American money. Meanwhile, staff members at the Italian and French embassies in Washington are pooling money to buy duty-free canned food and wines from Europe. An Italian diplomat stationed on Embassy Row says Washington "reminds me of my last post in Ethiopia." Labor is weak and unaggressive, even in the face of payroll trimming. Membership in the Communist-led General Union of Italian Workers continues to fall.

The dollar is feared; nobody hates me. I'm continually grateful for this. Five years after World War II, when I was in Paris on a pauper's allowance, you'd have thought that we—and not the Nazis—had been the enemies of France; I remember men, and women, too, in Paris, going out of their way to bump into me when I was carrying parcels. I was nineteen. And in Nuremberg a baker's family assailed me with stories of blond, blue-eyed girls, who would have been my age, killed by American bombs—and I cried, until I remembered that it was not I who was guilty, not we who had started the war. Marked by those memories, I am immensely well disposed toward the Milanesi, even if their behavior springs only from the habit of civility.

Because civility does govern casual conversations, any lapses are sharply anomalous: the travel agent who is too haughty and too blasé to secure you a smoking seat on the train to Stresa (she files her long tangerine-colored nails; she sighs); the bookstore clerk who feigns ignorance of anything and everything (all these young, pretty girls of Milan, dressed like a million, for whom work is play); the museum attendant who, asked if there is an elevator—all those museums in palazzi, flights and flights of stairs, how do the elderly and the infirm cope?—slams his fist on the counter and spews forth: "You stupid Americans—we'll have one built for you when you've finished seeing the pictures!"

Almost always when non-English-speaking Italians met in the course of a day's activities discover your Italian is not fluent, they (unlike Parisians) exhibit no contempt and happily hear you out as you mangle their beautiful language. But when they speak in return, they give no quarter; faster and faster they go. Is this the Italian equivalent of Americans' speaking louder and slower to foreign-speaking people, as if to idiot children? Is it a form of homage to your intelligence? What it probably means is that it is utterly incomprehensible to them that anyone cannot understand their language. In Rome, *"Buon giorno,"* you say to the cabdriver. "Ah, signora," he says, "how beautiful your Italian is. Your mother must be Italian. Maybe you live in Argentina?" How they do love to please, how far a little flattery can go. In Milan, if there is a hairline flaw in a vowel, a Milanese will know you are not Italian and will let you know that he knows. A woman who has lived here twenty years of her adult life tells me that she is obliged to explain to taxi drivers that she is from Egypt, so keen is her consciousness of not yet having perfected her Milanese Italian.

The bones of St. Ambrose kept performing a danse macabre in my head. What was needed was the hair of the dog. I went to the Cimitero Monumentale, in which funeral plots cost upward of a million dollars. On the way

I asked my taxi driver if it was safe to walk in the cemetery. He slammed on his brakes and asked, *"Ma perchè?"* But *why* would it not be safe? That anyone should disturb the peace of a graveyard was unbelievable to him. *"Bestiale! Bestiale,"* he alternately moaned and shouted, hitting his forehead with his hand as his bewilderment increased. "Have you no respect for the dead in your country?" he asked. "Are you barbarians, then?" When we reached the black iron entrance gates, he bought a white rose from a flower stall and presented it to me on account of my having to live among barbarians. . . . I can still see him, standing beside his cab, shaking his head, attempting to understand a phenomenon beyond his grasp (blessed is his nature or his fortune).

The Cimitero Monumentale is the ugliest, most flamboyant, outrageous, vainglorious burial place I have ever seen. Were it not for the absence of plumbing, one could live in almost any of those ostentatious mausoleums, mausoleums in the shapes of pyramids (accompanied by sphinxes); glass houses and conservatories; obelisks; "Mussolini architecture," brave-new-world monoliths; monstrous urns. I felt as if I were visiting a colony of summer bungalows for the dead erected by a demented architect. Who in life can have done anything to warrant so much in death? All monuments to human vanity; and nothing is lacking but whimsy, which might have redeemed the overwhelming vulgarity of the *cimitero*. . . . Is it really necessary to place the honorific "Dottore Ingegnere" on a tombstone? . . . Why are two Art Nouveau angels weeping over a medieval knight in armor in honor of a man who died in 1916, and why are a stone Jesus and bronze lambs part of this insane century-leapfrogging tableau? . . . What is the meaning, on a "Mussolini" mausoleum the size of a spacious cottage, of a woman hovering over men pulling two yoked oxen, her legs as thick as trees; why is an attenuated Christ figure standing next to her?

Against my will I am touched, softened, by the sight of women (the caretakers of the world, the keepers of the garden) tending graves—a flick of a handkerchief here; a spray of orchids there.

A simple grass circle lined with bricks. Stone slabs on which are carved these names: Buchenwald; Dachau; Belsen; Auschwitz—and names of those who fell there. So simple that at first I thought it was a signpost. And it is. A sign pointing to human evil and to human goodness:

"Blessed are those who hunger and thirst for justice . . . who suffer persecution for the sake of justice . . . fallen in the Nazi extermination camps."

I am glad I came. On the way out, I see coffins still on trestles, unhoused in memorial bungalows. They say: "Remember that you shall die"—the message the *cimitero* tries so insistently to deny. They are testimony to the lost life of the dead and to the human compact we make through burial.

Bethany's house was built over one hundred years ago for railroad workers. Across the street, red flags flutter from the local Communist headquarters, a storefront next to a pasta shop. On the corner is a three-story building, its discreet sign—HOTEL—designating a brothel. (I have learned to watch cabdrivers' faces when I give them Bethany's street address. They know the hotel. Sometimes they smile; sometimes they smirk; sometimes they look bewildered; always they shrug.) Bethany and Giancarlo have painted their house according to city color specifications; gray and sooty-yellow houses line the street. With its coat of fresh yellow paint, the house is sweet and pretty; in its high-tech kitchen, designed by Giancarlo, we have a light lunch of mild cabbage soup, cold chicken cutlets, cheeses, and scotch. . . . We are going to the supermarket, Esselunga.

I buy porcini, mushrooms still redolent of forests; blood oranges; apples, cheeses, and salamis; tortellini; pesto sauce; "Sicilian" sauce—meat and spinach and ricotta and tomato—fifteen dollars. Food for weeks of dinners. When I pronounce the word for bag—*borsa*—the checkout girl asks the world at large why I can't roll my *r*'s; she has been to hotel school, she says, her imperfect English matching my slovenly Italian. Bethany is not charmed. "Why does everything in Milan become an occasion for exercising authority?" she asks rhetorically. "Why is everyone jockeying for position? In every transaction must someone be right and someone be wrong?"

"Non toccare, non toccare [Don't touch!]," mothers call out to their children as pudgy hands grab, and Bethany's look is eloquent, authority being today her perceived foe.

Outside Esselunga there is a flower stall—mimosa; tiger lilies; canna lilies; lilacs; orchids; daffodils; yellow, purple, white freesias—and Bethany's temper is refreshed as she wanders among the spring flowers in her mink coat, her quarrel with Milan forgotten. Then, her arms full of dried lavender, she steps on a used syringe.

Laura LePetit says the main wish of her heart is for Esselunga to be open all hours—even, though this seems utopian to her, on Sundays. "Ah, Sunday!" she says, clutching her throat. "Every Friday I feel choked. Will I have bread in the house on Sunday?"

"I used to wonder when I first came here," I say, "how easy it would be for feminism to take root in a city where it took an hour to shop for an egg."

"Oh, and are you not still wondering?" she asks.

Laura LePetit is the head of a small feminist publishing house called La Tartaruga, one-quarter of which is owned by a fashion designer. On the Tartaruga list she shows me are these contemporary American writers: Grace Paley and Adrienne Rich. La Tartaruga has published four books by Virginia Woolf—who I sometimes think did more damage to women with her Bloomsbury airs and her vapors and her mad affairs than Norman Mailer in his wildest imagination could ever do—and one biography of Woolf. Dorothy Parker, Jean Rhys, Gertrude Stein, Stevie Smith, Edith Wharton, and Jane Austen are also represented. There is also a two-volume cookbook. This is not exactly the cutting edge.

Where in Milan are the passion and the freshness and the bravery that once infused American feminism? I am told that there is a bookshop in an arcade across from the Galleria in which I will be able to find feminist tracts— "broadsheets"—and translations of de Beauvoir. This information is delivered to me so lethargically—I imagine women both cozy and embittered among the bookshelves—that I always find I have something more pressing or pleasing to do than to search out the bookstore/meeting place, which I imagine to be cluttered, narrow, and—I don't know why—badly lit. There is a lesbian discotheque in Milan; that is not what I had in mind.

Ten years ago, LePetit says, feminism was—how easily this word springs to Milanese lips—"fashionable." ("Do you really find beauty in anything that is not *fashionable?*" Stendhal asked.) Then feminists marched for abortion rights in Rome, many crying because of their ambivalence. But feminism became "sloppy; everything we did as women was OK, they said," and now, LePetit says, feminist magazines like *Noi Donne* and *Effe* come and go, appear and disappear: "The product is not so good." LePetit gives me to understand that Italy's feminism, such as it is, is compounded of abstract "philosophical and cultural" discussions and what Americans call networking. "Networking" LePetit regards as "pragmatic." Activism she regards as déclassé, and in any case, "economic issues are not easy to dramatize." Her sympathies reside with Italian and American teachers, writers, lawyers, businesswomen. When I tell her of cutbacks in American social welfare programs that affect women and children, she regards me wide-eyed. Italy's fate depends on America's, she says, as a child depends upon its parents: "America has such a big responsibility to Europe. . . . Italy is a poor country. We close in the middle of the day. It is uncivilized. Milan has no parks, it has unbelievable traffic problems, it is not functional. It is *underdeveloped.* We have a protected economy. We can't sack anyone, there is no part-time work for women, we live with thousands and thousands of forms, thousands and thousands of taxes.

"There is no professionalism or competition here; there is an entrenched bureaucracy and no mobility.

"When economically we become truly capitalistic, when we have advanced capitalism, it will happen."

"What *it* is that?" I ask.

"Oh," LePetit says, "we are so much more cynical than you are. We have to be, in order to survive terrorism, the Mafia. . . ."

The Communist party espouses the rights of women, she says, but she questions its motives. As for the Holy Father, "nobody listens to him. . . .

"More and more women are taking over businesses, but you have to hide being a woman. An emancipated woman has to become a neuter." (The importance of presenting *la bella figura*—the proper image—takes different forms in Milan at different times, but it seems never to go away.)

"To be a woman alone is so difficult. One is *compelled* to have a husband around—for a job, an apartment. . . . Single women are not economically viable.

"These women who have children alone, without a husband—'I will do it,' they say; where is their sense of reality?" (Their sense of reality may stem, in part, from glossy magazines, like *Il Piacere,* which glorify unwed pregnant Hollywood stars.) "After six months they are desperate and shattered. Where is our day care? Our schools close at one. You have to be with a child all day and all night if you can't afford servants. This is a country that loves children and has no facilities for them. These women: They have the machinery—the plumbing—to make babies, so they think, Why not use it? A disaster.

"And the women of the South," she says (I was bound to hear it, sooner or later, this northern disdain, hatred of the South, this pronounced sense of racial superiority), "they still have five or six babies. The South is a reservoir for breeding. . . ."

My family comes from the South. My paternal grandmother had twelve children, seven stillborn. In Milan good breeding is what counts; to be well bred is not to breed "excessively." Breeding babies at all in certain quarters is unfashionable.

How dispiriting this conversation is, as dispiriting as a conversation can be when premises are not shared. Laura LePetit speaks English, but we do not speak the same language. "Oh, well," she says, as if reading my mind, "what does it matter? If there is a war—*puff!* It will all be over anyway."

"Feminism," literary agent Luigi Bernabò says, echoing my thoughts, "is not in the air here.

"Some single professional women have or feel a kind of proximity to success. But it is almost impossible for an Italian woman to imagine herself *not* as a mother. Everywhere you look there is a picture of a Madonna and Child. But so many are disenchanted with what they see of marriage. And Milan is a city people *come* to, a city of mobile people, so the famous Italian family system—grandparents, uncles, aunts—breaks down. . . .

"This is the contemporary dilemma: If you have children, you want to give them your best; but if a husband and wife are both working, which you have to do to give them the best, you *can't* give them your best. . . . Sometimes my wife and I wish—this is ridiculous romanticism, of course—that we were simple working-class people who had children unthinkingly. . . .

"This is not a good world for children."

I had children unthinkingly. Laura LePetit might say it was my southern blood—born to breed. It was the best thing I ever did.

In a way Bernabò starts where American feminists have taken years to arrive: Who will take care of the children? In America, this question took a backseat to abstractions and to arguments about the Equal Rights Amendment, pornography, and abortion rights.

Children hold us hostage; they represent our commitment to the future. Twenty years ago Luigi Barzini, in *The Italians,* the book from which so many Americans derived their ideas about the nature of Italians, called the Italian family self-sufficient and invincible. "There is still no divorce on the law books, and there never will be," he stated categorically; "not only is the Church against it, but the people themselves rightly consider it a barbarous and ruinous institution; the necessity to preserve some solid bulwark against the impermanence of things will always prevent its adoption." The family was "the sacred ark." Barzini saw this as a mixed blessing—or as a chicken-and-egg riddle: "Do political institutions flourish only where the family is weak, or is it the other way around? Does the family become self-sufficient only where the political institutions are not strong enough?" Unable to answer what he called the central riddle of Italian history and political life, he believed that law and institutions in Italy were only make-believe and that only the family—which "corroded and destroyed" political regimes, which is to say, corrupted them—was real. Now Italy has the unspeakable, divorce, and the unthinkable, abortion. And few would argue that political institutions have as a consequence of the waning influence of the family changed or improved. This is a time of great cultural dislocation in Italy, a time when women on trains twist their rings on their fingers and tell you how divorce—which they fought for ardently—has ruined their lives economically and socially . . . and tell you, too, how they would not want to go back to the old ways, for which, however, they have an unbearable nostalgia.

The Romans defined marriage—"a chaste and carnal union"—as the "unbroken companionship of life"; marriage, Giambattista Vico said, was "the first kind of friendship in the world."

Never give the Devil a role in a book or a play, Dorothy Sayers said; the Devil will always make himself the most interesting character. The Devil had the leading role in a strange and feverish event I witnessed in the spring of 1981, and this is (in part) what I wrote about it then:

> For three days this spring I . . . experienced that sense of disequilibrium that comes of seeing people being goaded and psychologically terrorized, and of not knowing to what exact purpose. To say that I was watching a funny little man from Calabria attempting to take over, or remake, a culture—or that I was watching an experiment to determine how many people could be bamboozled in the space of seventy-two hours—is perhaps to sound over-wrought. But I've thought a lot about it since then, and I remain unshaken in my conviction that what I saw was an elaborate scam, all the more appalling because its exact nature continues to elude me.
>
> All I know is that it was bad. . . .
>
> I interviewed him (a dream discourse), *him* being Armando Verdiglione, thirty-six-year-old darling of Milanese nihilists, bête noire of those European intellectuals who have not his alchemical power to transform opaque ideas into a thriving industry, founder and leader of the Movimento Freudiano Internazionale, and arguably the worst thing that has happened to Italy since

Mussolini addressed his people from that little balcony across from the Victor Emmanuel Monument.

I ask you to suspend disbelief and take my word for it that the following conversation took place on an evening in May, in the Baroque Room of the Plaza Hotel, on the third day of a Movimento happening billed as the "International Congress of Psychoanalysis: Sex and Language," at a time when I was in full command of my senses. Extraordinary circumstances call for extraordinary measures. In the ordinary course of events, I do not pose such questions as: "What would you give a starving Somali: a piece of bread or a sentence?"

"Mankind is fed by language."

"Yes, but what *would* you give a dying man?"

"I cannot talk in generalities. I do not behave uniformly. I would have to make a separate decision for each man. I would have to ask myself certain questions first. Every act is a failed act. . . . *Altri questioni.*"

"I'm not at all sure I understood your answer to my first question. . . . Is hunger something that concerns you?"

"Your questions stem from an outworn mythology. There is no such thing as class. There is no such thing as rich and poor. There is only language."

"I see." I did not, of course, see.

"But language is not a tool of communication," he goes on to say.

"So what are a thousand people doing here at a congress called 'Sex and Language'?"

"We are here to listen to one another through misunderstanding. We understand through misunderstanding. We are listening, hearing, but not understanding."

"Am I meant to understand that that is a good thing?"

"You are meant to understand nothing. I do not recognize such categories as good or bad. Logic exists outside of good and evil."

"So perhaps you'll tell me where all the money comes from to hold this conference."

"That is a question that stems from demonology."

"I understand from that that you accuse me of being a demonologist. Would you care to be more precise?"

"I do not believe in you. I believe in nothing. God is an empty point. The empty point exists in language only. . . . *Altri questioni.*"

"Is sex good?"

"Sex is neither good nor bad. Sex is sex."

"And is the body an instrument of love?"

"The body is not an instrument of anything. . . . *Altri questioni.*"

"If sex is 'just sex,' and if language is not a means of communication, why have we been listening to people talk about sex in three languages for three days?"

"Dante danced in the sky with the Devil."

"I beg your pardon?"

"Altri questioni."

He is a totally unprepossessing guru: squat, square, an oiled pompadour, a shiny mohair suit, three-toned ventilated shoes, unlit cigar in his mouth; a joke-person.

What kind of power does Verdiglione have? He is the head of a publishing house, the author of hundreds of articles and dozens of books (all on display at the Plaza), the president of a glossy monthly magazine called *Spirale,* and the publisher of four bimonthly journals of psychiatry, clinical theory, logic, and mathematics. If to be entrepreneurially busy is to be powerful, he is very powerful.

Ugo Stille, the distinguished American correspondent for *Corriere della Sera,* says: "Every morning, hundreds of Milanesi wake up and curse Verdiglione and wish that they were Verdiglione. Ah, lucre! And all those pretty young boys and girls." (All those pretty young boys and girls, according to sources who are reluctant to be quoted for attribution, are the kids of rich Milanesi with recognizable family names.)

Ah, hedonism! Ah, nihilism! . . .

Gurus are in business to offer people something—salvation, success, riches, contentment, enlightenment. But Verdiglione offers his followers nothing but incomprehensible lectures out of which they can occasionally salvage a phrase, "the impossibility of living" being one such phrase, and his only hard offer. A hatful of rain. Like other gurus, Verdiglione claims that his philosophy (if it can be called that) serves neither the left nor the right; it is an essence uncorrupted by politics or by what you and I might call "current events," which trouble Mr. Verdiglione not at all.

Nothing troubles Mr. Verdiglione because "nothing matters."

If nothing matters, then every act is like every other act, everything is possible, and everything is permitted—which, for some people, must sweeten considerably "the impossibility of living."

Ah, hedonism! Ah, nihilism! . . .

On Thursday, May 1, a day before the congress was open to the public, a press conference was held at the Plaza. It was composed, in equal parts, of press camaraderie, nihilist chic, and jabberwocky. French, Italian, and American journalists drank Moët champagne, indulged their appetites for croissants and brioches, and meanwhile tried to decipher the material contained in the press kits, of which this is a sample:

"Sex permeates language and language permeates sex."

"Sexuality and politics are neither translatable nor interchangeable."

"New York Congress is a determinant moment in the Freudian Movement proposing the invention of a culture, starting from the indications which comes [*sic*] from the psychoanalysis; a non-ontological practice, being aware of time."

Verdiglione's people mingled among the crowd, repeating certain words: *the void . . . the conjugability of signifiers . . . the un-number . . . Cartesian assumption . . . Husserlian assumption.* And certain names: Roland Barthes, Claude Lévi-Strauss, Michel Foucault, Jacques Lacan.

Verdiglione stalked the room (never without a trail of pretty attendants). He smirked and shrugged off questions with a wave of his cigar: all would be made clear in the fullness of time.

"Is Verdiglione a structuralist?" I heard someone ask.

"He's not saying."

"Is Verdiglione a semiologist?"

" *'Io sono Verdiglione'* is all he'll say."

No questions are invited; no questions are asked.

Later, comparing notes with other journalists (why *didn't* we bombard them with questions?), I found that, almost without exception, they'd felt bludgeoned; their bodies hurt, as did mine. . . .

A New York psychoanalyst said: "This is not a cultural gathering at all, but a quasi-religious event in Verdiglione's honor. He wants to be a great intellectual on a world scale. The man is some sort of maniac. Possibly psychopathic." I wondered if he was overreacting. (I wondered if *I* was overreacting.) "Let me ask you this," he said. "Does your body hurt?" . . .

"A group," Freud said, "is subject to the truly magical power of words." For three days participants and observers were held hostage to words, as they darted from conference room to conference room, hoping, I suppose, to find an insight, or a comprehensible sentence.

I had breakfast at the Plaza with a friend who has studied structuralism and semiotics. "You're overwrought," she said. "I'm sure all they're trying to do is break down conventional categories. They're stirring passive people up, shocking them into forging new connections. . . . Who the hell are these people listening in to our conversation?" Verdiglione's people were all around us in the Palm Court. "They're bad," my friend said. Robbe-Grillet passed our table. His latest film—undistributed in France—was being shown at the NYU Dental School auditorium.

In the Savoy Room, Lina Wertmüller informed a dense crowd that in the good old days one always had "a childhood accomplice, a friend, against one's mother." Now children have "only an ugly luminescent box—television—a paid accomplice, to act against their mothers, against the family, against authority." Inconceivable that a child might actually *like* his mother. Inconceivable that the family is not necessarily a microcosm of Hitlerian or Stalinist authoritarianism. "Fascinating," Wertmüller said, commenting on her own words. "I don't know what I'm saying, I'm blind. I hope you don't understand a thing." Not to worry. . . .

A woman who represented herself as a German feminist said: "I want to insert this in the mind of the audience. There is no penetration in the sexual act, there is only engulfment. Has that penetrated your minds?"

And so it went. Silly, you might say. I say evil. After all, it is possible for a thing to be dangerous as well as funny, sinister as well as silly. I say evil because people were being toyed with. When Verdiglione says, for example, that philosophers support "the religion which believes in the universe and in its moral order," one doesn't know whether he is defending a moral order or implying that no moral order exists. Like much of the conference's rhetoric, this is designed to breed confusion; it makes people crazy. What is one to make of a statement like this: "Where there is truth, there is oppression. I believe in truth."

"The body," mathematician Jean Toussaint Desanti declared at one point in the conference, "is that which appears and disappears. The body has the unity of zero. . . . To verify that wine has body," Desanti said, "one must taste and swallow it. It must disappear. What remains is the body of the wine. The wine remains to be consumed; it exists for disappearing." It sounded like a parody of a Black Mass.

"For all the talk about sex," Peter Blom, a Dutch psychiatrist, said to me, "did you ever get the feeling that anyone was talking about sex as human beings actually experience sex? Did you hear anyone say sex was fun, healthy, loving, good, warm?" I didn't. . . .

I prayed for the Lord to deliver me. I got Philippe Sollers instead. Sollers: "I am asked: Is this show business? A circus? I am asked: How is it possible to formulate in a hotel any theoretical consideration of sex and language? I am asked: Where does the money come from? All questions from money fetishists! We are Martians. We are paid by a secret organization. This congress will mark an important stage in the destruction of analysis. I am too tired to speak of the plague."

At last Verdiglione invited questions.

"Where does the money come from?" No answer. . . .

"What issues are being debated?" (Hisses.)

A young woman took the floor microphone. "I am a dance therapist, and I am having separation anxiety," she said. . . .

"Why, from the moment this conference began, has the conference itself, and not the substance of the speeches, been the issue? Why has language been paid more attention to than what was being said?"

"Altri questioni." . . .

"How can we keep the plague from New York?"

"Why won't you tell us where the money comes from?"

At last Verdiglione (speaking so loudly into a microphone that almost adhered to his lips that his translator could salvage only isolated phrases from the wreckage of his ranting) began his peroration: "The bottom of the night is zero. . . . Between the path of night and the path of day, there is dusk. . . . Once upon a time there was a sophist. . . . I came down out of the sky. . . .

"Thieves!" Verdiglione shouted. "Dante existed in solitude. . . . There exists a contingent of walkers in the sky! . . . Armando Verdiglione now goes to Milan. . . . Walk in the sky!"

And people cheered.

Incantations, Voltaire said, will destroy a flock of sheep if administered with a quantity of arsenic. "They call it the spirit of the age to seduce and be seduced."—Tacitus

In Milan, I accepted an invitation to visit Verdiglione's people. . . .

I go to their office on the Via Torino; in and out flit pale young men who seem to have been born to wear boutonnieres; their cheeks are splashed with pink.

Executives from Olivetti are just now meeting in the conference rooms on the Via Torino, the better to learn, I am told, about the connections among "Art, Computer Science, the New Technology, and Psychoanalysis."

Christina Frua, a female lieutenant of Verdiglione's, speaks to me; the effect is to obfuscate.

"Here there is a private psychoanalysis, a new science—a cross between art and science. You don't need to be ill or to have problems or neuroses to be psychoanalyzed," Frua says. "You need only to have a scientific interest." And, one supposes, money. Frua, the rich gleam of zealotry in her eyes, says, "Soon there will be a transformation all over the world—a second Renaissance." Well, Milan could do with a second Renaissance, the first having left a minimal physical impression on it.

Frua is immensely pleasant. "It is difficult to have an idea in Rome," she says, from which I infer that it is her belief that beauty and antiquity interfere with the thought processes. "In Milan the politics of work and of art intersect with international culture." (They do so unhindered, in this cloudy endeavor, by the ghosts of the past; poor Milan, with its little scraps of sunken Roman walls, the sixteen Corinthian columns of which it is so proud. . . .) "Here," Frua says, "you create yourself all the time; whenever you think you can rest, you are on the wrong way."

My eyes and my attention stray to a window-framed view of the Duomo. Where else in Italy but in Milan—a restless city with little claim to beauty— would such a movement originate and hope for any degree of success? Certainly not in Rome, the city of visible history. Answering my unspoken thought, "We are all fragmented and hungry," Frua says. "This movement sprang up in the wake of terrorism. The Church should provide a context, but it is busy with things eternal. And Milan is not so much a Catholic city as a Calvinist city. . . ."

"A context for what?" I ask, inwardly rejoicing that the Church is busy with things eternal, of which Olivetti is not one.

"Where does fashion intersect with video, design, new technology, computer science, psychology?" is Frua's answer; in fact, it is a good question, though not responsive to my own. How I would love to eavesdrop on Olivetti.

"Are you talking about environmental psychology?" I ask. After all, it is sometimes desirable to enter with brio into a nutty conversation, why ruin a good day?

"The movement will be big business," Frua says, "as the world changes in a good and interesting way. Feminism is not important here," she says. ". . . The Virgin appears in Catholic culture to teach us that every time is the first time; there is no sin. Virginity is not of the body, a woman is always a virgin if she is a mother. But no woman should accept motherhood as a category. The story of the Virgin Mary is very beautiful, but it is only a story. . . ."

My eyes stray to the golden Madonnina of the Duomo, golden sunlight playing on the gold of her substance. *Virginity is not of the body.* Frua has a point. There has always existed the concept of the virgin mind: Each time a woman falls in love it is the first time; it is always the same love reembodied.

Which is all very well; but I want to know where the MFI gets its money.

Every week visitors from Tokyo and Germany are flown into Milan. A Tokyo congress took three years to prepare, and in that time Frua made twenty-five trips to Japan: money. Everything circles back to money. As we speak, Olivetti is planning a link with Japan's Toshiba corporation, a move of strategic importance that will enable Olivetti to find new markets.

"Ah, the Japanese are so close to the Europeans," Frua says; news to me.

"This is a psychoanalysis that does not start off with sexuality, but sexuality is the subject at the Tokyo congress, and one Japanese said, 'It is the first time I talk about sex at nine in the morning.'"

I am afraid to ask what sexuality has to do with the new technology, computers, etc.—afraid of what new tangent Ms. Frua will take off on.

"The money?" I repeat.

"Happiness," she answers.

Frua has been with the MFI since 1974—the year many Italian women began to agitate for abortion—and she invested, she says, all she had in this project, and she expects to realize her investment. Frua is a well-known name in Milan, an old, large, important industrial family. No one is paid by Verdiglione; all MFI members are "associates"—three thousand associates, Frua says, many of whom are investors.

"Investors in exactly what?"

"Happiness. The new technology. The movement. Happiness."

Ah, yes; well. I accept an invitation to lunch with Verdiglione in his villa near the small town of Seregno, an hour from Milan. A villa is a palazzo in the country. I could do with a visit to the country.

Lunching with Luigi Bernabò (deer steak; shrimp in seashells with fennel; crème de caramel), I discuss the Verdiglione phenomenon.

"Isn't he silly?" I say.

"Yes; so was Mussolini. You don't know if a thing is dangerous till it proves itself to be dangerous, do you?" The speculation is that the MFI is neo-Fascist; on the other hand, money from the Socialist party is said to be funneled to Verdiglione; that may or may not rule out its being neo-Fascist. Bernabò says: "No Freudian knows what they are about, except, of course, power." So deep is Bernabò's suspicion of Verdiglione that he will not allow any of his authors to be published by Verdiglione's small publishing company. Where does this sense of unease come from? Verdiglione makes people cranky and nervous. He makes people envious, too. Milanesi want to be part of an elite. Nobody can figure out whether Verdiglione's rich followers constitute an elite or simply an aberration.

In moments of immersed contemplation of beauty, pure adoration of beauty, one's self is simultaneously enhanced and forgotten; one becomes what one sees; one is simultaneously stupendously alive and oblivious of oneself—as one is when one is in love. I have not experienced this abdication of the self in Milan. Perhaps a trip to the country will do me good. . . . And I want to see if Verdiglione makes me nervous.

St. Charles Borromeo—who in all portraits looks sad and avaricious—is entombed in the Duomo. The Borromeo family owned Isola Bella, an island in Lake Maggiore famous for its palace and terraced gardens; and Armando Verdiglione owns the fifteenth-century Borromeo villa near Seregno. To this villa the Borromeos repaired to escape the plague. HERE IN THE GOOD AIR AND FERTILE FIELDS WE REMEMBER OUR ANCESTORS—this is inscribed on the facade of the villa.

Seregno is a Communist stronghold. Its main piazza is called Hiroshima; next to Piazza Hiroshima is Piazzetta Tiziano—past and present collapse into each other in Italy.

I was driven to Seregno by a young woman called Francesca Gobbo, whose exertions to be charming, when I met her for the second time, produced fruit. I could not understand my previous aversion to this delightful young woman, who was studying psychoanalysis with Verdiglione while teaching adolescent psychology at the University of Padua and who had received her master's degree at the University of California at Berkeley. She didn't seem sinister or silly at all.

It is almost impossible not to feel churlish and ungrateful if you harbor animosity toward anyone with whom you are breaking bread. Verdiglione's servants unsmilingly brought us paper-thin slices of Parma ham; pasta with fat shrimp cooked to baby pink in parsley butter (a little cold because of its ascent from the ancient kitchens below); a simple grilled veal chop accompanied by puree of artichoke; pear belle Hélène (a fresh pear, vanilla gelato with chocolate chunks, chocolate sauce . . . I'd always failed to see the affinity between pears and chocolate before); a white wine; a red wine. Verdiglione, who now aspires to elegance, is on a weight-loss diet, color-coded: no meat, a parade of vegetables—*carciofi;* carrots smothered in a puree of fresh tomato; heaps of some white root vegetable shredded; white and brown grilled lettuce. I don't grasp the principle that governs the color coding; and I don't understand the conversation much better.

The villa is beautiful in spite of the addition to the formal gardens of nineteenth-century statues and fountains; fountains inside, too—one under the stairwell, as was the vogue (and charming, if somewhat gratuitous) in the nineteenth century. We walk through countless rooms; on many wood-beamed ceilings frescoes are being restored to their original splendor; acres of parquet floors are being mopped (no harm is done to their soft waxy luster, the patina of years). I see a bicycle made of ash, modeled after a Leonardo design; and (lust rises in my acquisitive heart) seashells collected over the centuries by the Borromeos, each unique, each with its own magnificent geometry, each with its own history. Paul Valéry said: "A shell stands out from the usual disorder that characterizes most perceptible things. [It is a] privileged form that [is] more intelligible for the eye even though more mysterious for the mind than all the others we see indistinctly." I want to fondle seashells, not to play with disordered ideas.

In the ballroom red and white desk chairs are arranged for a conference. In the apartments in which the princely Borromeos once lived now reside "candidates for psychoanalysis." Except for vague references to Jacques Lacan, nobody will explain the system—either of learning or of psychoanalysis—to me. Elie Wiesel comes here for summers, Verdiglione says. (Does he? Why?) Here is Marek Halter, the respected French-Jewish writer of the New Right, born in the Warsaw Ghetto, his family the oldest printing family in Europe, once employed by Gutenberg. I want to ask him about his life; I want especially to ask him why he is here; he is courtly and gentle, but Francesca hovers, and I cannot.

Verdiglione, a thoughtful host, is not at all defensive, not at all incendiary. "America is old and dying. Japan is the Milan of the Pacific," he says, and smiles benignly. "In four years [in 1989] Italy will have another Renaissance." I cannot be troubled to question this certainty, or to spin conspiratorial theories; and the food is so good, also the wine. The families of Verdiglione and of one of his guests attempted to make an independent state of five regions of Calabria in 1945; is it from this frustrated revolutionary activity that his messianic impulses spring? Touching, really, his softheaded belief in technology, his belief in progress; just so did men think of the Industrial Revolution, which seemed to them the agent of salvation, no more famine, no more plague. "No more terrorism," Verdiglione says. No details are supplied. Technology and hybrid psychoanalysis have replaced God in the MFI; Verdiglione is a heretic, but that is no business of mine. "Rome," George Eliot said in *Middlemarch,* "is the city of visible history, where the past of a whole hemisphere seems moving in funeral procession with strange ancestral images and trophies from afar." Rome also interprets history. Verdiglione has set himself up in opposition to Rome as the interpreter of the world. Verdiglione's is the dynamic of despair, the dynamism of artifice; babble and jabberwocky. All these people are pale, and all their ideas are pale;

poor little Verdiglione, poor little man. America—Henry James's bright new innocent world—may now be old and dying, but only an exhausted culture, a distressed city, could produce Verdiglione.

Poor little man. Four months later, on the Sorrentine Peninsula, I learn of his arrest and imprisonment on charges of fraud, theft, embezzlement, and tax evasion.

It was the money of Cardinal Borromeo that made possible the foundation of the Pinacoteca Ambrosiana in 1618. Imagine an exalted jumble sale, and you are near to comprehending the organizing principle of this museum: sculpture; Botticelli and Brueghel Madonnas (so many Madonnas look sly and smug, and with their secret, who wouldn't?); and Lotto Madonnas (lovable because they don't simper); paintings by Tiepolo, Veronese, and Titian; a 1973 portrait of dancer Carla Fracci; photographs of Toscanini (who is buried in the Cimitero Monumentale); Caravaggios; the famous profile of Beatrice d'Este, the wife of Ludovico il Moro, who employed Leonardo da Vinci, to whom this painting was once ascribed (her young eyes stare off into adulthood as if to a far country); and—my favorite juxtaposition—a lock of Lucrezia Borgia's blond hair next to a glove worn by Napoleon at Waterloo, memento mori, both; a ceramic bootie; cartoons by Raphael; works by Leonardo.

One of the pleasures of a small, compact museum like the Ambrosiana—a museum one can easily walk through in a day—is that the mind automatically catalogs and makes lists; and lists are magical. Lists are litanies and incantations; they can soothe or arouse or bemuse.

The *Dictionary of Christian Botany,* under "Periwinkle," says: "Reader, study the periwinkle in detail, and you will see how detail increases an object's stature." This observation, which echoes in different forms in all of literature ("a handful of sand is an anthology of the universe"), leads Gaston Bachelard to say, "Miniature is one of the refuges of greatness. . . . The man with the magnifying glass . . . is a fresh eye before a new object. The botanist's magnifying glass is youth recaptured. . . . We have only to imagine [miniaturists] for our soul to be bathed in peace. All small things must evolve slowly . . . a long period of leisure, in a quiet room, was needed to miniaturize the world. . . ."

There are hundreds of enchanting miniatures at the Pinacoteca Ambrosiana: exquisite eighteenth-century mosaics, fretted ivory, enamel; miniature portraits on enamel dating from the French Revolution, one a ringer for Madame Defarge; Limoges boxes with figures representing Heaven (a young woman, how nice), Purgatory (a young man, why?), Hell (a shrieking old man, flames of gilt); a miniature glass slipper. Almost everyone is drawn to the miniatures, which, however sophisticated their execution, seem to speak of a certain naiveté. To contemplate them is to be enlarged, to see the universe in a grain of sand. The desire to miniaturize the world is not the same as the compulsion to reduce—as anyone who has ever owned a dollhouse, a manageable world, knows.

As I wander through the Leonardo rooms, an American lady clutching a Michelin greets (accosts) me. She has heard me joshing with a guard in English and in Italian. "Oh," she says, "I am so happy to hear an American voice. I've been in Italy four months, and it has been the loneliest time of my life." She can speak no Italian. Her husband, an engineer from Pittsburgh, is here to lecture in Florence—"the opportunity of a lifetime," she says, "and the weather! All it does is rain and I spend most of my time crying and I hate it." In Milan for several days, she "couldn't find the metro and didn't know I was two blocks from the Duomo, which I wanted to see, and then it was thunder and lightning. . . ." Her loud voice follows me from room to room. Her voice sounds strained, as if she were unaccustomed to speaking. I like to take paintings in alone; still, "Won't you have lunch with me?" I ask; she is so eager. She calls her husband, screaming into the phone: "Well, I can't *help* it, Sidney, *I can't hear you.* . . . I don't *want* to meet you for lunch. I want to eat with an American woman. . . . Why *not?* . . . Where? P-a-a-o-l-a? P-o-l-i-a? How do I get there? . . . Can't I take a taxi? . . . Well, I get *lost* on the way to the metro, Sidney. . . ." Thwarted, she asks if I will have a quick cup of coffee with her before she descends into the metro. On the way to the café I find a shop that sells batteries, and I stop; and she—all too evidently used to being rebuffed—takes this as a dismissal. She wails pugnaciously: "Scholars can get to see a manuscript by Virgil with notes by Petrarch at the Ambrosiana. I didn't do *that,* either. Good-bye, good-bye." She trots off, sensible shoes, Michelin, sad face.

I take with me these lasting impressions: a Brueghel panel of six scenes in which angels rain posies and petals over a wintery landscape; a young, reposeful Brueghel Madonna in a ring of bright flowers, holding the Child and caressing one of his fat feet; a Caravaggio—one thinks his soul must have been so sweet, and yet he murdered a man—called *Basket of Fruit,* translucent grapes, light shining from and through them (light unto light, the grapes are without sin); and an engaging Brueghel of a mouse, a caterpillar, two roses, a butterfly *(Mouse and a Rose)* that answers Clive Bell's question "Does anyone feel the same kind of emotion for a butterfly or a flower that he feels for a cathedral or a picture?" As the Brueghel is both a picture and a butterfly and rose, the nice answer is Yes.

I also carry away with me from the old palace postcards of three fifteenth-century Arab miniatures, all of them bestiaries, my favorite a sweet-natured crocodile, prettily named *A Bird Polishing the Teeth of a Crocodile;* in the mouth of the scaled and sleepy beast a white bird solemnly pecks away. ("The human imagination never invented anything that was not true, in this world or any other"—Gérard de Nerval.)

My dinner of scotch and chocolate and fruit may have ill disposed me; on the day I visited the Pinacoteca Brera, no painting—neither brooding Madonna nor pale Crucifixion—would come alive for me. I found myself paying more attention to schoolchildren, fresh and lively in their responses, than to a Mantegna *Dead Christ* I had particularly wished to see. In the museum bar I fell in love again with Italian faces. But back in the galleries I felt once more what Hawthorne in *The Marble Faun* calls "the torment . . . in greater or lesser degree . . . of those who seek to enjoy pictures in an uncongenial mood . . . that icy demon of weariness who haunts great picture galleries. . . . A picture however admirable the painter's art, and wonderful his power, requires of the spectator a surrender of himself. . . . There is always the necessity of helping out the painter's art with your own resources of sensibility and imagination."

Resourceless, I climbed down flights of stairs crablike, my ghastly fear of steps returning, thinking a phobic's inflated thoughts, thinking of Christ's suffering and presuming to see in it an image of my own as, sick with vertigo and nausea and breathlessness, I slowly descended; then I argued with myself—for if Christ is my brother as well as my Lord, am I not allowed to join my sufferings to His (but to what end?)—and sick of myself, my phobia and folly, I wandered blindly down alleys and experienced a sudden change of mood: inner courtyards, their doors flung open. The Brera is the bohemian section of Milan, and, drug addicts notwithstanding, I felt a return to happiness and sanity. (Insanity is a lack of proportion.) I found a Tuscan restaurant with pots of tulips and dimity curtains where I ate tagliatelle with a sauce of tomato and cream; and giant crayfish; and a cream custard. However exquisite a cream custard is, it is always nursery food, which is why it is always good food.

Whenever, as at the Brera, I feel deficient in my responses, I remind myself that Montaigne had not seen fit, after his passage through Florence, to write a word about Michelangelo, Correggio, Leonardo, or Raphael. An ardor for art can't be wooed into existence; the sweet melancholy of reverie that looking at pictures requires and induces is not a state that can be summoned on demand. I had visited the Brera on a day when the pleasures it held out to me were too exalted to match my mood.

The Poldi Pezzoli Museum is not the product of an orderly mind, and in that lies its wacky charm. Gian Giacomo Poldi Pezzoli di Albertone was a nineteenth-century gentleman with a mania for things. He began by collecting Greek, Roman, and Etruscan arms and armor, and soon his bachelor apartment in an ocher-colored mansion near what is now Publishers' Row bristled with objets d'art. On August 15, 1943, the day before bombs partly destroyed the refectory housing *The Last Supper,* a bomb eviscerated the apartment of Poldi Pezzoli, destroying frescoes and walnut-and-ebony inlays; the museum was reopened in 1951. Only pictures of the ruined rooms—richly festooned, encrusted, embellished, crowded beyond logic or grace—exist now. The pictures are black-and-white, but they manage to suggest a deep blood red—crimson enlivened by the glimmer of crystal and gold and the white of porcelain or of bone.

The Poldi Pezzoli has a large collection of armor, crucifixes, and clocks, which have in common death and the passage of time, and so I imagined the leisured gentleman whose legacy this was to have been a connoisseur of Thanatos, and I wove stories in my head about a lonely death-obsessed Milanese—until I read that his apartments had been the center of "fervid intellectual activity" . . . and that the clocks had been donated after his death. This may or may not establish the supremacy of fiction over nonfiction, but it's a pity we are not able to see only those things amassed by Poldi Pezzoli himself, for then we would have had a picture of a single, singular nineteenth-century man instead of a contrived composite, and our imaginations could have played about him more fully. (An aggregate does not inspire musing.) But the intimate Poldi Pezzoli is engaging, an occasion for happily reflecting upon both the meaning and the poetry of objects, a pleasure not unlike having a leisured, exquisite meal.

Under the well of the elliptical stairway (a romantic, tickling fusion of the Baroque and Liberty styles), resting on tiles of black-and-white marble, is an elaborate fountain (cherubs and seashells crowned improbably with aspidistra), goldfish swimming therein. This excess prepares you for excesses—Venetian glass and Limoges enamel, silver and coral, alabaster, precious wood and gold, velvet and cloisonné, all hodgepodge—to come: tapestries (an altar cloth attributed to busy Beatrice d'Este, who seems to have conceived of Christ as a saturnine jack-in-the-box); sixteenth-century Greek folios; swords; seventeenth-century mirrors ornamented with chiseled bronze and rock crystal (it would take a great deal of vanity to say "Mirror, mirror on the wall" to this pair of mirrors, clearly of more importance than anyone whose image they might reflect); Flemish miniatures; porcelain (the curators exhibit plates peculiarly: They look like they are defying gravity or awaiting an astronaut's dinner); inlaid console tables; Islamic tiles; beer steins; a Botticelli Pietà; a collection of witty bronze satyrs; skulls; a Lotto Madonna (in it St. John regards the Infant, but Lotto loved Mary—and by implication all women—so our eyes go not to the Child but to the oval face, the deep-set hooded eyes and high cheekbones of a beautiful Mary, who is self-possessed and unperplexed); Persian rugs; a Mantegna Mother and colicky-looking Child, which is reverently called *Madonna and Sleeping Child,* but which is more suggestive of a child with a bubble of gas on his pouting lips; Lucas Cranach paintings of Martin Luther and of his wife, both looking so stern and homely one wonders what pleasures conjugality could ever have held for them; a fifteenth-century Florentine triptych of a sweetly surprised Mother and Child, and on the other side of the panels, leering, toothless skulls; and timepieces and clocks—timepieces built into opera glasses, bejeweled clocks, enamel clocks, clocks of crystal, watches set in rings, clocks with pastoral scenes and religious panoramas and mythological bas-reliefs, a pocket watch on the lid of which a woman impudently offers her lover her right breast, he already having taken possession of the left, a clock set in a crucifix, which is gratuitous (as time does not exist in eternity) as well as redundant (as we need nothing more than the death of Christ to remind us we are rushing toward Judgment Day). Perhaps its designer thought its owner might be enabled to count his long hours in Purgatory, or perhaps he believed that every day is Judgment Day, a proposition that modern life inclines one more and more to believe.

I was reflecting upon the clock in the cross as I drove to the house of friends for dinner. J., my host, comes from a Jewish family that converted to Catholicism after World War II; no explanation has ever been proffered J. for this conversion, but J. does know that his father was never devout. On one of the rare occasions that his father actually went to church, he turned to J. when the celebrant of the Mass elevated the Host and asked him what *that* was all about, sincerely ignorant, according to J. So one supposes that J.'s father converted for social reasons (or because he thought his survival depended on it) rather than for pietistic reasons. If this is the conclusion he has come to, J. is, on the subject, understandably reticent. "I am Jewish and I am Catholic," J. says if directly asked, but his circumstances have given birth to an odd streak of blank withdrawals in his cordial, garrulous, and pleasant personality. It is impossible for him to answer a question directly. I asked him (for example) whether he preferred to be called by his full name or his nickname. "Nobody ever asked me that before" was his reply.

J. remembers having been given a picture of a heart, on which, every time he told a lie or did a bad thing, he was obliged to make a black mark, until at last his heart was obliterated, black with sin.

This anecdote J. tells in the presence of a Jewish-American who was a member of the armed forces that liberated Dachau.

We are eating a dinner prepared by a chef from Emilia—tagliatelle with a sweet, delicate meat sauce; rolled fresh turkey breast stuffed with sage and parsley and mortadella; a salad green I have never seen before with an anchovy dressing; and hazelnut cookies. The wines match the food in excellence; but the evening—the combination of elements—makes my stomach sick, and I cannot sleep all night. J. says it must have been the sediment in the wine that kept me awake and irritable; I think it is the talk of camps and conversions.

I am having lunch with an American priest from a North Italian city. He asks me to meet him at Rinascente (across the piazza from the Duomo), suggesting that the food there is much better than the food one finds at "Italian restaurants," twenty years in Italy not having reconciled him to the fact that in Italian restaurants Italian food is served.

In the windows of Rinascente are mannequins dressed in black, and, in black letters on white silk banners, the words FASHION VICTIMS. The Italians do look facts—even lucrative facts—in the face. How much I like this.

On the phone Father V. sounded strained and jocular—as if he had seen *Going My Way* once too often and felt an imperative to be that movie phenomenon, a priest who is a "regular guy" with a heart of gold and a touch of the old blarney. "You'll expect to find someone six feet tall and handsome with blue eyes," he says, "and you'll find a little old man. . . ."

Before I meet Father V., I go to see Rinascente's exhibition of Marcello

Dudovich poster art, executed by the artist (1878–1962) in bold clean lines, to advertise the department store's wares. In posters drawn from 1939 to 1945, there is no hint that a war was being waged (smartly turned-out women in hiking clothes and evening clothes; geraniums). In a poster drawn in 1946 (swimsuits) there is no hint that a war is over. As I circle the room to view with tainted pleasure dozens of Deco posters, I see only two that suggest there ever was a war in Italy (though Milan was regarded as a stronghold of partisans): a 1941 poster of a heroic woman wreathed in chiffons soaring against a background of smokestacks; a 1938 poster of a young boy whose toy drums and toy guns may or may not suggest war.

This is not the first time I have noticed an eerie absence of history in Milan.

In one poster a woman casts her shadow the wrong way.

Father V.—neither very little nor very old—is a man who knows how to enjoy himself. He talks loudly, and in the sound of his voice he takes delight. He drinks from a wellspring of bitterness, and this nectar nourishes his sense of superiority. Standing on the cafeteria line, he asks if I have read "a book, written by some Jew, I think it must have been written by some Jew, that's what I think, some Jew—*In God's Name,* that's what I think it's called, about the death of Pope John Paul the First. Says he was murdered." (This last sentence he utters in a stage whisper.) I agree to send this book to him; I have no intention whatsoever of doing so. His bigotry not having yet exhausted itself, Father V. moves on to politics. (The only thing that keeps me from committing suicide by falling onto the steam table is that he is speaking in English.) "In my hometown they had two good Irish boys fighting each other for mayor, so it went to some black boy—oops! I can't say black boy anymore," he booms, *"colored man."*

I have already dipped my spoon into my pasta e fagioli when he begins to pray ostentatiously; he has presumably never heard of silent prayer.

I receive balefully his boast that he derives all his information and all his opinions from the English edition of *L'Osservatore Romano;* he reads just enough to justify his own sour views: "What's all that nonsense about priests going around in blue jeans? And those girls in blue jeans, who'd marry them? Priests with workers' hands [his own are white and soft and flabby], dressed like hoboes, bums, revolutionaries! Now, Cardenal [he pronounces the name of the Nicaraguan priest as if he were referring to a bird], good for him he got kicked out, the bum. Do we have a law or do we have a law? Do we have a Church or do we have a Church?"

"The American bishops—" I say.

"There is no American Church," he says. "There is only one Church. These Italian priests, I'll take them any day—they're more sophisticated, they don't spend their time sporting. And that liturgy you have in America. . . . You go to a church in *Greenwich Village?* Dancing around the altar. Disgraceful. We have a book; we go by the book, simple and dignified. The Americans who come to me, they're professionals; they're business people. Dignified. They have heads on their shoulders. They do what I tell them. Now, these worker priests, these revolutionaries. Why? I'm above you. You want to look up to me, right? Why should I come down to your level? I don't mean *your* level; you're all right. Why should I come down to your level?" He is spraying spittle on me. "We have to have dignity," he repeats, eating and talking about "ex-patriots." "We call them ex-patriots," he says, his mistaken grasp of the word suggesting that expatriates have lost their right to salute the American flag. To these people he ministers, and to Filipinos hired by Americans. (Any maid in Milan, including an Italian one, is likely to be called le Filippine.)

"A nun and a woman," he rambles on, "double trouble. Here they're good girls—not like your American nuns, always agitating, breaking God's law. They wear shorts! Shorts! And the women here on the beach—invisible bikinis, nude. Of course, I don't go to such beaches, but I hear, I hear. . . . Two fellas of my order, they were married. I guess two of your kind trapped them, eh?"

Perhaps, I say, it was the priests who trapped the women, or perhaps they fell in love and there is no blame, ideas which are to him novel and heretical; wasn't it Eve who offered the apple to Adam? And he pronounces, leaning back in his chair away from me, away from my cigarette smoke, from my Rinascente rings and my womanness, that there are three things that are keeping people out of the American Church: "The nonsense about contraception—do we have a law or do we have a law? And abortion. And divorce. Once you're married, you're married, that's it," he says grimly. Then he grills me about my own marital status and my religious devotions and those of my children, from whom may God keep such a man. His sisters all have more than six children; by these standards I am next to barren. When I say—stretching a point—that my daughter goes frequently to Nicaragua and is a friend of Cardenal's, he looks at me as if he has seen the face of evil.

"Nobody prays enough, nobody prays enough," he says, occasioning sympathy in me—the impoverishment of his life!—and also causing me to consider, unfruitfully, the uses of prayer to enlarge the soul. Halfheartedly, rather in the nature of a test, he asks if I will be coming to his church. Nothing could be further from my mind.

The impoverishment of his life. . . . He has never been to Florence or to the lakes or to Venice. A first-class train ticket from his city to Venice is sixteen dollars, and one to Lake Como under ten dollars; he will never love Italy.

I tell him I will remain behind to smoke a cigarette when he goes—I can see the friendly rooftop of the Duomo from where we sit—but the thought appalls him. Perhaps he has some outdated notions of chivalry, or perhaps (he has glanced more than once at my long red nails and at the rings I am wearing today) he is afraid that any breach of etiquette might lead onlookers to believe that ours was an illicit assignation. In a cafeteria of a department store.

On the elevator he continues to discourse about women in jeans (I am wearing a sober black dress), and I say good-bye to him sadly. Everything mean and small in my Church saddens me—and all in the shadow of the Duomo.

I try to think, as I watch his figure retreating, that there is something gallant about the poor old man cycling around his city on what he must construe as errands of mercy; I cannot.

BERGAMO: COMMEDIA DELL'ARTE

The next day I drove thirty miles with Bethany to Bergamo (where for lunch a pasta called *strozzapreti*, which means "strangled priests," recommended itself to my attention; and the waiter later brought us in goblets with green stems moscato d'Asti, a golden Piedmontese dessert wine, a wine that is capable of cheating one temporarily of unhappiness).

To get from the modern provincial lower city to its parental upper town, Bergamo Alta, one takes a funicular, which, against the background of Alpine slopes, makes a very nearly perpendicular ascent, though the ride is deceptively gentle, perhaps because it affords glimpses of the houses of the rich, some with loggias to dally on, and centuries-old frescoes intact. Then one hikes to the Piazza Vecchia, the historical center, wherein are contained and compressed five centuries of history. A maze of cobblestoned streets betrays the market origins of this lovely town: Via delle Scarpe, Via del Pesce (Street of Shoes, Street of Fish). Every third Sunday there is a flea market here. One can fortify oneself for the walk by pausing to rest at the Sala del Thé (where English voices flute among teacups).

Bergamo is beautiful. Full of medieval churches and palaces, towers and belfries, squares and green terraces and recessed wall fountains, it seems to dream over the plain below. It is girdled by massive sixteenth-century walls; and one feels enclosed in it as if in a crystalline bell jar, far above whatever is soiled and trite and brittle. The crisp mountain air is sweet. Stendhal, who admittedly became infatuated as often as a silly girl, called it "the most beautiful place on the earth and the most enchanting town I have ever seen."

Bergamo is lyrical (and Donizetti was born here). But its beautiful square was designed with practical intent, designed as an assembly place—and still it breathes, it is not a museum. . . . In Italy history is never stale.

In the harmonious Piazza Vecchia stands the Palazzo della Ragione, the oldest communal palace in Italy, perhaps one of the oldest town halls in the world. This building, symbol of the medieval free city, boasts an outside roofed staircase supported by five Romanesque columns, and a bas-relief of a winged lion—a reminder that Bergamo was once a possession of the maritime kingdom of Venice. Rising theatrically from the angles formed by the palazzo and the fourteenth-century staircase is a twelfth-century bell tower, the placement of which seems like the happiest accident—like New York's skyline, which no one could with such felicitous effect have planned. Opposite the Palazzo della Ragione is the marble-sheathed Palladian palace that closes the square to the north; the Civic Library (Biblioteca Civica), it is said to hold two hundred thousand books (twice as many books as Bergamo has citizens). In the center of the square (so prettily paved, worn bricks intersecting with worn stone) prettily stands a low fountain. The basin, its modest single jet emanating from the mouth of a sphinx, is surrounded by animals—half serpent, half lion—with facial expressions like those of devoted puppies. ("Obviously," says H. V. Morton, "no unworthy thought, much less a bloodthirsty one, ever entered their heads.") Each holds part of a heavy uniting chain in his mouth.

The piazza contains shops, a taverna, and several houses; it is not a stage set . . . young boys play soccer; it *is* a stage set . . . a fat priest with a bald pate, his brown tunic belted with rope, waddles by.

According to a local guidebook, jazz musician Ben Webster was sitting on the staircase below the bell tower several months before he died, ravaged by dope and drink, when he told an Italian journalist that in Bergamo he "left the world, my damned black world in which, deaf and blind, I have been living too long. . . . I sprang into this square and I discovered all these stones, the churches that stand over there, this fountain; perhaps I had never seen such a beautiful place and I felt my music spring up again inside, the music I played with Duke, when my saxophone used to play tireless, and I felt lonely, my aimless life. I started weeping. I'm sorry, maybe a man wouldn't have wept. I wept with emotion for joy and then with shame and rage. Because inside, believe me, I'm still the one I used to be. But my hands are trembling. I can hardly stand. My eyes are veiled. I'm finished; yet, in a square like this one, maybe for the last time, I could play my music and laugh and weep as a man does, not as the wretched man I have become." I knew Ben Webster. I used, with my first lover, a jazz drummer, to go to the Metropole bar to hear him play. (That the Metropole of the fifties is gone and the ancient bell tower remains is a short essay on the difference between two cultures.) I had never thought him wretched, I had only laughed and been gay with him, and these quoted words sound far too operatic to have been spoken by the funky, sweet-natured man I knew and liked. But if it is true that he was so deeply unhappy and if it is true that Bergamo gave him surcease from pain, that is reason enough to love Bergamo.

The arches that support the Palazzo della Ragione frame another piazza, Piazza del Duomo. The arcade formed by the arches offers more than vistas; it offers a feeling of safety and well-being, and for one beautiful piazza to unfold into another, even more beautiful piazza seems too good to be true. In this small piazza are the Colleoni Chapel, a baptistry, and a basilica. The Colleoni Chapel, with its trompe l'oeil facade of pink and gray and white and pale blue marble frosted with sculptures and medallions and surmounted by a pillared loggia and lit by a rose window—so gorgeous you almost don't want to go inside because it is difficult to believe that whatever is inside could surpass it (but inside there are frescoes by Tiepolo and panels of glowing inlaid wood depicting the life and passion of Our Lord by Lotto). On the steps of the octagonal baptistry of multicolored marble with red-marble statues of the Virtues were a pair of yellow roller skates. They looked at home, maybe because a small octagonal building seems very much as if it were made to suit a child's fancy. In fact, the octagon establishes the connection between the square shape, which symbolizes the earth, and the round, which symbolizes Heaven; the octagon symbolizes eternity, to which children, in an odd way, seem to belong more than do adults, who belong to time; to square a circle has been called the prime example of illogical effort—but that is what the octagon does. The Romanesque Basilica of Santa Maria Maggiore, as golden and light, inside, as summer wine, hasn't an inch that is not decorated by paintings, frescoes, and tapestries; it ought to be too "busy," but to say that is to say that the heart of a multifaceted diamond is too busy—and who could not find irresistible those frescoes and a Last Supper attributed to the school of Giotto, which look, amidst this richness of art and Baroque confessionals, almost primitive, like a Grandma Moses, so sincere and eloquent of integrity? It doesn't seem credible that Augustinian hermits reproached Giotto for producing things more for the sake of pomp and pride than for the glory of God. His people look so human; they have physical presence; they tell a true story. What Boccaccio said of Giotto appears to be true of his disciples (if one leaves some room for loving hyperbole): "Nature can produce nothing he has not painted equally like and even identical with it; as a result men are often mistaken on seeing the things he did, taking the painting for the truth." One always feels that Giotto's paintings are the truth, even if they are not the literal truth.

As we left the church, an old woman on a red motorcycle zipped in and out of the arches; she wore mourning black, but she was made up like Elizabeth I—chalk-white face powder and scarlet circles of rouge.

A madman with an aquiline profile, high-heeled boots, a cape artfully and arrogantly tossed, stalked us—but only in order to strike poses in doorways and arches. Bergamo is, after all, the birthplace of the commedia dell'arte, and the madman embodied its spirit of spontaneity and caricature; he was benign.

In all this Bethany and I took appropriate pleasure; we liked the boutiques of Bergamo Alta, too, though one is supposed to deplore them. Those who deplore them are those whose presence created them—tired Milanesi, world-weary rich—and soon they will be saying Bergamo is ruined.

Frank Lloyd Wright said it was impossible to visit Bergamo without being stunned and astonished.

I felt—and feel—somewhat false in relation to Bergamo: I saw, much more than I felt, its beauty; I trumped up the appropriate feelings. This I took for being jaded.

On our way to the lower town, Bethany and I stopped at a dim church, St. Pancrazio. There we saw a waxen image of St. Anna, worthy of Madame Tussaud; also two tiny, misshapen skulls (whose?). Bethany has a superstitious horror of relics. Italians may have an intellectual revulsion for relics, but relics hold no terror for them. This is because they know that they will die. They know this in their marrow.

The next day I took a train to Stresa, on Lake Maggiore.

* * *

It's as much a mistake to be indiscriminately enthusiastic about Italian train travel as it is to damn it for its inefficiency.

When I was twenty-five, a quarter of a century ago, I started off from Paris, my destination being Florence, and I had to change trains in Milan. I had made the mistake of traveling on Holy Thursday. The crowds on the train platform were dense with southerners going back home from their jobs in the industrial North; I could not hold a container of coffee in my hands without getting jostled and scalded. (I was so tired I forgot the Italian word for milk.) I let several trains and several hours pass by, I purchased a seat reservation. When my train rolled in, the eager waiting men threw their suitcases into open windows; then they scrambled on while the train was still in motion and ran up and down the aisles of the moving train in an effort to find their tossed belongings. They ripped off all the reserved-seat signs, and they clogged the entrance to each compartment. When I got through this wall of human flesh, I could find neither my seat nor any other seat unoccupied. I stood outside a compartment. I'll cry, I thought; that always works in Italy. Why are you crying? a man asked from the compartment nearest me. Because I'm pregnant, I said, which, although I didn't know it, was true. He ordered a young man to stand. I sat next to my savior, who wiggled his hand under my thigh. (Well, he deserves *something,* I thought; that was a quarter of a century ago, when pretty young girls always thought they were on the debit side of the ledger.) At Florence the aisles were so crowded with bodies and valises I could not get off. I traveled all the way to Rome, where I had, for Good Friday, Holy Saturday, and Easter Sunday, no hotel reservation. (At a *pensione* improbably called the Bellavista Milton, the manager set up a cot for me behind the reception desk, where, from twelve at night to seven in the morning, I was able to sleep. The manager was deranged; she insisted she was having an affair with the Pope. In all other respects she was sane, and she was very pleasant.)

I concluded from this experience that the train station in Milan was Hell.

The station was, this time, as I boarded the train for Stresa, only gloomy and (within Italian limits) orderly. In my second-class compartment a well-dressed young man offered boldly to sell me gold chains, "eighteen karat." The arrival of a young woman sent him scurrying, with a wink and a shrug, away.

The young woman was called Antonella. (She was twenty; why can't I call her a girl? Why does feminist usage demand the sacrifice of this springtime word? Would anyone dream of describing a Botticelli maiden as a young woman? And Mary was a girl.)

Antonella tells me all about her family. I tell her all about mine. (This telling is a ritual on Italian trains.) She comes from a village in the foothills of the Alps—no tourists! she says, half rueful, half pleased. She watches "Dallas" on TV, and she thinks New York must look like Dallas, and that Brooklyn, where I live, must consist of houses like J. R. Ewing's ranch. I try to disabuse her of the idea that I live on a ranch, as a result of which, when we pass a dreary suburb of Milan, she dimples and says: "Brooklyn!"

Antonella examines my makeup kit as gravely and frankly as a child, calling out the Italian words for lipstick, nail polish, rouge. Antonella—in her first year of medical school—has never seen Naples, Florence, Venice, Rome; but she is young, she says—ten years younger than I must be, she says, dimpling (what happy fictions Italians invent, and how gently and far they take us into intimacy). Antonella knows only one sentence of English; she does not remember where or why she learned it, or whence it derives, or precisely what it means. The sentence is: "The virtues that attach to your youth are the virtues that attach to your age."

STRESA: HÔTEL DU LAC

You pay a double tariff for great hotels: Hauteur goes with the cosseting. Or so I thought when I walked through grand and silent rooms to a small dusty-rose and blue dining salon and was received with what appeared to be bemused contempt. I was told (but not for several awkward moments) that I had entered a working school for employees. The employees were embarrassed, not contemptuous, though the same could not be said of the clerk who deposited my traveler's checks in the safe-deposit box in apparent disbelief that I had no important jewelry to leave with her.

It is out of season, and the Hotel des Îles Borromées, a splendid Victorian heap, is empty: I dine alone in whiteness whiter than the white Alps: three layers of silken white curtains on windows that overlook the lake, icy white frosting on a warm white ceiling, milky white Venetian glass wall sconces. Homely white daisies on my snowy white table linen gently mock the Victorian opulence.

Before I sleep, I prowl—from the carpeted hush of my wing through swinging doors to a long corridor of varnished doors; halls tiled in a pattern of fleur-de-lys, no sign of life. This part of the hotel must be where the servants of emperors and queens once stayed. I would welcome a ghost, but instead, curled under down quilts, I watch television: "One Life to Live," dubbed; an Italian documentary about Oxford and Cambridge—how foreign the British look when the narrator's voice is Italian! How snowy my bed linens are, how soothing the splashing of the lake. On late-night television Marilyn Monroe is eulogized.

Palm trees and Alps—this juxtaposition amazes me, as does the fact that there *are* Italian Alps, the effect of reading *Heidi* having been to convince me that the Alps belong only to Switzerland.

After lunch (three businessmen eat yogurt, reinforcing my obdurate belief that I am really in Switzerland), I walk alone on the grand esplanade along Lake Maggiore, alone except for scuttling lizards and one old man taking a dignified stroll. All around me hotels and shops are shuttered and shut. Voices ring long away and hollow in the solitude; where do they come from? Only dandelions are thriving now; magnolia buds are tightly curled. The lake water is clear. I would love to swim in that water fed by Alpine streams. I am warm in my light coat. But when I bend to stare into the water's depths, my face feels very cold.

In the late afternoon the lapidary waters turn plum-colored; the Alps turn rosy, and then they recede into mist. On Isola Bella, the Borromean palazzo is sternly and arrogantly gray, impervious to sunlight . . . a gray, sooty wedding cake, like Miss Haversham's. At night the lights of the mountain town across the lake sparkle like a queen's necklace, flashing against snow like rubies, sapphires, emeralds against snowy white fur.

Perhaps it is the loneliness and theatricality of an empty grand hotel, perhaps it is the rock music I hear on my bedside radio: I find myself thinking of other voices, other times—Italians dancing on raised platforms, dancing gaily to Italian popular music under strings of colored lights in small towns in Libya, dancing against borrowed time, time borrowed from a sick old man, King Idris, who lay resting, dying, in an American hospital on an American air force base on the Mediterranean—the sun was setting for them, too; soon they would be sent away from Tripoli and Benghazi and from the oases they had made their own, sent "home" to a home they only dimly remembered or remembered not at all; their nostalgia for what they knew, knew slightly, or knew not at all warred with their fear and they danced. . . . In the pre-Islamic oasis of Gadames, I slept in a bed that had once accommodated Sophia Loren, in a hotel built for a movie company, a hotel that had one permanent guest—an Englishman who shot pigeons—and a dirty barefoot waiter and a never-visible cook. The sheik of Gadames had once seen Josephine Baker dance in Paris; this memory was to him something in the nature of a sacrament. And I, he said, was even more beautiful than

Sophia Loren. O sad world . . . thinking of that long-ago Libyan gallantry I fall asleep, dreaming of the Englishman armed with a rifle to shoot pigeons for our lunch.

The mountains are like white bunting, and I sleep secure.

Morning, six-thirty, and the sun makes an orange path from the sky to the lake and gilds the white chairs on my balcony outside the snowy white curtains of my window. Sun. After all the dreary days in Milan. My room is flooded with light; I feel as if light is an element I could swim in.

My waiter used to be a ship's steward; now (he looks at Lake Maggiore as if it were an impertinent puddle) he has a wife and children, he is landlocked. What he liked best about New York, his favorite port of call, was "Broadway Times Square," where (he marvels still) every newspaper in the world could be bought; I don't have the heart to tell him it is no longer so. He liked best to see Marx Brothers movies on Forty-second Street; he liked the smell of popcorn—a smell that recalls innocence to me. He likes the feel of certain English words. He exalts the merits of porridge—"porridge, porridge, porridge," he says; "it is a nice word, no?" Yes. And he likes to say Palermo—"Palermo, Palermo, Palermo, Arab gold," he says; "Milan is Austrian gray." On the sideboard there are dragon lilies and Parma ham, the flesh of meat and flower equally delectable.

Long, echoing walks in Stresa are bracketed by meals. Lunch is mozzarella in carrozza—fresh white mozzarella cheese melting between two pieces of golden batter-fried bread, an anchovy at the center to redeem it from blandness; dinner is calf's liver, razor-thin, sautéed in onions and parsley and white wine. . . .

"I will make you a good price," the concierge says, which words, usually disingenuous, usually preface avarice. But when *il capitano* arrives in his blue canopied motorboat to take me to the Borromean Islands (very gay the boat is, and it looks almost lakeworthy as well), the price—fifteen dollars—*is* good; and *il capitano*'s manners are lovely, and I am all alone to tour the Borromean Islands, which suits me.

On Isola Bella the Borromean Palace is closed. Dead wood burns, giving the island a pleasant, nutty aroma; the season has not yet begun. Two pink peacocks strut on the terraced grounds of the palace. It is a feudal world, but the houses, with rotting wooden balconies on twisting alleys, all lead— the view is the same for commoner, serf, or prince—to the lake, hence to the Alps. The islanders, in preparation for the tourists to come, are in a flurry, sweeping and washing narrow streets, setting up stalls. *Il capitano* helps a villager set up a pegboard for his stall while I wander; later I find him sitting in his boat, grinning and making mock bows to grinning workers—*"Sono un turista* [I am a tourist]," he says, and he good-naturedly invites me to join in the joke as we make for the neighboring Isola dei Pescatori.

One looks for an occasion to rise to, just as one wishes to be taken out of oneself (the impulse is identical), and Isola dei Pescatori provides it. ("What can one say of Lake Maggiore, and of the Borromean Islands . . . except to pity people who do not go mad over them?" Stendhal asked.) The Island of the Fishermen has its own little esplanade, and its own dignity, dignity not borrowed from the grand signore of the palazzo of Isola Bella, but dignity owing to pride in honest work. Stalls have already been set up by people with kind country faces. (Wooden Pinocchios abound.) From balconies hang fishing nets, some plastic—lime green, pale pink, electric fuchsia—some old rope intricately knotted. No hands are idle. Women sit outside; they watch the show and are part of the show. They knit; men repair their fishing boats. The fresh smell of lake water mingles with the rich, dark smell of alluvial soil. The first daffodil shows itself. A man turns over the black soil of his garden. Beds are made; in the newness of the day, straw mattresses are flung on windowsills to freshen. There are more cats than people here, say the two ladies from whom I buy chocolate in a cool shop on a narrow street; in winter the cats sleep in empty houses. How *brutta* that one is, says one signora; *povera gatta,* it has no *padrone*—and ugly it is, scarred and embattled and mean; ranks of cats just sitting, cats in packs pouring out of alleys, feral, untouchable; twin black cats sit unblinking near the village Church of San Vittorio, its white belfry rising above the red-gabled tumbledown houses. Ancient floor mosaics, the bleached newness of wooden pews—a small church, but its bell has a great silver tongue, to warn of disaster, to sound hope. Sprays of hot-colored flowers are scattered all over the altar and against the pale gray stone, such perfect sprays I thought at first they were of wax. Red and tangerine zinnias big as tea plates on their fleshy, springy stems. Here, in a fishermen's village, frescoes by an unknown artist, candelabra and crucifixes of silver, gold, and coral, all unguarded. What a good place to pray . . . bearing in mind that Peter was a fisherman before he was a fisher of men.

Up and down flights of worn stone steps—no fear, here, of getting lost or harmed. . . . I see what I think is a private garden, its gates hospitably open. It is a tiny cemetery, Alps looming over a few dozen tenderly cared-for graves. The same half-dozen names appear over and over, the pictures inset on tombstones show a resemblance of features; this is an island of relatives. The first hyacinths of the season bloom on the grave of Felice Zaccheria,

1892–1976. *Felice* means "happy." On the tombstone of someone named Ugo there is a picture of a young man sweet and sober in a turtleneck sweater; 1935–1972—a cutoff life. On his grave is a simple bronze sculpture over which grows wandering Jew. Sometimes one is moved to grieve for someone one does not know. Who is the real object of this cleansing grief? Is it he, Ugo? Or is the griever grieving for herself? In a cemetery on a sunny day, grief is almost indistinguishable from happiness.

I hear a voice call, *"Guten Tag!"* A German tourist, so relieved to hear her own voice speaking German she assumes my Germanness.

In the window of a shop I see a wooden box covered with lentils sunk in resin. It is so inventive in its ugliness I almost buy it. I have the feeling that the Italian who made this atrocity has been to America. In Little Italys all over America these things, or things of equal ugliness, are sold; what happens to people's aesthetics when they are uprooted?

In the Unione restaurant to which *il capitano* directs me there are vases of cherry blossoms, also a coal stove and a fireplace, on its hearth copper pots that are put to use. (The signora yells out over the balcony to a passing boy to get me some cigarettes.) I have a simple *aglio e olio* (garlic and oil) pasta, and—the bartender at the hotel has told me to ask for this—a huge plate of *arborelli,* tiny fried fish, each two and a half inches long (I think there must be thirty-five of them); they are sprinkled with coarse salt and lemon and their skin is crunchy and their flesh is sweet and their bones are unthreatening, as are their edible fins. But there is a bitter aftertaste. I am convinced the bitter aftertaste comes from their little round eyes. I wash this down with a headache-inducing Piedmontese rosé wine. Aftertaste and headache notwithstanding, this day has been an occasion for rising.

The entire village has been put on the alert to watch for me. I am thoughtlessly an hour late for my captain, who has sent a friend to meet me. *Il capitano*'s colleague takes me back to Stresa in his boat—in which there are several pictures of Marilyn Monroe.

Her vanilla-and-honey sexiness in a land of sun-ripened olive beauty, her white, whispery, beckoning sultriness, the promise of accessibility, availability, readiness, the baby innocence and the adult heat; always ready, always vulnerable: The Italian infatuation with Marilyn exceeds our own. A Milanese designer makes a sofa in the shape of red lips slightly parted and calls it "Marylin."

When I arrive at the hotel, I find *il capitano* seated in his parked car, his forehead creased with worry: Where have I been? He is dressed in a nautical blazer and white sharkskin trousers; I love it when a man richer than I am worries about me. I love it that a man I took to be a simple villager drives an Alfa Romeo.

Because it is my last day, Giuseppe, the concierge, wants to show me the hotel's new and unused exercise and fitness center. Looking like a stage Italian in his silly cutaway suit, he takes me over vast expanses of mirrorlike parquet; he is like a sacristan showing me a hidden Titian.

"Who will come here?"

"Only Americans and very rich Italians," Giuseppe ("call me Joe") says; and then he takes me to the pool, in a room of blue and white tiles, a warm virgin pool. Joe reads my face, mouths *"Mezz'ora,"* and slips out of the sanctuary. I undress and dreamily swim, buoyant, abandoned, floating half asleep for half an hour till Joe knocks discreetly and I leave the receiving warm water.

Bethany and I want to go to the Triennale, the Palazzo dell'Arte, an insolent building of Fascist design, in the Parco Sempione, to see an exhibition of furniture design called (from a title of Goethe's) "Elective Affinities."

("Are you married?" Bethany's housemaid, a lame woman in her forties, asks me. "No, not now," I say. "Are you?" "Ah," she says triumphantly, "me—never. I am unchained.")

Sometimes it seems that everything functional that Italian designers put their hands to is beautiful. But I remember an exhibit of Milanese "environments" at the Museum of Modern Art over a decade ago. These "environments" were touted as a solution to what we used to call the overpopulation problem; they ended up not in the service of the poor but as playthings for the rich, tucked in corners of grand salons, like jungle gyms or monkey bars for grown-up rich kids. My memory of them may work to caricature them, but not, I think, to exaggerate their fatuity.

Once America had a good space-saving idea called the Murphy bed: You pressed a button, and the bed, cleverly concealed, fell out from its hiding place in a false wall. The Murphy bed lent itself to lots of sight gags in forties movies, but no one doubted its usefulness. Imagine a mad genius enlarging and going haywire with the concept of a Murphy bed and you get some idea of Milanese "environments." In bright primary colors, the compact plastic units (none bigger than an average-sized walk-in closet) were composed of several parts, each of which became something else as need dictated: With the flick of a button a bed became a table; a stove doubled as a desk; a commode doubled as a reading chair, from which a light sprouted; refrigerators were nestled under bureaus, which also served as bookcases . . . and *ooh!* and *ah!* everybody said, *how clever!* "I hope I die before the world turns into that," said my young son. "It's all right if you want to live in an airplane cockpit," said my younger daughter. Some things you couldn't imagine in these sterile environments were: clutter; a baby; a flower pot; a cat. They are still much praised in Milan as prototypes. (But prototypes for what?) While Rome, devoted to spectacle, may in its least successful aspects be regarded as subject matter for Mel Brooks, Milan might be more appropriate subject matter for Woody Allen.

"Elective Affinities" once again set itself the grandiose task of "proving its commitment towards the major problems arising from the historic evolution of economics and society, and from the new technical and scientific revolution . . ." and while I was captivated by such whimsy as a multicolored chest of drawers with big brass handles that had WILLIAM AND MARY written on it in bold black script, I did not see, quite, how this witty and decorative bureau (by American architect Robert Venturi) fulfilled its mandate to "offer a rational solution for problems connected with our life and existence." Many pieces—there were twenty-one, not all by Italian designers, though all produced by the manufacturers and craftsmen of nearby Lissone— were witty; the inflated rhetoric accompanying them was only funny. ("This exhibition may be considered a long voyage to the discovery of ideas and feelings and into the realm of the operative niceties. . . .") "The City of Affinities" was arranged on two levels, approached through "computer-generated" arches and ramps.

Here, on the lower level, purporting to represent "memory . . . the DNA, the genes of designers," is an Esso gas station, a floor of white and green. Above it on a raised platform is an étagère/cupboard/desk chair, pearlized, laminated, by Ettore Sottsass, dean of Italian designers, leader of the Memphis group, producers of instant camp. What do gas pumps have in common with Sottsass's furniture? Sottsass says the "more or less Arab flooring" represents "the value of the culture of the South, the soft color, the long vaporous nights. . . ." And the gas pumps represent "the scents of contemporaneity." But what either the gas pumps or the "Arab" flooring has to do with an étagère made of garish pearlized plastic laminates and fake woods remains a mystery. It was a mistake to try to forge a connection between the lower level, called by the curator "the evocative dimension," and the thing—the design—itself. To insist upon evocations is a form of bullying, as one does not wish to be told what one is looking at or what it should evoke in one, and also as an artist's unconscious is, except to a clinician, far less interesting than the tactile and conscious and tangible work of his hands. In any case, an artist's unconscious is not always available to him *except* through his work, and all verbal attempts to explain it usually are crashing bores or, at best, inadequate.

If one succeeded in ignoring the words and the cacophonous music that blared unceasingly and if one didn't on principle disapprove of the flamboyant and nonfunctional, pleasure—even a measure of enchantment—was to be had. One does not, after all, have to capitulate to Sottsass's imperative to idealize the outrageously gaudy and the kitschy (and the expensive); Sottsass doesn't have to be taken up on his dare, though fashionable Milan dictates that he must.

I don't know designer Emilio Ambasz, but his unconscious—which I have no desire to be privy to—must reveal itself in dreams in the form of poetry. Ambasz created a "Library in the Garden"—bookcases of precious woods and beveled glass that, acting as doors, swung open to reveal leather-bound books and old photographs in a house made for daydreams and repose, a house roofed in latticework densely covered by green leaves. No one, seeing that house, could possibly wish not to crawl into it for green and leafy shelter. From another aperture one sees, inside the house, a chair facing a bookcase. Books are stories, and an empty chair facing a bookcase tells a story: Someone is coming; someone has left—stories within stories . . . and stories are for consuming . . . a house one could eat, like a gingerbread house, or wear, like a skin.

Swiss Mario Botta designed a "Transparency"—a piece of furniture designed for two persons sitting opposite each other, "a kind of transparent lay confessional . . . a bosom-space." The gorgeously crafted sculptural piece made of elegantly thin strips of beechwood was so romantic and amusing it almost supported the weight of Botta's words. It had no practical function—no one would really want to sit in a beechwood cylinder for very long—but it could be taken as metaphor for intimacy or as metaphor for isolation—and it certainly made one wish to rush to Lissone. It was, in the words of another designer, Rafael Moneo (who constructed a very sensible Cubist desk), one of "those small, complete, self-sufficient universes in which things live happily together as if they had found their natural habitat"; it was chrysalis and nest, and like old-fashioned porches, it offered a gentle barrier, permitting the sitters to feel secluded from the world and, at the same time, permitting the gaze of the world to enter the secluded space. (A porch on a summer night is one of the most potent images in the language of remembrance.) It was wonderful, though I do not think it will solve the problems of the future.

In a smaller exhibition of theoretical design at the Triennale, I found a table, electronically controlled, on which one could create, by body warmth, a doily—the *word* DOILY. The old-fashioned word *doily* leaping out of a table of futuristic design was a marvelous conceit. By means of this conjunction, I was struck with the notion that Milan exists somewhere between the future and the past—but not exactly in what I understand to be the present.

The odd mixture, not just of nostalgia but of reverence for nostalgia and determination to provide the world with prototypes (the lower level of the exhibition became more "readable" if one saw in it not the "unconscious" of the designer but his conscious yearning for what was past), is a melancholy mixture. The melancholy of Milan may be dressed to kill, it may be almost unrecognizable, but it is as pervasive as the diesel fumes, the staccato tapping of heels on marble.

The well-known journalist has just moved into a new apartment; we sit on crates in her living room. The elaborate security system is in place; a Warhol Monroe is on one white wall; nothing else is unpacked. "What famous people have you seen? Do you want to see famous people?" She punctuates her remarks with these questions, trying to place me by the people I have seen. "And who are the new important writers in America?" she asks, answering her own question. "There is Tom Robbins," she says, "and there is Joan Didion, who is the new Susan Sontag, who is the new Mary McCarthy, who is not so good anymore. . . . N. didn't answer my phone calls," she says, referring to an American writer whose first novel went directly to the best-seller list. The journalist's ego is bruised. "Once, she said she was asleep, and another time she told me to call again at ten. She must have thought I was a little nothing, and I had written a big review of her book. I review everything fashionable from America. I create the fashion. What do you think of postfeminist writing? Do you agree that all that feminism accomplished is that now you have to go to dinner Holland treat? . . . D. didn't answer my calls either, but one knows she is a very sick woman, she sent me a nice letter. Tell N. when you see her I am not a little nothing." The journalist is credited with having introduced Hemingway to Italy (a documentary of Hemingway, who is again in vogue here, is being shot in Venice as we speak), and Kerouac, too—"whom the literary establishment here doesn't appreciate. . . . How well do you know N.? As you can see, I am not a little nothing."

"What is Milan about?" I ask. "Fashion?"

"Money," she says.

"Design?"

"Money," she says.

"Publishing?"

"Money," she says. . . . "How does N. get Meryl Streep to star in her movies? Are you on good terms with N.? Are you well known to each other?"

In an attempt to get her off the sore subject of N.—for she genuinely wishes to help me, though she doesn't get the point of me at all—I tell her what it was like to live with first-generation Italian immigrant parents. She seizes upon my parents' use of language.

"How did they say 'bathroom'?"

"Back-ouse—because, you see, they had an *out*house and so they were saying 'backhouse' with an Italian accent. I thought all the time I was growing up that was the word for bathroom."

"An *outhouse?"*

"Yes; and *on-gup* was their corruption for 'upstairs' and they said *on-bash* for 'downstairs,' because *on-bash* meant 'basement,' and they said 'open the light' and 'close the light,' which is a transliteration from the Italian for 'turn the light on' or 'turn the light off.'. . ."

"I don't understand about the light."

"Well, it doesn't matter."

"They were from the South?"

"Yes. Abruzzo and Calabria."

"Oh!" says the journalist, happy at last. "You are writing a book about WOP."

"I'm sorry?"

"About WOP. About the WOP language."

"Yes, I suppose you might say that."

I go with the journalist to the Caffè Milano on Piazza Mirabello. Food is not the reason people go to the Caffè Milano. A small bowl of greasy penne with ricotta is set before me. The journalist says, "I am protected here. . . . And if you came in alone, they would glare at you."

M., a woman with pink hair, joins us; she is described as a punk architect, and I am introduced to her as an American writing a book about WOP. "Do you want to go to an alternative disco?" she asks.

A long parade of people passes our table. Some greet the journalist, some chat, some sit; all are introduced as "famous." Famous editors, architects, writers, painters, famous heads of failed publishing houses. Everybody is carefully dressed so as not to look carefully dressed.

"Do you know Bob Blackman?" someone asks.

"Who?"

"But of course you know Bob Blackman, he lives at Thirty-nine Central Park West!"

"No."

"But you must! He is a great graphics designer."

"No."

"Ah, well," says the former head of a collapsed publishing company, "I wish to move to New York City—I *do* know Bob Blackman—or if that is too expensive—of course, you are richer than we will ever be in our wildest dreams—to Westport. Do you know Paul Newman, who lives there?"

"No," I say.

"She hasn't met Calvino," says the journalist, who is really very kind to me, considering that I haven't met Paul Newman or Italo Calvino or a graphics designer who lives at 39 Central Park West. Her husband, a famous designer, left her years ago for "A SLUT A WHORE SHE WORE GOLD LAMÉ AND RED DRESSES." "I always wore *this* color," she says, fingering my fawn-colored tunic. "Where does Woody Allen eat dinner? Where is Elaine's restaurant? . . . My husband had male menopause. In Italy men want a mother or wife—the same thing—until they grow up. Then they divorce and marry a daughter. They don't grow up till they're sixty, and then where are you, where is the wife? . . . Perhaps you could write down on this napkin the address of Elaine's. Is Woody Allen known to you? . . . Verdiglione is a madman, a Fascist; also, our prime minister is a Fascist. . . ."

A sweet-faced man married to an editor says, "Milan is so boring, there is no fun. It is like the Duomo—all that work, all that restlessness, for what . . . Politics? *Una commedia.*" That morning Ezio Tarantelli, a forty-five-year-old university professor who advocated union reforms to curb inflation, was killed by the Red Brigades with twenty shots from a submachine gun. . . . "So boring."

"Verdiglione put Burroughs here in a freezing room, poor man, with no blankets and no drugs. A very bad man, Verdiglione, but unimportant."

"The alternative disco is called Plastic."

"No one reads Moravia anymore."

"You mean Morante."

"I mean Moravia."

"Hemingway hated museums till he got to the Prado. He wanted *Death in the Afternoon* to be like a Goya. . . . Will you write down the address of Elaine's?" My slowness is owing to the fact that I do not know the address of Elaine's. . . . "Write it! Write it!" I give up and scribble an address in the general area of Elaine's. . . . "Are you known there?"

"I traveled with friends to Russia, they said I must not act as if my life were over because that bastard left me . . . and then the flight was canceled and everybody ran off to telex or phone and I had nobody in the world to phone. Good fortune I don't have children, because they would all grow up to be on drugs or they would be terrorists or they would be kidnapped."

"You think we are cynical? We are."

"How were the Caravaggios?"

"I hate curators."

"Yes, but how were the Caravaggios?"

"Italy is a wonderful combination of anarchy and chaos."

"Everybody believes he can write; everybody believes writing is a communal endeavor."

"It is because of the Communists."

"It is because of the Fascists."

"We have a Socialist government. It is because of the Socialists."

"The Socialists *are* Fascists."

"The Caravaggios were very diffident."

"You mean the curator was diffident."

"No, I mean the Caravaggios were diffident."

"This is a famous American journalist."

"Ah, yes, I saw her walking in here looking as if she had a grip on things."

"There is an alternative disco."

"Do you have a grip on things?"

"That girl has a very famous Italian surname," the journalist whispers to me. I look up from my gin and orange to see a woman with enormous gray-green eyes dressed in a red raw-silk suit, a red scarf, wooden beads; no makeup. She has just written a book about the journalist's ex-husband, "that bastard." She is "very very rich and has a famous name," the journalist whispers, and she beams upon the biographer of her ex-husband, "that bastard."

"And what is your new Rajneesh name, dear G.?" she says. "One forgets."

G. smiles. She takes my hand captive and says: "I used to be very aggressive and fuck a lot. I went to Brazil and I went to Turkey and Tibet and I found nothing—"

"Nobody goes to Brazil," says someone in a Valentino dress with green hair who appears to be snorting cocaine.

"—And then I met a very kind man with very kind eyes who told me to go to Poona, and so I did. When I met Rajneesh, I knew not one word of English. He was in any event not speaking one word that year, it was his time of silence. He looked into my eyes and into my soul. He knew me. When he began to speak, every word he said was meant for me. Every woman at this café is embittered by men—"

"Let me tell you who is bisexual and who is sleeping with whom," the journalist says. "These are facts a journalist must know—"

"—So much better than Catholicism, which is all mystery and dogma, and Buddhism, which is fundamentally unacceptable. Rajneesh would say the most profound thing and the next moment the filthiest, filthiest jokes. Americans cannot understand this playfulness. . . . In Italy weird things will happen to you. But you must be positive. My biography is positive. I don't write about flaws. . . . Weird things will happen. . . ."

Not the least weird of which (considering that she has just in fact placed a curse on me) is that the next evening G. arrives at my residence unannounced with a friend—the picture editor of a popular glossy—as I am preparing to settle in with cheese, scotch, and *The Confessions of St. Augustine,* having given sufficient thought to the small, incestuous world of the Caffè Milano, where being a Rajneeshi does not prevent G.—given her famous surname—from being a regular. Milanesi like their playthings.

We walk a mile to G.'s Mercedes. Then we drive a quarter of a mile to an expensive restaurant called Rigolo near the Caffè Milano, and then we park on the pavement. G. disregards the COMPLETELY OCCUPIED sign and is given precedence over others waiting in line. Her parents, she says, as we eat a beautiful pasta coated with the thick green-black ink of squid, were among the first to be divorced in Italy; she went, she says, "from revolution—I had a left-wing lover, very violent"—she pauses to see what effect this has on me; I regard the squid ink, which is forming into little green-black beads—"and then when that was over, I took up masturbation and then feminism, and then I was part of the gay movement"—another pause; I try to arrange my face so that I can appear to look neutral and nonjudgmental, which I am not—"and then I took a male gay lover—and then Rajneesh. And I have been with him for six years. . . .

"Sannyasis—his followers—are sixty percent Jewish, so of course they're clever and that's why the Ku Klux Klan hates them for having taken over in Oregon. . . ."

"Well, I don't think that can be exactly right," I say.

"We are given complete freedom of fucking!" (Nobody in the restaurant wishes to give the appearance of having noticed this outburst.) "But when AIDS happened"—what am I doing with this woman?—"Rajneesh said for the good of the community we must fuck with condoms and gloves. OK. I always fucked a lot. I got my identity from men. All the time crying. There are no real men. Look at poor P., acting like a widow for ten years because her husband left her, all the time crying. This city is dead. Communism is finished. Feminism is finished. Florence is for the English, Naples is Mafia, Rome is bureaucracy, Milan and Turin and Genoa are for Calvinists, and the South is lazy and stupid. . . . I will not come to America and be treated like a stupid WOP. Will they open restaurants for me in New York? I will not trade on my family's name. . . . Perhaps you would like to see my stepmother in Rome? She is after all only a contessa, quite poor, but you will see how ordinary people live. . . ."

The night porter at my residence has got it into his head that I have come to Milan for the season at La Scala, and whenever possible he commiserates with me because the house is closed. The day before I am due to leave Milan he delivers with heartfelt happiness the news that the strike is over—his city has not entirely failed me or mortified him.

Bethany, with great industry and application, has been able to secure for me tickets for *The Magic Flute,* which Stendhal, who drank iced sherry here, saw, and which he didn't particularly fancy (nor do I); the Italians of 1828 liked Mozart's opera even less: "Their eyes seemed to say, 'Is there really another music than that of Italy?'"

La Scala, which holds three thousand people, has the quality shared by all great theaters: It is both intimate and grand. It is a treat to stand in the lobby, with its busts of Rossini, Bellini, Donizetti, and Verdi, and watch the brilliantly dressed expectant audience. The house is full of children, as if *The Magic Flute*—which has not been seen here since the 1955–1956 season—were to Eastertide what the *Nutcracker* is to American children at Christmastide. I have a house orchestra seat on the aisle, to which I am shown by ushers dressed in black wearing heavy silver medallions on chains (they look like wine tasters). Sitting in the orchestra is like sitting inside a candy box. The six tiers of red brocade and gilt boxes are like receptacles for jewels, and the house whispers of silk, and there is an enveloping green fragrance, like a mingling of rich and expensive scents and oils—perhaps the fragrance of new silk itself.

It is almost impossible to believe that all this has not been here forever, or at least since Stendhal and Byron disported themselves in boxes where picnic hampers were brought; in those days, protocol demanded silence only during the singing of major arias (not such a bad thing—opera then may have been for the rich, but it was not for the stuffy). In fact, the house was leveled by a bomb during World War II and is another example of the Italian genius for restoration.

When the houselights dim, faces—pale ovals—glow dimly in the recesses of the boxes, and then the boxes go dark, and only the enormous stage is lit. This is magic—the lights subdued and then the absolute dark, the boxes the last to go black. An afterimage of faces floats before the eyes. There is a few seconds' pause in the darkened house before applause greets the invisible orchestra . . . and it is this time I most love, the anticipatory hush before the confectionary music begins. I keep thinking of Anna Karenina sitting in that hush and faint rustle, the object of hissing. But all is decorous now; Milan is not nineteenth-century Petersburg, it isn't even nineteenth-century Milan, and propriety reigns in boxes where scandals and feasts—the original floor plan included kitchens, pantries, and a pastry shop—once provided the real action, opera being merely a backdrop to and a diversion from the real spectacle and tableaux of social life.

At the final choral scene the boxes blaze; this sudden immersion into light causes at first some consternation and then a murmur of approval; we are all part of a giant wedding reception for Tamino and Pamina, singers and audience united in the victory of love over the Queen of the Night.

The Madonnina glows, shedding her light over a city impossible to love.

One never knows what one will carry away from a place. I find Milan impossible to love, but whenever I think of Milan, an image of a vigorous old man in a red scarf being toasted, on the occasion of his ninetieth birthday, by his young granddaughter flashes before me, and I feel affection I must after all attach to this place.

I no longer believe one has failed a city that one has failed to love.

* * *

The porter who takes me through the labyrinthine underground tunnels of Milan's train station to the underused elevator (the choice is between winding dark tunnels or daunting flights of ceremonial stairs) tells me I am beautiful. I feel old. "An old hen makes good broth," he says. He asks me if my rings are gold. They are, but I lie. He raises my hand in a courtly gesture as if to kiss it. He bites a ring and stirs the air with his finger to reproach me for having told a silly lie. Then he congratulates me for having the wit to tell a lie—"the South is full of thieves" (I am going to Venice)—and then he carries my luggage onto the train.

Chapter II

VENICE:
"MIRROR OF WATER"

The very contained man sitting across from me is listening to a Sony Walkman; from his earplug emerge the faint squeaky sounds of British English. The book he holds *(Streamline English)* is open to Lesson IV, "What to Do at the Racetrack." His lips form the words *horse* and *jockey*. He turns the volume up: *Win-place-show.* The recorded sound of horses clopping on British turf keeps the train wheels company as, from the window, the remains of the network of canals that once linked Venice to Verona slip by.

Across the aisle a little girl is filling in an outline of Mickey Mouse with an acid-green crayon. I smile at her, and on the strength of my smile and her answering smile, her father hoists my three suitcases off the train when we reach Venice, and then he swings me onto the platform. He embraces me, his wife hugs me, they all kiss me—everybody smells slightly and not unpleasantly of fan-dried sweat, and we say thank yous and good-byes, the first words we have exchanged. How good people are.

Soon I am sitting in a mechanized baggage cart alongside my valises as the porter drives me from the train platform to the quay, from which I have my first thrilling glimpse of striped mooring poles and Gothic palaces with lacy arches resplendent in the enlivening spring air—the air that is almost tactile, the air that coats the worn stone with a silken glaze. "Signora Gucci," the porter calls me, because the cart is designed for luggage, not for humans,

"Signora Gucci," he says, "you enter Venice like Cleopatra, you are a good one, you." He deposits me in a sturdy blue motorboat belonging to his "cousin," a boat which, from the look and smell of it, has lately been used to carry fish from the market and which is more closely related to a barge than to a gondola. The tightness I felt in Milan leaves my neck and shoulders and my stomach as I take in drafts of air—the air has the tang of the sea—and we chug past silently slipping gondolas, their steel prows creasing the waters like a knife, down the Grand Canal . . . which is just as one has dreamed or remembered it and which inspires, as it always does (every time you see it, you see it for the first time), a most improbable joy. These are the works of man, whose will made a fairy tale of a swamp. These palazzi, splendid and proud in decay, their arches and loggias, their rusty-red and soft green and brown stone and white marble shimmering in the water-light, are the offspring of avarice and of longing, and they evoke commingled pride and pity—pride in the human endeavor to create paradise (a quasi-Oriental paradise) on earth, pity for the human need, the temerity to conquer nature and time, which pride and pity are indistinguishable from love. In this way stones teach us to love men. The boatman weaves his way to a tiny canal and fetches up against a dark landing stage between sweating walls, and sets me on my feet just yards away from my hotel in the Campo of La Fenice.

The unselfconsciousness of Venetians is as amazing as the unselfconsciousness of animals.

I've read somewhere that the average length of a stay in Venice is eighteen days. Henry James said that after two weeks in Venice one becomes as restless as if one were on shipboard. I sometimes think that there are two ways to see Venice. One is to let it have its way with you for three days, time in which to glide up and down the Grand Canal, thereafter to make for the open sea; time to sail to the lovely island of Torcello, mother city of Venice, zigzagging through pales (exaggerated twigs) in the water, an experience which defeats the most stubborn unhappiness; and time also to sit for leisured hours in St. Mark's Square, which for good reason has been called Europe's greatest drawing room (a "piazza of pure stone and pure idea") and which not to take pleasure in is absurdly snobbish and pretentious. The other way to see Venice is to stay at least six months, to know intimately its watery streets and its painters, and, in long months, to allow the initial stunning impact of the water kingdom to be replaced by the more enlightened affection of understanding. The trouble with staying in Venice for a week or ten days is that the seductive city is likely to betray you; you may feel at first, as Goethe did, that you are lord of the Adriatic, but you may later feel that you are a denizen of dark alleys, lost in a sinister maze.

My own advice notwithstanding, I have never stayed in Venice for more than ten or fewer than seven days. For the first three days I have lived in a state of serene exhilaration, experiencing the unique liberation of sensibility that comes from knowing you are surrounded by and in the midst of water. To contemplate the ocean seems to immerse you in life's origins. Every small canal in Venice is a gentle pulsating thread, a pulley, that leads to the sea, which is ever constant in the imagination. "The ocean is a powerful drug," Ronald Blythe writes; you are dragged into its pull, "and the draining is exquisite." And while the ocean drains, it also replenishes: Life lived on or near water holds the promise of life without end; the contours of one's emotional life conform to the expansiveness of the sea. Venice opens the floodgates of the heart. But there is danger.

After three days the magic may wear off and a dull disenchantment set in. Water, the element that seemed so emancipating, begins to feel constraining; Venice becomes claustrophobic and—worse—trite. Turner's paintings of the place—a fusion of light and dancing water in which solid objects are hinted at and float—seem more like the place than the place itself, the actual touristed Venice a collection of snapshot clichés. And one grows weary of the tourists (of the other tourists, for of course one sets oneself above them) and of their aggressive cameras, which, imposing tunnel vision, get between the object and the seeing eye and intervene between the traveler who comes unequipped with a camera and the world that traveler can trap only with her senses. For the first few love-smitten days in Venice, you think, whenever the intricate geography of canals and bridges delivers you to a dead end, Never mind—to be lost in Venice is to find. But then there comes a moment when you think: I do not want to climb another small bridge over another small canal; I want to be able to walk from A to B without having to hopscotch over lilliputian bridges; I do not want my field of vision criss-crossed by arterial veins, canals. And, one thinks, I have seen the glorious facades, and I have had the slightly perverse thrill of seeing the slimy back and belly of Venice, the backwaters; I would not have this kingdom—this city of masks and mirrors—for a gondolier's song, a feeling known to Oscar Wilde, who said, after a ride in a gondola, that he had been through a sewer in a coffin. "I never mind being lost in Venice," says a character in Nicolas Roeg's film *Don't Look Now,* in which Venice is palpably sinister. "I never mind being lost in Venice"—and then she sees the water rats, and her *pensione* seems to vanish from its street, and as she tries vainly to retrace her steps, echoes bounce off the water; there are too many shadows; Venice seems then to her like a city in aspic, left over from a dinner party—and all the guests are dead. And then she notices the unique "twinning" in Venice that Mary McCarthy has commented on: Nothing exists that does not have its counterpart; the city itself exists twice over—in its solid weight and in its reflections . . . like the tremulously shining light on my bedroom ceiling that sometimes gives me the odd sensation of swimming in air. But it isn't only material objects that are reflected in Venice, it is emotions and experience. In Roeg's film a child dies and its father finds a rubber doll in a canal, water pouring from its blank eye sockets; a blind twin has second sight.

Leone Battista Alberti, the great fifteenth-century Florentine Humanist, regarded Narcissus as the first painter; his image, reflected in water, was an exact likeness of himself on a flat surface. Leonardo da Vinci called the reflection in the mirror "the true painting." In this case, all of Venice is a painting—which is how it exists in memory. Memory turns the wheel again. In memory Venice is always magic.

My shady bedroom in La Fenice et des Artistes overlooks a small canal. From the doorway of a red house with green shutters across the canal two cherubs grin at me conspiratorially. Fleets of gondolas glide by. I like to see the boatmen of these elegant vessels duck their heads instinctively as they pass under bridges, and I like the charming discordance between the elegant black boats and the jaunty straw hats of the boatmen; it is like going to a funeral in a bathing costume. I like to hear the gondoliers sing in their liquid, lisping Venetian dialect—although the famous Venetian songs have yielded to spirited renditions of "O Sole Mio," a song from the South, or "Arrivederci, Roma," a song from the movies, the better to please tourists . . . who look dazed; to be serenaded at noon embarrasses them; the jocular exchanges of boatmen and their accompanying accordion players contribute to their disequilibrium. Venice is more than anyone bargains for. And less, too. The gondolas, evocative of perfumed nights and solemn processions, of honeyed love and Black Death, now carry tourists oddly matched; from my window I see a boatful of Japanese girls carrying gay parasols followed by a gondola bearing middle-aged men dressed in Hawaiian shirts, and a third gondola is full of bare white flesh—boys and girls in cutoff jeans and (it is deliciously cool) winter jackets. They are in their own way charming, but one wishes for dresses of white lawn, for ball gowns at dusk. . . . I think of Sebastian and Charles Rider, here, in Venice, so fresh in their affections—and so immaculately dressed. The gondola requires an elegant simplicity of dress or the luxurious excess of Carnevale; anything short of these extremes seems an affront.

Peggy Guggenheim, it is said, had the last private gondola in Venice; and she is dead.

Byron called Venice "the masque of Italy."

One feels that one could slip so easily into stylized mannerisms here, an exaggerated show . . . or spiral downward, at some point ceasing to care, into physical ruin and moral decay; one walks with a certain wariness.

In almost every shop there are masks for sale.

In the morning I wake to mist and to the early cries of boatmen. "Oy!" they cry, or "Always!"; it sounds as if they are crying "Always" with a mouthful of marbles. Barzini says the boatmen call out "Pope!" when they turn a corner, but I have never heard that. When they sing, the top notes are pinched, the vocal equivalent of the closed, pinched-off streets, the narrow alleys.

I am very tired when I arrive, but not to walk to St. Mark's is an impossibility. The first time I came to Venice I was bustled past St. Mark's Square by a porter—La Fenice is a five-minute walk from the square—and I didn't even know I had passed it. The square's main opening is through the Piazzetta that fronts on the Grand Canal. If you do not arrive at the great square by this means, you come to it through one of a number of narrow entrances in the covered galleries that surround the square. (If you were to regard the square as L-shaped—the Piazzetta, with its two granite columns surmounted by the Lion of St. Mark and St. Theodore spearing a crocodile—you would see the Piazza San Marco as a salon, the Piazzetta as its foyer.) Because you can enter the piazza by means of narrow entrances, it is possible to arrive without immediately understanding where you are. A sudden change of light precedes understanding—a long, slow take—and one of the most glorious spaces in the world is before and around you. Venice is a city of arrivals. You cannot arrive by train or plane without traversing water with immeasurable delight; you cannot arrive at the Piazza of San Marco without feeling that you have made your way not only to the world's greatest drawing room but to the heart and soul of a kingdom; wherever you stay in Venice, wherever you wander, St. Mark's remains the place upon arriving at which you say: I am home. (I knew a man who wrote a guide to Venice, a series of walking tours; his source of pride was that he did not lead his readers through the square more than once. I do not regard this as a great accomplishment. Not going to San Marco every day is like having a unicorn in your living room and ignoring it.)

Giddy with fatigue, adrenalized with the jolt of pleasure San Marco immediately provides, I pay my respects to the square and to the glittering Byzantine splendor of St. Mark's Basilica, and receive a confused but happy impression of ascending waves of pigeons, of crowds of tourists perambulating or taking their ease in outdoor cafés, listening to the tinny sound of string orchestras not quite in tune; bright flags and bright laughter. Then I make my way home past a house where Mozart lived (a little boy in an orange raft is making circles in the canal in front of it, which would have made Mozart happy), and because it is the season of Lent, I stop at the small Church of San Fantin, where a wooden image of Christ crucified upon the cross is stretched upon the floor. The little church has plastic holders for plastic flowers—and a painting ascribed to Tintoretto. Past shops with chocolate fish and chocolate eggs, past showplaces for good Murano glass, past collections of masks and collections of fish—silver, pink, mottled fish, fish with lemons in their mouths, crustaceans whose antennae quiver feebly. Lemons are the symbol of fidelity in love.

At night the Campo of La Fenice is dramatic, contained, lyrical, and peaceful. Seen through the silk curtains of the restaurant La Fenice, people entering the *campo* with its strings of colored lights are like players entering a stage; this could be the setting (in Venice it is impossible, as Goethe moaned, to escape the obvious) for *La Bohème*.

Minutes away, on the Riva degli Schiavoni, the grand esplanade of Venice, exasperated tourists mutter their disapprobation of other tourists.

Luigi Barzini said Venice smelled like rotting cabbages. "Phew! Phew!" German tourists say as they cross an especially rank canal on their way to the Accademia. I like the dank smell of canals. The smell of the one we are now crossing mixes with the sugary aroma of candy shops that line our path—a Coney Island, cotton-candy smell.

The large wooden bridge leading to the Accademia—one of three bridges that cross the snaking Grand Canal—is being restored. Dozens of cats prowl in the workyard. Cardboard boxes of kittens line the steps of the bridge.

Some optimist has put them there; they will go untaken, they will become feral. The clean new smell of sawdust mingles with cat smell and canal smell and cotton-candy smell. The line to the Accademia is long. An English couple behind me takes turns going to the toilet. (There must be a certain facial expression one wears when one has to use the toilet, because it isn't even necessary to open one's mouth before a café proprietor says *"Toletta?"* A street with a free toilet near the Accademia is nicely called Via Toletta. Times have changed—all public toilets are kept spotlessly clean by impassive old women—since Goethe asked an innkeeper where the bathroom was and was pointed in the direction of the courtyard. But where in the courtyard? Goethe asked. Anywhere you wish, the innkeeper replied.)

Yesterday the English couple waited three hours to see a Soviet exhibition of Van Goghs in St. Mark's Square. Why, when all of Venice is a museum, would they do this? When I display my impatience and make to leave the line, the Englishman—who has a handkerchief secured to his thus-squared head by means of four corner knots—says, "You'll have to get used to this." His assumed superiority and his condescension needle me; I hate tourists like poison. But I am a tourist, too, and so is every tourist who complains of every other tourist, and we all know this; but we complain nevertheless. So I head for my *campo* and my hotel, circuitously, past the Campo Santo Stefano and the Conservatory of Music (the strains of Stravinsky vying with those of Vivaldi), past impromptu shrines and past fountains—fountains in Venice being a true example of gilding the lily, as well as an example of the way Venice echoes and reflects itself. This city that has no dearth of lovers makes love to itself.

Five-thirty A.M. Venice is washed in golden, unambiguous light.

According to one esoteric view of Creation, concentric rings of water girdled the earth before the Flood; in Venice, where the water reflects the sky and the sky is aqueous, this theory is almost credible.

Sometimes I feel like I am living inside a milky pearl.

How can living on water not change one? Everyone says it does—Goethe said that "the Venetian was bound to develop into a new kind of creature"— but no one says in what way it changes one.

My body and my mind experience this lagoon life as a prelude to a mystery, but I don't know what the mystery is.

When I go down a dark, narrow street by way of a deserted *campo* and find myself at water's edge, I feel that I have reached the end of Venice; but

Venice has ended only in the topography of my mind—in fact I am at a vaporetto stop (where lovers meet and kiss). At night the chandeliers in empty palaces gleam suggestively through leaded glass, catching light from water. In heavy fog the yellow warning lights on the canal, the lights of gondolas and water taxis, combine to create a rose-blue haze over the Grand Canal; you are sailing into and through a Turner painting. The garish neon lights that illuminate a restaurant near the Rialto Bridge are cold and cheerless and seem in some obscure way to mock the human cargo on the oily waters. The mournful cry of boatmen—*ooh-ee ooh-ee*—echoes in the mist, the mist composed of all the residue of all the gold dust and silver and pepper and spices that Venice ever traded or looted.

I leave the vaporetto where I started, at the landing dock of the Campo Sant'Angelo; but I make a wrong turn. No light is diffused by single bulbs that create only puddles of watery light in the clinging darkness. Walking through narrow alleys, trying to retrace my steps in the fog, I hear wreaths of laughter, distant voices that are echoes of voices. I am on the Street of Three Assassins, lost. I stop at three hotels (the symmetry is eerily perfect) to ask for directions. Are they hotels? They seem, in this menacing dark, to have some more sinister reason for being. At each hotel—all of them have empty, threadbare, brightly lit lobbies—different directions are given me. I turn a corner to see the black shadow of a man against a gray wall, which causes my heart to stop. Someone has painted it there—which is somehow worse than if it were a real man, but at the same time a relief. I pass another dark *campo*—a florist shop with sprays of Easter orchids, a confectionary shop (chocolate fish)—where three girls, lost, huddle and for my benefit feign indifference.

The Hindu word for a sudden bright vision, for a glimpse of the hidden god within, is *darshan*. I turn another corner, and I see—a bright vision—the light of the Campo Fenice. In the Teatro bar, cheerful people are eating pizza and drinking beer, leafing through magazines and playing video games. The Grand Canal is not the river Styx. Nor is it Constantinople, though sometimes, in its indifference to human atoms, it seems more of the East than of the West.

PER I POVERI—PANE . . . "Bread for the Poor." There ought, I suppose, to be irony in the hand-scrawled sign above the poor box in this basilica that shrieks of loot. But the bulbous-domed and spired church—which Ruskin called "a treasure heap . . . partly of gold, and partly of opal and mother-of-pearl"—can't inspire nasty thoughts. "Why such an intensely foreign building of great size should exert this power of welcome I cannot say," wrote E. V. Lucas at the beginning of this century, "but the fact remains that St. Mark's, for all its Eastern domes and gold and odd designs and billowy floors, does more to make a stranger and a Protestant at home than any cathedral I know."

Why this should be so it is difficult to say. Perhaps the very thing Protestants might be expected to hold against it—the fact that Constantinople was sacked in aid of Latin Catholicism—is in its favor: St. Mark's may be welcoming, but the welcome does not appear to extend from the Pope of Rome. It is a stone fantasy garden, genial, suitable for pleasure or for prayer; for all its Byzantine authority and its immensity, it seems beautifully to float in the air. It has been remarked that the basilica seems to conform more to the rules of music than to those of architecture. I agree with this perception, though I do not in the least know how to defend it.

Standing inside the five-domed church, contemplating the geometric floor marbles and the mosaics, so intensely colored, that tell the scriptural history of the world, one has the most agreeable and childlike sensations; one feels no obligation to decry what one official guidebook blandly calls "decorative elements . . . from the entire ancient world, Greek, Roman, Syrian, African, brought a few at a time to the basilica as an act of homage by the citizens to their patron Saint"—in other words, loot. Here are stylized birds, waves, and trees, peacocks, Christ crucified, Salome presenting the head of John the Baptist to her mother, Noah's animals—so exotic, so charming—coexisting, uniting East and West, Byzantine mosaic and Romanesque sculpture; one can enter history—or God's universe—at any point, work one's way, say, backward from the Last Judgment to the story of Abraham, Hagar, and Sarah, thus defeating time. The doges who ruled the Most Serene Republic attended Mass here privately, arriving by means of the adjoining ducal palace (a dreary, graceless place), an experience roughly akin to having the Atlantic Ocean to oneself for a bath.

The remains of St. Mark, the patron saint of Venice, are said to reside beneath the high altar. How the evangelist's venerated bones got there is anybody's guess. A guidebook sold in the basilica says, with Venetian diplomacy, that in 828 the body of St. Mark was "transferred" from Alexandria to Venice. Some say he was smuggled past Muslim border officials under cover of cabbages and pork. At any rate, an angel is said to have announced to him, when, in life, he was shipwrecked on an island in the lagoon that was to become Venice, "Here you will find peace, Mark, my evangelist"—a pretty story.

The central doorway of St. Mark's (there are five) is surmounted by four bronze horses rearing over a golden mosaic of Christ glorified. The horses, once thought to have been the work of Praxiteles, predate Christ by about three hundred years. They are not, however, the original horses taken from Constantinople; they are reproductions. The original horses—which are not, however, bronze but are in all likelihood an amalgam of copper and silver and gold—repose in St. Mark's Museum, which is attained by a steep stairway entered by a small door near the main entrance. From the museum one has the double pleasure of seeing the real horses and their twins. It does not in any case matter that the horses we see over the entranceway are not "real." What matters is that they are intelligent, magnanimous, and, above all, unselfconscious creatures, impossible not to feel affection for.

Whether one can feel affection for the Byzantine Pala d'Oro—the gold altarpiece of St. Mark's—is another matter. It screams *booty*. Whether it was made in Constantinople in the tenth century and restored in Venice in the eleventh, as one version of history goes, or composed in its entirety by the Venetian goldsmith Giampolo Boninsegna in the fourteenth century to replace the earlier gold altarpiece (as another story goes), it is universally acknowledged that many of the enamels set in the jewel-studded block of gold were booty of war from the conquest of Constantinople in 1204, during the Fourth Crusade. The eye and mind cannot take in the thousands of rubies, emeralds, amethysts, garnets, diamonds, sapphires, and pearls embedded in the gold. The effect is stupefying rather than dazzling, and it is asking too much of any mortal to "read" the enamels for their religious significance when precious stones the size of a baby lamb chop compete with narrative. At the center of the altarpiece is an enamel of the resurrected Christ. Lord of Lords and King of Kings He is—but the Second Adam, who gave the preferential option to the poor and whose first followers were humble fishermen, looks as surprised to find Himself amidst such splendor as any poor carpenter would.

The modern predilection to deplore the loot of Venice was not shared by Alberti, whose measured approach to commerce is described by Anthony Blunt: "Architecture . . . the art most closely connected with the practical needs of man . . . serves commerce, of which . . . Alberti speaks in the highest terms; it enables the city to defend itself against its enemies, and, by inventing aggressive machines of war . . . helps to extend its dominion. From architecture the city derives its splendid public buildings, its private houses, and the monuments which keep alive the memory of its great men." Without wealth, Alberti argued, neither experience nor wisdom (the wisdom required for the making of laws and for the supervision of religious life) could be functional. (It is a nice irony that these capitalistic views were forwarded by Blunt, once adviser for the Queen's pictures and drawings, and, along with Philby, Burgess, and McLean, a spy for the Soviet Union, the "fourth man." . . . But, then, most of Venice's contemporary cultural administrators are Communists—albeit Italian Communists, very different from their Soviet comrades; and one can make what one wishes out of that.)

San Marco places before one the terms of a theological argument: Suger, the twelfth-century monk, adviser to Louis VI and Louis VII, justified the use of gems, crystal, and enamel (he saw God as a symphony of light). "When the enchanting beauty of the house of God has overwhelmed me," he said, "by the grace of God [and by "the charm of multi-colored gems"], I can be transported mystically from life on this earth to the higher realm." St. Bernard, on the other hand, regarded all ornament as vanity, "and folly even greater than the vanity. The church sparkles and gleams on all sides, while its poor huddle in need." Suger contended that the poor found, in the light of gold and of translucent materials, the light that was Christ. . . . This quarrel will never die.

Ruskin, who beautifully said that the Square of San Marco opened up from the basilica "in a kind of awe," also said that "you may walk from sunrise to sunset, to and fro, before the gateway of S. Mark's, and you will not see an eye lifted to it, nor a countenance brightened by it. Priest and layman, soldier and civilian, rich and poor, pass it by alike regardlessly." Perhaps, though it seems unlikely, this was true in 1851, but it could not have been true during the Renaissance. In Gentile Bellini's famous painting *Procession in St. Mark's Square,* the True Cross, escorted by priests all in white, holding candles, is carried in a golden casket beneath a rich red canopy; and a very orderly, dignified, gorgeous procession it is. The Campanile had not yet been built when Bellini depicted this pageantry, but the Doges' Palace had. (The original bell tower collapsed in 1902, injuring no one, and was restored, with fairly miraculous speed, by 1912.) The white-and-pink geometric facade of the Ducal Palace is charming. In Monet's painting *The Ducal Palace at Venice* (which is in the permanent collection of the Brooklyn Museum, adjacent to a neighborhood in which there is a replica of a Venetian palazzo, the friezes of which depict American Indians and frontiersmen—a witty, remarkable, but, in this context, not a beautiful building), the palace is *blue* and white, and it casts white light slightly tinged with lime-yellow unto the waters; nothing could be prettier. (But the inside of the Doges' Palace is so austere that having seen it once, I wish never to see it again. The slime and decay and rot of Venice teach us that time and earthly life are not forever; to while away a spring day at Caffè Florian is to make better use of life and time.)

No one would call the crowds of tourists and the souvenir hawkers in St. Mark's Square orderly today; but the great square seems almost infinitely expandable and congenial. To sit outdoors at Quadri in the sea-cooled breeze on a day of brilliant sunshine, observing all the mad and joyous intersections and juxtapositions of the sacred and the profane, the solemn and the gay, is one of life's great pleasures. There is something wonderful and slightly mad about waiters dressed in formal black and white under a blazing sun. It is no accident that *al fresco,* the term we use for eating or drinking outdoors, is taken from the Italian; Italian food is well suited for outdoor consumption, and the Italian temperament is uniquely qualified to enjoy the processional.

The sundials are inscribed *"Horas non numero nisi serenas."* The hour is struck by two giant bronze Moors in the clock tower. String orchestras play, with minimal attachment to notions of harmony, at Florian and Quadri. . . . And I read these melancholy words from an old guidebook: "What if some terrible natural catastrophe, an earthquake or a deluge, had wiped Venice off the face of the world, say about the year 1500?" It is unimaginable to think that the unimaginable city should not exist.

Ruskin, whose own marriage was unconsummated, wrote of Venetian communally celebrated marriages in these yearning words:

Let us consider for a little the significance and nobleness of that early custom of the Venetians . . . that there should be but one marriage day for the nobles of the whole nation, so that all might rejoice together, and that the sympathy might be full, not only of the families who that year beheld the alliance of their children, and prayed for them in one crowd, weeping before the altar, but of all the families of all the state, who saw, in the day which brought happiness to others, the anniversary of their own. Imagine the strong bond of brotherhood thus sanctified among them . . . the greater deliberation and openness necessarily given to the contemplation of marriage, to which all the people were solemnly to bear testimony; the more lofty and unselfish tone which it would give to all their thoughts. It was the exact opposite of stolen marriage. It was marriage to which God and man were taken for witness, and every eye was invoked for its glance, and every tongue for its prayers.

Sansovino, who sculpted the bronze sacristy doors of the basilica, wrote that when the espousal had taken place—to the sound of pipes and trumpets—the bride, dressed in white, her hair thrown over her shoulder and interwoven with threads of gold, danced serenely, bowing before the guests—a custom which ended (alas) in the Year of Our Lord 943.

It is easy to picture these lovely celebrations, this exquisite and happy formality, taking place in the great square—where now there is not even a beadle, as there was a quarter of a century ago, to keep men in shorts and women immodestly dressed from entering the basilica. We are meant to regard this as progress. When I remember Venice, I think of these weddings—"the exact opposite of stolen marriage"—and I am enchanted and sad, sunnily desolate.

Goethe, whose heart was tender, tells us how the women of the Lido used to sit on the seashore while their husbands were fishing, and sing songs by Tasso; and their men replied from the sea, a form of conversation that no longer exists: "It is the cry of some lonely human being sent out into the wide world till it reaches the ears of another human being who is moved to answer it."

Once, when I was sick with love in Venice and inconsolable, a Venetian said to me: "If you did not come here with lovesickness, you would develop it here. Venice is a city for lovers. Everything here comes in pairs or multiples of pairs. Go home."

In New Orleans it is a crime to wear a mask except on the day of Mardi Gras. *"Boo!"* a little American boy calls out, craning his neck around a corner, holding a mask to his face. I loathe masks. They are the crudest form of disguise and mockery. They say: To lie and to dissimulate is acceptable, and more than that, it's fun. They establish an inequality between the observer and the observed. I don't like puppets—another form of trickery, gross and transparent—either. Masks and puppets frighten me. They are hostile; they take on pseudohuman characteristics in order to hold human feelings at arm's length. Children are frightened by the story of Pinocchio, and are meant to be.

Seen from a vaporetto: a gondola with a liveried gondolier carrying a middle-aged woman and an elderly man. She is standing; he is reclining against pillows. His face is painted charcoal. Is he covering the marks of a dread disease? Is this a private game? What game is it?

Men, women, children,
Masses for the gas chambers
Advancing toward horror
Beneath the whip of the executioners
Your sad holocaust is
Engraved in history
And nothing shall purge
Your death from our memories
For our memories are your only grave. . . . *The City of Venice remembers the Venetian Jews who were deported to the Nazi concentration camps on December 6, 1943, and August 17, 1944.*

—*Plaque in the Campo of the Nuovo
Ghetto (New Ghetto)*

Pots of begonias bloom in the Ghetto; there are gay red awnings over shops that sell sweets and cakes and the unleavened bread of Passover; in restaurants with mezuzahs on their doorways there are—just as there are in restaurants all over Venice—special menus for tourists *(Menu Turistico)*. No Italian's death goes unmarked; here, in the Ghetto, death notices posted on walls bear not the Cross but the Star of David; and there are plaques to commemorate the lives and deaths of Israeli martyrs.

It is different here.

In the peopled desolation of the Ghetto, history is a heavy weight; history is visible and tangible. The business of living goes on. Laundry is strung from the tall, narrow buildings—six-storied skyscrapers with steep, cruel steps. "This is the way we wash our clothes, wash our clothes, wash our clothes"— the sign of an ordered, domestic existence. The tourists who come here cry. One-fourth of all Venetian Jews were killed by the Nazis. They were the poorest of the city's Jews; the others had moved to other quarters, more spacious, less severe, less haunted. Three centuries have passed since Jews were forced to wear a distinguishing yellow circle and remain within the Ghetto gates from sunset till dawn. You can still feel the grooves into which the Ghetto gates were fitted. You finger them, a form of communion.

Holy Thursday. Bells toll. When is a mirage not a mirage? When it is an island oasis in a brackish lagoon: Burano. The sunlight bounces off the canals of the fishing village and shimmers on the pastel houses. Actually the houses are no more or less pastel here than they are in Venice proper, though they are always referred to as splashes of pastel; but because they are simple, almost pastoral, the adjective is appropriate here, as it is not for Venice: It is a synonym for *benign,* perhaps for *pretty,* which word we tend to shun. Burano calms the eye. The houses are small, and in fact, the colors—rusty red and powder blue—are brilliant, the more so as they provide background for dazzling white laundry that festoons them. These are the colors Italians of my parents' generation tried to transplant to Newark and Brooklyn, with remarkably unhappy results.

The palaces of Venice are secretive; here on Burano, private life is on perpetual display. Street doors of these houses—cottages, really—open onto formal dining rooms (stuffed furniture and antimacassars), immaculately clean, polished, proud.

In some of the doorways, black-shawled women do lacework, their faces lined as with a network of canals. The streets that border the sluggish canals are the Venetian equivalent of our backyards. The women's pudgy fingers fly; when the women pause, they chat. Gossip is the way they knit the world together, with random bits of news and speculation. (Burano calms the eye and inspires a respect for traditional ways. These women do their needlework and tend their world. In India the women gather together and beat their clothes on boulders to wash them; in Guatemala the women wash their clothes in communal tubs—how often I heard young brides giggle and older women proffer advice! It is we who deprecate the value of manual or physical work, not they. Work and social life are inseparable for these women, who make a good thing of a necessary thing.)

In the center of the village is a lacemaking school (Scuola dei Merletti) that has been described (in 1914, by E. V. Lucas) as "an oasis of smiling cleanliness," where "thousands of girls . . . all so neat and happy" work, and (by Mary McCarthy, in 1963) as "a long double room, with rather poor light, where silent rows of little girls," whose sad eyes shoot "poisoned darts

at charmed tourists, sit on benches, presided over by a nun and a crucifix."
The school was closed in 1972. The art is dying. I saw only a few cheerful
middle-aged women, of the type one refers to as "respectable," sitting in
front of the long windows, demonstrating their art, working on hoops or
on red rag cushions *(cuscinetti di stracci)* to which were attached patterns
drawn on paper—subtle patterns; this is an art that makes crocheting look
coarse. I was prepared for a sweatshop. What I saw was infinitely more
appealing than the sight of women at video terminals, and the work infinitely more creative—flowers, stars, animals, peacocks, swans, abstract designs, a Last Supper (no craft is immune from kitsch).

Fishermen's nets were made and darned by women; Burano lace, which
appeared in paintings by Carpaccio in the fifteenth and sixteenth centuries,
was a natural evolution.

Here is a story told to me by one of the lacemakers: A young girl was
given a token of seaweed by her lover when he left Burano for the Crusades.
Afraid that the perishability of the seaweed was a bad omen, the girl
re-created it together with a sea urchin, with the thread of her father's fishing
net, and lace was born.

The school of lace functions now as a museum. Encased in glass are creamy
lace masks and fans (one that belonged to the Sun King); foamy lace parasols
with ivory handles, parasols that could never have been meant to screen out
the sun, but to throw dappled light on the face of beauty; an eighteenth-
century wedding dress of gossamer lace—no bridal night was ever so delicate
as this.

For men must work and women must pray. Men fish; women, waiting, make
lace. It is said on Burano that the art of needlework died the year it was too
cold for men to go out on the icy waters to fish. They are, whether this story
is true or not, complementary activities.

There is a park, an esplanade, on Burano. A little girl tries, without much
enthusiasm or success, to sell glass from the neighboring island of Murano.
The trees beneath which she walks look like Art Nouveau drapery. It is
impossible in Venice or on Burano not to describe things in terms of other
things. A ship glides through the lagoon; it looks like a child's toy, it looks
as if a child were pulling it effortlessly by a slender thread. The traveler's
eye miniaturizes this island world, which is, however, the whole world for
its island people.

The bell tower lists. At four forty-five the bells peal and the world goes to church. On the Church of San Martino there is a plaque commemorating St. Barbara, virgin and martyr, imprisoned in a tower by her father, who contrived to have her sentenced to death when she became a Christian; he was struck by lightning. St. Barbara, as a consequence of her father's sudden death, became the patron saint of those in danger of sudden death (miners and gunners in particular). One might think that, given her father's cruelty, she would have dispensed largess in another direction; perhaps we are meant to understand this as a lesson in forgiveness. According to other sources, at a time when her father was absent she added a window to the two-window bathhouse she occupied, in order to honor the Three-Person Trinity, and so she is the patron saint of architects and builders. (In the first version there is a kind of mystical turning of the screw; in the second, there is logic and charm—St. Barbara's legend accommodates different casts of mind.) One of my earliest memories is of being told that St. Barbara, for whom I was named, cut off her breasts in order to escape marriage. I do not know why I was told this; I can find no evidence for it. St. Barbara is now thought not to have existed at all. (A round tower, a narrow window—this is still the stuff of dreams: Rapunzel.)

An aluminum ladder leans shakily against the church; a sacristan retrieves rubber balls from the roof's gutter. Girls—their arms linked through those of a fair young nun—count the balls; there are fifteen. An altar boy wearing sneakers under his robes disputes the count. The nun maintains a careful neutrality. The children tell us not to go into San Martino, which is being cleaned for services; but from the window of the adjacent rectory a handsome, ascetic-looking priest smiles down and calls, *"Avanti!"* Inside, five women in aprons and floppy felt slippers are engaged in housekeeping of a high and solemn order—they are preparing for Holy Communion. When people think of the Catholic Church, and speak of it in fear, admiration, condescension, or anger, they never seem to be seeing *this* Church—the Church of family, community, simplicity, anchorage, and ease.

The children are learning their Easter lessons: "What is the meaning of this meal? What is the meaning of the bread? The wine?" The pulpit all but engulfs the boy who reads the Scriptures; only his towhead can be seen. Each child who enters is greeted playfully by one of the old smiling nuns: A cheek is caressed; heads are patted, hands squeezed. But: *"Mea culpa,"* the children recite, *"mea maxima culpa."* Children do no harm; of what sin can they possibly be guilty? . . . Except, of course, the original one. *"Tu sei la mia vita, altro io non ho / Tu sei la mia strada, la verità,"* they sing. "You are my life, no other do I have / You are my path, the truth." Will they believe these words, which their high, sweet voices imbue with such fervor, ten years from now? It is strange to hear the name Judas in young mouths; what do they know of betrayal? They know everything, of course, but they will know that they know only years from now. The priest is so kind and earnest, so young. He addresses each child gravely: Serena, Cristina, Alessandro, Gianfranco. . . . He reminds me of the Protestant minister who taught me my lessons when my father, before he became a vociferous atheist, briefly enlisted with the Presbyterians because the Church of his mother was both too womanish and too harsh for him. "Listen to the pin drop," the Presbyterian minister said at Sunday school; and I never heard it, and I thought that only I couldn't hear it, and so Gentle Jesus Meek and Mild wouldn't love me, nor would my father. What will these children not understand? Who among them will feel unloved? (Lace petticoats dip beneath the mended wool of the girls' skirts in delicious, provocative waves.) And in what mysterious way is grace operating in their hearts, these children who speak of betrayal as if it were something they came home to every night?

The greeting of peace is exchanged. Everyone makes for me; perhaps they think all Americans are heathens. Everyone is kind. I am the only one who receives the Host in her hands. I hold God in my hand; but they address Him in the familiar: *Tu.*

In the Trattoria Da Romano, to which it is understood every tourist must be directed, under Venetian chandeliers and pink neon lights I eat spaghetti with butter and cheese and *canocchie*—fish in a pale lavender spiral shell— and tiny clams and mussels, and an orange Bavarian cream. The menu has the names of famous diners the restaurant has entertained, conveniently categorized for reference: painters, poets, and writers; athletes; personalities and politicians. Sinclair Lewis ate here, and so did naughty Ezra Pound and so did Ernest Heminguay. Katarin Hapburne! Matisse ate here—this does wonders for my mood—and Farah Fawcet Mayor.

In a front room at Florian, on the south side of St. Mark's Square, four people admire themselves in one of the smoky mirrors on the apple-green walls. They contrive to look famous. It is not possible to decipher the nature of their couplings. One of the men and one of the women are dressed like Moors; they wear turbans threaded with gold. The Moor-woman wriggles out of her velvet cape to reveal a purple togalike garment and a braided gold collar that extends from her collarbone to her chin. The younger man wears a black leather-and-zipper costume (more zippers than leather) and daintily eats petits fours. The younger woman—whose nipples, large as thumbs, press against the pink silk of her dress—drops a diamond ring into her wineglass. "A gesture learned from the films, *cara*," the Moor-woman says, whereupon the younger woman licks the cheek of the older man and then his long white hair.

Venetians (and their dogs) all ride the vaporetti, but if you ask any Venetian if your destination is within walking distance, he will say Yes. Usually he will say, "No more than twenty minutes, no more than half a kilometer." (It is explained to me that this pleasant fiction is maintained "so you will like us. . . . So you will know we like you. If we told you you couldn't walk there, you might think we didn't want you to get there, no?" And why portray life as it actually is? Why not dress uncomfortable facts in agreeable colors?)

I simply can never get used to the vaporetto as a normal means of transportation; I keep thinking these egalitarian water buses are provided as a convenience for tourists.

After the third or fourth day in Venice, small pools of light in the side canals—lights filtered through shuttered windows—are ineffably sad. The magic of Venice contends with the accumulated sadness of centuries—Crusaders, loot, sighs, prisoners, laments. . . . So to a hamburger at pink-and-clubby Harry's Bar. Blood-red orange juice and vodka. Chocolate ice cream. American voices, a view of the Grand Canal. If discontentment or ennui entered these precincts, the maître d' would sweep it out with a broom. In Dallas a journalist has just won the International Imitation Hemingway contest with a send-up of *For Whom the Bell Tolls*. The judging was held in Harry's American Bar and Grill, a replica of Harry's Bar, in Century City, a suburb of Los Angeles. His prize is a trip to Florence.

Venice has no dust. There are no dust motes dancing in the shafts of light that pierce the cool dimness of the churches. In St. Mark's a choir is rehearsing a Bach chorale. Outside, there is the sound of Prince, acid rock from transistor radios.

From my hotel I hear Japanese girls serenading a gondolier: "Edelweiss forever," they sing, and they clap their hands. In another gondola, an accordionist sings a ribald Neapolitan song, a song sung to bridegrooms by older women of the family on wedding days. Nobody can tell me why Venetian boatmen sing Neapolitan songs with lewd lyrics. Goethe heard boatmen "chant verses by Tasso and Ariosto to their own melodies. . . . Something between chorale and recitative. . . . The singer sits . . . in a gondola, and sings [at] the top of his voice—the people here appreciate volume more than anything else. His aim is to make his voice carry as far as possible over the still mirror of water. Far away another singer hears it"—images of a noble, faded world.

Morning coffee. Frank Sinatra is singing "New York, New York."

My hotel is wedged pie-shaped into a *campo* that is a village unto itself: a foundry (*getto,* in Italian; and it is from this word that our word *ghetto* is thought to have derived); a barbershop; a beauty parlor; a pizzeria; a restaurant; and, through a vine-covered passage, a theater—La Fenice—and a church.

On Good Friday, a day of mourning, I go to the beauty parlor, a one-woman shop, which serves as an informal information office. Carmela pokes her head out of the curtained opening to give directions, in Italian and English, to tourists whose flagging footsteps she is alert to hear; Carmela is forty-four, and her son Marco is four—she issues many instructions to Marco, too—and with what is left of her attention, she snips my hair. I have searched for years in New York for a hairdresser I could bully as effectively as hairdressers bully me, and now I am being bullied in Venice by Carmela, whose hair—Anna Magnani, circa 1945—is exactly what I would like mine not to look like. She says she wants me to look *moderna.* After the brushing and the teasing and the gelling I grow drowsy under the hair dryer; I jerk awake when I remember that I have missed making the Stations of the Cross. My hair is black. It is not supposed to be black. . . . My concierge, to whom in my tardy zeal to join the processional I apply, tells me that he is "not informated" on these matters. Then he asks me if I am Irish. Then he asks me if I have a brother who is a priest, a sister who is a nun. These questions disturb me. He cannot take his eyes off my hair; perhaps he thinks I have had it colored black in honor of the most solemn day of the liturgical year, which I have spent—to ridiculous effect—with Carmela's brushes and gels.

On television children talk with a professor about the meaning of Easter. One girl says: "Christ was born in October, not December." She is a Jehovah's Witness. My mother was a Jehovah's Witness; I was raised to be one, too. I wonder if I was as smug as that little girl is. I think I was—and underneath it very scared. The professor receives her statement with an eloquent shrug of dismissal. Nothing new can pose a threat to him. Jehovah's Witnesses are the fastest-growing religion in Italy, but new religions come and go, whereas Catholicism is bred in the bone and marrow of Italians; it is the air they breathe.

Little Marco brings me a chocolate Easter bunny, which I accept as reparation. He stares, bug-eyed, at the watered silk of my hotel room walls, at the expanse of watered silk on my bed, which, giggling, he jumps upon. Carmela is as good a disciplinarian as she is a hairdresser.

There are no church bells today. Their absence is another form of sound.

Today, in Rome, the Pope wears a mask. His mask is anonymity. He dons the garb of an ordinary priest and, in a chapel at St. Peter's, hears the confessions of thirteen of the faithful.

On Holy Saturday there is an antiques fair at the Campo of San Maurizio: fountain pens—gold, chased silver, mother-of-pearl, ivory (the metallic pen is thought to have been invented in the fifteenth century by apostolic notary Cola di Rienzo, himself a collector); fans—pastoral scenes on parchment, lace, fretted old ivory; dolls; scraps of old lace; walking sticks with handles of horn and silver and ivory, the most romantic of all masculine accessories (oh, Mr. Rochester!); Tiffany glass; pendants of diamonds and rubies and bluish pearls; illuminated manuscripts; anatomical and floral aquatints; opera glasses; clerical vestments in all the colors of the liturgical year—all the colors of the rainbow; junk from India; tin replicas of body parts (ex-votos)—hearts, lungs, breasts, legs—offerings to God, a tangible form of request that he might cure the fleshly counterparts thereof. . . . My head is buzzing with stories—each object has and is a mute story—and also with avarice.

Strolling through networks of streets not densely populated with tourists, or, for that matter, with natives, I reach the Church of San Trovaso, near which there is what looks like a series of log cabins or an Alpine ski resort. This is a boatyard, and it has been here since the Middle Ages. Gondolas—looking most unromantic with their green undersides exposed—are being caulked and repaired. A gondola seen on the water—even if its human freight disappoints—is both mythic and invulnerable. When they are seen like this, you feel for the proud things almost the kind of pity you might feel for a human being robbed of his defenses, caught naked and surprised, or for a sleeping lover. (It may not be true that one must be in love to appreciate a gondola, but it is true that one has to be in love—and paired—to loll in one without self-consciousness or embarrassment.)

On this walk I also see, spray-painted on a white wall, ELVIS LIVES and, on a nearby building of Titian red, RASTA MAN—the only contemporary graffiti in Venice.

At the Antica Locanda Montin I sit at a table covered with oilcloth and eat an artichoke with a long, elegant stem and wonder how I will ever reconcile myself to living in America.

I call a *motoscafo,* a water taxi, to take me home. The mercantile life and the domestic life of the city go on in the back canals, and the camaraderie and rivalry of these boatmen please me more than the perfected performances of gondoliers. The boatmen have no patience with amateurs. They call out imprecations when someone makes a clumsy move; an amateur in control of a boat is treated like an adult who has chosen not to learn how to walk.

A woman with a stupid young companion shrinks into herself more every day. She has suffered revulsion from having revealed to me her unhappiness; she now cannot meet my eye. Her companion, in her desperation to please, acts jollier and jollier—to no effect.

It is sad to be alone on Easter. But exasperation and irritation are harder to bear than unalloyed sadness. Sadness or loneliness can be the gateway to felicity or to exaltation; jangled nerves cannot. Alone you can form a lover-ly relationship with a city, with the material world. Casual human gestures delight. But irritation, which has to be masked and managed, clogs the pores of human feeling. If you are traveling alone, sadness or melancholy can be the means of discovery, of simultaneously burrowing inward and reaching out. It takes so much energy to skate on the grounds of superficial good manners—energy that deoxygenates the brain and hardens the heart. Sometimes, here alone, I have the odd but agreeable feeling that I am sinking into the air around me, that I am invisible, a part of the landscape, which I, in turn, take into me.

A friend has come to Venice, and we go to the nearby Church of San Moisè for Easter Mass on Saturday night. Its elaborate Venetian Baroque facade looks as if it had been made by a soft-ice-cream machine gone haywire—a glob here, a trickle there, here a whirl. Its shiny granite altarpiece, portraying a wrathful Jehovah and a quivering Moses with tablets of stone, is full of grotesque excrescences.

It is cold. I can feel the chill of marble through my sandals; my breath hangs in the air. San Moisè has an organ in need of repair and an unaccomplished violinist. The few tourists who wander in find the Mass insufficiently theatrical and leave, after shuffling their feet for a few moments, with embarrassed grins.

The bone often thrown to practicing Catholics by people who cannot believe that they have found themselves in the same room with one is that while the Church itself is . . . "Well, darling, *you* know," it's "*awfully* good theater, I do admit." This is an attitude I intensely dislike. Either the Church is the true Church or it is not; it does not exist to entertain us . . . which no doubt is evidence of my own reprehensible snobbery: As God speaks to us through our individual temperaments, He may, for all I know, call people to Him through theater. It is possible that people substitute the word *theater* for the word *community* because the word *community* makes them shy. Worshipers united in common purpose that transcends otherwise preserved differences—that is part of the meaning of the Mass, an unusual (and maybe scary) phenomenon in a world that celebrates individualism. The use of the word *theater* may be a way to diminish a dynamic the longing for which is sensed but, because of fear or convention, not acknowledged or articulated. The Mass is communion among men and women united in communion with God. That this—and not dumb show—might be what is happening is in part terrifying, in part thrilling. It is the ensemble playing that is in part feared, in part envied.

The celebrant of the Mass is an old man who has seen many changes in his lifetime (a young woman in slacks, her head uncovered, reads from the Book of Genesis), and, in spite of the familiar and familial way in which we address Our Lord, when I cup my hands to receive the Host—the Body of Christ—he is for a moment nonplussed. When he was ordained, one received the Host in one's mouth. It is an awkward moment; but then he smiles sweetly, and I move among the others—Italians love to mill around in church—and then we borrow light from one another's candles, in symbol and praise of the risen Lord—though as this is Italy, He defers his resurrection to 1:00 A.M., He is an hour late; and then we walk home through rain-washed streets.

These were small fires we lit, in a small church, but they dispersed the gloom. Soft fires, they wavered in the hard, cold air, but they were not extinguished. *Light unto light.*

On Easter Sunday we go to St. Mark's. "Not a very good cathedral," says an Englishman. "Well, perhaps if there weren't this *ceremony,* one could *see* it," says his wife, the ceremony being the Mass; "quite nice gold," she says.

Dickens, writing about Easter Sunday in Rome, said that "the ceremonies, in general, are of the most tedious and wearisome kind; the heat and crowd at every one of them, painfully oppressive; the hubbub, and confusion, quite distracting. We abandoned pursuit of these shows." Here is Dickens on Holy Thursday, perfectly candid in his bigotry (which, of course, he did not recognize as bigotry): "There were . . . a great many priests, walking two and two, and carrying—the good-looking priests at least—their lighted tapers, so as to throw the light with good effect upon their faces. . . . Those who were not handsome, or who had not long beards, carried *their* tapers anyhow, and abandoned themselves to spiritual contemplation. Meanwhile, the chanting was very monotonous and dreary."

In one of the chapels of St. Peter's, Dickens saw the Pope wash the feet of "thirteen men, representing the twelve apostles, and Judas Iscariot. . . . The Cardinals, and other attendants, smiled to each other, from time to time, as if the thing were a great farce; and if they thought so, there is little doubt they were perfectly right. His Holiness did what he had to do, as a sensible man gets through a troublesome ceremony, and seemed very glad when it was over."

Because Dickens, in common with all nineteenth-century travel writers, did not trouble to disguise his biases, his praise, when it is forthcoming, has the unmistakable ring of sincerity: "Easter Sunday was a day so bright and blue: so cloudless, balmy, wonderfully bright . . . that all the previous bad weather vanished from the recollection in a moment. . . . On this Sunday morning [Rome's fountains] were running diamonds. The miles of miserable streets through which we drove . . . were so full of color, that nothing in them was capable of wearing a faded aspect. . . . Every squalid and desolate hut in the Eternal City . . . was fresh and new with some ray of the sun." And at night, in St. Peter's, "what a sense of exaltation, joy, delight, it was . . . to behold one bright red mass of fire, soar gallantly from the top of the cupola to the extremest summit of the cross, and the moment it leaped into its place, become the signal of a bursting out of countless lights, as great, and red, and blazing as itself, from every part of the gigantic church; so that every cornice, capital, and smallest ornament of stone, expressed itself in fire."

Dickens mocked, scorned, and railed—and who can take umbrage?—but he saw the great point: *Light unto light.*

> I was happy, such a rare thing: Not in Venice, I don't mean that. I mean on Torcello. When I walked about Torcello in the early morning alone I was happy. I wanted to stay there forever.
>
> —*Harold Pinter,* Betrayal

"Once she did hold the gorgeous East in fee. . . ." After the sensual decay of Venice, a day in the country—through the marshland on Easter Sunday to lovely lost Torcello.

The central piazza of this lagoon island is grass-grown, and the grass— dotted with anemones and tulips that are already overblown and ragged, though spring seems hardly to have come—is comforting to the eye that has grown accustomed to water. There are only a few small, simple houses on Torcello, which went into malarial decline in the ninth century; the island is home to no more than a hundred fishermen.

Italians from Venice picnic here: love among the ruins. A pungent melancholy pervades the island. This is the fate Venice escaped; this is what Venice, which, compared with this simplicity, is a painted courtesan, given a change of tide and fortune, may become long after we are gone. From atop the campanile of Torcello, Ruskin cried: "Mother and daughter, you behold them both in their widowhood—Torcello and Venice." Chronology aside, a city less maternal in aspect and feeling than Venice has never existed.

It is strange for the eye accustomed to the consummate artifice of Venice to see the flowers and farm animals of Torcello, the peach and pear and apple trees in bloom, the weedy artichoke fields, the pheasants and parrots—and the caged canaries that Italians offer up to the Angel of Death, so that if he comes, he will take the smallest and least significant of the household, the yellow bird. Here on Torcello it is marvelously clear that the Angel of Death is no respecter of persons, or of civilizations.

Venice is shuttered. Torcello is open. There is almost a superfluity of flowers here, as if to remind us of what Venice so gorgeously invites us to forget: that we are dust and that to dust, to earth, which has seemed for days an alien, almost arbitrary, element, we must return. In Torcello you remember that it is as possible to be land-starved as it is to be water-starved; and you take in great breaths of sweet grass-green air. Children from Venice play in the grass and with it, as if grass were something amazing. This is how landlocked children respond when they first see the ocean.

Standing with a forlorn pride on the grassy piazza, the ruined Romanesque Church of Santa Fosca—its brick unsheathed by marble or shiny stone—inspires great tenderness (the octagonal is such a sweet, unthreatening shape, a circle frozen in the process of being squared). It is the bones and skeleton of a church; stripped bare of adornment, its timber vault naked and exposed, it is eloquent of a kind of purity. Near Santa Fosca, in the Cathedral of Santa Maria Assunta, a graceful elongated Byzantine Madonna floats above the stalls of the golden-tiled apse, holding a solemn baby in her willowy arms. She weeps mosaic tears. (For Him? For us?) One thinks of *her* as orphaned, though it was her son who died. Mary's color is lapis lazuli; blue is her color because the pigment, made from lapis, was the dearest and most precious of all. (I always think lapis lazuli should be the name of a place—a lost continent, perhaps. . . . "Blue as a vein o'er the Madonna's breast," Browning called lapis. . . .) This floating Mary is ethereal, long-necked and supple, the arches of her slim feet high and elegant; but in my imagination, the girl to whom the angel Gabriel announced the most terrifying and exalting news is a peasant girl, sturdy, with a wide pelvis and short peasant's feet and a shy and sun-warmed open face, a girl who did not swoon but accepted her fate with gravity, wonder, humility, and a calm and sturdy joy.

Elsewhere in Santa Maria there is a huge fresco of the Last Judgment. In and out of the eyes of the skeletal remains of the damned slide cannibal snakes, feasting on brains. It is no wonder Christianity, so various, provokes such various responses: Mary weeps; the reptiles gorge. (My companion turns her eyes away.)

Because it is Easter Sunday, we eat kid, which is not as good as it sounds and which, in fact, seems on this day cannibalistic.

Up and down the tiny lanes of the tiny island, and then we leave the felicitously poignant place, walking alongside a willow-lined canal to the ferry dock. This is the dog's end of a holiday; I am reminded suddenly of the frayed endings of bright summer beach days when we came back from Coney Island on the Sea Beach train, which was as crowded as we were cranky. (No matter how often this happened, we always forgot that we would come home cranky; only the sparkling blue hours of sun remained in our memories.) Everybody at the ferry dock is cranky. The ferry is too crowded to take us all on; the ferryman, making light of our accumulating distress, spreads his arms and calls us all, male and female, "brides who can't wait for love." He exhorts us to wait for another, smaller boat that is just in view; but when the smaller vessel arrives, its boatman won't let us on, something to do with rules and routes. So the ferryman who has assured us that our patience will be rewarded shouts to the operator of the smaller boat across a stretch of water: "I left thirty-five fat behinds here waiting like brides [he exaggerates by twenty], and I promised every ass it would have a place to put its rear end!" The ferryman prevails, and a major incident—his loss of face—is averted.

(On the way to Torcello, not wishing to be late for our al fresco lunch of spaghetti with eggplant and mozzarella, and kid, at the Locanda Cipriani, we took a water taxi. The driver of the *motoscafo* made a rude gesture to a passing boatman, a gesture that implied that we were suckers—in both the monetary and the sexual sense. Taxi drivers will be taxi drivers, even in Venice, even on the sea, and this is nice, because Venice has a reality aside from the perceptions of visitors and is not exotic to those who live here.)

I love the cultivated gardens of Torcello, I love its weeds and scrubby fields. My grandfather always had gardens. He had a Victory Garden in Brooklyn during World War II; he planted sweet basil for the Allies while he sang the Fascist youth anthem. I·think of all Italians as having gardens. I know that Venice has gardens—tiny gardens, spilling over with azalea and bougainvillaea and lantana and sweet peas—but gardens don't leap to mind when you think of Venice, they are not part of the Venice unconscious.

The crowds on the Riva are oppressive when we land at Venice. I feel slightly giddy, as if the ground might not be there to receive my next step. We go to the Danieli for drinks. In the hushed, ornate lobby of the fourteenth-century palazzo (a lobby where Dickens, D'Annunzio, and Wagner sat), a group of Texans are discussing their insurance policies. "Mama's *eighty-five* and *blind!*" one jeweled lady shouts. "She's on her last legs, honey, and *deaf*, too." "*Speriamo*," says her faintly smiling waiter, "*speriamo*" ("Let us hope so"). She takes this to be an endearment.

One year I went to the terrace of the Gritti, the other great hotel on the Grand Canal, to watch the regatta. An old lady wearing a hairnet and white socks and oxfords and a housedress engaged me in conversation about her grandchildren—her gift to the future, she called them—and my children. Children are the good people, she said. When it came time for him to put the tablecloths on the tables, the maître d' asked me to leave, as I had no reservation. I was sad. The parade of all kinds of vessels, some manned by beautiful young men and women, others by very old hands, is one of the gayest and prettiest sights in the world—everything sparkling and all moods buoyant—and I regretted having to leave the pleasant old lady, too. The pleasant old lady addressed the maître d' sternly and nodded to me beneficently, and I was allowed to stay and made to feel welcome. When the first gondola pulled up to the Gritti, the gondolier ceremoniously handed the old lady a sheath of roses, addressed her as Contessa, and kissed her hand, as did subsequent boatmen. I never learned the name of the contessa/grand marshal; but this incident—the woman's kindness, the not impersonal negotiations built on the slender thread of mutual affection for the young and on family feeling—enabled me to think of Venice in a new and happy way: not as a bazaar or mercantile arena or as a museum but as a place of shared human responses, a place where people trade in goodness.

There is a ragtag sign hand-lettered on the door of the Accademia: CHIUSO PER RIPOSO SETTIMANALE. Evidently Easter week has proven too arduous for the museum guards, who feel themselves entitled to a little rest. Oh, my negligence makes me sad; no Titians, no Bellinis for me. (The only Bellini a drink named after the painter at Harry's Bar—peach nectar and champagne.) No Veroneses, no Carpaccios (the only carpaccio a dish of paper-thin raw beef named after the painter), no Tintorettos, no Giorgiones. I would come this far just to see Carpaccio's *Dream of St. Ursula,* which, having once been seen, can never be forgotten: The young girl lies sleeping upon her bed—so still—while the angel brings tidings of her future martyrdom. Her head rests on her cupped palm, her eyes are closed, she sweetly dreams the angel in the muted morning light; scarcely a wrinkle in the red and white bedclothes to show for the sad tidings. The canopied bed is solid and untrembling in the presence of an angel. Poor Ursula, whose slippers, neatly placed, do not protest this imposition of trumpets. And I wanted to see all those paintings of camels in St. Mark's Square, the Annunciation and the Ascension taking place in St. Mark's, and Jesus suckling on the Grand Canal—for how could they have imagined that Bethlehem looked different from Venice?

Sometimes I think I do it on purpose, leaving places unseen—my form of insurance. I must see Ursula again; I must come back again to see the early-morning market at the Rialto Bridge, bounty in crystalline light and gondoliers calling "Oy!"; and next time I will go inside the Ca' Rezzonico, the most splendid of all the palazzi, and perhaps I'll even enter the Arsenal, swim in the Lido. . . . All the time I was eating the oversalted food of Venice (which cannot seem to retire its obligation to the salt that helped to make it rich), and liver and onions with polenta, and fish fries and spider crabs, and hamburgers at Harry's Bar, and plate-sized pizzas and risi-e-bisi at Al Teatro, and pasta with four cheeses (which is actually only three cheeses: Gorgonzola and fontina and mozzarella), and confections made of zuppa inglese and sponge cake and semifreddo and chocolate cream, I could have been getting better acquainted with the Ca' d'Oro (its tarted-up lacy Gothic archways), the white-domed Church of Santa Maria della Salute at the entrance to the Grand Canal. . . . I don't regret any errors of omission, I don't think they are errors: These things and places unseen are amulets I hold against time, the common enemy.

A long time ago a courtier of the Nizam of Hyderabad gave me six Venetian glass goblets, pale summer-green crystal with cut-glass cascades of grapes and rims of hand-painted gold. He could not put an age to them, but they were very old and very fine. One by one they broke. In those days I owned little that was beautiful, and what I had I needed to touch every day. When I think of those tall goblets now, I think with sadness that I once held part of Renaissance Venice in my hands (sometimes my babies drank milk out of them); and my sadness is informative. It tells me that love and greed, tenderness and acquisitiveness, can coexist—in the human heart . . . in Venice, too.

Chapter III

"LOVELY FLORENCE"

SAN GIMIGNANO:

"CITY OF FINE TOWERS"

When I dream of houses I have lived in, I am reclaiming the past. When I dream of rambling rooms and intimate corners, I am staking a claim on what the dream allows me to believe is a possible future. I collect houses—teapots in the form of English cottages, green vines curling around chimneys and doors, tiny windows lodged snugly just below overhanging thatched roofs; and sugar pots and cream pitchers in the shape of cottages, too, and one cup; and salt cellars, miniature bisque towers with mullioned windows and gray turrets; and a cookie jar with violent-orange trees thrusting cozily in crazy logic against a manor house door. When I look at these houses, I feel safe.

When I ride on a train and see the backs of houses, the minutiae of daily life fascinate me; daydreaming, I own the houses, I feel safe.

Estruscans made funeral urns in the shape of houses.

Dreaming through the noble Tuscan landscape, the terraced hills crowned by churches and towers and blessed by vineyards, and everything—stone houses, silver-green olive trees, blue-green undulating fields, triangles and bowls of wheat-green land bordered by dark exclamatory cypresses and shaded by beneficent umbrella pines—everything bathed in the austere, uncompromising Tuscan light, I feel that life is altogether bounteous and good, lovable, manageable, sweet.

This landscape is unchanged since the nineteenth century, one of my trainmates remarks (and indeed it is a landscape Victorians loved); but because so many Florentine painters set Christ among the cypress groves, Mary among the olive trees, it seems centuries older: a dream of Bethlehem.

Our *pensione*, the Pitti Palace (named for the museum, which is a five-minute walk away), is on the Oltrarno, the left bank of the Arno, on Via Barbadori, just over the Ponte Vecchio, the jeweler's bridge, which was before the sixteenth century the butcher's bridge, and the only one to have survived World War II. Several streets intersect on this side of the busy bridge; they form a *piazzetta* (a newsstand, a café, a taxi rank). If you turn sharply right after you cross the romantic bridge, lined, on each side, with red-tiled shops, you pass a wall fountain—a charming satyr spouting diamond ribbons of water into a basin—and you are at the pleasant establishment of Amedeo and Mary Ann Pinto. In this nest of narrow streets one finds again that familiar and felicitous Italian phenomenon, a village within a city.

I spend late afternoons drinking Aperol, the honey- and orange-colored Florentine aperitif, on the roof garden of Amedeo and Mary Ann's hotel. The rooftop, which bristles with the telephone and television antennas that somehow never show up in pictures of the sloping, projecting roofs of Florence, is an ad hoc affair. There are pots of sweet basil and rosemary and thyme and dill, and tomatoes in old tins, and pansies, a few scattered tables and chairs, strings of laundry, perennially blooming climbing Tuscan roses *("le rose d'ogni mese")* . . . and there is Florence: the pink-black-green-and-white-marble candy-striped Duomo; Brunelleschi's white-ribbed red dome; Giotto's Lily Tower; the sober gray-and-white Uffizi Gallery making its ordered geometric statement. Paintings have so accustomed me to seeing the Annunciation take place in the hills of Tuscany, I half expect to see flights of angels every time I sit here. (I would not be the first to wait in happy expectation: Citizens of the Republic of Florence believed their sacred city would be redeemed by armed angels descending from the skies.)

Vespas are credited with bringing people from outlying districts into the city center and helping to tear down class distinctions; it has been said that, small and friendly, they are more like household appliances than automobiles. When you walk down the narrow streets of Florence, Vespas (and cars) whiz by so closely you can feel the hairs on the back of your neck stand up. There are designated parking stations for Vespas, and one of them is outside the windows of Mary Ann and Amedeo's *pensione*. Their noise has sent more than a few tourists flying to a hotel in the hills of Fiesole; for me, the eccentric and happy hominess of the Pitti Palace is more than ample recompense for belching motorscooters and motorcycles (for which Vespa has become the generic term).

The dull-green Arno smells. The lobby of the Pitti Palace hotel smells. *Lobby* is a courtesy word for the ground-floor hallway that accommodates the *pensione*'s lift, which has a mind of its own. The *pensione* occupies the third through the sixth floors of a postwar building that is otherwise occupied by psychiatrists and mysterious others with equally quiet pursuits. On the fifth floor are the reception area and a lounge that is full of yellowing old books and plump sofas and easy chairs covered with chintz, from which one can see the crenellated tower of the Palazzo Vecchio, gaunt, beautiful, and "too stony," Henry James says, "to be brilliant." The airy yellow breakfast room has the slightly sour smell of damp linen—a smell like that of yeast, a good, morning smell. Two of the gilded chairs in this room are wobbly, their legs uneven. Every morning one of the wobbly chairs is propped up by a folded napkin—but always only one, and one never knows which one it is to be.

From the window of the lounge I see into an office in a red-tiled building: A man, pensive, chain-smoking, sits surrounded by tree stands of rubber stamps. He is elegantly dressed. With the hand that does not hold his cigarette, he stamps paper after paper all day long. He is a living caricature; he says: Bureaucracy.

Some of the rooms in the Pitti Palace look like something the Red Cross set up in an emergency—offices with cots. Some of the rooms are palatial; they have oriels and deep-eyed windows and chaise longues and beautiful old furniture and views of medieval towers. The elevator that services these rooms cannot handle more than one set of instructions at a time. It will, when it is occupied, not stop in its descent or ascent to pick up a waiting guest. In Italy one learns patience.

Mary Ann, who has lived in Florence for nearly two decades, speaks perfectly grammatical Italian with an American accent so heavy as to obscure her earnest meaning. Amedeo speaks unidiomatic English with a perfect American accent. Mary Ann and Amedeo miss each other when they are a floor apart. He brings her breakfast in bed and calls her sweetheart and darlingheart.

I love this place.

I share a bath with an elegant elderly couple who wear lavender water like an aura and have cornsilk white hair—they speak to no one but each other and bestow smiles on all; and with a middle-aged German man and woman—are they lovers? father and daughter?—who dress exactly alike (black suit, white shirt, bow tie, black-and-ivory walking stick). One of these people—I don't know which—does not flush the toilet. It's not so much the not flushing that I mind (though I do) as the not knowing. Why this should trouble me so much I don't know.

A guest grumbles that the manservant at the Pitti Palace must be cousin to the elevator. Agostino shuffles slowly back and forth to the pantry; he never makes one trip when two will do. Two requests, two trips; two guests, two trips—his logic, though limited, is impeccable; his appearance is not. His hair stands up like a brush. Either his slightly soiled white jacket or his slightly soiled white shirt is buttoned askew. He seems to take a kind of pleasure in this, as he takes a saturnine pleasure in all minor misfortunes accruing to him: Sporting an egg-splotched ascot, he stops at the threshold of the roof garden and croaks that he has a sore throat; this saves him the work of walking five feet to carry our drinks to us, and it also allows him to luxuriate in self-pity ("What is life for a poor thing like me?"). But just when you think this fellow is altogether dark and withdrawn—when you think that he hates his life and you, too—he displays an almost feminine curiosity, his gloomy uncommunicativeness dissipates. He hovers over your easy chair and examines your purchases with the soft pleasure of a child.

Glaring: "Caffelatte," he says at breakfast, as if to warn anyone who might have the temerity to ask for anything else. "Some want lemon, some want milk," he says, singsong. This business of choice greatly afflicts him; he rolls his eyes heavenward, flicking at imaginary dust motes with his stale towel. Trying to affect disdain, he avidly listens to breakfast conversations, uncontrollably grunting to express understanding, approval, or disapproval; he moves his lips in silent soliloquy. One morning he listens to an American who is on his way to Venice; while English spinsters stare, he bursts into song—a gondolier's song—holding a four-minute egg aloft in his hand. "Poor old thing" that he professes himself to be, Agostino would rather be Agostino than anyone else in the world. *"Meno male,"* he responds to inquiries about his well-being—which means, literally, "less bad," a frugal Florentine way of saying: "I am as God wishes me to be."

Old Giulia is older than stone, she has been here forever, longer than Mary Ann, who is intimidated by her. Giulia looks like a frog. She and Agostino have not spoken to each other in years. Giulia grunts, too. Her main function is to spur the young cleaning women on to greater activity. One evening I find her sitting on my bed. She has taken it into her head to bring me a pot of hot chocolate and a plate of biscuits. She greets me with a grunt. She elicits from me the fact that I am divorced; she wants to know all about my children. *Brutto,* she says, *brutto* (ugly)—her judgment upon divorce, upon bringing children up without a father. She likes me. I can't begin to satisfy her greed for detail. She points to the rings I wear and communicates mutely that she wants to see my jewelry. I have been through this ritual before, other times, other places. It is about stories, it is not about jewels ("and my husband gave me this, and this was my mother's"). "If commodities could speak . . ." Marx said. They do. Poor Marx, he couldn't read the language of jewelry, two women sitting on a bed. "Cultural anthropology reconstructs the systems of social life from objects," Umberto Eco says. The labor of poetry, Giambattista Vico wrote, "is to give sense and passion to insensate things; and it is characteristic of children to take inanimate things in their hands and talk to them in play as if they were living persons." This is what Giulia does. Giulia is on an anthropological dig of my psyche.

Now every day Giulia greets me in the breakfast room (Agostino glares), her hands on her ample hips. Sometimes she utters, sometimes she does not. Sometimes she sticks out her tongue at me; this is a gesture of affection. She nods solemnly: "The Pitti Palace is *magnifico,*" she says. She says this every day. She includes me and Florence in this encomium. She tells me that she loves chocolates. I extend a box of chocolates to her, and with one of her brown paws she makes to grab them all; she grunts. Every day I bring her Perugina chocolates, which she tucks into her apron; her grunting acceptance of the gift is her only form of thanks.

Giulia prays to St. Zita. St. Zita was for forty-eight years a servant girl in the house of the Fatinelli family of Lucca, disliked by the other servants for her pronounced piety. One day, when Lucca was under interdict, Zita had to choose between baking the day's bread for the rich family of wool dealers she served or going to church to receive Holy Communion. She went to church. When she came back, she found bread baked by the angels of the Lord. Zita's feast day is celebrated with chocolate cake. She is the patron saint of servants and especially concerns herself with their lost keys and with their safety when crossing bridges or rivers. This comes in handy in Florence.

"I make myself small," Ruth says.

Ruth is a guest at the Pitti Palace hotel. She has come to Florence, as have so many before her, to find peace on a limited income. She is in her seventies. Age has rendered her orthodox beauty exquisite. Her aristocratic bones are close, now, to the surface of her milk-white skin; the whites of her eyes are only slightly less blue than the irises. "I am not managing well," she says. She longs for the luxury of breakfast in bed but cannot bring herself to ask for this concession to her age and fragility. (*"Povera signora,* do you have fever?" the maids ask when they bring me breakfast in bed. *Fever* is their term for all nonspecific maladies, including laziness and self-indulgence. They make my bed while I am still in it.) Disappointment has not dulled Ruth's intellect; she talks with lively wit of art and history and metaphysics, but more often than not she doesn't know what day or what time it is. "I'm not managing well," she says quietly; there is no belligerence in her. She cannot bring herself to get on the bus to Siena or Fiesole or San Gimignano; she is afraid the peace she is looking for will elude her even in those beautiful hill towns. Ruth wanders about with her map and her guidebook, looking for gardens, looking (where are her children, whose pictures she clutches?) for a place to lay her head. "Florence is not a romantic city anymore." She sighs. The young drug addicts nodding in the sunlight of the lovely Piazza of Santo Spirito; the scuttling Gypsies everywhere, their babies in bandoliers, their hard, darting eyes shooting poison glances at foreigners; the Hare Krishnas and the Senegalese selling gewgaws on the Ponte Vecchio, where once mendicants and friars walked in peace: they all frighten Ruth. "Make yourself anonymous," Mary Ann warns. Ruth keeps herself small.

Elsa is twenty-seven. She is adorable, slightly decayed, sweet-sour. She is in transit from Kuwait, and she is embittered by all her ephemeral love affairs, and eager to start another. She complains: Men lunge at her in train compartments, at coffee bars, in trams. She would be indignant if they did not. Elsa wants a boyfriend, not just a lover, desperately. But she is willing to settle for heat and play, though she talks about babies, babies, babies. She is a doctor. One night we walk across the Ponte Vecchio together; she is wearing tight black corduroys, a black leather jacket open to a blouse that exposes one shoulder with a perfectly round beauty mark; all her clothes are old and worn; she has moody blue eyes and a dimpled, pouting smile, her frizzled hair is streaked, blond on blond. She is stalking a man with an interesting back: black silk pants, a creamy shantung jacket—and white cotton athletic socks. We see a couple embracing, and she bumps her hip—grinds it—into mine; "Oooh," she says. Her grind is a sexual reflex; she would include anyone next to her in her muzzy lust. She hastens toward the man with the interesting back, who circles around and behind her. "Don't make me follow you like this," he says. "Where are you from?" An exceedingly banal conversation follows; it means: Bed. He is not in the least to be trusted, she is making a mistake. She feels responsible for me because she has invited me for a walk. I think I should protect her. Irritated by her silliness—from which I feel obliged to protect her—I signal that I am bowing out. She is supposed to leave tomorrow morning for Capri. Off she goes with her predatory boy. In the morning she knocks on my door; she reports that he has asked to marry her; he wants to take her to Lebanon, he is Lebanese. She says he folded all his clothes—"he undressed more slowly than any man I ever knew"—as carefully as if he were packing for a final happy voyage. "It's his hunting suit," she says. "Oh, when will I ever have a baby?" She leaves for Capri.

For years Florence endeared itself to expatriates (to English expatriates in particular, complaints that it was "overmonumented and underbathroomed" notwithstanding). Hawthorne said of Florence that "the intellect finds a home [in it] more than in any other spot in the world and wins the heart to stay in it," and John Singer Sargent, who was born on Via Guicciardini, around the corner from the Pitti Palace hotel, said Florence was the only place where he felt perfectly at ease. Henry James, with his great and casual Anglo chauvinism, his equation of dark beauty with deceit, said that Englishmen were seen to particularly good advantage in Florence: "In the midst of these false and beautiful Italians they glow with the light of the great fact, that after all they love a bath-tub and they hate a lie."

Montaigne thought the cathedral and the bell tower, "all faced with black and white marble . . . one of the most beautiful and sumptuous things in the world," but he declared that he had "never . . . seen a nation where there were so few beautiful women as the Italian." When he met the scandalous intriguer Bianca Cappello of Venice, he pronounced her "beautiful by Italian notions, an agreeable and imperious face, big bust, and breasts the way they like them." (He had nothing but praise, however, for the large and luscious melons of Tuscany.) At first he found little to like in Florence, and much to complain of: dirty earthenware vessels, grievously cumbersome shutters, filthy and expensive hostelries, peculiarly small drinking glasses. He was at the time, however, passing gallstones, which, in a fit of justifiable irritability, he blamed on Tuscan wine. Florence eventually brought him to his knees.

He was at last obliged to confess "that Florence was rightly called 'the beautiful.' "

British-born Iris Origo, who has brilliantly re-created the world of a Tuscan merchant *(The Merchant of Prato)* and of a Tuscan saint *(The World of San Bernardino)* and who has lived the large part of her graceful life in Tuscany, farm wife to a farming nobleman, says that "the established Anglo-Florentine . . . felt himself to have become as much a part of the city life as any Tuscan. Some of these residents sank roots so deep that when, at the outbreak of the Second World War, the British Consulate attempted to repatriate them, a number of obscure old ladies refused to leave, saying that, after fifty years residence in Florence, they preferred even the risk of a concentration camp to a return to England."

Many of them came because Florence was cheap. Many of them came because they believed that Italy was a paradise where the sun never ceased to shine. (But the South is sunnier as well as cheaper; and even on the Mediterranean, kerosene stoves are used against the winter chill.) Many of them—like Robert and Elizabeth Barrett Browning, whose unprepossessing palazzo, the Casa Guidi (in the cellar of which Elizabeth's dog, Flush, is buried), is across the street from a *latteria* that neighborhood people say has the best gelato in Florence, and across also from the Pitti Palace Museum—came to Florence to escape domestic entanglements. They found themselves embroiled in new ones: Elizabeth dressed their son, Pen, like a girl until her death (the boy was ten when she died; his long blond ringlets, which were like those of a fifteenth-century Italian boy, occasioned much comment on the streets of Florence), and she got awfully enthusiastic about spiritualism, an eccentricity her husband was obliged to tolerate.

They stayed, many of them, because the design of God–the–Artist seemed nowhere so visible as in Florence. "Nowhere else," Anatole France said, "is nature so subtle, elegant, and fine. The God who made the hills of Florence was an artist. How could it be possible that this violet hill of San Miniato, so purely and firmly designed, be by the same author of the Mont Blanc?" By comparison, all else was gross.

The dialectic between the narrowness of street and the sunny stone expanse of piazza creates an elastic tension that soothes as it thrills. "And there is almost no space here; and you feel almost calm at the thought that it is impossible for anything but the large to hold in this narrowness." Rilke was not speaking of Florence when he wrote this, but he might have been. Florence is contained in its hills, and it is a stone nest in which we are cozily contained (the stones are the color of warm earth; the spirit rises). Florence—

even more than incomparably beautiful Rome—because of its compactness, because it is knowable, entices and allures with names alone: Michelangelo, Brunelleschi, Dante, Savonarola, Machiavelli. We walk their streets, we eat where they ate, our hands touch what they have touched. We live history and breathe art and feel ourselves not to be strangers. (In the eighteenth century Vico said of the Romans that "their word for hearing was *audire*, as if *haurire*, for the ears drink in the air which has been set in motion by other bodies.") You can see Florence from Florence—it encapsulates you; and you always feel that you are never more than a few steps away from a vantage point that will offer you the view of the quintessential Florence of dreams and remembrance. Benvenuto Cellini tells us that "Caesar decided to call the . . . city Florence (Fiorenza), as it was a very beautiful name and very apposite, and it seemed, with its suggestion of flowers, to make a good omen." Caesar did well. Florence does suggest—as magnificent Rome does not—the sweetness of flowers. The Florence of memory and imagination is an ineffably perfumed city. In April metaphor becomes fact; Florence puts on a flower show. The Loggia della Signoria and the courtyard of the Palazzo Vecchio and the Uffizi Gallery are banked and circled by pots of brilliantly colored plants—azalea, tuberose, bougainvillaea, wisteria— resplendent against gray stone, brown stone, and cityscape. "The very *sweetest* among cities," Henry James called it, the "rounded pearl of cities," revising his earlier estimate that the narrowness of the streets and the "vast cyclopean structure of many of the buildings is rather gloomy." Its sweetness, its "delicate charm," restored him—as it restored, at last, even poor suffering Montaigne "to perfect equanimity."

Beautiful and imposing, efficient, neat, "combining usefulness with grace" (Goethe), a "delicious mixture of beauty and convenience" (James): Is there not an element of condescension in these raptures? The British, after all, once acted almost as if Florence were a colonial outpost; many of them seldom troubled to talk with Florentines other than their servants, but they were able, nevertheless, to say they "loved" Florence. Unlike disturbing, ambiguous Venice, Florence could be encompassed, mentally and physically; one could walk from hill to verdant hill without taxing oneself unduly; Florence was a small town. It did not intimidate one with layers and layers of visible history, as Rome did, nor did it force one strenuously, as Rome did, to confront one's religious beliefs. Rome was a city of profound and passionate encounters; Florence gentled one. Florence existed to charm.

Florentines are generally thought to have the virtues of small-town dwellers, about which qualities we are of several minds. "In Florence," Stendhal said, "the people are very logical, prudent, and even witty; but I have never seen men more devoid of passions; love itself is so unknown there that pleasure has usurped its name. The great and deep passions inhabit Rome. As for the Neapolitan, he is the slave of the sensation of the moment." The narrowness of Florentine streets invaded Stendhal's thinking about Florentines: "Florence people are sometimes narrow-minded; they busy themselves too much with little things." Every Italian will tell you that *his* city is the most beautiful in all of Italy; I have never met anyone who broke that rule. Italians to the north and to the south of Florence are fond of repeating that "the streets of Florence are narrow and full of shit, and so are its people."

But for those who have an enduring love of Florence, it is incomprehensible that anyone should wish to call another place home. Mary Ann, at the Pitti Palace hotel, has beautiful manners, but she permits me to see that in my love of Rome—sprawling, splashy, untidy, layered, passionate, spectacular Rome—she sees something that partakes of the vulgar. For lovers of Florence, disdainful of exuberant Baroque, unmoved by explosions of color, there is no place on earth at once so charming, dignified, straightforward, gentle, and kind.

There is something magical about the way the Ponte Vecchio shuts down in the early hours of the morning, shuttered doors—secretive, like jewel boxes ("nail-studded like dungeon doors," H. V. Morton says)—closed against the glittering contents, the unmistakable gleam of gold. One would like to think Dante met Beatrice here. He didn't. One would like to think a fine sensibility is required to appreciate the Ponte Vecchio. It isn't. The Ponte Vecchio, with its shattered sundial so nicely placed over the Arno as to remind us of time and tides, its bust of Cellini on which a pigeon, as if by fiat, permanently perches, was Hitler's favorite bridge. Hitler called Florence the jewel of Europe and said, after half a day in the city, that his joy in Florence (odd to think of Hitler experiencing joy) eclipsed his joy in Rome. (This was not a sentiment shared by Mussolini, who, during the Führer's first visit, was heard to mutter, as he trudged behind him at the Uffizi, *"Tutti questi quadri!"*—"All these damned pictures!") Florence returned Hitler's favor by greeting him enthusiastically.

Hitler is said to have given orders to blow up the bridges of Florence, "saving only the most artistic one"—the Ponte Vecchio. Buildings on either side of the Ponte Vecchio were demolished to make access to the bridge impossible; a score of palaces, perhaps a dozen medieval towers, and fifty medieval houses were so destroyed. Dante's Florence was eviscerated.

It rained on the occasion of Hitler's first visit to Florence. In old pictures he can be seen in a sea of umbrellas on the Ponte Vecchio. (It is strange how these newspaper photographs call to mind the very peopled paintings of fifteenth-century Florentine artists—people of all classes minutely observed, craning and posturing.) By the summer of 1943 Germans were in full possession of Florence, and they had removed all the gold and silver from the shops on the Ponte Vecchio. In old photos pretty girls hand flowers to German soldiers. Short years later other pretty girls, who look like the same pretty girls, applaud British soldiers. (In pictures of those war years everybody looks exactly the same; my mother, a pretty girl, is interchangeable with thousands of other mothers, or so I always think.) Florentines who had welcomed Hitler greeted the liberators with equal enthusiasm; railing against the mystical languors and cynicism of Fascism, they marched toward the Duomo, singing songs of the Risorgimento.

In terrible and eloquent photographs the Ponte Santa Trinità, which died hard—three charges of explosives were required to demolish it—looks as if it is sighing as it goes down in exhalations of smoke. From a design by Michelangelo, carried out by Ammannati, this slender bridge, strong and delicate, with its three great looping feminine arches—arches that conform to no known geometrical shape—supported by two strong, masculine pillars, was reconstructed in 1958. All the bridges we so much admire are, as things Italian go, new; the last wooden bridge was swept away in the great flood of 1557. The Ponte Vecchio was built in 1345.

Just as Londoners looked, every morning, to see if St. Paul's was still standing in the City after air raids, the first impulse of Florentines was to look, after bombardments, at Brunelleschi's dome, which, in pictures of these sad times, rises serenely from the wasteland of rubble.

On Via Guicciardini, where the torturer and informer Carità found and seized arms parachuted into Florence for the Resistance Action party, there is a jeweler, Niccolò Forte, who was born in Naples and is loyal to his memories of that city; his remarks about the war are astringently Florentine: "The reason the Germans didn't destroy the Ponte Vecchio was not because of the goodness of their hearts or for reasons of aesthetics. That is sentimental nonsense. The Ponte Vecchio is the only bridge with shops. The Germans knew the Allies would simply make a new bridge out of the rubble. So they blew up the other bridges—less rubble.

"One day we awoke to see posters—proclamations—advising us all to leave the quarter until the last German soldier was across the bridge. It seemed quite reasonable and civilized not to interfere with troop movements, but many Florentines thought it would do just as well to stay at home. So they were killed. Because what the Germans didn't tell us was that they were going to destroy the houses on the Lungarno.

"I was a young boy. I can remember what sounded like bombs. When people went back to their homes to retrieve their possessions and to collect family members, many were killed by unexploded mines.

"Now, if I were French, I would say we were all partisans. Have you ever met a Frenchman who was not part of the Resistance? All hypocrisy and lies. There were more Fascist bandits than there were partisans, you may believe. We were all Fascists; it's how we grew up. [According to the best estimates, two hundred partisans were killed in Florence in 1945.] And Mussolini wasn't bad for the laborers; he gave us pensions and half-day holidays. He and his family died poor, surrounded by thieves. He made one major mistake—to join that madman Hitler."

It is necessary for man's view of himself to believe that war is at least as ennobling as it is brutalizing; as another Florentine said to me, "We believe in the Resistance, so we have therefore to believe that goodness matters—or we believe in the Resistance *in order* to believe that goodness matters. But the reality is that exhaustion determines the outcome of most wars, and most people, having been sinned against in time of war, sin." Less than a month after Signor Forte delivered himself of remarks that a sentimentalist would call cynical, faced with a series of suicides and murders in the Apennine town of Bargagli, Elvizio Massai, deputy leader of a band of partisans, said that the ranks of partisans under his command—in actual fact fifteen hundred fighting men—was inflated to number twenty-six thousand toward the end of the war. "If there had been that many partisans in the area," he said, "we could have taken the Germans by the hand and led them out like children." Inquiring into postwar murders (five by hanging) over a looted Nazi treasure left in the forest near Bargagli by retreating Germans, state magistrate Rosario D'Angelo said that the Italian National Partisan Association "behaves as though the Resistance were the Immaculate Conception."

Italians may be shocked but they are not surprised, and they are not plunged into despair nor do they go into frenzies of denial when people they supposed were good turn out to have acted badly. Italians believe in Original Sin. As they have also been taught to believe in the ultimate triumph of good over evil (the Incarnation and the Resurrection—whether they profess to believe in those events or not), they do not go into paroxysms of surprised joy when people behave well. This measured view is, depending on one's own theories of human nature, seen as cynicism or realism.

"We could not be bothered to kill the Jews. We lack the energy for sustained hatred, and we lack the stomach. [Bernard Berenson said that the Nazi persecution of the Jews was "incomprehensible to Florentines."]

"We knew we would lose the war after Pearl Harbor. Americans are our cousins; there are so many of us there. . . . The English, of course, are snakes. They have always acted in concert with our enemies and ruined our economy. [Signor Forte's memory goes back a long way: to 1339, when Edward III went bankrupt and brought down with him the two great Florentine banking houses of the Bardi and the Peruzzi, thus effectively ruining Florence as a world banking power.] The Austrians ruled us. The Spaniards ruled us. The French ruled us. But what reason could we have to kill an American?

"It was good that we lost the war. It is appalling to think we might now be ruled by the Germans. The Japanese, now . . . so kind, so lovely to do business with. . . .

"Ah, it was so long ago. We Italians survive everything."

Signora Forte says: "My husband is a Fascist."

At the end of World War II the bell of the Palazzo del Bargello tolled, as it does for the end of the century . . . and as it did on the day of November 4, 1966.

Florentines behaved beautifully during the devastating flood of 1966, "with a courage, an absence of self-pity, a kindness and a sense of humor beyond all praise," Iris Origo writes, "digging in the stinking mud and rubble, distributing food and water and drugs, blankets and clothing, salvaging works of art and precious manuscripts, saving old people and patients in hospitals who had been marooned, Communists working beside parish priests, Red Cross nurses beside young students. . . ."

Italians love a good joke, especially when it's on them, and all the better if it is illustrative of human folly, and so they often give the flood of 1966 as proof of the incompetence of civil workers, who (in the now compressed, popularized version of the events of November 4, 1966) opened the sluice gates to regulate the roaring waters and then "forgot" how (or when) to close them. The waters of the swollen Arno came hurtling over bridges at fifty miles an hour and covered eleven and a half miles, spreading over two-thirds of the city. The Pitti Palace hotel, without electricity, got its water from the springs of the Boboli Gardens. Giulia—whom it is impossible to imagine having ever been young—carried the water up six flights of stairs in green hand-blown glass urns that were used to transport oil and cheap wine; they were half her height and must have been half her weight. (One seldom sees these elegant containers nowadays; they have been replaced by plastic. I owned two of them when I lived in Libya in 1961—I used to love to regard their beautiful imperfections—but then I moved to India and the servants didn't see the point of them and they got broken, and I was very sad.) In many shops there are plaques to indicate the waterline of the flood; in some it is over six feet from the ground. All over Florence there are plaques commemorating floods—in that dignified, decent, and delightful Italian way whereby everything public is publicly named and cataloged: the flood of 1333, the flood of 1547, and the flood of 1740 (and now the Arno is jaundice-yellow/green and sluggish). In the flood of 1966 lizard handbags and gold chains were embedded in the mud near the Ponte Vecchio. . . .

Streets paved with gold. That is what my father, ten years old when he came to America from southern Italy, expected to find here. He didn't, he was later fond of saying (defying the women of his family, whose memories of raw poverty had been laundered by moderate success), even find streets lined with cabbages. Before dawn, my father, Dominick, and his brother, Lenny, went to the produce markets of New York equipped with long spiked poles with which they impaled lettuces and cabbages that rolled off the trucks (and some that didn't roll off trucks); they took these home in burlap sacks slung across their shoulders. (America, Toynbee said, is the worst country to be poor in.) When I tell Signor Forte this story, he says, "Italy is the real America—there is gold in the air, in the light." The amber light is turning to soft blue streaked with rose, and the Gothic cypresses and the inverted bowls of umbrella pines are making dark statements against the definite sky; who am I to disagree?

The barren interior of the Duomo, vast Cathedral of St. Mary of the Flower, astonishes without delighting. It is easy to sympathize with the English tourist who, gazing at acres of gray Gothic, says to her companion, "They don't heat churches here," and easy, even, to agree with Stendhal, who said, "Only the Gothic style is in harmony with a terror-inspiring religion, which says to the greatest number of those who enter its churches: *Thou shalt be damned.*" The Duomo is cold, inimical to worship. It is not a place one wishes to enter again and again, either for spiritual refreshment or for aesthetic pleasure. But I have never known anyone who did not love the candy-striped facade of the cathedral, white, green, red (like sumptuous Christmas wrappings), or Giotto's multicolored Bell Tower, which Longfellow called "the lily of Florence blossoming in stone," and which James called "the graceful and indestructible soul of the city made visible."

The Duomo, the octagonal green-and-white Baptistry, and the Bell or Lily Tower form the spiritual heart of Florence.

The Duomo stands where once stood the Church of Santa Reparata, a twelve-year-old martyr who rendered military assistance to the citizens of Florence in the fifth century, miraculously appearing in the midst of Vandals and Goths with a lily and a blood-red banner in her hand. She is the Joan of Arc of Florence. The fate of female saints with military proclivities is either to be forgotten or to be burned.

The magnificent dome of the cathedral is 348 feet high. When the wardens-of-the-works of the cathedral were ready to proceed with the construction of the dome, Brunelleschi was in Rome, playing hard to get. Upon their beseeching, he returned to Florence, only to be greeted by artists and masons and wardens who assured him of the impossibility of achieving a means to support so massive a cupola as had been envisioned. Employing the same double-edged modesty that allowed Florentines to proclaim Christ the Ruler of Florence and to name Jesus Christ King of the Florentine People, Elected by Popular Decree *(Jesus Christus rex florentini populi s.p. decreto electus),* Brunelleschi, a canny fellow, appealed both to their faith and to their inadequacies, simultaneously giving the glory to God and advancing his own cause: "When I remember that this is a church dedicated to God and to the Virgin I am confident that since it is being built in her honor she will not fail to give us knowledge which is lacking and to grant strength, wisdom, and understanding to whoever is responsible for the work. But how can I help, since the project has not been entrusted to me? All I can say definitely is that, if it were, I would be bold and resolute in finding a way round the difficulties in order to vault the cupola." He suggested that architects from Germany, France, England, and Spain be consulted— "more," says Vasari, that gossipy and charmingly hyperbolic chronicler of the life of artists, "because he wanted to prove his superior intelligence than because he thought they would be able . . . even to undertake the task . . . rightly believing that he was the only one who could do it." Then, with the instincts of a showman, he returned to Rome to let everyone else have a go at what he knew only he could do. When finally all the experts, including Brunelleschi, convened in Florence in 1420, many schemes were proposed for the construction of the dome, the most fanciful being "to fill it with a mixture of earth and coins so that when it was raised those who wanted to could be given permission to help themselves to the earth [which is to say, to the coins], and in that way they would quickly remove [the earth that supported the cupola], all without expense"—in other words, a kind of earthen plum pudding. Brunelleschi proposed making the vault double— "one vault inside and the other outside so a man can walk upright between them"—a sophisticated play of weight and counterweight, and not a cumbersome wooden framework, to sustain it. For his pains, Brunelleschi, who alone among the architects took into account such details as stairways (should frescoes ever be required) and rain conduits, was called an ass and a babbler and carried out by ushers. He was greeted on the streets of Florence by cries of "Madman!" Undaunted, he refused to submit a model. Instead,

> he suggested to the other masters, both the foreigners and the Florentines, that whoever could make an egg stand on end on a flat piece of marble should build the cupola, since this would show how intelligent each man was. So an egg was procured and the artists in turn tried to make it stand on end; but they were all unsuccessful. Then Filippo was asked to do so, and taking the egg graciously he cracked its bottom on the marble and made it stay upright. The others complained that they could have done as much, and laughing at them Filippo reported that they would also have known how to vault the cupola if they had seen his model or plans. And so they resolved that Filippo should be given the task of carrying out the work.

This story is as satisfying as any fairy tale.

But it doesn't end with Brunelleschi's triumph in 1420 (Vasari's genre was the moralistic soap opera, not the fairy tale). Poor Brunelleschi—who found a way to calculate the vanishing point, and so has the very great distinction of giving the world a new understanding of geometry and of optics—had to endure the humiliation of being assigned a coarchitect, the great Ghiberti, one of the sculptors of the bronze doors of the Baptistry; on the verge of madness, comforted by Donatello and Luca della Robbia, he feigned illness—colic—in order to prove that only he could issue instructions for the erection of the cupola. Then other artists competed with him to make models for the lantern of the cupola. Finally, Vasari tells us, as if this were the last straw, even a woman made so bold as to enter the competition. Brunelleschi, who did not, alas, live to see his lantern constructed, laughed at the presumption of one and all. When the dome achieved a great height, he arranged for kitchens to be provided on site, so no one would have to descend for food or wine. Workers ate, drank, and slept on scaffolding. "As for how beautiful the edifice is, it is its own witness," says Vasari, who, being a prudent Italian with no wish to attract the Evil Eye, cannot help adding an aside: "Indeed, the heavens themselves seem to be envious of [the dome] since every day it is struck by lightning." It is not.

Vasari, the architect of the Uffizi Palace, thought of himself as a critic, not as a teller of tales. But it is for his colorful stories—in what proportion true to false it is impossible to know—that he is remembered. In his roisterous *Autobiography,* Cellini, a man who possessed the quality he most admired (which must be one definition of happiness)—"a soul that was never broken"—tells an acid story about "little Giorgio Vasari." Cellini entertained Vasari in Rome, and for his troubles had his house turned topsy-turvy: "This came of his having a dry-skin disease, and he was always tearing himself and scratching away with his hands. He had slept with a good-natured young man I had, called Manno, and thinking that he was scratching himself he had taken the skin off one of Manno's legs, with those filthy little claws he never cut. Manno had left my service and sworn to kill him. I made it up between them and then got Giorgio a position with Cardinal de' Medici, and I never left off helping him in one way or another." Vasari's architecture, so orderly, and his writing, so romantic, do nothing to prepare us for Cellini's breezily mean story (that the work and the worker are not the same is a lesson that has to be learned over and over again).

If the Piazza del Duomo is the spiritual heart of Florence, the Piazza della Signoria is its secular heart; D. H. Lawrence called it "the perfect center of the human world." But even here it is not possible to forget that this was a God-filled world: The Florentine fleur-de-lys suggests the Triune God; the fountains remind us of a God who gives Himself and returns to Himself. Florence, and the Piazza della Signoria in particular, reminds us of the special charm that attaches to belief.

This noble square is now in part a parking lot. Someone—perhaps one of the greasy-haired guitarists the carabinieri listen to with bemused courtesy—has scribbled on the wall of the Uguccioni Palace FLORENCE THE BEAUTIFUL IS FULL OF FASCISTS BE ON GUARD! But in my memory it is a perfect place, and I am sitting at Caffè Rivoire, surrounded by potted lemon trees and drinking chocolate or amber Aperol, gazing at—never tiring of—the fourteenth-century Palazzo Vecchio, the seat of government, often the home of tyrants, the heart of the heart of republican Florence. Why the massive crenellated clock tower seems airy remains a mystery to me; boldly rising from the battlements of the solid, cube-shaped building, it ought not to give the appearance of floating; it was, after all, designed to be forbidding.

Doing nothing in Italy is almost never doing nothing. From my table at Rivoire (the inside of which is all polished mahogany and gleaming brass), I watch the world and see great art, without having to parade up and down corridors to do so. This fills my heart with gratitude.

I see Ammannati's *Fountain of Neptune* with its base of bronze nymphs and satyrs, a fountain that draws a crowd of delighted children because the water that splashes into the marble basin and onto the rearing horses' heads that adorn it seems in its downward course to emanate from Neptune's penis, and as the wind carries and throws the water onto the surrounding cobblestones, the giggling children have all the pleasure of naughtiness while experiencing all the virtue of viewing art. And they are being rained upon on a rainless day, a double blessing, as a summer shower is always a miracle during the long, long summers of childhood.

I see, near the entrance to the Palazzo Vecchio, a copy of Michelangelo's *David*. The original is in the Academy of Fine Arts; another—there is no such thing, for a Florentine, as too much Michelangelo—is on a promontory above the city, the Piazzale Michelangiolo. How differently a copy would be regarded if it were the original, one has only to hear the intaken breath, and to see the posture of humility and homage suddenly adopted by mistaken tourists, to understand.

To the right of the warm and sandy-colored Palazzo Vecchio are the two gray wings of Vasari's elegant Uffizi with their red slate roofs, a building that lengthens the Piazza della Signoria as it joins the Palazzo Vecchio to the Arno, which closes it on the other side. It is lovely for the eye to traverse this corridor (although this exercise requires leaving one's place at Rivoire; in Italy it is so difficult to choose among pleasures); it gives one a sensation very much like that of looking at the ocean; one feels as if the eyes have muscles one is being given fresh permission to stretch, and that these muscles are directly connected to that of the heart.

Also to the right of the Palazzo Vecchio is the arched Loggia della Signoria, or the Loggia dei Lanzi, in which the Medicis once had hanging gardens. Framed by one of the gray Florentine Gothic arches is Cellini's bronze *Perseus Holding the Head of Medusa*. Full-blooded Cellini loved a battle of wills as much as he loved gunpowder (he tells us, sweet-hearted, boasting man, that he applied himself to the fury of the guns "with unimaginable energy and zeal"; his braggadocio amounts to a kind of innocence). When Cosimo de' Medici commissioned Cellini to sculpt a *Perseus,* he replied, "There are works on the piazza by the great Donatello, and by the marvelous Michelangelo, and those two men have proved themselves the greatest artists since the time of the ancients. But . . . let me say that I have it in me to produce a work that will be three times better still." Thereafter he had nothing but trouble with Cosimo ("a flimsy little fellow with his tiny spider's hands and a small gnat's voice"), but he completed his *Perseus* (as he completed his life), giving thanks to God, rejoicing in the ways of God and man and in his own genius, "sound as a roach."

"What God and the world allowed me to earn, I concluded, was good enough as far as I was concerned." So said Benvenuto Cellini, who went on his way rejoicing; and every artist should commit these words to heart before he takes up pen or brush.

This does not complete the catalog of wonders contained in the Piazza della Signoria.

On the occasion of the visit of Prince Charles and Princess Diana to Florence, torches were lit on the battlements and tower of the Palazzo Vecchio, and on that blazing night the palazzo, dressed as if to kill, seemed truly barbaric, even the banners seemed brazen. One could well imagine the fanatical Dominican Savonarola lighting his Bonfire of Vanities—cosmetics, false hair, statues, paintings, books, jewels—in this piazza. On the night of the royal visit, that which was meant to be festive, but which inspired unreasonable awe, was in direct contradiction to the spirit of the lovely and serene fifteenth-century arcaded courtyard of the Palazzo Vecchio, to enter which is to step into the Renaissance: its richly decorated gold-and-white columns; its charming fountain (designed by little Vasari) of a porphyry winged infant standing upon one foot, beatifically cuddling a baby dolphin with one hand. Florentines call him *genietto* (little genius), and, so sweet, he might be the genius of happiness.

When Prince Charles and Princess Diana drove by the Pitti Palace hotel in an open carriage, one felt—the narrowness of the streets making every encounter an intimate one—that one could touch them, and some of the maids tried to. Even Giulia was all atwitter.

* * *

137

In the same place where he had earlier lit his bonfire, Savonarola was arrested, tried, hanged, and burned at the stake in 1498; there is a stone memorial to him set in the pavement. In a painting of him in his cell at the Monastery of San Marco, the reformer, enemy of the Medicis, looks like a hanging judge, a man at war with his appetites: He has a fleshy nose, a thin, curled upper lip, and a pendulous lower lip.

It is hard to find sympathy in one's heart for a book burner and a man so violently opposed to the pleasures of the senses; but no less a writer and a sensualist than Stendhal called Fra Girolamo Savonarola "a man of lofty character and great insight, who attempted the role of Luther. . . . When with two of his friends he was tied to a stake above the pile of faggots prepared to burn them, the bishop of Florence declared that he separated them from the Church. 'From the militant,' replied Savonarola softly, thereby giving to understand that in his quality of martyr he was that moment entering the Church triumphant (these are the terms of theology). Savonarola said nothing more and perished thus at the age of somewhat less than forty-six. Michelangelo was his friend." Michelangelo read and reread his sermons; he found them refreshing.

(Savonarola's followers were called the *piagnoni* [the weepers] because they cried for the sins of the people; partisans of the Medicis and Savonarola's enemies were called the *arrabbiati* [the angry ones]. There is a southern Italian pasta dish called penne all'arrabbiata, so called because of its red, hot, spicy—angry—sauce, a mixture of tomato, olives, capers, garlic, and red pepper; there is no dish named for weeping.)

Savonarola's sermons were thunderously delivered at the Cathedral of St. Mary of the Flower. Anthony Blunt says that Savonarola feared the evil effects that might come from the "wrong kind of art," mundane art, but that "he had the greatest faith in the good which could be done by the right kind." It was not—and is not—remarkably clear what "the right kind" might be; it never is, in arguments of this sort. In one sermon, Fra Girolamo told his hearers to read the Scriptures, "and you who cannot read, go to paintings and contemplate the life of Christ and of his Saints." Art has been called the Bible of the illiterate; Savonarola said "figures represented in churches are the books of women and children." But what kinds of paintings? Savonarola's teaching was "a protest against the worldly papacy of Alexander VI; he wished to restore the 'purity' of medieval life and doctrine. His conception of Beauty," Blunt says, was based on "the assumption that the spiritual is superior to the material." But this dichotomy between the spiritual and the material is bound in some degree to be false and always to be subjective, if we believe—as Catholics are instructed to believe—that God reveals Himself through the material world. And it is certainly at war with the perception that beauty is pleasure objectified. As Blunt himself says, "since the forms of all created things proceed ultimately from God, beauty in the material world is a reflection of the divine." (Therefore Dante was led to greater love of God through Beatrice.) It would be interesting to walk through history with Savonarola as one's guide to the "indecent and the mundane." Would his views agree, say, with those of Michelangelo? Oddly enough, they might in some ways coincide. Michelangelo, who in his thirties and forties came to believe that love of physical beauty was a cheat, expressed the belief that a painter of religious subjects needed to be both skillful and pious: "Often badly wrought images distract the attention and prevent the devotion, at least with persons who have but little; while those which are divinely fashioned excite even those who have little devotion or sensibility to contemplation and tears, and by their austere beauty inspire them with great reverence and fear." Fra Girolamo also protested against paintings that aroused laughter by reason of their mediocrity, thus setting himself up as an art critic as well as a moralist. (All art critics are moralists.)

Savonarola, who lived during the splendor of the Renaissance, has been called "the gravedigger of Florence"; he was not so much an aberration as a throwback. Florence has always had its share of ascetics and reformers. In the twelfth and thirteenth centuries the Patarine heresy flourished. Like the Albigensians, members of this sect believed that matter was evil; they must have had a sorry time of it, as they were not only vegetarians and pacifists but eschewers of marriage who did not believe in the Sacraments of Baptism or the Eucharist or in prayers for the dead or in veneration of relics or inanimate objects. What they did believe was that the world was ruled by the Devil, a belief that would sour the beef broth in anyone's stomach. In the fourteenth century, when three-fifths of all Florentines were killed by the Black Death, flagellants who made their first appearance in Germany spread southward, preaching simplicity and poverty, undermining the power and authority of the Church, scourging themselves. Penitent pilgrims paraded through the streets; they fasted and slept on straw. It has been suggested that the Misericordia—which provided the first public ambulance service in the world—was originated by these penitents. During the Middle Ages members of the Misericordia dressed like a benign Ku Klux Klan; they wore red robes and hoods with slits to look through, to preserve their anonymity. In the nineteenth century every member of the royal family was a member of the Misericordia, which, anticipating death, the great leveler, has always had an open-door policy; if one were dying of the plague, one could not know if one were being taken to the hospital by a shoemaker or a king. In this manner, praise went to God and not to man. At the time of the flood of 1966, robed Misericordia volunteers went through the ruined streets of Florence carrying a banner emblazoned with the Red Cross of Mercy.

It is odd—and good—to think that this ancient society can today be reached by telephone. Its number is 21 22 22.

The headquarters of the Misericordia is across the street from the Cathedral of St. Mary of the Flower; it is very pretty, and it smells—unlike any hospital I have ever been in—of freshly varnished wood and dried flowers.

One day as I was strolling toward the Piazza of Santo Spirito, I stopped to look at a frescoed palazzo and saw that it was the headquarters of the Testimoni di Geova—Jehovah's Witnesses. It seemed strange to me that a fundamentalist apocalyptic sect should set itself up for business in Florence, but I reminded myself that Florence has historically attracted religious extremists, and not just in the distant past. In the 1870s a Catholic evangelical movement broke away from Rome. Heaven knows what they would have thought of Cellini, who trafficked with demons and necromancers. (It seems to have done him no great harm.)

Quel che non ammazza ingrassa, Italians say. "What doesn't kill you fattens you." Savonarola longed for the purity of the Middle Ages; the fact is that anyone who could afford to be a glutton in the Middle Ages was one.

My friend Bethany calls Tuscan panforte "truly medieval and cruel." I see what she means. Literally "strong bread," panforte, as dense as it is flat, is made of flour, butter, eggs, almonds, walnuts, candied fruits, and lemon, orange, or rose water. (There is chocolate panforte, too; impossibly rich.) Eating it is like chewing on a spongy rock impregnated with gravel, an ordeal.

Italians' relationship to food is loving, informal, and gay; as Waverley Root points out, while "French cooking has become professional cooking even when it is executed by amateurs, [Italian cooking] has remained basically amateur cooking even when it is executed by professionals . . . human, light-hearted." And so the tendency to anthropomorphize food and to use it to express a blithe irreverence: A variety of plum is called "nun's thighs"; a kind of sausage is called "the priest"; when cooked rice is semiliquid and creamy, it is given the feminine, *la risotta;* there is a kind of pasta called "little cupids," another called "clowns' hats" and one called "priests' hats"; there are at least three tubular pastas which for obvious reasons are called "bridegrooms": ziti, ziti rigati ("grooved bridegrooms," ziti with ridges), and zitoni ("husky bridegrooms," a larger version of ziti). Italian food is the product of improvisation and inspiration: "Order béarnaise sauce in two hundred different French restaurants," gastronome Enrico Galozzi says, "and you will get exactly the same sauce two hundred times. Ask for Bolognese sauce in two hundred different Italian restaurants, and you will get two hundred different versions of ragù." It is characterized by abundance.

Abigail Adams sometimes served her guests cornmeal pudding as a first course—because it depressed their appetites. In the sixteenth century the first course of a Tuscan feast might have consisted of pastries made with milk and eggs; prosciutto cooked in wine with capers, grape pulp, and sugar; sliced salted pork tongues cooked in wine; cold roasted songbirds with their tongues over them; and sweet mustard.

In the fifteenth century, when Savonarola set the moral tone for Florence—gluttony is one of the Seven Deadly Sins—Sumptuary Laws had been introduced to impose limits on consumption. Florentines ate two meals a day, and at each of these meals "only" three courses were permitted. Italian ingenuity circumvented and made nonsense of the laws: One of the three courses allowed was "roast with pie"—which meant in practice, if not in theory, that anything that could be stuffed between two layers of pastry was, in peculiar alliance, joined. A roast with pie might therefore consist of pork, chickens, ham, eggs, dates, almonds, flour, spices, sugar, and saffron.

Well, life was short, and who can blame Florentines for wishing to eat their fill so long as it lasted? They could always eat "white food," such as pounded chicken, if their stomachs rebelled, and women had special recourse for gas pains, which were called *mal di madre* (mother's complaint): They could pray to St. Elizabeth, who is said to have been afflicted with gas until the angel Gabriel announced to her the birth of John the Baptist.

The passage of the Sumptuary Laws probably wasn't the first, and certainly wasn't the last, example of Italians going haywire over food. Maybe a people that behaves so sensibly and without folderol about food has to go nuts (or bananas—it's interesting that we use food metaphorically for insanity) about what they eat from time to time. In 1930 in Milan the Futurist poet Marinetti called for the abolition of pasta, "an obsolete food . . . heavy, brutalizing, and gross"; he said that its nutritive qualities were deceptive and that it induced skepticism, sloth, and pessimism. Italians took this idiocy seriously enough to squabble over it. Naples is a pasta-eating city. The enormous popularity of pasta in Naples seems to have started in the late 1800s; prints of that time show Neapolitans eating pasta without sauce (a kind of finger food) as they strolled along the streets. (Macaroni was mentioned in Boccaccio's *Decameron* two hundred years before the tomato was known in Europe, and lasagne was mentioned by Cicero and Horace.) The Duke of Bovino, Mayor of Naples, contending with Marinetti, asserted that "the angels in Paradise eat nothing but vermicelli al pomodoro." *Vermicelli* means "little worms"; perhaps the mayor was having his own little joke; he could have made his point more nicely had he used *capellini d'angelo* (angel-hair pasta). Marinetti, only half in jest, inveighing against all established forms of cooking, proposed new dishes, which in 1954 British cookery writer Elizabeth Davis called "preposterous . . . founded on the shock principle of combining unsuitable and exotic ingredients (mortadella with nougat, pineapple with sardines, cooked salame immersed in a bath of hot black coffee flavored with eau-de Cologne, an aphrodisiacal drink composed of pineapple juice, eggs, cocoa, caviar, almond paste, red pepper, nutmeg, cloves, and Strega)." What Elizabeth Davis called preposterous in 1954 we wouldn't be terribly surprised to see on a nouvelle cuisine menu today. Anyone who dislikes nouvelle cuisine may take comfort from the fact that Mussolini contributed a preface to Marinetti's *Cucina Futurista,* calling the Futurist his "dear old friend of the first Fascist battles."

THREE MEALS

1. *Antipasto*: Tiny portions of peccorino (sheep's milk cheese) with fresh peas; mixed-cheese soufflé; smoked mozzarella and fresh mozzarella (made from buffalo milk); ricotta (made from cow's milk); cold tripe dressed with hot pepper and olive oil; crisp green pepper with a grainy stuffing of ricotta and ground beef.
Minestra: White-bean and artichoke soup (pureed).
Main Course: Duck (a circle of sweet, succulent flesh and crisp skin with a rich stuffing of its own liver, *pancetta* (bacon), veal, Parmesan cheese, pine nuts, tarragon, and wine); lightly cooked asparagus.
Dolce: Slivers of two chocolate cakes, one dense and crunchy, the other spongy with a creamy frosting; a sliver of lemon torte.
2. Florentine T-bone steak brushed with olive oil and grilled; *insalata di campo*—salad of wild and cultivated greens, sweet and bitter, including dill, mint, parsley, arugula, radicchio, dandelions.

3. *Antipasto*: *Polpette* (meatballs); artichoke hearts; frittata; fried zucchini, toasted polenta (corn meal); prosciutto; salami with fennel; crostini.
Pasta: Spaghetti alla carrettiera (a brisk sauce of fresh tomato, garlic, and fresh basil).
Main Course: Mixed roast—pigeon, chicken, turkey, lamb, beef.
Dolce: *Vin santo* (a dessert wine) and *biscotti* (biscuits).

"The Florentine," says Marcella Hazan, author of indispensable Italian cookbooks, is a "careful and calculating man who knows the measure of all things, and his cooking is an austerely composed play upon essential and unadorned themes. . . . Florence takes a T-bone steak of noble size and grills it quickly over a blazing fire, adding nothing but the aroma of freshly ground pepper and olive oil." She goes on to observe, as does everyone who writes about Italian food, that Italian food doesn't exist: Italian cooking is regional. This is not absolutely true. In Florence, as in Milan and Rome, and to some extent in Venice, one can find food of many regions prepared with integrity, true to the region that gave it birth. It is possible to find such food, which makes no concessions to palates that have been corrupted by "Italian-American" restaurant food, in small, family-run trattorie as well as in large dining rooms. As one travels south of Rome, where the climate is warmer, as are the tempers (and the sauces), regional food predominates. Tastes become less subtle, more intense, even violent; you encounter more tomato; butter all but disappears, and red pepper comes on with a vengeance, and as food becomes spicier and more pungent, the onion gives way to garlic. I would be surprised if in the small villages of the Abruzzi and Calabria where my family lives, the kinds of food available, and the ways of preparing them, had changed very much in the last hundred years. (Some people speak of Italy as having two great civilizations: that of wine-and-olive-oil and that of milk-and-butter. In Tuscany, according to this view, the gastronomic civilizations meet.)

The romance of food never fades. Someone once told me that capers were the hearts of nasturtiums, and this was such a pretty notion I chose to believe it; in fact, caper shrubs grow from ancient walls and castles and rocky ground in Chianti villages. They flower in the summer, and the bud must be put in wine vinegar before it opens. This story is just as pretty as the apocryphal one.

Florentines drink an intense dessert wine called *vin santo,* which no one outside Tuscany seems to have any great desire for; it is related to sauterne, though I think it much lovelier and meatier, and with it they eat hard, dry cookies, *biscotti,* a perfect complement. Amber-colored *vin santo* is made from white grapes sun-dried on straw, stored in oak barrels under terra-cotta roofs, and allowed to go through four yearly cycles of hot and cold before it is bottled. There's very little I wouldn't give to have *vin santo* and *biscotti* under Florentine skies; I had my wine merchant get me some, and it was very nice indeed, but not so lovely as it had been in Florence, and I am inclined to think that that is not because some wines do not travel well but because we are transported when we drink them under their own skies.

Food evokes place. To remember meals I ate in Florence is a way for me to "locate" myself in Florence—just as to think of the remembered rooms of childhood is to remember childhood itself. (An exercise in sentimentality, a litany of delectable variety, this will, I hope, dispel the idea that Florentine cooking is all about entrails and innards and onions):

Burnt sienna–colored pepper soup with beads of raw green olive oil and herbed croutons

Fagioli all'uccelletto, white beans cooked in sage, tomato, and garlic (so called because small, wild birds [*uccelli*] were once routinely served with the beans)

Tripe cooked with tomatoes and Parmesan cheese

Pappardelle (broad green noodles) with ragù; veal sautéed with red, yellow, and green peppers

Zuppa di panna, a pureed soup, served tepid, of sweet, fresh tomatoes and cannellini (white beans) with a hint of bitter cabbage and chunks of rough, Tuscan country bread; a thick pork chop roasted with aromatic herbs; zucchini lightly dressed with olive oil, garlic, and raw tomato

Light-as-air ravioli filled with spinach and served in a cream-and-tomato sauce

Fresh spinach with olive oil

Fresh spinach with butter

Tender young asparagus with chunks of Parmesan cheese and butter

Taglierini al limone, pasta with a hint of garlic, cream, and a strong taste and fragrance of lemon; veal scaloppine; radicchio salad

Cheese ravioli with a sauce of tomato and cognac; puree of artichoke; orange torte

Rice, each grain separate, with brilliant green spinach and wild mushrooms; grilled trout with oil and lemon; strawberries big as a child's heart in a bowl of lightly sugared water, eaten with a fork and knife

Salsiccia di cinghiale, dried sausage made from the meat of wild boar

Calf's liver covered with Parma ham and cooked in a clay oven for two and a half hours

A Leonardo, fresh strawberry juice with sparkling spumante wine; chicken curry; apple pie with cream; coffee (at Harry's Bar, of course)

Marcella hasn't eaten out since 1978, on which occasion she became ill; she is afraid that "the cream might go off." She is in no other respect odd.

Italians are at their most mystical when they think they are being their most rational. Clarissa has asthma. Her cure for an attack is to stand in front of a closed window and look at a green garden while drinking a white wine, preferably Lacrima Christi (tear of Christ). She is in no other respect odd.

A tourist asks Marcella if churches are open to view on Sunday. Without missing a beat she says, "But, yes, madame . . . with pleasure. . . . Heathens," she mutters under her breath, "fools."

At Harry's Bar. A cultivated waiter with impeccable manners. He looks like an ascetic monk. He speaks perfect English. He is serving two women from Taiwan who have upper-class British accents. He brings all his charm to bear on the older and less beautiful of the two women and on the little girl of nine or ten who is her charge. He asks the child where she was born. "In a hospital," she says. "Which one?" he asks, and he lists the hospitals in London where she might have been born. He appears to have an intimate knowledge of St. John's Wood, where they live. "In a cheap hospital," the child says. "All English hospitals are cheap," he says. "Do you know why? Because you were born without clothes." In fact, as Italian babies are swaddled with clothing that weighs more than they do from the approximate moment of birth, he is making a fine point. Later, when I remark that the little girl was charming, he says, managing not to be offensive, managing an almost elegant leer, "The young woman was charming, the child was a chatterbox." "But you were kind to her," I say. "If one is not kind to children, one is not kind," he says. "Children can do no harm."

"The indulgence with which we now treat our young children," Giambattista Vico wrote, "produces all the tenderness of our (modern) natures." It is pleasant—and probably accurate—to think of tenderness proceeding from indulgence as opposed to indulgence proceeding from tenderness.

At a restaurant near the Pitti Palace a man and a woman are having an argument in two languages—he in Florentine (which is true Italian, codified by Dante in the *Commedia*), she in British English (a plummy accent, a moneyed voice). On the face of it, the argument is about architecture. They have the look of a couple who have been married for years and who have had this argument for years. It is not about architecture. "You have a marvelous sense of color, darling," she says, "and a great gift for textiles"— gifts that she clearly thinks are of small account—"but you know absolutely nothing about form." "The blood of Donatello flows in my veins," he says. "The blood of brigands, darling," she says. "In which case, our children . . ." he says. They have the look of people who have exhausted sex long ago, perhaps he is gay. "What can you do," she says, now speaking in Italian, "with a country that cooks hare in tomato sauce?" "What can you do with a race of women who interrupt?" he says. He makes meticulous drawings on paper supplied by an obsequious waiter. She smiles and talks through clenched teeth. "Interrupt!" she says. "You are forever expostulating, you with your *dunque*s and *allora*s. . . ." An elderly American spinster seats herself to my right. On my left are the arguing couple, I am invisible to them. Over my head they talk to the spinster, pleasant as morning. (The Englishwoman's hands are shaking.) They ask the spinster about someone called Julie. "She must be enjoying the country—the flowers," the Englishwoman says. "Julie is sated with the country, she likes the city," the spinster says. "Yes!" the Englishwoman says. "She must be enjoying the flowers." Her husband shrugs. The waiter, so recently obsequious, winks at him. While the Englishwoman carries on about flowers—"fhlars"—and the spinster talks (in large part to herself) about the utter impossibility of her going to Leeds for a family wedding, the elegant Italian man lightly, discreetly, pats the waiter on the ass. A large lady wearing many pieces of reproduction Etruscan gold jewelry enters. We have been introduced before. She has told me she has read reviews of my books; this is meant to be a great compliment. I like her; I like her zeal for Florence: She offered her services after the flood, and now she feels, having waded in muck, that she is a citizen of Florence, and that gives her very great pleasure. (The Englishwoman married to the Italian snubs her.) I tell her in the course of conversation that in six months' time I will go to Calabria. "We don't like the Calabresi," the waiter interjects (I have done nothing to offend him). Caught off guard, "Why?" I ask. "They are lazy, dirty," he says. "Do your parents live there?" "Cousins," I say. "Oh, yes," he says, "you will have many cousins, they breed. We do not like even to go to Rome."

Later: "But that is absurd," Signor Forte, the jeweler, says. (It is he who has sold the large lady the gold jewelry she wears; Florence is a small town.) "No one of refinement would despise the South. You must keep your distance from waiters, they are servants with the opinions of dolts. The man was uncultivated—perhaps Sicilian," he says.

Da Pennello (Paintbrush) is said to have been a restaurant since the fifteenth century, the offspring of a failed artist who loved food and drink more than he loved art. If the poor fellow had lived a century later, he could have joined the gastronomic society Il Paiolo, members of which were Mannerist painters and followers of Michelangelo, himself a gastronome who sometimes used the ink of squid for his drawings and who counted lamb brains among his favorite foods. Da Pennello is near the house in which Dante once briefly lived. Florentines like to eat here of a Sunday; the food is robust— roast suckling pig; veal with rosemary, cooked in its own juices till its skin crackles—and the Florentine families that come here (men in shiny black suits, plump women in flowered dresses) are robust, too; they speak loudly and use broad gestures; they do everything with gusto. Sometimes the waiters sing—to themselves—not to amuse the guests but to ease their task.

There is a soccer playoff the night I eat at Natale, on the Arno, between the Ponte Vecchio and the Ponte Santa Trinità. The restaurant is empty except for me, a friend, and a family of Venetians, who sit quietly, with a flashing of ringed fingers. Comes a hunchback with a battered case to exhibit mechanical windup toys he says he's made. A dog with a tail that whirls like a helicopter's rotors dances among the dishes of spaghetti alle vongole the homesick Venetians have ordered. They take no notice. The waiters take no notice. He is tolerated; he is invisible; he belongs to the Italian landscape—a stock figure from a comic opera.

> . . . When our mind, more of a wanderer from the
> flesh and less prisoned by thoughts,
> in its vision is almost prophetic. . . .
>
> *—Dante, "Purgatorio," Canto IX*

In the early hours of the morning (when dreams are true), from my little city-village on the Oltrarno I cross the Ponte Vecchio and zigzag my way past medieval towers through narrow passages to the Piazza di Parte Guelfa, a place of shaded repose where a great deal is going on architecturally: a mélange of styles from the trecento to the quattrocento, and graffiti—incised drawings of cherubs and flowers—from the fourteenth and fifteenth centuries, all congruous and pleasing.

Here a lone merchant stands with a wire contraption that resembles an abbreviated hatstand. On the "arms" of this peculiar vending machine are oranges and coconuts and watermelons, onto which, from curved spouts, water flows. No one buys his fruit.

This is the heart of Dante's Florence, about which a visitor is likely to feel more sentimental than the poet ever did; Dante had for Florence—a city he considered corrupted by florins, a city he compared to a sick person "who can find no rest . . . but by turning about, shuns her pain"—reproachful pity, mingled shame and affection ("Purgatorio," Canto VI). He was a victim of civil war. The Guelphs, members of the merchant classes, people governed by business, banking, commercial, and guild influences, supported the Pope. The Ghibellines, for the most part members of the feudal nobility, supported the Holy Roman Emperor. They battled during the thirteenth century with seesaw results, till the Ghibellines were defeated in 1266, after which the victorious Guelphs split into two parties: the Whites, who sought to maintain the integrity and independence of the Republic, and the Blacks. In 1348 the Black Death put an end to internecine warfare by putting an end to the mortal life of three-fifths of the townspeople of Florence. Dante was exiled from Florence in 1302 by the Black Guelphs; he was thirty-seven, and he never returned to the city of his birth. It is not surprising that the man who tasted the "salt-bitter bread" of exile placed "Traitors to Guests" in the Ninth Circle of Hell. ("Ungrateful land," wrote Michelangelo; "as his exile has no parallel, never walked the earth a greater man than he.")

While we sometimes think of august poets, when they've been dead long enough, as sanctified creatures who drank air and lived in mists, *The Divine Comedy* is full of contemporary political and antipapal allusions. (Indeed, Vico calls it history and not poetry.) And yet to think of Dante as living in a concrete place and in a particular time, and to immerse oneself in the political history of that time, is in a way to do Dante and oneself a disservice. Dorothy L. Sayers understood the problem well. "If we look upon Dante," she wrote, "as a man totally explicable in terms of a vanished period, we may succeed in forgetting that he is a man like ourselves. If we account for everything that he said by the consideration that, being born when he was, there was nothing else he could very well say, we shall have provided ourselves with an excellent excuse for not applying what he said to ourselves." Sayers, who translated Dante after she wrote the celebrated Peter Wimsey mystery novels, hailed him—across the negligible gap of six centuries—as "a fellow-poet, a fellow-lover, and a fellow Christian," and she tells this story about her contemporary and fellow Dante scholar Charles Williams:

While Williams was having a haircut one day, his barber told him the story of his own love affair. "When my girl's about," the barber said, "I'm that happy I don't feel as if I had an enemy in the world. I'd forgive anybody anything."

"My dear man," said Williams, jumping out of his seat and pumping the barber's hand, "that's *exactly* what Dante said." And of course he was right, Guelphs and Ghibellines being, for the barber's purposes—and for the theology of romantic love—beside the point. What both the barber and Dante understood was the sanctity of the flesh, "holy and glorious flesh"—*la santa e gloriosa carne.*

Dante begins *The Divine Comedy* with an intense, and intensely personal, experience: *Nel mezzo del cammin di nostra vita / Mi ritrovai per una selva oscura, / Che la diretta via era smaritta. / Ahi! . . .* "In the middle of the journey of our life I came / To myself in a dark wood where the straight / Way was lost. / Ah! . . ." And because it is so personal, and because Dante's journey was—and is—the journey of our life (that wonderful pronoun: the journey of *our* life), we are, with him, adrift on the "great sea of being." Dante is our brother.

To our bodies turn we then, that so
weak men on love revealed may look.

—*Michelangelo*

Many men have found peace in a woman's eyes. Dante, who saw the divine and human nature of Christ reflected in Beatrice's eyes, teaches us that human love leads us to love of God: "The splendor of her laughing eyes . . . strengthened him for heaven" ("Paradiso," Canto X); human love prepares us for the time when no excess of delight will be beyond our joyful grasp—when "light will not baffle us" ("Paradiso," Canto XIV). Dante was drawn into the light of God by the light in Beatrice; she "imparadised his mind." . . . Through human love, one of Dante's translators says, it is sometimes possible to experience a portion of the joy of the redeemed— "where every *where* is here and every *when* is now," and when joy no longer needs "the stimulus supplied by the fear of losing it or the effort to retain it."

But what of poor Paolo and Francesca, the lovers Dante consigns to the Second Circle of Hell, where the Lustful are "battered by opposing winds . . . a place where every light is muted" ("Inferno," Canto X)?* Dante himself fainted when he saw them in that dark, malignant air. What was their crime? "Love," Francesca says, "led the two of us into one death . . . love that releases no beloved from loving." The beauty of Beatrice led Dante to God; the beauty of Paolo led Francesca, by way of gentle thoughts and deep longing, to Hell.

It doesn't seem fair.

(They were alone; they "suspected nothing." But time and again their eyes met, their faces paled, till, enlivened by the story they were reading—"One day, to pass the time away, we read of Lancelot"—Paolo kissed Francesca's lips: "That day we read no more.")

Why were they damned? Dante himself is in an agony of doubt. It does not satisfy him to be told that one must refuse to love all things that are speciously attractive, to scorn love that cannot be affiliated to the love of God. Dante believes that in love all things are safe; it confuses him to be told by Virgil that love is at the root of all evil conduct as well as of all

---

*This and the following translations in this section are by Allen Mandelbaum (New York: Bantam Classics, 1982). All other translations of Dante are from the Dent edition listed in the Bibliography.

good conduct; it maddens him to be told that love, which springs from absolute necessity, must be arrested by power of will. . . . It maddens me; no one was ever happy to be invited to suspect the goodness of his own love. . . .

Francesca's tragedy is that, though forever lost, she longs to know God. This is Hell.

Karl Rahner says that when a human being expresses "genuine, personal love for another human being, it always has a validity, an eternal significance. . . . Man is boundless. Every sin is at root merely a refusal to entrust himself to this boundlessness." A lesser love, which refuses to become the greater, "is no longer love at all." By the greater, he means that love "so constituted as to be a way of actualizing the love of God." Paolo and Francesca bound themselves together in life; in doing so, it is suggested, they negated their potentially boundless love for God. . . . My sympathies reside irresistibly with them.

They had eyes only for each other; a form of idolatry—and the punishment agrees with the sin. "Love that releases no beloved from loving," Francesca says, "took hold of me so that, as you can see, it has not left me yet"; Paolo is "this one who shall never be parted from my side." The fleeting moment when the lovers bound themselves solely unto each other will endure throughout all of eternity.

I wish them well.

Nowhere does God, in His grace, reveal Himself to me more clearly than in some lovely human form, which I love solely because it is a mirrored image of Himself.

—Michelangelo

Michelangelo dissected human bodies to learn anatomy. He seldom used models. He cherished human beauty, but you'd never know from the female figures on the sarcophagi in the New Sacristy of the Medici Chapels that he cherished the female body. His women are in many cases not women at all. The figure of *Night* on the sarcophagus of Giuliano de' Medici is a long-haired man without a penis; its breasts are afterthoughts—marble blobs like prosthetics—and its forearms and thighs are so massive and muscular as to lend credence to the theory that Michelangelo had mentally prepared a sepulcher for the bones of Dante, interred in Ravenna, and, having been cheated of the poet's remains, applied his genius to the tomb of the undistinguished Giuliano instead.

I cannot find it in my heart to call the Medici Chapels sublime or even melancholy; the jewels and wall-to-wall frescoes of the stagy octagonal chapels of the gouty, nouveaux riches Medicis have an oddly blanketing effect on my senses, like Muzak. Behind the main altar, though, are two small rooms that are more wonderful in their way than grand and marbled tombs. They contain rare and precious relics, quite horrible, fascinating, and repulsive. Bones of babies—one visitor took them to be the bones of a small bird, a pigeon—in a richly ornamented crystal urn; a baby's skull wreathed with pearls and precious stones in an urn of silver, gold, and crystal, richly embellished. Terrible. Singularly ostentatious, these memento mori don't say "Remember you must die"; they say "Remember we were rich."

Built in part by Brunelleschi, San Lorenzo, parish church of the Medicis, of which the chapels are a part, is one of those naked "anatomical" churches one comes across so often in Italy, partly unsheathed by stone and marble, and somehow the more exuberant for it. Its airy bulk sits on the Piazza of San Lorenzo, a happy place with its large outdoor market, its blue and orange and white and green umbrellas and open stalls nestled up against the church—clothes, leather goods, and bow ties in every possible color displayed. God seems so domestic in Italy—this marvelous juxtaposition of bow ties and architectural grandeur. The cloisters of San Lorenzo—Brunelleschi's—are serene, as by definition cloisters are; outside is hurly-burly. The message we receive is that bow ties and human vanities belong to God as much as worship and as death do; and a very nice thing that is, Savonarola notwithstanding.

The triple staircase leading from Brunelleschi's cloisters to Michelangelo's Laurentian Library in the Church of San Lorenzo is the most perfect staircase in the world, its columned vestibule in gray and white a dynamic statement of simplicity and nobility—and very brave, too: a declaration of enormous strength in an intimate space.

Michelangelo's *David,* washed in lovely light at the Accademia, is a different matter from the hefty women resting on the Medici sarcophagi. His youth and slim, tensile beauty are so much more than the sum of his parts—pendulous testicles, scrolled pubic hair, supple wrists, purposeful hands, curiously small ears, the tender line of his jaw, the very nearly coy tilt of one hip, the look of blank inward concentration. . . . Sublime, but not necessarily lovable. And one does wish one didn't know that Martha

Graham once told her male dancers, "Now, dears, I know you've all just come back from Florence, but I want you to forget that" . . . because one does know exactly what she means.

(Michelangelo's *David* is uncircumcised, as the David of the Holy Scriptures could never have been. This strikes one as an odd—perverse—artistic and theological statement.)

Mary Ann says: "Your uncle is here." As this cannot be a prank (Mary Ann is incapable of mischief), it must be a mistake. I rule out the possibility of a death in the family. I don't know why I rule out the possibility of a death in the family. There are members of my family who would be pleased if I were an ocean away from death; my absence would—I have had years in which to study the workings of their minds—be proof to them that my moral character is slack, which is what they already believe to be true.

I have three uncles. I see my Uncle Tony at family funerals. He tells me to write "nice things," by which he means that I write "bad" things, though I doubt he has ever read anything I've written. I have a picture of Uncle Tony taken when he came back from the War, or perhaps when he was on leave, I don't remember. He is holding my hand, we are caught in mid-stride—my pigtails are flying, and I am smiling a huge gap-toothed smile; I am wearing a ruffled, striped pinafore and he is wearing his soldier suit. When I look at this picture my heart turns over and I hear a music box play "Amapola, My Pretty Little Poppy," which must mean I had a crush on Uncle Tony, though that is inconceivable to me, as he lives too much in his body and not enough in his mind. . . . Of course, that may be why I had a crush on him. . . . We are walking down a street of dilapidated row houses near the old Brooklyn Navy Yard. Grandma and Grandpa DiNardo live here. Grandpa was handsome and Grandma was beautiful, and they were unhappy. Grandpa once took an ax to the player piano (I loved the player piano), no one knows why. When Grandpa got his first television set he turned it on to a picture of Arthur Godfrey shot from the waist up. "Where's his legs, son-a-ma-beetch-television?" my grandfather said. We told him that the camera was shooting Arthur Godfrey from the waist up, but once Grandpa got angry he couldn't be deflected from his course, so he threw a hard bosc pear at the television set, which exploded. This gave Grandpa an obscure calming pleasure and gave Grandma an excuse to light a candle and kneel before a plaster statue of the Blessed Virgin, which made Grandpa mad all over again.

We are not an anecdotal family; I don't know who told me this story: Grandpa had a rich relative in Campobasso from whom Grandpa's older brothers borrowed money to sail to America; their collateral was Grandpa, who was left behind to care for the rich relative's sheep. Grandpa lived alone in a shepherd's hut, an indentured servant, and had his food brought to him by a house servant; he did not converse with a living soul for ten years, until he was twenty, when his brothers paid their rich relative back. Before he sailed, Grandpa married Grandma, the prettiest girl in the village. He was so handsome.

This is how I received the story; it seemed whole to me, and it explained why Grandpa was always angry, though never at me. I was not afraid of Grandpa, who was violent; I was afraid of Grandma, who prayed and sighed, prayed and sighed.

Uncle Tony told me he would mail me the ear of a dead Jap, which also I believed. At funerals he talks about the War in Burma, and he cries. His tears are for himself.

Uncle Tony is my mother's brother. My father's brother, Uncle Leonard, looks like a wizened old monkey and colors his hair with black boot polish, which fact he denies. Once Uncle Leonard didn't come home for dinner and my grandfather Grizzuti told my father to go out and look for Lenny and not come home till he found him; so my father got a job on a freighter and sailed through the Panama Canal to California because he couldn't find Uncle Leonard—in those days my father was a boxer and made his living anywhere. Two years later he came home and climbed up the fire escape and stuck his head in the window and asked Aunt Lee: "Is Lenny back yet?" At family funerals—the only times we meet nowadays—Uncle Leonard always wears the same disreputable black suit, and his fly is secured with a large safety pin. Nobody knows how Uncle Leonard hears of family deaths because nobody ever knows where Uncle Leonard is. He has an old car and an old dog, and he lives on the road. Years ago, before his wife, Aunt Esther, died, Uncle Lenny was an oil-burner man, and he worked in the basements of rich Long Islanders, which may account for his having had a collection of antique fans and a silver service for thirty-six, with soup tureen, and for his occasional presentation to me, when I was a child, of bits and pieces of pretty things he called "hair looms." I wish the natural order of things could be reversed so that Uncle Lenny could cry at my funeral, because when he cries it is for the whole suffering world, he does not act as if it were he who had had the bad fortune to die, as most people do at funerals when they are not (perhaps your family doesn't do this) telling crude and dirty jokes to relieve the gloom. The jokes do not relieve the gloom.

Actually my first reaction upon hearing Mary Ann's news was fear. I was afraid that someone had come to scold me. It took me forever to learn the things my cousins, and my brother, seemed to know by instinct. For example, I did not know till my own father died that you were supposed to come to family funerals with an envelope filled with cash (fifty dollars with adjustments for inflation) to give to the bereaved. Also, I got divorced. I did things that were "not nice." My brother, who loves me and who does not think "you–could–eat–off–her–floor" is the highest compliment that can be paid to a woman, takes pleasure in my being the family rebel and even greater pleasure in his ability to love me because or in spite of misdemeanors. The truth is, my childhood rebellions were more often than not a case of my mind's being somewhere else, they weren't calculated to provoke. If I could have figured out what "nice" was, I probably would have done it more often. I'd like to have been able to please in small ways, I didn't know how.

"Haven't you taught that kid how to ride a bike yet?" That's the first thing Uncle Pat, brother to my Uncle Tony, said when he came back from the War (in my mind it is the first thing he said); he thought my childhood was being mismanaged. His kindness evoked in me more sadness and confusion (feelings akin, actually, to terror) than the busy scolding of all my aunts and the reproaches of my Uncle Tony, onto whose lap—to my own great surprise—I once emptied a tray of my nail clippings together with hair gleaned from my hairbrush, a gesture that was not interpreted by him as one of love. The beating I got as a consequence seemed to me insanely unjust. (It still seems to me insanely unjust that so few hearts—mine is not among them—are capable of the genius required to interpret the apparently random gestures of a child.)

I was a flower girl at Uncle Pat's wedding to Aunt Mary. I cried that day because my hair looked funny. Aunt Mary cried because her Sicilian family would not speak to our Abruzzese/Calabrese family and our Abruzzese/Calabrese family called Aunt Mary "the Arab." Now everyone has forgotten that but me and Aunt Mary, who likes me as a consequence of my remembering. Most members of my family think some things are best forgotten.

Uncle Pat is the ugliest man I have ever known. His eyes are blue. He once during the Depression asked my mother for three fried eggs for breakfast and because he is as charming as he is ugly, he got them. (This is one story the family delights to tell.) I have always liked cops because Uncle Pat was a cop, and when I see a cop I want to pull his gun out of his holster.

My imagination does not take me further than this: I pull out the gun; I do not know what happens next.

There are two hundred *pensioni* and hotels in Florence; how, I ask Amedeo, is it possible that my Uncle Pat—I am by this time convinced that it is my Uncle Pat, my luck has been good so far on this trip—should have found me? Amedeo, flipping through a ledger, gives me what is for him an obvious answer: "Blood calls to blood."

I heard Aunt Mary before I saw her. Her laugh is like the wine of my childhood, the wine Grandpa made (the dark house seemed to rise like dough with its fragrance); it is good-natured, lusty, chewy, raw, ingratiating. When I was a child, the radio said a cop called Pasquale DiNardo had shot his wife and three children with his service revolver, and the family, thinking it was he, went to Uncle Pat's house, a procession of cars. Uncle Pat stood on the steps of his house in his bathrobe, hands on his hips, saying, "You bastards, you bastards." Inside, Aunt Mary laughed.

There is an indentation—a kind of cave, a hollow patch—in Uncle Pat's forehead, over which the skin is taut; a pulse throbs visibly here. I am fascinated by this unexplained physical anomaly, but not repulsed. Uncle Pat wears his mortality so close to his flesh. If flesh were wax, a thumb could make this indentation; it is like a primitive signature, God's signature.

We are sitting in the lounge of the Pitti Palace hotel, and Aunt Mary is telling Uncle Pat's old patrol partner, John, and his wife, Rita, about me. "This kid was smarter than me when she was five years old," Aunt Mary says, "and spoiled rotten." Who spoiled me? What can she mean? This is not the story of my childhood. "She drank from a bottle till she was five years old." But I remember an emerald-green glass frosted with white cattails and flying geese, a glass from which I drank in the big bedroom of the house on Long Island before I knew what sex was, the house the ivy blanketed and held together in all its parts, green mortar and insurance against collapse. This ivy my mother caused to be cut down. My favorite story was Rapunzel, I lived in the castle, and if I was good Daddy would come home and smooth my long blond hair. On the underside of the green glass my mother pasted pictures—kittens, flowers, red lips and hearts and cottages—to get me to drink to the bottom. This memory is the only proof I have that she once loved me. Aunt Mary says: "She'd carry the bottle up the stairs and say she wasn't going to bed, she was going to Germany, she was going to Egypt. 'Tell me a story,' she'd say; 'I know that one,' she'd say, and I'd feel so stupid." "She wasn't spoiled," Uncle Pat says. "She's the only sane one in your family," Aunt Mary says. Oh, adults are quarreling over me, I understand this. How fascinating I am. I am invisible and fascinating and I am thrilled. "Tell me the gossip," Aunt Mary says. But Uncle Pat can understand the present only in the light of the remembered past, he will countenance no talk of family adulteries and contested wills, he does not want anyone painting for him different pictures of the gallery of family members in his mind. I turn reluctantly from Aunt Mary's lively superficiality, her grit and glitter, which I like. Uncle Pat is crying. I feel a frisson, distinctly sexual, at the sight of his tears. Grandpa, he says, worked like an animal, and worked because he loved. This is not the story as I know the story. My mother, herself a great beauty and so sad, said Grandpa broke the nose of each of his five children in anger. He slammed an iron against my mother's face, that is what my mother says. When Uncle Johnny got polio—I was four, then, and I drank milk from an emerald-green glass—Grandma forced him to sit up and broke his back, that is what my mother says. Uncle Pat says: "Your grandmother said the rosary for all of us every day." For me, too? I ask; I am greedy. Yes. Grandma's heart was broken when your mother became a Jehovah's Witness, Uncle Pat says. And I broke my mother's heart when I became a Catholic, I say. "You are the only sane person in your family," Aunt Mary says; "you and me." "You know what your mother was like?" Uncle Pat says. "If eight people were coming to dinner there'd be eight pork chops, that's what your mother was like." When my mother broke Grandma's heart by becoming a Jehovah's Witness, Uncle Pat, baffled and angry, turned a furious silence in her direction, and my mother said, "Why are you treating me like a harlot?" ("What's a harlot?" I said.) John and Rita assess me as if to determine proof of sanity. How strange that they should be in the story.

Uncle Pat has come to Florence at the end of his journey and at the beginning of mine. He has come from Abruzzo, and he entreats me to go to Abruzzo, which has been my plan all along. "It's your past," he says, "it belongs to you, it's your right." He says this angrily, as if dark forces were at work to keep me from executing my purpose, which they are not. I deduce that he has tried to wrest meaning from the place and has failed and this failure will stay with him for the rest of his life, and whatever is incomplete in his story of his hard, proud father and his beautiful mother, whose invincible stupidity frightened me when I was a child, will remain incomplete and there will be no bright truth for him to point to and say: Look. It is there.

("What will you do there?" my cousin Peter, whose mother was my grandmother's sister, asked. He thinks I am frivolous and dangerous to myself. "What do *they* do?" I ask. "They work and they eat and they sleep," Peter says. He is a new immigrant. My daughter believes that he carries a gun.)

"They are dirty, greedy people in that village," Aunt Mary says, "and the women do all the work."

"The women do all the work," Uncle Pat echoes.

They make cheese and olive oil, "and they are so greedy they wanted my Swiss watch," Aunt Mary says.

One branch of the DiNardo family is called the "toad" branch, Uncle Pat doesn't know why. Uncle Pat never met the toads, he met only the other branch; and when he asked to see the well that figured in his mother's stories, they said No. And they wouldn't direct him to the toad branch, either.

"Were Grandma and Grandpa cousins?"

"They're all cousins, everybody's a cousin, they only want to sit and talk," Aunt Mary says.

Why are the cousins Uncle Pat met angry at the toads? Something about corn left unharvested, wheat unreaped, something long, long past. They forget; they never forgive. The source of their ancient animosity is lost. Departures, betrayals, a divorce in the family. For Uncle Pat all this is an algebraic problem that must be solved, it is a chronicle in need of an interpreter and a narrator—"And where is the meadow?" he asks, the meadow his mother talked about; he saw no meadow that corresponded to the meadow of her story, the meadow in his mind; no meadow at all. And now he is going back again to Abruzzo—another journey of love and of curiosity in which there is nothing prurient or casual or clinical; he is going back to tell them to expect me, "and don't change your ways," he says, "you have a right to your questions and your red fingernails."

"Oh, they'll love her," Aunt Mary says; "they'll pull the rings off her fingers and the clothes off her back; why can't we go to Sicily?"

"Your mother never made me three eggs," Uncle Pat says. "If there were eight people for dinner, she made eight pork chops, she never made nine."

"Your mother," Aunt Mary says; "when she joined that crazy religion! . . . What a brat you were, honey."

When do we rework the past? start to forget, to revise? When is the truth lost? In the moment, in the twinkling of an eye? If the past and the future exist, where are they? I do not wish to receive new information about my mother though I am hungry to possess her. I have always been hungry to possess her; I want *my* Her, not Uncle Pat's Her. I hear my mother's voice in Uncle Pat's, this is too close for comfort. Sometimes my own voice sounds like this—the voice of someone with a permanent grievance against the universe. Oh! I am tired. We have been excavating the past too long. On the roof terrace of the Pitti Palace I imagine I hear the faint bleeping of bats, a beating of wings.

I take Aunt Mary and Uncle Pat and Rita and John and my friend Alice—poor Rita, poor Alice, poor John, not meant to be in this story—to the Square of Santo Spirito, the place of my heart; and we eat gelato at Ricchi. Aunt Mary, Uncle Pat, and poor Alice and Rita and John and I talk like pleasant strangers.

Sitting next to Uncle Pat in Ricchi's *gelateria,* I am suddenly reminded of a movie house and a man who sat next to me one Saturday afternoon and offered me popcorn at the kiddies' matinee; his eyes were bright; I shrank away. And then—is this a story or a metaphor?—Uncle Pat appeared in his cop's uniform with his shiny badge, and the man like an animal cowered, and Uncle Pat took my hand and led me into the dazzling light.

I have fallen completely in love. Uncle Pat's pulse visibly throbs.

Look! Till the end of the world, it is there. The immaculate beauty of Brunelleschi's Santo Spirito is inviolable.

In a sweet city of impressive and beautiful churches—Santa Maria Novella, holiday-wrapped in white-and-green marble, near which, at the Hotel Minerva, Emerson lived; Santa Croce, in which are buried Michelangelo and Machiavelli and Galileo, whose ashes stir to the gay music of the Communist party rallies held in its huge oblong piazza; the Romanesque San Miniato, whose green-and-white geometric facade gleams rosy on its hill outside the city walls at sunset—none is more radiantly pure than this Renaissance church, the exquisite lines of which would make adornment superfluous.

During World War II the area around Santo Spirito was declared off limits to the liberating armies; more recently, carabinieri walked these streets four, not two, abreast. But the presence of the young soldiers and police who now sometimes guard the piazza is remarkably discreet. They chat with people quietly, they examine papers with no bluster—almost apologetically, bashfully—and their actions inspire no contagious fear.

They are there because of neighborhood concern: Drug pushers and young addicts and foreigners who want to smoke marijuana congregate on the steps of Santo Spirito. Heroin is processed in Florence; the same pushers who deal in soft drugs like marijuana also deal in heroin, which is by our standards cheap. The streets here are littered with disposable syringes. Sometimes one steps over vomit. (On the side of the piazza facing Santo Spirito, there is a pharmacy that refuses to sell disposable syringes; it has everyone's admiration and respect. This is the same pharmacy where I was given sympathy and sulfur over the counter for a stomach ailment by a pharmacist who urged me to go to a nearby trattoria for a "white meal"; and when I got there, I found the pharmacist had ordered my dinner in advance of my coming: spaghetti with olive oil and garlic, chicken with sage, coffee and Sambuca.) And yet, in spite of addicts and posturing, sandaled, grass-smoking tourists, it is peaceful here, not threatening. Night after night in the quiet and gracious square I sat under the old trees—I never thought to ask their names, Italian trees seemed to me at the time to be so Italian as to have no American counterparts—and, listening to the splashing fountain, felt no fear, no dismay. At night when the lamps are lit—dramatically, as if for a play—the perfect proportions of Brunelleschi's church seem to impose a hush on human activity (I remembered an old Wesleyan hymn: "Be Silent, Mortal Flesh").

Sitting at Ricchi, I looked up into the hospitably open windows of the palazzi that line the square (if God is in the details, it is worth a detour from the North Pole just to see the doorbells of the palazzi) and saw ceiling frescoes, and ate the best ice cream (raspberry gelato, chocolate mousse semifreddo) in Florence.

Ice cream is said to have been given to the world by the Hindus, but this would be a hard proposition to defend in Florence. Giuliano Bugialli, master of Italian *alta cucina* and food historian, says that ice cream emerged in its present form in sixteenth-century Florence and was taken to France in that century by Catherine de' Medici (who also introduced forks to the French court). Primitive forms of sweet frozen drinks were probably brought to Sicily in the eleventh century by invaders from North Africa. Linguist Mario Pei, in his introduction to Ada Boni's *Talisman Italian Cook Book* (an out-of-print masterpiece to which Marcella Hazan pays homage, and which is the one cookbook I would have if I could have only one), says that both ice cream and ices (sorbetto) originated in Italy, "whence they spread to the rest of the world." (Gelato is made with egg yolks and milk; semifreddo is made with egg yolks and frozen whipped cream; sorbetto may contain whipped cream and egg whites and is a kind of frozen mousse; traditionally, American ice cream is not made with eggs.)

The piazza is approached through narrow, winding streets. It's a gorgeous kind of pilgrim's progress: Watery, thin shafts of light penetrate the comfortable, permanent half dusk . . . and then one comes into the piazza as if into an explosion of light.

The church presides over one end of a great rectangular square lined by dignified palazzi; within the rectangle is an oblong framed and shaded by ancient trees, and within the oblong there is a fountain.

The Piazza of Santo Spirito, once home to the School of St. Augustine, has often been called a theater and was perhaps intended as one. Even when the piazza is not the stage for political rallies or avant-garde mummers, it is a theater and, in spite of its size, an intimate one: In the morning produce is sold from carts under striped umbrellas, and in the afternoon used clothes are sold; and lovers stroll all the time, old people warm their bodies in the sun, children play ball (in spite of a plaque dated 1639 that forbids playing ball). The square has always served a communal function.

For one of the most beautiful of all churches to gaze with its single deep-eyed window over such homely activities is the very essence of sincerity and charm.

Santo Spirito has thirty-eight semicircular chapels; in one of them is a Virgin by Filippo Lippi, in another a marble Last Supper by Sansovino, in others minor Renaissance masterpieces—and in another, an insipid plaster Madonna with a halo of light bulbs; and in another, in front of a sixteenth-century mural of a stern Jesus chasing the money changers out of the temple, a cloying representation of St. Joseph (plaster), holding an even more cloying Baby Jesus, who is holding the world, on top of which is a gold cross. Poor St. Joseph—he wasn't even widely venerated till the fifteenth century—is bound to be thought of as a cuckold; and cuckolded by the Holy Spirit. . . . We know that isn't true; but bad attempts at art lead to other kinds of blasphemy, and it's impossible not to see in him something fundamentally absurd, if not ridiculous.

. . . Jesus holds the world; the world is a ball. . . . Six balls appear on the Medici coat of arms. . . . Soccer is thought by some to have first been played in this piazza. . . . The piazza is familiarly known as the Piazza della

Palla—Ball Square. . . . Only a place that is old and that is imbued with the recognition of the shadowy nature of mortal life can have such echoes. This piazza strikes one as wise. . . .

It is a miracle that the Catholic Church has survived its own iconography. I grew up in houses of simpering, suffering, Madame Tussaud Madonnas, houses in which the eyes of a blood-eroticized Christ followed me; and I was first received into the Catholic Church in that time which, for the sake of convenience, we call the sixties, when floppy felt banners drooped about altars, "like wash," as one *Commonweal* observer wrote, "on a Marrakesh clothes line . . . inscribed with Gospel messages or those of some latter-day prophet (e.g., Kahlil Gibran)." From one form of kitsch to another, and both insults to the God who became man. And yet the virility and directness of Catholic art is to be found not only in the great paintings of the past but in the street shrines one sees all over Florence (all over Italy); these shrines transform and add a spiritual dimension to daily life at the same time that they tell us that God belongs not to churches but to people. On one wall at a busy intersection, a crude, strong chalk drawing, not in the least sentimental, of a suffering Christ, a rag (a loincloth) stretched from hip to hip to hide his genitals. . . .

Which invites a question: Why is the sexuality of Jesus more often than not obscured? In *The Sexuality of Christ in Renaissance Art and in Modern Oblivion,* Leo Steinberg writes that:

> Renaissance art . . . produced a large body of devotional imagery in which the genitalia of the Christ Child, or of the Dead Christ, receive so much demonstrative emphasis that one must recognize an *ostentatio genitalium* comparable to the canonic *ostentatio vulnerum,* the showing forth of the wounds. In many hundreds of pious, religious works, from before 1400 to past the mid–sixteenth century, the ostensive unveiling of the Child's sex, or the touching, protecting or presentation of it, is the main action [an action often accompanied by the Infant's chucking the Mother under the chin], and the emphasis recurs in images of the Dead Christ, or of the Mystical Man of Sorrows [as in Andrea del Sarto's sixteenth-century drawing for a Pietà]. . . . The Child's lower body concedes its humanity . . . the divinity in the incarnate Word needs no demonstration. . . . The humanization of God . . . becomes the set theme of every Renaissance Nativity, Adoration, Holy Family, or Madonna and Child. . . . Sooner or later someone is bound to notice what the Madonna's left hand is doing. . . . [What the Madonna's left hand is doing is pointing to or fondling the Child's genitals.] The rendering of the incarnate Christ ever more unmistakeably flesh and blood is a religious enter-

prise because it testifies to God's greatest achievement . . . that God once embodied himself in human nature is to confess that the eternal, there and then, became mortal and sexual.

It is a matter of faith that Jesus was, as St. Augustine declares, "complete in all the parts of a man" and, as Tertullian writes, "a man entirely virginal." And it is a matter of fact that while Michelangelo's *Risen Christ* was utterly naked, sixteenth-century copies of the *Risen Christ* (drawings, woodcuts, engravings, bronze and marble replications or adaptations) represent the figure as aproned; the original statue, in the Cathedral of Santa Maria Sopra Minerva in Rome, is now similarly girdled. In Fra Angelico's *Crucifixion,* in the Monastery of St. Mark, the sex of Christ is hidden by a diaphanous cloth. But Fra Filippo Lippi, Bellini, Andrea del Sarto, and Veronese present the blameless sexuality of the Child: We come naked into the world, and so did the man/God who shared our human condition. It might have been better for us all—it might have substantially altered our view of human sexuality—if false notions of decorum had not vitiated this truth.

All such considerations are irrelevant before the luminous facade of Santo Spirito. That is the function of visual art—to erase questions . . . not *to mean,* but *to be* (a function which, Archibald MacLeish notwithstanding, poetry cannot fulfill).

Before Brunelleschi gave the world the science of optics, it was believed that the eyes sent out rays to illuminate everything one looked at. (That is why we say it "hurts" us to look at something beautiful—for example, Brunelleschi's Santo Spirito.) Brunelleschi's theories went into a kind of limbo, to be resurrected much later by the Impressionists. In 1744 Giambattista Vico wrote that "the eyes are like a sieve and the pupils like two holes, and as from the sieve sticks of dust issue to touch the earth, so from the eyes, through the pupils sticks of light issue to touch the objects which are distinctly seen. . . . Things [are] actually taken possession of by sight." This is poetically (and phenomenologically) true: When we close our eyes, the world is dark; the light is within us, we contain it.

A long, long time ago, when the six Balls of Purple occupied the celestial borders with the superb geometry of the space ships, . . . the lion that was both prisoner and guardian of the Florentine townwalls stopped roaring and turned into marble. And the balls invaded palaces and churches, silky sails and bales of wool. They were imprinted on soldiers' shields and on merchants' escutcheons; they were the insignia of arts and crafts; they untied knots and joined rings.

"Balls! Balls!" the population cries at their sight, vulgarly mixing swears and prayers, since everything comes from the rolling spheres. . . .

—Piazza S. Spirito*

One golden afternoon I walked into Ricchi for a gelato, and some serendipitous instinct (the muse of grateful travelers) prompted me to ask the cashier to turn on the light in a darkened inner room; and I found one of the happiest places in Florence. I had not seen the sign above the door— ARCHIVIO—nor would I have known what it meant if I had.

This is what I saw: A coffee room—bulbous briarwood tables, like mushrooms with flat caps, or like balls on stems, balls that have been sliced in half, each with a belly button (a ball-like indentation); and the frolicky motif of balls, and balls within balls, is repeated and repeated, and it is a conceit one does not tire of—built-in briarwood benches with armrests that echo the curves of Brunelleschi's facade (a ball atop each armrest); and three hundred twelve-by-twelve-inch framed photographs of Brunelleschi's church elaborated upon with facades given it by artists—whimsical, iconoclastic, irreverent, good-natured puns and fantasies; what delight!

In 1792 Florence wisely thwarted a plan to gussy up Brunelleschi's facade. In 1980 artist Mario Mariotti felicitiously conceived of having a competition for "decorating" the austere facade of Santo Spirito without defacing it. Its starkness would seem to invite the mischievousness of graffiti; it's a kind of miracle that this natural slate has not been scrawled upon, a miracle that stems from its incorruptible beauty. Mariotti's colleague, archivist Sergio Salvi, says that "everybody was allowed 'to restore,' 'to finish,' 'to renew' the facade of Santo Spirito, not only the traditional, qualified image creators but also . . . the nonartists who had the chance to become such in the exchange of roles."

For two months the piazza became a living theater for avant-garde cinema, dance, and poetry readings, and the audience gave extemporaneous performances, too.

"The ball, sneaking out of the geometry of the coat-of-arms and out of the composed equilibrium of history, rolled in the field of the square to start the game. . . . The facade of the church became the 'game.'" The inspiration for this

*Assessorato alla Cultura, Comune di Firenze; Firenze Estate, 1980.

"game" may have come from the drawings, in Santo Spirito's sacristy, of Bellincioni, who endeavored fruitlessly to present an elaborated facade to the people of Florence, who loved Santo Spirito exactly as it was. Onto the facade, in 1980, were projected images of the facade as conceived by various artists. These superimposed images are preserved for us in photographs, which were then displayed in Ricchi. This is as nice a case of eating your cake and having it too as I have ever encountered; how pleased Brunelleschi must be to see his church take on so many new aspects while forever remaining the same.

And how lovely the spirit of harmless, not wicked, mischief that prevails.

Three hundred satirical, inventive, loving, sly, punning facades are too much to take in at one time; and each time I came back to Ricchi, I was drawn to different ones:

The church becomes an overstuffed armchair, upholstered in a pattern of bright red cherries, on which sits a fat, surprised tabby cat.

Brunelleschi's single, simple, recessed round window becomes a doorbell (with a brass nameplate—Brunelleschi's—under it); a ghostly finger pushes the bell.

The verb *to be* is conjugated on an otherwise unembellished facade. (This conceit, so simple, is really the most elaborate metaphysically, and very happy-spirited, too.)

An arrow points to the central doorway: VOI SIETE QUI! (You are here!)

(It is unimaginable for this project to have taken place in America, Ireland, or Spain, the nature of the Church in those countries—what a happy, human Church the Italian one is!—forbidding it.)

The church becomes: a stuffed owl; a harlequin's mask; a crocheted doily; a map of Florence; a baby swimming in amniotic fluid; a bar; a gas station; a man's rear end clad in blue jeans; a collection of sandbags; a Hindu deity; a jack-in-the-box; a leering general; a bull's-eye; a peacock spreading its tail; a frog; a Christmas tree; Madame Tussaud's wax museum; a still life of fruits and vegetables; the New York skyline; the Piazza of Santo Spirito; a necropolis; the Italian news agency; a tenement building; a circus; a hanging garden.

Three words are projected onto the facade: QUI SONO FELICE—"Here I am happy."

Another artist projects these words onto the facade: COSA PENSEREBBE BRUNELLESCHI DI TUTTO QUESTO?!—"What would Brunelleschi think of all this?!" (As Brunelleschi was himself a practical joker, he would probably have loved it.)

Two artists find pleasure in the idea of serpents: In one projection a stylized serpent weaves its way around the inspiring window, and in another, a realistic serpent with protruded red fangs seems to be choking the spirit out of Santo Spirito—nice little essays suggesting the sins of the Church. And two artists are equally infatuated with watermelons (not so odd; a melon is a ball). In one, a watermelon is stretched across the facade like a smile; in another, melons like balls frolic over the facade.

A picture of naked starving African children is superimposed on the facade, together with one word: AMEN.

Brunelleschi's apparently irresistible window becomes a clock, and the facade is given Baroque embellishments and the words BAROCK AROUND THE CLOCK.

A Devil with red horns and a long red tongue is superimposed in one projection; a scantily dressed girl with a pale pink tongue licking two joined ice-cream cones (a cigarette in one hand) pictured in another.

A Crucifixion takes place in one projection (disaffection with the Church expresses itself in church images in Italy); a merry pattern of lipstick kisses on another.

Simple geometric designs: The church becomes a field of fleur-de-lys; Gucci projects his red-and-green logo and the word GUCCI.

Satan is in the garden with a pretty little girl.

Tuborg beer cans obscure the facade.

Coca-Cola cans dance on the facade.

A man sits in a beach chair on railroad tracks that merge into a vanishing point; the vanishing point is Brunelleschi's window. He is stolid in the face of magic—perspective is magic—and he is, according to the artist, "contemplating and continuing the project of my life."

A Goyaesque nude sprawls across Santo Spirito.

One projection says NON.

Another projection says IO! (!)

Together they constitute a statement on Florentines' feeling about the Church and about tradition: affection and exasperation, familiarity, rebellion, heady flirtation, an inevitable return to the Source.

Qui sono felice. Here I am happy. . . . I am happy sitting inside at Ricchi, and I am happy sitting outside at Ricchi, drenched in the luminosity of Santo Spirito. The choices here are between happiness and happiness.

When Prince Charles and Princess Diana were in Florence, I thought how lucky I was not to be they. They were at a state dinner; I was in the Piazza Santo Spirito.

To walk to the piazza from my hotel is itself a pleasure, a pleasure I prolong by stopping at a Jolly café for *vin santo*. On these twisting streets artisans work; they disregard me—which is the way I like it—as they drink their *vin santo;* their clothes smell of their work, a sharp smell overlaid by a dusty smell pervades the cool Jolly. These men polish and make brass artifacts; they are woodworkers and carpenters and restorers of antiques and creators of instant antiques. Their shops are hospitably open, allowing me to postpone the ultimate pleasure of Santo Spirito. In one shop there is a lithographer, Viviana Sarubbi, who reproduces old engravings; I like to watch her work with acids and immerse zinc plates in ink baths and hang them up with clothespins to dry. I stop by on days when she is running her press. I love the romantic smell of ink, my father was a printer. I love this part of the Oltrarno with its *latterie* and *gelaterie* and wine bars; I love what I think of as the bohemian quarter—though strictly speaking there is no bohemian quarter in Florence, there are artists scattered all over—narrow, sleepy streets with Napoleonic streetlamps, uniform yellow houses, streets that seem to have come to drowsy life from one of Viviana's engravings. At the busy intersection of Borgo San Jacopo and Via dello Sprone there is a curious triangular-shaped building that projects onto the street like the prow of a ship; high above is a partially boarded loggia, beneath it the Medici coat of arms with its six balls, and beneath that, at street level, there is a scalloped basin into which (whence onto the street) a marble satyr spews forth water. This house figures in my dreams.

And once I found a garden.

Memory, memory mixed with desire, often betrays us into believing we have had glimpses of secret gardens (Vico: "Imagination is nothing but extended or compounded memory"), so when we dream of gardens, we hardly know if we are dreaming of something once seen or something always longed for.

This garden is real.

I do not know how I was drawn into it—perhaps some hint, a foretaste of sweetness on the crowded street, a fragrant courtyard, a series of arches (arches are the architecture of dreams) that beckoned. In this garden, pots and pots of azaleas bloom—it is too early for azaleas in Florence—and only here and nowhere else has wisteria come to life against sienna-colored walls. There is a wall fountain—ruined pillars and cracked urns and armless and decapitated statues, a pool of black water in which dead leaves float and bloated orange fish and slim silver fish swim. Mossy steps from the black pool lead to hedges twelve feet tall. Behind the hedges looms ethereal the bell tower of Santo Spirito. There is an oval of grass planted with verbena; a magnolia in bud, waxy green leaves. In the center of the oval there is a cylindrical brass sculpture. Benches. On the gravel cars are parked.

This garden figures in my dreams. The cars have no substance. I am in an unpeopled world.

> *À la porte de la maison qui viendra frapper?*
>
> *—Pierre Albert Birot*

> "Is there anybody there?" said the Traveller. . . .
> "Tell them that I came, and no one answered,
> That I kept my word," he said.
>
> *—Walter de la Mare, "The Listeners"*

An American in Milan told me to be sure to see the Davanzati, something I might not otherwise have done. She seemed, when I met her in the Pinacoteca Ambrosiana, such a strange mixture of practicality and perturbation—sturdy shoes and reference books, a wailing voice that surprised itself by the intensity of loneliness it conveyed—she might have been credited with an excess of imagination or with none at all. The Davanzati is imagination's domain.

Near the fourteenth-century Palazzo Torrigiani, converted in the nineteenth century to the Hotel Porta Rossa (a mysterious twilight oasis of lace half-curtains, stained-glass windows, tarnished gilt lettering on old glass, old servingmen in rusty black uniforms), at 13 Via Porta Rossa, is the fourteenth-century Palazzo Davanzati, commonly referred to as a museum of decorative arts. It is more useful to think of it—bearing in mind that objects speak—as a family house to which we have privileged entry.

When life was short, those who could do so lived in a visually complex universe: Every inch of every room of the Davanzati is frescoed with heraldic images, images drawn from nature, from Scripture and myth. The shutters that close against the meager light, provided by narrow recessed smoked, beveled, and leaded barred windows, are a maze of geometric patterns; they are dependent upon a superfluity of decorative hinges.

A child born to the Davanzati merchant family in the great four-poster bed where generations mated, birthed, and died opened his eyes to a magical world of knights and ladies dallying in tame forests, of wantonly clad men and women exchanging lazy embraces, of men on horseback and men playing chess, of men and women in bed—in the very bed that first received the infant's wail.

A house of fireplaces and generous hearths and absurdly narrow frescoed hallways and low entranceways, of beamed and frescoed ceilings, all alcoves and nooks and angles, convenient to daydreaming, it is a house of such cupboards and coffers (the drawer had not yet been invented) as one might see in a painting by Titian.

These chests or coffers, with their extremely intricate and beautiful machinery—locks designed to defy indiscretion—are, as Gaston Bachelard says, "veritable organs of the secret psychological life. Indeed, without these 'objects' . . . our intimate life would lack a model of intimacy. . . . A wardrobe's inner space is also intimate space, space that is not open to just anybody. . . . Chests and caskets . . . are very evident witnesses of the need for secrecy, of an intuitive sense of hiding places."

But the jewels and the bridal linens and the secrets the coffers and the cupboards once contained are gone; and this makes one sad, for cupboards and caskets epitomize the need for order, and are containers of history and memory as well as of things. (I once bought, in a junk shop, an eighteenth-century jelly pantry; and there still remained in it, under layers of newspapers, under layers of paint, slips of paper: "Peach preserves, 1798." . . . This moved me so much the pantry became almost an object of veneration.)

Whenever I think of houses in which I have lived, whenever I close my eyes to "read" the rooms I moved in, I stop inevitably at secret hiding places—the musty attic crawl space where I hid slips of paper on which were messages from me to an unknown future (and from me to the football captain of my school); the locked box on Aunt Betty's vanity table that she sometimes opened to show me fabulous jewels (I have them now, they are all glass; but each piece tells me a story of my childhood, reminds me of a word, a gesture, a person loved or dead or gone or so changed as to appear to have gone); the linen closet that smelled of lavender, where my aunts kept a silver box of sugar cubes. This box, from which in thrilling solitude I ate till my teeth ached with sweetness, was always, when I found it, full, replenished by adults, and this convinced me, against all other evidence, of the goodness of grown-ups, and hence of the goodness of the world. And I needed convincing. My daughter once, in a fevered delirium, cried out for a room with shutters and flowered wallpaper and screamed that a mantelpiece would fall on her and kill her. She has forgotten she dreamed this. This is the room in which she received the news that her father and I were going to be divorced.

We walk too swiftly through the Davanzati to read the rooms as lovingly as they deserve to be read, and this makes me sad.

But the Davanzati house was so constructed and decorated as to keep unhappiness and disorder at bay; it still does. I never thought a lavatory could be lyrical, and I distrust people who make pleasure palaces of bathrooms; but the fourteen-foot-high beamed, closeted lavatories are inspired. (Inside, and comfortable, are wooden or stone benches, and on the sanitary openings there is something that resembles the cover of a pot.) One lavatory is frescoed in what a fellow tourist accurately called Gucci stripes and Gucci colors, and another (my favorite) is densely covered with red and green lollipop flowers—like a Laura Ashley pattern, or a happy child's dream. . . . Three hundred years later Versailles did not have toilets.

The crimson dining room of the Davanzati—the Room of the Parrots, with its wide view of Florence and its frescoed designs borrowed from medieval tapestries—is one stone flight of stairs up; the kitchen—pity the servants!—is on the fourth, or top, floor. In some ways it is the most interesting room of the house because it looks, with its open hearth, bellows, and spit, caldrons and looms and clay oil-burning lamps, its witty ceramic hand warmers in the shape of shoes, as if it were peopled still. (In the fourteenth century the spit was hand-rotated by means of pulleys; it wasn't until the fifteenth century that dogs were used to control the mechanism—which may have been bliss for the servants, but which seems like an evolutionary step backward into barbarism to me.)

There are no servants' rooms; servants slept just anywhere. In the extended family of the late Middle Ages, slaves, servants, and children were treated very much alike; patriarchal merchants like the Davanzatis were responsible for members of a vast tribe—poor relations, even families of business partners. (In my experience, it is not so much male authority that women mind [women have a right and a need to be protected because they are mothers or prospective mothers]; it is the posture of authority [which requires a complementary female posture of submission] without the graceful substance of authority, the substance of authority being duty fulfilled.)

The Palazzo Davanzati is built around a central courtyard and a well; the loggias are lovely, and even the plumbing pipes that snake down toward the tiled courtyard are decorative; but the outside stone steps are cruelly narrow and steep. The whole house combines charm with ruthless defensiveness: lollipops and barred windows. . . .

"Elevators," Bachelard said, "do away with the heroism of stair climbing so that there is no longer any virtue in living up near the sky." I would gladly exchange heroism for ordinariness and comfort. "What do old people do?" I asked the Davanzati guide, a question I frequently asked in Italy when confronted with an infinity of steps and no elevator. The guide, choosing to misunderstand me (or perhaps understanding me too well), said: "*You,* old? *I'm* forty-four. If all old women were like you, life would be heaven for men." (With your looks, life must be a Muslim heaven on earth for you, I thought; but of course I refrained from saying so.) The good man, with an air of cleverness to which he was clearly entitled, popped me into a creaky old elevator ("built by Mussolini") hidden by a tapestry, with instructions to the other tourists to stay put. As he repeated this performance on each of three stories of the palazzo, he was obliged to run down the stairs three times to collect the waiting tourists and then to march up the stairs three times with the tourists in tow. I would have sworn this was a disinterested act of kindness, except that somewhere between the third and fourth stories his wedding band disappeared from his ring finger.

I had been giving thought to my having escaped a clichéd infatuation with a beautiful Italian man, a problem I solved to my own satisfaction after several months in Rome: I was so enraptured with Italy, my heart and mind so completely engaged, that a love affair would have been redundant, as well as trite. . . . What this said about my need for intimacy, which seemed to have grown sluggish under Italian skies, did more, however, to trouble than to reassure me; I would not have thought temperament and emotions could owe so much to geography.

I never returned to the Davanzati because, so far as I can make out, the guide was too beautifully present, and I had set myself to inhabit realms of the past. . . . The past can be tamed and controlled.

My Aunt Ann had a miniature alabaster fountain with little alabaster birds perched on it. They swung to the touch of a finger and dipped their tiny beaks into the water in the basin. I was enchanted by this object, I loved it.

This is how taste is formed. We love the alabaster fountain forever; or we rebel against it and form aesthetic judgments that deny our past love; or we translate our love into campy raptures over kitsch; or we love it because we loved it and not because of what it is—we call it charming because it charmed. . . .

One thing that can be said about an alabaster fountain with birds on it is that it tells us no great truth. . . .

Every morning in Florence I read the *International Herald Tribune,* which I buy steps away from my hotel at a newsstand in the *piazzetta* just off the Ponte Vecchio, and which I read in a café with the cup of cappuccino that is my second breakfast. After months in Italy I find myself living as if by habit, following routines; the daily rituals are, like all good ritual, both exciting and comforting, and they leave room to accommodate fortuity and serendipity.

One morning my eye was caught by an article about Judy Chicago, the American feminist artist, who had designed something called "The Birth Project"; executed by 150 volunteers from drawings by Chicago, the project consisted of embroidery, quilting, petit point, weavings, crochet, and other forms of needlework, representing women's experience of birth. Ms. Chicago was struck, according to the account, by the "changeover from matriarchy to patriarchy" in Creation stories: "The idea that a male God created man is such a reversal of the reality of how life comes forth. . . . I started looking for images of birth, and I didn't find any. There were almost no birth images in the history of Western art, although I found some from preindustrial societies." Ms. Chicago's volunteers began to believe, they said, that their needlework was "special," not "ordinary," not busywork or a craft, but "an art form that women have created over the centuries and that they've had no recognition for."

These tendentious remarks sent me hurrying to the Pitti, thereafter to the Uffizi. I wished to rest my eyes on paintings of the Madonna and Child. MAIDEN GIVES BIRTH TO GOD is what I call front-page news.

It is not true that women have received no recognition for needlework. In the sixteenth and seventeenth centuries Venetian women were admitted into the Compagnia della Calza—the pinnacle of artistic and social life—as a result of their highly valued knitting. The *compagne* wore a coat of arms decorated with gold and embroidered in pearls, and the red-and-blue stockings seen in Renaissance paintings (and worn by Henry II of France when he married Catherine de' Medici). Cencia Scarpariola, who revived the art of needlework in Burano in the late nineteenth century, is revered. If the needleworkers of Abruzzo, Sicily, and Burano labor anonymously, so did the builders of the great cathedrals.

Such works of art as Piero della Francesca's *Madonna del Parto,* in which a perfectly beautiful woman wears a light-blue maternity gown unbuttoned down the front, to a belly she musingly caresses, might not satisfy Ms.

Chicago, as they do not graphically represent blood and placenta, which Ms. Chicago's workers rendered in "vibrant blues, reds, purples and earth tones." The agony of labor is not their subject. People do seem to forget that the point of having a baby is to have a baby—not simply to have an Experience. But the *Madonna del Parto* is, magnificently, both the theater of action and the action itself, theater and protagonist. The painters of the Renaissance were able to keep both the baby and the mother's experience of the baby securely in mind.

Nowhere is it written that Mary suffered labor pains (in fact, whether her hymen was broken has been a matter for debate); but it can't be proven that she didn't, and there's a theology to support the conjecture that she did. God didn't, after all, snap His fingers and send His son down amidst clouds; He joined the human family in a human way. When Jesus began to witness in the temple, the response was: What's that neighborhood kid doing here? It is possible to believe that Mary, though she was free from sin, had a delivery like that of other women, including her sister, Eve.

Here, at the Pitti, is Raphael's *Madonna of the Chair,* the exquisite Oriental-looking mother and the fat baby so closely entwined they give new meaning to the words *one flesh;* he seems a part of her still. . . . The naked eyes of Raphael's *La Gravida,* and the set of her fleshy jaw as her pudgy fingers touch her stomach in tender expectation, contain all the complex braided emotions, the ambivalence experienced by a woman bearing a child—something celebratory, something defiant, something shy, something triumphant. "I've got a secret," she says, a secret like no other, both hidden and visible; her fertile belly visibly says: "I have a secret inner life."

The beauty of Raphael's paintings cannot tell false stories.

And at the Uffizi, Leonardo's mother, in the *Adoration of the Magi,* is like any neighborhood mamma. One knows that look; she is showing her new baby off; she is, with one stupendous exception, exactly like us. . . . In Leonardo's *Annunciation* she is, as we were, when we first knew we were pregnant, surprised/not surprised. . . . In Correggio's *Adoration of the Child* she is, as we were, playful and in awe—in awe of her own body and of that other.

Tuscany is not the place to nourish resentment against men (as Georges Duby saw): "It was in Tuscany, at the dawn of the quattrocento . . . that a stoic Christianity offered a release from the anxiety and guilty shivers of erotic festival, that female flesh appeared in its fullness for the first time, in bronze and marble. Woman was not resurrected here, she was born. She brought new man the tranquil pleasure of her body." On the door of the

Baptistry, Ghiberti "portrayed the creation of woman. Here the flight of angels which until then had borne only one carnal body to heaven, the Virgin of the Assumption, supports the soaring figure of Eve. She is saved at last, justified. Confirmed. She belongs to purity and splendor. Her beauty ascends toward divine light, victorious over all remorse." Angels support this loved Eve (Ghiberti's art erases any notions one might have of a Madonna/whore dichotomy) by the neck, the shoulders, the arms, the mound of Venus, as she soars. The Virgin and the original sinner are sisters.

Nineteenth-century painter Robert Walter Weir said his life was changed forever by a poem of Du Fresnay's that led him to Raphael: "See Raffaello, there his form celestial trace / Unrivaled sovereign of the realm of grace...."

If one were to spend all one's time looking at Raphael, one would feel nothing but serenity and sweet repose. But:

"FUCK!" is written inside the elevator at the Uffizi; the world intrudes upon our dreams.

T. has an enchanting accent and the bitterness that comes of being a permanently displaced person—that, and some deeper sadness beyond the cynicism, the wellsprings of which I do not understand. When World War II broke out, T.'s mother and father, Italians who had emigrated to Scotland, were arrested in their Glasgow home and transported to Canada and interned for the duration. Her father's "crime," T. says, was that one of his daughters had been seen in the company of Fascists. In fact, it was government policy to intern Italians. Perfectly blameless people were swept up in this way, caught by surprise. T.'s father did frequent an Italian "social club" (as did her mother—to learn to sew); but T., who was born in Canada and returned later to Scotland, is convinced that he would have been a partisan had he remained in Italy. (The past can be tamed, reshaped, controlled.)

T. lives in Florence now, saddened and made cynical by her recently ended relationship with an Englishman. "The real English vice is sadomasochism," she says, "but very quiet sadomasochism because they care so much what people think. I didn't mind, so much, being tied with a drape sash. I minded being told to *shhh* so the town of Lucca wouldn't hear me, especially as I wasn't saying anything."

But—poor T.!—if Englishmen are bad, Italian men are worse, "impossible." In a country of Madonnas and *bambini,* she says, "mothers have their sons by the balls." They are always their mothers' boys. This view is not unique to T.; the phenomenon she describes is called *mammismo.* Luigi Barzini said without qualification that "woman is the predominant character of Italian life. . . . What other people call for their mother in time of stress or danger? Do the Germans say *'Mutter,'* the French *'Maman,'* the English *'Mother of Mine,'* when faced by a disappointment or an emergency? Wounded Italian soldiers in front-line dressing stations moan *'Mamma, mamma, mamma,'* almost inaudibly, like hurt children. *'Mamma,'* say men condemned to death as they wait for the firing squad to fire."

It is difficult, as it always is in diatribes of this sort, to know exactly whom T. despises—Italian men, Italian women, or herself.

"Italians are lousy lovers," she says, "superficial and careless. You can't tell them about your orgasms—it would wound their precious manhood. Provided they have any." Florence, T. says, "is gay—the San Francisco of Italy" (which fact had escaped my notice). "They all get married, all the gay men, and then they have their nights out with the boys, and what do their wives care, as long as they have status and their precious position and babies? . . . Let them screw anybody, who cares?" T. is as vociferous as Savonarola was on the subject of Florentine homosexuality; her anger extends to the dead—to Michelangelo and Leonardo, to the last of the Medicis (whose inclination toward men made it impossible for them to procreate and ensured the extinction of their line). As it is very difficult to nourish hatred for the dead—in my experience it is impossible—it is a measure of T.'s rage that she cannot speak the name of Lorenzo de' Medici without a shudder of aversion.

We are having this discussion, in which I am a silent partner, as we stroll, stopping in shops that catch our fancy. Across from the Pitti, a paper shop, Giannini e Figlio, with gorgeous marbleized and patterned Florentine paper (suitable to be framed, hand-dyed with herbs and vegetable roots), puts a stop—as this art knows no gender—to rancorous chatter. We cross over the Ponte Vecchio to Via Por Santa Maria, a street of dress shops and boutiques; and T. says contemptuously, "Florentines wear their money on their backs," a view of Italians shared by Luigi Barzini, who says, "Apparently the things they want above all are the show of prosperity and the reassurance they can read in the eyes of their envious neighbors. . . . The last thing they spend money on is better food. Better food is invisible." This perception confuses me, as it is so outdated and so much at odds with my own; but I don't take it upon myself to quarrel with someone who is enjoying a go at self- and cultural hatred.

T. is miserable today. T. may be feeling anti-Italian (antiself) today, but her reflexes don't correspond to her cynical judgments. In the New Market, which smells so wonderfully of leather and straw, she pats the snout of the brass boar, Il Porcellino, just like any other Italian, just as if she were in love with Florence, which today she is not. We wander among the stalls, and T. becomes increasingly Italian (she speaks Italian or English according to her mood) as she watches tourists attempt to haggle with storekeepers who would dream neither of offering them merchandise at the labeled price nor of bargaining—they are the sole arbiters, there is no contest, and they are happy to give you a moment's pleasure by offering you a price lower than the one with which the merchandise is marked, but haggling is not their game. I love these elegant arcades (Cellini worked here), the marriage of art to commerce—the holiness of daily life. . . . In celebration of which I buy a multicompartmented leather purse exactly like the purses Italian train conductors wear slung over their shoulders, which I have coveted for their insouciance and practicality. . . . On the little Square of San Martino, near the house where Dante was born, there is a small chapel; old ladies—and T. and I—sit on benches to rest. It is the Chapel of San Martino, patron saint of the poor, among whom T. is today counting herself, and there is an opening in the wall of the chapel where bread for the poor was once offered and received. The old ladies who sit on the wooden benches that line the chapel smile. "We are all poor," one of them says, including and sweeping us up into her loneliness; T. softens and smiles. In the small Chapel of San Martino, Dante married Gemma Donati. This does not delight T. . . . The beautiful Church of Orsanmichele, once a granary, later an oratory for craftsmen and guildsmen (the scene of many summer-night concerts), is closed for restoration, which infuriates T., who is going out of her way to be infuriated. *"Chiuso per restauro* are the most used words in Italian." She takes me down a flight of stairs into a cavelike studio where a sculptor works, unconcerned by our arrival. T. flings her arms out as if to say: Here is proof! Here is certainly proof, revolting, that there are men who hate women. There is a monumental Barbie doll; she is menstruating and wearing a filthy rag. There is a woman impaled, upside down, on a cross. A rubber head protrudes from a plaster woman who is giving birth; in place of her nose and mouth is a penis ("red and glistening like a dog's," T. says, and then: "What good have divorce laws done women?" she blurts out. "They have only allowed men to abrogate their contracts. *Porci!*") . . . Perhaps shopping is the answer, it often is. But the young thin-as-a-dime and haughty salesgirls in the fancy shops on the Via Tornabuoni are rude; T. glares at me, not at them: "You see? If blue is the color this year, if it is *fuori stagione,* out of season, you have to go to Switzerland for black shoes." . . . My affection for Florence is a thorn, today, in her side.

Later that night, to pamper her unhappiness, "Let's go to the café Strozzi to see the *borghesi,*" T. says. The Strozzi is closed. So T. takes me to the Piazza della Repubblica—"the ugliest square in Florence"—built on the site of the Old Market in the second half of the nineteenth century. But I like the big square, its many busy cafés side by side, people strolling to watch the show (they are the show). Sometimes at night under the strings of colored lights, when tourists from the South join the string orchestras to sing ribald songs, I feel as if I am in my family village—which I have seen, as yet, only in my imagination, which presents it to me as one long wedding scene from *The Godfather*—and I am happy. T. has no wish to sit outside, where the mood is honeysuckle-gay and Italian tourists sip sweet drinks and guzzle raw wine; and she takes me to the sawdusty recesses of a café where habitués sit silently and strike poses. They are a sorry lot, dressed to the nines in that casual blowaway beautiful Italian style and cultivating unhappiness, a trendy ennui. T. struggles with herself, she can't decide whether to join them or to assert her superiority to them; so she propels me into her car and we drive, she won't say where to.

I begin to feel Dantesque. We are, or seem to be, in the middle of a dark wood . . . Felliniesque, in fact. Along the broad avenue down which we drive are women of all ages and shapes; they are selling themselves. I have never seen such a display of thighs and heaving bosoms and black-lace lingerie. One of the women, under one of the poison-yellow lights, is wearing a red-lace Merry Widow corset and cowboy boots; another, a *belle époque* ball gown and towering high heels—her long hair is bright green; another wears a gingham apron and carries a whip. T. is driving me through the Cascine, the vast park where Shelley wrote "Ode to the West Wind" and where children play by day. . . . I see merry-go-rounds, children's rides, behind the women, who, seeing that we are two women in the car, curl their beckoning fingers into fists, swear at us, and spit. We pass a six-foot-tall blonde wrapped in leather, and "That is the most beautiful woman I have ever seen," I say. T. laughs for the first time today. "That is Carlotta, she is famous." I see what I had not seen before: All the "women" are men.

Late that night T. comes to my hotel room. Without preamble she says:

"I had an abortion last year. First I went to a women's health center, then to a hospital near Florence. They told me to wait a week to 'think it over.' I had to fill out a million papers. Imagine going to the post office, only a hundred million times worse—and that's just the forms, not the abortion. They told me I was past my first trimester—a lie. They told me I would have had little boy twins. So now I hope they die, the sadists, why did they tell me little boy twins? They showed me the sonogram. *Women* doctors did this to me!

"I don't want to talk about it. I want to sit on the roof garden." So we do. T. drinks a pint of scotch whiskey. "If you write bad things about the Cascine, I will never forgive you," she says. "I love this city."

In the Piazza della Santissima Annunziata, an old man sneezes, hawks, and spits. Passersby cluck their tongues in disapproval. He flings out his arms, hawks and spits again; he raises his hat. This time, the second time, it is a performance, calculated. He looks around for applause, and gets it. "Bravo! Bravo!" shout the same Italians who have just expressed their disapproval. He bows.

This spectacle takes place in a square dominated by the oldest foundling hospital in Europe, Brunelleschi's Ospedale degli Innocenti. On the portico of the hospital are fourteen ceramic medallions by Andrea della Robbia, with backgrounds of the blue that has become inseparable from his name. The medallions are representations of abandoned babies in swaddling clothes, each in a different beseeching pose. (Oh, poor T.! To have had an abortion in this country of Madonnas and *bambini!*)

Until 1879 mothers placed their unwanted babies through a window onto a *ruota* (wheel), near which was a bell rope to call attention to the precious deposit. Under the window are carved these words by the Psalmist: "When my mother and father forsake me, then the Lord will take me up."

I am not particularly charmed by della Robbia, or by this piazza, in which there are two Baroque fountains and far too many cars; there's something almost cynical about those cars and Vespas racing by perpetually yearning babies . . . but I like sometimes to stand here because if you peer down one street from its center you have a view of the many-sided Duomo; and if you peer down another when the light is soft at evening, you see what appears to be a country lane. This combination of the rustic and the sophisticated is in many ways emblematic of Florence, and the square is a favorite of Florentines.

RUMMAGING IN FLORENCE;
or, Incidental Pleasure

Pharmacies and Apothecary Shops: My favorites are the elaborate old, scented, hushed emporiums of La Farmacia del Cinghiale, near the New Market; La Farmacia di San Marco, on Via Cavour; La Farmacia Inglese, a perfumery near Doney's pretty tea shop on snooty Via Tornabuoni (the Tornabuonis were one of the great banking families when Florence was a banking city-state); and La Farmacia di Santa Maria Novella, once a Dominican chapel, which opens onto a cloister.

Here one finds "natural" cosmetics made of everything but yak butter—extract of lettuce, wheat germ, carrots, ginseng, chamomile, cypress, turtle oil; hand, breast, and face creams and tonics made of milk and honey, of clay, rosemary, sage and rosewater, and—a concession to the twentieth century—of collagen; hair remedies ("nutrients," "sustainers," and "refreshers," almond shampoo for baldness); perfumes (gardenia, lavender, magnolia, sandalwood, violet, freesia, narcissus, tobacco, verbena, acacia, tuberose); a fruity scent named for Dante's Francesca (at Cinghiale); and (at Santa Maria Novella) Marescialla, a perfume named for the wife of a Florentine marshal, Marquise d'Aumont, who applied this essence to her gloves; she was said to have been a witch, and was burned at the stake. There are also herbal potions for hangovers, cellulite, poor circulation, stress, the vapors, *meteorismo,* a pretty word for flatulence, and, of course, potions for liver problems; *zodiacali* bath powders (mine, a cloying gardenia which is said to be appropriate for Virgos, is a fragrance I very much dislike, whereas I do like the scent of heliotrope [it smells like tropical sex] and strawberry essence and bottled "extract of milk and honey," perhaps because it is irresistibly named).

Abundance, in America, often gets translated into waste. Our utilitarian society is one of disposable goods (and people). One has the reassuring sense that this is not so in Florence, where, for example, old clothes find their way to the Mercatino delle Pulci, and then, if they are not sold, to the town of Prato, where old fabric is rewoven to become new cloth. This little rag market lives in the shadow of the nineteenth-century food market of Sant'Ambrosio, where, one morning, I counted twenty-four kinds of salad greens; this made me very happy, and I gave out before the salad greens did. On marble counters are heaps of bright-eyed fresh fish; and in other stalls there are mountains of waxy peppers, yellow, green, red, bluish purple;

vine-ripened cooking tomatoes so fresh that parts of their pulpy green stems are still attached to them; pale red salad tomatoes streaked with blue-green, with a kind of nipple on the stem end; zucchini with their fragile yellow flowers still attached. There are separate stalls for cheeses and for organ meats, for poultry, game, beef, pork; watching a butcher cut a side of pork with economy, pride, and precision is a morning's occupation.

Near this noisy but orderly place of abundance is the flea market of Florence. I am drawn to flea markets more than I am to antique shops, and this is not simply a matter of economics and the thrill of discovery: I accrete; I like jumble and clutter and everything every which way, as in old cellars and attics where treasures can be found. I found no treasures in the flea market that had market value. But I found that comforting feeling that steals over me when I walk through graveyards—I found myself reconciled to the past and to the future, to death, by looking at faded photographs (I form "a compact with the human race"). Where are they now, the stoic women in black shawls, the laughing young men in woolen bathing suits and bathing caps like helmets, the pretty girls in their First Communion dresses? Gone; but still here, their eyes crinkled against the intrusion of the camera. (If the past and the future exist, where are they?) Something about this whole complex of markets—the abundance of food, the bedraggled gaiety of cheap perfume and plastic jewelry, the lost but found faces of the photographs— filled me with an almost treacly sentimentality, from which pastel emotion I emerged as I walked through warrens of shops selling World War I and World War II memorabilia—helmets and flasks and ugly gas masks and medals (base coin, now)—and no pictures of Mussolini, none at all.

There are no new answers, only new questions.

When Pope Clement refused to give Benvenuto Cellini a paying post, he did so on the grounds that "if I gave it to you, you'd spend all day scratching your belly, lose all your marvelous skill, and get me blamed for it." Cellini replied that "the purest-bred cats made better mousers when they were fat than when they were starving . . . honest craftsmen did much better work when they had plenty to live on. . . . Princes who enabled artists to prosper were watering the roots of genius, which to start with were weak and diseased."

Cellini looked upon his exertions as "a kind of relaxation." I asked my friend Signor Forte to take me to his workshop, where goldsmiths make eighteen-karat gold reproductions of Etruscan jewelry and where the lost-wax designs of the sculptor Germano (whose works are in the Kremlin and in the Vatican) are executed, to see the manner in which goldsmiths work today.

On the way from his shop on Via Guicciardini to the studio nearby, where he employs fifteen people, Signor Forte tried, as usual, to educate me. "Which Bellini?" he asked querulously when I mentioned a Bellini I'd seen at the Uffizi. "It is very important to be precise in these matters, as painters have sons and painters' sons have fathers, and in Italy genius runs in the blood. A goldsmith does not give birth to a stockbroker. No one can be taught how to master the lost-wax process, the means are in the blood." Thus was I chastened, but not enlightened. Signor Forte holds to the principle that "poor people are more precocious than sophisticated people. In southern Italy, the poor have less, they use what comes to hand and are therefore more clever." When I quote Cellini on the negative virtues of poverty, Signor Forte harrumphs and calls into evidence my paternal grandfather, a master mason and carpenter about whom I've told him (this grandfather built foundations of stone without mortar and an outdoor oven in which my grandmother once baked twelve different kinds of pizza and a turkey at one time). "If he had been rich," Signor Forte says, "he would have asked other people to build the foundations of his house, and it would by now have crumbled."

Signor Forte's shop is a happy place; he does not act on the principle that poverty inspires genius. Much has changed since Cellini's time; much has not. Workers still keep the gold shavings swept from the floor and use the proceeds for a bang-up weekly dinner. Finished goldwork is still immersed in tubs of sawdust to be cleaned and dried. (These tubs, into one of which, at Signor Forte's invitation, I plunge my arm, are like fantasy plum puddings or the ultimate Cracker Jack box; my "prize" is a huge emerald set in white gold (which, alas, I do not keep). Cellini threw off the dross by hand, with a *fionda* (slingshot); now, that work is done by means of a machine using centrifugal force. But the lost-wax process is unchanged: The sculptor works in wax, which is placed into a cylinder; plaster and then liquid gold are poured over the original wax sculpture; this results in rough gold sculptures (which must then be refined) and in the "loss" of the wax.

The sculptor Germano, whose work Signor Forte compares with that of Donatello, became famous for his work in miniature; he made crucifixes with tiny agonized Christ figures; gold copies of a Raphael Madonna and

Child (I admire the exquisite workmanship but do not see the point of a copy of a Raphael); representations of Charon, boatman of Hades (ruby-eyed), ferrying damned souls to what may be a longed-for Hell—figures expressive of lust, desperation, or resignation. Dante tells us that some souls wish to be in Hell, they desire their punishment—which makes it seem awfully obliging of God to put them there—and that some souls, like Francesca, yearn, in their misery, for God, Who one might hope would weaken, considering that Francesca has been there yearning for so long (but this is reckoning time as humans do); Germano sculpts Paolo and Francesca, arrested in that very moment when their eyes met and they read no more.

I wear a gold cross made by Germano and also a copy of the pagan Bocca della Verità (Mouth of Truth), the stone original of which is under the portico of the very pretty Church of Santa Maria in Cosmedin in Rome and is said to bite the hand of anyone with a lie on his conscience. I wear it to remind myself not to lie, as lying is a sin to which writers are particularly prone. Writers lie out of the best of motives (though they are always carrying on about their obligation to tell the truth): They want to make order out of chaos and bring shape and form to muddle. It is hard to bear witness to the truth and at the same time to shape messy experience in such a way as to make sense of it. The process is analogous to the art of lost wax: Something gets burned away, lost; something is refined, found.

Cellini suffered from eyes so painfully inflamed he "almost died of the agony." A friend of Clement's told him to bathe his eyes with irises—petals and roots and stalks—distilled over a slow fire; he did so and was healed. Germano, alas, also suffers from eye problems (but not as a result of what Cellini calls "the French pox," caught from a servant girl); his optic nerve is damaged from working in miniature, and he now, in his mid-sixties, works large, in bronze. "Blood and suffering," Signor Forte says, "forty years of working, twenty of success, and then eye damage." It is no wonder that some artists swagger; every artist lives with the terror of losing the gift he has worked so hard to refine. (That this terror can coexist with the joy of creating is the miracle of every artist's life.) Artists are the only people I know who believe you can forget to ride a bicycle; their swagger cloaks their terror. The swagger is also a way of dealing with the coincidence of opposites, the fact that the impulse to create art springs from wonder, wonder that is contingent upon humility, and that, nevertheless, it takes an enormous amount of arrogance to order a moral universe and to offer one's vision of the world to others. Only a very rare artist, like Cellini, is able to achieve a happy equilibrium, to praise God and love the world for the portion assigned to him, to love his work and accept his gifts and his rewards and to go on his way rejoicing.

No landscape has ever lent itself better to pictorial depiction of the life of Christ than that of Tuscany, as Fra Angelico's frescoes in the Dominican Cloister of San Marco amply demonstrate: Here are Joseph and Mary among gentle hills and slopes, ribbons and swatches of cultivated land; the Annunciation takes place in boudoirs nestled among dark groves of cypresses and palms as camels wander by medieval towers; the Garden of Gethsemane is a place of silvery gray olive trees and chestnut trees.

Fra Angelico's heavy-lidded aristocratic Madonna cradles the crucified Christ as gently as if He were a baby; but the artist, called Beato for the mildness of his disposition, for all his legendary sweetness and in spite of the delicacy of his paintings, represents evil and damnation as if they were no strangers to his imagination—as perhaps they are not to anyone who is genuinely good. Fra Angelico's Judas is a small and perfect study in cringing hypocrisy; Hell, in these frescoes, is peopled with monsters and ragged-toothed whales and serpents like chains; bodies are strangled and devoured amidst dishes of toads and caldrons of fire and blood, all in heavenly soft blues and pinks and reds.

There should be another word for *cell;* our word sounds so harsh. The small white vaulted rooms of San Marco are made for contemplation and sweet secrets; in such places all thoughts simultaneously expand and contract into one thought, the thought to which we give the name of God. I slipped my shoes off in the monastery, the tiles underfoot were so silky, smooth. I wonder if the good monks allowed themselves that sensual pleasure, I wonder if Savonarola did. Onetime prior of San Marco, he wrote his fiery sermons here; Michelangelo never forgot the sound of his voice. It must have occurred to Savonarola, the enemy of adornment, that all of architecture is the adornment of an idea, the embellishment of a concept. It is strange to see his rosary here. He was executed a hundred years after Fra Angelico's birth.

How might it change one's life to live, day after day, every day of one's life, in close white quarters with a fresco of a crucified Christ, blood spurting out of His side . . . or with the placid infant in the manger, the animals alert and knowing, the angels rejoicing . . . or with the risen Christ extending a benediction, His radiant blessing casting out all fear? And was it by the luck of the draw that a monk was assigned his cell with the fresco with which he would have to spend his earthly life? (We all live in cells, some of us in boxes, some in prisons. Some rooms are larger, some whiter, than others. Is mine the result of the draw?)

In one cell there is a fresco of Christ wearing a crown of thorns, seated on a red throne on a white pedestal; He is holding a staff in one hand, a ball in the other. In this fresco disembodied hands surround the Christ—one holds a staff, one extends an empty palm, another adjusts the nimbus that circles Christ's crown. In another, a tonsured monk studies a book of maps, maps being a Florentine preoccupation; a woman consults her thoughts; a black man wearing an Alpine hat looks toward a blindfolded figure on a stake—from his mouth comes spray (breath? the Holy Spirit?); his dismembered hand lifts his jaunty hat. . . . I could consult guidebooks to see what these frescoes, so tantalizingly mysterious and enigmatic without text, mean, and what time may have done to them; but I have forbidden myself to do so, I want my imagination to play with the unknown.

St. Dominic, founder of the monastery, was the enemy of the Albigensians, who believed not that the body was good but that matter was evil; these heretics denied the Trinity and therefore the Incarnation, as, given their premises, they were logically obliged to do: If matter was evil, God could scarcely have become flesh, and if the Father and the Son were not two Persons in one, Jesus Christ was not God incarnate. (The mystery of the Trinity was strongly affirmed by the fifteenth-century Council of Florence.) St. Dominic, kind, thoughtful, and logical, was a most pacific enemy; his weapons were instruction and prayer. He started a new form of monasticism by joining action to contemplation, and it was his idea that there should be centers of sacred learning, members of which taught and preached (for the sake of the world) as well as prayed. St. Thomas Aquinas is his spiritual descendant. He is seen in Florence with a dog—a pun on his name: *Domini canis.*

In the enticing outer cloister of San Marco children play boisterously (and do no dishonor to God, flesh being good); in the inner cloister, enticing and discreet, all is silent—an oasis of nature in a city of men. What a beautiful, inspired form of architecture this is: What is closed is open and what is open is closed; sweet, womblike, maternal. Or seen another way, not necessarily mutually exclusive, a pleasure garden (close your eyes, smell the musk); it is a seraglio. Lucky monks, in their secret white cells, their cloistered gardens, their Spirit-filled world.

How obliging God seems some days (blue skies; a rosebush twines around a cedar of Lebanon); how indulgent.

SAN GIMIGNANO: "City of Fine Towers"

A tower is the creation of another century. Without a past it is nothing. Indeed, a new tower would be ridiculous.

—*Gaston Bachelard*

There are places one comes home to that one has never been to: San Gimignano.

An English spinster, almost deaf, attaches herself to me on the bus to San Gimignano. She tells me of her adventures and misadventures in Spain, Portugal, Italy—all having to do with trains nearly missed, roads not taken, the kindness of strangers. I am not feeling particularly generous or kindly, except toward the green hills and the fields of yellow flowers in which I wish to lose my thoughts. "Rape, I think those flowers are," she says, "horrible name. I think they make oil of it." I think it is saffron, perhaps crocus. . . .

Butter-yellow flowers bloom from the medieval towers for which San Gimignano is famous. They are variously called wallflowers and violets (and said by townspeople to grow nowhere else on earth). The small and fragrant flowers sprang up on the coffin of St. Fina (among whose gifts was the ability to extinguish house fires) and on the towns' towers on the day of her death. (On that day bells tolled; they were rung by angels.) St. Fina is sometimes called the Saint of the Wallflowers. (*Wallflower,* in addition to its botanical meaning, in colloquial Italian means, as it does in English, a "girl who is not invited to dance"—*ragazza che fa da tappezzeria.*) She died when she was fifteen. She was loved for her goodness and beauty, she had butter-yellow hair, she once accepted an orange from a young man at a well, and she died on an oak plank in penance for what seems to have been an entirely blameless life. In paintings by Ghirlandaio in San Gimignano's cathedral, she is so slender and delicate, so attenuated, as to cause one pain.

Modest St. Fina, a silent slip of a girl, might seem an odd choice for veneration in a walled city of military architecture—proud ramparts and aggressive towers built by suspicious patrician families to hide treasures and to assert the will for power. (Alberti railed against towers, regarding them as antisocial; in the sixteenth century Cosimo de' Medici ordered a halt to the expansion of San Gimignano, forbidding the commune of Florence to allocate to it "even the slightest amount for any need, be it sacred or profane.")

There is a wrinkle in time in San Gimignano. There is no such thing as a mellow or lovable skyscraper, but the towers of San Gimignano, glibly called the skyscrapers of Tuscany, seem to have been born old . . . or at least to have anticipated the day when gentle St. Fina would, like Rapunzel, who also lived in a tower and whose hair was also gold, seem the perfect anointing presence. One imagines her—one imagines both Rapunzel and St. Fina—at the top of a steep, narrow, spiraling stone stairway, breathing silently in a slender shaft of brief light from a narrow window . . . everything military has retreated from this fairy-tale place.

There are fourteen tall towers in San Gimignano; there were once seventy-two. They are surrounded, on the narrow city streets, by palazzi and modest houses, all higgledy-piggledy, with projecting Tuscan roofs. They stretch from earth to sky and are built on shifting soil; and they speak, as Georges Duby says, two languages: "on the one hand the unreal space of courtly myth, the vertical flight of mystic ascension, the linear curve carrying composition in to the scrolls of poetic reverie. And on the other, a rigorous marquetry offering the view of a compact universe, profound and solid." They have one peculiar property: Their stones remain the same color—a gray-gold with a suggestion, a faint pentimento, of black—whether wet with rain or hot with sun. The little guidebook I bought in San Gimignano is quite lyrical and accurate about the walls and towers of San Gimignano, which embody, as its author says, the contradictions of the medieval mind, a mind "reserved and hospitable, bold and fearful. Fearful of enemies, of strangers, of night-time, of treasons." The walls kept enemies out; they also kept people in; they imparted, to those within, a "sense of community, of common interests and ideals never denied." San Gimignano is formidable in its beauty; every description of it I have ever read makes it sound both forbidding and delightful. Forbidding it once was, in the days of fratricidal warfare, when families threw collapsible wooden bridges from the window of one tower-fortress to that of another (the days when it traded with Egypt, Syria, and Tunisia and men vied for great wealth); now it is simply delightful. And sheltering. The walls cup and cradle (as, in Niccolò Gerini's painting of St. Fina, she cradles the walled city in her slender young arms). The towers exist not to keep enemies—the Other—out, but to house the soul warmly; one has a sense of great bodily integrity in these spaces; one feels safe. When St. Fina drove the Devil out of San Gimignano with a gesture of her long and lovely hand, she did it for us.

Because one yields, in San Gimignano, to the fancy that the world is created anew each day, that time does not, in the way we ordinarily understand it, exist, it is exactly right, and so lovely, to find in a deserted piazza a small thirteenth-century church dedicated to St. Augustine, whose reflections on the nature and measurement of time so profoundly informed his love of God (and anticipated the existentialists):

> But if the present were always present, and would not pass into the past, it would no longer be time, but eternity. Therefore, if the present, so as to be time, must be so constituted that it passes into the past, how can we say that it is, since the cause of its being is the fact that it will cease to be? Does it not follow that we can truly say that it is time, only because it tends towards non-being? . . . How, then, can . . . the past and the future be, when the past no longer is and the future as yet does not be?

On the chancel wall of the church are lively fifteenth-century frescoes by Benozzo Gozzoli of the life of the great theologian. I am surprised to see St. Monica plump, peasant-sturdy, and careworn; I always imagined that one who prayed unceasingly, as she did, for the salvation of her son, would find one's flesh melting in the process. (I think of a life of prayer as inimical to fat.) Of all the charming frescoes, the most charming is that of Augustine chatting with the infant Jesus about the Mystery of the Trinity (that which might be remote and austere Gozzoli rendered immediate and intimate); the Child attempts to empty the sea into a puddle—much as any child might at the seashore, with a pail, or a shell—the impossibility of which convinces Augustine that the Trinity cannot be comprehended by reason alone.

Everything You have made is beautiful, Augustine said to his God, but You are more beautiful than anything You have made. In the cloister of the Church of St. Augustine, that beauty is palpable; one feels one has entered the light and peace of God. The cloister is divided by box hedges into four quadrangular plots of land in which grow irises and tulips and palm trees and white and yellow dandelions and pink and blue wandering flowers. . . . How sweet, these enclosures within an enclosed opening: open/close, close/open; a cypress punctuates each of four corners. A loggia—pots of yellow flowers and geraniums—looks out over a central cistern; the scent of lilacs is pervasive, the lilacs swarm with bees. The fragrance of lilacs mingles with the fragrance of woodsmoke. I walk beneath a tree the leaves of which are the color of China tea; a cobweb brushes across my forehead.

A jet plane streaks across the fragrance of lilacs; an orange-and-black cat mews piteously in the garden.

(Were mazes an outgrowth and elaboration of these enclosures within enclosures? Why would anyone wish to complicate and convolute so simple, satisfying, and sweet a design?)

The sacristan plucks tenacious thorns from my coat. He is listening to a popular love song on his transistor radio in the sacristy. I light a candle and the sacristan extinguishes the flame. Even God has a *riposo* in Italy at lunch hour.

My hotel, once a palazzo, is in the Piazza della Cisterna, in the middle of which is a thirteenth-century cistern. From this piazza, through the battlemented archway, I can reach the square of the cathedral with its seven towers. I like the feel of the herringbone-patterned bricks under my thin sandals. I wander up and down steep hills, arched alleys, passing old men and women with canes. I never want to leave. My terraced hilltop room looks out over roofs and towers and blessed hills to the Val d'Elsa. I am beginning to believe the Annunciation did take place here. Art plagiarizes nature. I want to fly, as Cellini wanted to fly, "on a pair of wings made of waxed linen." And I want to stay here, rooted, forever.

At dinner a baby boy crawls through the tunneled legs of diners, to the cooing delight of waiters. A woman lights a cigarette, over which a British man and woman make a great disapproving fuss. "There is no remedy for death," the smoker says, coolly addressing the room at large. She says this in English and then in Italian.

After dinner, in a dim lounge, I watch *Two Women,* a movie with Sophia Loren. I am joined by the Italian woman who smokes. Out of an abundance of feeling I cry, not so much because this is the story of a rape, not because of the girl's loss of innocence and the mother's rage and grief, but because the injured girl is singing, her voice frail, a song my grandmother used to sing: *"Vieni, c'è una strada nel bosco* . . . I want you to know it, too . . . *c'è una strada nel cuore* . . . There's a road in my heart. . . ." The woman who smokes is crying, too. I am thinking of my daughter. When she leaves, the woman kisses the crown of my head. We have exchanged no words. Men have stood on the threshold and not come in. I never see her again.

I cross the piazza to sit in a brightly lit outdoor café. It is late. I am the only woman in the café. I fend off three approaches. I won't be denied the pleasure of seeing the light and shadows of the lovely square, the purple night sky. Inside, male voices are raised in a sentimental love song; they sing to the strings of a mandolin. Their singing is saccharine, their laughter is boisterous, and there are no women here. I wonder, with some little anger, what it would be like to be part of their sentimental, prideful, tough and tender world. I put on dark glasses. A little boy eating a gelato plays hide-and-seek, covering his eyes with sticky fingers (hide), waiting for me to smile (seek). A policeman strolls by apparently without purpose. I am an anomaly. I remove my glasses, thinking that if I can't see men's faces, they can't see mine.

What pleasure does it give men to sing of the beauty of women when there are no women in the café?

I find myself thinking of the handsome guide at the Davanzati who held the elevator for me.

The bed linen smells of lilacs. The air vibrates with the aftersound of bells. In San Gimignano the birds sing all night long.

In the morning I drink my coffee from a mug bearing the words OLD TIME TEA.

In the Piazza della Cisterna there is a *sala di giochi*—video games. Is it possible that the children who grow up here—young men with studied, languid poses—think they are living in a hick town?

On the Via San Martino, away from the cathedral and the Cisterna, there is a café peopled entirely by old men. The café is part billiard parlor; newspapers are bought and read in common. I am accepted here in the morning light of day; I would not have been accepted here last night. I am served my morning coffee with old-fashioned gallantry by a man in a shiny black suit. With great difficulty he recites something he has been taught by an English-speaking cousin: " 'We shall sit upon the ground and tell sad stories of the death of Kings.' Is sad?" he asks.

To leave a walled city is to feel evicted, cast out—cast out of paradise; no matter that the countryside outside the walls is paradisiacal.

The bus, full of high-spirited schoolchildren, that stopped at Porta San Giovanni was the wrong bus, but the driver took me on anyway, avuncularly advised the children to be more calm in the presence of *la bella signora,* and deposited me at the right bus stop. We went by back roads, and I had the sensation, for the first time in Tuscany, not of passing but of being in the countryside, part of (not merely an observer of) a gorgeous (and calm) crazy quilt of silver-green olive trees and flowering peach and cherry trees; the yellow-and-red bus wound its way through the intricate sensual folds of hills dignified by cypress trees: "And you, O God, saw all the things that you had made, and behold, 'they were very good.' For we also see them and behold, they are all very good."*

The bus went slowly, like a swimmer who loves the water too much to race and challenge it, and the world unfolded like a child's picture book: gardeners turning over soil with gnarled, patient hands; bronzed youths of Etruscan beauty casually strolling by the roadside as if here were just anywhere and everywhere was beautiful; showers of wisteria framing old women shelling peas in doorways; lovers picnicking in a vineyard; laughing nuns pushing children on orange swings, their heavy habits floating on magnolia-scented air: "Your works praise you."†

Confessions of St. Augustine 13/28; 13/33.

†Ibid.

Chapter IV

ROME:
THE ART OF LIVING

What can one do here with a single pen? . . .
Everything is just as I imagined it,
yet everything is new.

—*Goethe*

I've seen Rome, and I shall go to bed a
wiser man than I last rose.

—*Henry James*

Rome is a pleasant place to live in. . . .
I never tasted air more temperate for me or
more suited to my constitution.

—*Montaigne*

This is fiction, an artifact; it is true, and it is real, but it is real only as people
and events in stories are real. . . . In Rome, the city of true sensation, I
understood that emotions had a geometry. (Also, it amused me, when not

in Rome, to think of people who are the exact antithesis of the spirit of Rome; this is the form [I grant that it is perverse] that longing sometimes takes):

TO BE

"Life is terrible," Joel said. This sentence gave him evident pleasure. "No, it is not," Laura said. He is indecent, she thought. "It is full of joy and delight and our troubles are of our own making," she said. She did not entirely believe this, how could one? But it vexed her to see Joel sitting in his sunny kitchen, rolling his own cigarettes—he could well afford to buy cigarettes—discoursing with relish on the terribleness of life, his own life in smooth working order. He sits at a round oak table and sleeps in a brass double bed, how can he say life is terrible, Laura thought; he would probably declare against happiness in the Pantheon. Laura had been wont, in times past, to judge people by their response to the Pantheon, which she had experienced as a place of perfect happiness and safety, as proof in fact that the world was good. She would like to have skated on a sheet of thin ice over the marble floor of the Pantheon while clouds drifted over the round aperture above. Joel said her aesthetic appreciation—that is what he called it—was a matter of upper-class social conditioning; he put it to her that the Pantheon reminded her of the dome of a Wall Street bank. "Why don't you read the *Autobiography of Benvenuto Cellini?*" Laura now said, giggling—a Wall Street bank!—"it will inspire you with joy." She had herself just reread the *Autobiography of Benvenuto Cellini,* and it had inspired her with joy. Miriam, Joel's wife, who was chopping scallions at the marble counter, looked at Laura with pity. The line between pity and condescension is a fine one, Laura thought; and, the last thing Miriam and Joel wish to have brought to their attention is that happiness is generally available, she thought. They pitied Laura because, in their company, she professed to believe in the availability of happiness, a profession of faith which did not jibe with their own peculiar ideology. Laura herself was in fact unhappy.

"What?" she said.

Joel was talking, as Laura contemplated her unhappiness, about some recent manifestation of Class Oppression and—this was a new one—Tribality. Laura declined to talk about Tribality, whatever that was. "The world does not consist of conspiracies," she said, hoping to fend off the inevitable discussion of who was in league with whom to destroy the Third World, of which Miriam and Joel—for reasons that Laura had heard many times but refused to make an effort of the imagination to comprehend—considered themselves satellites. Miriam and Joel sighed in unison. "The world does not consist of people conspiring," Laura said. Actually Laura was not quite sure she wished to fend off a discussion of conspiracies, as, while she herself made no great claim to sanity, she liked, from time to time, to receive proof that Joel and Miriam were crackers. At least, she thought, I am not smug.

"They're all the same people," Miriam said.

"Who are all the same people?" Laura said. "Is Benvenuto Cellini in on the conspiracy?" she said.

Miriam and Joel exchanged glances. Miriam was scraping ginger with which to season a sirloin steak.

"For example," Joel said, "could you argue that the old lady downstairs visits her troubles upon herself?" This rendered Laura mute. The old lady downstairs was about to be evicted, her children having abandoned her, which event Joel laboriously traced to the far-reaching tendrils and the cunning contrivances of the multinational corporations and in particular to southern bankers. "I hate Freud and Marx with an equal passion," Laura said; "perhaps we could give the old lady downstairs a share of the sirloin, it might considerably lighten her oppression."

"The Israeli Mafia is in league with the Soviets," Joel said, "and the role of the multinationals is clear when you consider—"

"Why don't we invite the old lady up for dinner?" Laura said.

"The steak is ready," Miriam said, setting three places.

"What you lack," Joel said, "is a world view." That is true, Laura thought; and this plunged her into depression.

Laura had had a falling-out with Joel months before. He had tried to establish himself as her mentor at the community college where he held, tenuously, a post in the sociology department, and where Laura taught Freshman Italian. In addition to lacking a world view, Laura lacked a mentor (she was also, at this time in her life, short on friends); and for a while she amused herself, while trying simultaneously to take their preposterous views seriously, by listening to Joel and Miriam carry on about the impossibility of achieving happiness in a class-ridden society. Then one day she had said, "You are truly preposterous, you have no idea how real people live in the real world, the real world is not made up of oppressed and oppressors, it is made up of people—more or less happy, good or bad depending on their degree of ignorance—of whom I am one, and why I listen to you at all I can't imagine." "You have been conditioned," Joel said. . . . "Yes, at the beauty parlor," Laura said, after which they had not spoken.

This evening she had met Joel at the butcher's, and he'd invited her to dinner, and, her unhappiness having taken the form of lethargy, she had consented to go with him. This obliged her to walk up six flights of stairs to Joel and Miriam's shabby-by-intent apartment; and this predisposed her to anger, inasmuch as Joel and Miriam could well have afforded to buy the building in which they lived, all this laboring up stairs being an affectation in aid of exactly what Laura could not be expected to understand.

"Living in Italy disqualified you for understanding real life," Joel said.

Joel thought real life was that which he lived.

Laura had lived in Rome, quite happily, for ten years, until she had been robbed and raped in Trastevere. There she had lived in a six-flight walk-up—and what cruel steps they were—but the reward for her exertions had been a view of St. Peter's and a terrace on which jasmine and oleander grew. "Rome, however," she said, "is the real world, why is any one place any less real than any other place?"

"I thought you liked bean sprouts," Miriam said; "have some more."

"He pays lip service to social justice but he supports Opus Dei," Joel said, "he" being the Pope.

In Rome Laura had seriously considered the demands of the Catholic Church and had judged them outrageous. Were I a Catholic, she thought now, I should have to love Joel and Miriam, an impossibility. Then she thought of these words of Blake: "To love thine enemies is to betray thy friends / That is surely not what Christ intends." She saw the point. Seeing the point ruled out having a world view—at least one that emanated from Rome; and, having spoken the truth when she said she hated Marx and Freud with an equal passion, where exactly did that leave her?

"Have some more steak," Miriam said; "the dog doesn't like ginger."

Laura went home to find her daughter reading Edith Wharton. "How's Edith Wharton?" Laura said. Laura's daughter looked up from her book and crossed her eyes. "When you were fifteen months old," Laura said, "you spoke English and Italian. How is it that now you hardly utter, can you tell me that?" Laura's daughter vouchsafed no reply. Perhaps she's forming a World View, Laura thought; God help me.

At two in the morning Laura decided to write down randomly ten things she loved:

Baroque churches—the Gesù, Sant'Agostino, Sant'Ignazio. (She counted this as one love.)

Granita di caffè.

Penne all'arrabbiata.

Caravaggio.

Frank Sinatra.

I Know Where I'm Going, a movie circa 1945 in which Wendy Hiller and
   Roger Livesey live Happily Ever After, she a fiercely independent,
   prickly bank clerk's daughter who aspires to wealth, he a tender, impoverished Scottish laird blessed with exquisite manners and dedicated to
   the concept of noblesse oblige. ("A wartime propaganda film that
   conveys subtle messages about class," Joel had said when she taped this
   movie on his VCR; "a way to lull the British working class into
   believing the war would unite all classes." "I don't receive subtle
   messages," Laura had said; "subtle messages are lost on me. They loved
   each other and that's good enough for me.")

The New York skyline.

Her daughter's flesh.

Her father, dead.

Jasmine, white.

The Piazza in Piscinula. She thought of the three masked men who had
   robbed and raped her in an alley in Trastevere, crossed off "Piazza in
   Piscinula," then, after some consideration, reinstated it.

Her list had come to eleven. She crossed off "penne all'arrabbiata." Then she
added: "Bittersweet chocolate and the Pantheon."

She looked at her list. It did not in her opinion add up to anything approaching
a world view. Laura reckoned it might be therapeutic if she now made a list of ten
important questions, important to her: Can stupidity ever be harmless? Is sensation
more important than intellect? Is the one contingent upon the other? Her heart was
not in it. Bored by the puerility of what she had caused to appear on paper, she went
to her daughter's room. The child was still reading Edith Wharton. "How would
you like to go back to Rome?" Laura said. Laura's daughter dropped her book and
ostentatiously feigned sleep.

The next night Laura received a call from a friend of Joel and Miriam's, a man called
Steve, whom she intensely disliked in spite of the fact that he'd been hospitalized
for schizophrenia, which fact, Laura thought, ought to have triggered her compassion

but did not. Can one be latently compassionate? she wondered, as Steve babbled on. In Italy there was a law that declared there were no insane people, as a result of which schizophrenics and other crazy people freely roamed the streets, a contributing factor to her returning home to New York, where also crazies roamed the streets. Steve wanted her to join a protest march, something to do with a blind man with a German shepherd who was being evicted from his apartment. "I can't make it that night," Laura said, "sorry." "I haven't told you what night," Steve said; "it's day." "I can't stand crowds," Laura said. "There probably won't be more than four or five of us," Steve said. "In which case it will do no good," Laura said; "look, I'm very sorry, I'm busy marking papers." This was a lie.

Laura called Pan Am and TWA to find out what the airfare was to Rome. She made six separate calls to six separate agents, booked six tickets, two in first class, two in business class, and two in economy class (which she refused to call coach).

At school the next day she avoided Joel; this was made easy for her, as Joel seemed bent upon avoiding her. In her afternoon class she conjugated the verb *essere:* To Be. *I want to be in bed with Joel.* This thought darted through her mind. It surprised but did not alarm her. She scrutinized it with interest. Laura had not been to bed with anyone since the night of the three masked men—two years. Joel, to whom in the early days of their friendship she had related the events of that night, had explained it as a function of Class Oppression. Laura, he said, was merely a symbol to these men of all that had made their lives mean, and their violence had had little to do with her—"per se." A function of my walking down a dark alley, a function of my being in the wrong place at the wrong time, she thought. She had not felt like a symbol at the time. But she had permitted herself to draw some comfort from Joel's words; they gentled her into believing that neither had she, Laura, been chosen, nor (by her congenital woolly-mindedness which sometimes gathered itself into an orb—this is how she imaged it—of flaming concentration, but which had not done so on the night of the attack) had she, Laura, chosen her rape or her rapists. Laura thought of her mind as a series of twisting dark alleys in which were contained memory and desire and which sometimes led to a round place of blazing light. She often saw herself walking around in her mind; but she could never anticipate the coming of the light. What an idiot, she thought. Then she examined the sentence she had spoken silently, and thought: Who is the idiot in that sentence, Joel? Or me?

Laura invited Joel and Miriam to dinner, the origins of this impulse being obscure to her. It seemed in some way connected with her daughter, Laura did not know how—Oh if life consisted only of conjugating verbs. Joel and Miriam would expect

Italian food, Laura was an excellent cook. She decided to cook Indian food, curry being a mystery to her; she wanted to see Joel eating with his fingers, for reasons she thought might become clear to her sooner or later.

The curry, of repellent texture, color and odor, dribbled on Joel's beard. He pronounced it too mild, which was the least of its problems. Laura watched in fascination as the yellow-gray stuff mingled with the black-gray of his beard. Miriam ate fastidiously insofar as that was possible. Laura's daughter ate with *Portrait of a Lady* propped up against her water glass. Joel began, as he helped himself to more of the mess, to expound upon the reasons for hunger in the Third World, a turn of events Laura had anticipated and in equal measure dreaded and hoped for, as she knew it would provoke her to wrath, an emotion she had, since the night of the ginger-steak, wished very much to experience in Joel's presence.

"I'm going back to Rome," Laura said, aborting the conversation about hunger, which had not succeeded in making her sufficiently angry.

"What do you think about that?" Miriam asked Laura's daughter.

"Ask her what she feels, thinking is not instructive in this regard," Laura said.

Laura's daughter turned the page of her book with her left hand.

Joel proceeded to talk about the origins of Tribality on the subcontinent.

"I don't suppose anyone cares to take me seriously," Laura said. "I'm going back to Rome. A fact. A real fact. Hello? Anybody there?"

"How do you feel about Henry James?" Miriam asked Laura's daughter.

"Oh my God," Laura said. "Ask her to conjugate *to be* and *to feel* in Italian," she said. "Do you know there is no exact equivalent for the English *to feel* in Italian? I find that more interesting than Pakistan and Lord Mountbatten, to tell the truth."

Steve called while Joel and Miriam were helping themselves to thirds. "I'm afraid you have the wrong number," Laura said, disguising her voice with facility.

Laura's daughter said, in her clear, high voice, "My mother lies."

"That is true," Laura said. "I see you've found your voice, however."

"Sono, sei, è, siamo, siete, sono, sarò, ero, eri, era, eravamo, eravate, erano," Laura's daughter said.

Laura was suddenly immensely happy, and immediately began to question from which direction her happiness had come.

"What is the difference between happiness and joy?" she asked.

"It comes and it goes," Laura's daughter said.

"Which does?"

Laura's daughter crossed her eyes.

Laura asked Miriam to name ten things she loved—"or eleven." Miriam gave this request such earnest and prolonged attention, never once looking at Joel, that Laura was moved to silent mirth; her happiness expanded, as a result of which she pinched her daughter's thigh. Miriam was still pondering when Joel said, "Laura, may I see you alone? About that business at school."

Laura was on the point of asking, What business? but did not, and allowed herself to be led into the living room. There Joel kissed her, a very wet and very garlicky kiss which Laura entertained but did not return.

"Don't go," Joel said.

"We can't stay here forever, there's salad and dessert," Laura said.

"Don't go to Rome," Joel said.

"Forse che sì, forse che no," Laura said. "Wipe that goo off your beard."

In the kitchen Laura's daughter was singing. She was singing "Giovenezza," the Fascist youth anthem. Miriam, who did not know it was the Fascist youth anthem, was smiling benignly upon her.

"Dear me, where did you learn that?" Laura said.

"Grandpa," the child answered.

"Naughty of him," Laura said.

"Why was it naughty?" asked Miriam, handling the word naughty as if it were itself suspect; it was not in her vocabulary.

"I prefer my mother's lies," Laura's daughter said. Laura correctly interpreted this sentence to mean that her daughter did not like Joel and Miriam.

"What I want to know," Laura said, addressing her daughter, "is, do you have a world view?" Laura's daughter crossed her eyes. Joel dipped his napkin in his glass and applied it to his beard. Miriam asked for a finger bowl.

"Finger bowl!" Laura's daughter said. She tugged at Laura's hair, letting her hand rest for a moment on the nape of her mother's neck.

Laura's feelings went on a collision course. Her feelings were: pity for Joel and Miriam, a pained love for her daughter's flesh, and—oh let it not be fleeting, she prayed—a clear and unmistakable roundness of joy.

There is, sometimes, a bleeding, a time when by some peculiar combination of elements all of Rome is flat and overexposed, a time of light without shadows, a still white light that is more like the seepage of light than light itself: a vampire light. Rome is then breathless, withdrawn. If you are with a Roman when this phenomenon occurs—everything against the bleached and empty sky assumes a singularity and integrity, and nothing trembles but the heart of things—you will hear him sigh; an agitated fatalism like a little whirlwind will possess him, and—Romans like to define themselves, it is a form of forgivable narcissism in a city of regarded artifacts; his city is not only its intimidating stones—perhaps he will choose the ephemeral occasion to tell you that Romans are a "meteorological" lot. And so they are, like necromancers attuned to weather; perhaps it comes of growing up so intimately under the sign of the Cross, of pledging oneself in the name of the Holy Spirit, the Spirit of God that moves across the waters (as children blow bubbles, as angels blow clouds). The Romans profess themselves to be governed by the spirit of the winds that play across their sweet, grand city—the *ponentino,* a pet of a wind, the westerly sea breeze that cools the hottest August day on afternoons when help is needed and despaired of; the *tramontana,* the steely northerly winter wind that threads the air and stirs the palms with Alpine cold and searches into every place (the wind is *brutto,* it incites to murder); the *scirocco,* the siren wind of Africa, hot, suggestive, weakening.

One afternoon in May—Henry James says "there are days when the beauty of the climate of Rome alone suffices for happiness," and May is the loveliest month of all—I stood on a promontory overlooking the Forum in one of those reveries one is always falling into in Rome (a nourished melancholy), and a fierce hot wind sprang up like an assailant and slammed me. It ripped the glasses off my face and they flew high and landed on the lap of a souvenir hawker below me. "Ah, signora," he called out, looking complacently upon my distress, looking oracular, too (and also lecherous), "there must be an earthquake in Sicily." He made this sound like an invitation to licentiousness; and there was an earthquake, in Messina, I saw it in the paper the next day.

From the bluff upon which I stood, traitors had, in ancient times, been hurled to their death.

Mattina	*Morning*
Millumino	On the edge of night
d'immenso.	I fill with the light
	Of Immensity.

—*Giuseppe Ungaretti*

I met Eva in a restaurant near the Piazza di Spagna. We were obliged to share a table. This did not suit her, for she has an icy Swedish reserve. But it is not worth the effort, in Rome, to hold on to an idea of oneself, and soon she was quite merry, and from time to time we saw each other; and she did brave things: She rode on Vespas with beautiful young strangers; she strode through the Borghese Gardens alone at night, never fearing the thieves who lurk in that once-malarial expanse ("where fever walks arm-in-arm with you, and death awaits you at the end of the dim vista"*). Every six months or so this Valkyrie sends me a card: "Have you caught the light? . . . Do you remember the light? . . . Will you write about the light?" She longs for that light. I do, too.

The light shatters reserve.

The skies are endless; the trees define them: "These trees are magnificent, but even more magnificent is the sublime and moving space between them, as though with their growth it too increased."† Solemn, ornamental, and eternal, the cypress and the umbrella pine enlarge the Roman sky.

From my balcony I see across the Tiber to the Aventine. There, in the Piazza dei Cavalieri di Malta, is a green door with a tiny keyhole, and through that keyhole one can see, at the end of a long avenue of mingling branches, the dome of St. Peter's. From the dome we should see the world; instead, from the keyhole we see the dome. The keyhole is bigger than we are; the large is contained in the small. This strange and wonderful inversion of perspective is magic—and a metaphor, perhaps, for Catholic Italy: "Experience," wrote Santayana, "is a mere peephole through which glimpses come down to us of eternal things." That is what Rome has been for many; and for me: a glimpse, an intimation, as glorious as the empty thrones that Giotto imagined in Paradise.

On the crest of the Aventine, umbrella pines frame the intimate immensity of sky, their graceful sobriety a necessary counterpoint to the wasted grandeur of Rome's ruins. Two decades ago it was feared that a blight might destroy them, and the cry went up that had been sounded so often before: Rome will be ruined!

"You'll like it," Henry James's Osmond says to Isabel. "They have spoiled it, but you'll like it."

"Ought I to dislike it, because it's spoiled?" she asks.

"No, I think not. It has been spoiled so often," he says.

James, who in 1869 reeled through Rome in a liberating fever of delight,

*Nathaniel Hawthorne, *The Marble Faun.*

†Gaston Bachelard, *The Poetics of Space.*

three years later pronounced the city hopelessly modernized, and foretold that it would soon become "a lugubrious modern capital." Dickens, whose superstitious horror of relics often made him bellicose and cranky in Italy, fumed and called Rome "the Dead City . . . no more my Rome, [but] the Rome of anybody's fancy, man or boy: degraded and fallen and lying asleep in the sun among a heap of ruins." Hawthorne thought even the ruins were ruined.

We are all proprietary toward cities we love. "Ah, you should have seen her when I loved her!" we say, reciting glories since faded or defiled, trusting her to no one else; that others should know and love her in her present fallen state (for she must fall without our vigilant love) is a species of betrayal.

Rome seems perpetually perched on the very edge of ruin.

In the last century it was the Vittorio Emanuele Monument on the Piazza Venezia, silly and pompous, white as an operating room, bombastic and ridiculously at odds with its neighbors—a failed attempt, at the time of the unification of Italy, to reanimate the spirit of Imperial Rome—that was said to be emblematic of the decline of Rome. It hasn't worn well; it hasn't, in fact, worn at all. The distinguishing white Brescian marble of which it is made continues, unlike Rome's honey-colored travertine, to blind but not to dazzle. It refuses to be anything other than white. It is not a morally illuminating building.

Nineteenth-century writers invariably capitalized *Beauty,* and as in Rome Beauty is a boon companion, not abstract but corporeal, this was more than sentimentality. Rome, as one romantic traveler observed, not only cultivates Beauty as other countries cultivate corn but tolerates all things without defilement. (This is said of the Catholic Church, too: that it elevates, conse-crates, and dedicates all things to God's glory. Rome, like the Church, is a living organism, an example of Darwinian principles at work.) It is now possible to regard the foolish Vittorio Emanuele almost with affection. That which makes it deplorable—its brazen conspicuousness—also works to re-deem it: It serves as a landmark; if your path takes you, as mine often did, up the traffic-clogged Corso and beyond the Piazza Venezia to the Tiber and Trastevere, you find the sight of the funny old thing not only reassuring but bracing. Now, when I close my eyes to receive one of those lantern-slide memories that hold me in love with Rome, I see a grouping that has arranged itself without my advice and consent: I see, from a café on the Via del Teatro di Marcello, the dignified amber-brown brick Church of Santa Maria d'Aracoeli with its two Gothic rose windows, a building sensual in its severity; and Michelangelo's peach- and honey-colored Capitol buildings;

and—it has become part of the landscape of memory—the Vittorio Emanuele, Rome's colossal "wedding cake."

More recently it was Mussolini who "ruined" Rome, not nearly so much by building (his sterile and spooky "garden suburb" built for an exposition that never happened—Esposizione Universale di Roma [EUR, pronounced "ay-ur"]—is too far south to impinge upon that part of Rome that we think of as Rome) as by excavating the odd Roman ruin, here a ruin, there a ruin, tearing down belonging buildings, peeling back visible layers of history to do so. Romans' respect for ruins is fabulous. When I entered Rome for the first time, years ago, by train, I practically swooned with gratitude when I saw that fragments of an Etruscan wall were an integral part of the structure of the railroad terminal. I immediately saw what the texture of Rome would be. Many of the landmarks of my youth were being torn down in an orgy of building that my own city, New York, was at that time undergoing, and having entered adulthood recently and tentatively enough to need all the outward and visible emblems of my childhood firmly in place, I was feeling like a displaced person. Rome is kind to its past; and to grow up in a city that reveres history must make one feel that history—the world's, and one's own—has a point.

In the Piazza Augusto Imperatore, Augustus Caesar's jostled bones lie buried near one of the restaurants that vie for the title of the "original Alfredo's," and next to the sunken ruins excavated by Mussolini is a fatuous Fascist building with this inscription: THE ITALIAN PEOPLE ARE THE PEOPLE IMMORTAL WHO FIND ALWAYS THE SPRINGTIME OF HOPE, OF PASSION, OF GRANDEUR (which springtime for Mussolini did not last long). It is a strange juxtaposition . . . but Rome is full of unexpected juxtapositions, most of them felicitous; this one is not.

While time has not effaced the architectural damage the Fascists inflicted upon Rome, time—helped along by the Romans—has softened it. The massive Fascist government building near the Circus Maximus on what used to be called the Viale Adolfo Hitler now serves as offices for the United Nations Food and Agricultural Organization; the *viale* has been rechristened Viale delle Fosse Ardeatine, in memory of the 335 souls, including 100 Jews and a boy of fourteen, massacred in 1944 by the Nazis in the Ardeatine caves beyond the Catacombs.

Time has humanized ruins which somehow, under Mussolini's patronage, tended to look like visual aids for a dreary civics lesson. On the Piazza Fiume, for example—a busy piazza to which one goes for the pleasure of shopping at a Roman department store—there is an extrusion, perhaps once a fortification, from a Roman wall (and growing from the broken wall, a tree as ancient as the ruin). People, perhaps squatters, live here—their laundry proclaims their existence; they revivify the ruins. We are not far from the Baths of Diocletian, and in the neighborhood of the Porta Pia and the Porta Salaria, two of the fifteen gates that pierce the encircling Wall of Rome—a monument itself, though so much an integrated part of the landscape we don't see it in that light. Beyond these gates once lay the vast Campagna, miles and miles of waste and grass-covered ruins: "an undulating flat . . . where few people can live; and where, for miles and miles, there is nothing to relieve the terrible monotony and gloom. . . . So sad, so quiet, so sullen; so secret in its covering up of great masses of ruin, and hiding them; so like the waste places into which the men possessed with devils used to go and howl and rend themselves, in the old days of Jerusalem. . . . Nothing but now and then a lonely house, or a villainous-looking shepherd: with matted hair all over his face, and himself wrapped to the chin in a frowsy brown mantle, tending his sheep." This is not long ago as time is counted in Rome; Dickens wrote this of it.

There is not, on the other hand, much to be said for the Via della Conciliazione, the broad thoroughfare that leads to the Square of St. Peter's, or for the two raw-looking end buildings that link the thoroughfare to Bernini's colonnade. The Borgo is the area around St. Peter's; surrounded by Leonine walls, it is bordered by the Castel Sant'Angelo on the west and the Vatican on the east, two strongholds that are connected by a *passetto,* or fortified corridor, through which Clement VIII escaped during the Sack of Rome; its residents call the Via della Conciliazione "the gash," an ugly name. It was begun in 1936 and not finished until the Holy Year of 1950, and it replaced a cluster of medieval streets. God save Rome from reckless city planners who want to "open the city up." The beautiful *piazze* of Rome always take one by surprise, *especially* if one knows they are there; one comes from dark and narrow streets, hoarding and postponing pleasure, into a bath of always surprising light. Some liken the effect of this tunneling in the dark toward light to the Resurrection. The Via della Conciliazione, with its absurd obelisk lamps, its shops with their souvenirs poignant and execrable in equal part (*articoli religiosi, oggetti sacri*—pictures of Christ with tearful eyes that follow you lasciviously), robs the pilgrim of surprise. (And to add insult to injury, there is not even a good café or restaurant along this avenue, a most un-Roman state of affairs.)

Now it is the roisterous traffic or the proliferating American-style fast-food restaurants that will "ruin" Rome.

The fast-food restaurant near the Fountain of Trevi, where "in a narrow little throat of a street," Dickens saw "a booth, dressed out with flaring lamps, and boughs of trees . . . a group of sulky Romans round smoky coppers of hot broth and cauliflower stew; trays of dried fish and . . . flasks of wine," is of course not admirable. But Trevi, once a basin in which to rinse wool, a fountain that barely escapes lunacy to achieve an incarnation of joy, still shelters lovers in its hollows late at night. Poor Trevi; its water comes from Agrippa's aqueduct, Acqua Vergine, built nineteen years before the birth of Christ, but someone is always having a brand-new idea for this fantastic wall of sporting gods and goddesses and cascading water which is set, improbably, in the junction of three tiny streets (hence, *tre vie*). When leaders of the Italian fashion industry wanted a removable Plexiglas walkway placed across the riotous fountain in order for models to parade the season's wares, the city said No, it would be unbecoming. And shortly after this contretemps a judge banned the use of ancient monuments for "cultural extravaganzas"; he suggested that even outdoor opera at the Baths of Caracalla might be illegal, and considered, in the interest of safeguarding the historical and artistic wealth of Italy, halting the sale of refreshments at the Colosseum. A former mayor of Rome called a city-sponsored circus at the Piazza Navona the "sign of a fallen civilization."

Quod non fecerunt barbari, fecerunt Barberini (What the barbarians didn't do, the Barberinis did): We can't reasonably expect to see the elevation, purification, and consecration of the sleazy fast-food restaurants near traffic-throttled Piazza Barberini (or, for that matter, the [discreetly archless] McDonald's near the Spanish Steps). The Barberinis, for their sins—they stripped the Pantheon of its bronze—gaze upward or downward, as the case may be, from the place assigned to them by God, to see that Bernini's lovely Triton Fountain and the piazza named for them has become a traffic rotary.

These new food establishments (of the one that faces the Pantheon it is too awful to speak), because they are less inexpensive than the unpretentious *rosticcerie* and *tavole calda* that have served Romans and visitors adequately and sometimes brilliantly for years with simple food (cold meats; roasted chicken; plain or grilled sandwiches [*panini*]; salads), are an affront to logic as well as to aesthetics. It's a shock to see a Benny Burger on the Viale di Trastevere; the Roman youngbloods on Vespas and on foot who frequent it look pleased with themselves and defiant (and Benny Burger as a consequence has a rakish, speakeasy air), which suggests that they are doing something naughty, as perhaps they are. . . . But no one is so beautiful, taking his ease, as a Roman; and at night, on the *viale,* it is lively and gay, and Rome is not "spoiled," only minimally altered, immensely lovable, pleasing not in every part but steadfastly beautiful as a whole. It remains in its essentials unalterable.

One soft May evening a taxi was taking me to a dinner party; when my driver came to the Piazza of Santa Maria Sopra Minerva, he slammed on his brakes (this is a frequent occurrence in Rome, one grows inured) and sang out curses and imprecations which, to give him the benefit of the doubt, he didn't realize I would understand. He wasn't, although his curses were deeply felt, unconscious of the effect he was having on me. His curses were magnificent; he supposed I'd understand the music, if not the lyrics. When he grasped that I understood both, he apologized by saying one didn't "get the benefit of cursing" unless it was strong, like coffee, black and evil; "small curses are of no use," he said, holding up traffic for this exegesis; "better none at all." He had slammed on his brakes in a fury of aggrieved civic pride: An Egyptian obelisk "rides" the back of a marble elephant in this piazza—it is a witty idea, and it was Bernini's pretty idea—and the trouble was, the cars parked around the elephant obscured it.

My driver loved his city—this is one of the most attractive things about Romans, that they love to be where they are—in token of which he took the fare off the meter and showed me what cars had done to Rome: We crisscrossed the city—from Minerva to the spacious Piazza del Popolo, so spacious it has been turned into a legal parking lot ("and you lose all the benefit," he moaned), and then to the Ghetto and the lovely Turtle Fountain—Fontana della Tartarughe, composed of boys and dolphins and tortoises, water, rock, grace, and joy and, in the moonlight, surrounded by cars. He wanted me to see the city through his eyes, as it had been. He harangued, he beseeched; this was an act of spirited love.

"In New York the traffic is anarchy," a taxi driver says. He is a maniac. He is zipping around a blind corner on two wheels. He is flapping his arms and gesturing toward his middle, describing his waist with his hands—something about a money belt. In fact it is not about a money belt, it is about a hernia operation and his straps and bandages. Just this morning I have asked the porter in my hotel/residence for a ball breaker *(rompiscatole),* instead of a can opener *(apriscatole);* this is not my day to understand Italian. Language comes and goes, like Roman moods. It is also not my day to be understood:

This morning two giggling maids ask me why I have a police whistle. (My son has given me a police whistle as a joke, and also for dark-alley emergencies.) Is your brother a policeman? they ask. Are you a member of the secret Italian-American police? The *guardia?* The *vigili?* They offer their confusion over my police whistle and my identity as reason for their not cleaning the toilet: They are afraid to touch anything—Roman logic at its most picturesque.

Some people think all Roman taxi drivers are maniacs, but this is not true. They speed and they stop on a dime and sometimes you get the impression that their day is made by a *"coincidenza"*—a head-to-head confrontation with another car. They speed and they brake and they have their eyes and their stout hearts examined every six months, as well they might. But: They do not drive with hostile intent, they do not want to kill you; in this they are different from New York cabbies. They seldom try to cheat you, and when they do—"Wait, I am going to have coffee now," a driver says, his meter running—their attempts at larceny are so transparent as to be disarming. "You smell like violets," they say, "you are beautiful, how many children do you have? You are a grandmother? Impossible." I am not a grandmother, but I am old enough to be one, and I think this will cool a driver's ardor, which it does not. "A divorced grandmother," I say; this is a mistake. (In America it would cool anybody's ardor.) "You are bad, *cattiva,*" the driver says; "you don't believe in love." My noncompliance is an insult to a sunny day. But Roman men, obliged by glands and custom to make a pass, invariably remain pleasant when they are turned down. "Well, I tried," their shrug seems to say, and the attempt satisfies manly honor. "Your Italian is perfect," my herniated driver says, though I have understood little and spoken less. "Your mother must have been born in Italy." This is all nonsense. But it lightens the day.

Exasperation, amusement, resignation, and, finally, the kind of pleasure one feels in the face of the nonthreatening ridiculous: You're caught in traffic behind a truck that could not possibly have forced its way into a street as wide as a wrinkle but has. And then eight brawny men in shirtsleeves lift the truck up to make it possible for cars to squeeze around it, and what can you do but laugh?

Much of the city's historical center is off limits to unauthorized cars (the pots of azaleas that used, so exuberantly, to line the Spanish Steps are now put to practical use: They are used in the piazza, to act as a barricade against cars); but people make mistakes, and police are loath to give out tickets. They're greeted with heckling if they do. "Fascist!" onlookers cry. (How comradely Roman drivers are. In New York every motorist is every other motorist's enemy and takes pleasure in his humiliation.)

Carabinieri; polizia; vigili urbani; vigili municipali. Lots of police; what's the difference among them? No one seems exactly to know.

B. and I are driving through the historical center, searching for a café I have often found on foot. This is tricky business. Suddenly—by what black magic we can't think—we find ourselves in Piazza Navona, ablaze with light, where cars are not permitted. The horseshoe-shaped piazza is dense with human flesh. It is the hour of the *passeggiata,* the evening stroll. Camels will go through the eyes of needles before B.'s car will find a way that isn't lethal through this parade. We become the mark of every peripatetic peddler in the square. Young men in blue jeans thump our car good-naturedly. "All very well," B. says, "but what if the carabinieri should come?" Her license is, as she delicately puts it, "not quite in order," which is to say she drives without one. Of course the carabinieri do appear; a stage like this attracts the necessary players. A truckload of them, rifles slung over their shoulders. This *"coincidenza"* is not amusing, though the half of Rome that is in the Piazza Navona stands ready to be amused. Two "honeybunches"—B.'s word for all Roman men under eighty, and these appear to be under twenty—examine the floor of the car, in fact it is our legs that they are examining, having already cursorily examined our faces (which met with their approval); they do not examine B.'s license, thank God.

They ask us to meet them later tonight, in a nightclub in Trastevere. B., who is willing to rob the cradle but not the womb, also does not wish to be arrested, so: *"Mi dispiace*—I'm sorry," she says (from her intake of breath I can tell—she is an actress—that she is about to lie). "My friend and I . . ." She makes a dumb show of her hands and eyes. "You don't like men?" one of the boys—years away from manhood—asks. "No," B. says, *"un gran peccato"* (while I, somewhere between anger and hysterical laughter, burn, for never did woman love man more than B.). "Never mind," says the older boy cheerily, "we are lovers, too. But we like you a little bit enough. I go with you, my friend goes with your friend, why not?" "My husband forbids it," says B., continuing to invent. "Foreigners! *Ma che pazze*—how crazy!"

the sweet younger boy says (hoping). Before I can decide whether to burst into tears—I can produce tears at will, a talent which served me well when I was a pretty young girl in Italy but which I'm not sure I can rely on in middle age, considerations of morality aside—the truck driver is backing up, a path is cleared through flesh, and B., who is triumphant, says (as she finds her way into the Piazza della Rotonda, also forbidden to cars, but by this time who cares?) that she will stay in Rome forever because nothing really bad can happen here, especially if you have a talent for the stage.

In a bad mood, it is easy to believe that Rome is a perpetual chariot race to which hapless pedestrians are incidental; certainly the traffic lights have nothing at all to do with pedestrian crossings and everything to do with the flow and merger of cars. Even two cars in an empty piazza can look as if they are an accident about to happen—like bumper cars at Coney Island; a game. Any attempt to walk across so wide a street as the Via del Teatro di Marcello (engineered by Mussolini to "open up" the Piazza Venezia) is bound to curdle smiles. I am frequently obliged to cross this street, I change buses here. So many lines of traffic debouch into the piazza that crossing it requires the courage of crossing a highway—which it resembles—blindfolded. There is no longer a smartly dressed policeman in white operatically orchestrating movement from a pedestal (the picture memory of him comes from a gentler, more leisured time); there is only a harassed cop directing cars. Sometimes there is no guard at all, only blind faith; it is as implausible to negotiate these streets by car as by foot. Even Romans cross with fear and trembling. I've seen grown women stand for fifteen minutes before they can bring themselves to take the plunge into the stream of cars to get to a traffic island, which will in any case bring them only halfway to their objective. I looped many loops to find a way to get from the bus junction to the Campidoglio or to the Teatro Marcello without the small hairs on the back of my neck standing up; to no avail. One day, after I'd taken three steps forward and two back into the Via del Teatro di Marcello, I closed my eyes for the plunge and found my arms seized by a French man and woman who I thought must have smelled my fear and sensed my vertigo. They had their own fear, and they depended on me to make a phalanx with them; we sputtered at one another in English, French, and Italian to keep our courage up until we reached the Campidoglio. If someone is keeping a ledger, I am now entitled to at least one act of that civility and succor in Paris that I take for granted in Rome.

* * *

There is a persistent rumor, too good not to believe, that stolen cars find their way into unfrequented parts of the Catacombs, out of which bands of car thieves operate.

I am hailing a cab, my right arm upraised. A man wearing a good three-piece suit and carrying an attaché case, the picture of probity and sobriety, hits me over the head, hard, with his rolled-up newspaper. "Heil Hitler to *you,* bitch," he says. Afraid to catch the attention of this ambulatory crazy man, everyone on the busy street averts his eyes. This is New York.

If this had happened to me in Rome, everyone who witnessed it would gather around me in seconds—to proffer comfort and advice, to question and to analyze, to relate this event to what happened to their-uncle-the-crazy-man, their-daughter-the-victim. They would direct their comments to me, to God, to the universe. B. is wrong; bad things do happen in Rome. But you don't have to experience them in isolation. Strangers—or perhaps you are not strange to them, perhaps they have taken note of you all along—volunteer information in the neighborhoods of Rome. "Two muggings today in Trastevere," a man will tell you on the *viale* confidingly. Minding your own business has not become a virtue in Rome. A restaurant owner sweeping the pavement will cry out: "The bread is rising! The strawberries have just come in!" You are part of the city. Rome adopts you. In New York we act as if public acts were private acts—watch the impassive face of a fireman. In Rome private acts become public acts.

I was not lonely, not one day, in Rome.

For the first five years of its existence, there was no felony crime committed on Rome's fifteen-mile subway. This is a helpful, orienting fact.

You can't go reeling unwary through the streets of Rome: There are hard-up drug addicts and roving bands of thieving Gypsies whose children vociferously, threateningly importune; there are purse snatchers on Vespas. But it's salutary to remember that a century ago travelers were inveighing against the "night hawks within and the brigands without"; Goethe professed himself to be astonished by the number of murders in Rome. . . .

Rome is not ruined.

Its Beauty is not spoiled.

* * *

In the nineteenth century the same scribblers who capitalized *Beauty* railed against "idol worship" and popery and in general gave their raptures and their biases free rein. We have become more reticent and more polite. No one (alas!) would dare express in writing the Protestant revulsion Dickens felt for graven images or allow himself to say, as Dickens did, that in Catholic Rome the true faith and the false were merged into a "monstrous union." It's now the fashion to shrink as decorously from ecstasy as from ejaculations of horror. Love and passion and idiosyncrasy are sacrificed to a false gentility that goes by the name of tolerance. Maintaining a careful neutrality, we write about Rome good-manneredly, as if we came to it with no religious baggage of our own; we are like the tourist who asked if churches were open on Sunday, basing his question on the assumption that churches are museums. We think it is all very well for Goethe to say that in Rome all the dreams of his youth came to life (and "a new life begins"), that he found a peace that would last him all his life; Goethe is, after all, dead and beyond embarrassment. . . .

This is ludicrous. If you are constrained from expressing your feelings about Catholic Rome (Catholicism is not confined to the churches, it is in the air Romans—and you—breathe), if you approach a church in which the bones of dead monks are arranged in pretty arabesques as if it were merely an artistic aberration and leave your feelings out, then I (a Catholic in Catholic Rome) must for parity's sake leave my feelings out of it—which I cannot do. . . .

Goethe was born again in Italy.

This is not susceptible of proof, but it is true. Galileo's error was not that he said the earth revolved around the sun but that he accorded science a sacramental authority. The perversion of science lies in elevating empiricism to a moral principle. Science is empirical, but not objective; scientific findings are an artifact of the research design. If I say to you, "I love you," you will—unless you have reason to think I am a pathological liar—believe me, but if I say, "I love you I really do don't you believe I do? I love love love love you I love you I really really do honest I do," you might feel I am fraudulent; but scientific facts rest on establishing proof by just such repetition and duplication (which is counter to the way we "know" things in real life), to which science then assigns the name of unimpeachable truth. The "sin" of science is to presuppose that all of reality is knowable and to deny that which we know not theoretically but from direct experience.

And yet: Goethe's rebirth in Rome has the ring of "scientific" as well as of emotional truth, and this is why: Science tells us that in our memories we rehearse the years of our childhood and of our early adulthood. Experience buoys this research. Reveries and wandering memories take as their subject matter not the events of our majority, our middle years, but the events of our early lives: the source. (Do you remember any room so well as you remember the rooms of your childhood? Has any kitchen ever been so sunny as the remembered kitchen of your childhood? There is a clearing in the woods where rays of light congregate: This memory comes from childhood.) Our memory knows that childhood is the cause, and everything else—including memory—is the effect. Rome has an incalculable gift to impart: Its Beauty provides us with a new reserve of memories. It is literally rejuvenating. We have in our emotions grown crusty, scaled, indifferent; but Rome is a bottomless well, it provides us with the stuff of ineradicable memories, communal dreams and private visions: a source. We live again because we have been granted—how amazing that it should happen twice!—a new beginning where beginnings matter: in the heart. This it bequeaths us through "a charm inexpressible, indefinable . . . which, once deeply felt, leaves forever its mark upon the sensitive mind, and fastens it to Italian soil throu' all its future wanderings by a delicate chain of longings and regrets." By what Forster called "the thousand little civilities that create a tenderness in time," Italy offers one the most priceless of all one's possessions—one's own soul.

In his old age, Goethe—who lived to be eighty-three—complained that he had been happy for only four weeks in his entire life. Those were the weeks he spent in Rome.

How can one cease to be grateful?

I see a courtyard, a doorway, a door seductively ajar (Rome is a city of thresholds, not a city of revolving doors; revolving doors don't know where they are going, they give you ambiguous messages; Rome says: "Come in!"); I am on a cobblestoned street, accompanied by the fragrance of yellow roses, walking toward a murmuring fountain, a lonely and obedient water-driven clock; here is a secret street, cool and mysterious, that leads into a familiar piazza—into an explosion of light; I feel again the piercing sweetness of strangers who find themselves at a dinner party organized according to no

known principle, and—under white umbrellas, gazing across the rooftops of Rome, picking from the rosy darkening sky the merry corkscrew steeple of Sant'Ivo alla Sapienza—find, in the sunset, that they are friends; swallows wheel against the lantern of St. Peter's at dusk; cascades of green and star jasmine on ocher buildings, a flight of warm and curving shallow steps; unexpected, unexplained fragments of white statuary, marble busts, in bowers of oleander (apricot, rose, lavender) on terraced rooftops on the leafy Lungotevere as I drive by on a moonlit night, the Tiber smelling green; a small burnt-sienna house, green shutters, a cozy flight of outside stairs cluttered with the impedimenta of daily living—a broom, a mat, empty tins—and home to pots of straggling basil, thyme, geraniums, an umbrella turned inside out (inanimate objects declaring a principle of Roman life: Inside is outside, outside is inside); fountains: water patiently following orders for a thousand years; a wheelbarrow in an ancient square piled high with new fruit . . . the grand and the domestic present to the senses, at ease with each other and at once, as they are in dreams; the wild and comfortable logic of belfries and multilevel roofs; a blanket of rosemary in a ruin; "proletarian terraces with lines for drying laundry and with tomato plants growing in tin cans directly facing residential terraces with espaliered plants growing against wooden trellises . . . the surface of things is inexhaustible"*
. . . honeysuckle, clumps of weeds growing from the Pincian wall, anointed by moonlight; and none of these things alone but all of them together, each separate part declaring the permanence of beauty. . . .

The light ravishes.

I am happy here; when I or others have bruised my life, I close my eyes against the hurt and think of Rome: as possibility, and hope. And I feel more related to my environment and to my circumstances in Rome than I do anywhere else on earth; I am blessed, intensely delighted, satisfied, and reconciled. The world is lovable when the world is Rome. Everything good in my nature is nourished here. My body feels safe here. When I love the space around my body, I love my body. For the rest of my life I will love Rome and think better of my life for having known Rome. Rome, rooted and ethereal, stretching from earth to heaven, casts aside so little and embraces so much—there's room for me. It is everything; it is elegant, robust, common, spectacular, vulgar, exquisite, and above all rare. It is Gregorian

*Italo Calvino, *Mr. Palomar*.

chant in Sant'Anselmo on the Aventine; it is the gestures of the Trasteverini, their games—*morra,* a game my father played with ferocious patience (he taught me, too, though girls were not supposed to play; when the ancient Romans played it—they called it *micare digitis*—it was always played by two men): Two men stand facing each other, and each throws out one or two or three fingers, shouting out the number of fingers he expects, in sum, to see. This game is deceptively simple; I think it is a show of manhood in which guessing—feminine intuition—secures the victory.

Rome is all things high and low. It is like God, it accommodates so much.

My friend Jane tells this story: She was dining with her lover, a Calabrian nobleman, in a little restaurant on the Campo dei Fiori, and, "Oh, wouldn't it be lovely if we could eat outside," she said, it being February, and she in love. "So in five minutes the waiter had a table outside and linen and cutlery and candles [candles being essential, in Rome, to worship and to love], and we were all alone in the Campo dining just outside the Farnese, Michelangelo's palace; how they love a spectacle," she says; her mouth turns down. "How they love love."

"What a nice story," I say.

"The Calabrian left me," she says.

What Jane means to illustrate is not just that Italians love spectacles but that the love of a spectacle somehow compromises true feeling or masks an absence of feeling, perhaps both—in proof of which Jane gestures toward the fountain we are sitting next to (in the eighteenth century the bathtub of a princess), and to the pergola wound with grapevines overhead. We are having lunch at Otello, a trattoria in a cobblestoned courtyard on the Via della Croce, a block away from the Piazza di Spagna and its fancy shops; it is always cool here, the fountain murmurs green music all the time. Against the wall and in the basin of the fountain are pyramids (red, green, yellow, white, purple) of peppers, pears, tomatoes, grapes, cherries, eggplants, peaches, squash (their green-yellow trumpetlike flowers intact). I cannot comprehend Jane's objection to this cornucopia. It is not typical of her; and if we want a peach, the waiter will pluck one from the pyramid and dip it in the fountain and bring it to us, droplets icy, flesh warm. Nothing is lost, it is not an economy of waste . . . and yet the Romans are somehow taken to task for this and similar displays, how odd. . . . Of course, the Calabrian did leave her.

If Romans were "all surface"—as, for example, Milanesi say (but I do not believe them)—why would it matter so much? How graceful the surface is (how lovely the dance). "They prepare a face for the world to see." So do we all. They do it well. That the taxi driver who slammed on his brakes in the Piazza of Santa Maria Sopra Minerva was *acting* his feelings there is no doubt; he was also *feeling* his feelings.

Things are always happening to Jane. Late one night she calls. On her dark street a man has approached her from behind and seized her breasts. She swings around and hits him with the remains of a watermelon she has brought home from a dinner party. As he sinks to his knees, splattered with watermelon like blood, "Oh, your blond hair," he moans, "your beautiful long blond hair." . . . The police have come, they are sympathetic and engaging. They will keep a watch on Jane's flat from Monday to Friday.

"What about Saturday and Sunday?"

"Oh, we don't work Saturday and Sunday," they say.

"Who does?"

"Nessuno [no one]."

It's just as well Romans are not perfect, one would have to give up family and children for Rome.

"It's just too much to bear," Jane says.

"What is?"

"I could never go back to Chicago again," Jane says.

Well, no.

They have seen so much, perhaps too much, they know so much, nothing shocks them. Cynicism and pragmatism are notoriously easy to confuse. Italians look facts in the face—chosen facts, of course; anyone who looked every fact in the face and gave every fact equal weight would immediately slit his wrists. To the extent to which Italians are not idealistic, it is because they believe in, or have been inculcated with, the idea of Original Sin; they look it in the face. This does not mean they do not want the world to be a better place. It means they have never shared our innocent, cloud-cuckoo-land belief in the inevitability of progress; Italians know that while public morality may be legislated, perfection of intention cannot.

Italians know they are going to die. (Americans have not quite got used to the idea.) You cannot have lived your life in Rome without getting used to the idea—without breathing in the idea—that to dust you will return. This knowledge oxygenates the blood of Romans, and it is this knowledge that animates the living dust we call flesh. The beautiful young men and women at the café Rosati in the Piazza del Popolo live so beautifully in the moment because they know they are *of* the moment; they are probably not, are almost certainly not, consciously considering the Four Last Things— Heaven, Hell, Death, and Judgment—but they know they are going to die.

Romans are invariably more attractive than their detractors; the accused are so much less cynical than their accusers.

Still: "How cynical Italians are!" I heard this time and again in the course of a guided tour to the Catacombs of Santa Domitilla and the Basilica of San Giovanni in Laterano. In the Piazza of San Giovanni in Laterano is the Scala Santa, the staircase which is popularly supposed to be that which Christ climbed for his interview with Pontius Pilate. Our guide was quick to say these stairs are not in fact the stairs climbed by Christ. The prudent Vatican (slow to attribute miraculous properties to venerated objects) has so decreed. (This does not prevent Catholics, including Italian Catholics, from climbing those cruel steps on their knees, from which it is not to be inferred that their penance is in vain. If their pain is an offering to God, then God, it must be supposed, will scarcely reject it, as no gift is unacceptable to Him, even if it is based on a misunderstanding; so we are taught.) The Catacombs, the guide pointed out with forgivable relish, were not in fact a hiding place for early Christians; their Roman persecutors would hardly have failed to notice a mass exodus to the suburbs of Rome. The idea that Christians ritualistically met in the Catacombs derived from Metro-Goldwyn-Mayer. Well, so crest-fallen were tourists—including American Catholics, including Protestants and Jews—upon having their beliefs tweaked, you'd think someone had told them that the Trinity was a fabrication of Louis B. Mayer's imagination. (One American Catholic ostentatiously crossed himself.)

Why should Catholics need to have their Catholicism shored up or jazzed up by pastel fictions? To believe in the Holy Trinity is a lot more difficult than to believe that early Christians held powwows in caves. Out of what he must have considered a noisy and bothersome curiosity, I asked the guide if he believed in the Trinity. He looked at me as if I were mad. *"Sono cattolico,"* he said: "I am Catholic." The question answered itself.

May 10. Today I went to an anniversary of the American Women's Association at the Grand Hotel: penne with fresh tomato sauce; American ham with canned pineapple, mashed potatoes (which the woman seated next to me piled high on Ritz crackers: Homesickness takes curious forms); strawberry gelato and cake. "I hope that cake is Betty Crocker," said a very pleasant

woman from Indiana; and it almost certainly was. There were speeches.
When the speeches went on too long, as of course they did, the contessa
brandished or thumped her silver-handled cane, her personal comfort out-
weighing her fear of embarrassing herself.

The contessa is old, she has a steel hip as well as a chased silver cane. Oh,
to be a wicked-tongued rich old countess in Rome! She has lived in Italy
for fifty years in style. "Loved Rome, married Naples," a Neapolitan count
to be precise, and she loves her life although the count died long ago and
now her dog has died and her maid of twenty-two years has left her—"a
Communist, of course"—and the English girl who rented her fashionable
apartment denuded it of "every movable . . . worse things have happened,"
and she has sold one of her apartments but not her villa to ———, a
politician, who had the effrontery to bargain her down two million lire, but
she maintains a house in Washington, too, never mind. The contessa wears
a fur tippet and she chain-smokes and her fingernails, ridged with age, are
painted scarlet, and during all the long and boring speeches she talks politics,
which isn't done among overseas Americans; never mind. (When I lived in
Guatemala, I was invited to a meeting of the American Women's Club and
asked what my life had been in America and I said something about the
antiwar movement and the civil rights movement, and: "Oh, we think the
Peace Corps is doing a wonderful job," said the wife of the ambassador to
break the ensuing dreadful silence, which, I was given to understand, was
a result of my boorishness; overseas wives are not meant to have independent
opinions.) The contessa isn't buying that, she is too old for pretense; when
you are her age, anything left to fear, if you have lived any kind of life at
all, is not of this earth.

She has worked for NATO, says the contessa, and as a journalist, and
during World War II her husband served on Italy's side, as also he did in
World War I, but she was sent to America in an "exchange program," she
says—"a joint American-Italian venture." In Lisbon her ship was stopped in
the harbor because "they found two spies." . . . Who did? Spies for whom?
"Never mind." In Lisbon she managed to extract nuns from a brothel where
Americans had managed to billet them; and in America so full of praise was
she for Italy's part in this venture ("What venture?" "Never mind.") that
she was followed, they thought she was a spy. ("Who did?" "I've just *said.*")
So she didn't see her husband for three and a half years. ("But I had his name,
which is after all what counts.") The contessa's stories are short on factual
detail and long on ribaldry. Oh, the dances, the parties, the candlelit villas!
she says; but "I could never write a book about that time before

the war, everyone in Rome is writing a book with her *toes*. I'd have to leave out all the best parts. One of my suitors was a nephew of Pius X, and another . . ." (She whispers a name that is good for a gasp in all the Christian world.)

"I dream of black boots," says a cadaverously thin, sharp-featured woman sitting at our table. She looks as if she is about to shield herself from a blow. There are widening circles of sweat under the arms of her very good, very well-cut, not very fashionable wool dress. "I am always afraid except on Columbus Avenue." Lala—that is her name—was living near Anzio when the war ended, a child; she was "liberated by colored soldiers from Morocco, Tunisia, and Egypt," and her dreams are invaded by men wearing black boots.

"I, however, was in Lisbon," the contessa says. The contessa has a niece who appeared in B movies of the forties and fifties, almost always as what used to be known as an executive secretary, elegant in black, her ash-blond hair sleek in a chignon, a gold pen worn on a necklace around her long but humble neck. I used, sometimes, to consider being this person, having this life, the life of a secular nun: disciplined, omniscient, subservient, aloof, asexual, and unimpeachable. Because she has a niece who figured in my fantasy life, I feel that there is a bond between the contessa and me.

"I dream of bombardment," Lala says. Lala married an American; she misses delicatessens. She hates Rome now, it is so sad, so many cars, too many people, she hasn't been to Trastevere—she lives in a remote southern suburb of Rome—since 1976, and then only to change buses. Lala has not become so Americanized as to have lost her Roman talent for instant disclosure; she has come back to Rome out of duty to her dying mother—"and now I am a divided soul, not Italian, not American, what shall I do with my life?" She is like a damaged doll. How her accent must have charmed her husband (of whom she does not speak).

Before the war what the contessa wished to do with her life was to write a cookbook—"but nobody in America cared for Italian food then," she says, looking at her canned pineapple as one might look at a cockroach. "The war made people hungry. . . ." This sentence strikes her as being oddly constructed, as susceptible of more than one meaning; the contessa can almost be seen to look at her sentences after she has spoken them.

Julia—"I should have married a German, the Germans love slightly overweight blondes"—is married to Massimo, an Italian set designer who has a toothache today, "so of course he wants to jump out the window. In New York he behaves perfectly reasonably, but in Rome he carries on as if life were an opera. Today he is Dying Fatalistically. If you're crying in Rome it's assumed you're dying, but if you are really dying, they shrug their shoulders and turn their backs and then they 'opera-ate.' " Julia divides her time between New York, where she teaches voice, and Rome, where "after my husband married me because I was independent and more interesting than a housewife, he proceeded to turn me into a housewife. He is ruled by the women of his family, his sisters and his mother," she says. "They have him by the balls; Italian women control the money. I, being American, do not. He asked me for twelve thousand dollars the day we were married in New York in order to get his mistress out of his apartment in Rome. His mother cleans the toilet with a toothbrush. I didn't have twelve thousand dollars, I only had a mink coat, that was his mistake. Italian women have no power after they're thirty-two—the younger ones fuck from twelve in the afternoon until four. Wives have to keep their husbands teased. I control Massimo by withholding sex. . . . Of course I can't work here, it's all nepotism and influence, and Massimo won't let me out of the house. . . ."

The contessa, who looks apoplectic, does not deign to call attention to the fact that Julia—whose light soprano voice makes her confused diatribe sound almost pretty—has in fact managed to make it out of the house today; instead, with her left hand, she clasps her glass of pink champagne (at which she looks most dubiously), and she raises the third (arthritic) finger of her right hand. *"Sempre dritto e figli maschi!"* she calls out, to the perturbation of the pleasant woman from Indiana and to the sweet amusement of Julia, whose coloratura peals interrupt yet another speech. *Sempre dritto* —"Always straight and your sons will be male!"

Lala has been listening to a self-important woman who is "compiling a biography" of Pope John Paul II and of possible successors to his office; it is feared that on a trip to the Netherlands—the compiler says this with palpable glee—he will be assassinated. Lala, worldly and by reason of her several marriages a lapsed Catholic, says: "This man who lives by faith, not reason, will die a bloody death, the Virgin has saved him more than once, and since he believes he is under sentence of bloody death, he is bound to preserve what has for centuries made the Catholic Church the Catholic Church."

"Hear, hear!" says the contessa.

"No one has had a new idea in this country since the Renaissance," says Julia (that being, as far as I am concerned, one of the reasons to love this country).

"I will pray for you all," says the contessa, her inclusive glance horrifying the pleasant woman from Indiana, "and for the Holy Father," she says.

"Hear, hear!" says Julia, who has been to est.

"You have become so tolerant in Rome it almost amounts to a vice," an American friend says. He means that I have become Italianate in my affections. For Romans, people are either *simpatici* or *antipatici;* one responds to another on the basis of immediately formed instinct. As no system for choosing friends—or for being chosen—is foolproof, this suits me under sunny skies. Here I trust my instincts better than I trust my words on paper (words on paper do not always make contact with instinct), a novelty.

The morning after the American Women's Association meeting, Julia comes to visit me; I have given up cigarettes and am, as a consequence, too shaky to cross the *viale* to buy the cigarettes I dearly want. She brings me cigarettes, a newspaper, wine; she is so kind, so eager not to offend. She tells me all about corruption in the movie industry and about lots of things that, under ordinary (New York) circumstances, I would not wish to hear about at all—reincarnation, for example, her husband's past life being the reason, or so she thinks today, for his present infidelities. She also delivers herself of the opinion that Romans do not have logical minds. I smoke and drink red wine, my eyes on the Aventine.

"I am going to the Forum today," I say to the contessa (we are having our early-morning phone chat). "Oh," says she, "I did that once seventy years ago." Perhaps she meant to say in 1970, or when she was seventy years old; no matter—the contessa is always adjusting her age upward or downward for effect; and I am tickled by her breezy implied disdain.

"All those rocks," says an American friend of mine who dislikes Rome, "all that stone!" I know just what she means. ("Ah!" says Zola; "if you had strolled over the Palatine hardly fifty years ago! There were only vines, little gardens, low hedges, a veritable compagna [*sic*], a real desert where one never met a single soul. And then to think that all those palaces were sleeping underneath.") I spend no time in the Colosseum, preferring to see it—always amazing, never friendly—from a taxi.

Rome's architecturally mixed messages induce a kind of schizophrenia:

Ancient Rome and Christian Rome convey totally antithetical messages. "If the Colosseum falls, Rome falls, and if Rome falls, the world falls." Yes; but here is the Roman Forum and it *has* fallen, and in its desolation is the message that man and his works are perishable, mortal, destructible: futile. And here, on the other hand, is Christian Rome, the message of which is that in God nothing is lost, that our flesh and the works of our hands may perish but our souls will not, that God broods over us gently, regarding our follies, our sins, and our feeble attempts at goodness with a loving, merciful, impartial eye. . . . Here also is synthesis: a church (so many churches) built upon, or incorporating, the ruins of ancient Rome. Out of decay and despair, this message: Christ has died, Christ has risen, Christ will come again. The Pantheon is celebrated as a perfect space; it is, and it is more: It is a reminder that from human conceit and arrogance may arise the humility of belief, the generosity of belief. A pagan edifice elevated, consecrated, dedicated to the God we imperfectly serve, it says: Forever; *secoli dei secoli,* world without end.

Those rocks, that stone, those mixed messages—Rome seems designed to provide violent mood swings; but in the end it is the message of the Pantheon that prevails, it is happiness that predominates.

All the time I was in Rome I felt as if I were tipsy, slightly drunk, and being lightly tossed in a very agreeable blanket.

An American writer says offhandedly that he lives in a flat on Largo di Torre Argentina overlooking the Area Sacra del Largo in order to witness the end of the world in Eternal Rome. My gift for irony does not extend that far. I go to Argentina (excavation on which was begun in 1926, and part of which was a public lavatory), not to look at the long, narrow sunken ruins Mussolini excavated, but to change buses (and sometimes to stop at Delfino's to bring half a deviled chicken home). But sometimes I am arrested by a winsome sight: young lovers embracing unselfconsciously, his hands seeking the warm vivid flesh under her blouse, in the pretty reconstructed loggia that overlooks the remains of four classical temples, which are among the oldest in Rome. . . . A girl with outstretched sunburnt legs, reclining on steps that lead to the ruins, reading, oblivious of ghosts. . . . Someone has tied, with wire rope, a plastic container to the guard post of the ruin, and in it are anemones and red carnations; this gesture—this need to pay homage to the past—warms my feeling for the ruin itself (and vandals will not disturb this offering, as a gift of flowers is a form of prayer).

Time has ruined all; ivy covers the walls that once were clothed with tapestries and golden draperies; thorns and scrub flourish where once sat purple-clad tribunes, and snakes infest the queen's chambers.

—Pope Pius II, 1451

"All is death, there"; the Forum frightens me. To get to it, to the place to which all roads once led, I walk from the Capitol down the Via della Consolazione, a road that becomes a leafy path; I like it, the damp earth smells like tea. . . . I liked it until I saw a sign that said DERATIZATION GOING ON. DON'T TOUCH THE BAIT. Well, who would? But where is the bait? . . . And I find myself soon in the cradle, heart, and graveyard of the ancient world. To walk where Caesar walked and feel no thrill is strange. I need much less—I can read history and mysteries into an object I can hold in the palm of my hand—or much more. For some, the absence of detail—the very lack of obelisks, fountains, roofs of hammered gold—acts as a spur to the imagination. Stendhal's advice, tongue in cheek, was to "imagine what is lacking, and disregard what is there." But my imagination can't reconstruct the Forum as it once was, nor can it disregard the mutilation that is there. . . . The statues are forever fallen, the columns smashed, the roofs ungilded, the narrow streets peopled not by hundreds of men in tunics and togas, smelling of garlic and pomade—they have all stepped over the brink into the great chasm—but by enervated tourists with guidebooks (maps to a bomb site) at a loss to know if they are looking at a prison, a theater, or a temple. There is no consolation to be derived here from the transitoriness of things. The silence of the distant world is deafening.

We can never know how objective we are being about an inert object or an artifact. I remember scrambling through tunnels of sand to a newly excavated amphitheater in Leptis Magna years ago, and that was thrilling; but Leptis Magna is on the Mediterranean Sea, and the sea is always an aid to the imagination; and both the ancient cities of Libya—Leptis Magna and Sabratha—are (or were) almost perfectly preserved, houses, and pavements of mosaics, glittering under the North African sun. One was always alone there, with only the sound of the waves. I wonder how those brilliant stones and those domestic interiors, so mysterious and yet so familiar, have, under Qaddafi, fared.

By comparison, the Roman Forum is taciturn.

As I traversed the Via Sacra—only eight hundred yards long, such a narrow place for such mighty intercourse as once had been—I wanted to find something to love, or to quicken my imagination, and I found my way to the Temple of Vesta, where Vestal Virgins kept alive the Sacred Flame. The circular foundations alone remain. If a Vestal allowed the fire to go out, she was stripped, and beaten in the dark by the Pontifex Maximus. If a Virgin broke her vow of chastity, she was buried alive. This building is said to have been the prettiest little temple in Rome—"a gay, delightful circle of marble with white columns around it connected with lattice work" (H. V. Morton), conferring such dignity upon its surroundings as to make them "the most fashionable neighborhood in Rome." I think it is a horrid place of leprous sadness and decay, unhallowed littered ground. All that remains of the ruined two-storied House of the Vestals, in which these cloistered women, recruited when they were no more than ten years old, served out their thirty-year sentence (which was regarded as a great privilege, but perhaps not by them—although Giambattista Vico tells us that emancipation was regarded as "chastisement or punishment"), is a grassy place, broken brick walls around which huge scentless yellow roses climb . . . they ought by right to be red; but nature doesn't accommodate our feelings or our fictions. In this grassy place are two walled oblong ponds. The water looks stagnant, but occasionally little bubbles rise to its surface and spring up in the air, so perhaps beneath the slime, goldfish still swim; generations of travelers have fed them bread, and told about it. Where once there was also a colonnade, there is now only a row of white statues, monuments to the chief Vestals, the *Vestales Maximae;* on one statue the name and inscription have been erased, and this is thought to be the statue of Claudia, a convert to Christianity, whose punishment for desertion from the ranks was to have been ignominious obscurity. Here grow roses, orange, yellow, crimson, without scent. If one could only think of this as a garden of an English gentleman, one might call it sweet (indeed, one nineteenth-century chauvinist credited the work of excavation to the Duchess of Devonshire!).

So many men, good, interesting, and kind, have written of their love for the House of the Vestals, as it must once have been (an architectural prototype for cloistered nunneries; a place where the presence of a man once guaranteed his death): white, and those within it noble, peaceful, gentle, pure, and disciplined. We are left to wonder at the persistence of male desire for the perfect priestess of the hearth. The fate of a wayward Virgin, the sorrow and the terror which these travelers dutifully deplore, seems to them an aberration; they have in the forefront of their minds the Sacred Flame symbolizing perpetuity and stability, the purity, the dedication white as snow. Whereas, in fact, the barbaric punishment was inherent in the vow.

Women may desire to be cloistered, to bid a cool good-bye to Vanity Fair (as, from time to time, weary of the hurly-burly, do I); but there is a difference between a cloister and a jail. Those Vestals who transgressed their vows were gagged with leather straps before they were brought to their burial place in covered hearses and made to descend a ladder to their tombs; a seal was placed over the trenches in which they were so horribly buried, conscious of their fate—and no one received their cries. It saddens and alarms me to think that men are a little thrilled by this.

What I felt, on a day of hot winds and threatening skies at the Forum, wasn't "meteorological" apprehension. It was foreboding: The world can die. The scentless roses, the invasion of rats in what was once a field where cattle grazed, the fallen pillars—the Forum mocks our hopes. Who wishes to be dust to feed a yellow rose?

"Whatever is fortified will be attacked; and whatever is attacked may be destroyed." Sometimes, in the midst of joy in this city of joy, one is afflicted with ennui which might go by the name of terror.

I think that what I hate about the Forum is that everything that has happened there has already happened.

Sometimes at night, restless as bells rang out the time, I dreamed of the Forum—the severe grandeur of columns rising high into a vampire sky; a heavy white moon hangs above the columns of the Temple of Castor and Pollux—this image dominates all other images of my dream; but I can't, asleep or awake, go beyond the image to meaning. The Forum over which the columns reign is a sepulcher; tiny, inconsequential bodies—here flesh has no weight or meaning, fragrance, grace—rummage in the ruined gardens, the desolate fields.

Just over the Libyan border in Tunisia, on the coastal road, there is an amphitheater alike in size to the Colosseum. One comes upon it unprepared, and it is like a blow to the heart—the sea, the desert, its naked and tremendous solitude.

To get to the Pantheon—than which there is no more potent antidote to unhappiness, gloom is exorcised within these walls—my path took me, from my residence in Trastevere, on to the Viale di Trastevere, past the Church of San Crisogono, through the Piazza Sonnino, over the Ponte Garibaldi, up the busy Via Arenula, into the Piazza della Rotonda. Coming back, bad humors dispelled, I drove through a section of the Corso, into the Piazza Venezia and past the Capitol and the Teatro di Marcello and the Piazza della Bocca della Verità, the Church of Santa Maria in Cosmedin, the foursquare Temple of Manly Virtues, and the pretty round temple often called, but incorrectly, the Temple of the Vestal Virgins, looking innocent, on the banks of the Tiber, in a grassy plot; over the Ponte Sublicio, through the Porta Portese and the Viale delle Mura Portuensi, hugging the ancient wall—and home.

This is a litany, comforting and thrilling only to me. I am disregarding all but those landmarks that I see when I close my eyes; this is not a road map; it is a different kind of directory.... Sometimes when lovers of Rome get together, they just say the names of places ("Santa Maria in Cosmedin, ah!"); shorthand for rapture—the word we all, because we are "modern," avoid.

From my terrace I can see, in the distance, the Ponte Garibaldi, the orange buses, the yellow taxis. I always know when there is a *sciopero,* a transport strike (*sciopero* is one of the first words you learn when you come to Italy); I adjust my plans accordingly. Living near a bridge gives me the sense that I live in a navigable world.

No matter who or what is on strike in Rome and for whatever reason— sometimes a strike is simply a means to remind Romans that no worker is expendable, that workers have human faces—life goes consequentially on.

(It is often said that Rome and Romans are inefficient, and there are ways in which that is true [that is why we go to the Vatican City post office to post our mail], but it is also true that their not taking it upon themselves to organize the world makes Romans in some ways trustworthy. "They had no 'machine' to capture or kill Jews, they were too lazy," says a Jewish friend of mine; to charge Romans with laziness in this context is a compliment.)

The Viale di Trastevere, which takes me to the bridge that crosses the Tiber, is busy with the traffic of office workers and housewives, but seldom with tourists, for the majority of whom this part of Trastevere gains importance only on Sundays, when the Porta Portese flea market extends its dubious charms. In fact, there is little that is remarkable about the leafy thoroughfare (such charm as it has lies in its ordinariness), always excepting its several cafés, in one of which, on the Piazza Bernardino da Feltre, near the Ministero della Pubblica Istruzione (an ornate weathered-pink, declaratively tropical building surrounded by oleanders and palms, the function of which no one is quite sure of), can be found the best granita di caffè (dark, sweet coffee, frozen, and crushed into ice, best with *panna,* cream) in Rome.

Rome is a city in which life exists in the midst of death, death in the midst of life. On the way to the Piazza Sonnino there is a wall at which I often stop to refresh my spirits; it is a shrine to the Virgin—in the midst of clamor, salubrious naiveté: a collection of pictures of those in peril saved by Mary; ex-votos, tin or silver representations of body parts for which Mary's healing grace is asked; and testimonials to her efficacious intercession. (I am at the post office, I always think, when I stop here, the post office where the Virgin collects her mail and simple sprays of flowers.) Each day there is a new thank-you note, a new request; it makes one quite happy to have left one's house.

On the Piazza Sonnino I buy cherries; the explosion and the trickle of dark-red sweetness their firm flesh yields feels as if it should be illicit. The gray Church of San Crisogono is next to the green umbrella stands where I buy black cherries, greengage plums. The fruit is chosen for me, one doesn't select one's own in cornucopial Rome; and I never have a cherry that is overripe or one that has soured; and this is explained to me: The fruiterer gives his "secondary produce" to women with large families for one-third the price. This makes the fruiterer an amateur sociologist, and Rome, Montaigne's city of artichokes and roses, a very human place in which to live.

I like at all times to visit the happy Church of San Crisogono, with its classical columns and its atrium, its mixture of the Romanesque, Baroque, and Mannerist; I like especially to visit it with Lala, who, convent education notwithstanding, treats every church as if it were a drawing room. Lala beams at the Baroque cupids on the blue-and-gold Rinascimento ceiling. *"Cattivi,"* she calls them, "naughty, mischievous . . . like cupids and satyrs," delicious. Lala would walk on her hands on this floor if she could; she has a special love for the Fratelli Cosmati, the medieval family of marble cutters who scavenged ruins for pretty marbles—especially rare red and green porphyry—and cut them into circles, squares, and cubes with which to make infinitely varied hand-set geometric patterns. Lala scampers about San Crisogono like a child, amused even by the *spingere* candles—candles with electric flames activated by buttons (*tsk-tsk,* the tourists say). I link arms with her, confident that her unconventional piety, if not her interior-decorator sensibilities, will not be offended before a statue of the Madonna locked behind plate glass, festooned with jewels: a simple string of coral beads such as one might find in any souvenir shop; a nineteenth-century brooch of seed pearls and diamonds; many gold rings; a gold cross; a tarnished silver watch and watch fob girdling Mary's waist.

When people say that Catholics in Rome are not "really" Catholic, I wonder what they think these manifestations of thanks and supplication to the Virgin mean.

Lala says, "They think the rules are foolish and restrictive, and they castigate us for not following them, and they want us to be more Catholic than the Pope, whom they despise. They think that we are primitive and superstitious and repressed and that we are worldly and sophisticated and have illicit sex all the time—which we are and which we do, so what?"

"Which of it?"

"All of it."

Lala makes the sign of the Cross.

(San Crisogono, martyr, was a Roman official imprisoned by Diocletian and beheaded; his body was recovered from the sea.)

I like, when I cross the Tiber, to think of the teams of white buffaloes that towed boats centuries ago; Montaigne saw them.

On a hot day on the Via Arenula, cars belching noxious fumes, "The wind was sent by Qaddafi," a driver says, "the birds in the trees of Trastevere were sent by the Russians to fly into people's houses, and the traffic is mad because Rome is Communist and any policeman who would try to regulate it is a Fascist, furthermore." There are days when one understands why Ezra Pound found Rome congenial. In fact, swallows arrive from North Africa in May; the wildest flights of fancy sometimes have a tenuous connection to fact. (This is a principle my paternal grandfather exemplified. Toward the end of his life, he believed that he had flown across the Atlantic with Lindbergh, "but I got no credit because I was Italian." The truth was that he worked with Bruno Hauptmann, the convicted kidnapper of the Lindbergh baby [a ladder built by Hauptmann rested against the loft window of my bedroom in Grandpa's country bungalow, and this was an object of terror to me; children do not believe death puts people out of reach, and I thought Hauptmann, executed, would get me next], so there was some link between him and Lindbergh, and he so much preferred his version to the truth it soon became the truth for him.) This driver sets himself to please; he points to every spigot, to everything that might conceivably be called a fountain and says: "Bernini." And: "Ah, the bats," he says, "Qaddafi sends them, full of Arab blood."

I am describing my road to the Pantheon.

Just before the Via Arenula meets with the Via di Sant'Anna (I am almost at the Pantheon now), there are three green flower tubs. I know this because this is how directions are given when buildings jostle on narrow streets in a city not built on a grid. "Turn left at the green flower tubs, right at the first café . . . up 194 steps." The number of stairs is always included in an invitation to a dinner party; one wishes to know the worst, and it gives the indisposed a reason to decline. . . .

. . . And soon I am at the Pantheon, the home of my delight.

Sometimes I think the ragged Gypsy girl curled up, somnolent, in the doorway of the dignified palazzo near the Alemagna pastry shop on the Corso will be there forever, she will never grow and never move, she belongs to Rome, as permanent as rock.

The Corso takes me home.

The Corso runs in a straight line from the Piazza del Popolo to the Piazza Venezia; it takes its name from the *corse,* the races that were run during the February Carnival initiated by Pope Paul II in 1466. The street is narrow—traffic is terrible—and the buildings squeeze it like pincers. An eighteenth-century writer called the Corso "one long tomb," and Stendhal thought it smelled of rotten cabbages. Dickens gives us a wonderful little picture of its buildings, now gray with calcified traffic fumes: "There are verandahs and balconies, of all shapes and sizes, to almost every house—not on one story alone, but often to one room or another on every story—put there in general with so little order or regularity that, if year after year, and season after season, it had rained balconies, hailed balconies, snowed balconies, blown balconies, they could scarcely have come into existence in a more disorderly manner."

Rome is a city of echoes as well as a city of layers: The races of the fifteenth century were meant to evoke the chariot races and games of ancient Rome; today's Romans, laden with shopping bags from the smart shops on the streets that branch off the Corso, of which the Via Condotti is not the least important, cross the street any which way—and, indeed, walk in the street—as if the spirit of Carnival still prevailed.

The Carnival was, even after its most barbarous customs were suspended by fiat, a peculiar mixture of glamour and cruelty. Even some of its participants were terminally divided between believing the Carnival was an occasion of innocent vivacity and condemning it as the epitome of masked wickedness. Horses were at one time whipped by little boys, and donkeys and buffaloes viciously goaded by men on horseback; and cripples and hunchbacks, naked old men, and despised Jews were made to run for sport. (Later, in the seventeenth century, after this repugnant practice ceased, the prizes for horse races were distributed by Jews.) In the eighteenth and nineteenth centuries revelers wore little wire face masks in order to escape being hit in the lovely crossfire and vertical fire of *confetti* (sugared almonds), oranges, and nosegays. From the balconies Dickens described, streamers and banners and draperies were hung: "The buildings seemed to have been literally turned inside out, and to have all their gaiety towards the highway. Shopfronts were taken down, and the windows filled with company, like boxes at a shining theater; . . . builders' scaffoldings were gorgeous temples, radiant in silver, gold, and crimson. . . . Every sort of bewitching madness of dress was there." It is difficult now to imagine these low balconies full of brilliant faces, the pealing laughter, the flashing lights at dusk, the fire spread from taper to taper till gradually the whole long street was one great glare and blaze of fire . . . and the instant hush that came upon the festivities, the silence when the "Ave Maria" rang from all the steeples. . . .

At one time, if Stendhal is to be believed, "all high class funeral processions" passed down this street. Stendhal might have been a native, so profoundly did he believe in and practice the proverb *Se non è vero è ben trovato* (If it's not true, it's to the point). A cheerful plagiarist, he was also a great inventor of facts to suit his fancy; he adds, for the sake of veracity, that all funeral processions passed "at twenty-three and a half hours"; this is just the kind of detail one would embed in fiction if one were trying to pass fiction off as fact.

(Stendhal wrote his *Roman Journal* in Paris, fifteen years after he had seen Rome. He was hard up for money; and the *Journal* is the result of research, memory, and the notes of a cousin who had just returned from Rome. It is in no way a "journal," and it will surely outlast most books written with scrupulous regard to facts.)

Stendhal was appalled (he said) by the sight of the young Marchesa Caesarini Sforza dead on a stretcher with her head exposed, surrounded by one hundred lighted candles—"an atrocious spectacle that I shall not forget so long as I live, but that makes one think of death, or rather that strikes one's imagination with it . . . a spectacle highly useful to those who reign in this world by making people fear the other." In this dainty horror he was not at all like a native, for Romans know that the spectacle of death is edifying, useful, not only for those who reign in this world but for all, for all must one day die, a salient fact of life. . . .

Milan's Duomo and great square. The roof is a forest of saints — hundreds, perhaps thousands of saints — on marble pinnacles, and one can walk among them.

Milan's Galleria, a shopping arcade with cafés, an outdoor/indoor living room.

Lake Maggiore. The beauty of the lakes notwithstanding, Italians have profoundly ambivalent feelings about them and invariably call lakes *triste,* sad.

Venice. Magic by day, sinister at night.

Giotto's Lily Tower and Brunelleschi's Dome. This is the sacred heart of Florence, and it is both gay — red, white, pink, green, black, white — and serene.

Florence, Brunelleschi's Santo Spirito. The immaculate beauty of this church, set in a large and lively square, needs no elaboration.

San Gimignano. These medieval towers — early skyscrapers — are warm and friendly, not forbidding.

A cloister is womblike, maternal, ordered, rectified, serene. It allows one to partake of the pleasures of the physical world without risk.

Rome, the Forum, Temple of Vespasian. There is no life here. These stones intimidate and inspire fear.

The Cemetery of the Capuchin Fathers, in the Church of the Immaculate Conception, Via Veneto, Rome. "As you are, so was I, / As I am, so shall you be."

Rome, the Pantheon. Perfect space.

Rome, the Ghetto, Porta d'Ottavia. The ruins of this Roman enclosure stand at the corner of a busy street. The gates to the Ghetto no longer exist.

Mussolini, his balcony.

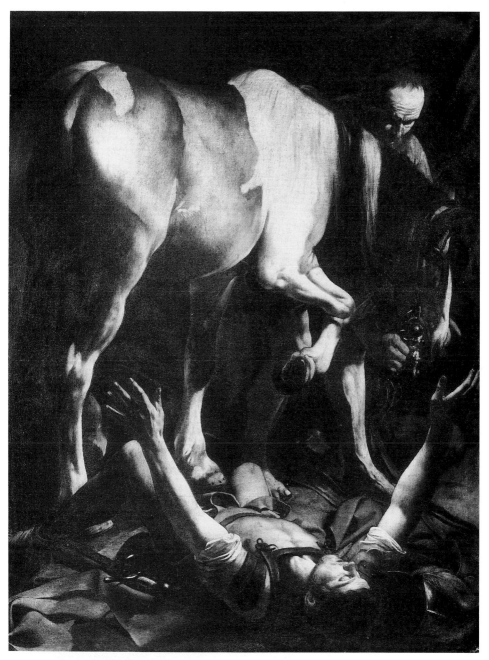

Caravaggio's *Conversion of Saint Paul,* in Rome's Santa Maria del Popolo. This radiant painting is an essay in the theology of light.

Rome, Piazza di Spagna. An orchestral flight of steps, a marvelously silly fountain.

Rome, a classical view: St. Peter's, the Tiber, Castel Sant'Angelo.

The oldest known easel painting of Mary. This hangs largely unvisited by tourists, in the Church of Santa Francesca Romana in the Forum.

The Church of Santa Francesca Romana. The pagan and Christian worlds juxtaposed.

In Naples the distinction between inside and outside seems at times to disappear completely.

The belvedere of the Grand Hotel Cocumella, Sorrento. The Etruscans cut steps, still in use, through these· cliffs to the sea.

Capri, the Faraglioni rocks, with their gorgeous inevitability.

Positano is a bit more built up now than it was when this picture was taken; its pastel houses still climb down in steps to the sea in a profusion of perfumed flowers.

Alberobello. No one knows how these strange houses originated. They take getting used to. These archetypal images are met in poetry and dreams.

Above: My welcoming family, my mother's relatives, cousins, in Vallecupa, Abruzzo. The houses that have been ruined by earthquakes are indistinguishable from those that have not.

Left: Cocullo, Abruzzo. San Domenico. Every year snakes are gathered in his honor. Remarkably pagan, the rite is accepted by the Abruzzesi unquestioningly.

Rocca Imperiale, Calabria, Castle of Frederick II, falconer. This rocky place of severe, wind-scoured beauty where my father was born is five miles from the sea and holi-daymakers.

Bronze men found off the coast of Reggio, Calabria. Who were they? Where did they come from? Where are they going? They seem on the very threshold of speech.

The riderless horses of the Carnival flew wild; their flight was halted by a huge white sheet suspended near the spot where the Vittorio Emanuele Monument now stands; and near this spot, on the Capitoline Hill, Caesar, dressed as Jupiter, placed sacrifices to his god.

The shallow stairs (the Cordonata) leading to the Capitol Square—Piazza del Campidoglio—in which there are three buildings (Palazzo Senatorio, Palazzo dei Conservatori, and Palazzo Nuovo, in the design of all of which Michelangelo had a hand)—should perhaps be called a ramp; they are less intimidating than the steps (122 or 124; agreement on this score does not seem possible) leading to the beautiful thirteenth-century Church of Santa Maria d'Aracoeli. In between these two purposeful flights of stairs (which are at surprising, witty angles to each other) is a third, easily overlooked, bucolic, decorative flight of stairs that appears to curve into a hidden garden—a grace note. To the left of all these stairs there is a tiny garden, which brings us back to human scale. Without such gardens Rome would be a rock-hard place.

When I first came to Rome, a quarter of a century ago, a bronze statue of the *She-Wolf with Romulus and Remus*, the twins sucking at her teats, adorned the square; it was a most charming sculpture (a little alarming, too, defying, as it did, the separation of thinking from nonthinking animals), and its presence here seemed to mark the Capitol as the heart of pagan Rome. Now the *She-Wolf* is in the Conservatori, a focus is gone. And no one seems to know the whereabouts of the *Equestrian Statue of Marcus Aurelius,* which once stood at the center of a beautifully simple geometric design conceived by Michelangelo. It is very present in its absence; the square needs a commanding figure on a horse to lend weight (and an emblem of continuity) to the exquisite pastel buildings, apricot and peach. Hawthorne felt its presence keenly; he called it "the most majestic representation of the kingly character that ever the world has seen. . . . He stretches forth his hand . . . a command that was in itself a benediction." In his absence, there is no benediction. There is the Church of Santa Maria d'Aracoeli, higher than the Capitol; the sacred broods over the profane.

When I first visited Rome, a quarter of a century ago, I sat at a café—the same one I sit at today—across from Santa Maria d'Aracoeli, and watched an old woman in black climb 122—or 124—steps (steps moved from the Temple of the Sun on the Quirinal Hill and placed here as an offering to the Virgin during the Black Death of 1348); she climbed them on her knees.

They made—how can one say this without sounding blasphemous and effete?—a nice picture, black against the Aracoeli's brown, a moving small-ness rising, silhouetted against an uncluttered sky; a dramatic reinforcement of one's belief that Heaven has an exact physical location and that, with preparation, it can be achieved. Although I was not Catholic at the time, I was not appalled by the old lady's exertions (it may, of course, be true that baptism—I was baptized as an infant into the Roman Catholic Church—is like a vaccination that eventually "takes"); but I was at that time with people who saw futility in every penitential act, for if God were good, they said, He would not want old ladies to climb stairs on their knees to Him. But I found it splendid to think of a God whose needs are intuited by old ladies in black, His needs, in this act of penance, being inseparable from theirs. . . . No one asks a mountain if it wants to be climbed. . . . From the top of the steps there is a view of St. Peter's, and of the Synagogue, too—very little exertion, really, for so much gain.

So I had thought. But as time went by, I began to fret about those steps, and all the steps and stairs of Rome.

We are climbing Jacob's ladder. They are beautiful. There are so many of them. The nursery school image, the illustrated-Bible image, of flights of stairs leading to God in Heaven above is based not only on our belief that God is above man but on the popular medieval conceit that the spiritual life is a ladder; thirty steps or rungs were required to attain religious perfection, and each step represented a trial and the acquisition of a virtue. I began, in Rome, to see the trial more than to apprehend the virtue; sometimes in Rome the sheer number of steps begins in itself to seem punitive. So many; not just the steps that are an unavoidable and magnificent consequence of Rome's being built upon hills, but all the steps in all the museums and all the churches. And what if one were in a wheelchair, eighty-five, not strong of limb or stout of heart? I asked. The answer, invariably, was a shrug. The answer was: In that case you must forget about visiting museums or getting on a bus. There is an Italian proverb disturbing for its acceptance of a brutal fact of life: *Il mondo è fatto a scale: c'è chi scende è c'è chi sale* (The world is made of stairs; there are those who go down and those who go up). (I have said that this is what I love Italians for—that they look facts in the face. . . . But I don't love this fact!)

While I was pondering this, I read the words of Eileen Marie Gardner, special assistant to then Education Secretary William Bennett: "The handi-capped falsely assume that the lottery of life has penalized them at random. This is not so. Nothing comes to an individual that he has not, at some time in his development, summoned. . . . As unfair as it may seem . . . a person's external circumstances do fit his level of inner spiritual development." Something can be said for this point of view (for example, if I am fat, I have in all probability defied the injunction against gluttony), but not very much. It is cruel. It is perhaps reflective of a muddled understanding of natural law, a belief that to deny the facticity of affliction is *contra naturam*. Secretary Bennett called Gardner's view of the handicapped "a fundamental doctrine of Christian existentialism." It occurred to me to wonder if Italy's lack of facilities for the elderly and the handicapped was owing to a similar understanding—which I should call heretical—of Christianity. (I cannot believe in a God less merciful than I am.)

One's conscience is not, unless one is a saint, a sponge for all the wrongdoings of the people and the institutions one loves. One is selectively vexed and aggrieved. My joy in Rome was not diminished by thoughts of the Inquisition; upon the corruption, nepotism, insanity, venality of dead Popes I did not dwell. I bore in mind these words of H. V. Morton (not himself a Roman Catholic):

> The Medieval Papacy produced more saints than sinners. . . . The blood and thunder of a savage age underlines the extraordinary ability of the Papacy to ride out storms and miseries which would have ended any other institution. Boccaccio wittily expressed this idea in the story of the Jew who went to Rome and was horrified to discover a squalid little city in which the throne of St. Peter was occupied apparently by Anti-Christ; but he became a Christian at once, his argument being that a religion which could exist in spite of the Papacy must have a divine origin! . . . It must be part of the mysterious process of God that so many a good deed has been achieved by a bad Pope, [while a Pope one might consider good] had no effect whatsoever on the times.

Yet I was worrying about the metaphysical implications of stairs.

Perhaps I worried about stairs because I am myself afraid of stairs; perhaps it all comes down to that: Everything that intellectually disturbs us in the external world is umbilically attached to our own failures, fears, and sins; the world is a mirror of our confusion.

However that may be, visits to Vatican City allayed any fears I had that Rome was motivated by "Christian existentialism." The Vatican Museums have elevators and wheelchairs; extraterritorial churches have ramps. The Vatican works, regardless of one's physical condition. I found this reassuring.

I was able to regard Rome's flights of stairs—as much a part of it as are its fountains—with uncontaminated pleasure. This did not mean that I was able to negotiate the stairs with ease: I was still obliged to ask for help at the head of long flights of stairs—I need only to touch human flesh, my vertigo is not physical in origin—and I frequently asked nuns, who smiled and offered me a hand, an arm; they are used to serving without asking gratuitous questions.

"Since the images of womb and tomb are associated with the earth, and images of resurrection and the afterlife are related to the sky, the vertical axis is . . . closely bound to the concept of transition through the cycles of life." To ascend and descend is "to enjoy the feelings of aspiring to heaven and then returning to earth."* If this is true, a fear of steps may represent a fear of achieving that transition, that is, a fear of death—which is, of course, what Freud believed, although he chose to call it a death *wish* rather than a fear.

The Aracoeli invites legend; this story is told about its steps: In the early part of the seventeenth century it was the custom of farmers to spend the night boisterously at the foot of the stairs; a nobleman who lived in a house nearby, Prince Caffarelli, having had no success in ousting them, filled huge barrels with stones and sent them rolling down the steps. With a terrible noise they crushed the bodies of farmers in the dead of night—and farmers come no more.

My people, the Abruzzesi, Italy's bagpipers, do come, though, from the mountains, on Christmas Eve; they come to serenade the Bambino, a Baby Jesus said to be made of the wood of an olive tree from Gethsemane. ("A little wooden doll, in face very like Tom Thumb, the American dwarf," Dickens called Him, "gorgeously dressed in satin and gold lace and actually blazing with rich jewels.") In these democratic days, even the Baby Jesus must ride in taxis; the Bambino is taken to the bedside of the ailing and the dying (where, said Dickens, He frequently frightened them to death), no longer in His own splendid coach, but in a cab. Even the Fascists knew enough never to impede the progress of the car in which the Bambino rode.

It was in the Aracoeli that Gibbon decided to write his history of the Roman Empire, "while the barefoot friars were singing Vespers in the Temple of Jupiter," and on the steps of the Aracoeli Henry Adams delivered himself of this delightfully provincial opinion: "Rome could not be fitted

---

*Kent C. Bloomer and Charles W. Moore, *Body, Memory, and Architecture.*

into an orderly, middle-class, Bostonian, systematic scheme of evolution. No law of progress applied to it. Not even time-sequences—that last refuge of helpless historians—had value for it." Rome did not evolve, he concluded; it simply existed. Another, less Bostonian way of saying this is that Rome is like eternity; time does not exist in it.

If I were driving back from the historical center to Trastevere, I should already have passed the Palazzo Venezia, its balcony. It is strange, I think, how little power that balcony, upon which Mussolini stood and blustered vile nonsense, has to horrify.

His office, on the second floor, was huge and unfurnished except for a desk and three chairs and an ancient map of the world. From the door to Mussolini's desk was a distance of twenty yards, and Mussolini never greeted visitors at the door. Most visitors—including the women to whom he "made love"—were required to stand in his presence. A small door next to a monumental fireplace led to his private apartment; of its furnishings there is no record; presumably there was a bed. What an unpleasant man he was, and not even complicated enough to sustain conjecture.

He kept a light on till all hours. He liked it to be said of him that he worked hard, which he did. When he became acutely lonely, as he deserved to be, he went out on his narrow balcony and surveyed the life of the city, supervised excavations, and forgot, no doubt, that he would someday die. . . .

My cab swings by the Theater of Marcellus. Begun by Caesar and completed by Augustus, it presents an inscrutable face to the world; broken and surrounded by broken marble columns in a field of poppies, it is an apartment building, having never ceased to be in and of use, as theater, fort, palazzo, marketplace, and, most nobly, refuge for the Jews from German occupiers. In one of the apartments there is a hanging garden. These are magic, sunny thoughts. . . .

I am past the theater now, I am in the Piazza della Bocca della Verità; sun slants off the Tiber; here is an open space where fountains calm and oleanders perfume the air, the cypress and the pines and the buildings—ancient, medieval, and Baroque—revitalize the word *picturesque*. . . . And here is the pretty Church of Santa Maria in Cosmedin, its elegant bell tower, its porch with the Bocca della Verità—the marble face with holes for eyes, an unkind slit of a mouth. If you have a lie on your conscience, do not put your hand in its mouth; it will chew it off (it probably came from a sewer, a manhole). And here is the Temple of Vesta, so called for its dear circular shape, on a slope of green, on the left bank of the Tiber; and here the Temple of Manly Fortune, foursquare and manly indeed . . . though it was probably a temple to Matuta, the goddess of dawn. This part of Rome was made for dawn and dusk; it receives light like a dream of light.

Now I am crossing the Tiber, and here is the boat-shaped Tiber Island, and soon I am at the Porta Portese, cars battling through a double-arched gate, and from this large and noisy space, before the spell of peace can be broken, into the green intimacy of the leafy tunnel formed by the Portuense Wall—it is amazing how much affection one can feel for walls—and home.

"I have a terrible thought," a friend says. He is rocking on his heels on the elaborate Cosmati floor of Santa Maria in Cosmedin. "I see this church in the Style Section of the *New York Times.* Some idiot of a designer has turned it into a country house. He talks a lot of crap about its perfect proportions. He turns the high altar into a kitchen."

I do not know if this is a terrible thought or not.

One day there is a wedding party at the fountain in the square near the church. My taxi driver cries; he has been married for twenty-six years— "with the help of God"—and he rubs two fingers together, there is no space between; two by two.

Foreigners in Rome say dogs "look different" in Italy. I don't know if this is true—dogs don't interest me—or, if it is true, what it means, or, if it is not true, what it means that they perceive it to be true.

"Povera signora," the taxi driver says, "you live on the only ugly street in Rome." This is an exaggeration—and I hear in his voice the slightly bully-ing, condescending quality that is sometimes part of Roman curiosity and kindness; but it is to the point: I do not love it here.

Anthony Burgess calls the years he spent "within rattling distance of the bones of the matron saint of music" on the Piazza Santa Cecilia, in southern Trastevere, the happiest of his life. I live in southern Trastevere, too—next to a bus garage, in a neo-Fascist apartment residence set among concrete office buildings and shops and housing complexes for the new middle class. Through a plate-glass window full of dirty silk flowers, in the first restaurant I see are sleek and bored-looking waiters putting antipasti in a microwave oven; outside, there is a tourist bus from Sicily. This is not the Trastevere of small medieval houses, twisting lanes, wisteria, and sunny sadness one dreams of; it is blighted, but not by the melancholy of things that have had their day. It is the Newark of Rome. I am sandwiched between the Viale di Trastevere—an impertinently grandiose thoroughfare—and the Porta Portese; in between is a warren of bleak alleys, a dank tunnel, an open urinal, a wasteland of long, naked streets. High, forbidding gray walls remind me of the walls that surrounded a convent I feared in my childhood: Shards of clear glass were embedded along the top of them, for me an object of fascination and revulsion—I feared contamination. Behind one of these gray walls, off the Vicolo dei Tabacchi, is a tobacco factory founded in 1863 by Pius IX to provide the Trasteverini with employment and himself with snuff. Sometimes the silence of these streets is punctuated by hollow metallic noises from shuttered shops that deal in spare car parts (the provenance of which is uncertain), in electrical supplies, and in all manner of things associated with maleness, hardness, secrecy, and sweat.

In fact, I am only ten minutes away from Santa Cecilia and from such evidence of questionable chic as English-language bookstores and hair salons with fake amphorae, architectural plants, faux Corinthian columns, marble nymphs that mock the real, plate glass, white leather and chrome, and British hairstylists. But I never can forget, walking unprotected here, that the Trasteverini, Gibbon's "pure and native race," proud of their descent from the ancient Romans (which is, however, dubious), for centuries were regarded as "the most addicted of all the people of Rome to carrying the prohibited knife" and to using the knife to commit murder "on the slightest provocation." Even cabdrivers warn me against "thieving." (The ladies at the American Women's Association, when they hear where I live, just say: "My *God!*") The Trasteverini, both warier and more talkative than other Romans, are perversely proud of being *cattivi,* and Romans are happy to assign to them crimes in disproportionate number. The Trasteverini refer to themselves as *noialtri* (people like us; we others). They used to refer to themselves as Eminenti. (It comes to the same thing, the pride in difference, exalted or debased.) There was a time when they were proud of never crossing the river to "Rome" . . . just as my family never crossed the river from Brooklyn to Manhattan. . . . Their tribal loyalty is strong.

I came here soft and eager to be beguiled.

The man riding with me on the elevator taps my teeth with a pencil and smilingly pronounces them the work of *il dentista*. His stupidity, presumption of intimacy, his ignorance and malevolence enrage me. I want to bite his forward hand; he sidles away, winking, bowing, at his stop.

In Rome it comes as a surprise when people are not nice. And the *portiera* is snippy, too, her accent a mystery to me; I never see her without a nail file in her hand, she answers questions with a flounce and a pout.

Dogs bark and howl all night. It is the kennels on the Tiber, the maids say; I had imagined worse.

Why do maids steal razor blades?

All night, in the apartment next to mine, a woman moans and cries, keeping me from such sleep as the dogs have not disturbed. A male voice answers her cries with false cheer; it is the voice of her husband, he speaks English with a German accent, he calls her Mother. If there are going to be sleepless nights, I am at least going to have the benefit of the drama; I hold an inverted glass to the wall so as to hear. . . . They have come to Rome to see their son and his wife, something has gone wrong, there has been some terrible disappointment, the families are not meshing; Mother will not leave the apartment. The man tells her to put a good face on it, they have planned this trip for three years and he "wants to make it work." She coughs and wheedles and whines and occasionally asks indecipherable questions, her voice light, eager, birdlike: "Are they coming? Where are they? Where are the girls? Did you call the clerk? Who has the papers? Has he gone? Has it run its course?" Sometimes he threatens to leave her; the door opens and shuts, opens and shuts. When he does leave to see their son, she is completely silent; the chanting-crying stops. What does she do then? In the hallway he passes me like a large, diffident gray shadow. Perhaps he does not support her in her woes. Who is the villain? I have known men who in the name of peace deny their wives' reality till their wives are mad. Is she insane? What has hurt her? Is he truly kind? One night, awakened by her gurgling cries from seamless sleep, I bang on our common wall. "Did you hear that?" he says. "Did you hear *that*? What will people say if you come back home not having seen Rome?" he asks. This sentence turns me against him.

One day their son and his Italian wife come to visit and everyone is hearty—Mother has swept her little balcony for this event—and everyone laughs. The next day she cries again.

* * *

When people ask me if I am going to "define the Italian national character," I think of my neighbors; how little I know. I am in Italy with my ear against the wall, listening through a glass.

In the absence of wisteria, I try food, which exists for solace. I cross the *viale* to a small trattoria with a pergola; a pergola next to a bus stop is absurd, but even a pergola next to a bus stop is ensnaring.

I have seldom, when I have had failed meals in Italy, questioned the establishment's good intentions; in this place, though, there is not only an absence of goodwill—and a superfluity of dusty pottery and fruit flies—but a studied boredom. This is extraordinary; in Roman trattorie one receives the impression that one's waiter dwells in the happy expectation that any new encounter may forever change his life, or at least his mood; you are in his play, and he is in yours. Waiters take your measure as you order: If you order imaginatively, your waiter will, in gratitude for your having spruced up his day, present you with an almost audible smile and perhaps an after-meal *amaro* (bitters). If, on the other hand, you offend the logic of food, your waiter's response will range from pained expressions to sighs to expansive advice, depending not only on his temperament but on his reading of yours. Waiters at trattorie do not cultivate fashionable ennui.

Whereas, on this day, my waiter, expressionless, brought me Bolognese sauce "without meat," an impossibility, as a Bolognese sauce for pasta is by definition meat cooked in wine and then in milk for velvety tenderness, to which tomatoes are then added; no two Bolognese sauces taste exactly the same (food purists say that no truly superb Bolognese sauce can be obtained outside Bologna, though the ingredients don't vary by much). A mess of pasta smothered in a tinny, oily tomato sauce was presented to me. Fried *fiori di zucchini* came to my table, not as the delicate yellow flowers they are, their integrity of shape maintained, as, in order to perfect the conceit of eating flowers, they must be, but as an unreadable mush that tasted most unpleasantly of fish. (Italian cooking releases, and does not confuse or subvert, the essence of the food.) Imagine serving squash flowers without a smile.

Gluttony is not a temptation when food is honest or exquisite, only when it is pretentious or gross. So then I had a scaloppina of veal, hoping at last to find something that would satisfy me; it came clotted with flour and with rancid butter, proving the maxim that the simplest dishes are the most difficult to do well; and then I ordered strawberries, as nothing can go wrong with strawberries (I was wrong): The luscious things came crowned with aerated "cream"—which I never saw before in Italy and never saw again. All of this I drank down with a carafe of white wine, which gave me a terrific headache, from which I deduced that it contained preservative. . . . Then I returned home to decide whether to open all the windows and the French doors, in which case bats from the neighboring belfries might fly in, or to close the windows and the French doors and swelter in the sudden May heat.

The last memorably bad meal I had in Rome, many years ago, was in a restaurant off the Via Veneto to which an albino bellhop directed me. I stayed, in those days, in a *pensione* called the Bellavista Milton.

Bellavista Milton is a curious name. Mussolini—who abolished foreign words from street signs—took against it and renamed it Bellavista Milton*e,* an even odder name.

My paternal grandfather also affixed vowels to names when it suited him. His favorite singer, a man called Tony Martin, became Tony Martin*o,* and, to the day he died, he was convinced, or pretended to be, that I was married to someone called Signor Harrisoni. My grandfather called Mussolini "Mus-solino"—for spite, he said, though against whom his spite was directed it was hard to know. *"Mannagge America!* [Damn America!]" he would say, in Calabrese; there seemed to be not vitriol but rue in his curse.

My grandfather kept Bruno Hauptmann's ladder leaning against his country bungalow to remind him that "we" were never entirely safe from "them"—"the Americans."

He sang the Brownshirt anthem while he planted a Victory Garden in Brooklyn for the Allied troops. He planted lots of basil, without which, he said, the Allies could not possibly win the war; challenged, "Did you ever see a Japanese who ate the basil?" he said. He was not entirely sane.

Mussolini tortured language as any ideologue does. He abolished the use of *lei,* the formal address in the third-person singular, fatuously calling the abolition of the traditional form of address "a small punch" in the stomach of the bourgeoisie. (In his defense, it might be said that the formal construc-tion—*Lei come sta?*—never made much sense anyway, as, literally translated, it means not "How are you?" but "How is she?" [or "She how is?"]. Under the Fascists, a servant had the privilege of being addressed in the second-person singular—*voi*—not so intimate and informal as *tu.* Almost nobody uses *voi* anymore as a singular pronoun.)

My grandfather thought chicken livers were brain food and stole some from the hospital in which he worked as a carpenter to bring home to me at night.

Someone's birthday, dinner in northern Trastevere at La Tana di Noantri, under yellow umbrellas: delicate ravioli, light as down, a silky tomato-cream sauce; roast suckling pig; strawberries. A night of sweet May rain. And no taxis. (The rain glancing off the illuminated gilt mosaic facade of Santa Maria in Trastevere makes the church "look like a tart," someone says irreverently; it is true, and it is not true.) A prostitute invites me to share the cab she has snared after waiting at a taxi rank for twenty-five minutes. We are going in opposite directions, but, she says, "justice is not served if you wait twenty-five minutes more, justice is not served if I wait twenty-five minutes more, and it is terrible to be thieved in the rain." I offer her six thousand lire when she drops me off, but she returns it because she has had a good night, and because Americans are good luck—"like hunchbacks." ("What is the worst thing about your job?" the driver asks. "Talking to fools," she says, *"talking."*)

Food has become an obsession, something that often happens—that or complete disregard, the other of the twin evils—when one lives alone.

I am having a lover's quarrel with Rome, that is what this is, a quarrel it is not possible to sustain, Rome is too agreeable.

Soon I come to regard this place as my neighborhood. I have made a series of reassuring purchases: paper clips and notebooks with pictures of Mickey Mouse on them at the *magazino;* mozzarella (sweet and smoked), fresh ricotta, *parmigiano dolce, acqua minerale,* butter, and milk at the *alimentari;* a monthly bus pass (unlimited use) at the *tabacchi;* tomatoes and strawberries from the stalls along the Via Portuensi; sfogliatelle and cannoli from the nearby *pasticceria.* And I've found Gino and Paula's, a coffee bar around the corner. A neighborhood coffee bar is an anchor to a life in Rome. Where else can one read one's paper and observe the passing scene, write one's letters, assured of privacy, and yet be part of a moving whole? Gino makes strawberry tarts, and Paula—an intensely Roman mixture of disinterested advice, friendliness, curiosity, and hustling—knits sweaters for sale. ("Everybody in

Italy has a sideline," Lala says, "except me.") They are complementary and symmetrical. Paula tells me which streets are safe to walk on, advice that is lost upon me, as I choose to be guided by feral instinct; her fingers flashing with rings, she tells me not to wear jewelry, not to wear a handbag the straps of which might be used to strangle me. If I were to take everyone's well-meant advice, I would look like a derelict and carry my passport in my boots or never leave my house. But here, where I hear echoes from my child-hood—a dispensation of love was never *not* accompanied by advice—I am at home. Paula's insularity, her sense that the world outside her family is menacing, is comforting to me. A long line of my aunts and uncles and my grandparents seem to stand behind her; at the head of the line is my mother, who was so afraid of the outside world she refused to wear the prescription glasses that would enable her to see it; she carried a red umbrella so cars would not strike her. Daddy is on that line (everybody on that line is wagging an index finger). "Be careful, little girl," he says. "The world will eat you up." He was a WOP. He came here Without Papers; I did not sort this out till after he had died.

I am at Ente Turismo, the state travel information office, where I am being helped to plan a trip to Calabria. After many calls to the regional Calabrian travel office and as many sighs and disavowals that I am causing her trouble, a helpful young woman assures me that there is no hotel in the village of Rocca Imperiale in Calabria, that in fact there is no such village, never mind that my paternal grandfather came from Rocca Imperiale, and never mind that my maiden aunts have stayed in the hotel, described it to me in detail. I have found it in the *Blue Guide to Southern Italy*—five kilometers from the sea, *"Rocca Imperiale,* with a castle built by Frederick II, stands on an eminence"—but this does not impress the helpful bureaucrat, who, after peering closely at the *Blue Guide,* announces triumphantly that Rocca Imperiale is not in boldface, it is only in italics, as if any town in italics might decide to spring off the map, off the planet. She gives me lots of names and phone numbers of doctors-of-this and doctors-of-that in Calabria—in case I should find myself in distress, which she is reasonably sure I will, as I insist upon believing in my map of southern Italy, on which Rocca Imperiale is clearly (if italically) marked.

"In Italy," the bureaucrat says, "the larger the problem, the larger the number of people who must act on it." Why is it that while this sounds reasonable, I have a sure feeling that her approach will lead to disaster? She has now called many people, an extraordinary number of people, in Calabria and Abruzzo, and Campobasso and Isernia, working, evidently, on the scattershot principle; all of them have promised to be as helpful as she. . . . But as to hotels? roads? She shrugs—*someone* will know, *speriamo*.

In between phone calls, the pleasant young woman asks me a series of questions (none of them to do with the matter at hand): Her father's *contadini* left the land and went to America and four years later returned and bought all her father's land. "How?" she asks. Her maid is now in New York with a maid of her own, she says: "How?" As these are questions the answers to which she might be expected to understand better than I, I shrug and suggest what comes to mind: Drugs? The Mafia? A shuttered look comes over her face. She has heard, she says, that 90 percent of all American men are impotent and 10 percent are homosexual: "Why?" Her friends tell her that American men are *"mushado . . . mush-a-mush"* (this is American-Calabrian dialect that means exactly what it sounds like). "Why?" she asks, and: "Why are Italian men so *maschili,* male?" she asks.

When I fail this quiz, which I cannot have been expected to pass, she and the other women in the office play a game. It is called the picture game: Signora A. is a Rubens (she is fat); Signora B., from Florence, is *tutta* Botticelli; and I am "a Bernini." *"Perchè?"* I ask. *"Perchè,"* I am told. (Is it a compliment to be called Baroque?)

The young woman's daughter calls. There is an explosion of tenderness. "She has become a woman today," she announces to her colleagues, whose reaction leaves nothing to be desired. It is *normale, naturale,* this nice lady assures her lucky loved daughter. "Eat, sleep, Mamma will come home." She longs to be home. Everyone sighs, no one's eyes are dry.

I leave with no practical information at all. I have enjoyed the morning very much.

Acne, a doctor says on TV, is "a matter of hormones that marriage will alter."

At 11:30 P.M., on commercial TV, following a documentary about AIDS—*"Sono omosessuale,"* a man says softly, instructively brave in this world of *maschili* men—there is a movie about prerevolutionary French clerical lechers; costumes do little to disguise the bump and grind of heterosexual anal sex. On television commercials there is female frontal and rear nudity; this juxtaposes strangely with commercials for the Christian Democratic party *(la famiglia).*

In addition to the three-channel state TV network, RAI, there are dozens of private stations available to Roman viewers. Sometimes at night, along with Romans seduced by "Dynasty" and "I Love Lucy," I watch TV; it is wonderful the things I learn: *A fifteen-year-old should be given his or her own housekey.* This proposition is extensively debated. This discussion could not possibly take place in any public forum in America, for a plethora of social and cultural reasons it is instructive to reflect upon.

FACT SHEET

There is 1 coffee bar in Italy for every 472 inhabitants—1 for every 460 inhabitants in the North; 1 for every 391 inhabitants in central Italy; and 1 for every 559 inhabitants of southern Italy and the islands.

Ninety-seven percent of Italians have a grocery store and a bar within two kilometers of their residence.

The average Italian watches TV four hours per day.

Forty-two percent of Italians think the wife should get up when the baby cries; 1.7 percent think the male partner should get up at night; and 56.4 percent think both should.

Seventy-one percent think women should clean the house; 0.8 percent think men should; and 27.8 percent think housework should be shared. Seventeen percent think men should shop for food; 55.5 percent think women should; 42.9 percent think both should. Seventy-two percent believe women should prepare meals; 1.5 percent said men should; 26.5 percent say both should.

Approximately seventy-two minutes per day are dedicated to the actual preparation of meals.

Women do 90 percent of the housework.*

According to statistics published in 1987, the French work fewer hours than the Italians, whom they have been used to call lazy: Japanese workers employed by IBM (for example) worked an average of 1,964 hours apiece in 1985; French employees worked 1,612 hours; and Italian workers, 1,716.

*Pietro Sartogo, *Italian Re-Evolution: Design in Italian Society in the Eighties.*

(West German employees worked fewer hours than Italians, 1,660; and Americans worked more, 1,873.)

According to the *International Herald Tribune* (1985), the black or underground economy in Italy accounts for 20 to 30 percent of the gross national product. This invisible, untaxed, nonunion industry is the source of such parts and components as "shoelaces, zippers, buttons, nuts, bolts," mattress stuffing, dolls' hair, fake designers' jeans, purses, shoes. These are regarded as legitimate cottage industries by those engaged in them, who would otherwise be on the dole. It is therefore impossible to say what the rate of unemployment is in Italy. The civil service is no longer considered the catchall for those who could not otherwise secure jobs; the underground economy is. "Gloomy as the picture often appears on paper, nothing is ever lost in a country where private entrepreneurs show a baffling capacity to avoid the evils of an inefficient and archaic political system.

"Contradictory as it may seem, in the environment the individual flourishes—and even prospers."

According to *Newsweek* and *The Wall Street Journal* (1987), Italy was the fourth- or fifth-largest economic power in the world, surpassing Great Britain. (This is an almost impossible fact for an immigrant's daughter to assimilate; it is hard enough—*without* the evidence of Italy's postwar economic recovery—to believe that anyone would willingly leave the Bay of Naples to settle in Union City, New Jersey.)

On a dry, hot day, Julia takes me along Margaret Fuller Road to the mournful garden of the Villa Sciarra, across the *viale,* up flights of undistinguished monumental steps leading to the Janiculum. The limestone fountains, home to lizards and to Fanta cans, do not play; they look spongy in decay; the satyrs and nymphs that adorn them are scabrous with age. We walk down avenues of listless trees, to a topiary garden in which old people take their rest. Au pairs and Filippinas sit on shaded benches with preternaturally decorous children. There is a redundancy of gazebos with tired ducks and pigeons here. A few intrepid children, dressed as if for church, make use of an imaginative playground—ropes and wood, slides, monkey bars—but adult hands are outstretched to catch them lest they fall onto the uncushioned concrete below. Under such circumstances, it is an act of rebellion to play. (Play is always an act of rebellion.) On a merry-go-round with an odd assortment of horses, a miniature locomotive cab, spaceships, and a coach-

and-four, only a teenager, nodding out on drugs, rides. Everything is dusty here; Julia likes it here. Next to the villa, dedicated in 1932 to the people of Italy in the name of Goethe (words of praise for Mussolini have been erased by chisel from the facade), is a shack with video games.

Only the caretaker's house—stone without mortar surrounded by blowsy red roses—has a country-green charm.

My grandfather treated stones with reverence and imagination and patience, reserving for them the respect and love he did not display for animate objects (including me).

Mussolini's daughter Edda tells a story of falling, bouncing, all the way down the stairs in their villa in Rome—and Benito Mussolini stood at the head of the stairs, swearing and not helping her. There is something I know and understand in this story. My grandfather would have done—did do— this *(Mannagge America!),* out of atavistic southern fatalism, cruelty, rage; the shadow of his childhood poverty and desperation would have fallen upon him as I fell, I was not real for him then, I was an unmanageable object in the unmanageable space of the world. . . .

In the Palazzo Venezia, on Christmas Eve, 1933, Mussolini hosted ninety-three of the most prolific women in Italy, one from each province. Among them they had given birth to more than thirteen hundred children. They looked old. "The strength of a people rests in its numbers," their leader said.

My Calabrian grandmother had twelve children. Five of them survived childhood. She was a midwife in Calabria when she was fifteen. "What do you know?" she would ask me when I carelessly defied her—when, for example, I dirtied my starched pinafore playing hide-and-seek, or, later, when I spent long idle afternoons in her company. "What were you when you were fifteen?" Nothing. She began making novenas for me when I was seventeen and no husband was in sight. None of her three daughters married (both her sons did); my grandfather was a sometime mercenary, and when he went off to war, he instructed his sons to look after their sisters, which they did, evidently, too well. My father never met a man he thought was good enough for any of the women of his family. I married in despair of pleasing him and in consequence failed to please myself.

In spite of everything I know, I often wished my father had never left Calabria, I wish I had been born in Rocca Imperiale and had twelve children. "The more children you have, the fewer questions you ask." I thought my grandmother told me this when I was a little girl, but when I asked her what she meant (had she said "the fewer questions you *have"?* that would have made a difference), she said: "You make up stories, pug nose, I never said that thing." She refused to talk about the children who died; she said she had forgotten their names.

Country women used to keep their babies wrapped in cloth on boards held next to them—next to their hearts. Italian babies are swaddled against every climatic and internal contingency. Years ago I sailed on Italian ships from Bombay to New York, a toddler on each hip. They were sweet and wild, my two- and three-year-olds, and had that funky, sweaty, talcumy-delicious smell one loves. The Arabian Sea was glass, the winds caressed, and in the grand ballroom of the ocean liner, my India-bred children, who did not see the point of clothes, took off their clothes and danced. The mothers of the babies in swaddling clothes, returning from Australia, where their meager fortunes had been made, were horrified. That my children's diapers weren't Alpine white was for them a cause of amazement in the ship's laundry room, where we were much discussed. On this ship there was a near mutiny because the supply of anisette had run out halfway to port; this behavior caused me to regard my fellow passengers and crew with affection.

In Genoa we disembarked. We walked through the old city, and women emerged from doorways to bundle Joshua and Anna up. The first restaurant we went to was closed, but waiters could not resist the appeal of two merry nut-brown children who smiled; the doors were opened, and the children were hustled into the kitchen, wrapped in aprons, to be fed. I had lunch—for the first time in years, it seemed, alone. "Come back! Come back!" they said. Later that day a woman called the police to complain that two poor little children were "unclothed and catching death." Aboard the *Michelangelo,* Joshua put on his little plaid dressing gown from La Rinascente and his red felt slippers and stole from our cabin while I was asleep "to see the moonlight on the water," he later said, after which, without my knowledge, the steward locked us in at night. This same steward brought me a carrot tied with a red ribbon because I would not respond to his advances; it took me years to get mad at him. I laughed, and even now I laugh. Anna tried every day to escape the confines of her bathing suit in the baby pool; a special steward was put on guard to keep her from offending the sensibilities of the other passengers. The nurses in the playroom asked me to write down the lyrics of American popular songs and taught them to Anna, who sang: "I love-a-you-o-oo-oo, whatsa matta you-ooo-oo-oo-oo?"

This mixture of love and claustrophobia, tolerance and severity was as familiar to me as rain.

"Proper *borghese* children" Julia calls the children of the Villa Sciarra.

"Have you ever seen an Italian kid dirty? On a bike?" Julia, whose husband has been (she says) overly mothered, sees what she wants to see. She sees the starched and well-behaved children strolling in the Pincio and in the Borghese Gardens just as their parents did, and their parents before them.

In the new elementary school near my residence, boys under twelve play ball at recess time, holds barred; girls cluster to talk. (Are they all being kept children? Or are they growing old—assuming adult roles—too fast?) In adolescence they seem more like their American counterparts. The *piazzette* belong to boys and soccer balls, no holds barred. In Trastevere, away from this concrete complex, boys do wheelies on bikes and shout rude words, gay as spring, in dialect—*fa 'ngule!* They are reassuringly rough-and-tumble. (The girls bloom in the dark; soon their beauty will overtake the boys'; they will drive them mad in all the squares.)

At Paula's a boy on the verge of manhood, assuming a studied pose of boredom, leans away from his mother and aunt, who fuss and fuss over him, touch him with their hands, their eyes, their voices. His younger brother looks at him adoringly. Soon he will be stalking girls, perhaps in the Piazza del Popolo, where Roman playboys circling in Lancias and Alfa Romeos and Lamborghinis honk their horns—once if they like a girl's legs, two times if they like a girl's breasts. Sometimes the whole square is an orgy of honking, like some primitive mating call.

The brothers pinch each other's cheeks.

A child accidentally knocks over a cream cake at Otello. The waiter reassures him—in Italy this appears to be not indulgence but a logical response—and gives him a huge slab of cherry cake.

I am talking to an acquaintance at the Jesuit Curia on the Borgo Santo Spirito. It has been a long time since a man has tried to pinch my bottom in Rome, and I tell him so. Italian men are no longer so crude as they were twenty years ago, he says. "They are very mothered, here, not the terrifying infants one sees in America." Perhaps he says this to save my feelings.

A baker emerges from his silent shop, shading his eyes against the sun, and says: "A door in a door." In an anonymous wall on a long lonely street in southern Trastevere is a small door set in a larger door, and beyond it— beyond the metallic clamor of the world—is an enclosed garden world, completely beautiful, enigmatic, in which everything seems symbolic, though sadly one does not know of what. We are enveloped in the fragrance of orange blossoms and jasmine. Red, yellow, and white birds fly, like birds in a child's picture book, through arches of red roses. An elderly woman is sprinkling the roses with a hose (the fat drops of water catch the liquid light) . . . what a lovely, useful occupation. Nuns in black robes embrace a little girl who is eating chocolate cookies. A strolling priest wears, on his white robes, a felt cross, one that a child might have made, the red and blue stitches untidy and irregular. On the loggias there are pots and pots of homely marigolds; vines twine around octagonal columns. We are in a cloister of a building that presents a blind face to a blind street; its windows open to the cloister; in one of them we see a domestic tableau: two women at a table; one is shelling peas. "Do you take guests?" Lala asks the custodian; he doesn't answer. No one will tell us. We greedily imagine having apartments in this building. A young man and woman holding hands swing down the steps and into the crystalline light. Do they live here? Mystery in this clear light makes Lala restless. In the center of the cloister is a well—a tabby cat sits on it—framed by two marble columns.

Trastevere was home to sailors as early as the first century after Christ (sailors from Ravenna worked the awnings of the Colosseum); it was also home to Jews who were for the most part prisoners of war who had regained their freedom from their masters. (It is estimated that around the middle of the first century A.D. there were about forty thousand Jews in Rome.) Trastevere had since Republican times been a port for the unloading of goods that came from Ostia; it was home, as a consequence, to dockers, warehousemen, carpenters, and businessmen.

This is the fifteenth-century cloister of the Convent of San Giovanni Battista dei Genovesi, built in 1481 as a hospice for Genoese sailors who entered the river port. (Rome's first palm tree was planted here in 1588; an inscription on one of the octagonal columns that support the double loggia commemorates this date.)

Entrance to this magic place is theoretically achieved by ringing the bell for the custodian from three to five on weekdays; in practice, it takes a certain amount of luck and persistence to get in. I have more than once stood before that door hearing the bell create its own silence.

All around this building are forbidding institutions for the mentally ill (sometimes when the dogs bark at night I imagine it is their cries I hear) and for young delinquents and the unemployed.

We are in a neighborhood where aggressive obelisks flourish—in wide and desolate space, and on the curious face of the Church of Santa Maria dell'Orto, which has (I think) six obelisks. (St. Mary of the Garden is the English translation of this name, such a pretty name; this section was—though now so bleak—once bountiful farmland . . . but I never see signs of bounty here; I see funerals, never weddings.)

Not far from the cloister of San Giovanni Battista—a cloister which suggests to me that this particular form of architecture is meant to remind us that God assumed human flesh, that He, born of woman, walked in gardens, that the road to Gethsemane is the road to salvation—is the tiny Via di Santa Cecilia, which empties into the Piazza of Santa Cecilia, home, beyond great iron gates, of the Church of Santa Cecilia in Trastevere. The church is built upon the house in which she lived with her mate, Valerianus, and was martyred. This places us on such intimate terms with her; it is as if our prayers were joined to hers from the springs of the earth . . . literally from the springs of the earth. Below the church are the remains of the steam baths in which St. Cecilia underwent the first stage of her martyrdom, by suffocation.

Patrician Cecilia, virgin, patron saint of music and musicians, was married against her will to Valerianus; her marriage was not sexually consummated. She converted Valerianus and also his brother Tiburtius, both of whom were beheaded. Thereafter, Cecilia, unshakable in her faith, was arrested and sentenced to death in her own sudatorium; she miraculously survived the steam (it is rather wonderful to be able to see the lead steam pipes that were to have been the agent of her death) and as a consequence was beheaded. Her head was severed incompletely from her body, and she lay dying for three days, during which time she brought two hundred souls to God.

At her wedding she sang in her heart to God, disregarding nuptial music and merriment. It is no wonder her husband, too—God is fair—became a saint.

. . . "No," Lala says; "she is patron saint of music because she sang after her head was *completely severed.*" I prefer this version myself.

"The church is like a ballroom," Lala says (she loves the refined extravagance of this Roman Baroque), "cupolas like meringues."

In the body of the church the overall impression is of pale blue, and gray columns delicately gilded; St. Cecilia is elegantly housed. Her body was found, next to that of her long-suffering husband, who apparently chose to have chastity as a gift, in a catacomb on the Appian Way. She was very small, only five and a half palms in length; she lay on her right side, wrapped in a golden robe, facedown as if in sleep. On her neck were wounds made by three blows of the executioner's sword. Her tomb was opened in 1599, and

Stefano Maderno was brought to see her. The sculpture he made in imitation of her body reclines under the high altar of Santa Cecilia in a black-marble recess. It is one of the most lyrical in Christendom. Some people profess to find it gruesome, but that is affectation or a superficial response. Some tender gesture seems called for: You want to push her marble hair away from her marble eyes. There is a hairline split between her head and neck. Her draped body is eloquent of the calm of an accepted death. One should like to assume that trusting posture in death; it speaks of a lifetime of trust.

Below the church—much and frequently altered since the fifth century, when it was a simple sanctuary to St. Cecilia—is an exquisite crypt, vaulted ceilings upheld by the slenderest of pillars. This crypt, an imitation of the Byzantine, was completed in 1901; it would be a snobbish mistake to allow this fact to spoil one's pleasure in its sea-green and turquoise-blue and gold mosaics (a princess of the sweetest disposition and most refined sensibilities would be at home here). To this crypt we owe the world of streets and rooms below; a whole world of fallen antiquity was discovered when it was excavated.

St. Cecilia was saved from suffocation by a healing dew.

In fact, little is known of St. Cecilia; all this is legend.

When we come up from the ancient world, music, sweet voices, fill the candle-pungent air; the music comes from a chapel behind a grille (though it gave me pleasure to think it came from Cecilia's house, below; one feeds on innocent fancies in Rome). Benedictine nuns are singing the Mass. The nuns, in white, are old; one is bent over double; their voices are young. They work the land. Lala says that going to their convent schools—where they teach "embroidery and graces"—is, for people of good family, like going to . . . "What is that school Jean Harris taught at?" Lala always brings me back to the present—for her time past and time present often seem to belong to the same dimension—when I am lost in mists . . . or healing dew. (But when I ask her if she thinks the priest who celebrates the Mass is handsome, she censures me.)

I fancy we have walked in upon a private rite—Santa Cecilia is a terribly romantic church—but the nuns are in fact meant to be heard; there are microphones and speakers throughout the church. Never mind. Sensation and spectacle can coexist with heartfelt prayer. The nuns look wise. They preserve an engaging and venerable tradition: They weave the pallia— narrow bands of white wool decorated with six black crosses—that only the Pope, as shepherd of Christ's flock, may wear. On January 21, the feast day of St. Agnes, two lambs are brought in blue-ribboned wicker baskets to the altar of the church bearing her name during the singing of the "Agnus Dei" ("Lamb of God . . . have mercy on us . . . grant us peace"). They are blessed by the Holy Father and kept by the nuns of Santa Cecilia until Holy Thursday, and then they are shorn and the pallia are made from them, symbol of Christ's innocence.

St. Agnes, like St. Cecilia, suffered martyrdom by beheading. Like St. Cecilia, St. Agnes came from a patrician family; she was beautiful; and she was denounced by a spurned suitor—she, like Cecilia, had resolved to live a life of purity and abstinence—and, at the age of thirteen, she was sent to a Roman house of prostitution. Miraculously she kept her virginity; but she lost her head. Perhaps she and St. Cecilia keep each other company in Heaven; I myself would find them admirable but not entirely congenial.

Among the old-fashioned raised beds of flowers in the courtyard garden of the Church of Santa Cecilia is a massive marble fountain in the shape of a classical vase; water rises from it in a thin jet and falls into a marble basin. The fountain urn is much admired. I think it is silly and disproportionate.

The garden is full of laughing children.

From the windows of the building into which the dramatic iron gates are set Lala sees jeans and underwear flapping. There are clotheslines and there are flats everywhere in Rome; here, too; Lala is appalled. "What will the tourists think?" Her convent-trained soul picks unexpected moments to be injured . . . and she is still mulling over the occupancy of the cloister of San Giovanni Battista; she is tolerant of unorthodox arrangements, but only if they are carefully explained to her. (I am enchanted, yet she, who is "lapsed," needs the old ways more than I.)

In one of the windows there is a canary in a birdcage; if the Angel of Death strikes here, he will take the smallest member of the household—the yellow bird. As if the spirit of St. Cecilia were not enough protection. I am appalled. Lala is not. "Even my name sounds pagan," she says, "and you have to remember I was married three times."

The way to think of Trastevere is that it is a village of small houses and that within this village there are villages. The center of village life is the piazza.

Milanesi live in *cortili,* in courtyards; Florentines live in *piazze;* Romans live on *le scale,* the steps; so an Italian anthropologist says.

Sunday afternoon: On the banks of the sluggish Tiber are the Mercedeses and the Volvos of Romans who have come to the Piazza dei Mercanti in a country-picnic spirit. The sleepy square, once the center of maritime activity, is guaranteed to give one a case of déjà vu. We have seen this piazza—or one very much like it—in old prints; it lacks only beggars dressed in picturesque rags and a black crone to complete the scene. Houses with outdoor steps, their landings extensions of living room and kitchen . . . Where I grew up, Italian girls got married and moved "down the stoop" (houses away, on the same block) from their families; all the mothers and the daughters sat on stoops; grandmothers kept vigil above on pillows draped across windowsills. We were doing the homemaking, the gardening, and the landscaping of the world; the business of births, deaths, marriages was in our hands; to men belonged the machinery of progress and of commerce, the business of business. . . . This is the Trastevere of one's imagining (sienna, ocher, rose, wisteria), oppressive with history, but alive with somber happiness. Or so at first one thinks. It is lined, however, with theatrical restaurants (several of which are said to be owned by an American who once understudied the funereal part of Judd in *Oklahoma!*). A few years ago chariot races were held here for the benefit of tourists, for whom the piazza was "restored." It seems meanspirited not to like it, though, in spite of its charm's being contrived. The Roman sweethearts and families eating in the noisy restaurant to which I go are having such a rollicking good time (singing with the accordion player, eating lusty food) that I decide to commit myself to liking it. On the wall there is graffiti—"seventeenth century," a waiter says. "This used to be a dungeon." Well, *forse che sì, forse che no;* the piazza is not entirely ersatz . . . and if it were . . . why not surrender to its sunny charm?

Lala, who is suspicious of the out-of-doors when it doesn't have a church in it, says, "How can anyone know exactly what they think all the time and write it down as if it were law?" These are the words of a woman trained in medicine who fears wrong diagnoses; she is speaking of Luigi Barzini, whom she calls "that Austrian who loved himself better than he loved Rome." She invites me to take her words to heart. I am of two minds about the Piazza dei Mercanti; this pleases her. One mind is never enough for her.

The sunken Piazza in Piscinula, on the Tiber in southern Trastevere, the narrow streets around it full of weathered gay houses, is more to Lala's liking: It has a church—San Benedetto in Piscinula, the smallest Romanesque church in Rome—and is, unlike Mercanti, a real focal point of neighborhood life—not just restaurants (under an awning: a very angry arrabbiata, carpaccio with chunks of *parmigiano* and *insalata verde*) but a *tabacchi,* a *gelateria,* a coffee bar. Across from the trellised restaurant where I often eat on Sunday afternoons after church, when this part of Rome is so contentedly at collective ease, is the Casa Mattei, a large building, front to the river, back to the piazza (public/private, grand/domestic), that has accreted since the twelfth century: terraces, courtyards, marble statuary, and (seen through barred windows) a chrome kitchen, high-tech. . . . When I think of this piazza, it is resting in a golden glow, and it smells of honeysuckle and of fish. On one of the streets leading to the piazza, there is a marble plaque of a fish; in the Middle Ages this was probably a fish market. Earlier it may have been a Roman bath. (Fortunately Mussolini never got around to excavating here, or this oasis, self-contained, would be lost to us.)

No one from *Oklahoma!* could have fabricated this piazza. One wouldn't wish to add, subtract, or change a thing. On Sundays it is perfect in its sleepy, unastounding way: On the restaurant terrace a man reads his newspaper, his wife drifts in a summery dream, once in a while they pull themselves back to each other and smile; a boy in shirtsleeves rides his bike on its back wheel, wide-eyed, nut brown, and self-absorbed. He looks as if he is on the verge of some enormous revelation, of some disclosure; this is how they seduce, these Roman boys: They give you to understand that they have secrets, and that they will tell.

At the *gelateria* tourists pore over maps and are indulged by appraising waiters. . . . The piazza purrs, it hums; there is a sense of family life, a million stories, all around; one is cocooned in others' stories but bears no responsibility for them; voyeurism is implicitly endorsed; this is ease.

What is most often said about Trastevere is that it looks like a stage set, and indeed it is hard to believe that the narrow alleys, the small ocher buildings with their projecting roofs from which wildflowers grow, the grapevines, the wisteria, even the "backhouses," were not so arranged for effect. At the same time, there is absolutely nothing one can isolate and say: *"This* was put here to produce *that* effect"; its separate parts are organic to the whole. Here is a stiff blue rosette on a sienna house: A baby boy has been born. Here is a wrecked building in which jasmine grows and a picture of St. Francis still stands. Here is life celebrated in the open: neighborhood bars where dark men in shirtsleeves exercise territorial rites; houses open for living, curtains parted—one knows what their inhabitants wear, what they eat, what music they listen to. . . . This is one definition of generosity . . . perhaps it is necessity; perhaps not yielding to necessity is always mean.

Here, in a small, unobtrusive building, is a hospital—for skin diseases, Lala says, but no one dares to say he is going to it because it is immediately assumed that he has syphilis. (I shall have to ask the contessa—who introduces me to barons, counts, all of them over seventy, and several of them syphilitic—what she has to say of this.)

Here are four men mincing menacingly toward Lala and me; they carry black-and-scarlet fans.

Here, set in a bucolic basin of a piazza, steps leading away from it up to the Janiculum, snuggled next to Porta Settimiana, hugging that ancient wall, is Romolo, the trattoria which, according to legend, was the home of Raphael's mistress and model, Margherita Luti—"La Fornarina," the baker's daughter. This is the story as Romolo—who tells us it comes from "a document"—has it:

"One day Michelangelo left St. Peter's by mule and came to Via Lungara to see what [Raphael] was doing. He went into the Farnesina"—the place where Raphael was painting wall frescoes for the Sienese merchant banker Agostino Chigi—"but there was no reply. The scaffolding was still up, also the ladder. Michelangelo went up and looked around. Perhaps he found pleasure in the virgin surface prepared to receive the paint but as yet untouched, for he took a brush and rapidly drew the head of an angel in black. Then he left.

"Returning, Raphael, climbing up onto the scaffolding, saw Michelangelo's unmistakable hand. . . . 'While we were at Romoletto . . . Michelangelo was here.'

"The lunette was not touched. It is the only one ever done in black. And it is still called the Visiting Card of Michelangelo."

Raphael—whose "grace, industry, looks, modesty, and excellence of character" Vasari attributes to the fact that he was "suckled by his own mother and . . . trained in childhood in the family ways at home rather than in the houses of peasants or common people"—is said by Vasari to have been "a very amorous man with a great fondness for women . . . always indulging his sexual appetites"; Chigi was obliged to move Raphael's mistress into the palace where he was working; "and that was how the painting was finished." Raphael's paintings are the paintings of a man who loved women.

The restaurant he is said to have frequented is all arbored and terraced and candlelit and full of tourists from Germany and groups from UNICEF and American priests with their mothers and sisters and aunts; North African waiters, to Lala's horror, serve us. Lala thinks every restaurant with an awning or a trellis is a tourist trap, not understanding that it is in just such places that tourists wish to be trapped; leafy green bowers inspire her to count her lire in nervous anticipation of being rooked; the addition of a guitarist is too much for her, she launches into a learned diatribe about salmonella. Prey to the specters of looming poverty and infectious bacteria, she is ordering only a *primo,* a first course; an American honeymooning couple ask for help with the menu, and Lala, convent-trained to be obliging, translates it in its entirety: six *antipasti,* four *minestre,* eight *pastasciutta,* three *bolliti,* eight *pesce,* two *fritti,* nine *arrosti,* sixteen *umidi,* eight *contorni, formaggi,* four *frutta di stagione, dolce* . . . and, with specials, all in all, seventy dishes . . . by which time Lala's own bucatini all'Amatriciana is stone cold, as are the expressions on the faces of the North African waiters; and the Americans give every appearance of contemplating action for divorce.

At Galeassi I sip my wine diverted by funky chic—men and women dressed stylishly, some casually, some whorishly; and Roman Rajneeshis. Next door, at Sabatini, radiant young girls, self-contained in lacy white, like flocks of birds, celebrate their First Communion with their families; they are enjoying the sweetest relaxation, that which comes after the enactment of ritual. (I know just how the pearlized, white, onionskin missals they hold in white-gloved hands smell. For me it once was the most romantic smell on earth, forbidden, exotic, singular.) They are resplendent with the consciousness of innocent achievement.

In the warmth of contemplation, I am in the Piazza of Santa Maria in Trastevere, the heart of northern Trastevere, full of light; the figureless fountain plays and catches light; the mosaics on the facade of the beautiful Church of Santa Maria in Trastevere shine, giving and taking light. The girls in white chatter, the fountain chatters; all is, at a level below and beyond the lovely push and pull of lovely ordinary life, serene. A blue-and-gold mosaic Virgin is enthroned among mosaic palm trees.

At night the cobbled square is illuminated by electric light (and, as a waiter tells me with every appearance of sincerity, "by the moon, which is more important than the sun because it shines when we need it more"). This is said to be the site of the oldest church in Rome, the first one dedicated to the Virgin, and also of a fountain of pure oil that sprang from the earth thirty-eight years before the birth of Christ (or, in another version, at the moment of the Savior's birth), to herald the forthcoming diffusion of grace and joy.

Lala walks toward me from behind Santa Maria. She, who has warned me against any display of wealth, is ablaze with jewels—"paste," she says.

"But how will a robber know it is only paste? He will drag you away by the straps of your purse," I say, mimicking her words to me. "What terrible logic Americans have," she says.

Lala takes me to a place called Mario, where we have baby lamb, grilled breast of turkey, spinach cooked in butter, white wine, mineral water, and coffee. The slattern who waits on us has filthy nails, the tables are covered with sheets of gray-white paper (stained), and the lavatory facilities are a hole in the ground behind a curtain. This immensely reassures Lala, as does the bill, which is ridiculously low. A hunchback comes in to sell lottery tickets, a local crazy man comes in and shouts meaningless abuse. Lala looks as if she has done something clever.

"It is amusing for you," Lala says. She cannot come to grips with the boutiques that have sprung up all around, trinkets from Africa and India, or, for that matter, the Chinese restaurants that are opened one week and closed the next, on streets that branch out from Santa Maria. "It is amusing for you to see a van try to make its way through a narrow alley lined with cars faced in both directions, for you it is a spectacle. For me, no; where there is traffic there is rudeness," she says, and as if to prove her point, a Fiat, in an attempt to park, climbs the pavement on which we walk, nipping at our heels. On the other hand, I say, Romans walk for hours every day. "House-wives walk for food," she says, *"punto."*

In front of Benny Burger the sidewalk is being swept with angry energy, and refuse flies in my face. The bright lights of the *viale* are like the sad bright lights of any provincial town.

Twin images of goodness: water and oil. Everything is soothed by oil; everything is purified by water. Think of Trastevere as innocence frayed; innocence renewable.

Sunday morning: The flea market at the Porta Portese, used car parts, peanuts, pens, panty hose, cotton candy, Tina Turner records, watches, nameless junk. Nuns pick through piles of scanty underwear. Used clothes, bicycles, kitchenware, prints, purses, jeans, army surplus goods. Stalls under gay striped awnings. Built high against the Portuense Wall are shacks of tarpaulin and corrugated steel (bikes are sold in them, and used car parts); they are reached by immovable ladders, and some of these ladders are old and useless, ropy vines have covered them; and some of the ladders, flat, not perpendicular against the wall, are so far off the ground one wonders if anyone is meant to gain entrance to these shacks by honest means. Shoes, sneakers, cigarette lighters, corsets, snuff. Dry goods and the stuff of daily living lined up against an ancient and beautiful wall, antiques displayed on the prosaic *viale*.

The crowd turns surly in the sun. Tourists groan. Short of a helicopter, there is no way out of this tunnel/funnel, the wall on one side, stalls on the other. This is not what they expected: priests shopping for used sweaters; nylons three to a box. "Four kilometers more," someone says, whereupon I have a violent coughing fit. A man who specializes in silk scarves produces a folding chair and warns smokers away from me (I long for a cigarette, in fact). "Is it your heart?" they ask. It is a muscle pulled as a result of coughing and of claustrophobia. "It is not my heart," I say. *"Speriamo,"* they say; their fatalism is not unkind. It is now one o'clock. "My son will drive you home," the stallkeeper says. A spasm of irritation crosses the son's face; he has other inclinations, I am sure; if I were a boy, he would adore to drive me home . . . as it is. . . . Four men confer. The oldest suggests the Red Cross, a helicopter. I would rather die. (I am of the same blood as a cousin of mine who died in the ladies' room of a hotel at a doctors' convention choking on a piece of creamed chicken rather than call attention to the embarrassing fact that she was dying, humiliation being worse than tragedy at almost any time.) "He will drive you all the way to Brooklyn," the father says, warming to his matchmaking task. "Brooklyn is full of bandits," the petulant boy says dismissively. "And Trastevere is not?" I say. His father pretends to think this is very funny; he does not pretend that he is not pretending. When at last I seem recovered, the four men tell me there is a way out of this treadmill—a hidden gate. Another conference ensues: Is the gate a kilometer away or a hundred meters away? On and on they go. My having been in extremis is forgotten. Italians love to argue about distances, directions (in my family, whole holidays are spent in discussions of the upper versus the lower level of the Verrazano Bridge); they send me on my way. I stop at a roadside shrine to "the Madonna of *noialtri*"; this is my Sunday worship.

It is difficult to tell, in Trastevere, what it is that apparent candor masks.

Nowhere else but in Italy would the Holy Father be vocally admired because he makes a *bella figura*—cuts a fine figure.

*   *   *

Italians have trace memories of the past, body memories. Not to eat well is translated here not to eat *molto*—not to eat "a lot."

There are two ways to drive to St. Peter's from Trastevere: along the leafy Lungotevere, lined with Renaissance *palazzi*—the result of the Papacy's impulse to cleanse and beautify the malarial swamps alongside the Tiber in order to provide a fit setting for the jewel of St. Peter's—and over the leafy Janiculum Hill along the Aurelian Wall. It is a toss-up as to which is more beautiful. If I were forced to choose, I would drive along the Lungotevere, where the sacred and the profane converge by papal design. I would drive this way (as I do so often in memory) because to do so is to pass the Bridge and the Castle of Sant'Angelo, the one exuberant, the other austere—ten Bernini angels on the elegant bridge, a single golden angel sheathing his sword on the castle-fortress; he is the archangel Michael.

Some days in Rome one is of the opinion that everything is in the approach.

St. Peter's is the most exciting square in the world to enter, in part (thanks to Bernini's elliptical colonnades) because of its spectacular, enclosing, embracing symmetry; in part because of its immensity (one day I counted twelve tourist buses in the square, they were swallowed up in space—but Moscow and Mexico City boast larger squares); in great part because of our preknowledge of it and its associations. The visible heartbeat of Christ's Church on earth, to which millions of pilgrims have brought their bodies and their prayers, is also a miracle of design; Bernini completed the square in two years (whereas it took the workmen hired by Donald Trump fifteen months to construct an Italian marble dining table for one of Mr. Trump's residences). And our great expectations—refreshed, not diminished, each time we visit—are enhanced by the brush of an alarming thrill that we may not be (cannot possibly be) "up" to this and by the even greater alarm that we may indeed rise to it—and be changed by it forever.

Stendhal, who called the Square of St. Peter's "the most beautiful in existence" and the Church of St. Peter's "the world's most beautiful edifice," was obliged to remark that "one cannot help worshipping the religion that produces such things" in spite of his conviction that he was witnessing "the ceremonies of a religion that is going to undergo change and die out." (We no sooner read Stendhal empathetically than we are faced with the fact that

he considered a lie the proper embellishment of the truth. We ask ourselves
if it can be true that he witnessed this in St. Peter's: "The Savior's blood [the
chalice of wine] was brought to the Pope seated on his throne behind the
altar, and he sucked it with a gold straw." How utterly barbaric that gold
straw makes the ritual sound. . . . Barbaric enough to account for Henry
James's calling the celebrant of the Mass in St. Peter's "the Grand Lama
. . . that flaccid old woman" [for once James did not go in for subtlety] and
for his turning away sickened by the "absolute *obscenity*" of the Mass.
. . . What a rascal Stendhal was, and how interesting it would have been
if William James had accompanied his brother to Rome.)

It has been said of Bernini's forecourt that while "the eye sees one thing
(a certain grand intimacy) . . . the feet feel another (unexpectedly great
distances)." Thus one sense is pitted against another "for a powerfully
unsettling experience."* The great square is "felt" as much as it is seen: the
obelisk that stands in the center of the piazza, on the spot where Peter was
once thought to have greeted his martyrdom; the four candelabra surrounding it; the generous fountains on either side of it; the saints—rapt and poised
for flight, or dance—so beautifully articulated on Bernini's magnificent
circular colonnade. . . .

Midmorning—ten-thirty—I came one day to post a letter here (Rome's
post office being, as James said, "the thing in Rome you like least"); and all
the lights all around were on, sun blazing, and the fountains were not
playing, the world was in reverse. "They have pushed the wrong button,"
the taxi driver said laconically, and I felt that the Square of St. Peter's was
home to magic, a feeling I get whenever I stand on one of the two stones
set in the pavement between the fountains and the obelisk, the stones from
which, by the alchemy of perspective, the rows of columns four deep of the
colonnades appear to be a single row. These tricks of perspective always seem
to me a kind of taunting of the rules of nature, a flouting of the rules, impish:
pagan.

The colonnades are smelly. They have a river smell: dank. Old men rest
in their shadows. Bernini designed the colonnades for processionals of cardinals and princes—the central aisle of columns is wide enough for coaches
to pass each other—but few people choose to walk here, even on a day of
killing sun. There seems to be a tacit agreement to give the space over to
the very old, the indigent, and the unhappy young, who sprawl and prowl
here, sipping warm soda, looking sullen and bored, a threatening combina-

*Kent C. Bloomer and Charles W. Moore, *Body, Memory, and Architecture.*

tion. Life is never boring, and it is particularly not boring in Rome, how discontented they must be.

In front of the *Pietà* (violent, personal, mystical): "It must be very hard to lose your son at that age," a woman says. "But He was God!" her male companion says, with more assurance than I have that His being God made it easier for Mary, who must have taken pleasure in His first step and first tooth and first word and all the ordinary things—even after, at the age of twelve, He went into the Temple (confusing and disarming her) to do His Father's business. "The most important thing," another man says, rapping his knuckles on the ugly Plexiglas that has distanced and protected Michelangelo's masterpiece since a madman took a chisel to it some years ago (providing us with definitive proof that the workings of an insane mind are conclusively opaque and that madness is never romantic and never instructive), "the most important thing is *muscles.* . . ."

In this light (is it the light?) Christ—a long, thin God—looks waxen; she who holds Him in her arms has the face of a girl and the body of a woman, a woman who has suffered the irremediable grief, the death of a child. It would have been kind for Jesus to appear first to His mother upon His resurrection, but He did not.

I am very glad that I did not know, when I first saw the *Pietà,* that Michelangelo was only twenty-five when he completed it, which remarkable fact would have absorbed all my attention.

For me it is impossible to experience the whole of the interior of the Basilica of St. Peter's without mediation. My head is full of arguments derived from literature: St. Peter's is absurdly vulgar, it is absurdly pretty; it is vast, it is disappointingly small; it is beautiful, it is pretentious. . . .

It is vast.

(My mind translates the unlovely wooden and cloth dividers that are used for traffic control into attempts to domesticate huge space. Necessity demands them; but one [very good] definition of a basilica is "an enclosed volume open to the daylight," and they play havoc with the mind's ability to perceive the basilica's space in that liberating way.)

If one were to have snapped one's fingers and said, "For the glory of God, let there appear something between the sterile Duomo of Florence and the loot-full Basilica of San Marco," the result might have been St. Peter's. Perpetual golden sunlight bathes and emanates from the high altar—honeyed light from Bernini's window, which seems to come directly from his depiction of the Holy Spirit, the dove; pellucid light from the windows in Michelangelo's perfect cupola. Light calls to the light of Bernini's bronze baldaquin. . . . This place humbles words and elucidates their meaning: "In the beginning was the Word and the Word was with God and the Word was God"; but, in the beginning: "Let there be Light!" The Word is God; "God is light, and in him is no darkness at all." This is an articulate light, an essay in the theology of the Word. (St. Augustine compared Jesus' birth to light passing through a window.) One comes away with one fixed and lasting impression: the glitter of gold, the dull gleam of brass. Light, imperial light, not the light of kitchens and gardens—the light Mary knew—but the sovereign light of God which she saw when her son was raised.

Beneath the baldaquin, on the balustrade that surrounds the sunken *confessio,* ninety-five gilded bronze lamps burn perpetually. The lamps are in the shape of flowers, and the flame is a flower arising from flower: leaf, flower, leaves, flame, light unto light.

A nimbus surrounds the bronze statue of Peter, too—poor Peter, the butt of so many good-natured Italian jokes, the Rock upon which the Church is built, but "a simple man and unlettered"—his toes shiny from the kisses of the faithful, his peasant body short and squat, his face fine-boned, aristocratic.

("You remember," Chesterton said, "Saint Peter was crucified upside down. . . . He saw the landscape as it really is, with stars like flowers, and the clouds like hills, and all men hanging on the mercy of God." He chose, in extreme humility, to be crucified upside down so as not to share the fate of Christ.)

San Marco is the glory of God reflected in man. St. Peter's is the glory of God.

Of course it is easy to feel atomized here—and even to lose sight of God in one's harried pursuit: He is here . . . He is there . . . He is here. . . . He seems architecturally to clamor for our attention, so many reminders of Him in archetype and image, metal and stone; He is almost, if that were possible, too much here, and our pursuit of Him—His everywhereness—makes Him seem peculiarly illusive, and results in spiritual exhaustion. . . . For which the remedy is steadfast immersion in one or another detail: the lovely blind, fat cherubs supporting stoups of holy water; the radiant side chapel of the Holy Sacrament, where the Eucharist is perpetually adored (radiance in a confined space radiates more). . . .

Sometimes nothing seems to answer to it. Dizziness is the result of one's exertions; one is jelly. In such extremity one must gaze upward at Michelangelo's dome—the still point of this dazzling world.

("A man jumped from the dome," someone says, conjuring up an image of torment with a smile.)

This is what remains: warm sun on cool gray stone, an essay in light, light from a source different from familiar elements, but not remote; light that is like water, one is buoyed in it; light that is tender, but not insistent; light of the world, light that says: Nothing separates you from God but Yes. Mary is His mother; she said Yes. Light that is gold, that is glass:

> And the city was pure gold, like unto clear glass.
>
> And the foundations of the wall of the city were garnished with all manner of precious stone. The first foundation was jasper; the second, sapphire; the third, a chalcedony; the fourth, an emerald . . . sardonyx . . . sardius . . . chrysolite . . . topaz . . . chrysoprasus . . . jacinth . . . amethyst.
>
> And the twelve gates were twelve pearls; every several gate was one of pearl: and the street of the city was pure gold, as it were transparent glass. . . .
>
> For the glory of God did lighten it, and the Lamb is the light thereof.
>
> —*Rev. 21: 18–23*

Belief sometimes precedes understanding; faith sometimes precedes scientific evidence. For centuries Christians have believed that Peter was buried on the Vatican Hill, underneath St. Peter's Basilica, near Nero's Circus, scene of theatrical obscenities—human bodies covered with pitch, set on fire, and used as torches to light the way for Nero's nocturnal promenades; dogs ripping apart Christians covered in animal skins—and of Peter's crucifixion on the south side of the basilica.

His tomb was found by chance, for which another word may be Providence. In 1939, in the course of preparations for the tomb of Pius XI in the crypt of the basilica, artifacts from Constantine's fourth-century basilica (upon which the Renaissance church is built) came to light; Pius XII ordered excavation and archaeological examination of the area called the *sacre grotte*— the chambers between the floor level of Constantine's basilica, which is approximately level to the *confessio,* and the floor level of the present basilica—and of the ground beneath the papal altar. (It would not be surprising, though it might be ironic, if it were for that act that Pius XII, controversial and in large part unloved, will be remembered; this kind of fact acts as a brake on certain kinds of perplexity.)

What was discovered under the Renaissance church, and under Constantine's basilica, which preceded it, was a buried open-air cemetery, a necropolis built alongside a road that ran along the northern side of Nero's Circus. What was also discovered, among the graves of the poor, was the tomb of Peter and what many believe (but the Church declines to state authoritatively) are his bones.

Here is a lovely mystery. The tomb was there—glimpsed—all along. Every modern pilgrim has passed it, unaware (except perhaps as something holy in the very air): Constantine enclosed the "trophy" or monument to St. Peter in a marble structure. Pope Clement built a protective wall around it. After the excavations of 1940–1949, the wall built by Clement was taken down, and the rear of the box (into which archaeologists bore holes) was seen. Visitors can see it now, a chest of marble and of porphyry. (Imagine a seed in a casket, like a hidden jewel in a fairy tale.) It has always been venerated, always taken care of, as though, as one visitor remarked, "each transformation (even the most demanding ones) seemed to want to respect the previous situation . . . to pass its essence on to subsequent generations." To Constantine's work, Calixtus added. And Gregory the Great raised the presbytery so that the highest point of the monument could be used as an altar. It is extremely difficult to grasp this tangled archaeological find, this complicated architectural knot, without looking at a model or a diagram. Picture a series of nesting boxes, the magical boxes of childhood, images of infinity.

This tomb is the heart and soul of St. Peter's; he is indeed the rock upon which the church/Church is built.

In this necropolis the frescoes are fresh and bright; the air is sweet. It is one of the most beautiful places in Rome.

One's explorations begin with a licit thrill that feels illicit: To visit the excavations, one must go past the Swiss Guards, who lower their lances upon your approach and raise them again when you say to them: *"Ufficio scavi."* And then one has the rather wonderful feeling that one has entered the heart of the heart of the walled city. Men have died for this place.

One descends.

The funerary inscriptions tell us that these were, in large part, the graves of former slaves, freed men, or, as our guide, on casual terms with the ancient dead, says, "nouveaux riches." The niches that hold the little monuments of the dead look like little houses; they are quite attractive, really; one can see why chairs and benches were carved out of tufa, hardened volcanic ash, for the use of celebrants at Roman *refrigerium* banquets, the occasions for reconciliation among relatives, for rehearsal of the memory of the dead and for the joy of the food that was the symbol of the invisible presence of the dead; one can see that the banquets might be pleasant, tender. There are inscriptions on the tombs; they are wonderful. For his epitaph a man called Valerio had this: "A jolly good person . . . always played jokes and never quarreled with anyone." (Lots of us would settle for less.) Pagans and Christians rest together here (though "rest in peace" is inscribed only on Christian tombs, a gift of the resurrection for which they wait; and pagans were cremated, Christians not). In this place of narrow streets and pretty winding walls of warm red brick, frescoes of Isis, Jupiter, Minerva appear, and so, in mosaic, gold and vernal, does Christ, driving a chariot like that of Apollo, surrounded by green leaves; he is the Sun, the light of salvation. The mosaics—of peacocks and quail (symbols, for pagans and Christians alike, of immortality, cousin to the phoenix, which rises), animals and fruit—are exquisite. It is like a day in the country to be here; it *was* a day in the country once. One of the nicer things about the Romans was their incorporating the dead into the life of the living—tombs in gardens, villas, and amusement parks.

The grave of St. Peter is under Bernini's canopy. He was buried looking toward the sunrise.

Is he here? Are these his bones?

This much is certain: This grave, a simple one, covered with terra-cotta tiles (which are very nearly indestructible), was constantly visited; the wall next to the monument is covered with hundreds of Christian graffiti (the names of Christ and Peter and Mary are identifiable); hundreds of coins have been found, from all over Europe, including Scandinavia, and imperial coins dating from Augustus. St. Peter's head is drawn upon the wall, presumably by a workman, in coal, together with this inscription: "Oh, Peter, pray that those chosen of the faithful be buried near you!" This evidence, and evidence more esoteric and less picturesque, has convinced Vatican archaeologists and scientists, notoriously difficult to convince, that this is the tomb of Peter.

The basis of some of the evidence is reassuringly homely; for example, the manufacturer's stamp on tiles used for water pipes dates the tomb.

Christianity is like that—concrete, just when we might expect it to be mystical. Our God did not come swooning among us in the clouds of some remote and mythical time and place; He came when Herod was king, when

Caesar Augustus sent out a decree that all the world should be taxed ("and this taxing was first made when Cyrenius was governor of Syria").

But are his bones here?

The bones of saints—*rest in peace*—were moved about a lot, Peter's, it is believed, to the Catacombs of St. Sebastian on the Appian Way, to avoid their being profaned. It may be that when persecution waned, they were transferred back to his tomb; if the idea was to hide them, it certainly worked, for they weren't discovered till the middle of our century. The head of Peter is supposed to be in the Lateran, the mother church of Rome. . . . Perhaps his trunk is buried here?

The question is moot (and, it can't be helped, a little ludicrous), for as our guide so nicely says, "that 'brain' is still down here . . . Peter himself? Why not? Peter as earth, foundation rock. . . . He is physically here in the impregnated earth. . . ."

"And if they are the wrong bones?" a tourist asks. He has all along been petulant, mysteries make him cranky.

"Fifty-fifty," the guide says, "perhaps, yes, perhaps the bones of an important Christian of the first century, perhaps, yes, perhaps someone unimportant." Our guide, an art historian, erudite and of ecstatic temperament, and funny, too, has been vexed by this fellow, who has insultingly and cynically asked him: "Are you telling facts or what you think? . . . But if it's just his *lower* bones . . ." he now says. . . .

"But each community would be glad to claim the fingernail of a much lesser saint. . . . It works. It doesn't matter. Peter is here."

It was Mencken, of all people, who said, "The Latin church has always kept clearly before it the fact that religion is not a syllogism but a poem." Peter is here as blood-impregnated dust, as overwhelming presence and idea.

We emerge into the sixteenth century, into the Clementine Chapel, the jewellike work of Giacomo della Porta. Above us is a grille. People walk above our heads. St. Peter is below. The ground moves beneath our feet.

Which is the real world?

Lala is high. She has never been to the *scavi* before; she is skipping like a girl. Up the Via della Conciliazione she goes, heckling shopkeepers of whose wares she disapproves. Whenever she sees one of those horrible pictures of Christ with moving eyes that follow you, she turns them back to front. "No wonder Protestants say we worship idols," she says, "to say nothing of that *other* group." By "that *other* group" she means Jews. Oh, Lala, how could you? How could anyone?

In Scripture Peter denied Christ three times. In folklore this is translated into quotidian transgressions: lust for the liver of a hare; the theft of a cabbage; a reluctance to confront the wrath of a woman.

"Once the Lord and St. Peter were going through a field, when out darted a hare from among the vegetable rows and bumped right into the Lord." So begins an enchanting traditional folktale retold by Italo Calvino.

In folklore St. Peter is a rustic, unable to deny his appetite for cabbages and hare livers, a conventional man, afraid of women, fretful, but aware of his weaknesses, a good friend and companion. The Lord forgives him. Empowered by the Lord, Peter brings blessings to the country people he meets; he promises he will not do anything to hurt the Lord again; of course he does.

"You are Peter and upon this Rock I will build my Church": permanence and grace built upon human imperfection, how comforting, and how magnificent.

It is absurd to see a garden from the tinted window of a bus, like making love with a sheet between. Gardens are not meant to be seen in the company of tired strangers. The poetry of the Vatican Gardens is no match for our German/English tour guide, who has the hearty and prosaic soul of a hockey-playing gamesmistress; she does not believe gardens are for lingering in. ("He's deaf," a woman says of her husband, jerking her thumb at him, confiding this information in a whisper to the guide. "Don't tell everyone I'm deaf!" he bellows. They bicker all the way, disturbing subtext on a summer day.)

Pius IX used to ride here upon a white mule.

It was he who defined the dogma of papal infallibility, and he who lost for the Papacy its political power. As a result of his labors, the Pope became "the prisoner of the Vatican"; it was not until 1929, under the terms of the Lateran Treaty, that the Pope was officially recognized as sovereign of the Vatican State, and not until 1958 that a Pope made pastoral visitations outside the principality. John Paul II—whom Romans call *il nostro polacco romano* (our Roman Pole)—is so peripatetic it is sometimes hard to remember that Paul VI was the first modern Pope to leave Italy.

Our visit among the calla lilies and the palms was perfunctory—though I marked well the sixteenth-century summer house, a series of small pavilions and terraces, where Leo X, amidst marble carvings of mythical figures, swans, pineapples, lobsters, lions, roosters, shells, doves, entertained and feasted. Poetry and music were heard then in these gardens—and ladies were invited, too; and also what Augustus Hare called "tricksome water works" (in particular an ugly Borghese fountain which we disembark to see; it seems to me the parent fountain of all those basins on pedestals I grew up [embarrassed] among in Brooklyn, shells and colored glass embedded in stucco, remarkable for the principle of accretion they exemplify).

The ridiculous self-important—and pleasing—little choo-choo train puffs, bloated with mail; iron doors bang shut on the frontier of a lilliputian state.

From exquisite courtyards and gardens, delicious fragrances waft up; on a June day the temptation to allow the window embrasures of the Vatican Museums to become the chief occasion for delight is overwhelming. The magnificent collections, so varied, rich, demanding—five miles of wall space, none of it neutral, architecture, sculpture, and painting a harmonious whole—are backdrop to a summer day.

No one loves spirals more than the Italians do; one enters the museums through an atrium at the foot of a lovely spiral ramp (actually, a ramp within a ramp—one for going up, the other for going down), which is itself a work of art.

Rush past the Gallery of Egyptian Art, so humorless. . . . Pause, in the octagonal courtyard of the Pio-Clementine Museum, to greet the Apollo Belvedere, and as you do so, if you are not much moved by this cold god who deposes that mortals must live in anguish while he remains untouched by pain, think how much more nineteenth-century writers preferred sculpture to painting. Consider why, in *The Marble Faun*, "To be a sculptor seems a distinction in itself; whereas a painter is nothing, unless individually eminent," Hawthorne said; in an essay on the paintings and sculpture of Rome, he wrote: "Yesterday we went to the sculpture galleries of the Vatican. I think I enjoy these noble galleries and their contents and the beautiful arrangement better than anything else in the way of art. . . . I saw the Apollo Belvedere as something ethereal and godlike; only for a moment, however, as if he had alighted from heaven, or shone suddenly out of the sunlight, and then had withdrawn himself again. . . ." Leonardo, on the other hand, argued for the superiority of painting over sculpture, as sculpture did not make use of "color, aerial perspective, or depict luminous or transparent bodies, clouds, storms." Leonardo, who argued that painting was superior to poetry because its images were more truthful, compared the mind of the painter with the mind of the Maker: "That divine power, which lies in the knowledge of the painter, transforms the mind of the painter into the likeness of the divine mind, for with a free hand he can produce different beings, animals, plants, fruits, landscapes, open fields, abysses, terrifying and fearful places."

Dorothy L. Sayers held out for the supremacy of words. Like Leonardo, she compared the mind of the artist-creator to the mind of God-the-Creator; she saw the act of an artist as "threefold—a trinity—experience, expression, recognition: the unknowable reality in the experience; the image of that reality known in its expression; and power in the recognition; the whole making up the single and indivisible act of a creative mind." Here we see in a mirror darkly; we behold only the images; we wait for that time when we shall see face to face—"in the place where image and reality are one." . . .

I know how to look at a painting—perhaps because I think it is looking back at me—whereas I think blind sculpture is blind to me and my concerns. . . . I also believe it is not unlikely that male writers of the nineteenth century gave the superiority to sculpture because painting was something "nice women," ladies, did. Sculpture was, or could be seen as, an act of male aggression or dominance over matter.

If you do not wish to think about these matters—or even if you do—stop in the Sala degli Animali (the Room of the Animals), a marble miscellany, a kiddie heaven, a stone zoo—eagle and hare and crabs of green porphyry (mosaics of asparagus, too); charming, they require very little effort (whereas, as Hawthorne correctly notes, a Transfiguration requires that the observer be transfigured, too: "It is the spectator's mood that transfigures the Transfiguration").

The square is full of cardinals and archbishops, purple and scarlet, and pilgrims from Calabria in native dress, hot in their velvet and lace, but pretty and gay for the investiture of a cardinal; banners and flags and bells.

On a pie-shaped building (part of the Apostolic Palace) beyond the right arm of the colonnade is a ceramic plaque of Mary, dressed in blue, her color. I love her, she draws the eye; she watches, she is very kind.

In the post office there are postcards of Pope Paul VI, and of his successor, John Paul I, who lived for the blink of an eye, and of John XXIII, beloved of all, and none of John Paul II . . . a curiosity (one has to assume that not everything means something; that is why stereotypes are useful).

On this day the Vatican post office becomes a town hall: An Australian priest is speaking up for American intervention in Nicaragua. I wish he would shut up. Someone else says: There is something to be said for South African whites, they have a point. Oh, go away.

I often fancy I can see the Pope move behind the curtain of his third-floor window; sometimes I think he sees me. But it is impossible, I find, to dwell long upon the private movements of a Pope; the prohibition against it is as strong as against incest.

Forty thousand square yards of space: Tapestries woven from cartoons by Raphael, which—graceful, elegant, powerful, and sweet—give the lie to anyone who dares to suggest his work is merely "pretty"; and his *stanze,* to which the eye must learn to adapt itself, as in these populous frescoes of the life of Christ, there is no "white space." . . . Trompe l'oeil ceilings, frescoed nooks . . . Filippo Lippi's *Coronation of the Virgin,* immensely dignified and romantic . . . Raphael's *Transfiguration,* which, in its controlled tumult and its luminosity, suggests that there is something mean, stingy, about the failure to wish to believe . . . Leonardo's strange and wonderful *St. Jerome,* the scholarly hermit looking more like a shade than a man, and the sketchiness of the unfinished work underscoring and adding to our impression of him as a saint who fasted and prayed, prayed and fasted; the penitent melds into the rocky landscape (a lion crouches before his feet). This painting was dismembered, its head found in an antique shop, the rest of it at a shoe-maker's. Even now, its parts assembled, it bears the scars of its suffering. . . . So many painters for whom the human soul is expressed as much through the human hand as through the human face (as it is in dance): Raphael, of course; and Giovanni Bellini's *Burial of Christ* (the Savior's hand rests so trustingly in that of Mary Magdalene), a picture of extraordinary stillness; and, in Caravaggio's radiant and symphonic *Deposition,* the hands of mourn-ers cupped, upraised, imploring, blessing; the hand of the livid Christ nerve-less and limp and Mary Magdalene bunches her knuckles to her tear-filled

eyes, an ordinary gesture from the ordinary world for which Christ died.
. . . And surprises: the small, moon-drenched canvases of the eighteenth-
century Donato Creti, representations of the planets commissioned by a Pope
that look like nineteenth-century landscapes . . . and sometimes, their light
not of this world, almost like Magritte. . . .

> I've grown a goitre by dwelling in this den—
> . . . My beard turns up to heaven; my nape falls in,
> Fixed on my spine: my breast-bone visibly
> Grows like a harp: a rich embroidery
> Bedews my face from brush-drops thick and thin.
> My loins into my paunch like levers grind:
> My buttock like a crupper bears my weight; . . .
> In front my skin grows loose and long; behind,
> By bending it becomes more taut and strait;
> Crosswise I strain me like a Syrian bow:
> Whence false and quaint, I know,
> Must be the fruit of squinting brain and eyes; . . .
> Come then . . . try
> To succor my dead pictures and my frame;
> Since foul I fare and painting is my shame.

> —*Michelangelo Buonarroti, "To Giovanni
> da Pistoia on the Painting of the Sistine
> Chapel, 1509," translated by John
> Addington Symonds*

The space itself is strong, assured, majestic. I find myself thinking not of
Michelangelo's *Creation of Adam*— the God who brought Adam to life is too
calm for me; I cannot think of Creation except as an act of convulsion
(perhaps because I am a woman and associate creation with the pangs of
birth)—but of the *Last Judgment* on the altar wall. This is the terrible work
of a man who, Anthony Blunt tells us, "is no longer at ease with the world,
unable to face it directly," a man no longer enchanted and seduced by
physical beauty. It is this man: "Led by long years to my last hours, too late,
O world, I know your joys for what they are. . . . I say now, having put
it to the proof, that he has the better part in Heaven whose death falls nearest
his birth."

One of the most powerful images in all of art is that of St. Bartholomew, fiercely jubilant on Judgment Day, showing his Lord the knife that martyred him, and holding in his hand the folds of his own flesh. His flesh is a discarded garment; but St. Bartholomew, judged fit to reign with Christ, is embodied, corporeal, too (how else could man depict martyred and rewarded man?); a conundrum: Flesh holds despised discarded flesh. In the folds of the flesh are the tortured features of Michelangelo.

This painting teaches us that the body is the body of the soul.

During the Counter Reformation the *Last Judgment* came under attack for its "filth" and for its supposed lack of orthodoxy—the naked figures of the damned, lumpish, heavy as sin itself. Lovers of Raphael, whose works are sweet, could not abide the *Last Judgment.* We are fortunate to live now, at this remove. We can love them, Raphael and Michelangelo, both. . . . If one waits long enough, many of the claims of ideology, always so coarsening, dissipate.

I love so much the Vatican Library. There are no captions or legends in English here; of all the Vatican Museums it is the least touristed. Sometimes they seem unreal—a necessary creation in the story of our lives, but dusty-dead forever, even before they were born: Jerome, Thucydides, Caesar, Justinian, Augustine. Here they are, here are works in their hand. For all the sculpture in the world I would not exchange a folio of Augustine's treatise on the Trinity; and I know nothing more terrifying than Botticelli's illustrations for Canto XV of the "Inferno": the damned free-falling into space. . . . Agoraphobia is a fear of Hell.

What is more satisfying than an illuminated manuscript, this intimate joining of ornate image to divine word? . . . Not always divine, sometimes deliciously profane: The first printed work of culinary art, *Platine de Honesta Voluptate et Valitudine* (called by the name *Platina's Book*), was written by Vatican librarian Bartolomeo Sicci; six different editions were printed after its publication in 1474.

The Vatican Museums have: Teleguides, listening devices in French, Italian, German, Spanish, and English; a self-service restaurant from which one can perfectly see the dome of St. Peter's; a post office and a writing room; a foreign-currency exchange; three first-aid stations; wheelchairs for the disabled; a bus service connecting the museums to St. Peter's. The museums are open (except for stated holidays), and never capriciously shut, from 9:00

A.M. to 2:00 P.M. and from 9:00 to 5:00 on specified dates. Color-coded itineraries are available. The shortest, coded violet, is said to take one and one-half hours; the longest, coded yellow, five hours. I find this kind and in its way efficient, but odd. Who has timed these itineraries? Who can say that I will not stand before a single Caravaggio for five hours? (My life would be the better for it.)

Michelangelo was twenty-five when he sculpted the *Pietà* and eighty-one when he designed the dome of St. Peter's. This is a marvelous fact to reflect upon.

Lala's anti-Semitism troubled me; I am not so young that I can afford to terminate friendships on principle (nor do I wish I were), but it is never comfortable to love less than wholeheartedly, so I was sad. She had called the Jews "those others." Soon the rent in the fabric of friendship was given another tug (we always know unconsciously that we have damaged the cloth).

Lala and I are strolling in the neighborhood of the Spanish Steps, having a perfectly useless, lovely afternoon, tea at Babington's and purchases of Swiss face creams, new Parisian lipsticks, when "Of course, *they* own all the shops," Lala says. Oh, dear. During the war Jews were sheltered in her convent school, she says, "and then, after the war, when I went shopping on the Via Condotti, they wouldn't talk to me. Why? My father was a Fascist"—this is the first I have heard of this—"but he did nothing, nothing," nothing wrong. Perhaps it is too much to ask a woman to despise and disown the father she adored in her youth, or even to hate the objective evil while continuing to love the evildoer; but Lala's thinly veiled hatred of Jews is displaced anger: If it were not for the Jews, Lala implies, she would not be obliged to defend her father; she—in all other respects a loving and emotionally generous woman—would not harbor this serpent of hatred. She hates whom she hates because she cannot hate whom she cannot hate; and this is, in a way, the history of the Jews, hated for no other reason than that they are hated.

Jews have fared better in Italy than they have in any other country in Europe. (But they have not fared well enough.) Often—as with so many laws in Italy—regulations regarding the Jews existed only in theory and were not put into practice. "In modern times," Laura Fermi writes, the Jews "never constituted a problem" (a weird inversion of syntax that suggests that the Jews, and not their persecutors, were "the problem"). Jews could, in fact, become generals and prime ministers, as they could not in other European countries. When Mussolini launched his anti-Semitic campaign in 1938 (after denouncing anti-Semitism in 1924), Italy's forty thousand Jews were immensely shocked and surprised.

Jews had come to Rome for sanctuary from Jerusalem after its fall in A.D. 70 (Roman Jews are proud of the purity of the Italian liturgy, which they claim is the authentic rite used in the Temple); they came from Spain, in 1492, after their expulsion from that country, from the Middle East and from North Africa, and, later, from Poland and Germany; after 1943, during the German occupation of Rome, Jews were hidden in monasteries and convents all over Rome, including the seminary of St. John Lateran, the seat of the Bishop of Rome (the Pope). Many, perhaps most, Italians, including priests and bishops, behaved generously and bravely, the silence of Pius XII notwithstanding. Jews in Italy suffered numerically and proportionately much less than Jews in other countries during World War II; approximately 85 percent survived. But we are right to concentrate our attention and our moral energy on the 15 percent who did not survive; to say that Italian Jews fared better than other European Jews—even to lay their destruction at the feet of the Nazis, who put into motion the rusty and unused machinery Mussolini had established—is cold comfort.

In Rome, where one is entirely disposed to love the entire world of God's creation, anti-Semitism seems peculiarly primitive and aberrational; for it to exist is vile and incongruous in a city where St. Paul, the apostle to the Gentiles, himself a Jew, brought Christianity to people *other* than Jews only after much dissension in the young Church. One has but to scratch the layers of visible history in Rome to understand that the Jews, from whose tradition, as the Vatican says, "salvific gifts" are drawn and to which our own is uniquely bonded, are at the very least in a familial relationship to Christians. So one would like to think anti-Semitism is a thing of the past in Italy; but one knows better: Anti-Semitism is nowhere a thing of the past.

("Anti-Semitism," Mussolini said in 1938, "has now been injected in the Italians' blood. It will go on circulating.")

One day I walk through the Roman Ghetto with my Florentine friend T.; I show her the seventeenth-century Church of San Gregorio della Divina Pietà, which, when this quarter was known as the "seraglio of the Jews," stood just outside one of the seven gates of the Ghetto, and on which is chiseled, in Hebrew and in Latin, these terrible words from Isaiah: "I have spread out my hands all the way to a rebellious people which walketh in a way that was no good after their own thoughts." I show T. a plaque nearby—Italy has no wish at all to suppress the tragic facts—in memory of the 2,091 Jews who were gathered here in October 1943, sent by the Nazi occupiers to an almost certain death. We pass the Church of Sant'Angelo in Pescheria, set into the ruins of the Portico d'Ottavia; in this church Jews were obliged, during the Counter Reformation, to hear sermons in which they were excoriated.

T. is young; World War II has almost as little reality for her as the War of the Roses has for me; but she appears to share my gloomy horror. Then, after walking for ten minutes in silence: "But why are they so aggressive?" she blurts. "Why do they speak always of money?" T.'s parents, Italian immigrants to Scotland, were incarcerated during the War, and now, the memory of their bewilderment and pain a blood memory, she turns her anger against the Jews.

Jews were condemned to live a segregated existence within a seven-acre area in 1555, by Bull of the Neapolitan Pope Paul IV, who, says Stendhal with nice economy and astuteness, "believed himself to be infallible and who feared that he would be eternally damned if he did not yield to the secret impulses that commanded him to persecute." Hawthorne, in a disgusting passage, called the Ghetto "the foulest and ugliest part of Rome . . . where thousands of Jews," upon the unwalled banks of the malodorous Tiber, "lead a close, unclean, and multitudinous life, resembling that of maggots when they overpopulate a decaying cheese." In 1848, under Pius IX, restrictions were removed, but it was not until 1870 that Jews exercised full rights as Roman citizens. The splendid neo-Byzantine Synagogue on the Lungotevere Cenci was built in 1904.

I come often to the Ghetto, but while the sadness of history informs current happiness, I do not come in order to feel, nor, in the event, do I feel, the gloomy horror that settled over me the day I walked with T., for the Ghetto (no longer a ghetto) is, though it seems in this context obscene to say it, a delightful place. It is lively; it is a gorgeous architectural jumble: Renaissance buildings next to medieval houses, Corinthian columns on sidewalks, in courtyards, even on staircases. And medieval houses gussied up with discreet and beautiful windows the better from which to see the green slopes of the Capitol; and narrow streets hung with laundry that debouch into sunny small piazzas, some little more than cul-de-sacs; houses draped in ivy, courtyards adorned with succulents and fountains. There is a sense, here, of life fully lived; the *passeggiata,* here, resembles a parade. There is also (ironically) a sense of safety: One is not afraid, here, subliminally or actively, of being "thieved." To walk here is a tactile experience—sun and shadow on your skin as you walk down dark, narrow streets crowded with tall, narrow houses and exit into intimate piazzas. Architecture feels like your skin's skin, and this makes a kind of moral sense.

Dickens called the Ghetto "a miserable place, densely populated, and reeking with bad odours"; he added that the people "are industrious and money-getting. In the day-time as you make your way along the narrow streets, you see them all at work: upon the pavement oftener than in their dark and frowsy shops: furbishing old clothes and driving bargains." But something quickened his interest in this part of the city—the sudden, exciting shifts and changes of scale (which seem, nevertheless, to have a kind of harmony and coherence): "Certainly it is of most unwholesome aspect, but picturesque withal in a high degree. It is strange that behind its squalor and filth it should hold treasures of costly stuffs and other articles of value. It abuts on to the gloomy walls of the Theater of Marcellus, whose ancient porticos are workshops of artisans and the stores of vendors of smoke-begrimed wares. Its cavernous arches are often reproduced on the canvases of painters. . . ." And Hawthorne, in spite of his repugnance for the Ghetto, was able to see, "here and there," the poignancy of "an arched gateway, a cornice, a pillar, or a broken arcade that might have adorned a palace." Montaigne witnessed a circumcision: "The boy's outcry is like that of ours when they are baptized. As soon as his glans is . . . uncovered, they hastily offer some wine to the minister, who puts a little in his mouth and then goes and sucks the glans of this child, all bloody, and spits out the blood he has drawn from it, and immediately takes as much wine again." What Hawthorne professed to hate—but was obviously moved by—is what we cherish: "houses, piled massively out of the ruins of former ages. . . ." This wonderful sense that life is all around us, beneath us, before us, behind us . . . every walk through a cool narrow street is full of delicious expectancy: Here there are pomegranates among the ruins. Life is within us.

I shouldn't call the Teatro di Marcello gloomy, I should call it thrilling (and not at all because of its bulk); and I should love to live in it, which, given that it was built in the year 13, is a peculiarly gratifying and energizing sentiment. (Rome makes me feel clever; cities one loves do that for one.) Built to hold as many as twenty thousand spectators, it originally consisted of three tiers of arcades (and three tiers of arches—Ionic, Doric, and Corinthian columns). The stores of which Dickens wrote were on the second tier. In the sixteenth century, after the theater had lived for a while as a fortress,

Baldassare Peruzzi built an elegant palazzo for the Savelli family on what remained of the third tier of arches, enclosing them; and today (this makes my heart exit from my mouth), this theater, built by Augustus, is a honeycomb of apartments, so labyrinthine that it defied the search-and-destroy powers of the German occupiers. The building is a living, breathing organism, a moral force.

In the gardens surrounding the theater are fallen columns, and two beautiful Corinthian columns from the Temple of Apollo, and among them fields of anemones (these are the flowers that Jesus was speaking of when he said: "Consider the lilies of the fields, how they grow; they toil not, neither do they spin").

On a slight prominence next to—among—the ruins there is a small house garlanded with vines; and oleander, and blowsy nodding flyaway flowers, and cats.

On one side of the theater is the Via del Portico d'Ottavia, the main thoroughfare of the Ghetto. The portico is arched, gated, dank; it feels, though it is on street level, as if it were subterranean, and as if the temperature might be ten degrees cooler there; yet it stands on a busy street of shops and cafés. This sudden change of mood—or, more properly, this encapsulating of a mood within a mood—is the essence of Rome, the abiding thrill of Rome. It was built in 149 B.C. for triumphal processions; now its marble columns rise casually from the sidewalk, and among them are set, in clement weather, the tables of the restaurant Da Giggetto.

There may be experiences more sensual than resting one's arm in mock indifference against a sun-warmed Roman column after a meal of deep-fried artichokes and mozzarella in carrozza, all the while gazing at the *teatro*—the almost unbelievable reality of it makes you feel real-as-real, rooted, grounded . . . and also as if you were on the verge of levitating—but it is hard to know what those experiences might be.

There is a house on the Via del Portico d'Ottavia that I particularly love, in which I am not alone: It is No. 25; it is perhaps the base of a thirteenth-century tower. Its splendid portal is now an entrance to a butcher shop (why not? Life goes on). To the left of the portal is a long window, flower pots. Very often in Rome you get the feeling that someone has arranged something just for you—that flower pot, that curtain, that moving shadow in the evening light in a building older than your knowledge of God. The world, Rome says, was created for you.

*   *   *

After lunch among the ruins: a walk to the Piazza di Campitelli, an example of what the spirit of the Counter Reformation could do when it behaved itself. Baroque, Mannerist, Rococo, it is very sweet, and harmonious, and along the way are the terraced apartments of the rich who have chosen to live in this quarter. (Why do the English get all the credit for being a nation of gardeners? Pots and pots, everywhere, in Rome.) The Ghetto is now—this is cause for celebration but also somehow queasiness—a chic place in which to live.

Here is a recipe for codfish as Giggetto cooks it: Soak one piece dried codfish, 1–1½ pounds, for 48 hours in 6 changes of water. Drain it; cut it into pieces 2 inches wide. Mix 2 cups flour, ¼ tsp. baking powder, 1 tbsp. olive oil with enough water to make a thick batter in which to dip the fish. Submerge the fish in hot olive oil and cook, covered, over a medium-high flame, till golden brown. Serve with lemon wedges.

Or: After soaking and draining, fry the fish, rolled in flour, in oil and butter (with garlic), and stir in mint, basil leaves, capers, olives, and marinara sauce; cook uncovered for ½ hour; serve over pasta—*lingue di passeri* (sparrows' tongues) is preferred.

Dried cod is called *baccalà.* As long as I can remember, someone in my family—most lately, in the wake of attrition by means of death, my sister-in-law Carol—has cooked it on Christmas Eve along with the twelve other fish dishes that constitute (I don't know why) the evening feast. As long as I can remember, no one has ever eaten it. It belongs to custom, more properly to superstition (superstition says: It's bad luck to alter custom!). Nobody likes it. I don't see the point of *baccalà,* as codfish can be kept refrigerated without salting now. But I love to see large, heavy pieces of *baccalà,* like planks, in a shop, it makes me feel at home, safe.

On the Via del Portico d'Ottavia there are many houseware shops—*casalinghi.* Julia goes quite mad when she sees these shops. Julia's husband, Massimo, is bored; that is what Julia says. Italy is a perpetual Mother's Day, she says, all Italian men want to live with both their wives and their mothers and the wife tries to become both and soon she is a nonerotic object; and on and on Julia goes. She is going to remove herself from Rome, she is going to make herself perpetually tantalizing and perpetually unavailable, let him play his man game, she will play her woman game, and they will see. This sounds exhausting to me. Julia's life, she says, is a nightmare of washing floors with Windex and newspapers, and all she can think of at St. Peter's is who washes the marble floors—"nuns," she says bitterly; "at least they're married to someone they like." Julia has an American friend she wants to introduce me to, she is "truly crazy, she has had thirteen Italian lovers and twenty-two abortions." I don't want to meet her. "Don't judge her," Julia says, "you must have a love affair with an Italian to understand Italy." "I don't undertake affairs scientifically," I say. Today Julia decides to end her marriage; but that doesn't stop her from shopping for tortellini.

Years ago, the first time I saw Rome, walking along the Tiber I was stopped by a shabby man on a bridge, he was gesticulating wildly. This was shortly after the War. "What have they done to us? What have they done to us?" he cried, over and over, and clutched my sleeve, and made me understand that he wanted me to see the Synagogue. I have never forgotten him, his witness—honorable and necessary and pained.

This time I will see the Synagogue when my daughter comes. I want her loving heart, her clear eyes, her fair and sorrowing face.

One day in St. Peter's Square I met a young American man who said, "Come to Avezzano for my nephew's First Communion, I will call and tell them you are coming, and they will say, 'Of course' "; so he did, and they did; and so I did.

Avezzano is a town of 35,000 souls in the Abruzzi, about 110 kilometers to the east, and slightly to the north, of Rome, one and a half hours by train.

There is no one in my car but me and a man who inspires first disquietude, then fear (pasty face, feral eye, stale smile fixed on me); I do not move lest to do so should precipitate an answering action. . . . His breath is ragged, it comes in little grunts; he is sitting diagonally across from me, and though he is unnaturally still, I know that I am being stalked. A little boy— Alessandro—comes in from another car every now and then, for which I thank God, and sticks his tongue out at me; then his harried mother retrieves him. The man across the aisle from me pays absolutely no attention to this child and the child shies away from him; this is proof the man is bad. Two stops out of Rome an old lady gets on with her lumpy daughter; she regards us both, the man and me, and then fires a volley of questions at me: Where am I going? to be with whom? by whom will I be met? are these people cousins? . . . She moves next to me, spreading her long rusty skirts over my lap to cover and as if to protect me; she clasps my hands in her warm and scratchy ones; and I feel safe.

I am met by Gary, my friend of St. Peter's Square, and by his Uncle Armando, a very handsome man, with scrupulous courtesy. The day is sparkling, and along the broad and pleasant treelined streets the *passeggiata* is in progress. When does it begin? I ask Armando, for the sun is still high in the sky. On Saturday and Sunday at 9:00 A.M., he says; it is captivating: men and women, boys and girls, boys and boys, girls and girls—every possible configuration—and not a mating game or a dance of sex at all, times have changed in Italy, but a town got up to enjoy the honeyed days of June, the grace. A little boy darts between my legs.

Armando is married, he says, "to one of four beautiful sisters, daughters of a baker who has done well." These words make me feel as if I am in a fairy tale.

We drive to Colle'lungo, Armando's little town nestled in the mountains. "In America," Gary says, "mountains are . . . just mountains." I know just what he means. (He means he is in love.) Here villages perched on top of green mountains seem to call out to you (like villages in fairy tales). Yellow wildflowers splash the hills. "The only sentimental poem Leopardi ever wrote was about these flowers, these hills, it was his last poem," Armando says; he is an environmental engineer. (*"Sempre caro mi fu quest'ermo colle. . . ."* "It has always been dear to me, this lonely hill. . . . The sweetness of being shipwrecked in that sea of flowers.")

The baker's house is on a *piazzetta;* to his house we go, and from the outdoor staircase directly to the kitchen, which is simple and unfashionable and warm (the refrigerator and freezer are sheathed in glowing wood, and a wood stove burns). This village was leveled by an earthquake in 1915 and rebuilt; this house has undergone many metamorphoses; it is the house of someone born to a humble station in life who has, as Armando says, done well. The bakery is around the corner. The baker is stolid and uncommunicative. His wife is solid, talkative, and demonstrative. We sit down immediately to a meal of beefsteak, spinach, strawberries, and coffee. All four daughters are there, and all four daughters are beautiful. Giuliana, Armando's wife, teaches handicapped children in Colle'lungo; she lives here with her mother and her daughter, Alba. *Alba* means "dawn"—"Delta Dawn," Armando says, to show that he is up on things. Armando lives in Ostia, near his office. He has recently come back from China and all the sisters are dressed up in China silk. Sister Pina is married to Franco, an official at Alitalia. How beautiful your daughters are, I say to their mother. "They don't have to be pretty anymore, they're married," she says, raising an eyebrow at the next-to-youngest girl, Loriana, who is not married yet.

Nicoletta is married to Angelo, who is the mayor of the town. He is a "Socialist, not a Fascist Socialist, a left-wing Socialist," he says; that is Italian politics for you. The way he talks about politics makes me feel cozy. Because we are all now so cozy, I go to Nicoletta and Angelo's house a mile down the hill; they do not seem to know how beautiful it is, everything white and all bleached wood. The four daughters and I are having drinks and making sandwiches for the townspeople who are not invited to the formal party tomorrow; to be specific, we are making three hundred sandwiches, and canapés of caviar, butter and walnuts, and prosciutto. Loriana, who is not married, is carving melon; she will make three hundred melon flowers. Loriana has designed the pastry her father is baking tonight; it is a cream puff in the shape of a peach, tinted pink and green and pale yellow, drenched in peach liqueur, bursting open to reveal a dark brown-and-white (chocolate custard) pit; it has candied stems of green. The whole town smells good. No matter what Loriana ever does, she will always be the baker's daughter, and he will always be the baker whose beautiful daughters married well. Life in a small town is immutable; that accounts for both its claustrophobia and its charm.

"Why didn't the American lady come to *my* Communion?" Luigi, the older boy, says. He has taken to me, and he sulks in that ravishing Italian-boy way, which I love. Angelo, Jr., whose First Communion this will be, watches these preparations proud and nervous as a bridegroom. Can these fat peaches be for him? *because* of him? Has someone come from America because for the first time he will receive a wafer and a sip of wine on his tongue?

It is sweet to go to bed in the baker's house on the *piazzetta,* the mountain air is like goodness; a tree of red roses grows outside my window, I hear church bells and the sound of jazz: Ornette Coleman. The baker and his wife have given me their bedroom, up a flight of steep marble stairs—tonight all night they'll bake, yeasty they will rise and shine—their bed is so high I must use a stepladder to climb into it; and into it I sink ("my thoughts drown"—Leopardi). I am a princess in a fairy tale.

Sunday: Mass. Singing: "Ave Maria." Clapping: "Now and in the hour of our death," how merry this is. The daughters are in China silk; the boys of the town are in jeans; old ladies, impassive, in worn black . . . together they sing: *Gloria! Hallelujah!* Old men, outside, on the beautiful cobblestone square, make a business of discussing politics. All is as it should be, nothing has gone wrong, what could possibly go wrong?

Back to Angelo and Nicoletta's; we drink *digestivi* before there is anything to digest. Armando whispers to me: "The vice-president of Italy's largest labor union is here." They have made a *bella figura,* good.

We go to a restaurant, five families and their children who have made their First Communions, and two hundred guests, and this is what we eat (each course is served separately):

> Melon and prosciutto
> Stracciatelle (pasta with broth)
> Lasagne with béchamel and meat sauce
> Spaghetti with shellfish
> Fish fry
> Quail with potatoes
> Green salad
> Spinach in olive oil
> Ices
> Fruit and cheese
> Gelato
> Fruitcake with white frosting
> Coffee

This six-hour meal has no logic. *"Credete e amate, pace"*—"Believe it and love it, peace," Armando says.

Afterward, in their white and shining house, Nicoletta, Angelo, and little Angelo—now puffed up with pride—greet guests (three hundred sandwiches and drinks). Little Angelo is no longer nervous. (Angelo, Sr., has a tic in his cheek.) How beautifully it's done. The townspeople pay homage to their friend and mayor, he receives them with a formal bow, an ancient, civilized form of respect. . . . In the city anyone can become anything at any moment. Here people are themselves forever, chessmen on their allotted squares. In the soft and fragrant dusk this seems like a good thing.

Everybody gets a favor, *confetti* wrapped in a lace handkerchief, a bronze box on which there is a bronze snail.

Gary and I walk down the streets of this shaken, battered, bombed, and resurrected town. "Ga-ry! Ga-ry!" the young girls call. We walk down a neat and tidy street, identical small houses, small front yards, orange street-lamps against a black sky. All is calm, it is as if agitation and nonconformity had been abolished by fiat; one's feet touch the ground very sure that it will rise to meet them, sure that betrayal does not lurk in inanimate things, that trust lies behind all walls. We open a gate, and (as in a fairy tale) one step and we are inside another's warm world. "Come in! Come in!" two voices cry. "Speak English to us, please. . . ." In the garden underneath their cherry tree, cords of firewood are stacked against the coming winter. Nina and Gina wait. Nina is a seamstress in Rome during the winter and Gina keeps the home fires burning, they are sisters, they have never married. This house received a direct hit during the War (the Germans used Avezzano as a headquarters), but it is nice, now, in this room with its tiled and open hearth, with its fat chairs and long table and their good china dishes on display—and on the wall a faded snapshot of an American soldier. They do not count themselves poor. Suddenly the memory of the Communion feast is burden-some to me, though how can one fault Angelo and Nicoletta, who act as if kindness and generosity were an ordinary thing? Nina and Gina have a First Communion present for little Angelo. "And how is the dear family?" they say. One sees the point—am I really seeing the point?—of feudalism.

In the morning Armando drives me back to Rome. We pass the dried-up basin (now farmland) of Lago Fucino, the ancient Fucinus Lacus, which, without apparent outlet, used frequently to flood the countryside. Armando shows me what appear to be stone arches in the hillside, carved, he says, by Nero, "to equalize the channel pressure." (I am not quite sure what this means, my mind is on other things.) Claudius tried to drain this volatile lake, and so did Frederick II, with no success. In 1852, English, French, and Swiss engineers aided by the Roman prince Torlonia did succeed: A tunnel linked the lake to the nearby basin of the Liri, as a consequence of which Torlonia claimed the land for himself. In 1951 the lake area—fourteen thousand hectares—was expropriated by the Italian government and distributed among eight thousand families, bringing prosperity to this region. (If this had happened forty years earlier, my family—half Abruzzese—might never have left Italy.)

This is interesting. But I am thinking more of Pietro, a young—much too young, and much too charming—man I have met at Angelo and Nico-letta's reception. He studies philosophy in Rome, but this causes him to become agitated over nothing—*agitato per cose da nulla*. "He's awfully young and pretty," I say to Giuliana, making it sound like a condemnation. "What else do you need?" she says. "It's not as if you were going to marry him." "He's a good boy," Armando says. I doubt this very much. I wonder what I will say to him when he calls.

I was drinking a screwdriver in the Caffè Greco on Via Condotti when Jane stopped before me, with an untroubled candid smile, sinewy, ocean-tanned, and beautiful in a yellow pinafore. "You're Barbara," she said, and—because Jane's beauty is like a character trait, it resembles goodness—I was glad she'd picked me from the crowd (we have friends in common; we had arranged to meet).

"These shoals of American fellow-residents with their endless requisitions and unremunerative contact are the dark side of life in Rome, they really abridge very much the sense of all that one comes for, and make one ask very often whether under such circumstances Rome pays." So Henry James wrote, making free use of pecuniary metaphors, articulating his own miserliness.

Most people harbor a deep suspicion of expatriates, which suspicion is often gratified, for as Hawthorne—himself afflicted in Rome by flu and fleas—wrote:

The years, after all, have a kind of emptiness, when we spend too many of them on a foreign shore. We defer the reality of life, in such cases, until a future moment, when we shall again breathe our native air; but, by and by, there are no future moments; or, if we do return, we find that the native air has lost its invigorating quality, and that life has shifted in reality to the spot where we have deemed ourselves only temporary residents. Thus, between two countries, we have none at all, or only that little space of either in which we finally lay down our discontented bones. . . .

Unhappiness makes beggars or accountants of us all.

I have sometimes been ungenerous in my mind to expatriates, and that is because I love another country better than my own.

I later came to see how sad Jane was—for she was in exile from a place she could no longer even think of as home—but I never had an unhappy time with her; she never allowed her unhappiness to become contagious, it was a great gift she had.

Jane lives in one room lined with suitcases near the Hospital of the Holy Ghost, far from the center of Rome, a room in which, she says, the only pieces of furniture are a table, a bed, and a chair. (I never visited her, she was too proud. Sometimes she'd call and tell me that a man had spent the night, and I'd wonder what bed was like when bed was the only place one could go to.) One would think she might be soured by her circumstances. She was sent to a Jesuit school in Rome by despairing parents in the turbulent sixties, and, her beauty smoothing the way, she willy-nilly stayed on; she isn't sour, though. Once she lived in Parioli with a Calabrian prince in a house with a swimming pool and tennis courts; he was terribly romantic; he was unfaithful. So reduced, she stays. She has been thieved in her apartment building and on the street thirteen times in the last four years.

Here she is at mazelike Caffè Greco, in one small (wood and marble) salon (warm and light), where she has greeted scores of visiting foreigners, seen the same penguin waiters for years, watched the haut monde and the tourists come and go (as they have come and gone for more than two hundred years, Buffalo Bill and several Indians among them, also Keats). Her unaffected curiosity remains eager: *Who is that man in sequins? Who is that boy in white? Look at that woman (is it a woman?) all in purple net and green fishnet stockings, a cascade of black hair; is she a starlet-whore or a starlet who only looks like a whore, what do you think?* and this is a mark of her generosity: She enters one's pleasure.

Gypsies sell roses; they never open, they are buds and then they die.

There are lovely dinner parties (an Egyptologist, a cinematographer, a left-wing documentary filmmaker, a right-wing baronessa, a cuddly man who draws pictures of ships, scholars, writers, will-o'-the-wisps), in restaurants near the Farnesina, in Piazza del Popolo, on terraces under white and yellow umbrellas ("Look! you can see the statue of Garibaldi on the Janiculum!"); everyone is witty, Jane draws people to her, no one is unkind, will we ever meet again, how good life is, how lucky we are; swallows whirl. Sometimes people talk about real things. There is lovely food—fettucini with black truffles, saltimbocca, marinated wild mushrooms; broccoli rape and frittate; rigatoni with artichokes; paillard of veal; spaghetti with zucchini and ham; grilled swordfish; a green vegetable that looks like fat grass, in season for the blink of an eye; crostini and bruschetta and improvised pasta with fresh *pomodoro* and *basilico;* artichokes day after day after day; chicken baked in peppers, lemon juice, olive oil, and parsley; celery in tomato sauce with *pancetta;* burning grappa or *amari* and *digestivi* that taste heavenly, like melted cough drops, and so make one feel like a privileged child on the mend (we are all on the mend from our lives).

One night—we are eating on the Via Flaminia, near the Ministero Marina—dozens of white horses canter by, almost silently (the night sounds are more multitudinous than they, and even the ordinary night sounds are muted, as sometimes happens when people are happy), and they have white plumes, and the men who ride them have helmets with white plumes and silver buttons that shine in the night. "Like a scene from a Fellini film," says my dinner partner; he is Fellini's cinematographer. Reminded that he is, "Well, I forgot," he says; and everyone murmurs, "Of course."

There is lovely chat and lazy gossip, perhaps true, perhaps not, no matter. . . .

When *femminelle*—male transsexual whores—marched in Rome, one was so inspired by his/her own rhetoric that he/she/it declared it was going to douse itself with gas and set fire to itself; the crowd roared: "What! And with the price of gas so high today!" A butcher in the neighborhood of the Pantheon was instantly smitten with one transsexual—as with Dante, love at first sight—and leaving his shop unattended, he followed the march, wringing and twisting his hands in his bloodstained apron for miles. . . . An American film crew from a morning news show wanted to film a café near the Pantheon and asked an American living in Rome: "Whose palm do we grease?" Now this is interesting because "Whose palm do we grease?" is the kind of question usually attributed to Italians, all of whom are, by people hard to please, thought to be on the bribe/dole. So the American writer asked the café's proprietor, who said, "Are you crazy? The sidewalk is free"; but the television people wouldn't believe this and thought somebody was laying a trap for them and gave the American writer five hundred dollars, which he turned over to the proprietor of the café, for which he now shall have free coffee in perpetuity, as well as the proprietor's prayers. . . . When Jean-Luc Godard's film *Je Vous Salue, Marie (Hail Mary)*—which portrays Mary as the surly teenage daughter of a gas station manager and Joseph as a science fiction–reading taxi driver and the Archangel Gabriel as a dirty old man, and which the Pope denounced as blasphemous—played at the Capranichetta, nuns of the Marianite order came out to protest (they had not seen the film), and then a Liberal senator came out to protest against the protesters, and the nuns threw lots of holy water at him and he called the carabinieri, who came and were followed by a senator from the Fascist party (the Movimento Sociale Italiano), who flung himself on the cobblestones, praying loudly to the Virgin, and of course the carabinieri did not know whom to succor or to arrest; and after that, as one filmmaker on his way to make a film in Katmandu says, "It was all take and no lines"—all gestures, no talk—and the moviegoers walked right in. . . . It is midnight, and we are outdoors in Trastevere beneath white umbrellas and fairy lights; the air is full of bells.

One night Jane drives me home in her beat-up Fiat, and we discuss who was the "spook"—the CIA agent—at the party; there had to have been one, something in the air. Fifteen minutes after she has dropped me off, Jane calls: "What was that all about?" she says. "Paranoia?" Or: We are too lucky and must invent an irritant. Because we are in Rome and when was life so good?

One night—I have left my house slightly tipsy, I have driven along the Tiber for what seems so long (in the moonlight, space is hard to judge) I think I must be in the country, in fact the restaurant I am entering is five minutes from Piazza del Popolo—I am falling in love, in large, slow spirals; my feelings (after the first course) are, however, still reversible: Perhaps he will say something stupid. (He doesn't.) Jane kicks me in the shins. We read each other's face; hers is glowing. Oh, dear. She is falling in love with him, too. Out of respect for her feelings (I choose to regard something he says as asinine), I rein my feelings in. I do not fall in love. Out of respect for my feelings, she reins her feelings in. He goes off with a third woman. "Well, who d'you think he'd have chosen anyway? You? Me?" We play this young girls' game. It's fun. This is what it must be like to come from a family that's not crazy, to have a sister. I feel great pleasure (and, in retrospect, I feel deprived).

Jane has allowed an impoverished prince to move in with her. Poor; and he doesn't bed her either. He is seventy and consorts with tarts in Sardinia, she says; he has wasted the family fortune and is proud of having achieved a singularly useless life. So, why? She wants to walk into Harrods someday and be called a *principessa* by the doorman, she says. But the prince has no idea of marrying her. Never mind; she wants to be called Your Highness— and lives in mortal fear of growing fat. She rides buses, her Fiat having expired and her means being on their way to exhaustion because of the excesses of the prince.

One day, near Piazza Navona, a salesgirl at a *tabacchi* tries to talk me out of buying cigarettes, she wrests them from my hand. "I must lay in stock for Sunday," I say.

"But it is a drug!" she says. There are needle tracks on her arms. She is American and has been here for twelve years, she says.

"Why?"

"Any place is better than Minnesota," she says. "Come back if you are ever in need," she says, how kind.

This is what I learn about her later: She has been here for twenty years. She has a parrot that flies freely across her living room; the unpleasant bird relieves itself at will. She is a talented art restorer but is spending her life collecting junk; she scavenges every day, and her apartment is so littered as to have caused her lover to leave in despair. When it came upon her that she had no money, she, who has a doctorate in fine arts, applied for a job as a dishwasher in a restaurant near the Piazza Navona. There were forty people waiting in line, of whom she was the thirty-ninth and the only American; of course she didn't get the job. She will economize, she says, by turning off the electricity, which she does. She has no garbage to speak of, she never throws anything out. She hunts for junk and turns piles of garbage over and why one piece of garbage/junk attracts her and not another nobody knows. She does not pay her garbage tax. As, in Italy, all paper chases begin with one's garbage tax, it is entirely possible that she has no legal existence— no factual existence here—which possibility gives her an obscure pleasure.

So much to-do about Godard's *Je Vous Salue, Marie*—the Pope has denounced its "abuses and insults" to the Virgin; he has publicly said a rosary in "deploration" of the film. I must go see it.

The Capranichetta cinema is near the Piazza Colonna, a piazza dominated by the Column of Marcus Aurelius, ninety-five feet high. I remember finding it—the column and the square—marvelous thirty years ago, when the piazza was ringed with cafés; now it is a car park, and no one goes to a car park to see a column in a square. (People are always saying it was Ingrid Bergman's favorite piazza, but I think they must be wrong.) In the Middle Ages this square was the home of blacksmiths and locksmiths. In the eighteenth century the Column of Marcus Aurelius "was surrounded with stoves where the entire city's supply of coffee was roasted. This extraordinary practice was dictated by law, and was due to the curious foible, then fashionable in Rome, of detesting any kind of scent or aroma, even flowers." (Julia, to whom I pass on this morsel, says, "Ha! Whoever wrote that"— Georgina Masson wrote that—"should smell the unwashed bodies on Roman buses." Julia is convinced that the smell of unwashed flesh clings to her clothes and to her hair.) In the nineteenth century the Piazza Colonna was full of fashionable cafés. "Dandies whisper compliments to the fair objects of their devotion," a nineteenth-century observer wrote; "the stalls where iced water is sold are besieged by the thirsty; the sellers of newspapers elbow their way here, there, and everywhere. The musicians are encouraged by much hand-clapping, and many a shout of *'da capo'* or 'encore.' . . . They are all good performers; and though concerts are given on many other of the Roman *piazze* they never attract anything like the praise they do here." And now it is a car park.

There are no crowds outside the Capranichetta, only one bemused-looking priest, and nobody in the theater to speak of. (I would like to have seen the synopsis of the film given to Pope John Paul, who has made a silliness of a silliness.)

I go to Giolitti for ice cream—watermelon (the seeds are made of chocolate); ricotta ice cream, too.

Giolitti looks as if it should be the scene of a *thé dansant*. Grandmothers and their small charges are there, and young Romans about whose beauty one can never cease exclaiming, and foreign cruisers and hustlers, and families; and here are some of the flavors of Giolitti gelati: almond marzipan, apple, apricot, champagne (made with spumante), chestnut, coconut, coffee, cognac, crema (or cream—the essence of gelato, creamy vanilla), date, fig, Grand Marnier, hazelnut, kiwi, lemon, lime, mandarin, melon, mint, nut, orange, peach, peanut, pear, persimmon, pineapple, pistachio, plum, prickly pear, raspberry, rice, ricotta, rum baba, rum nougat, rum raisin, sour cherry, strawberry, tangerine, torrone, watermelon, whiskey, zabaglione (egg and marsala). You can have gelato in chocolate-lined cones, gelato with whipped cream and shaved chocolate—and *acqua minerale* to revive you; gelato is made fresh every day; and, by law, syrups are never used (hazelnut, for example, is made from the nut itself). You can eat inside—dismiss all notions of an American ice cream parlor: Chandeliers descend from pistachio-colored ceilings; walls are painted blueberry-blue, raspberry, and cream; tables are marble-topped and hold floral bouquets. You can eat outside, where you will become part of the *passeggiata* (lean your chair against a gilt-trimmed faux Corinthian column); the streets are narrow, Porsches and Alfa Romeos shriek; the Pantheon rises dark and everlastingly beautiful behind you.

Tonight I learned from watching RAI that fourteen out of fifteen people questioned didn't know what the Nuremberg trials were, and the fifteenth, a woman, said it was too sad to think about. No one knew who Haile Selassie was. (It is almost exactly fifty years since Mussolini invaded Ethiopia.) But everyone knows about the Caesars.

A director who is making yet another movie about the life of Christ says: *"Gesù è sempre di moda* [Jesus is always in fashion]."

Julia takes me out to the old de Laurentiis movie studios, where her husband is designing a movie set. "What are SIWGER STAPLES?" she says to him. This is a low-budget movie; Massimo is painting the signs he designs; no unions. "SIWGER STAPLES," he says; "you don't know what means that?" "Hell, no," says Julia; it is baking in the sun. "SIWGER SIWGER SIWGER," Massimo shouts. "You mean SINGER?" Julia says. "SIWGER, SINGER, what difference?" "Well, Singer doesn't make staples, it makes sewing machines," Julia says. "I think it's chemical," she says. "What is?" I ask. "His infidelity." "What infidelity?" "He's having an affair with the prop girl," Julia says. "The prop girl is a lesbian, anyone can see that." "In this country that doesn't matter. Come on, Julia." "It's chemical—it's in the wiring of his brain. Like SIWGER. If you really wanna go crazy," Julia says, "go watch somebody make a movie in Abruzzo." "Why would I want to do that?" "Beats me," Julia says.

The main square of Castel Gandolfo is sunny, elegant, pretty, all buttery yellow and gray. It has an engaging air of improvisation, and at the same time it looks as if it had been here forever. (Fifteenth century; Bernini's hand is apparent in the charming fountain and the church.) The summer residence of Popes is on a ledge above Lake Albano, a lake intensely blue; and strewn on the slopes of the circular volcanic lake—on which pleasure boats, which from our rocky eminence look like plume-spraying toys—are wildflowers, especially poppies, and chestnut trees, white villas, olive trees, and roses: yellow, red. On a nearby terrace is a restaurant that juts out over meadows, vineyard, lake. It is vine-covered, and its red-and-white tablecloths flutter in the wind; but Jane, with whom I am spending this summer day in the Alban Hills—the Castelli Romani—says we must not go there, it is a tourist trap. . . . People are always trying to steer me away from tourist traps, it is a way they assert their superiority, but Jane has never done this before, the prince is making her cranky. . . .

The nearby Lake of Nemi is another and a gloomier matter. It is cupped by steep, dark, wooded hills. Perhaps—for here, in ancient times, were groves sacred to the goddess Diana—it exists in the Italian unconscious and provides Italians with a reason to fear lakes. Caligula sailed pleasure barges upon it; Mussolini, who detested lakes, lowered it, and for his pains the Nazis burned Caligula's boats.

Byron has the exact feel of the lake, Diana's looking glass:

> Navell'd in the woody hills . . .
> calm as cherish'd hate, its surface wears
> A deep cold settled aspect nought can shake,
> All coil'd into itself and, round, as sleeps the snake.

"Cherish'd hate . . . as sleeps the snake" is very good. (Mussolini was caught by partisans while fleeing from Lake Como.)

Nemi has odd resonances: It is sugary, and it is sinister. It is famous for its wild strawberries—there is a strawberry festival in May—but the spirit of the implacable Diana, even on a sunny, blameless day, rules over it; and from it Sir James Frazer took his inspiration for *The Golden Bough*.

In Diana's sacred grove day and night a figure prowls, he tells us: "He was a priest and a murderer; and the man for whom he looked was sooner or later to murder him and hold the priesthood in his stead." The office of priest-king was secured by killing the incumbent priest-king; "surely no crowned head ever lay uneasier, or was visited by more evil dreams."

It is too late in the season for strawberries, but not too late for hunters of wild boar. In the town, ropes of wild-boar sausages are hung outside to dry; shops display hairy leg and cloven foot of boar; and in one shop there is not an inch of wall or ceiling space that is not covered with hams and sausages of boar except for a fringe of red-white-and-green crepe bunting.

The sky is bled of light. This is vampire time (and Jane-unplain sinks into lethargy).

Grottaferrata: A Byzantine monastery, fortresslike outside, womblike inside; severity of concept, richness of execution—mosaics, gold.

Monte Cavo: Once the site of the Temple of Jupiter, later a convent, and then a restaurant/hotel famous for its view of the lakes. Now it is an act of trepidation to drive into this terrace of the Apennines: Link fences surround satellite dishes and antennas, and it has a vaguely militaristic and futuristic science-fiction look. . . . In this funny place, Jane has recovered her good spirits; the light has changed: Under young trees restored to green and buoyant light, she skips along the broad, flat stones of the Sacra Via, which once led up from the Roman Forum to the temple, where now there is a satellite dish.

On a summer evening, the custom in Frascati, which is famous for its wines, is to buy salami and prosciutto and cheese from an *alimentari* and to go with your waxed-paper parcel from cantina to cantina, where you are provided with fork and knife and you drink wine.

Near Frascati, in Montecompatri, we have, on a table set for us on the gravel driveway so as not to waste the precious light, the healing breeze, a late lunch:

> Veal, paper-thin, cooked in seaweed, charcoal-grilled
>
> Bruschetta al pomodoro (bread brushed with olive oil and topped with fresh tomatoes)
>
> Bresaola (air-dried salted beef)
>
> Baby artichokes in olive oil

Submitting to the chef's eloquence, we order a too-generous sampling of three *primi:*

> Bucatini all'Amatriciana, pasta in a tomato sauce both light and angry
>
> Gnocchi in cream and tomato sauce with *ortica,* nettle, which one cannot touch with one's bare hands but which is said to have medicinal properties when cooked and eaten
>
> Fettuccine con porcini (wild mushrooms)
>
> Roasted veal with myrtle
>
> Pork tenderloin in chestnuts (all the woods are covered with sweet chestnuts) and cream
>
> A salad of carnations and roses

This meal seems mythological.

Both of us say No to the chef's suggestion of a dessert composed of polenta, pecorino cheese, ricotta, and raspberry preserves (No also to prosciutto gelato); but he brings the polenta dessert that seems so ill conceived; and it is wonderful.

This restaurant is called D'Artagnan.

A young girl in a blue dress skips out, blond braids flying; she is talking to herself. "How good it is to exist," she says.

"Isn't she beautiful?" I say to our driver when we have dropped Jane off, for I am full of love for her, and she is beautiful. He pauses too effectively.

"None of us is getting any younger," he says, which I count mean.

My passion for a country villa whetted, I went to Tivoli, to the Villa d'Este; I went on a guided tour.

It is difficult to believe that these whimsical, extravagant fountains were ever silenced; perhaps, when, deserted and lordless, the lotus languished in the green water, the villa's theatrical magnificence was even more romantic (but who is here to say?). The tinkling, rushing, splashing, slithering, whispering, crashing, rippling, cascading sounds of water keep me company under a wisteria vine on the terrace, from which I see glimpses of fantastical pools and fountains I remember from long ago, a happy, dreamlike terraced waterscape created for Ippolito Cardinal d'Este, the son of Lucrezia Borgia, a cardinal "who bought his hat," the tour guide says neutrally (causing consternation). "These gardens were not made for nuns," he says rather sternly as he and the group disappear around the bend of a flight of mossy stone steps. (From the breasts of Egyptian sphinxes, water spouts.)

When I last came to Tivoli, I was newly pregnant, and at a dinner party I met an Alitalia pilot who fell in love with me; pregnancy was for him an aphrodisiac. But that which attracted him to me also put me out of reach, and we embarked upon a sentimental adventure rather than a love affair.

I had not thought of him till I came here and heard and saw the waters—obedient to orders received hundreds of years ago—rise and fall.

I don't know what we had in mind.

I did not understand my life as I was living it then and saw no path clear and right before me; I had never been mothered, and I was about to have a child; that is why I did not understand my life (I immensely wanted this child). Also, I could not remember my reasons for having married my husband.

What did we think we wanted? Fantasy—bittersweet is an Italian flavor—and no better place for fantasy than here.

We walked down the Avenue of a Hundred Fountains, a long straight green and mossy walk, water spouting and curling in on itself from all manner of things—boats and cabbages and lilies and lions' heads. Our mood, combined of anticipation and studied resignation—the very definition of romance—held as we passed the fishpond with its fat, lazy orange fish that suddenly darted, hid, in blue-green opaque depths; and the Oval Fountain, its slender maidens pouring dancing water from their water pots, shafts of water clashing. . . . We watched lovers whose love was accomplished pursue each other behind the waterfall of Rometta, their play presided over by an obelisk and a she-wolf, a male and a female principle, so appropriate (and so wonderfully silly); we didn't join them because our mood was restrained. But then we came to the final fountain, the Organ Fountain, whose hydraulic music is silenced, and—all those explosive jets and so many streams from so many spouts and breasts—our romantic mood (contrived by us in collusion) was shattered; we laughed. My sweet suitor sat on the ground and held his sides and laughed; this was a circus, and a suggestive one, and it was clear from that time on we would not have to engineer our moods. We held hands and behaved like happy children almost well behaved. (In all my happy moods I have thought: This is what it is like to come from a family that is not crazy . . . to hold hands like this is what sane people do.) Two months later he died in an air crash. I had not remembered this with force until I stood on the terrace of the villa leading to the garden, and, having remembered, I could not proceed.

So I sat on the terrace for the fifteen minutes it took the tour to survey seven acres of water at play, grateful, as one is, for the memory of someone who loved one when one was young.

In God's economy (so I am taught) nothing is wasted . . . as here, in the Villa d'Este, water from one terrace falls onto another terrace to be used—sculpted, as it were—anew. . . . But I couldn't help thinking that there was something wasteful about the way in which that brief love (love in a minor key) lost itself on a summer afternoon (and then he died).

It is summer, but my memories are autumnal.

Yesterday, at Castel Gandolfo, Jane said, "Why are you divorced?" (more tactfully than that, of course). And I remembered that I had experienced, in the Catacombs of Santa Domitilla, a premonitory chill when the man to whom I was married accused me there of sacrilege: The Catacombs inspire funeral-parlor giggles as often as they do excursions into piety, and I had seen the humor of something he had not, and he had punished me, and what was odd and disturbing was that he had no religious feeling at all, only a slavish devotion to appearances (especially to mine). I knew then that our marriage would not last, for he was profoundly unconventional in secret ways, but it was to be my part to fulfill the conventions and conform to creed; I knew what this meant: I would be punished for his lapses (and I was).

When this time our tour came to Santa Domitilla's, I did not enter; it seemed to be my day for paying for failures of love by incurring new ones of imagination. . . . For my sins I said a prayer in St. John Lateran, which basilica we next visited.

This church is the cathedral church of the Diocese of Rome, the seat of the Bishop of Rome, the Pope; only he may celebrate the Mass at the papal altar. One of the first official acts of a newly elected Pope is to take possession of the basilica. Popes used to meet this privilege and this obligation by riding on white mules, preceded by religious orders, cardinals, bishops, and Swiss Guards. At least until the thirteenth century the third versicle of the "Agnus Dei"—*dona nobis pacem* (grant us peace)—was left out of the liturgy, the Lateran being the symbol of the eternal temple in which Christ shall be the peace of the just, and there will be no more need of craving it.

(Dante considered the Popes' moving from the Lateran to Avignon a sin, punishable by eternal damnation. A special place was assigned in Hell to Clement V, in *The Divine Comedy,* and other Popes suffered hanging upside down in a travesty of baptism: They were purified with fire, not with holy water.)

The basilica, damaged and destroyed and rebuilt more than once, has a confused architectural presence; but it is formidable—as formidable as it is cold. One doesn't come here to chat with God. ("The odor of silence is so cold.") The costly colored pavements, across which it is dizziness to walk, shine with the fire of ice. The church is sober and vast. There is enough light here to read a book; there is no dark and scented intimacy.

Constantine—whom our guide brands a "political hustler," to the chagrin of those seeking the easy thrill of assumed piety—built this basilica to symbolize the defeat of paganism; it is "Mother and Head of all the churches in the City and in the World," the earliest home of the Papacy. But for all that, it isn't moving, except perhaps for one corner: an adorable, gleaming, glittering Gothic altar, where, behind a gilt grille, in silver reliquaries, are the heads of Peter and Paul—copies thereof. Montaigne claims to have seen, on Easter Eve, "the heads of Saint Paul and Saint Peter . . . which still have their flesh, color, and beard, as if they were alive."

(If these are copies of the jeweled copies of the heads of Rome's saints, where are the actual ones? The head of St. Peter is not, as we have seen, in all probability, in the necropolis underneath St. Peter's. This mystery deepens as one tries to solve it, unless one accepts the hedging of the guidebooks that say "part of the heads" of Peter and Paul reside in the reliquaries.)

The wooden door of St. John Lateran is open only on Holy Years; on this door the Pope—on every Holy Year, and only then—knocks. The Pope's throne is empty; his absence is declarative.

If there is little that is warm or tender about this church (even the gold ceilings fail to warm the pale interior light), the place has a mighty history: It has been the scene of five Church councils, one of which, the Fourth Lateran General Council in 1215, put to rest the Albigensian heresy. This tenacious and pernicious heresy (which surfaces, from time to time, in different form) held that all matter is evil and that it does not come from the true God and that, therefore, Christians must abstain from food, from marriage, and especially from conception. The Lateran Council affirmed a Trinitarian faith: If Christ is fully God and has a human as well as a divine nature, matter cannot be evil. It professed that there is "one origin of all things: The Creator of all things visible and invisible, spiritual and corporal." This was a moment of supreme importance—and of wholesomeness—in the history of the Church. . . . It would be inconceivable to worship a God who did not share human suffering.

Our tour guide, an iconoclastic and saturnine fellow, did not take us into the thirteenth-century cloisters of St. John Lateran, which are said to be among the most beautiful in Rome, presumably because we were going next to St. Paul Without the Walls, which has cloisters of its own; and that was too bad, because the embrasures of these cloisters might have provided respite from the glassy expanse of St. John.

In the Square of San Giovanni in Laterano stands the tallest Egyptian obelisk in Rome.

Icons of St. Peter and St. Paul paired abound; in the Church of Santa Maria Nuova next to the Roman Forum (also called the Church of Santa Francesca Romana) are two basalt stones from the Sacra Via on which are the venerated imprints of the knees of both apostles. According to one legend, Peter and Paul prayed on these stones as they were being led to martyrdom. According to another, more colorful story, here they challenged Simon Magus (the sorcerer, from whose name derives the sin of simony) to a feat of levitation; Simon was plucked by demons into the air but flung down again with a mighty crash as the result of the combined prayers of Sts. Peter and Paul.

Paul was decapitated on the same day Peter was crucified upside down— his beheading a courtesy due a Roman citizen. By virtue of their evangelizing and of their martyrdom, Rome is, to pilgrims now, the City of Peter and Paul. . . . "If Castor and Pollux, Romulus and Remus 'prepared' Christians," our guide says, "to believe in the 'twinning' of Peter and Paul, that doesn't undermine the tradition." (The British also "twinned" Peter and Paul; there are 283 English churches dedicated to the pair.) Catholicism is a kind of echo chamber, Christianity being full of foreshadowings; image and reality.

Someone once remarked that Romans were extremely logical in tracing the causes of their ill luck to others; their faults they call misfortunes, an act of moral turpitude an *accidente*. (Marcello Mastroianni attributes his philandering to his having been "marked" by the Madonna, and no one in Italy thinks that this is strange.)

On the night of July 15–16, 1823, a fire destroyed the better part of St. Paul Without the Walls, a church built in 337 by Constantine above the tomb of Paul.

A book I bought in Vatican City says that fire was caused "by the distraction of two workmen"; in fact, that "distraction" consisted of a workman's throwing a pan of hot coals at his companion on the roof. It is supposed that a red-hot coal smoldered in a crevice of the roof; at two o'clock on the morning of the sixteenth, a monk saw, from a nearby monastery, a sheet of flame rise into the sky as the roof of the church collapsed, with a mighty sigh, into the nave.

During the course of reconstruction, completed in 1854, windows in the nave were replaced by screens of alabaster, through which light filters to play on eighty granite columns, a forest of columns, and on rare malachite and lapis lazuli. What one remembers is the light.

Our guide told us that a munitions explosion in 1921 knocked out stained-glass windows in the nave and that only then were transparent amber sheets of alabaster put in. . . . There seems to be no proof of this, and all in all, the destruction of St. Paul's appears to be (still) as much a confusion of embarrassment as a tragedy. It was kept secret from Pius VII, who died on the seventeenth of July; according to Stendhal, Pius had a premonition that disaster threatened the church; but Stendhal is not trustworthy.

The light is honeyed, warm, exquisite, nourishing.

I remember thinking: I could eat this light.

Think of a shelter made of light.

Think of a religion constructed of pure gold, transparent glass, water, light.

The thirteenth-century cloister of St. Paul's is like a Moorish pleasure garden (sculpture from the pagan necropolis unearthed in 1823 is here; and Christian graves are here). It is graced by columns beautiful and varied— twisted, fluted, corkscrew, slim, milky-marble, and encrusted; the serpentine columns are the work of Pietro Vassalletto of the Cosmati school. They glitter green and gold.

The roses in the garden, against the dark-green box hedges, are purple, bruised.

A cloister, Georges Duby says, is a rectified island of nature, "separated from its wicked environment," which in this case is literally true, as St. Paul's is surrounded by noisy tram lines, factories. A cloister is an oasis wherein are recovered the freshness and innocence of the first morning of Creation. "The design of the inner courtyard expressed its participation in perfections which the earth has not known since the fall of Adam. . . . To those who had chosen to withdraw there, the cloister spoke the accomplished finished tongue of the other world." It is a place of retrieved, abiding, and accumulated peace; a definable center, safe, that triumphs over the outside world. It contains the large within the small; it contains the real real world: nature, self, and God. It is a universe: a great reckoning in a small place.

Inside the church are mosaic medallions, "medals" of all the Popes, from Peter to John Paul. There are thirteen empty spaces; when they are filled, the world will end.

In literature and tradition Paul is described as bald, bearded, bowlegged, and pale; in iconography he has a long face and deep-set eyes, and he is bald. Nothing to write home about. Paul is any case problematic; his letters to the Romans and to the Colossians are almost certainly misogynistic. It is difficult to know what to make of a man who says it is better to marry than to burn; he appears to be, at the very least, grudging, and at best, a divine grump. He has historically been problematic because arguments concerning justification through grace versus justification through works centered on him. He is in part stern, in part gorgeously lyrical; he is a man of many parts.

In the Church of Santa Maria del Popolo is one of those rare paintings that can change one's interior landscape; it has changed forever the way I think about St. Paul, the way I see him. It is Caravaggio's ennobling *Conversion of St. Paul*. It is Saul of Tarsus who persecuted Christians on his way to Damascus, breathing "threatenings and slaughter," caught in his moment of vanquishment—which is also his moment of glory. Stricken, blind, prostrate, his fingers splayed and arms raised in a tension of supplication . . . he is young! One never thought of him as young. A fine athletic Roman body; virile. His face, naked in its anguish, is tender from every angle.

". . . suddenly there shined round about him a light from heaven: And he fell to the earth, and heard a voice saying unto him, Saul, Saul, why persecutest thou me? . . . And he trembling and astonished said, Lord, what wilt thou have me to do?"

His conversion is a visitation of light. This Caravaggio is a visitation of light to (with, through, and in) a beautiful young man. This is what conversion is: One is new; one is oneself; it is the morning of the soul and the whole world shines; this light is morning light.

Caravaggio's Paul is the Paul who told us that in Christ there is no male, no female, no slave, no freeman; this is the man who told us beautifully to "rejoice with them that do rejoice, and weep with them that weep"; Caravaggio's Paul is this Paul:

Though I speak with the tongues of men and of angels, and have not charity, I am become as sounding brass, or a tinkling cymbal. . . . Charity . . . beareth all things, believeth all things, hopeth all things, endureth all things. . . . For now we see through a glass, darkly; but then face to face: now I know in part; but then shall I know even as also I am known. And now abideth faith, hope, charity, these three; but the greatest of these is charity.

—*1 Cor. 13*

This is the Paul who sings in his heart with grace.

In the Church of Santa Maria del Popolo is also Caravaggio's *Martyrdom of St. Peter,* Peter the Rock, nailed to the cross—an old man's weary flesh. In this painting the expected has happened, the unspeakable expected thing, the obscene expected thing; the terrible thing is happening, and in the imminence of death, Peter's muscles are lax, he has turned to flab (his beard is white and he is partly bald and almost certainly toothless). He looks like any old man dying . . . in the friendship of God. He seems, both bewildered and resigned, to be saying both Yes and Why? And, so great is the humanity of this painting, those who carry the stake, conspirators in his death, are hurting, too, straining against more than the weight of an old man's body.

* * *

The young men in the Piazza del Popolo are so fair it is easy to believe that the breeze that ruffles their hair was made only to complete them. Their existence argues for a moment of sweetness before we turn to dust.

Under Santa Maria del Popolo are Nero's ashes.

The Piazza del Popolo, in spite of its being Rome's largest parking lot, smells green because of its proximity to the Pincian Gardens above. It is nice to sit here, eating gelato at Rosati and regarding the "twin" churches of Santa Maria di Montesanto and Santa Maria dei Miracoli, from which fan out three streets, Via del Babuino, the Ripetta, and the Corso. . . . The churches, I read in a guidebook, "form a proscenium." They do—and it is no wonder that one feels so often caught up in a drama here, even when the conscious mind cannot reckon why.

In the seventeenth century Alexander VII caused to be inscribed, on the inner face of the Porta del Popolo, *Felici fausto ingressui* (For a blessed and prosperous entrance); in the eighteenth century there were still two troughs in the piazza, at one of which women washed clothes and at one of which cattle drank; in the nineteenth century Pope Alexander's inscription was mocked by the presence of a guillotine set up by the French and, later, by customshouse officers, nobody's favorites.

I always feel that I have reached the marked end of Rome when I come here; I think all cities should have gates.

An international women's club is having a luncheon fund-raiser at the Marymount Convent School on Via Nomentana. "Apple pies! Apple pies!" the contessa roars. But at the American booth there are no apple pies, there is orange Jell-O and chicken cooked in Crisco, which nobody, least of all an American, wants to eat. At other booths there are Spanish chicken with saffron and pine nuts, scented Indonesian rice, tandoori chicken, stuffed grape leaves, curries and kebabs and jugs of wine and a purple Thai fruit punch with white orchids floating in it. In the terraced garden of this villa on the outskirts of Rome, the ladies in floating saris look so pretty, and so do all the little girls in convent blue-and-white.

Today the contessa is wearing a polyester shirt adorned with moon and stars, a souvenir of a trip to Hawaii or to Bali, she can't remember which; also powder-pink polyester pants; also strings of lustrous pearls with a clasp of sapphires and an important diamond, also an Etruscan emerald ring and an onyx-and-silver-handled cane. She has walked here, a distance of two miles from her home, never mind her steel hip, taking with her her secretary-companion, who looks fit to faint and who is older than the contessa. The contessa has commandeered six folding chairs in order to hold court. She rejoices to give advice. "Never marry beneath you in this country," she says. "Here you must have a setup. All these mad American girls falling in love with carabinieri! You must have a setup," she says, "a setup." An American girl who is here to grub an inexpensive meal invents on the spot a prestigious career for her Italian lover, who is metamorphosed into a husband—and who is, in fact, a member of the *guardia*. The contessa bats her baby blues. She points to a ninety-year-old woman who from the back looks as if she might be in her twenties. "Who is older?" she asks. "She or I?" She is vain. Today is her eighty-fifth birthday. "In America you can bring your husband up to your class, here they will drag you down," she says. "Americans are all about sex, which isn't important here," she says. "All my maids left, and when I asked them why, they said my husband tried to get into their bedrooms. So at last I hired one I was determined to keep, and she said: 'Contessa, the count is trying to get into my bedroom.' The count denied it, of course. So I said, 'Well, Maria Angelica, lock your bedroom door, what's the problem?' I had the name, after all. Let him play the game, I have the name, after all. . . . A setup," she says, "a setup."

"When does sexual jealousy end?" she is asked, by a young American who has practical reasons for wanting to know. "Why ask me, how should I know, I'm only eighty-five," the contessa says.

Near to the Marymount School is the villa given to Mussolini and his family by Prince Giovanni Torlonia, which the Duce used as a summer residence (he and his wife, Rachele, had separate bedrooms) and occasionally in winter for official receptions. (Among the persons he entertained were Mahatma Gandhi and Ras Tafari, the future Haile Selassie.)

Here Rachele Mussolini raised her chickens and tended her vegetable gardens, and Benito Mussolini kept his pets: an eagle, young lions, and thoroughbred horses.

In 1974 Jewish catacombs were excavated in Villa Torlonia; on almost every monument was found an inscription of a shofar, an oil vase, and a menorah. These remain. But no trace of Mussolini here remains. *Dalla stelle alle stalle*—"from the stars to the stable," they say of him.

* * *

Four dollars is a bit steep for coffee, even at Doneys, particularly as the Via Veneto is no longer the center of smart life; even the Arabs have moved on. . . . Who buys all those high-priced interior-design magazines? Americans who miss their kitchens?

At the foot of the once fashionable, now used-up Via Veneto, near the Piazza Barberini, is the Capuchin cemetery, in the Church of the Immaculate Conception (Santa Maria della Concezione). In that cemetery—an underground passage, forty meters long, with six vaulted chambers—are arranged gracefully and elegantly, in Rococo floral and geometrical designs, the bones of four thousand religious who died between 1528 and 1870; there are also three small skeletons, framed by anonymous bones, those of two young princes and a princess of the Barberini family, grandnephews and grandniece of Pope Urban VIII; and in one chamber are skeletons clothed in their hooded brown Franciscan robes, standing or lying, one of whom seems to have died in terror; his jaw emits a silent scream. (This fellow gave Hawthorne—who invented a sinister Capuchin for *The Marble Faun*—the willies: "One reverend father has his mouth wide open, as if he had died in the midst of a howl of terror and remorse, which perhaps even now is screeching through eternity.") Soil was brought from Jerusalem to accommodate the righteous bones of those privileged to be buried here, and it used to be that when the cemetery got full up, the bones of the longest buried were disinterred to make room for the newest, but this custom no longer prevails.

It is remarkable how many patterns can be made of human bones; even the candelabra here are made of tibia and fibula, wrist bone and ankle bone, shin bone, fingers.

The Church has always invited meditation on the corruption of the body (which, in its relationship to love and together with memories of childhood, is the source of most great poetry and art); the image of a skeleton is an invitation to prudence and humility, an injunction against vanity. But this church is no longer on the pilgrims' path. Perhaps the Church, in its questionable wisdom, decided that the cemetery was almost too merry; it is, really, if one looks at it without the scrim of nervous morbidity, almost as pretty as a fried squash flower, than which nothing is prettier; so pretty it borders on insouciance, it runs the risk of mocking death. Few Italians would be inclined to joke about this cemetery; a more likely response would be a shrug. Americans invariably joke in this cemetery; it makes them nervous.

The cemetery is, of course, a visual pun: It doesn't cover up the evidence.

In Italy it is wise to cultivate a taste for memento mori.

Written on a tibia in Magic Marker: "Stanley loves Mary."

It is too easy to regard this as an anatomy lesson, a curiosity, a flighty arabesque of bones:

We were like you.

You will be like us. . . .

These words remind us of the pyrrhic victory of flesh over time:

"Chi eri? Quale il tuo nome?" the poet writes. "Who were you? What is your name?"

(The cemetery provides us with yet another way to meditate upon the vagaries of time, the ephemeral nature of fame, the leveling of death: When the Victorians came here, Guido Reni's *St. Michael Trampling on the Devil* in the church above the crypt was one of the major attractions of Rome. For years it was not easy to find anyone who remembered Guido Reni's name.)

The cemetery on the Via Veneto is many things, and many things to many people, but if one wants a romantic cemetery—and who, from time to time, does not?—the place to go is the Protestant Cemetery near the Porta San Paolo. Henry James called this place—which Romans call the cemetery not of Protestants but of foreigners—"divine—a place most lovely and solemn and exquisitely full of the traditional Roman quality—with a vast gray pyramid inserted into the sky on one side and the dark cold cypresses on the other, and the light bursting out between them and the whole surrounding landscape swooning away for very picturesqueness."

The marble-sheathed pyramid of which James speaks is the tomb of Gaius Cestius, an ordinary man; it is said to have been completed twenty-eight days after his death in 12 B.C., and not, for his heirs, a moment too soon, as his will provided that his legacies were not to be distributed until a suitable monument was erected to his memory, still warm.

The picturesqueness of the cemetery is mitigated by a mimeographed sheet handed one by its caretaker (who often chooses, grouchy lord of his sylvan domain, not to open its gates at all): One is advised that there is danger on this street from passing cars and pedestrian thieves, one is warned not to vandalize the graves or molest the cats, and governesses are abjured to keep their charges well in hand: "This zone is haunted by bag-snatchers, thieves, and others which she rides a motorcycle with any number plate or on board of cars with a false plate and always two of them."

Some people think this is the most beautiful cemetery in the world.

Oleanders (a plant so poisonous a foraging goat will pass it by), brooding cypresses, romantic palms, tidy box hedges; the dizzying sweetness of white jasmine arranged in bowers (almost nuptial) over tombs—it is the quintessential expression of expatriate angst.

What I like best about the cemetery is that it is incorporated into the Aurelian Wall, which seems to shelter it. The wall throws a comforting shadow over Shelley's tomb, under which, we are pleased to believe, lies Shelley's heart, snatched from his funeral pyre by Byron: "Nothing of him that doth fade / But doth suffer a sea-change / Into something rich and strange."

Shelley attributed Keats's death to the viciousness of English reviewers; but when Keats arrived in Italy, in 1820, on his twenty-fifth birthday, he was already dying of consumption. Irritable and nervous as a result of his sickness, he refused to stroll in the Pincio Gardens, for which he blamed Napoleon's sister Pauline, the Borghese princess; he was jealous of a tall English lieutenant with whom she flirted—he was short, and vain. Keats is buried under a stone engraved with a Grecian lyre with half its strings broken, a modest memorial designed by his friend the painter Joseph Severn at Keats's request. . . . Too modest; there is also this monument to Keats:

K eats if thy cherished name be "writ in water"
E ach drop has fallen from some mourner's cheek
A sacred tribute; such as heroes seek
T hough oft in vain for dazzling deeds and slaughter
S leep on! Not honored less for epitaph so meek!

Here, besides the famous two, are buried the three-year-old son of Mary Wollstonecraft Shelley and the poet; Goethe's son, August (whose stone leaves him, strangely, unnamed); and John Addington Symonds, who thought that Rome was feminine. Here also lies one William Beckfad of Surrey, to whom Mozart was tutor and whose ambition it was to build the tallest tower in the world. It is hard to find a grave that does not strike a chord: Bobbye Stephans, Beaumont, Texas, born December 19, 1939, died January 31, 1960, Tripoli, Libya—he died when I lived in Libya; perhaps I saw him there. What strange destinies took men and women from Kentucky and from Ceylon—from Libya—to die in the shadow of the pyramid and the wall?

"Returned to the eternal kiss of God through the soul is the earthly essence of the always loved son," says one epitaph. "Who loved much and was loved," says another. Even now I feel a connection to the souls for whom those inscriptions were written; and that is one of the purposes of cemeteries: to unite in love the living with the dead, to remind us that time does not exist in eternity, to create a necessary compact, to prepare us for death while simultaneously causing us to hug life.

"I always made an awkward bow!" Keats wrote his friend Charles Armitage Brown before he died (a "deadly sweat" on him) in a little corner room of a building overlooking the Piazza di Spagna, which is conveniently, if not entirely romantically, situated between the offices of American Express and Babington's Tearoom.

It is easy to convert even this most-touristed piazza to a village in your mind: a stop at the newsstand (the proprietress gets to know you after the second or third time, a miracle, considering the hundreds of foreigners who sit, loll, cruise on the Spanish Steps, where once thieves and murderers found asylum from papal gendarmes); a banking stop at American Express; flowers to buy, a splashy extravagance, at the foot of the steps near the Barcaccia, the Boat Fountain. (The Barcaccia, designed by Bernini or by his father—no one is sure—is a sinking boat, a barge, set in cobblestones at the foot of a sweeping orchestral flight of steps; it is so silly as to be felicitous . . . and it is entirely owing to the fact that water pressure at this place could not be got to rise in plume or jet.) Tea at Babington's.

There are times when only Babington's will do. Perhaps I do miss America after all, for here I am, wolfing down eggs Benedict and being served by waitresses, which makes a change, as does the determined gentility of chintz.

Lala today is distraught. She has sent for her son to come from New York, as a result of which she—and he—are lost in the thickets, the quagmire, the morass, the labyrinth, the metaphysics of Italian law. All that I understand are the wrinkles on Lala's brow; the Byzantine whys and wherefores of Italian law and of her son's standing in this country—his right to an education and his obligation to soldier (he is half American)—are lost on me. Lala calls me every time she finds a new law or a new clause in an old law that cancels, or appears to cancel, an old clause in the applicable law. It seems to me that with so many regulations and cancellations, there is no working law at all. That's just the trouble, Lala says; today a law clerk has found a new footnote for her edification. ("All ancient Roman law," Giambattista Vico wrote, "was a serious poem . . . and ancient jurisprudence was a severe poetry. . . . By its fictions what had happened was taken as not having happened, and what had not happened as having happened." The same might be said of contemporary Italian law.) Lala has invested all her money in an American nuclear power plant that has shut down; such bad luck seems hardly credible. (It is another's fault, her adviser has brought her bad luck.) She does not know how she will live, she is afraid of being poor. She wants her son here, he is her social security. Nevertheless, *"Gli Italiani si fanno all'estero,"* she says ruefully. "Italians make something of themselves only abroad." Poor Lala. She thinks she will grapple with the law forever. (Perhaps, like Alice, her son will disappear through it, or find an opening.)

This is one of the few dining rooms in Rome that choose not to be vivacious; at the next table a young American woman says: "Oh, us! Oh, us, too!" She cannot constrain herself. She and her fiancé are also caught in the coils of the law, and all for love. In an attempt to escape their large southern families and be married in simplicity, they decided to be married in Rome, and no one at the Italian Consulate could find an impediment. But here they have been for three months—in separate bedrooms, a gesture to the anticipated newness of their wedding day, now receding—in an attempt to satisfy yet another official, yet another regulation. Better large Texas families than this. "God bless America," Lala says fervently, nuclear plants notwithstanding. The young southern woman is eating quantities of whipped cream.

Louis Inturrisi has written one of the nicest descriptions of the Spanish Steps I have read:

> [The staircase] is not only grandly theatrical but stirringly musical as well. It swells and contracts in three exhilarating movements upward, three sets of flights and three landings, which allude to the Church of the Trinity at the top.
>
> The Spanish Steps do for space what a Baroque concerto does with time. The rhythms produced by the variations of intervals, angles, directions and landings suggest the irregularities and surprises of Vivaldi or Handel. Straight lines have been avoided in favor of curves and ellipses. The first three flights of steps in the first set flow outward in convex waves; the fourth is concave. The climber is directed from the center to the sides to the center again along 11 ramps that widen, then narrow, then widen again, while the curvilinear balustrades mark the intervals and separate the movement with pauses. Nowhere in Rome is the music of form so brilliantly illustrated architecturally.

* * *

On the Via Sistina Goethe planted a date palm from a "kernel" and lived to see it grow to the size of a man.

I seldom buy anything from the shops on the fashionable streets that fan out from Piazza di Spagna, but I love to walk here, because to do so evokes the magic I felt when I first came to Rome. On the Via Condotti, among the fancy shops, are the huge wooden doors of a palazzo, and inside, there is a cobblestoned courtyard—umber walls, green vines, a satyr's hushed and broken stone face, a wall fountain, a place where quiet reigns, a refuge (there are many; and the thrill is to find your own, and make it your familiar place).

Julia, on the other hand, spends hours in the bar of the Hotel L'Ingliterra off the Via Condotti. It is icy-cold air-conditioned, and she hears English spoken and forgets she is in Rome, which amnesia is the avowed purpose of all her days. It is not true that she goes there to pick up men.

On the Via Margutta, which leads me nicely from Piazza di Spagna into Piazza del Popolo (this was once the English "ghetto" of Rome), I collect many cards from many dealers in rugs, antiques, and curiosities. I know I will never return to buy anything on this romantic street of galleries and shops and artisans and houses that look like those of artists but that artists can nowadays seldom afford, and they know I will not return, and we maintain the pleasant fiction for the sake of saving face. It requires much less energy than digging in one's heels, just as being kind is infinitely more relaxing than being unkind. Through courtyards into sculpture galleries: *Originals, "Originals," and "Original Copies."* One can't escape the conclusion that the contemporary artists shown here are either self-consciously aping masters or going out of their way not to. How does anyone dare to sculpt in the land of Michelangelo? (Of course one might just as well ask, "How does anyone dare to write in the language of Shakespeare?")

How can a watercolor of a barren Sicilian square dominated by an ancient country church, with a single bent old lady in black, even if it is badly executed, fail to be dramatic?

I have lunch at Osteria Margutta; the waiter lights table candles for the solitary couple dining in the place—they are in love, or so it suits his fancy to believe—but not for a group of antique dealers, and not for me. These are the times it is hard to be alone. Among framed children's drawings— rough, crude, energetic—are mirrors framed in red in which, too many times, I see my solitary reflection (I am eating fettuccine and young asparagus). I once had a lover who asked: "Why do people have to *masticate* together?" He thought eating was more intimate than sex; no perversion surprises me.

Two thrones made of concrete and seashells (too self-conscious to be folk art) stand in the middle of the street; in one of them a man sits, snoring. It is that hour, dreadful to tourists, when the restaurants are closed and the shops are not yet open.

On a marble plaque on the Via Margutta, nicely engraved, is this sign: PER ORDINE ESPRESSO DI MONSIG. ILL. MO. REV. DO. PRESIDENTE DELLE STRADE SI PROIBISCE ESPRESSAMENTE A QUALQUNQUE PERSONA DI GETTARE IMMONDIZIE E FARE MONDEZZARO IN QUESTA STRADA SOTTO PENE DI SCUDI DIECE ED ALTRE PENE AD ARBITRIO DI SUA SIG.RIA. ILL.MA. IN CONFORMITA DELL EDITO EMNATO IL P.O. MARZO MDCCXXXXI. It means that it is forbidden to throw trash in the street and that offenders will be fined. Roman gestures are fervently succinct; Roman language is not necessarily so.

Rome is a city of signs and inscriptions, not all of them admonitory; one is tempted to believe that anyone who has said more than three words in public here will find himself immortalized; as a Victorian writer remarked: "The whole history of the Eternal City might be compiled from the inscriptions left behind them by the successive generations who lived their little day within its boundaries."

On the Via Caetani in the Jewish Ghetto is a plaque to the memory of Christian Democrat leader Aldo Moro, whose body was found here, murdered by his kidnappers, members of the despicable Red Brigades. All of Rome mourned. Every church in Rome was filled that day in May 1978. It is difficult to say why some deaths become symbolic. (On the anniversary of the death of Enrico Berlinguer, Communist party secretary, crowds gather to cry in the Piazza Venezia, and go to church, too; and "Liberation Day" is celebrated exactly as if the Romans had been on our side in World War II.) It is said that Aldo Moro was a decent man. There are always flowers, there, where his butchered body was found.

Lala has a strange custom: She writes the names of terrorists in a book. She says she does so as insurance against God's forgetting and being too kind to them. Today she writes the name of Barbara Balzerani, captured in Ostia, wanted for the murder of Aldo Moro. In her book Lala has also written "Moroccans" many times, for the Fifth Army Goums who came to liberate her village in the dying days of World War II and raped and pillaged. She was just a little girl; but she does not forget. In her dreams there is a thunder of black boots.

* * *

In the eighteenth year of his life Filippo Neri, born of a noble family in Florence, experienced a profound conversion and went as a result to Rome, the spiritual center and the interpreter of the world. He lived reclusively for two years, tutoring two sons of a wealthy Florentine, and then he studied theology and philosophy, and then he busied himself preaching on the streets and in the marketplaces to Romans of shaky and casual faith, exhorting them to abandon evil, serve the sick, and visit the seven pilgrim churches of Rome in his company. In 1544 an orb of fire entered his mouth and palpitated his heart (this he saw in a vision); he read the secrets of men's hearts. With his confessor, he organized laymen to pray and to minister to pilgrims, founding the Confraternity of the Most Holy Trinity, which became Santa Trinità dei Pellegrini Hospital. In 1551, at the age of thirty-six, he was ordained. He made many converts; he was shrewd, sweet-natured, and magnetic, and he had an immense following among cardinals, the nobility, the exalted and the troubled, the rich and the poor. The priest–disciples and the laymen he gathered to him became known as Oratorians, because he used an oratory above the nave of San Girolamo (it is from them that the name of the art form comes; Palestrina was his friend). In his community (whose dual aims were practical charity and personal sanctification through the development of individual gifts), music, service, prayer, discussion, and manual labor were given equal status. In Goethe's words, "with . . . mysterious spiritual graces he combined the clearest common sense . . . and an active charity." In him "the holy could unite with the worldly, the virtuous with the things of every day."

John Henry Cardinal Newman said: "Whatever was exact and systematic pleased him not; he put from him monastic rule and authoritative speech, as David refused the armor of his king."

He wished at one time to become a foreign missionary, but he was told: Rome will be your Indies (his America, his newfound land). He is known as "the apostle to Rome."

He was an- ecstatic but is said to have tried to conceal and control his ecstasies; he was alarmed by visionaries, especially if they were women. He liked to play practical jokes, sometimes to test the mettle of would-be followers. He was a happy man. Because he insisted on the absolution of Henry IV of Navarre, the former Huguenot, a conflict between France and the Holy See was avoided in 1593, and the balance of power with Spain was maintained.

At the end of an ordinary day in May, "Last of all, we must die," he said; and then he did.

He exemplifies the practicality of Italian spirituality—the mystical Spaniards were given to the fires of the Inquisition—during the Counter Reformation.

He is called the Apostle of Joy.

Off the Corso Vittorio Emanuele, not far from Piazza Navona, is the Palazzo Massimo, the masterpiece of Baldassare Peruzzi. The palace, which belongs to the Massimos, the oldest family in Rome, is composed of three buildings; the oldest of the three overlooks a small piazza in which a beautiful, palpable silence reigns. From the Piazza Massimo the fountains of Piazza Navona are visible; they play but make no sound. This is wonderful. In this palazzo, on March 16, 1583, San Filippo Neri brought the lifeless body of Paolo Massimo back from death. But the boy, safe in the bosom of his family, declared that he was ready to die, and San Filippo said: "Go and be blessed and pray to God for me." Every March 16, Masses are celebrated in memory of this miracle in the second-floor chapel of the palazzo belonging to this august family, and all who wish may come, from the humble to the high, a good and wonderful thing.

I hold J. up as an example of that which I choose not to believe is inherent in the Italian male: languid cynicism and lechery, and grubbiness disguised as fashion.

One day, strolling near Piazza Navona, past the ivy-covered Hotel Raphael, I stopped to look at a menu posted outside a clubby-looking restaurant, and a well-dressed man (he says he's forty-nine; I don't believe him) invited me in. Caution blunted (this is the heart of Rome, I love it almost jealously), I accepted coffee in an eggshell cup. "I bought this place from ———— [a famous American film director]," he says. Rich burgundy leather; brass; a stale scent of heliotrope lingering on chilled tobacco-heavy air; dark. And in the course of business, J. says, he met and now is on intimate terms with ———— and ———— (two famous American actors). "All Mafia," he says, "all Mafia . . . laundering money through films." He names two major distributors, who, he says, supply arms, for which the films are merely a front. "Can you doubt it?" he says, "given the quality of the films?" Unless he is lying, J. owns a well-known club on the Via Veneto. I don't think he's lying. I can see him, white hair and blue eyes, shoulders tailored to swooning point, Roman and self-contained, dealing with his colleagues in Vegas; cool. He entirely dislikes America. He believes, or claims to believe, that 60 percent of all Italians are somehow connected to the mob; he is Catholic, but—cynicism is so boring, it makes one stupid—he does not like priests; Socialists, Mafia, Fascists are "all the same people," he says; he has an invincible belief in the corruptibility of all. "And you?" I ask. "A simple honest businessman," he says, with a grin approaching a leer. "And you, are you a saint?" he asks. He wants to know about the Godard film and in particular about its nudity. (The boy wiping glasses behind the bar smiles, and makes me feel unclean.) "Is Godard's Maria a saint?" he asks; "are you?" The boy behind the bar is enjoying this very much; I know where this is leading to. "Jews have all the money in Rome," J. says. He is shifting—in heat—on the soft leather couch. I give him my phone number, out of courtesy (and, in small measure, fear); I give him one incorrect digit; he knows that I have done so. He believes in the venality of all; he suspects all passion, believing none of it to be genuine. I know absolutely that he does terrible things in bed.

He wants to be in a book.

In Rome you don't have to work for your pleasures. If you just stand still—at the junction of the Via della Pace and the Via di Parione, between Piazza Navona and the Corso (for example)—this is what you can see: an 1870s café (samovar, brass fittings, marble tables, sinuous hardware on glass double doors . . . push aside wisteria to get in past the tarnished gilt lettering . . . young Romans gather here, it is a neighborhood café, everybody in the neighborhood is beautiful and young and has long hair; the wooden floor is uneven, the cappuccino machine hisses, there is steam, like fine crystal dust, in the air . . . this café is set into a salmon-colored, pie-shaped building; above its doors is a romantic picture of the Virgin); fruit and vegetable stands; a wheelbarrow full of old prints; a shrine to the Virgin (yet another), over which is painted a red hammer and sickle; the lovely semicircular porch of Santa Maria della Pace, concave, convex, around which Pietro da Cortona designed this square, leaving no effect to chance (a nun is washing the portico, on which there is vomit; the abandoned of Rome and young American boys and girls huddle here, where it is cool and shaded . . . inside is a fresco by Raphael); an *alimentari;* a Chinese restaurant with red lanterns and gold lanterns; and—it can't be helped, Italy arranges itself so, "as if everyone were an extra," a friend says—a man in white carrying an enormous mortadella on his shoulder; an old man all in black with a black bird perched on his shoulder (a crow?). All this in one's field of vision—is Rome not too good to be true?

Behind Santa Maria della Pace rises a pretty and eccentric steeple that appears to be fashioned of turquoise-blue and yellow balls. Explore: through a small door (a rectory, perhaps?); the *portiere* shakes his finger No. But then a young man arrives and opens the door (No. 20, Santa Maria dell'Anima) to a courtyard in which are fragments of Cosmati pavement, mythological marbles, succulents. From this place—the courtyard of the German hospice/seminary—the German Church of Santa Maria dell'Anima can be entered; it is distinguished by stained-glass windows atypical of Rome, varnish, lemon oil, extreme cleanliness, and shining order. Built by Pope Clement in the thirteenth century, thirty years after Boniface declared the First Holy Year, it has been restored many times, as its Baroque ceiling and its central altar painting (school of Raphael) show; it is, however one looks at it, imbued with a certain Teutonic feeling, and it is, properly speaking, a chapel, not a church at all. (The young man who welcomed us in so charmingly is a priest from Tyrol.) Marble monuments to Crusaders are here, and so is the tomb of Pope Adrian VI—the last non-Italian Pope before John Paul II.

On Via Santa Maria dell'Anima, surrounded by antique stores and old-and-funky-clothes shops, is what may be the best gift and housewares shop in Rome. It is called Spazio Sette, and to get to it, you pass through a courtyard with trailing vines and climb a grand staircase to the *piano nobile* of a palazzo. I bought a wedding gift for a princess here.

In this section, dear to the heart of lovers of Rome, where Sansovino, Bramante, and Bernini so beautifully play in the fields of the Lord, everything humble unites with everything grand, illustrating, as perhaps no other place in Rome does quite so well, why it is impossible to describe the charm and impact of Rome by describing the churches and the monuments of Rome:

What does it mean to you when I say: a café, 1870 . . . a church? . . . Can you see this intimate and holy juxtaposition? Does it say to you: The material world—that boy scribbling furiously, tugging at his forelock, that pale young girl in black tights—belongs, as much as Santa Maria della Pace does, to God?

Santa Maria della Pace and Santa Maria dell'Anima form a whole and straddle two streets (the sun shimmers off the absurd blue-and-gold Gothic balls, a perpetual Teutonic-Latin Christmas), and a kind of tunnel is formed in which there are dark, ambiguous odors, mostly (if odor had color) opaque green, but an undertone of something other, not quite wholesome, almost threatening . . . and that has the effect of propelling you out . . . and, suddenly! an explosion of light: the Piazza Navona (which, like everything else in Rome, owes its aesthetic value, and its conveyance of glad surprise, to everything that surrounds it) . . . such light. And such preparation by stages for such light: piazza-tunnel-piazza-light. You feel the changes on— in—your flesh: You feel the dark on your skin; then you feel the light on your skin; you feel as if you have traveled enormous distances. All journeys, carried to their logical, their ultimate, conclusion, are safe journeys; they lead into light.

Tre Scalini: saltimbocca, spinach, and tartufo—a rich chocolate ball riddled with generous chunks of even richer bittersweet chocolate, a cherry in the middle, whipped cream on top, a baroque confection.

About the fountains in Piazza Navona—Bernini's riotous Four Rivers (rock, water, man, palm, horse: the Nile . . . the men are holding up the sky); the Fountain of the Moor; the Fountain of Neptune—and about Borromini's Church of Sant'Agnese in Agone, and the rivalry between Bernini and Borromini, much has and will be written, but not by me (I feel as if I carry the memory of this place somewhere just inside my skin).

The long and narrow piazza has had a long and happy history. It was, as its shape suggests, a stadium, Domitian's, for athletic contests but not of the bloody kind; it was flooded in the summer and used for water sports; a great deal of happiness has accumulated here. (We always know instinctively places where a great deal of happiness has accumulated.) At one end of the piazza, Mussolini's excavators exposed part of the substructure of Domitian's stadium, and they tried, at that end of the piazza, on Via Zanardelli, to "open the piazza up." They made a mess, but they didn't— they couldn't—ruin the piazza.

One day I was buying lipstick at the *farmacia* on the piazza near the stones and columns of Domitian's ruins, and the man behind the counter seemed to be having more fun than I was comparing shades. I caught his eye, and he said: "What can I say, signora? Il Duce made it a crime to be a man like me; the Pope, he thinks it is a sin to be a man like me . . . but me? I pray every night for the Holy Father that God should enlighten him, and Mussolini is dead, he gets no prayers from me, and look at this red—*bello*—it is a lovely job and I am still alive, too, I've made a good thing of it, I am not a ruin."

I watch a curtain move. Inside an old house is an old lady looking out. The house is umber, splashed with geraniums and sprays of roses. She leans her heavy breasts on soft pillows on the windowsill and looks out. What does she make of me and my perfumed friend? In another house vines grow inside on the ceiling; this is true.

One day: Around the Fountain of the Moor, actors mime; their faces are painted (masks are loathsome to me); they wear pantaloons, making themselves ridiculous. They strike Martha Graham–like poses; they squat, hands to brow. Their audience consists of three bland nuns; two inebriated men, one swigging and crossing himself and uttering blasphemy, the other cheering them on. This group calls itself part of a "Charismatic Renewal." They are Catholics who claim to be born again, evangelizing; their presumption takes my breath away. "Do you have a personal relationship with God?" they ask, so presumptuous. Their eyes are oily with fanaticism. They have come from Malta, New Zealand, Ireland to reform Rome. Those Italians who do not find them amusing and fit for light banter give them a wide berth. Imagine this sorry, arrogant little group, this dim spectacle, this shabby theater, trying to take Rome by storm. The police threw them out of St. Peter's Square; then they got permission from the Vatican to carry on. One gathers they are rather sorry they got permission; "persecution" suits them, as it suits all fanatics; it proves to them—in the positive absence of other proof—that they are chosen. The presumption of a blond California giant telling Italians how to be Catholic! They treat the Sacraments with derision: "Were you 'sprinkled'?" they ask. This is not charming. "You didn't expect to find us here, did you?" they say, as if their presence were clever in itself; how vain. They are all jerky energy and no substance. The Church has had its reformers—Filippo Neri disturbed slack Romans in the streets, and Savonarola thundered in the pulpit, and many Catholic Evangelicals, during the 1530s and 1540s, defected to Protestantism—but these children are brazen, superficial, silly. They will go away and no one will remember them.

I am taught by my Church that I must love them, that I must not call them lost. Everything about Christianity is, on the face of it, ridiculous: How can one love idiots, and how can one not call idiots idiots? In Rome I tend to forget the vileness of human nature; the physical world is proof to me, here, that God became incarnate . . . that He died for us does not seem so shocking (it seems only miraculous) because human nature, here, is so nice (by which I mean so much to my liking); I tend to forget the vileness of human nature—except my own. I know what my confessor would say. He would say, "By reminding you of the vileness of human nature those children did you a service"; and I would glare.

St. Eustace, first-century martyr, patron of the chase (a popular saint in England), was a Roman general under Trajan, a member of Empress Octavia's family, who was converted when, hunting in Tivoli, he saw a vision of Christ between the antlers of a stag. He served his emperor well, but refused to make a sacrifice to Jupiter, and so, with his wife and two children, was roasted alive inside a brazen bull.

Never mind that he did not, in all probability, exist.

This fairy tale (legends about saints are often both charming and gruesome) accounts for one of Rome's most wonderful visual surprises: the great head of a stag, a cross amidst the antlers, on top of the rather homely Church of Sant'Eustachio. It looks positively loony. . . . But, then again, not. "We can't hunt God," Robert Lowell says; "he hunts us" ("and his story is sad").

Near Sant'Eustachio, between Piazza Navona and the Pantheon, lies "the French Quarter," which is little more than a bookshop (with posters of Roland Barthes) and the "French church," San Luigi dei Francesi (next to the Senate building), in which, in the Chapel of St. Matthew, are three huge and radiant paintings by Caravaggio in a remarkably small space.

Death be not proud. Matthew is so clearly the winner, his executioners so clearly the losers, one is reminded again, through this glowing visual essay, that art is a form of visual propaganda, and one wonders, anew, at the difference (or the relationship) between the work and the worker, for the painter of Matthew's victorious martyrdom was well known to the police for misdemeanors: He once threw a dish of artichokes at someone's head (that is not what I would call a serious crime, unless the artichokes were out of season); he killed a man in a duel (and died, in exile from Rome, at the age of thirty-seven).

Hawthorne called this church (probably by Giacomo della Porta) "most shamefully dingy and dirty"; he did not love Caravaggio. (He almost never left his house; he considered that Rome had "a peculiar quality of malignity"; occasionally he went to St. Peter's, where he found he could keep warm.)

On Via Monterone, one of the streets that empties into the Piazza di Sant'Eustachio, is a rather extraordinary restaurant, behind a lacquered blue door, in the palazzo that houses the Republican party of Italy; it is called L'Eau Vive.

(When Julia says she is running away from Massimo, what she means is she is coming here, to vaulted, frescoed ceilings and discreet lighting, to eat French food to the strains of Vivaldi, surrounded by diplomats, moneyed priests, and cardinals. "Ah, Vivaldi!" she sighs, as if Vivaldi had come from her beloved northern climes.)

The restaurant is run by people who call themselves the Working Missionaries of the Immaculate Conception; tables are served by self-effacing laywomen—"Christian Virgins"—women of color about whom both Romans and expatriates are curious and skeptical. There are L'Eau Vives in Belgium; Buenos Aires; Ougadouga and Bobo-Diolosso, Africa; Oceania; Vietnam; Manila; Peru.

> A house aperitif
> Salmon soup, cream- and chicken broth–based, lightly flavored
>   with dill, fennel, and onions
> Smoked trout with strawberries
> Filet mignon with béarnaise sauce; French-fried potatoes
> Alsace wine
> Chocolate mousse
> Coffee

"If anyone says the Hail Mary, I'm leaving," Julia says. Sometimes at night, I'm told, they do. I am not in the least Albigensian, but I can't quite grasp smoked trout and strawberries and the rosary.

At Pina's house, Armando said this shining sentence: "I knew my wife—I comprehended her in three days—and I wanted to live with her forever."

Pina says: "Women command the night."

We are having dinner at Pina and Franco's flat in the suburb of Parioli:

figs, melon and prosciutto, lombata di vitello, cheeses, green tomato salad, pineapple with cherries and whipped cream. The men are holding forth on the subject of family power, so Pina says: "Women command the night." It is clear that her love life is bliss.

Pina, the baker's beautiful daughter, has come far, but in unimportant ways she is provincial. Her ingrained frugality has led her to make a gaffe: She thinks she has given us the season's first figs, whereas the season is ending, she has not bought figs before, they are a luxury, and she is saving for a child. This embarrasses only her. Franco, her husband, is incapable of being embarrassed by her, which is one reason their marriage is enviable. Also, Pina thinks the Art Deco doors and the brass fittings and the pink marble fireplace of her drawing room are "old-fashioned"; she wants to rip them out. I have just had a long conversation with a friend about the decorative arts, he thinks anyone to whom they matter has a frivolous nature (in one of my favorite fantasies, I occupy a small corner of a museum, honorably anonymous, cataloging objets d'art); when I hear Pina's plans for pruning her spectacular flat, I gasp. She receives this as proof that all Americans are crazy—*"ma simpatici,"* she hastens to add.

Now everyone piles into Franco's big car—Franco, Pina, dear Armando, their friend Tommaso—and we drive to Sant'Eustachio for coffee.

It works like this: We drive one-half hour; we park; we cannot park near the Piazza di Sant'Eustachio, the whole world is strolling. So we walk—one-half hour. We drink our coffee—thought by many people to be the best coffee in Rome—standing up. This—the drinking part—takes three minutes; then we walk back to the car. I am defeated. My sedentary bones do not understand an hour's walk for a three-minute cup of coffee.

This night we go from Eustachio to Navona, my idea, for ices; we eat them standing up, Pina's idea. *"Soldi, soldi,"* she says; it is cheaper to eat ices standing up. Tommaso, who has had two aperitifs, countless glasses of red wine, and a tumblerful of grappa, passes up the ice—he says it is bad for his liver. I love Italians.

The night is glorious. The dark sky glows, as if, above the layer of blue-black, there were another layer, of white transparent light. The streets belong to the people—grandmothers, young hustlers, and everything in between.

Sometimes, away from Rome, I feel that Rome exists in my imagination, that it is a rare and blessed state of mind.

After we have walked twenty minutes, "Where is the car?" I ask Armando. (We have taken a different route back; yesterday, near here, I saw, high on the wall of Filippo Neri's Oratory, an exuberant Virgin surrounded by a glory of puffing angels; tonight the Pantheon seems new to me—I have never approached it from quite this angle, and I see, bathed in moonlight, two columns, noble and at home, from the baths of Alexander Severus. . . . One is always, every day, seeing something new in Rome.)

"*Sempre diritto,* two hundred meters," Armando says. "But Italians *always* say '*sempre diritto,* two hundred meters,' " I say. "If we made it complicated, you'd think we didn't like you," Armando says. I love Italians.

Whenever I wake up and feel remotely as if a blue mood might be stealing over me, I go directly to the Pantheon, where unhappiness cannot exist; God has abolished it by fiat (that is what I think).

I toy with the idea of moving into the Albergo del Sole on the Piazza della Rotonda, into a front room, so that from what may or may not be the oldest hotel in Rome (in such winsome arguments are hours whiled away), I can day and night be in that cobblestoned square that dips slightly toward the most beautiful temple on earth. Surrounded by modest old orange and yellow houses made happier by pots of red flowers, there I will sit all night and every day, I will sit in a café that overlooks Ramses' obelisk and Giacomo della Porta's fountain—which are a gloss on the perfection of the Pantheon.

One day, sitting in this square, I had this thought: This is what a bun waiting to rise must feel like.

I toy with the idea of moving to the Albergo Portoghesi, an old town mansion in an operatic piazza, with its funny little suites of rooms, its faded gentility, yellowed lace curtains, sleepy staff, its roof garden—how fat the bees are in summer among the breakfast cups—from which one can see, above the rooftops of many different centuries, the Torre della Scimmia— the Tower of the Monkey, the medieval tower of a Frangipani fortress. (There is a famous treasure, "Frangipani's treasure," which that family— whose name is that of a delicate white flower—is said to have buried under the Colosseum in the Middle Ages.) Hawthorne placed his pilgrim soul, Hilda, in that tower; in it every night she lights a beacon lamp to Mary against the dark. (It's a pretty little story; poor Hawthorne, his Protestant soul so agitated by the Rome of all the senses, so enamored and frightened of the Virgin.) According to legend, there was once a monkey that climbed to the top of the tower with a baby in its arms; when, after the infant's father prayed to Mary for his safety, the monkey climbed into a window, and the child was restored to him, he vowed to keep a lamp lit on top of the fortress forever. The story may not be true—who cares? Any story, once told, has a certain kind of truth. From the Albergo Portoghesi that light can still be seen.

From that enchanting corner of Rome a five-minute walk would take me to the Pantheon, and every step would be a delight (I don't know why I try to avoid the word *rapture*. . . . And only two minutes to Volpetti, Rome's most wonderful *rosticceria,* on Via della Scrofa, but that's another matter: squash flowers fried in batter with mozzarella and anchovies to go).

Inside the Pantheon I feel (no other space bestows this blessing) absolutely safe.

A man I admire says he would like to die sliding into home base after hitting an inside-the-park home run; I do see the joy in that. . . . I would like to die in the Pantheon; I would like it to be an ordinary day; I would like just enough time for that gasp of praise that is indistinguishable from joy and then . . . whatever. NOTHING BAD CAN HAPPEN HERE. . . . Teilhard de Chardin's last words were: "The terrible thing is happening." (That has always disturbed my mind.)

(My son cried here when he was five years old. "Why are you crying?" I said. "Because it's perfect," he said. These are his earliest memories: opening a box of cereal and finding two toy tanks, one orange, one green, and deciding which color was best suited to a tank; bringing a toy boat to nursery school and being given a sheet of blue paper to put it on; standing under the dome of the Pantheon. He does not remember that he cried. This is a sentimental story, but it is true. He is a painter.)

The Pantheon was built by Agrippa in 27 B.C. and dedicated to all the gods. Damaged by fire, it was restored in the year 80 by Domitian. In the second century A.D. Hadrian rebuilt it. The first Christian emperors closed it; the barbarians sacked it—gilded bronze plates and precious marbles are gone—as did Emperor Constantine, who wished to enrich Constantinople; Boniface IV saved it, whereupon it was converted to a church dedicated to Mary; during the Renaissance it was denuded of remaining bronze by the Barberini pope Urban VII (the bronze was converted into Bernini's baldaquin in St. Peter's); Raphael is buried here.

It is a domed rotunda with a rectangular portico beneath a pediment, supported by sixteen granite pillars. "The structure is of monumental simplicity and great scale. . . . The circular interior is covered by a hemispherical dome 144 feet in diameter, the summit of the dome being the same distance from the floor. . . . The center of the dome is dramatically pierced by a round opening . . . 30 feet in diameter, which, left unglazed and open to the sky, is the only source of light from the interior."* There are deep recesses in the walls, round and rectangular (they are now chapels), and, around them, monolithic marble columns. The dome is coffered. The floor is slightly convex.

This is perfect space.

"The experience one has on first entering this tremendous, shaped space [is] a feeling not of the weight of the enclosing masses, but of the palpable presence of space itself. . . . It is a whole that encloses the visitor without imprisoning him, a small cosmos that opens through the oculus to the drifting clouds, the blue sky, the sun, universal nature, and the gods."†

"By far the most beautiful piece of ancientry in Rome is that simple and unutterable Pantheon. . . . It's the most conclusive example I have yet seen of the simple sublime."‡

"The Pantheon has this great advantage: it requires only two moments to be penetrated by its beauty. You stop before the portico; you take a few steps, you see the church, and the whole thing is over. . . . I have never met a being absolutely devoid of emotion at the sight of the Pantheon. . . . This immense vault, suspended over their heads without apparent support, gives simpletons a sense of fear; presently they become reassured and say to themselves, 'After all, if they have gone to the trouble to give me this powerful sensation, it is in order to give me pleasure!'

"Is this not what we mean by the sublime?"§

"Life is probably *round.*"‖

Perhaps, if one will be, in Heaven, only as happy as one was in one's happiest moments on earth—no more, no less—all the world should be taken to the Pantheon; perhaps Heaven is "the palpable presence of space itself . . . a whole that encloses . . . without imprisoning."# It will do for a hypochondriac and an agoraphobic (I am both).

No sense of beneficence can match this: clouds drifting overhead in a blue sky seen through the eye—the good, all-seeing, nonjudging eye—of that

Gardner's Art Through the Ages.

†*Ibid.*

‡Henry James, *Letters,* Vol. I.

§Stendhal, *A Roman Journal.*

‖Vincent van Gogh, as quoted in Bachelard, *The Poetics of Space.*

#Gaston Bachelard, *The Poetics of Space.*

dome. I want to dance. I want to be stiller than I have ever in my life been still. I want to skate on a thin sheet of ice across the marble floor of that temple . . . elevated, consecrated, dedicated to the Most High God.

Schoolchildren sing in Latin. PRAISE HIS NAME! they sing, testing one's heart to the limits of joy.

I sit here for hours. Dear God, let me be this happy in Heaven.

I sit at the café for hours. If Heaven rejects me, I have had this.

A crone—almost doubled over though her only burden is roses—walks down the slight incline to the Pantheon, a gray shawl draped around her hunched shoulders. She is older than old, older than the Pantheon. Old is older than ancient.

In an excellent trattoria off the square, I eat: pasta with lentils, a grilled veal chop, beet greens with lemon. . . .

If there is one lesson Rome teaches, it is that matter is good; in Rome the holy and the homely rise and converge.

There are always flowers on Raphael's tomb in the Pantheon; many artists inspire awe, but few such sweet solicitations of love. Stendhal pays Raphael the nicest of compliments: "It does not appear that he ever hated anyone, he was too much taken up with his loves and with his works." Goethe says he saw the skull of Raphael in the Accademia di San Luca—"a brain-pan of beautiful proportions and perfectly smooth without any of those protuberances and bumps which appear on other skulls"—but the bones of Raphael (put to rest when he was only thirty-seven) never rested there.

"Have you ever noticed," B. says, "how Italian men scratch their crotches when they're thinking?" They do.

B. and Lala and I went to Ostia Antica. We drank sticky orange drinks and Chinotto—which resembles Coca-Cola but is slightly, and pleasantly, bitter. I found a piece of a marble cornice among nicotiana and thyme and took it home with me.

First a military and then a commercial port, domestic Ostia, not splendid like the Forum, inspires a picnicky mood; it's nice to rummage through a ruined house, a shop, a cemetery, an apartment, a tavern, a synagogue, a church, a marketplace, in the grass-sweet summer air. Lala (who is, unless the provocation is extreme, sedate) stays on the pleasant treelined walks. B. climbs up and down and declaims: " 'The silence and the calm of mute insensate things,' " she pronounces; but her giggles are at variance with melancholy.

On the nearby Lido the sand is black and women of every age and size go topless. We eat in a seaside restaurant, a glass box; around us there are peeling Art Deco buildings and Victorian heaps, follies when they were built, now disasters, painted whore-red.

St. Monica, Augustine's mother, died and was buried here (she was fifty-five); his grief for her is as beautiful as her yearning for his salvation was. She is regarded as the model for Christian motherhood.

Lala is still waiting for her son.

I went to see a doctor because I had bronchitis and an infected finger from a manicure. He told me I had bronchitis and an infected finger due to my typing in a draft. He told me not to drink white table wine.

The bones of saints do move around a lot. St. Monica is buried in Sant'Agostino; she was shifted here from Ostia in 1430. This was the church of Roman Humanists. Courtesans—for example, Fiammetta, Cesare Borgia's mistress—worshiped and some were buried here . . . strange company for a model-mother saint.

The church has a Renaissance facade; it has been restored many times inside, and Romans often group it with the Baroque churches of their city.

If you do not love the agitated pleasure of the Baroque, you cannot love Rome. You do not have to love Roman ruins to love Rome, but you have to love the Baroque, otherwise you will think Rome is florid and vulgar and recoil from its extravagance.

Sansovino's *Madonna del Parto* is in Sant'Agostino. She is a sturdy Mary with a sturdy child; her foot is worn smooth from the kisses of the faithful, who every day bring her roses and calla lilies. This church is always peopled and always festive.

It is the spirit of the Baroque that prevails in Rome.

Caravaggio's *Madonna dei Pellegrini (Madonna of the Pilgrims)* is here. Two peasants (a young man, an old woman) kneel before a long-necked Mary, who has a profile that is almost Etruscan; she is a graceful peasant holding (or containing, for he strains with curiosity) a healthy child.

Caravaggio understands feet, was fascinated by feet, and was censured for making feet in holy pictures cracked and dirty, real. The foot is such a "funny" part of the body (humble, a source of jokes) and seldom understood as lovely or erotic or even particularly interesting. Mary's feet, in this painting, are arched and slender—not a sturdy peasant's feet, but the feet of the Queen of Heaven. Jesus' baby feet dangle in that awkward, trusting way babies have, against her draped and slender body. The young man's naked feet are dirty.

Caravaggio altogether understood extremities. There isn't a hand here that isn't a marvel, and, rather nicely, the old woman's hands, in an attitude of prayer, are more beautiful than Mary's. Mary's hands are competent, utilitarian—the hands of a mother holding a baby, hands that express milk, shell peas, diaper, and gird.

The intense curiosity of the baby, expressed in every line of his body and face, gives this painting spirit; one gets tired of passive Christ children; Christ was after all the Redeemer of the world.

As regards Baroque, there is no such thing as superfluity. The Baroque is the antithesis of the grave and taciturn Roman ruins. Its frank purpose is to delight (for which it would be ungenerous not to be glad). It is, and could only be, Mediterranean. Barzini says—and this is the commonly accepted view—that the Baroque style, "designed to envelop the faithful in a dream-like atmosphere, an intoxicated feast of *son et lumière* and fragrant incense fumes," was created by architects of the Society of Jesus; but A. G. Dickens, historian of the Counter Reformation, argues that the sumptuousness and make-believe—the rich visual puns, the trompe l'oeil of Baroque art—would have shocked St. Ignatius Loyola, founder of the Society of Jesus: "During the period of Bernini and Borromini . . . the religious orders themselves had little control over the decoration of their churches. . . . In these resplendent buildings we behold a reflection, not of the founder-saints of the mid-sixteenth century, but of a rich aristocracy in whose minds a pietized neo-Renaissance still held sway."

Ignatius Loyola himself was not a flamboyant man. "The Baroque was not a hymn of joy on the lips of reforming saints: even at its most religious it was a pantheon erected by a later age to commemorate dead heroes, whose lives were not accurately remembered."

(Dickens adds that Baroque art "has appealed to simple but well-conditioned minds," in which category, if he is correct, I must place myself; I do so unashamedly. . . . Barzini is too Austrian in his tastes for me.)

Anthony Blunt, on the other hand, argues that the Jesuits "set about making religion more accessible," a goal with which one can hardly quarrel, "by making it appeal to the emotions. . . . The neophyte is urged to use all his five senses to realize, almost to re-enact, the scenes of the Passion, the torments of Hell, or the bliss of Heaven. He is not only to acknowledge these things with the mind, he is to feel them through the senses. . . . Almost all the artists employed in the original decoration of the central church of the Jesuits, the Gesù . . . belong to that group of Mannerists in whom anticipations of the Baroque are most evident." Blunt calls them "artists . . . consciously opposed to the intellect"—from which, even if this were true, it does not follow that intellectuals cannot enjoy their art.

God speaks to us through our own individual temperaments and personalities and aesthetic sensibilities; we are not all required to love Baroque art, any more than we are all required to love tulips.

Perhaps these arguments matter only to those for whom the Council of Trent or the Counter Reformation—in part a spontaneous movement of the Church to cleanse itself, in part a reaction to Luther—is a theological or an historical stumbling block.

The fact remains: Roman ruins are indifferent to you, they do not need you. Baroque art and architecture, which changed the face of Rome, were made for your express pleasure and delight. They were intended both to overwhelm and in luxury to cosset you, which seemingly mutually exclusive aims they achieve with their voluptuousness. Baroque is happy art.

The Gesù, in which Ignatius Loyola, founder of the Order of Jesuits, is buried, is one of the sunniest, most exuberant churches in Rome.

The Ignatius Chapel, built by Andrea Pozzo, a priest, more than a century after the Council of Trent, is a triumph of the Baroque. Sant'Ignazio, soldier-saint, marble and silver, is stark, and the Christ Child holding a globe of lapis lazuli is small, compared with the allegorical statues flanking the chapel, in particular the boisterous *Victory of Faith Over Heresy* in its spectacularly rich setting—dragons, cherubs, saints, porphyry, gilt, green marble, white marble, bronze. The angels in this chapel look as if they need only your permission to fly.

Middle-aged men drop into the Gesù, exactly, and as casually, as if they were stopping for a cup of coffee; they kneel and pray.

"I can find God whenever I will," Ignazio said; he was a fortunate man.

The seventeenth-century Church of Sant'Ignazio stands on a picture-perfect Rococo eighteenth-century piazza of the same name, which frequently inspires the comment "It's not real"; but as it is there, it is real, and it is utterly charming unless one hardens one's heart in principle against being charmed.

There is a semicircle of ocher houses with pretty gray shutters; on the street corners the facades of the houses curve, so that they look as if they are protecting the dignified church. One of these buildings houses the local police (as if this piazza didn't have color enough without musical comedy uniforms). The streetlights here are in the form of candles . . . and if you can harden your heart against all this, I wish you joy, though I can't imagine where you'll find it. It is said that Raguzzini designed this piazza in imitation of a theater set, but I wouldn't hold that against him, or it.

The truly astonishing feature of Sant'Ignazio is Andrea Pozzo's trompe l'oeil ceiling (*Entry of Sant'Ignazio into Paradise*); he creates a dome where none exists.

Trompe l'oeil makes a lot of people nervous, they like their reality concrete; they don't like to feel they've been had—and trompe l'oeil offends their sense of their own dignity (poor things). Romans are practical, realistic people who love spectacle. This confuses a lot of people. It makes me feel at home. I don't say it's good or bad, I just say it makes me feel at home.

If one is going to put one's love for the Baroque to the test, the place to go is to Santa Maria della Vittoria, which might almost be taken for a small opera house (Stendhal, wicked man, said, "a boudoir").

Carlo Maderna's church is all over decorated—for example, there is a gratuitous balcony holding up a voiceless organ, which in turn holds up a redundant balcony, and that is upheld by men in armor, their genitals covered with luxuriant gilded waves.

But it is Bernini's Cornaro Chapel, his *St. Teresa in Ecstasy,* that is the culmination of the Baroque, his most celebrated and his most controversial work—and his own favorite.

Bernini was the great genius of the Baroque. It's tempting to think that his Neapolitan blood warmed him to his task; Dr. Reinhold Schoener, who in the last century wrote extensively about Rome, called him "the greatest master of Decadence" and said "his S. Teresa in the Church of Santa Maria della Vittoria is a notable instance of want of repose." That is certainly one way of putting it.

Eight (half-length) members of the Cornaro family gaze, on either side of the recess, at St. Teresa; they are seated in alcoves that look for all the world like opera boxes, and they look at her and at one another as if surprised by an amazing performance, which of course this is. Golden rays of light— gilt shafts—surround St. Teresa of Ávila: Bernini's manufactured sunlight meshes with the sun from yellow windows that bathes the saint-in-ecstasy and the angel that stands ready to pierce her to the quick. No one, after seeing this, would easily call marble—delicate flesh-toned marble, drapes of gauzy veiling wrought of marble, folds of coarse cloth fashioned of marble—cold; it seems the most malleable and variable of substances. Teresa's hands and feet are absolutely heavy, limp; as for her face: One doesn't see the love of God written on the human countenance often or recognize it if one does; only hucksters and charlatans arrange their features in the showy love of God. But if it is true that human love prepares us for divine love, then what we see is not, as some have thought, an orgasmic St. Teresa, but a saint who feels God in her body which is the body of her soul.

St. Teresa of Ávila was a mystic and some people think that that means soppy, but it doesn't and she wasn't. She wasn't entirely on good terms with her own visions, she was hardheaded enough to be skeptical of them; she loved the Church. She was acerbic. "No wonder the Church is as it is, when the religious live as they do," she said. When she was a girl, she liked trinkets and perfume. She wrote *The Way of Perfection* and *Interior Castle*. She was charming. She had an active life. She had a cozy relationship with God. Once, when she was traveling for Him, her carriage got stuck in the mud, and she said: "If this is how you treat your friends, God, it's no wonder you have so few of them." She was the first woman to be declared a Doctor of the Church (1970).

An apartment in a Roman palace is a very fine affair.

—*Henry James*

Bounded on one end by the Corso Vittorio Emanuele and on the other by the Tiber, on ground that was once part of the great green plain of the Campus Martius—land occupied in ancient times by barracks of charioteers; land that received slain Caesar's blood—is the neighborhood of the Campo dei Fiori.

This is the heart of Renaissance Rome (three great palazzi are here); but the last thing in the world one wants to do is approach it as a compulsory lesson in art history (though frescoed buildings swim into astonished view). Its appeal to the senses is immediate, varied, resonant.

(Picture a palace on a lane; it will make you smile. What is it doing there, on such a narrow path? The fact of it is undeniable. Where do palaces appear in dreams? On alleys or on broad thoroughfares? On hills? Why on hills? What is the difference between Paris and Rome?)

There is first of all the Campo itself, a large (to say "lively" would be redundant) rectangular piazza; this used to be a meadow, Field of Flowers Square; later it became a place of execution. (Dickens once attended a public execution in Rome. He says the audience at the beheading counted the drops of blood that spurted out of the neck of the executed man in order to bet that number in the lottery; he was naturally appalled.)

It is a morning market now; there is no sense of accumulated sadness here. (Half price for swordfish and for stingrays after noon.) If you make a little *giro* of four sides of the square, you will find: a newsstand; a café; a bakery where, in visible ovens, "white" pizza (olive oil, garlic, salt) is made; a movie theater; a café; a shop where fresh pasta is made; a café; a *latteria;* a wine shop/bar; a *confetti* shop; a café; stucco houses, a frescoed house that would be at home in a magic wood; a crazy quilt of tiled roofs and chimney pots; two trattorie; a café.

In the middle of the piazza is a black statue of Giordano Bruno, looking very grim, as well he might. A victim of the institutionalized cruelty of the Counter Reformation, he was burned here for heresy in 1600. He was a Copernican.

Just as, if the Gospels did not specifically call Judas the archvillain, we might have thought Peter—who denied the Lord three times, denial being a most bitter form of betrayal—was a, if not the, villain, with just a slightly different twist of history and thought, Copernicus might have become a saint, not an heretical figure; for Copernicus, by removing the earth and therefore man from the center of the solar system, reduced and rendered man less independent, more (one might think) dependent upon the God in whose sight he could not (by reason) matter very much.

People lay wreaths of flowers at Giordano Bruno's feet, as an unintended consequence of which he is an exemplar not of the terror of the Inquisition but of the tender, wholesome Roman disposition to honor the dead.

The Campo, into the life of which one is so powerfully absorbed one loses oneself and forgets to be unhappy, spills over into the Piazza Farnese, on one side of which are two fountains, water falling from stone Farnese lilies into baths of Egyptian granite from the ruins of the Baths of Caracalla; they are often called, not unlovingly, the "bathtubs."

The Palazzo Farnese is generally thought to be the most magnificent palace of the High Renaissance. Antonio da Sangallo designed it for Alessandro Farnese; when he died in 1546, Michelangelo took over; Giacomo della

Porta took over odds and ends in 1589. Sangallo did the first two stories, and Michelangelo the top; some Romans say that if you look at it long enough, the top appears to recede, Michelangelo's way of calling attention to himself.

This palazzo and the chastely classical Palazzo della Cancelleria nearby offer themselves as an argument against the Baroque. After immersion in the Baroque—sumptuous, jokey, sensational—one might be inclined to see the Farnese and the Cancelleria, yes, as noble, but also as austere; then one berates oneself for having florid tastes. This is what is meant when the Baroque is labeled "decadent, corrupt."

But this is not an argument I'd care to take up. The glorious thing about Rome is that one can have one's cake and eat it too. One of the functions of the great piazze—the Campo, for example, a contained world—is that they serve as decompression chambers. You can wander, loony-high on an extravaganza of the Baroque, for hours or for days; but then a piazza can claim and calm you—amazing how piazze both whet and calm appetites, and sometimes simultaneously—and you are ready for the Renaissance.

In the court of the Cancelleria the *portiere* offered me a seat on a conveniently placed decapitated column—a seat prepared for me by emperors and kings.

I think of the Farnese as Jane's palace, the one in front of which she dined al fresco one February night, on a table set for her as for a queen; she dined swathed in mink, with her prince, her real prince, the one she loved, from Calabria, not the prince she lives with now. . . . Even a Michelangelo palazzo can be appropriated and become part of the story of one's life (only the Forum remains intimidating; no one could domesticate it, or want to).

I love the Spada—though, stylish and sophisticated, it is Mannerist and thus apt to be considered a bastard child of the late Renaissance—best of all. . . . It is on the Piazza della Quercia—such a small piazza (a chestnut tree and a restaurant) for such a large palazzo. In the courtyard, above the shadowy recesses of the porticoes, the Spada is elaborately festooned—fauns and ilexes, gods and centaurs, in relief, the icing on that cake we can have and also eat.

It is somewhat offputting to have to pass guards with machine guns to enter this courtyard—the Spada is now the headquarters of the Consiglio di Stato, Council of State—but Roman carabinieri, unlike their impassive, prickly counterparts elsewhere, are famous for propping their guns against their thighs while helping tourists read their city maps; unless you positively bristle with belligerence, no one will prevent your passing.

Behind a wall of glass on the ground floor—you will be drawn to it from the courtyard—is a library, and beyond that, the Spada's little miracle: a long arcaded gallery at the end of which is a giant statue on a pedestal. This is Borromini's famous trompe l'oeil, which, even if one is prepared for it, comes as a delicious surprise: Only ten meters separate the gallery from the statue; the statue is not a giant but a dwarf. This is felt as well as seen. To understand the trick, you have to walk down the gallery (feel the mosaics under your feet), and even then—rising floor, descending ceiling, rapidly diminishing columns—you don't quite believe it, you think the change is not in art or nature but in you. You never, for one moment, have the sense that you have conquered space or bettered the giant (who is very sweet), and that is nice. You somehow don't have the sense that you've been gulled, either, and that's even nicer.

The *portiere* saw me looking through the plate-glass wall. He took me into Borromini's courtyard. He said: "If you will come and live with me, I will turn a rat into a dove." He lives in a penthouse here, on top of the Spada; from his terrace he can see the Tiber, the straight, hard line of the Via Giulia (the handsomest street in Rome), the Ponte Sisto, the Janiculum (fountains, light). The *portiere* is a poor man, but who is poor who tumbles out of bed and is solitary lord of a palazzo?

"If you touch the statue"—Mars, god of war—"you will have a life of love, not war," he says. He's not married, he says; he cooks his own *pasta-sciutta* and *verdura* in his cabin in the sky. Sometimes it is all in the approach in Rome, sometimes only in the approach; this charmed beginning will go nowhere (he has few teeth).

The *portiere* takes me up the grand staircase into the chamber of the Council of State. He says Jacqueline Kennedy and Elizabeth Taylor were presented here, to the *consiglieri;* now it is my turn—my turn to bow to the empty chairs. (This is not the first time I have been flattered in this manner; in Gadames, an oasis in the Libyan desert, the Italian proprietor of an hotel built for the housing of a film company [and built to last] took me to a bedroom that had been occupied, he said, by Sophia Loren. "You are more beautiful than she," he said. "Yes," the Arab sheikh amiably echoed. "You weigh more.")

In this room is the eleven-foot statue of Pompey at the feet of which Julius Caesar is supposed to have been slain:

Folding his robe in dying dignity . . .
did he die
and thou, too, perish, Pompey? have ye been
Victors of countless kings, or puppets of a scene?

Byron's question is impossible to answer; about this at least the *portiere* is honest. It is glamorous and exciting to believe that this is that dread statue bathed with Caesar's blood; but there is little evidence for this claim. The statue, which, however doubtful its claim to having witnessed thrilling history, excites a kind of awe, was found near the gilded Teatro di Pompeo, the ruins of which lie buried only blocks away. . . . Incompletely buried, for Rome is anatomical; one can always manage to see through surfaces; vaults and arches belonging to Pompey's gilded stone theater can be seen in the basement dining room of the restaurant Da Pancrazio on the Via Biscione nearby.

It is amusing to conjecture about the workings of a Council of State that meets in a room dominated by a statue of a naked man and surrounded by trompe l'oeil caged birds.

The *portiere* takes me through many reception rooms. He says there are rude cartoons (dirty pictures) by "masters," but—just my luck—invited in earnest to see someone's etchings, I fail to get the joke; even when he points and roars with laughter, I see only harmless bucolic landscapes frescoed on gilded ceilings.

He takes me down the stairs to ground level and through several locked doors, where I see a spiral staircase by Borromini, four floors of it, the tightest spiral I have ever seen. Pulling broken doors apart, he says that the staircase descends underground and that it leads to a tunnel—"not functioning" (two words indispensable in the Roman vocabulary)—to St. Peter's. Then we go for a turn in the garden that backs onto the Via Giulia.

He has overreached himself. If there were such a wonder as a tunnel connecting the Spada to the Vatican, we would know of it. It is documented that connected to the Church of Santa Maria dell'Orazione e Morte on the Via Giulia were underground burial chambers extending to the Tiber (they were miniversions of those in the Capuchin Church on the Via Veneto, decorative bones; one chamber remains), but they did not burrow under the Tiber. . . . I would love to have entered that tunnel.

The Via Giulia, one kilometer of straight, unwinding road (extraordinary for the labyrinthine center city, and superbly elegant), was meant, by Pope

Julius II, to be a monumental entrance to the Vatican, access to which would be attained from the Ponte Sisto, but this plan—the execution of which rested in Bramante's hands—did not reach fruition, because of lack of funds. At one end of the quiet, fashionable sixteenth-century street is an arched overhead bridge dripping with vines and charm; it was meant by Michelangelo to link the Farnese Palace with the Farnesina across the Tiber, but it went nowhere (except in hundreds of watercolors; no amount of overexposure robs it of its charm). It is wonderful how a thoroughfare so failed in its essential goals is so delightful and successful in its being.

A predecessor of Julius II, Sixtus IV (1414–1484), rebuilt the ancient Pons Agrippae; we now call that bridge by his name, Ponte Sisto. Sixtus V (1521–1590) connected the seven pilgrim churches of Rome and made way for the great piazze of Rome by placing obelisks judiciously. It was due to the efforts of Sixtus V that the wilderness within the Aurelian Walls was repopulated; in five short years he built so many roads and rebuilt so many aqueducts—we owe to him Margutta, Sistina, di Spagna, and much much more—that he deserves to be called Rome's greatest urban planner, the father of urban planning, perhaps the greatest urban planner the world has ever known. It was under Sixtus V that Rome, as city of man, began to rival Florence and Siena. This was done for the honor of—and the city of—God.

Months passed. My daughter, Anna, came. We strolled along the Via Giulia. Imagine giving your daughter a city. And then her giving it back to you all polished and shiny with love. We walked into the courtyards of many apartment buildings, and I found one—orange fading to gray, a cool dark vestibule, hints of Art Deco, terraces, and the loamy smell of geraniums—I wanted to live in. "Hmmm," she said, and picked for herself the building next door.

This made me very happy.

It will never happen that my daughter and I will live next door to each other in Rome; but I felt, at that moment, as Meg's mother must have felt, when, after Meg is pronounced married, "The first kiss is for Marmee!" she says. (*Little Women* was the first book I read after Anna was born: This is how memory works; it curls, it is baroque.)

Everyone I know wants to live on the Via Giulia. (That is the kind of sentence a Roman would say; it exaggerates, it is baroque. A Roman would know that you know that; you would not—if you were *simpatico*—challenge him.)

* * *

I see the green Aventine obliquely from the terrace of my *residenza,* and I can walk to it—of all the hills of Rome this is the one that feels most to my foot like a hill—by way of the Clivo di Rocca Savello, a steep, winding, overgrown path that leads into the Giardino d'Arancia, more properly called the Parco Savello, from which small and fragrant place there is a perfect view of St. Peter's and a splendid view of Rome. Here, on the verdant cusp of the Aventine Hill, are three pretty churches all in a row: Santa Sabina, Sant'Alessio, Sant'Anselmo, each in its small piazza (lime trees, chestnuts, and fountains).

Some people, whose tastes are refined, think the ancient Church of Santa Sabina is the most beautiful in Rome. Some people think Santa Maria in Cosmedin is the sweetest church in Rome, and as the *clivo* or slope that leads to Santa Sabina winds down to Santa Maria in Cosmedin, one is in the enviable position of having one's choice.

The fifth-century Basilica of Santa Sabina (restored) has a flat wood ceiling; cypress doors which are perhaps the oldest carved doors in the world and which smell new and aromatic; twenty-four graceful Corinthian columns. It is a study in pure line and mysterious white light. I find the light cold; I find the church cold; it is certainly chaste. (*Bella,* Lala says, cooing.)

Nearby Sant'Alessio, pink and blue and white (and *pretty* is the word for it), is a favorite for weddings, and one sees it often decked out, fragrant, floral, gay, beribboned. ("These weddings—look at those bouquets—must be like debutantes' balls," I say to Lala. *"Bella,"* she says, "the vessel of sweet hope.")

Sant'Anselmo, plain stepbrother to Alessio and Sabina, does what it can. On summer evenings candles are set out in pewter dishes all along the walk and court; they illuminate the way for concertgoers—Mozart; Bach. They remind me of decorations for Divali, the Hindu festival of light. (When I say this to Lala, who is decidedly not ecumenical, she thinks I am being facetious, *cattiva.*)

In the Piazza dei Cavalieri di Malta, designed by Piranesi, an Alfa Romeo and a Porsche are playing chicken: charioteers among the small obelisks and trophies of arms bounded by old walls. This is the piazza of the keyhole through which one sees St. Peter's whole: "a glimpse of great things small and small things great."

The Aventine was sacked by the Goths; it was the neighborhood preferred by the wealthy after the fire of A.D. 36; it is an area of large homes and gardens, some of which look fortified for another attack. Along its sloping tree-lined streets one sees servants carrying home the day's groceries from the broad tram-lined Viale Aventino; one is reminded of class differences here, as in the center city, where a laborer and a prince may live in the same building, one is not. Servants and au pairs wait for flocks of children outside convent gates. Parts of the Aventine look like an Embassy Row in a Third World country; the sense that Rome is semitropical is very strong here.

Julia, a young grandmother, does not like visible reminders that the family is the primary unit in Italy; she hated all the days she waited for her children outside New York schools (whereas I felt confirmed in my identity, secure, and eager for their voices, too, and for a blessing of flesh. We talk very little about these differences, we wish to preserve our friendship; and when Julia advises a friend to buy a cat and not to have a baby—"a cat is just as affectionate and much less trouble"—I keep my counsel). Julia likes to come to the Aventine but tries to time her arrivals to escape the children. She likes to take coffee on the pleasant terrace of the Hotel Sant'Anselmo (so do I), a villa tucked away in green gardens. . . . A German bumps into Julia and beerily kisses her hand. Julia says that because she's blond and just plump enough to satisfy a German's fantasy of a soubrette, men fall in love with her in Germany. They don't with me. We all have countries in which, for reasons usually indecipherable, we shine. Men fall in love with me in England, though it is Rome I love. . . . Can you think of anything worse than picking a kid up from school? Julia says. Yes, I can, I think it's pretty—and it's *over* so soon, too soon, soon they are galumphing over your life in great big boots or, worse, leaving you alone. Julia says the calcium in Rome's water is leaving deposits in her hair and pitting her fine fresh Nordic skin; but those are small irritants, the real one being Family, and Massimo's ironbound commitment to his, "and what can I do?" she says; "I am without leverage—no money, no children to hold Massimo," who is younger than she. A beery kiss from a German tourist is like a vacation to Julia.

Lala was once one of the innocent convent girls waiting at a gate. She waited till the Nazis came, then her family moved to Anzio. What bad luck she has, investing in nuclear plants, moving to the Allied landing stage. Lala's bad luck is legendary; she wears it like a cloak.

There is a hill among these hills called Monte Testaccio. It is an artificial hill made of shards of Roman pottery; whenever an amphora—of oil, wine, honey, olives—was broken in transit from North Africa or Spain, it was thrown here; and when Lala was a little girl, she was occasionally allowed—

though it was not a proper occupation for a convent girl—to go hunting there for Roman pots. Now such scavenging is forbidden; and Lala gives this as evidence of the ruin of Rome.

Sitting in the Piazza Navona, eating a gelato, I am reminded of the Trinity: A fountain is an archetype of a self-giving, self-renewing God. It is as absurd to think one has to go to church to think of God in Rome as it is to think one has to go to a museum to see art in Rome. But I am Roman Catholic, I need and want the necessary discipline of praise, the rhythm—the great swinging movement of dark to light—of the liturgical year, and, most of all, the Sacrament of the Eucharist (life's food and blood). I am not happy when I do not go regularly to church, and not (I think) because I am oppressed by the consciousness of wrongdoing, but because I am weightier, having missed the opportunity to meditate, express adoration, contrition, thanks, and supplication in loving and dignified communion with others.

One wishes it could be simple; one wishes one could go to one's parish church and return refreshed. I often think that the heroic Catholics are those who do just that. But one is greedy and sometimes irritable; the Mass is always the Mass, but, the Church being fragmented, one finds oneself, inevitably, shopping around for that which is congenial, beautiful, satisfying to heart and mind.

In Rome I found myself under compulsion to "shop." . . .

"You are becoming so tolerant in Rome," a friend says. "It amounts almost to a vice." Perhaps; but I wasn't tolerant of the Catholic evangelicals I saw on the Piazza Navona. The sacred and the profane in Italy often seem indivisible to me; but that becomes a sterile formula if one does not put it somehow to work. For me, Catholic Rome was a "peephole through which glimpses come down to us of eternal things," but that did not go all the way toward solving the problem of where to go for Sunday church—or how to find a community of like-minded, agreeable souls. I want a lot. This is a great deal to wish for, a luxury of experience; but one is stuck with one's nature; and one has an intractable wish to feel at home. So, I shopped. Rome is every kind of candy store.

On Ascension Sunday, the day on which Christ ascended to the right hand of His Father, a week from Pentecost, I went to a Charismatic prayer meeting at the Gregoriana, the Gregorian University. I went with mingled curiosity and reluctance.

Charismatic Catholics, like Protestant Pentecostals, lay claim to having been "baptized in the spirit" and, as a consequence, to have experienced a new and profound sense of the powerful presence and working of God in their lives, which usually manifests itself in one (or more) charismatic gift—such as speaking in tongues.

I have been told that sometimes, after singing, the Charismatics gathered here speak in tongues, and (to allay my nervousness, for I distrust public manifestations of ecstasy including glossolalia and am afraid that someone—conceivably me—will lose control) I have been told it will resemble plainsong or Gregorian chant, which, in the event, it does; it takes the form of humming, rather like the buzzing of honey-intoxicated bees. No one translates the exotic words that emerge from the web of sound, so though it is so restrained as not to give rise to alarm, it also seems pointless to me, word-besotted person that I am.

("Seen in its most positive light," Richard P. McBrien says, "the gift of tongues is a form of discursive prayer not unlike the protracted 'A' sound at the end of the chanted 'Alleluia' or the spontaneous but unstructured communications of a child who has not yet learned to speak." It has been compared with the gift of tears, and likened to healing expressions of the subconscious in dreams or art.)

The Catholic Charismatics meet in a bare room dominated by a crucifix. There are perhaps seventy-five people here: Indian and Dutch nuns; priests; Americans traveling or living abroad; Englishmen; very few Italians. They seem, as a group, no more broken or sad than any group of people in any church or restaurant or café or hotel. I am prejudiced, I look for madmen; the only person who has that look of rapt inner communication which can be read as madness is sitting behind me, wearing a shirt with KANSAS CITY printed on it. (Why is it a rule of life that the crazy person is always sitting near one?)

Led by a guitarist (I do not—ever—wish to be led by a guitarist), they sing simple songs: "Gentle Jesus, Meek and Mild" . . . "Jesus Is My Friend." (I hope he may be, but I'd rather hear a Bach oratorio; Palestrina wouldn't be bad either.) They pray—spontaneous prayer, arms raised and hands cupped to receive the Spirit. After the songs there is some handclapping, but people seem, in spite of their prayers for the wide world, to be lost in private devotions. No one touches. I don't know if I am relieved by this or sorry; it seems a lonely kind of enterprise.

There is emphasis on Marian devotion, and on the discipline of fasting, and an air—worrisome—of that self-congratulation which comes from existing in willed opposition to or tension with the mainstream of belief.

A sister from Bangalore prays for "simplicity, chastity, transparency, and complete trust," a limpid state of soul I doubt that I shall ever achieve.

There is something sexual in this experience, I feel as if I were about to go under anesthesia and reveal the secrets of my libido. . . . Oh, why can't one leave one's restless intelligence behind? I like those simple songs and the humming that is like a coda to them, but when prayers or comments are offered, I mentally dissect. During the singing I want to lie down and rest. I am moved by the simplicity of the singing—and tension is gathering in my shoulders. I keep thinking. The trick, of course, is not to think—to relax, to yield.

My thoughts fly elsewhere.

This morning I read in the *Herald Tribune* that Jane Fonda said before a congressional committee that things had not been so bad on farms since her father made *Grapes of Wrath* . . . . Oh, these film people—all their references are not to the thing itself but to the filmed expression of the thing. . . . Why do I have these thoughts? . . . "Lighten the corner where you are / Someone far from harbor you may wave across the bar." Oh, dear, I am going to cry, my father sang that to me when I was a child, I'd forgotten it; why am I thinking of it now? . . . A reading from Romans, Chapter 8: "All things work to the good of those who love God." St. Paul was very sure of himself. Why do I sometimes think that prayer is a form of arm twisting? (Whose arm?) . . . These people are looking inward (not at one another) or upward— toward God—which may be the same thing, the Holy Spirit dwelling within us . . . well, in them, presumably. I am simply looking inward—and finding apprehension and confusion and a thwarted urge to analyze.

A well-dressed American woman, one of three women present wearing makeup, comes up to me. "I love you," she says. "I loved you the minute I saw you. I feel I should ask for your autograph, you look so dramatic." I am wearing a simple black dress and a black summer coat purchased on the Via Condotti. (I always feel under- or overdressed in Italy, even here.) So I say, feeling that she has given me permission to leave, as I cannot stand indiscriminate professions of love: "Call me sometime," and she says, "Oh, I'm so busy, come next Sunday, it is Pentecost."

I have cried during the singing, but I won't come back again.

Sunday night I go to the Chiesa Valdese to hear the great Bach Mass in B Minor. The contrapuntal music soars: *Gloria in excelsis Deo, et in terra pax hominibus bonae voluntatis. GLORIA! . . . Cum sancto spiritu in gloria Dei patris, Amen.* I manage what I have not achieved at the prayer meeting: I forget my restless wretched self.

334

*　*　*

Lala says: "What did you do with the Protestants?" (by which she means the Catholic Charismatics).

"Sang 'Gentle Jesus, Meek and Mild.' "

"What else?"

"Remembered a dumb song my father used to sing to me—'Lighten the Corner Where You Are.' "

"Don't do that, *cara.*"

"Don't lighten the corner where I am?"

"Don't try to think of what your father said to you." Poor Lala, she loves her Fascist father so, she loves her dreams of him, her memories are pictures without words.

When I present Father O'Neill at the Jesuit Curia with the hoary idea that Italian Catholics are "merely cultural Catholics"—a stereotype that delights and titillates foreigners, who seem to find in it a great and delicious irony—he (dry and humorous) says: "But is it not true that there are 'Catholics on wheels' in America? Baptized in baby carriages, marriages in limousines, funerals in hearses?" He invites me to look around, at the *edicole* (street shrines): "Folk religion is not synonymous with superstition," he says. "In folk religion, the believer gives the initiative to God, whereas the truly superstitious believe in magic and believe that they have a grip on God—that they can initiate God's action." Does this mean that my idea of prayer has all along been a superstitious one, that I believe prayer is a way for me to wrest the initiative away from God? (No wonder my fondest prayers are not answered or, if they are, are answered in forms I do not recognize.) How primitive and unpleasant. "I shouldn't think," Father O'Neill says, "that prayer is a form of twisting God's arm—except in the minds of the superstitious—any more than leaving flowers or jewels for the Virgin is a form of bullying. One would have to ask the person praying; and one still wouldn't know." (I do sometimes wish that Jesuits were not quite so reasonable and rational.) Perhaps superstition is a primitive form of faith, I say. "A step on the way to faith," Father O'Neill says. "Catholicism is truly a part of Italian culture; it isn't of ours. When a coalition government is being formed here and a prime minister or president is not acceptable, one hears: 'There is black smoke today, no white smoke,' just what one would hear at the election of a

Pope. When a criminal has an alias, it is called his 'name in the world'—a play on nuns' changing their names. The vocabulary and cultural furnishings are derived from Catholicism here. But you make a mistake to think that all Italians—not counting Jews—are baptized Catholic. Many never belonged to any church, a legacy from nineteenth-century anticlericals. . . . "

Father O'Neill is working in a honeycomb of offices, with others devoted to the same task, on the history of Jesuit missions; his particular specialty is missions to Louisiana. How I wish that I were part of the scholarly endeavor; often I think that one footnote in such a work is worth infinitely more (it will certainly last longer) than all our flailings of body and of mind.

He directs me to Father Jacques-Guy Bougerol in Grottaferrata; he is a priest who used to fly with St.-Exupéry. This is a most glamorous fact. . . . Father O'Neill does not understand the juxtaposition of the word *glamorous* with the word *fact;* that is why he is a scholar (he is unlikely to be more overwhelmed by one fact than by another fact), whereas I come to facts as I come to people, ready to be charmed.

The poor you will always have with you. Just around the corner from the Church of Santa Maria in Trastevere is the little ocher Church of Sant'Egidio, easy to overlook. Lala, so surprising in her sudden excursions into faith, took me there. (But of course, as Lala says, "There is always belief, always faith, in the part of one that is rested; it is always there, underlying doubt. It is contained in doubt." "And doubt is contained in faith," I say. "That, too," she says.)

The community of Sant'Egidio is a lay ecclesiastical movement whose members have chosen to commit themselves to a life in the service of the Church and of the poor. Some of its thirty-five hundred members live communally, some with their families, some alone or with partners. Their dedication to "solitary old people, abandoned children, young drug addicts, those who have no home in which to live, the handicapped, beggars, strangers and immigrants from the third world" is personal, practical, concrete, and unswerving. I admired them, one couldn't not, but I found myself entering the caveat that they were uniformly pale and rather too earnest (whereupon I immediately accused myself of decadence).

They proselytize. If one believes the Church to be the repository of revealed truth, how can one resist the impulse to proselytize? On the other hand, is it not possible, given that proselytizing accompanied by good works can be construed as a form of coercion, to evangelize only by example? I don't know. I've never known. But I don't, perhaps because of my having been raised in a proselytizing sect, find it attractive or palatable; I prefer the Dorothy Day and the Catholic Worker model (that is, to bear witness to the Christ of the Gospels by feeding the hungry, sheltering the homeless, and clothing the naked, without a whole lot of gab). . . .

Nobody knows how these changes occur. One day I just stopped "shopping." I went—wherever I was—to church.

In Rome I felt, as I had never been quite so conscious of feeling before, that we are indeed made in God's image and that the physical world (and all of Church art) proclaims this fact, which, in Italy—radiant with humanity, abounding in good things that make for human happiness, ministering to the comforts of body and the pleasures of mind and spirit—seems incontrovertible. I don't know what quelled my restlessness; but at once my need to find a "place" in the Church seemed puerile and redundant, an unnecessary fretting, and the Church, which I objectively perceived as splintered and fragmented, I simultaneously perceived as a honeycomb (the Church itself is a mixed metaphor), as many-faceted, as particular and as unified as life itself. . . .

"You are *innamorata* [in love] with Italy," the contessa said to me (the Church for her is an occasion for barbs). Of course she was right; but as God expresses Himself to us through our individual temperaments and natures, "So what?" I said to her. "Of course. Yes," she said, dear contessa.

> I believe, not theoretically, but from direct personal experience, that very few of the things that happen to us are purposeless or accidental (and this includes suffering and grief—even that of others), and that sometimes one catches a glimpse of the link between these happenings. I believe—even when I am myself blind and deaf, or even indifferent—in the existence of a mystery. . . .
>
> —*Iris Origo,* Image and Reality

The reason I love Iris Origo and enter completely into the authenticity of her belief is that one unassuming, but magnificent, phrase: " . . . very few of the things that happen to us are purposeless or accidental (and this includes suffering and grief—*even that of others*)." She puts the suffering and the grief of others above her own so simply and so naturally, I love her very much.

One day I went with my friend Gianni to the Church of San Gregorio Magno, overlooking the Circus Maximus—the headquarters of the Missionaries of Charity, Mother Teresa's order, dedicated to serving the poorest of the poor: unwed mothers and their children, Gypsies (by means of a soup kitchen at the Stazione Termini. . . . I am afraid of abstracted-looking Gypsies at the Stazione Termini; I see determination behind their glazed eyes. . . . Lala says they chloroform lonely passengers who fall asleep in trains. The sisters are not, of course, afraid).

On this site Pope Gregory served food to the poor every twelve days; he is lovable for his hospitality. (He himself suffered from gastritis.) Gregory the Great, a holy and a sophisticated man, lovable also for wishing to be known as "the servant of the servants of God" (and for codifying plainsong or Gregorian chant), sent Augustine to convert the English. He is the "apostle to the English." The day Gianni and I went to this much-restored church, not an Englishman was to be seen; in fact, the church, which was locked, felt dreary and neglected. A trolley passes just outside.

Gianni and I are not feeling particularly devout; we have been perusing his 1939 guidebook, which tells us that "Fascists do not have mustaches and do not kill."

In a building adjacent to the church is a Benedictine monastery that houses homeless—filthy, ill, old, derelict—men. In a courtyard next to the church the Missionaries of Charity, many of them Indian, all of them young, were preparing a meal; they giggled as they cooked. The entire courtyard, in rooms off which the sisters live, looked and smelled like an Indian village (so I felt at home). In a small chapel in the courtyard the sisters—the purity of their young, unlined faces at touching odds with the dirtiness of their naked, work-stained, callused feet—sang Vespers. The chapel was decorated in the garish colors of the subcontinent—colors used, in India, to embellish temples dedicated to Shiva and Ganesh. I couldn't take my eyes off their feet.

One of the sisters asked me if I might wish to aid them in caring for the old men, and I, alas, said No, offering money in lieu of myself.

Gianni and I left the sisters and their plaster saints, and each of us searched the other's face. Without a word both of us examined the shrubbery, smelled the flowers—from which no fragrance arose—for what seemed a very long time. Fully an hour later, when we were sitting at a café on the Viale di

Trastevere, drinking our Chinottos, "What do you suppose goodness smells like?" Gianni asked. So I knew I had not imagined it: From the ground where the Missionaries of Charity walked—and nowhere else, only between the church and the courtyard—there had arisen a fragrance of ineffable sweetness; it was as if the air around us trembled with goodness; and that goodness perfumed the air.

Gianni has more common sense than I have; I have a more irritable intelligence than he has. Neither one of us could argue persuasively that we were not jointly hallucinating or that the fragrance that had overwhelmed and quieted us both did not have its source in some purely physical phenomenon. But there it was.

I often return to this moment in my mind—to moments of absolute quiet, when all questions become moot. Rome—this is its great gift to travelers—both excited and in some deeper sense rested me. Rome made it easier, and lovelier, for me to wait till God makes all things clear, not as in a glass, darkly, but face to face.

Lala says Tyrone Power married Linda Christian in the Church of Santa Francesca Romana at the Forum. Lala knows all kinds of things. One day she took me there. This is the church that contains the stones that bear the imprint of the knees of Peter and Paul, who prayed when Simon the Magician tried to best them at levitation on the Sacra Via and was smashed to the ground for his wickedness. It rises from foundations built by Romulus. The monastery of the Benedictines of Monte Oliveto attached to it is built into the Temple of Venus and Rome. Columns of porphyry and granite fan out from it.

The Baroque church is pink, blue, gold, white, gorgeous. The bones of St. Francesca Romana are buried here. This unexciting saint (who may have been a hypochondriac) spent her days in works of charity and had plenty of company, chief among whom was her guardian angel, who was visible to her for many years—far better than being glamorous. There is a painting by Guido Reni here, and once there was a bronze statue by Bernini here; but Napoleon stole it to make cannons, Lala says.

Lala has brought me here to meet Father Ambrose Fumagalli. She does not call him Father, however; she calls him Maestro. He is an artist, and particularly wonderful are his stained-glass panels, one of which is in the monks' choir at Santa Francesca Romana. Stained glass is a good medium and also a good metaphor for him, brilliant and sharp and fragmented and held together with conscious, consummate skill. (I particularly liked a Crucifixion, angry red and orange—peppery. Anger is the emotion one least thinks of in regard to Christ on the cross, but this seems not inappropriate; after all, he was a man.)

Father Fumagalli has lost the greater part of his faith. That is what he says. He is a Marxist, insofar as he is anything at all (that is what he says). He still lives in the monastery. It does not seem at all odd to Lala—she has been Catholic forever, nothing seems odd to her—that the order should not have expelled him or that he should not wish to leave. He is a dark and bony man. He has had exhibits all over Italy and in America. He greets us in a long white robe. He is slightly tipsy, as soon we, too, shall be. He washes the monks' dishes in exchange for room and board.

We reach the church by way of a cobbled incline, from which we see the Colosseum, which looms just behind the monastery.

That part of the church which the casual visitor sees was converted to the Baroque in the early seventeenth century, but the Maestro takes us into the cloisters, which date from A.D. 800. The bell tower, a fine one, is perhaps the oldest in Rome, tenth or twelfth century. We are making our way upward, and our way takes us through two pillared loggias, one thirteenth century and one seventeenth. In these loggias stand bases and capitals of Roman columns, chunks of statuary, gathered from the Roman Forum (limbs, trunks); and also pots of weedy flowers and clotheslines strung from arches between which are yellow, blue, and green ceramic medallions, and clothespins from which hang indecipherable bits of clothing. This is a domestic interior. It is very beautiful and very innocent. As we pass the monks' cells—the Maestro is making no attempt to keep his voice low, and when Lala is excited, she chirps, and she is chirping now—a monk, agitated but tentative, calls out: "*Sbaglio?* [Mistake?]." I am the only one of the three of us who is nervous about invading this male domain. Maestro Fumagalli says, of our female presence in a house of males, that it is "prohibited—but allowed." This is a quintessentially Roman turn of phrase.

When we reach the Father's private living quarters and studio, "Where exactly are we?" I ask (we have climbed), to which his answer is: "The sixteenth century." This salon is full of old velvet and brocades, damask and the exciting smell of wet paint. We drink scotch. There are pictures of Pope Paul VI, a friend of Father Fumagalli's; and ceramic plates by Picasso, a friend of his; and good reproductions of Caravaggio, one of Caravaggio's Trasteverini Madonnas. "Her mouth is like yours," the Maestro says—I think it is the best compliment I have ever been paid, and so much nicer than if he'd said: "Your mouth is like hers."

The Maestro rumbles and Lala chirps away; they eat each other's gossip up, the Maestro's idea of gossip being to tell scabrous tales of the conduct of dead Popes; he is at home in several centuries, including—very much— our own.

There is even gossip about the ruins; to someone whose home is in the middle of the Roman Forum, an excavator is of no little interest: It is in fact an amazing thing to see the past, the ancient world, as one stands there, bodily turned up with the spade. To that ancient world he takes us—through a window in his studio onto a terrace; and there is no need for me to ask where I am now, for we face the Sacra Via; around us and before us are the Arch of Titus, the Basilica of Constantine . . . and all the Roman Forum and the Palatine . . . and drenched in moonlight, too, as if in a dream. I could almost like the Forum now, in any case I'm not afraid of it. Perhaps the Father reads my thoughts, for he says: "*You* dominate from here." *Forse che sì, forse che no;* but it has lost all power to tyrannize, it is stone, not prophecy or ideology. (A flight of birds; bells; olive trees.)

In the chocolate-brown and dusty sacristy, where we part, is a painting hanging tipsy (just like us). It is the fifth-century easel painting of the Virgin and Child, perhaps the oldest icon of Mary, the first. It was discovered— appropriately for this city of layered and visible history—beneath a twelfth- century picture, which was, in turn, found beneath a nineteenth-century painting. Father Fumagalli straightens it and wipes his hands on his robes (he surreptitiously crosses himself; and winks).

Mary's eyes know everything. They are blue.

Chapter V

TO THE MEZZOGIORNO:
NAPLES, THE SORRENTINE PENINSULA,
THE AMALFI COAST . . .
"BRIGHTNESS FALLS FROM THE AIR"

One can be tired of Rome after three weeks and feel one has exhausted it; after three months one feels that one has not even scratched the surface of Rome; and after six months one wishes never to leave it.

I spent my last night in a fifteenth-century palazzo on the Via Sant'Eustachio; from the dining table I could see—I could almost touch—the Pantheon. I was full of envy for my host and hostess, she a still photographer for Fellini, and he a cinematographer; imagine living in such proximity to the Pantheon . . . and talking (as one does, as one must do) about ordinary things: food. Deborah says: "How bad Roman food sometimes is, gristly *abbacchio,* veal cutlets half overcooked and raw next to the bone, oversalted pasta, and overcooked vegetables." . . . If this is meant to reconcile me to leaving Rome, it is having no such effect. Deborah is serving chicken in a clay pot with lemon and white wine and herbs, and broad beans with a fresh tomato sauce, and arugula—and all this she bought in shops around the corner from the Pantheon.

Gideon's silverware catches light from the lights illuminating the Pantheon; in his knife he has captured, for a moment, a tiny Pantheon, which wavers and then breaks.

Our talk goes on against a backdrop of Fellini props: a net body garment from *La Strada;* life-sized cardboard figures of Fred and Ginger, vaguely sinister; "Indian-style" murals made for a Fellini dream sequence; and among the Fellini artifacts—almost a Fellini retrospective—a life-sized *presepio* (a crèche); and, from the Porta Portese, an Art Deco lily lamp (the lilies are obscene; they look like the organs of an hermaphrodite); also Victorian glass domes in which are immured dusty dead birds and dried flowers, baby dolls, bits of paste and gilt, miniature queens in moth-eaten robes of velvet and ermine—objects opaquely fetishistic—all within a forest of colored beads.

From the mossy home of the crèche, Mary, Jesus, and Joseph look over us all, no matter that they are gaudy. The room can contain them, Rome can contain them, Rome can contain everything; in Rome, as in life, nothing is strange and everything is strange, everything is what it must be.

Life was "not worth the living away from the Corso and the Pincio," Henry James wrote. "I should vainly try to tell you how one looks back on Rome and hungers for her again."

Fortunately I was traveling south, to the Mezzogiorno, the land of high noon, golden sun—and not to the "stupid unlovely North."

The *rapido* to Palermo stops at Naples. Naples is where I am going.

Lala and Gianni accompany me to the railroad station. Lala says I will be chloroformed by Gypsies in my compartment (I am not riding in a compartment), Gypsies carrying knives. Gianni, to whom parting comes easier, bets me five hundred lire that within five minutes of my boarding someone will be offering to help me with my bags because my Italian is "so charming," by which he means it is inadequate, and by which he means something more: He means that I feign helplessness, which I do—largely by the device of allowing myself to feel helpless.

Lala's son has not yet come to Rome.

This parting is hard.

The last words I hear Lala say are: "I am in exile."

Only two doors, one on either end of the train, are open. Lots of people have come without seat reservations, and the police challenge them—but not so rigorously as to earn the epithet *Fascisti!* The police challenge them directly in front of the open doors (perhaps on the theory that one battles on and not near the battlefield), which means, of course, that no one can get on—except for one ancient woman who swings her suitcase at kneecaps, clearing a path, and grins victoriously and toothlessly with pale malice from the train at the milling, clamorous crowd. The police put an end to the melee in Roman fashion: They shrug and take their leave. Their departure has the effect of calming everybody down, their absence imposes order of a sort. . . . Of course one could never go so far as to say Italians queue for trains, but one is reasonably sure of getting on.

The young mother of two young children, behaving sensibly, leaves her eight- and nine-year-olds on the platform and goes with her cases to secure a seat. The children are happy as mud. She peers out the window. There they are, stolid and unconcerned, ready to be handed up to her. But all at once she sees the dramatic possibilities inherent in this event. *"I bambini! I bambini!"* she screams—"the children! the children!—beating her breast, exactly as if someone had kidnapped them, exactly as if they were not obdurately and in plain sight there. The children, hitherto models of their species, begin to snivel and then to howl: *"Mamma! Mamma!"* Hearing this, the police return. Chaos is restored.

On board, two very nice American men, dressed in colors approximating the lilies of the field, hoist my suitcase for me. (I look for Gianni, five hundred lire in my hand, in vain.) What should I have done without them? "I should have stood and cried, were I alone, for weeks," says one, how sweet. He is wearing penny loafers. They are both wearing penny loafers.

The train is called the Settebello (the beautiful seven, derived from *scopa,* a game of cards in which the winning card is the seven of diamonds); H. V. Morton called it "the most elegant [train] in Europe, probably . . . in the world." Nothing is as it was, especially as regards trains, and leather and wood have yielded to plastic, but the Settebello is still civilized and comfortable. . . .

The young woman seated across from me—a fresh-faced, green-eyed beauty in almost boisterously radiant health—is wearing white cotton and has many Topsy-like blue ribbons in her cascading chestnut hair, ribbons which ought to look ridiculous but which serve instead to make her look like an engaging child. She is twenty-six—"old for marriage," she says. She is in medical school but she wants to be an interior decorator but she can't find a job, and: "Failure and success, it's all the same," she says, smiling her childlike smile, affecting a world-weariness and cynicism that accord ill with her sanguine beauty. Within thirty minutes we have talked about the Pope, divorce, the family, the Holy Family, her family, my family, drugs, higher education, the use of the pronouns *lei* and *tu;* it is always like this on Italian trains. Her name is Gemma Donati. Her brother is married to a Texan. She has very few words in English; among them are *River Oaks Country Club.*

The River Oaks Country Club is in Houston, and I was once told that I was the only person in living memory who had ever addressed another human being in its precincts without having been formally introduced. The River Oaks Country Club is about as different from Italy as Betty Grable is from Anna Magnani. Once, when I was visiting the apartment of a gentleman who was a member of the River Oaks Country Club, a man who had held high office in Texas rang the bell, and, when I opened the door, "Are you," he asked with no preamble, "Mediterranean on *both* sides?" "Yes," I said. "How . . . marvelous," he said; and then he turned his back and walked away.

Gemma's word for Texas is *strano* (strange).

She asks me, as the Settebello rolls through Campania, if I will come to her brother's wedding in Sorrento. Of course I will, how nice.

Gemma's full name is Gemma Donati Primavera Bettachi Piersansovini.

Vesuvius is shrouded. The subject of so many picture postcards, it has become domesticated in our minds, it has lost the aura of danger that gave its beauty a sharp and tragic edge. North Africa begins here. This is a matter of crowds, of architecture, of an indefinable sweet-acrid smell, of heat and dust, rotting flowers, spices, car fumes, flesh, and something more, a sum of intangibles. In Naples the street shrines are contained within locked glass cubicles, for here the thieves have fewer qualms about stealing from Mary's person. They could break the glass, of course, but perhaps the ugly, violent sound of shattering glass (much worse, and much more unmistakable, than gunfire) insults, too much, their idea of themselves—or their idea of the Virgin; who knows? . . . We drive past the ugly industrial suburbs of Naples, and past the magic road signs—Pompeii and Ercolano—and it is not until we leave the *autostrada* and are on the long Corso Italia, the narrow road that becomes, as it rounds the curve of the Sorrentine Peninsula, the Amalfi Drive, the Amalfitana, that I feel that I am on my way to Sorrento: Brightness falls from the air.

*   *   *

High above the town, above the Bay of Naples, nine ancient pine trees frame the hills, the crags, the buttresses, unshrouded Vesuvius shimmering in the haze, Capri and Ischia, the opal surges of the violet sea. The pine trees are pagan. This is where I live, sea breeze by day, land breeze by night, in lush gardens among flowers whose names I do not know.

The British do not transplant well, a horrid lot is here, horrid fake-genteel accents, horrid tribal customs, horrid children, horrid lunches of fish and chips and lettuce and ketchup, horrid shopping ventures that bring them back laden and noisily tired from the town; their unshakable Englishness: "Only a light lunch please, one can't eat as they do—can one?—and tea."

The pool at the Hotel President is fed from mountain streams, it is so cold only the British could swim in it, but I do, too, and my body behaves without its usual fear, without thought, without regard to consequences. This is how a fish feels; breathing has no jagged edges.

Old families in Naples used to employ English governesses. In those days, if you wanted to buy a Rolls-Royce in Naples—and many Neapolitans did—the dealer would oblige you only if you took an English driver with it. Neapolitans think of Sorrento as the Englishmen's "New World"; the English came to sketch and to adore, and to export oranges, lemons, and almonds. The British ruled Sorrento from 1806 to 1808, a fact they choose to remember and the Sorrentines to forget; there was a Russian colony here once, too: Lenin visited Gorky in Sorrento; Diaghilev owned three tiny islands in the Gulf of Salerno . . . Burton and Taylor tried to buy an island but could not.

At night the horrid kiddies watch soccer on the television in the writing room (nobody writes). How can they, when so recently Liverpudlians took thirty-eight Italian lives at a soccer match in Brussels? The Italians are so kind, poaching eggs and preparing mushy Anglicized spaghetti.

From my balcony I see the Marina Grande, a little cove below the cliffs, the small pastel houses, a dozen or so, of fishermen; a road between them and the olive groves, flat and soft and green, that separate the fishermen's houses from the umber, red-tiled houses of the town. Every day the women of Marina Grande climb the steep hill road with fortitude to sell their husbands' early-morning fish catch in the center of Sorrento. They pray to St. Anna for the safety of their men at sea. They marry one another in this community, it is an enclosed world. I have always wanted to live in an enclosed world; but when I did, I wanted to get out. St. Anna was the mother of Mary, who is the Mother of God. (Luther violently attacked her cult.) Anna is my daughter's name, she is in Rome, I have never heard her sound so happy, she is *innamorata* (in love) with Rome, soon I will meet her in Naples, she is staying near the railroad station with three strange boys.

The town itself is slightly seedy, there is a whiff, not unpleasant, of decay. It should be painted sepia. Paint flakes and peels on grand hotels. If I were genteel poor and wasting, I would come to a *pensione* here to die a genteel death, tea among the almond orchards and the olive trees. Wagner and Ibsen liked it here, and Homer did, too. What I like is to go to the Public Gardens, the Villa Comunale, close to but away from the souvenir center of town; there it is cool and orange-scented and steps lead down to the sea, and Italians swim in it, it is not fashionable, and in the peaceful outdoor café ENGLISH TEA is advertised.

In the ladies' room of the Villa Comunale, an old man with white hair, dressed (in ninety-degree weather) in an orange cable-knit sweater and cerise pants, sleeps, his unsleeping weathered palm extended for a tip.

In the center of the town there is a *farmacia* of Neapolitan Baroque; cherubs fly above the Dr. Scholl's.

In the center of the town there is a vaulted, frescoed loggia, Operaio Mutuo Soccorso (Society of Mutual Aid); men sit here in the open air. These privileged men are members of a confraternity, that peculiar institution about whose origins no one can be sure, part social, part religious, membership in which, passed from father to oldest son, is highly prized. Members of the confraternity pray for their dead brothers, securing for them swift egress from Purgatory; and nowadays, Purgatory being not very much on anybody's agenda, they concern themselves with the organization of religious festivals; and they play cards.

In the center of the town on the Corso Italia there is a restaurant called O Parruchiano, which I love. It is run-down in that restaurant-by-the-sea way, it always looks as if the season were drawing to a close (it might, for example, be in Veracruz); and it is many-leveled—indoor-outdoor rooms, gardens, arbors—and good food is presented theatrically: an evil-looking lobster next to baroque meringues. Fish gills are pried open for my (untutored) inspection; I drink a local wine that tastes interestingly of sulfur. Whiskey; figs and melon; penne all'arrabbiata; wine, arugula, caffè, *amaro*.

On the Corso Italia there are bookstalls that call to mind Paris. In the winter they are shuttered, or removed, they are for tourists, but the books are all in Italian; this is strange.

It is nice to go to the church and the cloisters of San Francesco (past the whitewashed house where Ibsen stayed); in them, bowerlike grapevines flourish, emblematic of Sorrentine luxuriance and Sorrentine frugality; from these decorative grapes wine is made. Tacked about are posters with letters of the Hebrew alphabet—"The language of the Prophets, the language of Today"—and pictures of the Holy Land. . . . For Ibsen *this* was the holy land, almond-milk and sun-kissed honey.

At the Hotel President, above the sea that Homer loved, the sea where Sirens killed with sweetness, middle-aged Englishmen are freezing in the freezing pool, their flesh, shaking like Jell-O, dimpled with cold. They hold their children on their shoulders, and the children, shaking, too, dive. The men are kind, and the children are happy. In the lounge two elderly English spinsters are apologizing to a bewildered young waiter for the stupid soccer slaughter. . . . How nice the English are, how much they wish to please and to be pleased.

Mimi and Nello D'Aponte come to take me to their house in Sant'Agnello, a town of six thousand, three-quarters of a mile away from Sorrento.

Sant'Agnello (Mimi tells me this) is the patron saint and protector of pregnant women and of farmers whose animals are about to give birth. The townsfolk are on intimate terms with him; they fear him, too: "Said Sant'Agnello leaning out of his little window, 'Now, you poor people, screw yourselves!' " Any pregnant woman who does not visit Sant'Agnello on his feast day may bear a malformed child. (The pine trees here are pagan.)

Mimi and Nello live above a Vespa shop on the Corso Italia, that heroic road that bears so much traffic of every sort. They live, when they are in Italy, on one floor of this house, and members of their extended family live on other floors, in self-contained apartments.

In this bedroom, in this massive matrimonial bed of wormy walnut wood that Nello's father made, Nello was born, and his brothers and sisters, ten in all. I move every six years, I always have; this kind of continuity is wonderful to me; to be born and die in the same bed is a narrative poem.

A modern clothes washer. Faded pictures; framed honors—a Cavaliere of World War I.

A simple lunch: young zucchini cooked in oil from the family's olive trees—Nello cooks them, he says a drop of vinegar is the secret of their sweetness; fresh country bread fried in that oil; mozzarella, *provolone dolce,* prosciutto, greengage plums.

The windows of this kitchen overlook a grove of lemon trees—we seem to be floating above them (the clothes washer hums); and on a level just above the lemon trees a choo-choo train flies by, one comes every fifteen minutes from Naples. This is like looking through a magic diorama made for a child.

In my dreams of Sorrento I am not in a grand hotel, I am buoyed by the sound of a clothes washer, in my body dreaming above the trees.

The choo-choo train is the wonderfully named Circumvesuviana.

The lemon trees are supported by a crisscross grid of poles; they are covered with black nylon against the hail. Mimi says hailstones big as grapefruits barrage Sant'Agnello for fifteen or twenty minutes and then the sun comes out again.

On Mimi's house there is a balcony, and she likes this balcony, she likes the Sorrentine Good Friday procession, which begins at two-thirty on the morning of the day; she likes it because (she writes): "There is something magical, not to mention theatrical, about being awakened in the middle of the night by a lamenting band and chorus, and about going out on the balcony (which is the spectator area of every house along the street) . . . in hastily found raincoats" on a day of driving rain "to watch and listen. In becoming a part of this balcony-bound, suddenly-awakened audience, a special sort of theater is experienced. One comes to this theater fresh from sleep and clear of daytime preoccupations. The significance of this organized, nocturnal wandering—the search of Mary and the apostles for the arrested Christ, who unknown to them has already been condemned to death— changes from an intellectual concept to an experienced action. Perhaps the unkind weather . . . adds to the impression of woebegone search. . . . This procession is like church bells—with or without so choosing, one is made a part of its perpetual action." In Italy one is always spectator and actor, player and audience; one is not alone.

In the evening the poles that support the lemon trees have a rosy glow, and as the sun sets, the fragrance of the lemons deepens and drifts up through the kitchen window and perfumes the pictures, the teacups, the bed, the faces of friends.

If Sorrento is slightly and endearingly seedy, somewhat late-nineteenth-century in tone, it is making determined strides, in thick workmen's boots, into the twentieth century. Orange and lemon groves are being cut down for new construction, one doesn't know for how long this will be a perfumed place; years from now it will seem like a dream, like the Sirens of myth. And true to human nature, the Sorrentines are, as Nello says, "bemoaning the progress for which they pined."

The facade of the Church of Sant'Agnello was ruined in the earthquake of 1980. The only house badly damaged in that *terremoto* was that of the town miser, notorious for his failure of charity. His house is uninhabitable. One likes to read moral lessons into such events; but nature—which sends children to their death in wells and good men to their death in mines—is (one feels in this paradise where the earth so often trembles, slides, falls) blind.

The Grand Hotel Cocumella is the oldest on the Sorrentine Peninsula. It was until 1700 a Jesuit monastery for men of rich and "good" families. (The small sixteenth-century Neapolitan Baroque buttery-yellow chapel is still attached to the Cocumella; Sorrentini pass through its double green doors to be married in its pale-yellow embrace; the cloisters, tufa arches blocked off, are used for large parties, the old cistern a giant receptacle for flowers. The cloisters still smell of silence.) Thereafter the Count of Siracusa, brother of the Bourbon King of Naples, used it as a residence; in 1822 it became an hotel (the most beautiful I have ever visited). The Duke of Wellington stayed here, and Murat, and Goethe, who wrote of a coast "the shape of a crescent moon . . . orange trees in profusion . . . a lovely green leaf as thin as vellum . . . jasper, quartz, porphyry . . . marble and green-blue glass . . . the waves playing before one's eyes with the splendor of an earlier world." Nello's grandfather and Nello's father and Nello worked here; one day Nello brought me here.

A cactus Nello's grandfather planted against the facade has grown to twenty feet, nearly bursting the terra-cotta urn in which it stands, reaching toward the lacy gray first-floor balcony. . . . In the south of Italy, where history is long, small actions have visible consequences. Does this change the moral geography of the mind? . . . Nello knows every piece of furniture in the long reception gallery, one pale-blue-and-white room opening onto another after another and another, rooms made for evenings of scented luxury and murmured conversation, women in long white gowns, languid flirtations. His father built the furniture, faux Baroque. He touches the pieces as we walk through the gallery. "This chair had to have a piece added—here—because the leg was wobbly." As if it were yesterday. Each object has a story and Nello's story is inseparable from that of the objects. ("Rent, never buy," says a Neapolitan acquaintance. "Ghosts come back to the houses they have lived in. And you must redecorate quickly; ghosts visit objects they have loved." "But are there no ghosts who have rented?" I ask; and if so, wouldn't they come back? "Rent, don't buy, and redecorate," he says again; Italians think reiteration is a form of argument, of logic, even. He lives in hotels, his family house in Posilippo is untenanted. . . . But Nello sleeps in the double bed in which he was born, a happy man.) Nello was a bartender at the Cocumella, now he works for the Italian government in America; his father was a furniture maker, his grandfather a gardener. This was Nello's stepping-stone to success, but sadness waits for him here; through his satisfaction runs a thread of bitterness, perhaps of anger.

We walk through the Cocumella's century-old park (banks of hydrangeas, marigolds, pansies, morning glories, olive and acacia trees, plumbago, Christmas roses, pepper plants), which leads to the cliffs that fall precipitously, spectacularly to the jetty and the sea a hundred meters below. (To get to the candy-striped cabanas, the concrete bathing pier, the black-sand beach, one, if one has total faith in progress, takes a lift, or—more reliable and more thrilling—a flight of stairs carved out of rock by the Etruscans, whose chisel marks can still be seen. In the tunnels that punctuate the descent, Cocumella cooks make pasta; in those cool grottoes fishermen clean their fish. The view from the bottom of the sheer cliffs is as beautiful as the view from the top, satisfying the requirements of great sculpture.) Nello says his father owned part of this land but ceased to own it after the Fascists took power. The story is unclear to me. Nello, away from America, is more playful and effervescent, more the paterfamilias, but also more opaque, superficially sunny, in fact a nest of darkness in which something obscure seems always to lurk; he closes down. By way of explanation, "The law has no reason, the smart always win," he says.

Every house we have lived in, every building to which our hands have lent their work, belongs to us by virtue of love or of regret.

Fried rice balls stuffed with meat (arancini); fish fry (small anchovies, calamari, squid, scampi); pizza . . . One night at dinner in a lonely square of muted charm in Sant'Agnello—the small towns along the peninsula are proud, they wish to remain autonomous, though as the crow flies, they are separated, one from another, by scarcely a mile—Nello says: "Roosevelt was buried at sea."

"But surely not," I say.

An elegant, dismissive shrug, and, "Did you ever see his body?" Nello asks.

"Well, no, but why should I have? I was nine years old. . . . Though the aunt of a friend of mine was painting his portrait when he died. . . ."

"At sea," Nello reiterates, his shrug this time expressive of skepticism (what friend? what aunt?).

Facts mean nothing to wounded feelings, and the War, in some way I have not been given to understand, wounded Nello. *"La voce del popolo è il voce di Dio,"* he says. "The voice of the people is the voice of God." Nello is almost oracular in Italy; it is strange and interesting to see a man out of context.

We are on the roof of Mimi's house, hanging out the wash, white sheets flapping against the blue Mediterranean, the Church of Piano di Sorrento high in the purple-hazed hills overlooking Mimi's exertions and my lesser ones. Pretty Mimi is rosy with steam and dignified labor (maintaining a difficult balance): "Love calls us to the things of this world."

Mimi takes me past decaying villas, past villas with spanking new paint, past cafés with hopeful red-and-white awnings, down the hill on Marion Crawford Street.

This is what Marion Crawford, in the nineteenth century, wrote about Sorrento (Surriento to its inhabitants):

It is a beautiful place. . . . A little place it is, backed and flanked by the volçanic hills, but having before it the glory of the fairest water in the world. Straight down from the orange gardens the cliffs fall to the sea, and every villa and village has a descent, winding through caves and by stairways, to its own small sandy cove, where the boats lie in the sun through the summer's noontide heat, to shoot out at morning and evening into the coolness of the breezy bay. . . . Far along through the groves echoes the ancient song of the southern peasant, older than the trees, older than the soil, older than poor old Pompeii lying off there in the eternal ashes of her gorgeous sins. And ever the sapphire sea kisses the feet of the cliffs as though wooing the rocks to come down, and plunge in, and taste how good a thing it is to be cool and wet all over.

So of course the Sorrentines named a street for Crawford.

We are on our way to the Cocumella, to swim in the sweet- and seawater pool in the orange-scented garden at the end of a long avenue of trees, to eat refined food—penne with a delicate brown sauce combined with cream and fresh strawberries, surprising and exquisite—and to drink good red Gragnano.

In the Cocumella's guest book there are entries starting from 1827. Before 1900, when hotel tariffs were regulated, rooms were rented by personal contract; it was not unusual for guests to stay for as long as fifteen months. . . . Clergymen, lords and ladies, colonels from the East India Company, counts and barons, guests from St. Petersburg, St. Louis, Berlin; the sisters Gish, Byron, Orson Welles, Trelawny. . . .

These are the faded entries I like best (such books are holy and not to be abused):

22 Nov 1836: Wm J Norton from Boston in America can whip his weight in wild-cats—dive deeper—stay down longer and come up drier than any man what has two legs on.

Across this entry by the delightfully boastful Mr. (Master?) Norton is scrawled, in a woman's hand (lavender ink): "a typical man," and "a goose or fool."

26 May 1858: . . . last but not least, the donkey of the Hotel is quite a model of good will and steadiness . . . and also the garçon.—Mr. A. F. Buscarlet

(Nello likes to bargain with the pony-cart driver [no more donkeys]. The driver sleeps outside the Cocumella all day long and rouses from his slumbers only to quarrel fiercely about the value of his time.)

Nov 5 1861: Mrs. Philpotts and daughters strongly advise anyone imprudent enough to go from hence to Capri in an open boat to profit by their dearly bought experience—take the landlord's advice respecting weather in preference to that of the boatman. [I like this because it is the scaffolding for a short story.] . . . Wondrous grand and beautiful.

I read this under oleanders—dusty rose, pale rose, deep rose—and purple bougainvillaea, drinking orzata, the almond drink that never tastes so good outside Italy, and contemplate the goodness, the luxuriance (to which more is added the farther one travels south) of the natural world.

Armando Verdiglione, whom I have found so enigmatic in New York and in Milan, is in the papers: The Guardia di Finanza is investigating his finances, he has been relieved of his passport, and his business interests throughout the world are under scrutiny. The families of young people from whom he has allegedly taken money—perhaps the same people who told me they were "investing" in Verdiglione's enterprise—reported him to the police. He has been charged with "associating with delinquents." Verdiglione calls this the "new Dreyfus case" and says he is being "persecuted by demons."

"They are civilized," Henry James said, "plenty of fireworks and plenty of talk. That's all they ever want."
It is absurd for a woman to be drinking alone on a terrace overlooking the sea when the drink is pink and in it is fruit salad on a stick, also a miniature paper fan and three rambling roses. It is like the first frame of a movie in which the woman (no longer young) will meet Rossano Brazzi and come to no good end, or, alternatively, *not* meet Rossano Brazzi and come to no good end. This is the drink the bartender, a man infatuated with pink and lime, has prepared for me. Absurd; but here I sit, happy, the sun having accomplished its daily miracle and plopped into the sea, listening to someone playing the piano and singing "Tea for Two" in execrable English. (Where do all the couples go at night? I wonder; "Tea for Two," he croons, and beams at me.) I can pick out the white Church of San Francesco; higher in the hills the Church of Santa Maria del Carmine is outlined in bright lights for a feast day. All along the coast the lights twinkle, like the just in Auden's poem exchanging their messages. The peninsula is a cozy place.
Sometimes—especially on feast days—the wail of police cars drifts up

from the Corso Italia. A *"coincidenza"* can block the Corso, and traffic halfway around the peninsula, for hours, and so can a religious procession.

The Feast of All Saints, on which occasion dead relatives are honored, for—who knows?—they may be becoming or may already have become saints, is celebrated by every town on the peninsula large enough to have its own cemetery. In Sant'Agnello, the bell begins to toll at one-thirty in the afternoon. It is answered for the most part by the faithful . . . in Fiats. Mimi writes that as the human procession—carrying gifts for the dead— "winds its way up the narrow road pressed between vineyards and tiny dwellings, it is itself pressed hard against the road walls to permit the automobile procession passage. . . . Every one hundred yards or so a new family group emerges from some tiny doorway and melts into the praying walkers, so that the procession grows to about fifty people by the time it finishes its half-hour walk to the cemetery's entrance." Fortunately the dead themselves, who are believed to be present, do not contribute to the crush. The dead are modest.

The Curia of Sorrento has seen fit to address itself to this problem, and so has Monsignor Nuzzi of Amalfi, who reminded the good people of the peninsula of that which they already knew or sensed: that the *feste,* by externalizing faith, allowed the grandeur of Christianity to appear alive "even to the most distracted man," and that "overly dry" and formulaic scholastic teaching takes on life through feasts, evoking "the final phase of God's reign: the meeting of the wandering Church with the Church that has reached the end of the journey." Nevertheless, he saw fit to warn his flock gently against "useless spendings in lights and fireworks." It is forbidden, he said, in language stern and nice, "to prolong processions for many hours, in order not to impede the circulation of vehicles, on national roads or [those] of great vehicular traffic, and to avoid causing discomfort to the users of the street. This duty is to be considered a precise act of charity and of justice toward those who are in haste to attend to their own affairs." (It is also forbidden to "attach money to sacred images," which news has not yet reached New York or, indeed, Naples. . . . When I grew up, Jehovah's Witnesses taught me to regard the pinning of paper money to ambulatory statues of Mary as evidence of the corruption of the Church, which perhaps it is, though I could not [and cannot] see the harm.)

The monsignor's reforms were, for the most part, taken seriously. Until 1969, for example, each of six towns had a separate procession honoring the common patron saint, Antonio Abate. The monsignor considered this excessive. Now the procession begins at one end of the six towns and moves to another, in a semicircular pattern that will continue "until each of the six mountain villages has both initiated and received a procession honoring its patron. And then the pattern will begin again." In this case, law has enhanced rhythm, drama, and human mutuality.

I would like to see fireworks.

I would like in particular to see the white-and-red fireworks symbolizing the Virgin's meeting with the Devil; I would like to see that pagan dance of color in the sky.

I never understand critics of the Church who say, as if the fact should put an end to discussion (or to belief), that the cults of the saints, and of Mary, are imitative and derived in part from pagan cults. So what? God uses what comes to hand. Can popular devotions hurt if they convey the image of a more brotherly, accessible Christ? If the people of Sant'Agnello wish to wind around the pagan hills as Romans did, with gift offerings for the dead, as pagans did before them, I should think one would be comforted by the continuity of things. For almost every Christian act there has been a fore-shadowing. . . . And "everything possible to believe" (Blake said this) "is an image of truth." (Of course he said it in "Proverbs of Hell.")

There are those who think that liturgy evolved from theater (as well as those who argue that the decay of religious faith is an impulse to the birth of art) and those who think theater originated in the liturgy. What I think is that God burns away dross:

The power of the Holy Spirit also truly takes what is purest, subtlest, highest, the spark of the soul, and bears it on high in fire and in love, just as with the tree: the power of the sun takes what is purest and subtlest in the root of the tree and causes it to mount to the branches where it becomes a flower. In absolutely the same way, the spark of the soul is raised into the light and into the Holy Spirit and borne thus to its first origin. It becomes wholly one with God, moves absolutely toward union, it is one with God more truly than food with my body.

—*Meister Eckhart*

I entertain a disconcerting image of a naked saint.

At a party for a newly married couple, I meet a young widow whose brief marriage "was like a dream," she says. Her husband died when her son was only two. She is very pretty; she sews. "Why don't you marry again?" her relatives ask: *Why?* "Because my marriage was like a dream," she says.

Everybody at this party speaks in an accent—Neapolitan—that I associate with my family, and with poverty. But this house has six floors, elevators, electronic devices to guard against burglary, a garden brightly lit (its bottom, in shadows, extends to the edge of a cliff), a gazebo (pink and white). I keep thinking they're all mugging: Why do they speak in the dialect of poverty? I think.

The invitation read:

> Il duca del Sasso Francesco Capece Minutolo e
> la duchessa del Sasso Laura Delli Santi Cimaglia Gonzaga
> partecipano il matrimonio della figlia Paola con
> Puccio Donati
> Il Dott. Forese Donati e
> Maria Luisa Donati Primavera Bettachi Piersansovini
> partecipano il matrimonia del figlio Puccio con
> Paola Capece Minutolo

In concession to egalitarian times, *duke* and *duchess* are lowercased.

I had not understood, when I was invited by Gemma on the train from Rome to Naples, that I was being invited to the wedding of the son of a duke belonging to one of the noblest and most illustrious families in Italy. (No one, least of all me, is immune to the glamour of royalty; I bought a Krizia dress. How often in one's lifetime does one get invited to a wedding of someone whose ancestors were painted by Mantegna?)

The Piazza of Santa Maria Annunziata, six kilometers from Sorrento, is near Massa Lubrense, the peninsula's pivot into the Amalfi Drive. Here, it has been suggested, the ancient cult of the Sirens evolved into the worship of Athena. (Norman Douglas believed that the Neapolitans' beloved St. Lucia was a direct descendant, by way of Minerva, from the Sirens.)

The piazza crowns a hill; the church, the remains of a castle, a belvedere that juts out over the ocean, Capri, so improbable, so infinitely seductive, in sight . . . and nothing but the wide sky more: "a serious place on serious earth it is" (if there is no God, why isn't the universe dark brown?).

The *principe* says it is Graham Greene's favorite piazza on the Sorrentine-Amalfitan peninsula. The *principe,* his American mistress, Dottie, says, is famous. One doesn't know what he is famous for. As for that, one doesn't know his name. "But he's old, old!" Dottie says. Dottie came to Italy four years ago, her eyes are buried deep in violet sockets. "He never tells me what to wear." Dear Dottie, why should he? Because he is her keeper; it is not the *principe* she is in love with; it is Italy—"and for Italy I have burned my bridges and sold my soul." She wears russet silk and canary-yellow diamonds. "He's so crazy!" Dottie and the *principe* have yachted in from Capri. There are guests from Dallas, Florida, New York, Austria, Milan, Rome. "I don't recognize my friends unless they are in bathing suits," says Dottie; it occurs to me she is on drugs. I don't recognize giggling Gemma; the demure schoolgirl has been transformed—jonquils woven into upswept, braided, pomaded hair, couturier black-and-white silk—into a voguish woman, self-possessed, vaguely intimidating. Oh, what I would give for an Italian sense of style, I always look the same no matter what I wear.

From the blank windows of the ruined castle are draped Persian rugs and blankets, bedspreads—lace, crocheted, embroidered; it's decorative, but it's atavistic, too. . . . My mother always believed my grandma Rosie—my father's mother—checked the sheets for hymeneal blood; about this Grandma Rosie maintained a canny and a bullying silence.

In the piazza there is an oom-pah-pah band. Burly men snake around, trumpets blasting Vivaldi and the theme from *The Godfather;* on their white T-shirts PAOLA/PUCCIO is stamped in green. On improvised lattices are flowers, neon lights, neon bells.

Bells.

Cars park at the foot of the hill. Gay little vans take guests up to the old church, weathered to the color of warm ivory. The priest takes his turn driving the canopied van, his vestments billowing. He is regarded lovingly by villagers and members of the wedding party, familiarly and familially; and he responds in kind.

The church, its gold and white interior splendid and intimate, is decorated with yellow roses and lemons and baby's breath. Titled Italians mingle with villagers, chatting and gossiping during the ceremony, treating the church as if it were an extension of their drawing rooms, or their kitchens. Altar boys lounge on the steps leading to the altar, while Puccio and Paola, Paola's face innocent of makeup, exchange the vows that will bind them, divorce laws notwithstanding, in one fashion or another for life.

Fireworks. Illuminating the Bay of Naples. Illuminating the world. The world, when one is happy, is the place upon which one stands.

On the terrace, suspended in space over the sea into which the wasted fire fell, we ate and drank: pigs' feet, pizza rustica, sausages, calzoni (pillows of dough stuffed with mozzarella and prosciutto); red wine and sulfuric white wine—Capri bianco—from the slopes of Vesuvius: the peasant fare of every Sorrentine feast; and Haut-Brion flown in from France.

And I had the sense that we were all part of a family, and that God Himself was a member of the family, as kindly and as gentle, perhaps even as diffident, as the village priest.

In the midst of magic (never wait till the magic ends), I search for someone to drive me down the hill.

"I need help, please," I say to an Austrian royal.

"Home? I cannot, I should love to, but my wife—I'm sorry—is here."

"You misunderstand. . . ."

"They are all old," Dottie says. "He is deaf." She will stay until the magic dies.

The priest drives me down the hill, silent, rosy, smiling.

Sometimes, in Sorrento, I have trouble climbing hills; my breath comes hard. Villagers stop and ask me why. They peer into my face. They place no distance between us.

When I was young this lack of space—my family's feeling that they had a right to enter my private world without knocking—made me feel I could not breathe.

They stop; they look, their faces cold; then, warming, they talk.

After these encounters I swim with perfect ease.

"Abandon entoure d'abandon. . . ."*

"Abandon surrounds abandon. . . ."

That is how, on the corniche road, the drive to Amalfi—and, higher and beyond, the road to Ravello—feels, climbing and curling in upon itself, fragrant, serpentine, Saracen, sunlit, kaleidoscopic, "so beautiful," Gide wrote, "that I had no desire to see anything more beautiful on earth"— intimate curves, deep gorges, bare mountains, soft, soft green hills into which are folded white villages naked to the sun and held safe in velvet green

---

*Rainer Maria Rilke, "The Roses and the Windows," translated from the French by A. Poulin, Jr.

embrace, bleached rock houses carved from cliffs on sandy coves; below, the motherly expanse of sea. A world of voluptuary sweetness.

It is Giuseppina who drives me. I met Giuseppina in the taxi rank in the Piazza Tasso. She drives a taxi, and she sews. She was engaged to be married once, but her lover married her best friend. She is pinched and sad. She lives, with her dowry furniture and her brother, on the second floor of the building she and her husband were to have shared. He, her once-lover, lives with his wife on the third floor of the same building. So they all lived for twenty years and not a word did Giuseppina and her once-betrothed speak . . . until the last earthquake; then Giuseppina said: "Help."

Giuseppina will not take coffee with me in Positano, it is not her place. "What nonsense, Giuseppina." Giuseppina relents. She sits up very tall and straight in her flowered dress in the flowered arbor high above the plum-blue sea.

This is the last door in the dream, the one that leads to scented paradise:

> Then, looking on the waters, I was ware
> of something drifting through delighted air,
> —An isle of roses—and another near—;
> And more, on each hand thicken, and appear
> In shoals of bloom; as in unpeopled skies,
> Save by two stars, more crowding lights arise,
> And planets bud where'er we turn our mazed eyes.*

This is earth—cars, buses, horns, imprecations, *"coincidenze"*— yet, traveling through that "wild air, world-mothering air/nestling me everywhere," twisting and turning, "I say that we are wound/With mercy round and round/As if with air."

Giuseppina drives two miles an hour. Everybody hates us.

> The world is charged with the grandeur of God.
> It will flame out, like shining from shook foil.

A fire rages in the hills above Ravello. Small planes bring water from the sea in red buckets; in the pools of the villas of the rich, people swim.

This is a painting by Brueghel.

*Verse quotations in this chapter are taken from the poems of Gerard Manley Hopkins.

*   *   *

Giuseppina will not go into the Grotta Verde, the Emerald Grotto, it is not her place.

"What nonsense, Giuseppina."

"No."

An elevator goes down to the landing platform, which is crowded—God and Italy know why—with new, unconnected commodes.

The grotto was discovered in 1926 by two young fishermen, says our boatman guide, which is not true, for accounts of it go farther back than that; it is irrelevant, but one wonders idly why the boatman chose 1926— perhaps it was the year of his birth.

It is emerald; and it is turquoise; and it is robin's-egg blue, an iridescent fusion of water and light; the light seems to come from underground springs of light; and I have never wanted to swim anywhere so badly—to be washed by hidden water that is fed by rays of light.

The coins on the ocean floor—tourists' offerings—look touchable, reachable, near; the water is thirty feet deep. . . . "And God said, Let there be a firmament in the midst of the waters, and let it divide the waters from the waters. . . ." There are stalactites in the cave. Look, says our guide: Garibaldi, Mussolini. There are stalagmites reaching up from under the water. Look, says our guide: Jesus, Joseph, Mary.

"Now *you* go to the grotto, Giuseppina."

"No."

Giuseppina drives two miles an hour, setting her lips primly; she has not allowed love to kill her, nor will the traffic on the Amalfi Drive, they can honk their horns against the starry sky forever. She takes me—around and around and down and up again—to her town on the other side, the Sorrentine side, of the peninsula: Sant'Agata. There is a *festa;* no cars are permitted on the road to Sant'Agata; the election of a mayor is being celebrated. Giuseppina has a long dry talk with a carabiniere. He lets her through. We sit, in a deserted piazza, under bright lights, in a café with tables covered in red-and-white oilcloth. Giuseppina smiles in triumph. She buys the coffee.

> Because the Holy Ghost over the bent
> World broods with warm breast and with ah!
>   bright wings.

St. Agatha's breasts were cut off, and she was rolled over hot coals when she scorned the advances of a Roman consul. In paintings she is often portrayed holding a pair of pincers or bearing her breasts on a platter, giving rise to some confusion: Some people mistook her breasts for loaves of bread; on her feast day loaves of bread are blessed.

Anna is here. Within moments her personality and her possessions are all over the room, she is on every surface, she is bouncing off the walls, her voice fills every crevice, there is so much of her, but never enough for me, I am an emotional cannibal . . . I am so happy.

At night, when she is sleeping, it is enough for me: the quiet rhythms of her breathing. I had forgotten this, forgotten what joy it is to be in a dark room with my child, listening to her breathing; heart's pulse, speech without word. . . . All is well in this spirit-washed universe. . . .

Anna loved Rome; Anna is prepared to love Naples—Anna is always prepared to love, thus lovable—but Naples doesn't make it easy. Naples doesn't open up its heart, flamboyant though it may be.

We are in the Hotel Santa Lucia, a first-class hotel on the Via Partenope on the sea. French doors theoretically open onto the harbor, but there is green netting draped around the balconies like a shroud; construction is going on. Never mind. No one can resist the invitation a balcony, any balcony, extends (pebbles shower on our heads); for a willed moment the view almost allows us to believe that Naples is, in Goethe's wonderful words, "gay, free and alive. A numberless host is running hither and thither in all directions, the King is away hunting, the Queen is pregnant and all is right with the world." The view: sailboats, yachts, rowboats, all manner of pleasure boats, bobbing up and down in oily water—but also four lanes of traffic. As we look, a boy on a bicycle reaches into the open window of a stopped car, comes up with a purse, and pedals furiously off (if the owner of the purse raises her voice in alarm, her cries are lost in the squawking of horns, the imbecile screeching of brakes). There is no "numberless host . . . running hither and thither." In this section of Naples, Santa Lucia, Italian matrons take off their wedding bands—for them an awful thing—to escape the depredations of roving thieves. Santa Lucia is dead. It has been suggested, by those who take the long, perhaps overly long view, that Santa Lucia is lifeless because of earthquakes (and the bombardments of 1943); but excellent hotels—now black, no lights at all at night, so empty and so sad—flourished here in the early 1960s; I know. The "death" of Santa Lucia (and of Naples) as a tourist center came later (perhaps as a result of drug traffic and drug use); only twenty years ago the Hotel Excelsior was ablaze with light; I remember well, because my babies got sick there and the doctor who came in response to my call asked what I thought I could expect if I brought espresso to my room and let them drink it (how like my family, believers in swift retribution). In Italy, and especially in Naples, nothing that concerns a child goes unnoticed. . . . What *would* a Neapolitan think if he didn't feel himself wedged between God and the Devil? . . . And when I asked the doctor for birth control pills, he nearly fainted dead away, overwhelmed with added proof of my perniciousness. It doesn't do to forget what country you are in. . . .

"The King is away hunting, the Queen is pregnant. . . ." The Castel dell'Ovo—Castle of the Egg—the huge medieval fort which we also see, was begun in 1154 by the Norman king of Sicily and Naples, William I; Emperor Frederick II completed it. It was a favorite fortress of the Angevins. In its dank dungeons one royal lady was imprisoned for eighteen years. This is history.

This is legend: On this spot Lucullus built his villa; on this spot Cicero met Brutus after the murder of Caesar; and (nicest of all) it is Virgil to whom the castle owes its existence—he built it upon an egg anchored to the bottom of the sea, and it shall stand until the egg is broken. . . . In a baroque embellishment of the story we are told that the egg—which in some versions of this story was placed inside a jug which was placed inside an iron cage—was broken during the reign of Joanna I, who (no fool she) simply replaced the egg with another . . . and so the fortress stands.

A castle moored to an egg is a perfect metaphor for continuity resting upon (or in spite of) fragility. It suits Naples, ruled by seven princely families since the twelfth century, French, Spanish, Austrian, Bourbon.

Anna doesn't care; Anna has no fear and Anna lives in the moment and at the moment we are outside eating spaghetti drenched with garlic-caper-and-tomato sauce at Bersagliera on the harbor. "They could all be from Staten Island or Bensonhurst," Anna says, speaking of their dialect and getting it in reverse; as I did once in London—how much these buildings look like those of Bombay, I said, getting it in reverse; it all depends on where one stands. The Neapolitan singers are down-at-the-heels, down-at-the-mouth, and disconsolate; people try to sell us things ("Lookee, lookee"). There are beautiful girls swinging their legs on the jetty; there are urchins carrying

huge and noisy radios; Vespas speed all around us. . . . The voices, the accents
do me in: We are addressed in the familiar; the voices are singsong or whiny,
sometimes both. I never learned Italian at home. On the lips of my immigrant family, that language which in Rome I came so much to love because
of its generosity, its round, open vowels, its rolling consonants, sounded
always angry (all final vowels were cut off, executed), crude, excitable,
abrupt, dismissive, and whiny, too. Not the language of affection, even less
the language of love. It sounded much like this, the language of the Naples
waterfront. This is a disorienting fact, it enlarges my idea of my family. Once
one begins to understand, one begins to forgive, and once one begins to
forgive, there is no end, one rewrites the story. . . .

Out of a combination of mischief and interest, "tell me about the Cosa
Nostra, what is it?" I ask our waiter.

"The Mafia, the Camorra, the 'ndrangheta," he intones, all these being
regional branches of organized crime. "Started after the Allied occupation,"
he says, a lie. "In the old days was not bad—just contraband cigarettes, like
that; now, drugs—bad. . . . It happened," he says, "because waiters were ruled
by rich Jews." This he whispers, and I do not in actual fact hear it—it does
not register—till much much later.

The streets behind the hotel are strewn with garbage.

A man stops us, he thinks we're hookers. Hookers! My daughter.

When Anna says she wants to go out "to buy a barrette," my voice takes
an escalator ride: "A barrette! Not on your life, not on these streets, you
don't. . . . OK, then find a post office, too." That is the worst thing, the least
attractive thing about being a mother to a grown-up child: You protest; and
when you yield, you take the opportunity to exploit.

The room to which we return is huge, the fake Persian rugs are threadbare,
the paint is peeling, the ceiling is high; the air conditioner blows out tepid
air, the ribbons attached to it, intended to be indicators of its functioning,
are faded and sluggish, failures as weather vanes; the air is in any case dusty,
it lodges in our throats.

Anna's bare feet slap the tiles, she hums in the old-fashioned bathroom;
my daughter washes her silks. . . .

"Anna, isn't this like a Third World country? Anna, do you hate Naples?
Is it my fault?"

"Cheer up, Ma, don't be a twit."

To this room come my friend Laura and her daughter, Lizzie, who is Anna's friend. We are symmetrical. Laura is prepared to be happy and to see the good.

Laura and Lizzie and Anna go for a walk along the waterfront. They come back angry, rattled, sad. Their walk took them to the Galleria Umberto (which, haunt of American soldiers in World War II, now has all the charm of a New York subway station) and past tables set up for the sale of antiques—no buyers, no tourists; and one could feel sorry for Naples, not for oneself, except that: Twenty cars have stopped, their drivers have hurled bad words at Lizzie, Laura, and Anna. Three men, one an ugly brute with a black eye, got out of a car and followed them; they ducked into a nightclub to escape; the men have called them "fishes, little fishes"—cunts, little cunts.

At the front desk I ask about these men so horridly on the prowl: "Why?"

"Because you are not ugly," they say. "A cultural misunderstanding," they say.

But the men have called the girls and Laura fishes, little fishes.

"Is this *quartiere* unsafe?" I ask.

"Is your subway safe?" they say.

All this they say with courtliness. It pains them to acknowledge that their city is broken.

If it's a cultural misunderstanding, why is there no *passeggiata?* Where are the Neapolitans at night?

"Afraid of thieves," they say; "television keeps them at home," they say; "the 1980 earthquake frightened tourists away, tourists just come in for the day from Rome or Ischia or Capri or Sorrento. . . ."

"But why?"

"Because your papers say bad things about us," they say. . . . "But there are bad people here," they say. "Very bad."

They are twisted, poor things, in their wish to defend and explain. The handsome desk clerk says German girls in particular come here for sex, "so you can't blame boys."

"*Boys?* These are *men!*" Laura says.

"When I was in Ischia with my wife and children," the handsome desk clerk says, "a German girl kept trying to go to bed with me. . . ."

"Oh, shit! Crap on that," Laura says. Her Lizzie is blond and blue-eyed. (Laura is tiny, flapperlike, and has amazing green eyes flecked with gold.) Laura says it's all about the sanctification of the Madonna, that's why Italian men treat women like this, and now I'm scared that I will have a fight with

Laura because this does not coincide with my belief, but of course we don't fight; our daughters, sternly watching us, implicitly forbid it; we have their welfare to think of.

Last night Anna made a date with a waiter at the Bersagliera, which now, chastened, she will not keep.

Everyone says that Naples is enjoying a renaissance, that art is happening here; but we can't breathe. We go to a restaurant where the service is crude and the clientele looks arty and slummers wear jewels and an old man reads his newspaper; and we can't breathe.

At the Capodimonte picture gallery the guards are dressed in spiffy white, they pick their teeth, they lounge against the walls, they sing fragments of Neapolitan folk songs; the paintings hang crooked. One guard says he has eleven children who collect American coins; we banter—we know we are being importuned—he gets the coins. And Anna gets the compliment: She is "a true Neapolitan—*allegra, vivace.*"

"Quick of wit and of unbounded impudence," Juvenal said Neapolitans were, "as ready as any orator and more torrential. . . . Experts in flattery and yet believed."

I have come in particular to see Mantegna's portrait of Francesco Gonzaga; but I am enthralled by his darkly mysterious *St. Eufemia*. St. Eufemia is pierced under her left breast by a dagger; she holds white lilies in one hand, a plume in another; above her head there is a bough from which peaches and grapes descend; a tiger holds her right wrist in his mouth; the tiger regards us kindly; St. Eufemia looks as if this—the dagger, the tiger—were an everyday occurrence, she looks bemused, she stares peacefully off into the distance. I want this painting to come to me in a dream: This painting can be understood only by the dreaming subterranean mind.

Many of these paintings are cracked, faded, and peeling, a disaster (Filippino Lippi's *Annunciation*—a painting of heavenly beauty—is not).

In the courtyard of the Capodimonte, four men are quarreling, quarreling quite happily, and jostling and kicking a packing case. They are singsonging one another about how to cut foam rubber to accommodate the picture two other men are holding languidly, carelessly. They stop to admire Anna as we pass; the picture they are holding slips a little from their grasp. Six men alone in a courtyard with a picture, no guard.

"*Mommie!* What's that?"

"Dear God."

It is a Caravaggio. If it had been a bowl of zuppa de pesce, they would have handled it more carefully.

My body is completely happy in Rome, only in Rome.

We meet Alfredo in the taxi rank. We choose him, he chooses us, who knows? Alfredo fulfills Juvenal's description: "If you smile, they split with laughter; if you shed tears, they weep . . . at any moment taking their expression from another's face." And yet he is genuine; and how can this be? St. Paul told us to weep when others weep, to cry when others cry; this is called empathy. Some call it guile. Alfredo, warm, exuberant, convinced (thank God) that he is an equal among equals—his place is quite as good as ours; as honorable, his expression says—proves himself to be a friend.

It is interesting to watch him make the decision not to cheat; he winks at us, for we have understood that his better nature (to say nothing of his long-range interests) has wisely overcome his greed. He wants, he says, to keep things *belle*. (Italians are born with the word *bello* in their mouths.)

Every day he has lunch with his brothers and his sisters, and every day his wife and their baby girl have lunch with her mother.

Alfredo has become our *cicerone* and our bodyguard.

He takes us to the marvelously exuberant elliptical Piazza of Gesù Nuovo and thence to Spaccanapoli, the old quarter of decayed medieval and Renaissance palazzi (that which you think of when you think of street urchins, Vittorio de Sica, clotheslines, and Sophia Loren).

I am past asking Anna's forgiveness for bringing her to Napoli. I am in Baroque heaven. (This heaven is hot pink, pale green, and gray.)

In the center of the piazza is a grand white frothing marble stupa or *guglia,* as self-congratulatory as any monument can be. Its happy elaboration is enough to inspire a maypole dance around it. This is the Guglia dell'Immacolata, erected in thanksgiving for the end of a plague; once a year a ladder is placed against it, and an intrepid boy climbs to place a crown of flowers on Mary's head (obelisks are frequently used to honor Mary). The "confectionary" obelisk, its phallicism mitigated by its curls and swirls, exists in counterpoint to the seventeenth-century Church of Gesù Nuovo with its facade of fortress-gray embossed so that it resembles hard gem-cut waves or battle-ready bristles; actually, says Laura, the facade looks like hardened sfogliatelle—the shell-like Neapolitan confection with layers of fine pastry like ridges or waves, filled with candied fruit, chocolate, and ricotta (we are having a wonderful time).

Inside, Gesù Nuovo is anything but fortresslike. No inch of it is undecorated, it is a riot of colored marbles; atop white marble and green porphyry, against red marble above a huge sphere of lapis ringed with gold, stands Mary—*L'Immacolata*—exceedingly pregnant.

In one side altar are tier upon tier of open gilt "boxes," or rectangles, in which are wooden busts of saints; separating the rows of boxes vertically are rows of dusty glass panels full of skulls and bones. These boxes—nests, honeycombs—receding into the dimness of the ceiling, are like toys, child-like, entrancing: a child's vision of God. . . . The bones of the dead, in this context, look like playthings.

"What's the difference between all this and worshiping Ganesh?" Anna says. Anna was born in India. She is twenty-one.

"The difference between worshiping a human God and worshiping an elephant is obvious," I say.

"I don't see a God who became human, I see Mary," Laura says.

"Let's have a pizza," Lizzie says. "Isn't there a Benetton?" Lizzie is sixteen.

An arm of the church leading to the sacristy is covered, floor to ceiling, with ex-votos, tin and silver body parts (offerings of praise for those who've found relief): hearts, limbs, lungs, breasts, intestines, feet, brains.

"Happy, Mama?"

"God, can't you see our families doing this?" (This is Laura.)

"Bensonhurst," Anna says.

We all know what she means.

"Meaning no disrespect," she says.

Gesù Nuovo was built by a woman, Isabella della Rovere.

Across from Gesù Nuovo is the convent Church of St. Clara (Santa Chiara) and its otherworldly cloisters, unlike any others in the world: The cloisters were commissioned by the Bourbon queen Maria Amalia and designed by Domenico Antonio Vaccaro in the eighteenth century; this cloister is an unrivaled marvel of ceramic design. Majolica tile columns uphold wisteria arbors; tile benches invite mingled excitement and repose. Some of the tiles are decorative—fruit and flowers in Neapolitan abundance (flowers never seen on earth, fruit no Adam could resist)—and some tell stories—pastoral, biblical, historical (within this paradise there are seas, fortresses, ships, mountains, men, trees, rocks, sheep, queens, cats, troubadours, pigs, wine). Within this Franciscan paradise there are only the four of us—and a father and his daughter, whose name, by happy chance, is Clara.

St. Clara was born in Assisi of a noble family. Having refused to marry when she was twelve, she heard a Lenten sermon of St. Francis, whereupon she ran away from home and, from Francis, took the veil. Her sister Agnes also took the habit from St. Francis, when she was fifteen; when their father sent twelve armed men to get Agnes back, Clara's prayers succeeded in making Agnes so heavy she was rooted to the ground. Eventually Clara was joined by her mother and another sister, Beatrice. St. Francis gave to Clara and to her relatives and followers, who had become numerous, the old Church of San Damiano in Assisi; for forty years she was Superior.

Thus began the Poor Clares. Their life was one of mortification, austerity, extreme poverty (like that of Francis), and—we are told—of joy. The absolute poverty of the Poor Clares was questioned by some of their number, who formed another observance; from her vow Clara never swerved. She owned nothing but her faith; her life belonged to God. She was canonized two years after her death, in 1255.

Her flesh is said in books to be incorruptible; but those who have seen it say her face is black and she is mummified and in her hand she holds an artificial lily.

She who lived in absolute poverty seven hundred years ago in a church called, by one observer, a more primitive place of worship than any in remote Coptic villages in Egypt now has an Eden of tiles named for her. CIGA Hotels is restoring the tiles, which are not incorruptible. Blisters, the cause of which is unknown, have appeared on their surface; they swell and burst and leave bald red patches.

The Catholic Church is very strange. St. Clara was a contemplative. She is the patron saint of television.

One whole wall of the Gothic chancel of Santa Chiara is devoted to an eighteenth-century crib (or crèche, or *presepio*). This is like a dollhouse but a hundred thousand times more enchanting: The "doll" is the Baby Jesus. The *presepio* is detailed and particular, and all its parts are wondrously carved, astonishingly real/not real, giving rise to fantasies as well as spiritual reflections. Here, in addition to the principals—Mary, Jesus, Joseph, the Wise Men, and of course the angels and the shepherds—are couriers and ordinary villagers. A man puts a loaf of bread (perhaps a pizza) into an oven; the oven is aglow. Lights twinkle in the domed, variously blue sky. A house, lit by tiny oil vessels: in it bouquets of garlic, ropes of onions. Donkeys pull carts; farm animals graze; cats stalk mice. Ordinary people play and work while the miracle of His birth goes on. . . . As indeed they did. Christ came while bread was put in ovens. Christ is the bread of humankind.

Jesus was born in Naples, Vesuvius watching over Him.

At the end of the eighteenth century Neapolitans contrived to turn their *presepi* into puppet shows. Sometimes humans took the place of dolls. There were two requirements for the child "Christ": that he be poor, and that he be fair of feature.

The *presepio* Cuciniello, in the Museum of San Martino, has been called the "translation of the Bible into Neapolitan dialect."

After Henry James saw the churches of Naples, he professed himself "sick unto death. . . . Their 'picturesqueness' ends by making you want to go strongly into political economy or the New England school system." One loves his manner of expressing sentiments one couldn't disagree with more.

On the steps of Santa Chiara, an old lady in black sits with bread and water for the pigeons. She comes here every day. She carries a satchel in which she keeps plastic dishes. The birds eat and drink from dishes, she eats from garbage cans. "Why?"

"Because it is in her mind to do it," Alfredo says. "One is who one is."

In the Piazza of Gesù Nuovo, on Vespas, are bare-chested men, tattooed, festooned with gold chains. They are undercover cops, Alfredo says.

Alfredo embraces and kisses us; there is nothing sexual in this. But he hugs Anna most of all. Then he shows her pictures of his little girl.

We are walking through Spaccanapoli. We walk circumspectly, avoiding alleys with their showers of dust motes, narrow side streets where dark silences reign in bright and sunny places. There are lone figures on all these streets that go—where? To some Neapolitan end-of-the-world falling-off place? They are always boys. Alfredo keeps us to streets on which there are cars, though every street is in fact too narrow for cars and we flatten ourselves against walls, our heels slipping in ripe garbage. When four hard boys approach, Alfredo takes Laura's hand and says we must make "a crocodile"; we obey, though it is hard to imagine danger keeping company with the fresh white sheets that flap overhead. Alfredo says this isn't the poorest part of Naples, there are worse; everybody eats now, he says, there are no empty bellies (he loves his city); and: so little restoration here, compared to Florence or to Rome, he says, it's politics.

Junk dealers; gold and silver stores; stores in which to buy the figures of a *presepio;* in every gap between buildings, heaps of red, yellow, green vegetables piled high; fish; postcards; old records; garbage; streets devoted to Communion dresses, wedding gowns.

The distinction between inside and outside here is almost nonexistent: Rooms open directly onto the street—a bed is flush with a cart of red tomatoes, we see a chair, a bureau, a plaster Madonna, a woman in a rumpled housecoat brushing her long black hair.

We stop at an ex-voto store. We buy hearts. I want to buy a silver ex-voto representing breasts. "One?" "No, two." "Two one-breasts or two two-breasts?" "A set." "A set of two? A set of ones?" "A pair of breasts. One pair of breasts. One ex-voto, one pair of breasts, two breasts." "Two pair?" "Two breasts. . . . *Alfredo!*"

No one ever leaves Spaccanapoli entirely behind. I remembered it from twenty years ago, when I walked its narrow alleys alone and unafraid. Is the difference in Naples or in me? I am tired of vexing the question; and now I will always remember and be grateful to the Piazza of Gesù Nuovo for reminding me that in the midst of human degradation, fear, and despair, God blesses us with abundance; in Naples, broken and decayed, it is possible to think of God as playful.

I will always see, on a creased street that leads only to a vanishing point, a young boy with hard eyes, a mouth still tender. He stands and stares; his passivity is a kind of invitation. I turn away.

We leave Spaccanapoli for the Via Roma, a broad thoroughfare that runs almost the length of the city, from the north to the south, from the business quarter to the harbor.

On the Via Roma (which Neapolitans call Via Toledo after Don Pedro de Toledo, viceroy of the Spanish crown, who caused eighteen thousand Neapolitans to be hanged), there are few coffee bars—life is lived outside in Spaccanapoli, perhaps cafés would be redundant (a woman braids her hair as cars rush by almost grazing her feet). There are no taxis and only one tourist. He is Japanese.

Alfredo leaves us at a pizzeria. We eat dinner-plate–sized pizzas, one each: mozzarella, tomato, *prosciutto crudo*. There is no other food, though the trattoria has a menu a mile long. There is no coffee, and nobody has the will or energy to go to a coffee bar for us. Alfredo drives up as we are consulting the bill, which seems exorbitant. We have been overcharged for mineral water; Alfredo shrugs, regards us sympathetically, but wordlessly suggests we pay it as it is; he retreats behind his newspaper, eloquently: This is no business of mine, his body says. This detachment is uncharacteristic, foreign to him. Alfredo seems not exactly easy with the detached view, so, perhaps as recompense, he takes us for a *giro* in the taxi: to the semicircular Piazza del Plebiscito, laid out by Murat. In niches on the Palazzo Reale which encloses the piazza on one side there are statues of Neapolitan kings . . . to whom Alfredo, the blood of the too-much-dominated flowing through his veins, pays no homage. Their absurd frigid poses, he says, the position of their hands and arms, tell this story:

FIRST KING: Who peed?
SECOND KING *(hand in air)*: Not I.
THIRD KING *(smiting his breast)*: I.
FOURTH KING *(sword raised high)*: I'll cut off your hand.

(I think Alfredo presented us with a bowdlerized version. I don't think the sword was meant for the king's *hand.*)

On the walls of the Carthusian Monastery of San Martino *(chiuso)* there is a plaque commemorating the expulsion of the Spanish. "So what?" says Alfredo, dwelling on the injuries of the past. "Then we got the French." Next door to the monastery is a shop full of impressive antique cameos. The shopkeeper, a Sardinian who is much taken with Alfredo, tells us that life is *dolorosa* because it is his thirtieth birthday; this brings Alfredo back into the present and into good humor, for he is not yet thirty, and he has a child; and the hands of the Sardinian are too white, he says, a woman's hands; it gives him pleasure to regard his own.

We have driven up a spiral course to get here—to white cloisters that are closed—and now we stand on a spur of the Vomero Hill, and the Bay of Naples is below us, and the city is what Keats said it was: a dream.

So now we wind again, up, down, around, and we are on the promontory of Posillipo—we have passed the villas of the rich, the nighttime pleasure palaces of men who have no need to grab for girls—and Alfredo takes us to a garden café from which we see the islands of Capri, Procida, and Ischia; green and calm and pleasant. . . . We sit on swings—whee! over the bay—and Alfredo pays for *granita di caffè* and we are in love with Naples and with one another, and we echo Keats: "I do not feel in the world."

The greatest compliment a Neapolitan can pay is to say one is like a Neapolitan. Anna, Alfredo says, is a Neapolitan. She must not cut her abundant brown hair, he says. . . . In Naples a barber is called a Figaro. . . . It delights Alfredo that Anna took home from a restaurant a jar of chicken soup to bring to me one night. It isn't done. Anna does it. Anna makes the world her living room, just as a Neapolitan does; Anna doesn't recognize boundaries; outside is in. Across four lanes of traffic she comes in her blue halter dress, bearing *pastina in brodo.*

We pass a street shrine—a picture of a mournful Christ behind heavy glass surrounded by fleshy red gladioli and by iron bars. It is lit with seven pink candles and with a harsh red neon light, and on either side of Jesus are apothecary jars filled with plastic flowers, the whole topped with a gold ribbon such as one might put on a Christmas present. *"Finalmente,"* Alfredo says: *"Gesù."* For this is Mary's town. Laura gets that I'm-gonna-take-you-on-about-the-Madonna/whore-syndrome-in-this-country look in her eyes; but we are too tired and too content to quarrel. Anna and Lizzie are snoring lightly, they have fallen asleep immaculately, like cream-sated cats.

In the eighteenth century, after street-corner oil lamps had proved ineffectual in curbing nocturnal attacks and halting robberies, Padre Rocco, a Dominican priest, philosopher, and theologian, "armed with three hundred copies of a sacred picture of the Madonna, and one hundred large wooden crosses bearing the painted figure of Christ . . . instituted the indirect lighting supplied by tiny street altars. Under his auspices, two thousand street lamps were eventually lit for the sake of Christ or the Madonna, and kept burning."

The Neapolitans are practical, they use God.

God has not, however, obliged them with their hoped-for safety and security.

In this hotel the palms are dusty; the dining room is always empty save for us; the decrepit waiter keeps heaping up more plates on the buffet table, but no one comes; the glass display cases are empty, and so are the halls. Nothing works.

On this day we have seen two weddings, one at Gesù Nuovo and one at San Domenico Maggiore, a Gothic church in Spaccanapoli with sculpture of the Tuscan school, which Anna prefers to flowery Baroque (which she insists on comparing to temples dedicated to Ganesh, Shiva, and Hanuman).

At Gesù Nuovo a long black car stops, and flowers are trundled to the altar. The wedding party consists of the bride, a beautiful woman with a Grecian profile (an "Arab," Alfredo says dismissively, sensing Saracen blood); the groom (wearing a silly bridegroom smile on his face and trying unsuccessfully to look serious); a bridesmaid in slutty yellow lace; the best man; a flower girl; two ring bearers (boys); the bride's father, a small, wizened man with a puzzled expression; a photographer . . . no other guests. The organ plays "Ave Maria" . . . and the flowers are trundled out again; it is all over in minutes.

A square-shaped woman who comes uninvited to weddings—her husband is dead, her children have gone, and this is her entertainment—says that she is *arrabbiata* (angry) because there are not enough flowers. She is used to leaving her house for magnificent weddings; these people (she glares at the wedding party) are depriving her of her pleasures. She is holding a rosary in her hand.

At San Domenico Maggiore the wedding party is equally small, the ceremony is equally brief.

Why?

"Perhaps the guests are waiting in a restaurant?"

"Perhaps," says Anna, "the brides are pregnant." Anna pronounces this word *preg-a-nant.*

Also on this day we have passed the Tomb of San Gennaro (St. Januarius), whose blood, conserved in two vials, liquefies and sometimes bubbles and boils three times a year, in May, in September, and in December, and has done so for four hundred years.

Of the two phenomena—the liquefaction of the blood of a martyred saint and the five-minute weddings—the liquefaction of the blood is easier to understand.

At night the lights of the harbor twinkle and insist, and Anna and I sing in our double bed. We sing the folk songs and the protest songs she was brought up with: "Puff the Magic Dragon" ("who lived by the sea"); "If you miss me at the back of the bus"—she'd sung it ("come on over to the front of the bus, I'll be sittin' right there") when she was angry with bad-boss-mommy-me, defiant, but I'd never known that till now, I'd always joined in with her ("if you miss me in the cotton fields . . ."), which increased her pleasure in her private ritual of sassing me; "Day Is Done" ("and if you take my hand, my son, all will be well when the day is done"); "Little Boxes" ("little boxes, made of ticky-tacky"); "Puff the Magic Dragon" ("in a land called Ho-nah-Lee"). . . . And Anna, weaving the tapestry of her childhood, wrapped in calm, sings Elizabethan songs ("Once There Were Three Marys"). . . . And then we sing Cole Porter, and then we sing Rodgers and Hart and Rodgers and Hammerstein and Jerome Kern. "Love walked right in and drove the shadows away. . . ." How can I think of leaving America? How can I live in Italy? With whom, twined in familiar tenderness, will I sing Cole Porter songs? Who will know with me the terrible fate of Puff the Magic Dragon?

Anna and I go to Capri by *aliscafo,* hydrofoil. Island of fantastic rocks, of fragrant myrtle, juniper, and heather, of blue butterfly and blue lizard, of lemon sun and radiant waters, audacious hills and embracing green gardens (and Vanity Fair in the piazza), it can never—let no one tell you other-wise—be spoiled. "*This* is the most beautiful place on earth," Anna says, looking at me in frank and delighted amazement, for since she has come to Italy, life has offered her everywhere cornucopia and paradise.

Straight from the *aliscafo* and the Marina Grande to the Blue Grotto (I want to give my daughter a sapphire present): from a motor launch to a small boat, and all the boats, too many boats, jostling and jockeying for position, the boatmen in bad humor. The boatman who hauls me from the large boat to the small boat—we must lie flat to enter the cavern, its mouth is small—gives my wrist a vicious twist. He has a bloodied nose, perhaps from propelling himself by means of a chain into that small opening.

It is a good thing Italy is not devoted to Freud, all this slithering in and out of cave-wombs, laden with freight.

In we go, to magic: vibrant blue so blue the liquid concentration of blue essence, and iridescent; it is as if the source of light were not the sky but the molten center of the earth . . . and God moves among the mirrored waters. And then out we go, to a communal intake of breath. Too short a time in silvered sapphire waters.

The boatman relaxes his anger (perhaps because of Anna's solicitations); he becomes not just a device for ferrying people (Anna does this; she sees people); "It's hot," he says, "it's tricky, and it's dangerous. What a life," he says, "all sad." Anna's hand, cool as a silver fish from trailing in the blue waters, rests on mine. The sun is hot. What a life.

Tacitus says it was not so much the perfection of climate that charmed rotten Tiberius, who spent the last ten years of his life in debauchery on Capri, as the seclusion and inaccessibility of the island. And one still feels it, feels cut off from the rest of the world—though cars careen on roller-coaster roads, on one side the rock, on the other the precipice. In the coolness of the arched streets (which echo a fantastic archway in gigantic rock, brazen but inevitable in the water), in those streets where sobriety and intoxication fight for equal time, one feels it. Among the confused shining of hot cliffs one feels it. One feels it mostly as a blessing, but occasionally as a haunting. From a promontory in Capri Tiberius threw his victims to the sea, and there a band of Roman men received them and broke their bones with clubs and oars.

Because of ill timing we miss my friend the *principe.* Life for the rich is ritualized—what to do but eat lotus?—the *principe* is at the Hotel Tiberio from eleven to twelve, the Hotel Palma from three to six. Perhaps I do not want to see the *principe* and his drugged lover, she who sings in her chains like the sea.

Having taken the funicular from Marina Grande to the piazza (almost never called by its name, Piazza Umberto, as for all practical and people-watching purposes, it is the only piazza in Capri), we drink silly drinks and watch the parade of the elegant, the funky, the bizarre—everybody looking dazed, as we must have done, too, when we first entered this yellow-and-white piazza, which could be the result of a joint effort of God, Tiberius, and Mr. Disney.

We walk to the Gardens of Augustus, from which we see the wide cerulean sea and the Faraglioni, huge rocks that cannot, one feels, owe their breathtaking placement to chance. One, La Stella, is connected to the island; and two, Lo Scopolo (home of the blue lizards) and the prosaically named Grotta dell'Arsenale, are joined by a natural archway, through which one sails in bliss. One feels that this rock is more than rock, that if one looks hard enough—or loves hard enough—it will yield meaning. One never forgets the Faraglioni; that is meaning enough. Perhaps these rocks are a lesson in the meaning of time and the intersection of time and space—it is impossible to imagine the world without this landscape—they obliterate time by looking as if they had been there forever . . . and also by looking sculpted, for which another word is created.

In the gardens there is an old man, white hair, white white shirt, blue blue eyes, listless, but vivacious the moment I smile, and after an exchange of pleasantries—he is gallant, courtly, formal, charming—"Life is *dolorosa*," he begins. Naples, where he lives, is a *disastro*. I say I remember Naples—the *passeggiata*, the spirit, *allegro*, *vivace*—from twenty-five years ago. Not to be outdone, he remembers Naples from before World War II; and he expresses himself on decapitation and capital punishment for drug offenses: "Cut their hands off," he says, "as the Fascists would have done." He is crying.

How *dolorosa* can life be for an elderly man who comes to beautiful Capri two or three times a week? my daughter asks, gazing out to sea; Anna has seen the glories of Macchu Picchu, Golconda, and Atitlán, but she has seen nothing more beautiful than this in her life.

Nevertheless, he is crying.

"Old age is terrible," I say. Even I am nostalgic for the horses and carriages that used to climb to Anacapri, now taxis; think how he must feel, his whole world changed.

"Fascist fart," Anna says, "poor old nice Fascist fart," she says, "he's crying. . . . His blue eyes . . ."

We are having lunch in a restaurant that is like a cool green cave.

We take the bus to the village of Anacapri (which might, compared with the piazza of Capri, be called sedate, even, in its prettiness, prim), bus driver fearless, Anna—from these spiraling heights—not fearless; when she is able to open her eyes, which vertigo has shut: "*This* is the most beautiful place on earth," she says. I am sated, content to rehearse memories in an arbored café; Anna is my eyes and legs, she walks the long mile to Axel Munthe's Villa San Michele, built on a fragment of Tiberius's villa. I am under no compulsion to see everything, Anna is tireless; the sight of her slight body sturdily climbing charms and braces me, the sight of me sitting among roses comforts her, we both feel we've had the best of the bargain.

It is lovely to say "Now, voyager!" to one's daughter when the journey will bring her back full circle; these small contained departures, full of dignity and repose, prepare us for what Americans call "achieving separation" and what Italians call "My daughter is getting married."

To Marina Grande in a taxi with a fringe on top—exactly twenty times the bus fare, but haggling is guaranteed not to work, and it's that or miss our boat. One mustn't let one's days be jaundiced by men who strike hard bargains ("I have to live, signora"). He has a family in California, he says, but why should he leave beautiful Capri? At night, he says, in Anacapri, rich women wear nothing but jewels, and the jewelry shops remain open all night because people fall in love and buy each other jewelry. *"Viva Italia! Viva amore! E viva maccheroni!"* he shouts, hands perilously off the steering wheel. I like comic opera.

On the ferry are American honeymooners—spoiled brats ("No more kisses," she says to him, coyly; he glares—kisses are not on his mind, he has not bothered to shave). "I'll be honest with you," she says, "we've been cheated all over, and nobody is nice. I tried on three dresses in Capri, and money isn't a problem, I can buy anything"—she is twenty-three—"but the shopkeepers are so rude. Of course, I'm so slim it's hard to find my size. I'll be honest with you, I'm going to tell all my friends never to come to Italy."

"Why do you bother talking to them?" Anna asks.

I don't know. "Are they nuts?"

"They're having bad sex," Anna says. Of course.

Anna has lived in shacks on Peruvian mountaintops, picked lice from New York bag ladies, slept in hammocks in barrios—and she adores luxury; her adaptability and her kindness are not a function of an ideology, she is one of the least coarse people I know, uncoarsened by ideology. So she loves the Cocumella—*whoopee!* Sometimes I think she ought to act more sophisticated (in order to support my apparent breezy acceptance of luxury, my act), but Italians love her enthusiasm—*allegra, vivace*—they ravish her with their eyes and ply her with the Cocumella drink: Aperol and vodka and champagne.

She walks like a princess through the reception rooms that unfold in an enfilade. This space calls for leisured dignity; Anna understands space. The floors of the arched hallways are red-tiled; along the halls are hydrangeas in alabaster vases resting on Nello's father's furniture, and carved wooden saints from the Cocumella's convent days. Our sleep will be made in two brass double beds, under oiled wooden rafters, creamy crocheted curtains stirring at our windows. . . . And after eating two fat veal chops grilled with basil butter at the pool, Anna takes it into her head to swim, but there are no lights on near the pool, the sun has set, and Anna, her sensibilities excited by the glamour and the goodness of this honeyed day, says: "What if there are monsters?," which question Aldo, the headwaiter, takes seriously, whereupon Anna sees its foolishness.

At 3:30 A.M. she has not returned and she is not in the pool; I call the desk. They say it is *normale,* but how can they know? At four I hear voices from the pool, I hear Anna's voice, and she comes back cool, wet, self-possessed, unscathed. She has been with two men and two women to a nightclub in Sorrento where they sing Hebrew songs.

"*Hebrew* songs?"

"*Shalom,* honeybunch, sleep tight, Mama."

Alfredo has negotiated with Hertz for the car that Laura will drive along the Amalfitan coast to Ravello. For this and many services and kind offices he exacts no payment, and we all—proper southern Italians—hug and cry. . . . We love you, Alfredo, we say. *Certamente*—of course you do, he says.

This is how Naples was described in the first quarter of the twentieth century, by a writer who called Neapolitans—so like my own people— "obscene" and Naples "meaningless": ". . . rather a pen of animals than a city of men, a place amazing if you will, but disgusting in its amazement, whose life is merely life, without dignity, beauty, or reticence, or any of the nobler conventions of civilization, a place so restless and noisy and confused that it might be pandemonium, . . . parvenu and second-rate. . . ."

"How can anyone hate Naples?" Laura says. She says this though she has just driven down a one-way street the wrong way (Moses parting the Red Sea was nothing to it), and she is shaking and living off her nerves. She is waved on by a traffic cop, who, infinitely courteous (or perfectly mocking), bows. "How *could* one?" Laura says. Modest Alfredo has redeemed Naples, modest Alfredo and intemperate Baroque.

*   *   *

It is said that there are more than a thousand bends on the Amalfitan drive, and Laura negotiated them all, and we were immensely proud of her, and she of herself; she glows.

And so, by way of Amalfi, to Positano, where square white houses in gardens of figs, plumbago, grapes, and broad beans and almonds climb in steps down to the sea and Byzantine domes glitter in the (always) sun and gay clothes hang from shops of young designers like banners of another age. In an arbor where the sun seems almost possessed of intelligence—the bars of light and shade it throws across our bodies seem to warm us from within (a blood pattern)—we are cool-warm-cool-warm-hot-cool-warm-hot-cool; our bodies dance with this felt light. Laura and I cry . . . because we are old and good friends, because we are in Italy, because we are Italian . . . and because our daughters sing.

> Nature is never spent;
> There lives the dearest freshness deep down things.

And higher, to blue-green heights, to Ravello, logically suspended between sea and air.

Days of lambent happiness followed—days in which we had to will nothing, cause nothing, days in which that which was minimal became, observed, that which was large.

We found an hotel on a street of steps lined with oleander, the Albergo Toro, a converted villa steps away from the piazza, the cathedral, and from the Villa Rufolo—a place of towers and cloisters, hot-colored flower gardens, and long, saving sea views, occupied once by Adrian IV, the only English Pope, and once by Wagner, who found in the villa *Parsifal*'s magic gardens of Klingsor (and once by Jacqueline Kennedy).

How lightly, easily, we spent our days: hours in the piazza, in one of the two cafés on either side of the white cathedral; one café is patronized by Ravellesi (over two thousand souls live here)—old ladies in silk, carefully made up, wearing many rings; very old ladies who sit in doorways, part of café life, though nothing is required of them (nothing is required of us)— children circling and children cycling—children are on wheels (harbingers of things to come) in Italy before they are able to walk; wearing orthopedic shoes, they cycle. In this café the service is nicely slow. The other café is patronized by an occasional tourist and by Italians on holiday. ("They must send all the ugly ones to Staten Island," Anna says. How well I know the feeling.) In this café—the fancier one—there is a special table for taxi drivers (who are underemployed). We watch nuns in black habits and red sneakers carrying red canteens, shepherding children with clucking, purring noises; we watch the old taxi drivers remove their belts from their pants to tie together the suitcases of hotel guests; we watch the yellow buses disgorge their passengers for a fifteen-minute stop; the postmistress making her rounds. What other entertainment is necessary? Sometimes some of us arrange ourselves at one café and others (or one of us) at another: We wave across the square.

Why should this simple gesture make us happy?

Sometimes Laura and the girls take a winding road, a goats' path, past deserted monasteries to a pebble beach. They take the bus to Amalfi and Positano and come back with arms full of bright filmy clothes, and dress for the *passeggiata*. They bring me presents.

In Amalfi Anna saw a man in a swimsuit with a huge erection; nobody paid any mind.

It is not a mistake to be old here.

The cathedral is used like a living room; Ravellesi pass in and out of it, for refreshment.

In this church, with its magnificent pulpit, a menagerie: Marble eagles decorate the pulpit; six lions, each with a different expression, uphold it on glittering serpentine pillars. In it is the blood of St. Pantaleon (patron saint of doctors), a hardened dark-brown mass conserved in a thirteenth-century ampulla. St. Pantaleon was a doctor who demanded no payment for his services; his name means "all-compassionate." Under the persecution of Diocletian he was beheaded, but the earth did not absorb his blood, which now liquefies (and "if in some year the miracle did not occur, some grave public calamity always did").

I sit in the garden of the Toro—hot red begonias against dusty-pink oleanders; tea roses—drinking fresh lemonade. From the tennis school next door, separated from the garden by an ivy-covered stone wall, I hear the ping of tennis balls; from the cathedral I hear the music of sung Mass. At eight o'clock the bells of all the churches—thin, full, sweet, round, profound, high—toll; they take me with them: swinging.

Laura says her parents had a garden like this, it makes her cry. It was the same garden, she says, although theirs was in a depressed northeastern American town; the gardens of our childhood are all beautiful.

Lizzie and Anna say they understand their mothers better now; we do not know what they mean. What can landscape explain?

In the Victorian parlor of the Toro, which Laura peoples with characters from Henry James, I look through the musty books of past guests—a favorite occupation, eliminating choice; a mystery, *Murder at the KO Lodge,* 1939 . . . *The Countryman,* Autumn 1977 . . . contents:

"Hotel Keeping in the Highlands" ("When I was younger, it would have surprised me very much to be told that a time would come when one of my principal preoccupations in life would be inn-keeping. . . ."—Sir Fitzroy Maclean.)

"Jubilee in a Yorkshire Village"

"The Case for Culling"

"Eye-Level Gardening"

"Crops + Oil = Food"

"Mooching for Blackberries"

"Bargaining for Beef"

"Goat on the Roof"

"Homage to Beatrix Potter" . . .

When Anna sees the gold-and-silver statue of St. Pantaleon in the cathedral, she says his halo and the disposition of his hands remind her of the Buddha. Anna's radical ecumenism sometimes exasperates me. But then I think of all those apparently stylized Baby-Jesus gestures and those of angels, in Renaissance paintings, the graceful articulations of fingers and dimpled hands, like flowers with their petals opening in freeze-frame time; and I think: Of course. Babies do this. Real babies. My babies. A sleeping child, a murmur, all of a sudden a hand upraised, the fingers in a graceful curl, so stylized—so absolutely natural. And the gestures of the Buddha, the mudras, are like this, too. . . . Everything is connected.

At night we walk under Moorish arches, a fragrant labyrinth, to Compa' Cosimo, Netta's restaurant, across from the small and beautiful Romanesque

Church of Santa Maria, where someone seems always to be playing the harp, an instrument that requires moonlight.

Netta cooks, and she helps plan and harvest her family's farm in the nearby town of Scala, too; she is an inspired cook; we eat: crespolini, polenta pancakes stuffed with Parmesan and prosciutto (which she cures); tagliatelle (made in the trattoria) with fresh squash; fusilli with fresh tomatoes; penne in a tomato-parsley sauce with ground beef and pork; split-chicken al diavolo; beefsteak seasoned with garlic and lemon; an amber *amaro* made in house, with flecks of bitter lemon floating in it.

Anna and Lizzie play with Danilo, son of Lucca, who waits on us. Danilo is five. He takes it into his head to get mock-angry (he has a crush on one of the girls, and his anger masks his choice); he spits at Lizzie and slaps Anna's legs, and then he laughs. When a young waitress takes him to task (languidly, this is not a severe offense), he spits at her and calls her *puttana* (whore). He pinches Lizzie and Anna on the ass; he runs after us: *Puttana!*

"Do you really think it's sexual?" I say.

"Are you kidding?" Laura says. "It starts when they're three."

"They're always scratching their crotches, too," Lizzie says; which is true.

We go to the piazza for gelato. Two men with pigs' faces, hands on hips (their faces are mottled, as if from unhappy drinking), say: "Come here!" *("Vieni qua!")* They say it angrily. A waiter waves them off with a broom.

In the café Anna says, "You know how you told me Sophia Loren came in second in a beauty contest in Naples, and who could possibly have come in first?"

"Mmmm?"

"Everyone here came in first."

The streetlights are on but it is still light. The lights on the winding hills wind round and round like those on a perfectly symmetrical Christmas tree, fairy lights.

In the piazza men are erecting a platform, stringing lights in preparation for the Feast of St. Pantaleon. Fireworks—a trial display—burst pale against the pale-blue sky. Men and women wash the steps of the cathedral. A band strikes up discordantly.

"Who were those piggy men?" Lizzie says. "Why do they hate us?"

"Nobody hates us, honey," Laura says. "Have some of my chocolate"— exactly as if Lizzie were five years old.

That night the heat climbs to ninety degrees, we have no fan, and the chemicals in the *fornellino*— the "mosquito cooker" Laura has bought to keep the insects from biting her to death—cause her suffering. In the morning her eyes are swollen nearly closed.

The lira has fallen, the rate is 2,020 to the dollar, and the *cambio* shuts down for the first time in ten years. The woman in the information bureau, angry about the lira, is on strike, she tells Laura she doesn't know where Abruzzo is, we'll have to find it for ourselves ("Of course you can afford to pay someone to read a map . . .").

Early the next morning a man in blue overalls, white gloves, a face mask, and a respirator walks down our street, spraying pesticide—clouds of the white noxious stuff—on pink oleanders.

We call the hotel in Venafro, where my family lives; it rings emptily, it is now a supermarket.

"I don't care, I want to stay in Ravello anyway, forever," Lizzie says.

"This is the most beautiful place on earth," Anna says. "Notwithstanding."

"We stay for the feast—the blood may liquefy—or we visit our families in Abruzzo," Laura says.

"Is there a Benetton in Abruzzo?" Lizzie says.

"So it's blood or 'the blood,'" Anna says.

"The blood," Laura and I agree: families . . . our blood, our families' blood, more mysterious than saints'.

Netta sends us off with six lemons and a bottle of sparkling wine for Anna's feast day.

Danilo jumps up and kisses Lizzie's breast and runs away.

The children are singing in the cathedral.

Four women in tears.

Chapter VI

MOLISE AND ABRUZZO:
THE MOTHER COUNTRY . . .
BLESSING AND BONDAGE

We come from where the forest skirts the hill;
    A very little cottage is our home,
Where with our father and our mother still
    We live, and love our life, nor wish to roam.

        —Franco Sacchetti, "Ballata," 14–15
        century, translated by Dante Gabriel Rossetti

A solis ortus cardine   From the portal of the rising sun
  A dusque terrae limitem   At the end of the earth
  Christum canamus principem Let us sing of Christ the Lord
  natum Maria Virgine.   Born of the Virgin Mary.

    —Molise hymn, 5 century

387

This is the center of Italy, heart, cradle, home of ancient races, oldest man, older than history. Here one sees the earth as it was after the last sigh of Creation, one sees it as if it were still becoming . . . and this seeing, which is a kind of sharing in the act of creation, inspires awe not unalloyed by dread. The mountains seem still to be groaning, pushing themselves up toward the sky . . . and then resting, falling off into highland plains and meadows, pastures of aromatic grass . . . hills sloping down to fertile basins . . . and in these basins there are lakes, and in these lakes of clearest emerald, turquoise, jade, there are islands. Snaking bridges span the lakes and straddle the islands, a daisy chain of Colossi. From one mountain chain we see another . . . bare mountains stony mauve, snow-covered mountains. . . . We ride from one summit to another. Sometimes the horizon is vast, sometimes we are hedged in by sharp ridges that sheer off to rocky gorges; sometimes green hills surround us.

And this is like riding waves of mountains to the beginning of the wild world. The place where the world begins and the place where the world ends is the same place. We are out of our world.

We are in dark wild forests, among pines, among beeches, oaks, chestnut trees, hazel, ash. Golden eagles soar.

We are driving through drained marshes, gentle land, land that supports beets and maize, tomatoes; on this land, now so unperturbed, serpents once coiled and goddesses provoked them.

In these mountains, history and myth are equally plausible, impossible to separate. We are riding the crests of the waves. In fact there is a kind of tingle in the air that always means: the sea; the sea is to the east of us, eventually the mountains find their home in it (an end to all travail), and the land knows it, and so, on top of this world, do we.

Snakes are charmed here.

Christianity found an early home here, where aboriginal man roamed.

This is a peaceful land, a violent land, harsh, gentle, rich, poor, a land of blessing and of bondage.

This is home.

Fortress-villages extrude from castles and cling to them on wind-scoured mountaintops. (If your mind were a hand it would scoop them up.)

A flock of sheep enters a ruined tower.

"This is the best peach I have ever eaten," Laura says, "the only peach, I think."

"What is existential dread?" says Anna. "I have always hated deciduous trees." What does it mean, I wonder, to be the person who gives voice to dread? What a strange sibyl Anna is (*I have always hated deciduous trees*), how funny; contained in her dread is the sweetness of the soul that experiences it.

In fact we are not out of our known world, we are in it, for we stop on the Autostrada del Sole that runs from Milan all the way to the Strait of Messina, perhaps the finest road engineered since the construction of the Via Appia and the military roads of ancient Rome. We stop at the restaurant-bars that are also gas stations and that are like small department stores, traveler's-aid stations, newsstands ("Look! Look at Joan Collins!"), gift shops; slabs of roast beef, lamb on a spit, and bowls of pasta and beans. Nothing like food to recall you to a knowledge of the known.

"I am only afraid," says Anna, "that your family—"

"*Our* family . . ."

"Your family . . . *our* family . . . doesn't want to see you . . . us. . . ."

I have called Amerigo, who is the son of Ernesta, who is my great-aunt Ann's sister. . . . My great-aunt Ann married my mother's mother's brother (he is dead). What this makes Amerigo to me I scarcely know. ("'The blood,'" Lizzie says, rolling her eyes; she longs for a Benetton.)

My cousin Peter in New York has given me a list of all my relations in the province of Isernia, which is in the region of Molise, which till 1963 was part of Abruzzo, and which has been divided, annexed, and reunited, linked—to Apulia and to Naples—so many times, its boundaries redrawn by so many conquerors, that my family says they come neither from Abruzzo nor from Molise but from Campobasso, perhaps because when they were children it was the only place at which the railroad stopped.

"It is very strange to me that we should be called Abruzzese. . . ."

"But it *was* Abruzzo when my grandmother and grandfather lived here, and for all intents and purposes Molise and Abruzzo are the same. . . ."

"When, according to the map, we come from Molise and our family says we come from Campobasso—"

"Lizzie"—this is Laura—"if you make up one more jingle about 'the blood,' I'll kill you."

"Absolutely right you will." (This is me.) "And furthermore, they call it Campobass', always cutting off the last vowel like executioners. . . . Can you tell me what we're doing here? . . ."

"*Lizzie!* Not a word!"

This morning when we drove into the outskirts of town, into Venafro, an ancient Roman city circled by massive cyclopean walls, we stopped at a truckers' café, exclusively male. "They came all the way from America for *Venafro?*" That is the sentence we heard. Repeatedly.

So what are we doing here?

Because Amerigo, on the telephone—he is educated, my cousin Peter says, that is why I must call him first—Amerigo has denied all knowledge of my grandmother, although his own mother's sister, his aunt, was married to my grandmother's brother. He denies all knowledge of Peter as well. Peter comes from Venafro, he was born here.

In fact I don't even know in what relation I stand to Peter. My mind balks at *cousin;* what is a first cousin, a second cousin, a cousin once removed? For some reason I have never grasped what everybody else seems to know about this relationship . . . "due perhaps," Anna says, "to your strange upbringing." . . . (Where is my *brother,* why isn't he here?)

"Well, everybody in Italy's a *coo-geen,*" Lizzie says, pronouncing *cousin* in the Brooklyn *walyo* (vulgar) way.

"*Lizzie.*"

It is all typed out neatly for me on paper: my mother's mother and father, he born in Vallecupa and she in Venafro le Noci, towns just here, separated one from the other by dirt roads and hairpin curves; my mother's cousins, also here; my Aunt Ann's sister and her son, Amerigo . . . who now denies knowledge not only of Aunt Ann and my mother and Peter but of *his* mother; either that or sense and language have deserted me.

When my Aunt Ann came to America she could not, she says, believe she had exchanged the beauty of her country for "this . . . *this.*" . . . *This* was a dark and smelly tenement, a husband not tender, and something so hated and so thwarting it was called only "the place"—the place where she sat and sewed, doing piecework, ill paid. From wide to narrow she had gone. But then when she returned, the first time, to Italy, to Vallecupa and to Venafro, it seemed to her the work of beasts to carry water from a well. . . . And she met Nick, who had fought with the Fascists in the War and who, courting her—a Liberal Socialist now—said, "no woman I have ever met smells as good as you"; she smelled "American," she thought. And so she married Nick, who liked her American smell and who was kind and who wished to come to America, and when, years later, they returned to

Venafro together, she said to her sisters, "Unless one of you puts an indoor toilet in, I will not come here again," and so they did . . . or so I am told. . . . It does not seem to me that I will ever meet any of these people, and to think this makes me despair of ever understanding my mother (when did my mind make this leap? what did I think landscape and "the blood" could explain?).

I have in my possession notes taken by me at family reunions. Two years before she died, my mother, still beautiful, organized a family reunion. Perhaps she knew, though she was practiced in every form and discipline of denial, that her final separation from those she loved was near. (Did she, so unlike them in consciousness, love them? Did she love me? When?) She snipped the edges of her cloth napkin off with her cuticle scissors and plugged her ears so as not to hear the noise at the family reunion she had organized. . . . And I have in my possession notes taken at a family funeral, my mother's; these notes are scribbled by me on money envelopes marked (in pink), "In Loving Memory." . . . These are notes I have taken from my Uncle Pat, who talks about this family incessantly; the notes are of little use to me, however; they are runic; they say: Four brothers. Two made their lives in America, one in Scotland, one in Italy. (Here. *Where?*) 1912. One works in a McDonald's in London. DiNardo-Nard-spikenard, an aromatic plant or oil. Dinarc race (?) = Slavish and Saracen. Family of "Toads." . . . This seems little enough to have come to Abruzzo for.

In villages nearby, Albanian is still spoken.

The fields smell of dried aromatic plants.

Nothing augurs well. The Hotel Vittoria in Venafro is now a supermarket; the Hotel Dora outside Venafro has no rooms; the Hotel Tequila in Isernia, near Venafro, gives Laura the willies: The 1984 earthquake hit this area hard, the hotel stands amidst ugly new construction, and the staff seems not to have heard that Abruzzo and Molise are famous for the friendliness and hospitality of their people, who are said to be *forte e gentile,* strong and gentle, tenderly ironic. Their accent—a *walyo* accent, Lizzie says, correctly, and also one with Arab semitones—grates on my ears. Everybody sounds like a punishing parent.

*   *   *

Ovid was born here.

It is a country of castles and monasteries. It is believed that Christianity was practiced here from the time of the apostles. Benedictine abbeys flourished and became seats of government and agricultural communes, hospices, centers for craftspeople, hospitals, and nerve centers for study and cultural exchanges with sister communities beyond the Alps. Blessing and bondage: In the feudal society of the eleventh and twelfth centuries the world spun around the abbeys and the bishoprics in whose hands the land, the only source of wealth, was held.

On this land occurred the last of the struggles between the ancient Samnites and the Romans.

The people of this land have always had to struggle—with the land, and with waves of conquering armies: Swabians, Angevins, Aragonese, Spanish, Bourbon.

It is the home of the original Italic people.

Its villages, seen from a distance, are carved from, wrested from, inseparable from rock.

We drive to Castel San Vincenzo, a mirror-clear lake in the Mainarde Mountains that reflects the Mainarde Mountains. On the slopes of the lonely lake, where all the colors of all the mountains—sandy-red, mauve, bleached gray—meet the greens of hills and the yellows of cultivated land, there is (Italy is obliging) a flock of sheep led by a shepherd with a pipe. His walk is stately; his dogs follow.

Around the lake are the crude huts of shepherds; and this is the story as it has come down to me and been received by me . . . for the stories we tell are stories about stories: My maternal grandfather, Andrea DiNardo, was the youngest of four brothers, three of whom were sent to America by a rich uncle (*rich* being a relative term); Grandpa was held in indentured servitude in return for their steerage fare. As a shepherd he labored for ten years, having little human intercourse; almost never did he hear or speak words. (This accounts for the rage he expressed—the rage he dwelt in—a rage which I, a loved grandchild, never experienced but which his children, who bear scars, almost daily did.) Then (here there is a gap) my grandfather, born in Vallecupa, married my grandmother, Concetta Fascia, born in the nearby town of Venafro le Noci; she was the beauty of the town. And he had five children, one of whom was my Uncle Pat, and grew to hate his wife, whose beauty was not a sufficient complement to his intelligence. . . . This story is not in Uncle Pat's story.

In Uncle Pat's story there is a meadow—a meadow of tall white grass. My grandmother lulled him to sleep (and herself into sorrow) by telling about that meadow. The DiNardos in Venafro le Noci will not show him that meadow, though he has implored. Perhaps the meadow is in some way connected to ancient internecine animosities rehearsed but dimly understood. Perhaps there is no meadow, perhaps there never was. My grandmother said it smelled of the sea.

Ours is the only car on the road.

We pass silent villages, stony growths out of the hillside ("so ancient and strange it looks," Hawthorne said of a village like those we see, "without enough of life and juiciness in it to be any longer susceptible of decay. An earthquake would afford it the only chance of being ruined, beyond its present ruin"); there have been earthquakes, the last great one in 1984.

Women in bunchy black dresses sit outside their doors, their feet planted firmly apart, unsmiling.

Weathered men sit shirtless in cafés. Haystacks, donkeys, everything primitive, a fusion of timeless beauty and decay. . . . And: Cage Aux Foules. A bar called that. Teenagers in blue jeans. Strange, witchy juxtapositions, reminding one that this was once the home of the ancient Marsi people, soothsayers, magicians, *serpari* (snake charmers), wizards, worshipers of Circe and of the goddess Angitia (caretaker of magic potions, Keeper of the Book), believers in witches, werewolves, amulets, *malocchio* (the Evil Eye). (My brother wears around his neck an amulet—a *corno,* a gold horn—to ward off the Evil Eye . . . Never let a witch see you give her the sign to ward off the Evil Eye, your troubles will be doubled, I learned that very young; put honey in the porridge of a witch and then stay clear of her.)

Near Castel San Vincenzo there is a camping ground and a cryptic sign nailed to a tree in front of a shack where pizza is sold; it says, in English and in French: THE YOUTH OF S. VINCENZO APOLOGIZE FOR BAD CAMPING CONDITIONS . . . LACK OF HYGIENIC FACILITIES, LOOSE SOIL. . . . THIS DOES NOT COMPROMISE FRIENDLINESS. Reading between the lines we deduce that there has been trouble between the villagers and the campers; this compromises our equanimity.

Laura locks our rented car, leaving the keys inside.

The waiter from the pizza shack—his hair cut Mohawk style and streaked orange—comes out and wrings his hands in his apron. "Pity there are no

Neapolitans here," he says. "They'd open it in a second—thieves, bad boys."
He is full of admiration for them.

From my childhood there comes back to me a curse my grandfather
uttered, only under the greatest duress; it was the Mighty Curse, the one that
scared us half to death (he used it when he was hacking the player piano
to death with an ax for some imagined [real? One never knew] grievance:
SMASH—the sound his knuckles made when they met his children's noses
in his rage), FAHNAHPOLA—that is how I heard the curse. *Va a Napoli*
(Go to Naples)—that is what now (my ear attuned to dialect) I know it
meant. The worst thing my grandfather could imagine—worse even than
saying someone "put it to" his sister in the ass—was inviting someone to
go to Napoli, city of glitter and crime: Abruzzo/Molise was an outpost of
the Kingdom of Naples, the feared and hated rulers were there; and the lure
of city lights was there. My laughter is one of recognition. No one is
interested. Laura greets my laughter with understandable consternation.

Five or six men appear as if from nowhere. There is much discussing, an
almost ritual circling around the car. This is a task—a challenge—the young
men like; the older men advise. Another car drives up—a matron, impassive,
her husband in tow. She surveys.

"But *why* did you leave the key in the car?" she says.

This imbecile question Laura answers patiently; surely if there is anything
an Italian can be expected to understand, it is an *accidente*.

"But *why* did you leave it in the car?" the woman says again.

Laura: "Shit."

For an hour, all the while urging us to be calm, be calm—*calmati, calmati,
non ti preoccupare,* don't worry yourself—the young men work, and they
succeed, after a fashion: They break open the trunk (we will now have to
drive through southern Italy with our luggage not secure) and crawl to the
front seat and present Laura with the keys.

"But *why* did you leave the keys in the car?" the woman, whose name
is Romana Vittoria Italia, asks, immovable in her conviction that all questions have acceptable answers.

Laura (sotto voce): "Fuck."

Romana and her husband lead us back to our hotel in Isernia on a less
hazardous, less winding, and minimally less beautiful road. . . . SCENIC
BEAUTY SPOT AHEAD, signs say, a matter entirely of arbitrariness; it is impossible to say in what way any one spot here is more beautiful than any other.

Many of the castles—pleasure palaces—in these Apennines were built by
Frederick II, the thirteenth-century Hohenstaufen king, *Stupor Mundi* (won-

der of the world). Grandson of Frederick Barbarossa, he ruled for forty-two years; he loved to hunt with hawk and hound. A sorrowful Dante professed qualified admiration for him. He placed him in Hell with heretics . . . and praised him for nobility of character. Pope Gregory IX regarded him as blasphemer, Antichrist. He kept a harem . . . elephants, eunuchs. He tried, unsuccessfully, to test St. Francis with dancing girls. He discoursed upon philosophy with Arabs in their own tongue. He permitted Muslims in Apulia religious liberty; the Sultan of Egypt was his friend. Gregory, citing the Book of Revelation, called him the beast which is like unto a leopard. Frederick retaliated by announcing from a pulpit in Pisa that Pope Gregory was the Antichrist. He was excommunicated in 1227. "Those who eat Popes will choke to death," the saying goes; when Frederick marched on Rome, the Pope placed his tiara on the preserved and sanctified heads of the saints of Rome, Peter and Paul, and called upon them to defend the city; Romans, encouraged by this act, rushed to defend their city walls. Frederick did not dismiss astrologers from his court; and he led a Crusade.

Frederick's first-born son, Henry, plotted against him and was tried by him and sentenced to house arrest, in which condition he remained for seven years, till one day in Calabria he rode his horse over a cliff and was smashed to death. Frederick, mourning him, checked nature's tears by remembering the "pain of injury" and by insisting upon the "inflexibility of justice." He buried his son in a shroud of gold and silver cloth in which eagles' feathers were woven.

Frederick died in 1250. He was buried in embroidered garments of red silk, spurred boots of silk; a Crusader's cross was sewn to his mantle; on the third finger of his right hand he wore a large emerald set in gold; and a Crusader's purse and sword were buried with him. He rests in Sicily. His castles had plumbing. He had red hair. He wrote a book on falconry, the most aristocratic and romantic of sports, one that requires that man be the servant of the bird (Frederick introduced the hood) and that man be poised—as he is here—between earth and sky. He was perhaps the first bird-watcher in the world; he wrote the first scientific book on ornithology (with special reference to the nesting habits of the cuckoo).

Of all the men in recorded history, this man of culture and contradiction cries out to be known; I should like to have known him.

Laura smarts. Romana and her husband are kind, but they recognize no boundaries. I smart; that *why* ("But why? But why?") brings back acid memories of childhood. *Why are you as you are?*—that is what I hear: *Why?* And Laura and I both feel ungrateful. Neither of us feels we are accepting kindness well. Perhaps I don't know how to receive kindness, perhaps one can understand—deeply and fully understand—only that which one was brought up on. Romana and her mate are kind. They have, for example, led us to the Europa Hotel, where, pleasantly, we are now ensconced, the only guests in a hotel that caters to weddings and offers rooms to revelers. It is true that Romana—prune-faced in repose—keeps popping up, with gifts, advice, invitations . . . the *all-overness* of them! Their love, Laura says (meaning, of course, her family's love, for they have haplessly become stand-ins for our families), "is like a goddamn sticky shroud."

Niccolò, the proprietor of the Europa (who made his money in a pizzeria in Berlin), informs Laura that she is *nervosa*—and shouldn't be. This causes Laura to glare from under her swollen eyelids. The *zanzare* (mosquitoes) here are terrible; Augustus Hare placed them in the same category as earthquakes and brigands.

A maddening simplicity: You are nervous; you *shouldn't* be.

Lizzie and Anna, exasperated by us, ask to share a room; neither child wants to sleep with her mother. "Well, you *should* want to," I say—to my own and Anna's astonishment.

Anna calls Amerigo. She speaks in a mongrel Spanish-Italian, which for some reason thaws him. Before he arranges to meet us at the Europa, he speaks two sentences that make our holding a grudge impossible. "My wife is gravely ill," he says; and, "I value spontaneity and kindness," he says. . . . "What a sweetie pie he is," says Anna, whose spontaneity and kindness have thawed him.

He is—we understand this immediately we see him—gentle, melancholy, nervous, sweet, these qualities undisguised by his girth, the brigand's mustache and sideburns he affects.

We drive to his town, Ceppagna, a suburb of Venafro, if *suburb* is not too absurd and arbitrary a word to use for such a little place—Venafro has ten thousand inhabitants, Ceppagna seven hundred. Nuances of place are important here, where for the most part people seldom leave the plots of space assigned to them at birth: In Isernia they tell us to beware of the people in Venafro, which is ten miles away, ten miles closer to Naples and to cataloged sin. In these hills five miles can mean the difference between amity and blood feuds. This is part of what my Uncle Pat found incomprehensible

. . . but one has only to think of Verona, the Capulets and Montagues, casualties of geography.

We drive along a dirt road lined by olive trees, happily impeded by a formal wedding procession, the bride's heavy satin train trailing in the dust, her pearl embroidery picking up the silver-green of olive leaves.

Amerigo lives on a narrow street in a wide attached house set in a scrubby garden, and there are two entrances, one to the kitchen and one to the living quarters of his home. There is a kind of formal charm to this arrangement, the separation of communicating spheres. It is into the living quarters that we are ushered. Amerigo, perspiring lightly—we are an ordeal for him, perhaps everyone is—takes us to his book-lined study; his soft eyes, under their fierce, thick eyebrows, confer a look of love upon his books; a look of inquiry is directed toward us. What he sees in our faces pleases him. These books are like children to him, he says, his words tumbling over his words. . . .

In this study he writes poems:

> Ceppagna,
> I have endured your indigence . . .
>   the people in between misery and simulated smiles,
>   between
> The sadness and the joy of living in an antiquated
>   world. . . .
> And your many centuries and my few years
> Are happy together.

He writes monographs about the ancient world just surfacing here, still waiting to be discovered, monographs about excavated Roman columns, the columns of a pagan temple (later a house of Christian worship), and pre-Roman tombs. These monographs are infused with a sense of futility and doom, over which scholarship is only icing (Amerigo is sad): "A series of tombs, almost intact, came to light the first time this land was plowed, and skeletons, and small votive objects. The tombs fell apart and were dispersed. Bricks went to the construction of the land's rich proprietor. His dogs amused themselves with the bones; the votive objects—who knows where they are?"

That Isernia/Venafro was central to the peninsula and to the empire, that it remains a treasure trove ready to be unearthed, scholars agree; they are not all so saddened by ghosts of past glories as is our cousin Amerigo, whose love is inseparable from his grief; why do his people leave this land, his poems ask, to live out an existence of "exile and work, hope and nostalgia"? To him, we are abandoners, the alien by-products of formal departures that were unnecessary, unwise. . . .

> Where are you, exile,
> When the moon
> Enters my room to
> Illuminate
> My sleeplessness?
> What are you doing
> When I get up in the morning
> to reenter the monastery
> Of just another day?

Weep for the children that return old, sick, strangers. . . .

And sometimes he writes prophecy—though prophecy is often indistinguishable from nostalgia—about the coming of the road—"the coming and going of trucks that load the sand from the mountain quarry—to make someone else wealthy: Destroy and ruin. Perhaps in a century our Italian landscape will resemble the Gobi Desert. . . . This, they say, is uninteresting because we do not know it for a fact. . . ." In the South of Italy there is always a *they,* a careless, damaging other.

This is the man we thought was cold. He is afraid we will not see the beauties of his country, we will despise his little house; and he is *mortificato* because his wife is in the hospital and he cannot serve us food; and he is afraid his proud and stubborn love for this place will seem to us an aberration. He loves the old ways, he says; he feels "removed."

He teaches stenography in a secondary school.

He is part of a fellowship, a small band of Esperanto advocates—that impotent, contrived, "international" language of hopeful isolates, designed to unite all the world in one loving tissue of sound, designed with solidarity and communion in mind, practiced by solitary people exchanging lonely messages.

If it is odd to find an advocate of Esperanto here (Amerigo's car has Esperanto bumper stickers), it is odder still—perhaps Amerigo is right; perhaps our perspective is hopelessly warped, and this is not odd at all—to find a lover of the Pre-Raphaelites. (Remember that we are in a village, a village at the edge of the wild, and that we are urban, new.) Above all Amerigo loves the Pre-Raphaelites, and, as this is Laura's subject, the last walls tumble down. . . .

With whom does Amerigo discuss the Pre-Raphaelites when Laura is not here?

Amerigo is *mortificato* because he is unable to entertain us (in their mother's absence, Amerigo mothers his children, Eva and Renzo, as so many Italian men do—casually, tactfully). His reticence and shyness are a compound of his shame and his inability to bear the separations of which we, children of those who have left the land, are visible and painful reminders. (Why haven't we come before?) Amerigo has a vision of the world in which members of a family stand always together on hallowed home ground. We are missing links; we have broken the chain of human communion. We have inherited the sins of our fathers; our punishment is exile. Now, softened by the fact and presence of us, he wants us; we are parts of a treasured whole, not alien objects in alien space. Amerigo wants to make things nice, good; that is what his Esperanto is about, too. His love, at first violently withheld, then tentatively awakened, is now in full flower.

"*Sono mortificato, mortificato, mortificato,*" Amerigo says. I, too, am obscurely ashamed. Laura, so happily engaged in Pre-Raphaelite chat with Amerigo, nevertheless sees in our stumblings a vision of what she will encounter with her own family, an encounter she is consequently beginning to dread.

How do one's brain and viscera come to grips with the mind-bending geographical accident? To say, "I might have been born here," while it presents a host of dazzling and disturbing possibilities to the bemused mind, is an exercise in syllogism.

Amerigo makes a *giro* of Isernia and Venafro. The stamp of the ancient past is on this land; it is coming to the surface slowly (in the course of earthquakes and of excavations), like superimposed images on film taking form and shape in a bath of developing fluid. In the beautiful gray old stone town of Venafro there are, on cobbled streets, unexpected houses with Renaissance windows, medieval arches; this is antiquity preserved (but not as a museum) and casually regarded. The market square is unmistakably Roman in its geometry. The graspable past lives on here, too (a kind of half life). On a man-made lake in the square is a Liberty (Art Nouveau) hotel, deserted, gone to seed, the music of its froufrou fountain dead. This hotel—a make-believe castle in a land of real castles—makes no sense in this landscape, it has wandered here from another dream.

On the main piazza there are two churches. One is a bastardized Romanesque. The other, built on a Roman arch, has the appearance of being built upon a Venetian bridge; the architecturally unnecessary steps simply call out to be climbed, they demand the passage of your feet, so that one cannot go from one part of the piazza to another without feeling in one's body the centrality of the church—and from every part of this piazza one sees a church (to hide from God is not so easy here).

Seven thousand years old, sleepy Isernia is the oldest village in Italy, some say in the world; it is also the first capital of Italy. . . . Shops sell picture postcards of aboriginals walking through the forests a million years ago. These aboriginals come in trinities—father, mother, child. The father holds the hand of a child, and in his other hand is a club.

Isernia is known for its onions and its lace, a lovable combination.

In the lower part of the city, the old town, a middle-aged man appears from a doorway to show us the Fontana della Fraterna, a public drinking fountain, which, according to legend, was built in Roman times with stone slabs taken from the mausoleum of the Ponzia family, of which Pontius Pilate was a member. He tells us that Pontius Pilate was born here; "then he went to Palestine, where he killed Our Lord." He shrugs, as if to say, "What can you do?," as if the Crucifixion had happened yesterday (a very modern theological point of view). . . . Italians dwelling in the land of Samnites, Italics, Romans, have, one is sometimes encouraged to believe, little sense of linear time; their sense of time—bound to seasons and to harvests—is cyclical. It is easier to believe in God if one's sense of time is cyclical; it gives one the very slight degree of fatalism that is necessary to belief without eradicating the sense of surprise that is also necessary to belief.

"South Brooklyn," the man says, grinning, tossing these words over his shoulder (he pronounces it "Brook-a-leen"). What do these words mean to him? "Wait!" But he doesn't; he disappears.

Three little girls appear from another doorway. In dialect (a dialect that resounds in me as if I were a plucked guitar) they ask us what we're looking for; they cannot imagine what there is to see:

A Roman arch. Two stone statues, one headless, unnamed, of unknown gods. Buildings damaged by earthquakes, shored up by two-by-fours. We walk beneath scaffolding as if through a maze. (Old people died of heart arrest and out of fear, most recently in 1984; they jumped out of ancient windows onto ancient cobblestones.)

Anna and Lizzie do not like this. It is the time of siesta. The squares are empty. "Too archaeological," Lizzie says, meaning that in this buffeted landscape she needs the ameliorating presence of flesh.

Little boys, aping their resting elders, walk like old men; they scratch their crotches.

A truck with the words SUGAR BABY, its cargo watermelons, lumbers up the hill on a Roman road.

From here, from this place innocent of tourists, one sees across plains and fields to feudal villages carved out of rock; they look like toys, like toys trying to be invisible, so as not to be stolen.

The bishop of Isernia (sixteen thousand inhabitants) is, Anna reads in a letter from her religion professor, "a cultivated ecumenist"; he makes annual pilgrimages to the birthplace of the Buddha. . . . Try to say "provincial" with this fact in mind.

Feature films are shown in Isernia on Saturdays and Sundays. On week-nights pornographic films are shown.

From Isernia we drive through fields of anise, chicory, oregano, and clover shaded by birch trees, past apricot, plum, and black-cherry orchards. Olive trees are as prolific here as weeds.

In Venafro we go to the restaurant-bar of my cousin Maria Fascia (Fascia is my maternal grandmother's maiden name). Maria and her daughter Patrizia greet us with unalloyed pleasure and with generosity—as if (ah, but we all know better) this meeting is but the first of many, as if this greeting will be renewed. Free drinks, free gelati. Why can't we stay, I wonder, just a while longer? Because our lives are not here. Because Laura must go to L'Aquila, because Lizzie must go back to school. . . . Because I can't drive? Are these reasons sufficient to explain our haste, our grabbing of love simply offered, our zeal, my zeal (amounting to panic) to press on? . . . Why did I love my mother only after she died? This terrible longing for her . . . do I create departures to replicate that central fact?

* * *

From Amerigo's house we pick up Michele and Adelina, Amerigo's aunt and uncle. Michele greets the world—and us, its representatives—with an open smile and glad and sunny surprise. He cultivates the land; he is proud of guardianship (the verb he uses is *governare,* the same word he would use to describe raising children): "To let the land lie fallow is a sin. To cultivate and not be beholden is a blessing." Adelina, his sister, looks like an Aztec. She looks as if she carries her own weather underneath her weather-hardened skin. She is impassive. Her ugliness borders on nobility. She looks as if she has been carved from earth. Her enormous eyes are hooded. From time to time the veil lifts, and she looks at us with candid suffering or curiosity. Laura thinks she is D. H. Lawrence's peasant—"self-possessed," not "other-aware." She has been to America to visit my Aunt Ann but does not see the point of America except that it contains Aunt Ann. She has never been married. She gives us this fact as if it were an offering. What we do with the fact-that-is-an-offering is up to us.

Amerigo takes us into the kitchen. There are murals on all the walls—shepherds, farmers, olive trees. He lets us see them for only a moment; they are the work of his hands, they look as if Grandma Moses and a Pre-Raphaelite painter had joined forces; and then, as if sorry that the impulse to be open has come to him, he quickly ushers us out, muttering, *"Mortificato, mortificato."* ("How do you say that in Esperanto, Amerigo?" Laura asks. She has a gift for being easy with him; they lie gently on each other's mind.)

To get to Venafro le Noci, we drive past fields where tobacco leaves are drying; there is a smell, pungent and pleasing, of hay, pine, manure, in the air.

Six boys run down a hill. They are running in a straight line, "like fugitives," Amerigo says. Amerigo reads bodies. A turn in the road, and we see what they have done. They have set a fire in the dry forest. Amerigo, corpulent but swift, beats it out with branches. Anna and Lizzie, their dresses tucked into their belts, their feet planted far apart, join him. They look like peasants, and this is a transformation, a conversion by fire on a sunny day. I stare: at the fire, at the girls, the idiot question ringing once more in my ears: *What if we had been born here? . . .*

* * *

My grandmother Concetta Fascia was born in Venafro le Noci; Bella Concetta, Concetta the Beautiful, she was called. I take her beauty on faith, as when I knew her she was formless and fat, her face a red pudding in which were little blue spaghetti veins. She had a mustache and the beginnings of a beard. Her teeth were foul and few. I make her sound ugly, a caricature. In fact she was not; some hint, some subterranean image of her former beauty did in fact inform her decrepitude. She always wore black. One imagined voluminous black underwear, musty. Her kisses were frequent and wet. Her bathing suit was black, too. Before I was nine years old, before my mother, Concetta's beautiful daughter Carmela, became an unordained priestess in a consuming lunatic sect, Concetta took me swimming, to Coney Island. Her flesh was pink, spongy. We stood waist-high in the water and she scooped water into the top of her suit and patted her mottled jelly breasts and held my hands and jumped up as the waves came, and she sang . . . what did she sing? It seems important to me to remember, but I cannot. . . . It was an American song, and that seems sad. She must have loved me, why else would she have taken me to the beach? She kept a chocolate cake in the icebox for me; no cake has ever tasted so good. I cannot think of her and my grandfather DiNardo as one flesh; indeed, in my memory they are totally separate entities: He is raging (but not at her); she is in her massive bed, supine, receiving someone's curses (but not his); I am the center of this world. When my Uncle Tony came back from the War in Burma—that war about which we hear at every family funeral and reunion—her singsong prayers filled the house and joined his screams (he screamed in pain, a bullet still lodged in his leg, but the pain was not located in his leg), and the prayers and the screams were met by my grandfather's curses. This cacophony did not frighten me; silence did, my mother's silence: Even rage she withheld from me, my silent mother withheld everything—prayers, and screams of pain. "I never had a mother," my mother often said, using this tautology to beat me with . . . and she called herself my "relative," so beautiful and young she could not claim me as her child, yet when I graduated from high school, my mother, who claimed never to have been nurtured by her, took me to Grandma's house, some pride in me, some love for her mother (what other motive could she have had?) prompting her. That day I was dressed in emerald-green silk. Soon after that I fashioned myself anew. By the time my grandmother lay dying her final death, I had forgotten the beach, the chocolate cake, the wet and frequent kisses; and when my mother and my brother's wife went to see her in the hospital for the last time, I sat in the car, using my sick cat (vomiting in her carrying case) as an excuse. I felt no guilt. I was new. I had an apartment, a cat, a lover, I wore black leotards. For years I felt no remorse. My Uncle Pat, Concetta's ugliest and favorite son, says Concetta said a rosary for me every day. I never knew she prayed for me. Who loved her? Her husband didn't (his love in any case did not act like love); my mother did/did not. Uncle Pat did, the ugly son, her blue-eyed son. Perhaps her other grandchildren did—Pat's four handsome sons. . . . They are my cousins. I do not in any real sense know them. So why am I in Venafro le Noci looking for cousins whose relationship to me is even more tenuous?

Does one carry landscape in one's body, in one's genes?

"Try to act as if you're on *vacation,* Barbara," Laura says.

This visit takes on the trappings of a charade. My mother's cousins in Venafro le Noci are wearing my American Aunt Mary's clothes. She, Mary—Uncle Pat's wife, who has brought them a suitcase of worn clothes— has expressed herself tersely but eloquently on the subject of the inhabitants of Venafro le Noci—a hundred people, most of whom have never left their village or felt any need or desire to: They are, in the case of the men, "shiftless and dirty" and, in the case of the women, "hardworking and dirty." They will steal the rings from my fingers. They will insult me. They are stupid. This is the village where my grandmother Concetta danced in the tall white grass. . . .

"Did you ever *see* that meadow?" Aunt Mary says. "Did they ever *show* it to you?"

"No."

"Well?"

What this quarrel is about, Uncle Pat says, is that he didn't take Aunt Mary to Sicily, where her people come from. When Uncle Pat married Aunt Mary, Concetta wailed because her blue-eyed son was marrying "an Arab."

Aunt Mary never met Amerigo. Perhaps she would have liked him, his house full of horsehair furniture, oiled wood, crocheted doilies starched in sugar water. Which cousins one sees or does not see is all a matter of fortuity; at best one hopes only for partial revelations here. Knowledge is a matter of caprice; truths are farmed at random. Perhaps when Uncle Pat talks about blood feuds—which it grieves him to speak of, but which alone can account, in his mind, for the lack of a coherent community of loving relatives— perhaps what he means is, simply: The past is not whole, the present is rent. Past and present coexist and cannot illuminate, even in this land of sun, my future (his storied past). Perhaps it is wise to take the meadow of the tall white grass—the meadow that smelled of the sea—on faith.

Lizzie says the houses of Venafro le Noci are like secretive dollhouses; one cannot tell, till one has crossed the threshold, whether one is entering a hovel or, as in the case of my cousin Paolo, a tidy refuge, well organized against the world.

In Venafro le Noci no one speaks of my Uncle Tom, who was married (but not sweetly) to my Aunt Ann. Though Tom was Concetta's brother, it is Ann they claim. . . . No one speaks of Concetta either. They speak of my mother, of her great beauty. They have never seen her. My mother has attained the status of myth in a village of a hundred souls. Perhaps her beauty was the central fact of her life (this gives me something new to think about).

Had Uncle Pat been born eight months earlier, he would have been born here. This fact disturbs him.

My cousin Paolo says—he says this immediately—"My wife is not Italian, she is French." This has the effect of focusing all attention not on his wife, Maria, who is nowhere to be seen, but on him. What can he mean? It is a riddle, and we must guess. I hated this game when I was little—riddles that had unsatisfying, illogical resolutions, Cracker Jack boxes without prizes. "She comes from a village ten miles away!" Paolo says, triumphantly. The rules of the game never change: The guesser is always the disadvantaged; the poser of the riddle, no matter that his solution lacks all sense, is God.

"You are a bastard," Paolo says to me, "not Italian and not American." He says this with a smile. I am waiting for him to pinch my cheek hard with his dry, gnarled fingers (a vicious use of flesh); this, too, is part of the game.

He tells Lizzie: "I am sixty—too old for you to go off with me."

"I hear bells," Lizzie says, confused.

Church bells.

"Donkey bells. I go to get my ass." He goes, and comes back with his wife, Maria. (I will tell this to Aunt Mary. "His *ass!*" she will say.)

The kitchen fills up with people, a confusion of bodies, of voices; coffee in flowered cups is put on the table, and biscuits. Maria runs her finger across the yellow tiles of the hearth and they squeak: clean. Maria is walleyed. "Why do you stay only for a few hours?" they say, assuming the inevitable. Why do you love my mother, whom you have never seen, and not love Concetta? Why is Aunt Ann taken to your hearts and Tom never mentioned? I want to ask. "When are you coming back?" they say, over and over (though we have not yet prepared to leave). What they want from us is more than rings and clothes and tools (Uncle Pat brought a suitcase of tools, out of duty, and thinking it could purchase affection), and less than rings and clothes and tools. What they want is nothing more or less than love . . . justification. . . . We are the braille of their blindness; why did we leave? . . . That it was our parents who left is inconsequential. We are the answer to the riddle we pose: What is America? What is the world? Are we the world? Are they the world?

Are they the braille of our blindness? These surfaces are alien to me. I draw no meaning from their touch, from voices that assault.

Will you come back? *"Speriamo,"* I say, *"speriamo"*—we hope so. Anna kicks me in the shins; it hurts. She wants me to tell the truth her instinct has discerned: We are not coming back. . . . Never? Are we never coming back? That is what those departures—Concetta's, Tom's—must have said to them: that *never* was real, was true, that a moment in time is not replaceable; what they know of irrevocability is present to them in our foreign flesh.

Paolo says: "When you are old you will be *brutta"*—ugly—"like Pasquale," like my Uncle Pat. . . . The other three—Lizzie, Laura, Anna—are *belle,* he says. Have I traveled all this way to feel—again—that sin is present in my flesh, a stain that God and others (God and mothers) see but I, in chosen ignorance, cannot? ("We are on *vacation,* Barbara. . . ." Self-pity, I remind myself, rubbing my shin, which stings, is a vice, a vice belonging to a child.)

Amalia comes. She lives across the road, her dollhouse is perched on a rise in the road; it sits prettily in a garden. She has a washing machine, a bathroom, and cosmetics from America. Her husband is in the mountains herding sheep. She tells us this. (All we know of shepherds comes from Christmas carols; they are poor. Amalia is not poor, that is the point she wishes to make.) We are to have coffee with her. But we have already had coffee. (And we have expended our store of scotch, Sambuca, lemons, and mortadella.) *Why do you come at all when you come for so little time?* Amalia gives us cheeses to take home. Not to be outdone, Paolo, who hates me, gives us olive oil, three liters, from the first September pressing, oil of the finest quality. (Anna will leave this oil in a parking lot.)

"Soon, soon," we say, as we drive away. We mean *never.* Anna wears a look she has when something is unjust. ("Is it me, Anna?" "Not everything is about you, Mama.") Laura and Lizzie look abstracted, "anthropological," Anna says. Anna looks sad. Adelina is wearing her impassive Aztec face.

Amerigo, twisting down the mountain road—asphalted only last year—brakes. He points to a field of tall grasses: thistles, weeds. "There," he says, "there is where Concetta lived." Covered in vines (some of the weeds are white) is (I walk to it, nettles scratching my legs, briars pulling at my dress) . . . what? A cave? the foundation of a house? a building destroyed by an earthquake? by a bomb? refuge? walled-in madness? buried mystery? "Concetta's house," he says. Stones held together without mortar, an opening like a mouth, a ladder bleached white by the sun leading to the sky; no roof. A hut that satisfies one's fantasies of living like an animal in a hole? I peer within, expecting, though there is no roof, to see darkness; and I do. Before I can crawl in, Amerigo takes me by the shoulders. "It is enough," he says. "One never knows what one will find."

"Did Uncle Pat see this?"

In front of the house (hut and cave, bombed building open to the sky) is a slab; 1786, it says.

"Did Uncle Pat see this?"

Uncle Pat is, for Amerigo, an abstraction.

"It is where Concetta lived," he says. Concetta is for him an abstraction meaning more: She left (with Uncle Pat in her belly and my mother, the Beauty who is myth, years away from her first breath). She left his known world behind. "Come." He treats me like an invalid.

Anna waits for me in the car, apprehension and sorrow written on her face.

"It's all right."

Do I know that it's all right? I am at that intersection of pain and happiness called melancholy. . . .

"I say Mother. And my thoughts are of you, oh House."—O. V. Milosz.

I say House. And my thoughts are of you, oh Mother.

At night Laura, Lizzie, and Anna go with Amerigo to see a play by Pirandello in the amphitheater of Pietrabbondante, one thousand meters above the sea. Torches light their way. The ancient Roman-Italic semicircular theater and the ruins of the Samnite civilization "look like Jerusalem," Anna says. "You expect to see Jesus," Laura says. "At a Pirandello play?" For all our quarrels about Catholicism, all their references are to Christianity.

We take Adelina, Ernesta, Michele, and Amerigo out to dinner. Adelina and Ernesta are dressed respectably from the waist up. They are wearing old tattered skirts, Adelina's is held together by pins. Ernesta's shoes are mismatched, one is the red of blood pudding, the other dusty black. Adelina has sheep's wool in her hair. It crosses my mind that they have never been in a restaurant before. Awkwardness hangs over us like a fog. I can see *mortificato* written behind Amerigo's eyes. *"Non è bello,"* says Ernesta; one doesn't know to what she refers. "They asked us to come," says Adelina, apparently in response to Ernesta's cryptic phrase. They are, elliptically, in shorthand born of years' intimate knowledge of each other, referring to the problem of the bill. With sudden peasant directness, Adelina (like Italian children who don't think twice before addressing you almost as if you were an abstraction of yourself) says: *"Tanti soldi"*—much money to come here. I embark on a long story about my work and expense accounts, which story is incomprehensible to her. The immovable fact is that I have more money than she does. "A thing given they regard as a thing found," Norman Douglas wrote, "a happy hit in the lottery of life; the giver is the blind instrument of Fortune." This may be true; it does not follow that "this chilly attitude repels us" or that they regard us as good-natured strangers, "weak in the head." We have broken through the wall; we are not strangers, we are family (and, as even Douglas, who thought of southern Italians as little better than beasts, says, "they will do acts of spontaneous kindness towards their family, far oftener than customary with us"). Our acts of kindness they accept calmly, almost stoically. From each according to his ability, to each according to his need. Their act of kindness is to accept our act of kindness.

Once everyone has tucked in, everyone ceases to be *mortificato*. (Marinated anchovies and shellfish, cold calamari from the Adriatic; asparagus and spinach in lemon and oil; maccheroni alla chitarra with shredded lamb in a peppery, garlicky sauce; braciole—rolled round steak stuffed with pine nuts, currants, parsley and prosciutto and breadcrumbs.) Everyone, that is, but Amerigo, whose relationship to food is one of distrust. Amerigo cannot look at food without thinking of farmers, cannot think of farmers without thinking of the economy, cannot think of the economy without thinking of the North, cannot think of the North without thinking of the government, cannot think of the government without thinking of the Church, cannot think of the Church without thinking of love and death and art (and Esperanto). It is a miracle that he manages to stay alive. Adelina and Ernesta are happy, buttons bursting, hairpins flying; their relationship to food is simple and direct. Michele eats—as he does everything else—with pleasure, sunny grace.

MACCHERONI ALLA CHITARRA. The old traditional way of cutting pasta in the Abruzzi . . . is to "play the guitar." This pasta cutter does indeed have strings strung across and the strings are actually tuned in a fixed pattern as in an actual guitar. It is both interesting and mysterious that the folklore surrounding the instrument, such as why it's tuned in a particular way, has never been passed along with the tradition. The imagination drifts to thoughts of old rituals and cults, but who can tell? There is a different set of strings on each side of the guitar which is separated by a board. By flipping the guitar over, you can change from one set of strings to the other. . . .

—Giuliano Bugialli's Classic Techniques of Italian Cooking

Venafro was praised by Horace for its olive oil. "Olives nourish me," he said.

The food at the Europa is said to be the best in Isernia, and this is not difficult to believe: *pesce spada;* scampi; mussels; risotto with red fish sauce; good rough bread; beefsteak; lamb in spicy paprika sauce cooked in terra-cotta bowls; kids' heads baked with oil, wine, parsley, ewes' milk, cheese, egg yolk; mushrooms in oil; trout; white truffles; fresh pasta made of durum wheat— which the girls do not like because they say it tastes "fat." (Once the notion of fat pasta is introduced, the act of eating it becomes slightly obscene; one's teeth and palate and tongue become very conscious of the enterprise.) Almost all the diners are men. The functional rooms that lead off the mustard-, brown-, and salmon-colored hallways generally accommodate the wedding guests to whom the Europa caters. At one wedding of 360 people, Mendelssohn is played off-key while the TV flickers and the Terror Kids watch. Marco and Antonio, local truck drivers, their chests bare and hung with gold chains, thread their way in and out of the crowd, everyone drunk, the two exceptions being the sweating priest and the shy bride.

The Terror Kids, the children of Niccolò, the proprietor, play in the kitchen and in the TV lounge and on the terrace; they treat the staff and us as if they and we were members of an extended family, which is just as well, as their mother is never to be seen and it is to Niccolò that the job of mothering falls. These children, like so many Italian children, ask questions about one as if one weren't there. Their faces two inches from one's own, they say (to whom? one wonders), "Why is she fat?" or, "Why is her hair yellow?" or, "Why are her teeth so straight?" or, "Why does she wear these *brutti* clothes?" These questions are never discouraged and seldom answered. It seems an inefficient way of gathering information about the world, but they are quite as tolerable and as coherent as other children, if very much more *there,* leaving no space between themselves and other people. Will they come to believe that an accumulation of facts is tantamount to intimacy?

Niccolò gives us many brochures and each of us a Lucite clock with the word *Europa* stamped on it in blue; but who will come here? The clocks cannot be made to work. (The fountain of plaster nymphs does not play.)

The terrace on which we sit fronts directly onto the secondary road that carries all manner of traffic between Venafro and Isernia. It gives us a cozy feeling to sit here and watch the small world go by.

All day long a woman named Jackee watches television. Sometimes—she has had, in many subtle and refined ways, to be assured of her welcome— she joins us for coffee. She is black. She is from the Dominican Repub- lic. She is here (she says) "on work contract," words that fall chillingly on our ears. She dances at a club called Bali. Sometimes she helps out in the kitchen. Perhaps more. Her high, round breasts show above and through her sheer white blouse. The Terror Kids dance a wide circle around her. *"La vita è brutta* [Life is terrible]," she says.

One day two New York girls come with a wedding party to the Europa. Married to Italian businessmen, they live in Isernia, which they compare to Westchester: "No blacks, no Jews." Lizzie and Anna, caught off guard, cannot think of an appropriate response. Anna offends the waiter, when he arrives with her gelato, by saying, in a voice intended for the girls (who don't hear her): "That's a bunch of shit." The waiter has a difficult time understanding Anna's prolonged apology. He is a cowering boy.

We have a problem. We need a part for our rented car. Niccolò comes with us to the garage in Isernia. There is no part; the part is available only in Campobasso. From the terrace Niccolò flags down the pullman bus to Campobasso, hands the defective part to the driver, who will bring it to a Ford dealership in that city. In the event: no part. Not to worry, says Niccolò—*non ti preoccupare*—it is safe, *tranquillo,* here; the part will arrive tomorrow. Whatever *tomorrow* means, it does not mean tomorrow in the Gregorian or in the literal sense of the word. The part has been passed on to yet another bus driver, who is on his way to Termoli. "So when will it be ready?" *"Domani, dopodomani* [tomorrow, the day after tomorrow]. Italians are not precise." This is a source of pride.

Into this scenario Romana and her husband, Vincenzo, inject themselves, issuing well-meant but useless exhortations, Romana repeating the question of which she is so enamored (what does she think it will yield?): "But *why* did you leave your keys in the car?"

They live in an apartment with a wraparound terrace, seventy thousand dollars American, Vincenzo tells us. It is furnished as if from a store for immigrants on Mulberry Street: Lamps sprout cherubs; cherubs sprout lamps; heavy perforated plastic covers bulbous gold-and-white velvet furniture. Here and there an old poplar Deco piece survives, relegated to an odd corner, which it defines by its cleanliness of line.

On their terrace sits Vincenzo's old mother, of whom he takes loving care. She is ninety-four, her eyes are blue. It is possible only to admire Romana and Vincenzo when the evidence of their love is visible in this old lady, sitting happily among pots of basil with her rosary.

Vincenzo's brother was killed by a German bomb. Vincenzo was standing ten feet away. This fact colors and informs his life. After the bombs came the earthquakes.

Fabiola, the oldest of their three daughters, is eighteen; and she is matronly. "Duran Duran," she says. "To be or not to be," she says. . . . "Truth is beauty, beauty truth. . . ." The girls go with her for the *passeggiata;* "nice," Anna pronounces Fabiola, "like the 'nice girls' in Latin America, pale and bloodless." She knows *The Faerie Queene.* Romana can't control her harrumph when she sees me in skintight jersey pants, colored tights. We are what she has brought Fabiola up to fear.

And yet they desire our company, from which nothing material can be gained. Is this a form of love? We are—we feel we are—being taken over; silken tentacles of kindness hold us. Then we feel petty. Then Romana bullies us ("But *why?*") and we feel justified in our irritation.

There is a *festa* in Scapoli, the center of the *zampognari,* the bagpipe players. The *zampognari* travel in pairs; one plays a reed pipe, the other a bagpipe made of sheep's bladder—or of automobile inner tubes. They can be hired to perform in piazze and in shops, and go as far afield as Sorrento and Rome. This is what Stendhal said about *pifferari,* bagpipers:

> These people are enough to disgust one with music. They are crude peasants covered with sheepskins, who descend from the mountains of the Abruzzi and come to serenade the Madonnas of Rome on the occasion of the Nativity of the Savior.
>
> Nothing is so infuriating as to be awakened in the middle of the night by

the lugubrious sound of the bagpipes of these people; it grates on one's nerves like the bleat of the harmonica. Leo XII . . . enjoined them not to wake his subjects before four o'clock. . . . The *pifferaro* with whom I dealt in my small apartment told me that he hoped to take back with him thirty scudi (161 francs), an enormous sum in the Abruzzi, which will enable him to spend seven or eight months without working. . . . He told us a song that the young bagpipe players sing to the fair Roman ladies:

Fior de castagna,	[Flower of the chestnut,
Venite ad abitare nella vigna,	Come and live in the vineyard,
Che siete una bellezza di campagna.	You who are a beauty of the land.]

That which is generally called *folclorico* I generally dislike, as it seems to fossilize lifeless customs; exhibitions of *folclorico,* self-conscious and contrived, remind me of all those stilted junior high school skits in which we played at dressing up as Pilgrims (or worse: "Hello, I am Bolivia, and I produce tin") and felt like fools.

This *festa* (which, to cover all bases, has a local rock band) has no saint to justify its existence (saints' days are integral to these wilderness communities, organic, thus good), but it has something almost as good, in a campy kind of way, to account for its being laid on: Willie Cochran, the man in kilts (with a bagpipe) on the Dewar's scotch bottle—that's who he says he is—is here. What Cochran—"Scotland's Ambassador of Goodwill"—wants to discuss is his appearance on "Lifestyles of the Rich and Famous."

The men of the town, most of them shepherds, their faces carved and closed by weather, are wearing T-shirts with a Dewar's logo.

I am the only woman in the bar where they are sampling the ambassador's product. (I feel a disjunction of time and place.) The bar is set upon a spur so tiny it makes an immense statement; there are two street signs here: Via Aldo Moro and Corso J. F. Kennedy. Drunk old men sing. They sing "This Is My Country."

The mayor and the village priest genially attend stands set up for food and for the sale of four-hundred-dollar lace bedspreads made by women of the mountains; glass beads; wooden gewgaws all looking as if they were carved with a left hand and half a mind; combs; candy; shoes; plastic flowers; pirated tapes; rug beaters; umbrellas; cheap toys—a dispiriting array inappropriate to this time and this place.

We eat caciocavallo and scamorza cheeses. We eat cornmeal pizza baked in a hot oven under chestnut leaves and covered with potatoes, tomatoes, garlic, and wild greens that have been boiled in salt water with pigs' feet, ears, and snout. It is delicious, and of this time and place.

Who am I, romanticizing, to say what is of this time and place?

I have not seen an American or an English-language newspaper in sixteen days.

I leave to sit in the car, this lethargic planned revelry not suiting me. The breeze sings and stirs the olive leaves, which I watch—a pleasant occupation. Not one person who passes does not peer in to look at and appraise me; I am discussed as if I were an inanimate object.

Snaking down the mountain, led by Romana and Vincenzo (who always know a better path), we find, in village after village, other feasts. Pedestrians claim the right-of-way, and so do cars, Laura is scared of committing vehicular homicide. (Whereas I am scared of getting killed by walkers studiously oblivious of our presence.) Our windshield, as the mountain road tips and turns, is a landscape of blue-jeaned and flowered bottoms; they form a wall. The carabinieri stand by ineffectually. There is nothing to be done about this; we crawl all the way home.

I want to sing Cole Porter songs with Anna, but Anna wants to sleep in Lizzie's bedroom.

Tomorrow we go to Vallecupa, where my grandfather DiNardo was born. All this—the feast, the *folclorico*—has been a form of treading water.

This is my story. This is not Uncle Pat's story or my mother's story, and I make no claim to its being the true story. It is the story as I know the story. There are as many stories of a family as there are members of a family. This seems obvious to me, but not to Uncle Pat, who searches for an absolute truth, for revelations. I search for clues, for intimations. My way is my way only because it is my way, not because it is a better way. In my mother's story of the story, Grandpa was a cruel and angry man, he broke her nose with an iron when she was a little girl, he slammed it across her face; her beauty survived this assault.

In my memories he smiles at me. He never pinches my cheek, he never violates my flesh. He smells good.

He smashed the player piano with an ax. He smashed the television set (I have told this story) with a hard bosc pear.

After my grandmother died, Grandpa lived alone in the house near the waterfront, the house that smelled of ground-in poverty and wine fermented years before. The toilet was in the hall. The tub was in the kitchen. The walls were painted muddy green and brown. All the floors were covered in linoleum that rose in huge blisters to meet one's feet.

It was in this house, in the box room off the kitchen, that someone sat on my bed and asked me what I did under the covers with my hands at night. I cannot remember who this was—or what, exactly, his hands did next—though sometimes a face seems just about to swim into view. It is hot, it leers, and it is frightened; most of all it is frightened. The face is not my grandfather's face. It was not my grandfather.

This—the business of the hands—must have happened after my Uncle Johnny died. Uncle Johnny was my oldest uncle, born in Vallecupa. He died of a heart weakened by polio. In my mother's story of the story, Concetta, my grandmother, broke his back by forcing him to sit up when he was stricken with polio. This happened in the box room, too. It does not seem likely that my grandmother Concetta broke his back, but this fact which is not a fact has become part of the story, and if I try to move it out of the story, the story falls apart in my hands, in my mind. (This fact means: My mother hated her mother. On the day of my grandmother Concetta's funeral, my mother—whose name was Carmela, a beautiful name—wore a yellow satin dress; later that day she was matron of honor for her best friend, Alice, and she danced.) What I remember of Uncle Johnny is that he sat in a chair in front of the window looking out into the backyard. He wore red suspenders, which he allowed me to pluck. He was kind. He was buried wearing a good suit and a gold watch, two things he had never owned in life. I do not know how old he was; he could not have been more than thirty-five. On the day he died—I was five years old—my brother was born, from which I drew certain comforting conclusions.

What I remember best about the backyard is standing there with Uncle Tony after he had won the War. In pictures I look (I had a crush on him that I felt in parts of my body I had no name for, and in my nipples) as if *I* had won the War.

My mother's younger sister was my Aunt Louise. She knew about movie stars whose names no one remembers now. Frances Langford was one. She had a friend who had one date with Rudy Vallee. She was married to a man who beat her—this man, when I asked him how a car went backward, which is to say, in reverse, refused to answer me; he laughed—and she was very kind, she loved me. In later years my mother expressed bewilderment (a form of anger) at my friendship with Aunt Louise (Aunt Lou). Aunt Louise had peroxided hair, wore miniskirts when she was sixty-five, retained the violent diction of her youth, and went to bars and was never lonely; men liked her,

and she liked them. Her interest in them was not pecuniary and not obsessi
either, which was one of the things I admired about her, though most of
all, I admired her large, undiscriminating heart. "Bahbie" she called me.
When her first husband, he who beat her, died, she married again, and she
died, not long thereafter—she had terrible luck in husbands—of sclero-
derma, a disease in which the skin and organs harden and the pores can't
breathe; the night before she died, she asked her daughter, my cousin Patricia,
to walk her around and around and up and down the room, she wanted so
much not to die. I love my Aunt Louise and honor her in memory.

Grandpa was ninety-two when he died. Several years before he died, the
old house changed; it was as if, after all these years, he had decided to grow
a new skin. All the old furniture went out—the frowsty old bed, even the
Victorian bookcases with the glass doors that slid so cunningly into the
shelves above. In came chrome, Formica, and lamps that sprouted cherubs
and cherubs that sprouted lamps. Off came the linoleum (its blisters by this
time cracked). Floral rugs appeared. The smell of wine and incense and
candle smudge faded. All this was the work of Grandpa's companion, a
forty-five-year-old Puerto Rican woman, whom the family variously called
"nurse" and "slut" and "money grabber," and though I saw little of her—I
was living overseas most of this time—it was clear to me that she was none
of these, that she loved him and he her. In any case there was no money to
grab.

Grandpa had a throat cancer. The day before he was taken—raging—to
the hospital, he told his companion to pick the hot red peppers growing in
the backyard and berated her, hoarsely and loudly, for handling them carelessly. He scolded me, too, though the peppers were a gift to me, for not
knowing how to grow or pick them—and this I found bracing.

He put on his one suit, shiny with wear and age. In the hospital he sat
up in a chair, refusing to wear pajamas. That is how—having also refused
sedation—sitting up, staring with calm interest into a space just above our
heads, he died . . . like the turning of a page.

I wonder now, if then, if ever, he thought it good to have come to
America, so far from the trembling grasses, the thyme, the rosemary, the
mountains, wind, and rue.

It is said that in one Abruzzo town, Castel del Monte, the dead were buried,
in caves underneath the church, seated on rush chairs. A schoolmistress,
trying to illuminate the caves with a paper spill, set fire to the skeletons. This

The caves—the contents of which had appalled bricklay-
ed with earth and lime.

after my grandfather came to America, thirty thousand
in an earthquake in Abruzzo.

Amerigo, driving, looks at his white hands, the hands of an office worker
and an intellectual, and says: "They are simple country people." He means
the people of Vallecupa—fewer than one hundred of them, and many of
them tied to me by blood, not on Amerigo's side, but on my grandfather's.
The lineaments of the feud my Uncle Pat has tried so desperately to decipher
have not yet, and will not, appear. Perhaps there never was a feud, perhaps
a slow and gradual sundering of bonds, a weakening of connections by
attrition. . . . Perhaps also this is what my Uncle Pat most fears: atrophy,
like unto death.

We stop at the small church, into which there is set a commemorative
plaque: CADUTI DURANTE LA GUERRA [KILLED IN THE WAR], 1940–1945. The
names of six men, four of them family names: Agostino DiNardo, Giovanni
DiNardo, Antonio Fascia, Vincenzo Matteo. *(Pace.)* Anna is learning to
honor dead men.

An old man approaches (in fact he is not far advanced into middle age,
in fact he is close to my age), and Amerigo says, "These are the relatives of
Andrea DiNardo, do you know of him?"

The man's answer is to kiss us each in turn, no haste; it is the friendly,
warm kiss of a satisfied and gratified child, a child satisfied and gratified in
advance of satisfaction and gratification. My skin tingles: the white stubble
of his white beard.

He is wearing a soft felt hat, the brim of which sits low on his brow (it
rises to a dimpled pyramid); a white dress shirt cut off at the elbows; dirty,
beltless black pants; sandals.

"I am Domenico," he says. "I am the last of the DiNardos."

History has in a way ended here—that Domenico looks a hundred but
is only ten years older than I am is just a small part of it; the land and hope
itself seem to have ended here, in gray rubble and listless vegetation. Houses
have been bombed, have been reduced to piles of stone by earthquakes, and
it is impossible to tell the results of one calamity from the results of the other,
indeed to distinguish the inhabitable from the uninhabitable. They all look

so much the same. The road where my grandfather lived is impassable, it is a vastness of ruin; I can't walk there.

Domenico is the son of my grandfather's brother, Raffaello. He, Raffaello, worked with my grandfather. This is not part of the story as I know the story—as I know the story, Raffaello (lovely name) is not in the story—but here rocks are the story; human beings seem altogether intrusive.

Not a soul in Vallecupa was killed in the last earthquake, in 1984, says Domenico (whose sweet good nature shines through his pale-blue eyes); they were all praying at the church, the little Church of Maria Santissima degli Angeli, where my grandmother and grandfather were married. And when the bombs fell on Milano, on Torino, Domenico was praying to his patroness Mary, and look! he is here.

Domenico, happy, pliant, unquestioning—in this he is different from my other Molise relatives, he does not ask, "Why, why are you here? How long are you staying? Why did you go away? When will you come again?"— takes us to his house; and this is hard to take in: We are in a cobblestoned courtyard of noble and felicitous proportions. Dramatic stone arches lead into cavelike spaces where sacks of meal and flour and olive presses are stored and hams are hung for curing and cheeses ripen (all indications of prosperity), and animals take refuge (this, a cave, is absolute refuge) from the cold. On some of the arches numbers are stenciled, as if, in the not so distant past, this building (this accumulation of buildings) had honor or at least administrative significance. Several staircases, each with wrought-iron rails (a sign of wealth, which word is relative), lead to landings off which are sleeping chambers. On these steps are plastic containers, cans of olive oil, children's toys. On these landings there are rudimentary balconies, roughly hewn of wood, and on them pots of tomato and basil, and over them grapevines. The cooking is done either in the open—where are distributed, for the use of the extended family, mismatched chairs—or in one of the caves. Children, animals, chickens, adults, plants, stone, shovels, pots, laundry, tools—the coexistence of animate and inanimate things.

The whole is shored up against earthquake damage, past and future.

If there is wariness or trepidation underlying the simple dignity and friendliness with which we are received, it does not reveal itself; we are learning how to be (we learn how to be, anew, every day, but the lesson we learn here seldom comes our way) among hearts that are pure, bordered by a known world, self-possessed but other-aware.

Domenico says: "We have been waiting for you."

(For how long? And what was in your waiting heart? And *why?*)

Domenico's wife, Silvia, is almost toothless; she is wearing Aunt Mary's cast-off clothes and what remains of a pair of Gucci shoes. She looks vaguely Oriental. Her body is stunted, deformed by early years of poverty; she is almost dwarflike (though in fact she is Anna's and Laura's size).

Silvia's robust brother Pietro, bare-chested, wears shorts and a floppy cotton sun hat. He worked in Leeds, selling ice cream, till he was felled by a mysterious illness, which resembles, in all its symptoms, homesickness. "Yesterday," he sings, "all my trahbles seem-ed go-away," a song he evidently associates with Leeds. (A giggle forms in Lizzie's eyes but does not dare to make it to her lips.)

Silvia and Pietro have blue eyes. Like my mother's, like Uncle Pat's.

Domenico's sister Anna, with whom I have fallen in love, is eighty, her skin is translucent; she has the bluest eyes I have ever seen and she is one of the most beautiful women I have ever seen. Though nothing could be whiter than her white skin (across which, watercolor rose and ice-blue shadows sometimes surface from within), her hair is white whiter than white. She is dressed head to toe in black (the black of her garments is beginning to turn to rusty green): black kerchief, black high shoes, black patches on all her clothes. Her blue eyes trouble her immensely. ("White" the Abruzzesi call a cloudless day, and "white" they call the color of these eyes.) The name of the malady that afflicts her is unknown to her; a doctor prescribes for her, he comes to the village once a week. She shows us her *scatole* of medicine. She tells us this and shows us this, not in the expectation of concrete consequences or practical advice. Our presence here is felt as shamanistic; in our mysterious presence—mysterious to us as well as to her—resides our power.

They look alike, my Anna and this dear Anna; old Anna's gestures and her features seem to have found a home, an echo, in my Anna, to whom old Anna says: You will keep alive my name.

We do not know her surname.

My Anna does not understand how all these people are related to one another; the courtyard is filling up with people called Cosimo, Luigi, Gino, Maria, all "cousins." . . .

Domenico does not remember my grandfather, his uncle.

This does not matter to our love.

It is love; sentimentality washes off, this will not.

Amerigo has disappeared.

It is difficult to kiss the old women, their breath is terrible, as if it, too, has been living in caves.

Goodness is a phenomenon rarely encountered, but impossible not, for the willing heart, to recognize. . . . This teaches me our hearts are not yet too hardened or too bruised for new lessons of love. This is the gift they give me, their love, a respect for the resilience of my own battered heart.

The women bring us glass after glass of Domenico's strong red wine. They hover—Silvia uses a broom made of twigs to sweep the gray earth; the men sit, pressing upon us ripe pears from their trees and oranges (which they call *portoghesi*) . . . more wine.

(What were the battles Uncle Pat spoke of, what were the fights?)

What did we talk of, what did we say? (They expressed no interest in America, save to ask whether it was hot there, too.) We spoke of the soil, of the land, of Mary the Protectress, of the fabled beauty of Concetta. One old woman takes my face in her hands: "You look exactly like Concetta, the Beauty—*la bellissima*," she says, which makes me absurdly happy; we speak of earthquakes and of journeys, and of God, God not as an abstraction but God as He affects the fate of Vallecupa (His role is somewhat murkier than that of Mary; He is like a distant planet exercising an unknown tug and pull). Domenico shows us the beautiful spoons he carves out of maple and ash.

And this is how Norman Douglas describes Abruzzese peasants (he wrote this the year my mother was born, he could have been writing about Concetta and Andrea):

> Their life is one of miserable, revolting destitution. They have no games or sports, no local racing, clubs, cattle-shows, fox-hunting, politics, rat-catching, or any of those other joys that diversify the lives of our peasantry. No touch of humanity reaches them, no kindly dames send them jellies or blankets, no cheery doctor inquires for their children; they read no newspapers or books, and lack even the mild excitements of church *versus* chapel, or the vicar's daughter's love-affair, or the squire's latest row with his lady—nothing! Their existence is almost bestial in its blankness. I know them—I have lived among them. For four months in the year they are cooped up in damp dens, not to be called chambers, where an Englishman would deem it infamous to keep a dog—cooped up, amid squalor that must be seen to be believed. . . . The most depraved of city-dwellers has flashes of enthusiasm and self-abnegation never experienced by this shifty, retrogressive, and ungenerous brood, which lives like the beasts of the field and has learnt all too much of their logic. . . .

Norman Douglas's ethnocentric fairy tale does not satisfy the facts or me, nor does it accord with our happiness and harmony. . . . While I am making up my own fairy tale (perhaps this was once a hunting lodge for Frederick II, a falcon's lair?), in walks, shattering all reflection, a dazzling man . . . the twentieth century. He is Ilio, cousin to me (but this word has lost all meaning). His eyes are sapphire under dark gothic eyebrows, his hair is black and curly, and his brigand's mustache frames a tender mouth; his hard, supple body, to which Laura, Lizzie, Anna, and I all viscerally respond, is covered with a fuzz of fine, black, curly hair; he is wearing a red T-shirt and jeans cut off strategically; he is perfectly elegant; his elegance (having nothing to do with costume) is worn lightly.

"Well," he says (he says it just like this), "you must tell me all: all about American feminism, pacifism, progressive Catholicism, and your American family, the Jehovah's Witnesses."

His elders beam.

Ilio says he likes Jehovah's Witnesses because they are "fabulists," and he dislikes them because they "brainwash" (a neat summation), causing his elders to beam more brilliantly.

Ilio has a two-year-old son; he has been married one and a half years; nobody is disturbed or embarrassed by this, he has done the honorable thing.

Ilio says, "Yes, yes," to feminism. "All must work together for peace with hands and hearts," he says.

"Why are you wearing two rings?" Lizzie says. "One is an engagement ring, and the other a wedding ring," Ilio says; "they are heavy." This has a double meaning.

The next day Ilio takes Anna for a *giro* in his car; he takes her to a Gothic church in the mountains.

"So what's up, Annabanana?"

Anna crosses her eyes.

"His wedding rings are 'resting heavily' on him," she says. "There's no such thing as a cousinly *giro* in this country."

"And?"

"He respected my bodily integrity," she says, her face daring us to laugh.

In the middle of the night she says: "Ma? Lizzie? Laura? He drives a *hearse.*"

"A hearse, why?"

" 'Cause that's what he does, he's a teacher and he's the hearse driver for Vallecupa."

"Oh."

So then we all laugh, Anna has given us permission.

* * *

Living in the house that is joined to Amerigo's is Antonella; her parents emigrated to Scotland, where she spent most of her life. She came to Venafro to marry an Italian who is related to Amerigo's wife. It is odd that no one ever speaks of her. That lovely soft burr. She almost never speaks her own language anymore, she says. "It was lonely and hard," she says, "at first" (this "at first" is an afterthought, to fend off our pity). Next door Amerigo speaks Esperanto and writes of a mystical solidarity among men and longs to speak with someone about the Pre-Raphaelites. Two lonelinesses not joined.

Some travelers think Abruzzo resembles Scotland—especially in a thin drizzle, such as the one in which Antonella now stands.

Dopodomani (the day after tomorrow) we've said we'd return to Vallecupa, and the day after our first visit we do. Silvia serves us platters of boiled chicken and boiled beef (skinny boiled chicken) in broth, with chunks of rough bread. The chicken population in the courtyard has noticeably diminished. Anna valiantly chews flesh, family feeling overwhelming squeamishness. Flies abound and are, except by us, ignored. More pears. (More flies.)

Domenico carves his beautiful forks and spoons with the same knife he uses to cut the bread; it is difficult to believe that the man who is sawing at bread held between his knees carved these intricate, hand- and eye-worthy, useful forks and spoons of maple and ash. Naturally we want to buy some, and naturally this presents us with problems of delicacy and tact; we do not want to risk offending him. Laura negotiates. It takes Domenico three or four days to carve one spoon. He gives us many. The amount of money Laura gives him seems ludicrously small. He keeps giving us more spoons and forks.

"You are sad," Domenico says to me.

He is absolutely right; and this is a statement that could proceed only from absolute simplicity, from immediacy; between stimulus—a look, a glance, a knotted shoulder—to response, no system or structure or ideology mediates or intervenes. Amerigo reads bodies—to this extent he has retained simplicity—and so does Domenico.

One wishes always to avoid, in describing peasants, the word *simplicity* . . . for two reasons: One feels like a romantic fool (or a condescending one), and one feels guilty of idealization or of reduction (two sides of the same coin). But here we are, for these moments of time out of time, drawn, not kicking and screaming, into this condition of complete simplicity (which feels like blessedness); of what does it consist? For Domenico, for Silvia, for old Anna (but not for Ilio, who is the World), it consists of knowing (as the marrow knows) that the unconscious cooperates with matter. For them, a pot, a broom, a child, a chicken, a spoon, a relative from America, America itself, a plastic container, a cured ham, a pot of basil, stone, water are all the furniture of the world and of the mind, they are all *there,* and being all there have not to be individuated. They all belong equally and with the grace of existence to the world—and present themselves so to the unconscious: as a unity. The hand that holds the knife is one with the knife that carves the spoon that is one with the hand that holds the knife which is also one with the bread which it also carves, and into this we fit perfectly and completely; nothing is alien.

This simplicity is also synchronicity . . . as in ancient Chinese histories in which, in the Year of the Dragon, a king sets out to pursue the Emperor of the West. The empress miscarries. A phoenix is sighted on Mount Yu. Three roosters are seen sitting on a roof. . . . There is no cause and effect, no causality, in these events; they are. What unifies them is (only) that they took place in the Year of the Dragon.

For the primitive man, firm, simple, the collective and collectivity predominate over the individual and the individuated. Loyalty is to the tribe. The family exists in a psychic as well as a cultural continuum.

But while *primitive* can be understood to mean our own "real" nature— that which partakes of Original Sin but which also remains untouched, unmarked and unmoved, uncorrupted by the refinements of civilization and by institutional sin—the primitive is also that into which civilization may fall, sink, and be degraded; to be a primitive is to run the risk (without the knowledge of the risk) of seeing the nation as a family. It is not difficult to understand how these good, firm, simple farmers—these good people— could have become those bad Fascists. . . .

What does it mean to belong to a family, a family like mine, like the one in the courtyard, the courtyard that is like a womb?

Part of what it means is that for Uncle Pat I am always Bobbie. Bobbie who was nine when the War ended and didn't know how to ride a bike or swim; Bobbie who was precocious, sassy (scared). I will always be that Bobbie, that Bobbie who in part is a projection of my mind and in part of Uncle Pat's, that invented Bobbie upon whom Uncle Pat's story of Bobbie— and my story of Uncle Pat—rests. I can always go home to that Bobbie—go home, that is, to myself—and to Uncle Pat and to all my family, but there is a way in which, with my family, I can never be anything *but* that Bobbie.

I am as they defined me then, as tribal loyalties and strictures required them to define me, as I was "fixed." And this is in part comforting: I am known, held, accounted for. In part it is claustrophobic and stultifying: I am not known, the *I* that I am now is not cherished, held, accounted for—it does not exist. . . . *I* do not exist.

Domenico says: "You are sad."

In response to questions no longer eager, now belabored, Ilio will say only, "There are different families within families, different times of immigration. . . ." This casual approach to a tangled history strikes me as a kind of wisdom.

Three roosters sat on a rooftop.

There are at least five dialects spoken here, perhaps it would be more accurate to say five distinctly idiosyncratic patterns that our ears discern. Anna understands Ilio and Amerigo. Laura understands the speech of Amerigo and that of the middle-aged and of Romana (whom she doesn't like). I understand Amerigo and the speech of the very old. To Lizzie they are all equally comprehensible or incomprehensible as the case may be. Is this a matter of will? of sympathy? or simply of brainwaves and ear? None of us knows.

Domenico has given us bunches of rosemary. The rosemary perfumes our sleep. We will never see Domenico again.

Romana and Vincenzo visit us at the last minute with confused and cacophonous offers of help. It would be generous of us to accept their kindness, but we do not. Romana cries.

We have left the green hills of Molise, the tender land that slopes to the Adriatic Sea, and we are threading our way through a mountain wilderness, riding on top of a very old world.

* * *

High in these castle-dotted ridges near the Gran Sasso is the small village of Alfedena, once the capital of the Samnites, of Sabine descent—warriors toughened for the cold and for battle and for the hunt by wrestling (and by the cold and by battle and by the hunt). Here, sitting in a folding chair outside a café, we meet a retired Floridian, a man of seventy years. He talks to us of earthquakes—as much a subject for conversation as malaria was a hundred years ago—and of the politics of earthquakes (during the earthquakes of 1980 and 1984 houses were damaged, here in the epicenter, for the most part inside, he tells us, and nobody died, as a result of which the government—adhering to some severe poetry of law—is withholding millions of dollars in aid). What we are interested in, of course, is *him,* the anomalous fact of him, *here.* He takes his being here for granted, his fate does not surprise him. He wears badger bristles in his hatband to ward off the Evil Eye.

The Pope took a three-hour walk in the Apennines, alone, without bodyguards. This is an engaging fact.

We are in the Apennines, too, engrossed in the beautiful logic of green plains leading to violet mountains . . . when we are not held tight among trees, our view is sweeping, grand, clean, offering a rare vision of an impossible freedom, an intimation of scouring truth. . . . "Poor lonely Pope," Lizzie says.

We are driving through the National Park of Abruzzo, home of wolves and golden eagles, Sardinian warblers, wild foxes and wild pigs, chamois, bears, and home to campers, hikers, and movie stars (houses like Swiss chalets). Here, in this crisp and singing air, among the forests of pine trees, among beech woods and stands of oak trees, near river gorges and lakes, are dusty villages, hardly villages at all, scattered houses, winding streets on which old women sit knitting and donkeys wander without apparent aim or curiosity. . . .

Anna is sick.

Perhaps we have been talking theology too much. . . .

"If you are right about religion," Laura says, "then we are wrong; you are making us wrong by being right." (The idea that I may be "right" seems not only lunatic but irrelevant to me. I am Catholic, that is all.) A discussion of right and wrong must rest upon religious or spiritual terms, terms that Laura rejects; it is a language that has caused her pain. Laura prefers the language of psychology, a blunt instrument in my hands, a blunt instrument altogether, I think. Is it our languages that are different, or our dialects? Anna says, "Oh, don't be Augustinian, Mom," a sentence that releases a spring of laughter in me; but when I ask her what it means, she won't say.

What she does say is that she hates trees. Only banyan trees and olive trees she likes; she has hated trees ever since the third grade, when she had to paste leaves in a book (for a moment my nostrils perfectly and tinglingly recall the smell of that thick white paste which was like spice-impregnated marshmallow icing) . . . this she says, and: "This looks like Danbury, Connecticut," she says (which, in its majesty and lucidity, it surely does not).

Anna has had five glasses of wine, three cups of espresso, a Coke, and pasta for lunch, also Robitussin for a cold. All this nonsense about trees, scarifying nonsense, is it a matter of blood sugar? "What does existential terror feel like?" poor Anna asks. Her pulse is beating wildly and erratically.

Perhaps we should have asked Romana and Vincenzo to lunch at the Europa, accepted their help; Anna thought so, she is generous.

Castles and watchtowers placed on flanks of hills do not delight her, nor do medieval villages; a string of burros silhouetted against the sky—a moving sight, the unselfconsciousness of funny-looking animals—does not kindle in her enthusiasm or response. She withdraws, curls into herself in her corner of the car; she is white, she looks haunted. She refuses touch. This is a mother's nightmare—not to be of use.

"Anna, do you think you're having an anxiety attack?

"Anna, do you think you're physically ill? . . . Anna."

Anna does not entertain these impotent questions.

We stop at the mountain resort of Pescasseroli (part Capri, part Switzerland, part Amalfi, part Rockies, part tourist-Vermont, part Liberty, part kitsch—and wholly Apennine Italian). . . . I can see this town, its cafés, its shops of leather goods, its happy families picnicking, with total clarity, though at the time I thought I had closed my senses to everything but Anna's pain. I take Anna to the *farmacia,* my own heart beating in such a hurting pattern I have difficulty walking, and, "Is her pulse too fast?" I ask; and the pharmacist answers—in that phlegmatic way with which Italians sometimes greet genuine emergencies—*"Abbastanza,"* which is to say, "Sufficiently fast . . . fast enough" . . . which is to say: *Dear God.* And what to do? *"Si riposi."* Rest. The absurdity of this prescription reaches even Anna; she almost manages a laugh.

We settle ourselves in a resort hotel. Anna's exhaustion is a boon. "It looks like the creation of the world," she says. "What does?" But she is fast asleep.

The next morning, rosy, calm, "I've got my period," she says.

"But, Anna, was it—your anxiety—partly because of my smoking? Are you afraid I'll die?"

"You are the vainest woman I have ever met," Anna Harrison says.

In the town of Aielli we have a wonderful dinner of tagliatelle (not "fat") with cream and Gorgonzola cheese; rare lamb chops; a bitter green vegetable we do not recognize, which acts, our waiter says, as "an astringent," and a sufficient amount of espresso (not what the French call "a tear," by which they mean a drop); our waiter has worked in Switzerland, so we do not have to plead for *caffè lungo e doppio o quadruplo in una tazza grande*—long and double or quadruple in a big cup—in order to get enough coffee to satisfy us. Nevertheless, our waiter thinks our practice is "barbaric." He informs us of this in the most charming manner possible.

Here, near L'Aquila, from which can be seen the highest peaks of the Apennines, each town has a gastronomic specialty, and a festival to celebrate it. There is a festival of strawberries; of lamb; of lentils and sausages; of broad beans; of chestnuts; of roast suckling pig; of artichokes; of mullet; of maccheroni alla chitarra; of mussels; of pine nuts; of grapes; of trout and crayfish; of chicken; of cherries; of truffles.

The Abruzzesi—like my friends in Avezzano—have extraordinary and seemingly endless ritualized banquets—thirty-five to forty courses—on festive occasions, a custom that stems from the time when the mountain people finished off their food supply in a glorious blaze of conspicuous gastronomic consumption. These mythic feasts, called *panarde,* have been described by more than one food-enthralled writer; one, Gian Gaspare Napolitano, says of the *panarda:*

> It is the Arabian Phoenix of the Abruzzi table, a dinner that starts again when it seems finally over, beginning again every time it arrives at the end, an avalanche of food . . . perhaps not refined, but above all abundant. Any pretext is good. And the *panarda* is not only eaten; it is talked about, it is looked forward to with anticipation; it is prepared with every care, with great searchings for and accumulations of food so that it might be abundant. It has survived famines, the ravages and invasions of war.

Waverley Root describes a *panarda* of at least thirty courses, which included mountain ham, country bread and mountain butter, double consommé, boiled meats, and mortadella (these are only the appetizers); mac-cheroni alla chitarra, fritters in celery sauce, grilled trout, roast kid, chicken in jelly, omelets, sausages, veal rolls, eel, mutton, artichoke hearts, broccoli, two kinds of artichokes, two kinds of veal, two kinds of chicken in addition to that prepared in jelly, lamb, pig's liver, partridge, cheeses, cakes, cookies, liqueurs, wines.

The lamb and beef are fed on sweet meadow grasses, the durum wheat for pasta comes from the highlands. . . .

And the distinctive *amari* of the Abruzzi make the heart glad: Aurum, Centerba (one hundred herbs), Mentuccia, Amaro Maiella, Doppio Arancia (double orange)—all unknown in America, some, alas, unknown even in Rome.

In the fragrant night we swim in the pool. Bats skim the water.

Laura's cousin Marco lives near Aielli, which is not far from the city of L'Aquila, a prosperous city that once had ninety-nine piazze, and ninety-nine churches, and is supposed to have had ninety-nine castles at the time of Frederick II; ninety-nine church bells once rang in this city; and it still has a fountain with ninety-nine spouts.

Laura first came to Aielli in 1977; it was poor then. Marco is rich now. This seems topsy-turvy to Laura, whose family emigrated to Auburn, New York, in 1922, when that city on the Erie Canal was a boomtown. There was a shoe factory, a rope factory, and a sausage factory; and Laura's family had a garden a city block long. (One must observe that as to gardens, memories are treacherous.) Auburn is now poor.

Marco takes us to his new house, four years old, which with his own hands and to his own design he built for the equivalent of one hundred thousand dollars. It is fenced and gated and for good measure guarded by German shepherds, and Marco has made use of every kind of stone, marble, and terrazzo known to the vulgar imagination. It is the kind of middle-class house one learns to get used to in Italy: beautiful crocheted lacework and beautiful ceramic tiles—and "decorative" bamboo guitars with blue grottoes in their centers, objects that one is always afraid will turn out to be clocks or lamps and that usually do. It is immaculate, it shines. The furniture is solidly and reassuringly comfortable, and ugly.

Thirty years ago Aielli had a population of thirty-five hundred; now, because of earthquakes and migration, it has a population of one thousand, but it is growing again.

In 1980 Marco knew an earthquake was happening when the garden gate moved and the rosebushes did not.

In this garden, over which the Gran Sasso is sovereign—and from which one sees soft wooded hills, gold-green hills, distant mountain peaks, the huddled houses of the old town, a medieval tower—there are peach trees and walnut trees, Dick-and-Jane hollyhocks, geraniums, snapdragons, sweet Williams, marigolds, myrtle trees, roses bred not for perfection but for fragrance—roses that smell cinnamony; peachy-creamy gladioli, pansies, African violets that bloom under the first snow, pine trees, wild mountain flowers. In it laundry (how delicious it will smell) is hung out to dry, for Sandra, the mother of Marco's three daughters (Clara, Alicia, and Cesarina), has not lost the old ways. . . . Bells chime.

"What do you mean, the mother of your children?" Lizzie asks Marco; "your *wife." Forse che sì, forse che no.* Marco lives part of the year in Toronto; we intuit an "arrangement."

It is interesting to hear Marco talk about money—which forms the staple of his conversation—bearing in mind that he comes from a culture of poverty. This is what he says:

When he first came to Toronto (he was twenty-one and an auto mechanic), he lived for two years without work; he "had no shoes." And then, for pennies, he did construction work, and now he is rich. (I have noticed how, in stories of this kind, the details of the climb to success are often sacrificed to drama; first, in the story, Marco was poor; and all of a sudden he is rich, just as in a fairy tale.) Italians now don't want to work hard in construction, he says; the prosperity of this land—the Torino of Abruzzo, rich in potato and sugar beet farms—has "spoiled" them. . . . Ah, yes, but southerners have always been castigated for their laziness—up to now, by northerners. It is, however, Pakistanis whom Marco absolutely deplores— "Sikhs, sheep, all on welfare, all in Canada illegally." He uses Portuguese labor. From time to time he is able to send for "ten good men" from L'Aquila.

This talk is dispiriting. Work on the land is deprecated by those who don't work on the land except when it's romanticized. But this talk is not dispiriting to Sandra (who is plump and has green eyes flecked with brown and gold). She is in a prosperous house, set among prosperous houses in a prosperous land. Each of her daughters will have an apartment in her four-story house when the time comes; they are her hostages to fortune. . . . But they are not entirely complicit in their fate. "The *passeggiata*," Alicia says scornfully, "nothing to do! *Passeggiata* only!" Alicia will not go gently into her good fate.

Laura has seen the bed her mother and father spent their wedding night in. Perhaps as a consequence nothing is easy for her now. She cannot, for example, decide what gifts to bring her relatives; everything she thinks of seems wrong—and no wonder, when Marco tells her she has spent nine dollars for a five-dollar bottle of brandy. (We got it in a sad café. All the customers were male. The customers, here, are always male.)

For all the questions Sandra asks—how much do you weigh? why were you divorced?—and for all the answers she volunteers, there is something she holds in reserve, something coiled, wary, unyielding. She is a peasant, sturdy, now rich. In fact, her curiosity has limits, fixed boundaries, just as her revelations have. If one studies her apparently guileless questions, one sees that she asks only enough to "place" us. This hospitality has more rules than grace. She does not care to know our natures (wanting to know but not to possess is a form of grace); she needs to know our status. Intimacy is not the desire of her heart.

Her kindness is indistinguishable from her pride. . . . How she feeds us:

Fresh ribbon pasta light as air with a dollop of tomato sauce and cheese; wild mushrooms and truffles from the mountains; new tomatoes with home-made mayonnaise and oregano; beefsteak cooked in the microwave oven of which she is inordinately proud. An aged Montepulciano wine. A beautiful *digestivo* she has made of mint—the color, green-gold, of a perfect summer day. (She herself drinks Baileys Cream.) Cold marinated broad beans with mint. A frittata with mint. Mint is for the Madonna's feast day: "When Jesus died, she needed mint in her stomach, *povera*." A creamy risotto with mozzarella and tomato sauce and basil. Basil, according to legend, grew at the foot of the cross.

Laura says I apologize in my sleep. What for? I wonder. One cannot expect others to be concerned with one's own earned or unearned guilt. But I feel sorry for that sleeping person who says, "I'm sorry."

* * *

The town of Celano rises from the plains, and the houses of Celano rise in concentric circles to a medieval castle lodged against a flint-bare mountainside.

Sandra and Marco take us there.

Red-tiled limewashed houses with green or blue or varnished maple shutters, doors ajar, curtains tucked back—just enough for someone to peer out/peer in; firewood stacked casually against the sides of houses (it will be bitterly cold here in the winter, the pots of red and white flowers that rest with precarious gaiety on windowsills will soon need to be given a home indoors, and the houses will present blank faces to a snowy world); vegetables and fruits piled casually on stands, awnings and bright umbrellas protecting and announcing them. Celano is a pleasant town. It used, as did many of these mountain towns, to be a center for lacework; it still is, but to the black-clothed old women sitting in watery sunlight on rush chairs outside their houses something new has been added: chic boutiques. Italy's young designers are everywhere. But here is a clash between new and old:

Sandra says to us, "Shut up. I will do the bargaining. Don't let them know you are Americans." This is surely a charade, for surely the shopkeepers, as polished and brittle as any in Milan, will know we are American. And they do. And when Sandra tries to bargain with a long-haired young woman in a miniskirt, the girl says dryly, "Times have changed, signora." Sandra sputters. She has lost face and can rescue nothing from this situation; and this puts everyone out of sorts, especially Sandra and especially Laura, whose smiles are strained.

I buy mulberries from a dark, cool store behind a turquoise awning. I don't know what I expect from this fragile fruit, juices already staining the bottom of the paper bag. . . . Mulberry trees seem to me a thing of the lovely ancient past ("Come to my house," an English writer once said to me, "we have little to offer you, but there is a mulberry bush Milton's tutor planted here"—a perfect invitation) and also of the past that includes my grandmother, under whose mulberry tree I sat when I was a child, as safe as I have ever been or ever shall be, lost in the happy delirium of sunny choice: This one is ripe, this one is not; my world was narrowed down to that leafy choice, and nothing I could do was wrong. . . . No one ships mulberries anymore, the berries are too delicate, and Americans never really developed a passion for them. . . . These berries are not even sweet. I think of Laura's garden in a factory town, so beautiful in her memory ("a whole city block long"). . . .

The castle we have come to see—Piccolomini—bristles with projecting battlements; cylindrical towers visually soften the corners; children are playing soccer under the drawbridge. A central courtyard of great simplicity in the keep and a loggia and mullioned windows present a female counterpoint to the maleness of the aggressive structure (like a castle a child would make of sand, H. V. Morton called it—almost definitely the fantasy building of a boy; the inner space belongs to women, who kept wait). Sandra does not understand our compulsion to climb to the loggia—for the view, for the sake of the climb itself. She has offered us Celano's best wonder as if it were her own; that ought to be good enough; volition on our part is—she communicates this with silence and with sighs—an affront to her proprietariness.

In the large and gracious square of Celano, Sandra acts like a tyrannical tired child. Pouting: "I am tired," she says, into which, we are to suppose, volumes must be read. Sandra does not dissemble, she sees no need. It is us she is tired of. She has taken to calling us all, even Laura and Lizzie, "the Americans."

We go at night—Lizzie and Laura and Anna and I—exhausted as a result of Sandra's having exhausted her generosity and Marco's helplessness in the face of this—to eat at the Ristorante al Castello Aielli, a hilarious—quite delightful—attempt to replicate the Piccolomini in miniature. We eat fried rice balls stuffed with raisins and meat; potato croquettes; prosciutto; homemade pasta with a sauce of tomatoes, cream, and sage—all very good. We drink a house *amaro* "of the Marsica." The Marsi—for whom so many towns in the central Abruzzi are named—were those ancient peoples renowned as curers of snakebite, wizards, alchemists, worshipers of Circe, of whom, according to myth, they were descendants. Here there is a mural celebrating the Marsi, and there is a written legend:

The goddess Angitia (of whom Virgil wrote) wrestled with the serpents coiled at the bottom of the lake, Lake Fucino (now so fruitfully drained, the largest drained lake in the world). From their aggressive mating, it was thought, would come a stupendous ruler, powerful and terrible. . . . The story dribbles off here, as no such goddess, evidently, manifested herself (and the Italians are a pragmatic people). . . . A candelabrum with five branches:

in each candleholder is the face of Angitia, or rather the two faces of Angitia, for she has assimilated the serpent and wears behind her human face a serpent's face. A turtle dove, a lyrebird, a ewer. These are votive elements in the life of the Marsi. . . . This is the first panel.

Lake Fucino is drained. The serpent-fish, sinking into slime, and the goddess have disappeared. In the basin of the lake are huge egg-shaped ferns representing fertility. . . . This is the second panel.

Combined with agriculture is technology: The Società Tele-Spazio has placed satellite dishes in the Fucense plain. . . . This is the third panel. . . . It goes without saying that the satellite dishes look more mythological than the serpent, more unnatural, less belonging.

Laura is tired. She has seen the double bed of her parents. She is ready to move on.

We say good-bye in Pescina dei Marsi—a lonely slag heap of broken towers and decayed medieval houses—to Ignazio Silone (born 1900, died 1978); we pay respect to his grave. Silone was a Catholic who left the Church, a Communist who broke with the party, an early sympathizer of Mussolini who was sent by the Fascists into Swiss exile. He was suspicious of the official Church because of its institutionalized power; he became equally suspicious of political ideology. As between the victim and the victimizer, he said (with Camus), one must always side with the victim. He believed in, and wrote of in his books (the most famous of which is *Bread and Wine*), an unofficial church, a Christianity informed by a theology of hope, small intense communities held together by love and by the Eucharist. He died—at the age of seventy-eight—in Switzerland, but is buried here, in his native Abruzzo. Above his simple tomb is an iron cross.

In Abruzzo, San Domenico is revered; he provides the faithful with protection from toothaches and rabies and snakebite (this is a land of continuity; that is one way of putting it). In the white and shining town of Cocullo is the six-hundred-year-old Church of the Madonna delle Grazie, characteristically flat and boxlike. In it there is a life-sized statue of San Domenico; he is bearded and haloed and robed in black; he carries a crozier in his right hand, a mule's shoe in his left—a mule was this saint's best friend, and the shoe protects sheepdogs from rabies. An enormous fat snake winds around the saint, his halo, his crozier, his face, his mule shoe. A sweet cherub rests incongruously at his feet.

Every May, *serpari* (snake charmers) march in procession with San Domenico through Cocullo, carrying with them sacks of snakes, which they toss—without fear or danger of snakebite, we are told—onto San Domenico (San Domenico is followed by one of his teeth, in a silver reliquary). Children are encouraged to handle the snakes.

In glass display cases in this church are coiled snakes. Faded gladioli surround delicate fourteenth-century frescoes and nineteenth-century plaster saints. In neon lights—red, yellow, green—are these words: AVE MARIA; MATER DOLOROSA; SANTA LUCIA. (St. Lucy is a favorite saint of Naples and of the South; virgin and martyr, she was placed in a brothel [but managed to keep her virginity], burned [but survived her ordeal at the stake], stabbed in the throat [and survived]; her eyes were torn out by an admirer who thought them beautiful [they were miraculously restored]; she was finally killed by the sword, by which time she must have been grateful for death. It is sometimes difficult to distinguish between the worship of Mary and the worship of Lucy in Abruzzo. Some scholars see in Lucy the direct descendant and heir to the worship of the goddess Athena.)

"Why are snakes used in worship here?" Lizzie asked a passerby, who, puzzled, said: "Because always!"

My people are very old.

My childhood perception of them as immutable, as having been there forever, as having no new or shiny edges, forever since the world began, as old and as primitive as earth and sky, has an eccentric connection to fact.

Along the winding road that follows the Sagittario River, there are crosses to mark the sites of fatal accidents.

On the road to Scanno, tunnels have been cut through the mountains. The marks of chisels are not smoothed over, and this is pleasing; it is a testament to manual labor. Technology has not overwhelmed humanity here; the mark of the personal—the mark of the human hand—is everywhere.

Near a jade lake a mile long and 3,450 feet above the sea is the lovely little town of Scanno, its houses Renaissance and Baroque, its medieval cobbled streets punctuated by homely water pumps. Its arched and mazelike alleys are like those of a North African souk. Romeo and Juliet might have lived here. There are cool streets of steps; there are external staircases on narrow houses, staircases that wind into dark living quarters; steps lead and disappear, red-tiled houses climb a mountain—dignified, staggering only slightly. The flat-faced women of Scanno are famous for their lacework, made on cylindrical cushions, and for their distinctive costumes: shoes like pointed Oriental slippers; long, wide skirts and short embroidered jackets; pillbox hats like turbans with gold and silver braids. We did not see the colorful traditional dress; we saw women dressed in black jackets, black skirts (eight meters of cloth), black slippers, black turbans. They were elegant and contained. We saw nuns on the spur of a hill above the busy piazza, singing Vespers.

Outside a coffee shop in a narrow, busy alley we met Andrea and Mario, two beautiful boys, cocky, show-offy, frolicky, nice. Andrea took us to his uncle's fifteenth-century palazzo, the oldest and the largest in Scanno. Through a graceful archway we walked into the palazzo from the new part of Scanno; and we walked down and out through the back entrance of the palazzo to the old part of Scanno. This is Abruzzo: old, new, high, low. . . . The palazzo has been divided into apartments, the private chapel that once belonged to Andrea's family has been deconsecrated.

On motorcycles Andrea and Mario took Anna and Lizzie higher, on a dirt road, than Scanno, to a treeless, silent place of rock where winds whistled among undistinguished ruins. Lizzie and Anna on their bikes with their princelike boys leaned against the wind and zipped around the ruins, stones skipping beneath their wheels. Anna and Lizzie climbed a tower and surveyed us and the world from the ruined blank window of a ruin: No ruin is undistinguished. They flung their arms out. "We are here!" they called; conquering the scrubbed world on red motorcycles, unafraid.

Chapter VII

PUGLIA:
FAIRYLAND

The oil refineries of Bari shimmered like a mirage in a haze of their own making; we bypassed this grotesque, oddly clinical landscape which from our car seemed almost antiseptic—cylindrical tanks and ladders of shiny metal against a gunmetal Adriatic crowded with ferries and steamers and freighters. We were bound not for prosperous Bari but for a landscape equally provocative and insinuating, not brazenly new and technologically glamorous but prehistoric and runic: the rich undulating plain and the long Murge Plateau of Puglia, on which are scattered (and, in the town of Alberobello, converged) dwellings of strange and singular shape—trulli—that have no counterpart elsewhere on earth.

Many theories have been advanced to explain these whitewashed buildings on the Murge—buildings of which the most remarkable features are cone-shaped roofs made, without mortar, of large, gray, flat local limestones arranged in overhanging rows like scales, rising in diminishing concentric circles, topped with eccentric and diverse decorative finials—but the fact of them, astonishing and dreamlike, other-planetary from a distance, amazing (inspiring both giggles and awe) when viewed close up, is far more potent than any theory about them. They are symbols, we feel, though we do not know of what; symbols speak to the unconscious, theories to the conscious mind. Alberobello is a kind of Oz, no less Emerald for being white.

. . . It is made for a kind of skipping gladness—a gladness threaded with an inchoate, and perversely delicious, fear.

There is something romantic, touching, one doesn't know why, about structures of stone without mortar.

Religious and folk symbols are brushed in white on some of the conical roofs. Some of them yield meaning readily; others do not.

Puglia is the heel and the spur of the Italian "boot," on the southeastern peninsula that thrusts out between the Adriatic and the Gulf of Taranto. Horace called it "dry" and "thirsty"; it is now richly cultivated—long, straight roads crisscross wheatfields, almond and fig orchards, and vineyards—and it has been so since the Apulian Aqueduct, said to be the largest in the world, a project thirty years in the making, was completed in 1939.

Alberobello, to which (mountain-weary, glad of flat land and gentle hills and unsurprising roads) we were now bound, has, I think, the prettiest name of any town in Italy; it means, literally, "beautiful tree" and derives from the great oak forest that once covered the area, Silva Arboris Belli. It is in this town that trulli are concentrated along winding lanes, in rows, another planet's equivalent of rows of brownstones; in mazes that end in cul-de-sacs; along streets of steps—*stradelle*—where vendors sell straw goods and gnomish plaster trulli to tourists, almost all of whom are Italian, Puglia not yet having been, in that remarkable process of accident and intuition amalgamated with salesmanship, discovered by the foreign tourist trade.

Italo Calvino says that Apulian folktales are informed by the "enjoyment of grotesque malformation," and that is no wonder, given the nature of trulli, which are both bizarre and cozy, fantastic and very much of the earth, organic. Racy Apulian folktales are full of witty transformations: A man changed by a wizard into a pigeon transforms himself by dint of cleverness into a horse, who then, to escape his wizard/master, becomes an eel, whereupon the master becomes a conger and the eel a dove, whereupon the master/conger becomes a falcon in order to catch the dove, and the dove becomes a ring which drops between the breasts of a princess, a ring by day, a man by night.

"Folktales," Calvino says, "are real." They catalog potential destinies, the trials of achieving maturity and a full humanity. They are psychologically apt, of course; but Italian folktales also owe a great deal to social realities, to history and to class. In the folktales of southern Italy there are frequent imprecations against Saracens and murderous French kings, for in common with the rest of the South, Puglia has had many masters—among them Romans, Swabians, Normans, Angevins, Saracens. The lives of Apulians, which must have seemed to them predestined, were formed by forces complex and (to them) unknown, alien (ogres and ogresses are everybody's next-door neighbors in these tales). They must often have felt themselves to be under a spell, for they were not free men. Freedom—salvation, triumph, and beauty—contingent, in these tales, as Calvino says, upon "fidelity to a goal and purity of heart," is the breaking of the spell: Men who are awake—fully human and fully themselves—are free.

The appearance of a falcon (always representing evil in Apulian folktales) is interesting; Frederick II, who had hunting lodges throughout the South, loved falconry. Caves and underground vaults also make frequent appearances in southern Italian folktales. One can easily explain them, as Jung does, as metaphors of a descent into the subconscious or unconscious; but it is also true that southern Italians in fact often do (or did, in less prosperous times) live in caves or cavelike structures, huts.

Norman Douglas writes of the anchorites "whose dwellings honeycombed the warm slopes that confront the Ionian," of rock hermits who distrusted sunshine and an ordered social life, "their foul dieting, their dread of malign spirits, their cave-dwelling propensities. . . . This retrogression towards primevalism," he says, "must have possessed a certain charm, for it attracted vast multitudes." He seems to have believed that living in caves or cavelike structures was a kind of pathology, whereas Bachelard says: "The hermit is *alone* before God. . . . And there radiates about this centralized solitude a universe of meditation and prayer, a universe outside the universe." Underground living was in fact governed in part by the rigors of climate and also in part by psychic necessity, a necessity that modern man shares: Why do we build houses with garrets and cellars? (Jung asks us to imagine the house—attic and cellar—as a kind of picture of our mental structure; the cellar, or the cave, is our unconscious.) One lives in cellars (caves, huts, underground vaults) for practical and for psychological (and not necessarily for pathological) reasons; and these factors converge in folktales, the staying power of which is that they can be read—as life itself can and must be read—on more than one level. Folktales are memory and legend, the unconscious and history, melded.

The roof of a cave recalls the dome of the sky; the Pantheon is a kind of cave—enclosed space open to the sky.

* * *

In every house into which my paternal (Calabrian) grandparents and their children moved, the cellar or basement was immediately transformed into heart and pulsing center; and this was true of every Italian family I knew (one didn't, at that time, say southern or northern Italian; all immigrants were, or were assumed to be, from the South). I did not think of this then, nor do I now, as a disinclination for sunlight. . . . The sunlight that filtered through the leaves of the mulberry bush into the slivers of windows was warming and prismatic. The hatch doors that opened onto steps that led to the cellar had a quotidian magic; they ushered one into a world inside the world. In Grandma Rosie's basement there was a stove on which the Sunday "gravy" (the tomato sauce) simmered, and taralli danced in bubbling oil (these ring-shaped cakes appear in Italy's version of "Red Riding Hood"; the Jordan River has a weakness for them and enjoys twirling them in his whirlpools). There was a Victrola: "Don't Sit Under the Apple Tree with Anyone Else but Me," the Andrews Sisters sang; "ap-pa-la tree," Grandma echoed. There were fat wicker chairs and a round oak table; the floor was stone. On the round oak table there was a lamp with panels of blue glass, yellow glass, and rose-colored glass; on each panel was etched a boy in a rowboat, fishing—fishing, according to which panel one concentrated one's gaze on, at sunrise, sunset, noonday. This lamp still lights my memory; by thinking of it, I recall the past. One day at that table Grandma's next-door neighbor spoke of her husband. "Mr. Smith . . ." she said, as someone might say in a book; no one in my family ever called her husband *Mister.* No one in Mr. Smith's family had a basement like ours. (This taught me that there were all kinds of magic.) Best of all was the room behind the door that led to the subbasement. Grandma stored overnight the fresh cheese she made there weekly—we called it Thursday cheese—and the buckets of blood for blood sausage, blood pudding. That room smelled musty, sweet. Old schoolbooks were piled high here ("Pasqualina, her book"), and sheet music and old magazines, yellow and brittle, that no one—I found this kindness to inanimate objects reassuring—could bear to throw out. I went here for comfort, the comfort of confronting a manageable world alone; for fantasy.

In the closet on the bedroom floor silverfish darted in and out of Grandma's high-topped shoes. My aunts' bedroom opened onto a vine-covered terrace Grandpa built, a terrace from which I could see Coney Island and the World's Fair parachute ride, a fair part of the world.

The living room and the formal dining room went unused. The furniture in these rooms was always shrouded in white sheets except when a special visitor came to call. I thought the furniture must be made of gold.

When Aunt Lulu died of rheumatic fever—she was twenty-three—she was laid out in that (quite commonplace) living room, heavy with the mingled scent of flowers and candlewax and incense, in a yellow dress. They would not let me come down to see her. The smell rose up to me, and the sound of wailing. I crept down the stairs one night. I do not know what governed my flower-overwhelmed, excited senses. Perhaps it was the memory of one sunny Sunday afternoon when I helped Aunt Lulu—who'd made my mother's wedding gown—pin to her dressmaker's dummy the yellow taffeta gown which she now wore. With one finger I touched the face on the satin pillow, and then I vomited.

Whenever I think of this, my mind runs from it, and for comfort's sake, I am down again in the basement, watching the little boy fish, sunrise, sunset, bright noon; the sauce simmers and the Andrews Sisters sing "Don't Sit Under the Apple Tree with Anyone Else but Me."

In folktales, deaths are matter-of-fact, trenchant, remorseless, unsentimental—and quick. (So are the harsh facts of unredeemed life: "They sat down and ate and drank their fill, while here we are, dying of thirst.") "Coat me with pitch and burn me to death in the center of the town square," says the ugly Saracen, her wickedness unmasked. "So it was done"—with dispatch. Pappy Ogre is stabbed by seven good brothers with seven bread knives till he looks "like a strainer." In an Apulian variation on Cinderella, the hard-working stepdaughter is rewarded by a family of cats (who live in a house in a hole in the ground) with rings for all her fingers. The lazy daughter's fingers are covered with grasping worms. When the bad girl tries to look up into the great world above, a blood sausage falls on her face and hangs over her mouth, and she is obliged to nibble it constantly: "And from eating blood sausage day in, day out, the girl died." Her good sister marries (for these tales never end until the hero or heroine achieves maturity) a handsome youth.

Everyone gets his just deserts, just as foibles, preferences, and harmless eccentricities—eccentricities that don't threaten the social order—are accepted without undue moralizing: "Whoever wanted to eat, ate; whoever didn't want to, didn't." (It is not possible to read these words without visualizing an eloquent Italian shrug.)

These tales portray an orderly universe. No ultimate consequences are arbitrary or decried. Bad things happen. Justice triumphs. This is a universe as comforting as a well-loved, loving house.

* * *

The day is fresh and clear; we are the beneficiaries of a cyclone that hit Bari a few days ago. We leave the *autostrada* at Gioia del Colle, a busy market town of pastel buildings and lacy balconies, and drive, as the sun sets, on roads of red clay through fields of myrtle and chestnut and vineyards and orchards; low walls made of stone without mortar divide small, tidy family farms; from these friendly gray walls rise gnarled olive trees, silvery gray, timeless, comforting—a benign landscape.

Ahead, on two hills divided by a hollow, is Alberobello, a forest of man-made cones making no threat to the sky.

It is generally supposed that trulli were built without mortar so that they could be demolished immediately—overnight—in case of royal inspection, and taxes could thereby be withheld from the crown, this upon order of Count Giangirolamo Acquaviva, the *guercio,* or "one-eyed man," of Puglia. This feudal overlord—who by this decree ensured that peasants and shepherds would be completely dependent upon him—was not a pleasant fellow. He often shot at the water pitchers women carried on their heads (he seems to have suffered from boredom); sometimes he missed and shot the women instead. He skinned monks alive. The trulli are thought to have evolved from tumuli, or mounds, under which prehistoric tribes of Asia Minor—whose rudimentary utensils and arrows have been unearthed in Puglia—buried their dead. A trullo may present itself to the imagination as a Pyramid domesticated and brought to human scale. . . . To numbers of visitors it has seemed, instead, like a fairy-tale dwelling; for them, neither the Pyramids nor the Orient but Snow White and the Seven Dwarfs come to mind.

A man in black sits alone in the middle of a scorched field.

At a crossroads there are two wooden signs, one pointing west, the other east. Both signs point to the same town, Putignano.

These minor but indecipherable oddities do not seem inappropriate in the land of trulli. When one comes upon them in the dusk, it is hard to think of trulli as inanimate shells. There are single trulli, trulli clustered in the middle of neat farms—a trullo house, toolshed, animal refuge—whimsical variations on a single shape. As we near Alberobello, the trulli appear in groups of two and three, sometimes linked by grape arbors, the conical roof sometimes surmounting a cube, sometimes a circular house; sometimes large cones unite a variety of whitewashed shapes.

The first trulli, so far as historians are able to determine, rose directly from the ground in concentric circles toward the summit. Now, in this land of ancient trulli, a newly constructed trullo might have mortar, shutters, or decorative ironwork; there is great and pleasing diversity within this uniformity; sometimes the top rows of concentric, irregular stones forming the cone are whitewashed, sometimes not; chimneys are sometimes whitewashed, sometimes not. The cylindrical keystone that caps the dome is sometimes unadorned, sometimes surmounted by stone carved in the shape of a ball, a pyramid, a multidimensional star, a quarter moon. The Trullo Sovrano (Sovereign Trullo) has two stories; it consists of twelve trulli under one dome, the highest (fourteen meters) in Alberobello. There are "gentrified" trulli—trulli incorporated into new buildings—and there are new buildings that are given an extrinsic trullo "skin"; a church, Sant'Antonio, tries prettily but unsuccessfully to assume the outward flourishes of a trullo.

Mock trulli are kitschy. Old trulli are dignified; they are also poignant— perhaps because the lower, whitewashed portion of the trullo is little more than the height of a man, which makes both man and building seem vulnerable.

One would expect, if one believed that houses conformed to the people who lived in them, people of grace and wisdom and fortitude to come out of trulli. Old ladies in black sit in front of the recessed window arches and stone doorways and natter; they shell peas. Boxes of detergent rest on recessed windows; girdles flap on clotheslines.

Laura says this is phallic architecture; she is thinking of the cones. I say it is maternal space; I am thinking of the rounded lower portions. In fact it is a combination of both male and female principles, a pleasing aesthetic.

On the southern hill of Alberobello are the Rione Monti and the Rione Aia Piccola; in these protected *rioni,* or districts (which have been declared national monuments), there are 1,030 and 400 trulli respectively, all ancient, pure, but also various. The government forbids the demolition or the defacement of these structures and decrees that any new building in these districts be constructed in the same style and with the same materials as ancient trulli.

Variety within uniformity—the trulli are a metaphor for that kind of unlimited freedom within strict bounds that is the appeal of religious discipline, the antithesis of the prison of absolute freedom.

There are groups of new trulli that one immediately classifies as "suburban." These trulli have garages. There is a lipstick-red trullo, and one—an art gallery—pretty and precious in its hollyhock garden, with doors of lime and windows of clover. There is a traditional trullo with a large sign: NO JEHOVAH'S WITNESSES WELCOME HERE.

A cone is a shape belonging to a witch.

Immaculate houses flanking narrow streets in an immaculate town—one would like to see the trulli covered with snow, Alberobello white on white.

Before we sleep, we wander through clusters of trulli; in the daylight we will wonder whether to call this place camp (and decide not to give way to our fear of liking what is quaint); at night the flower-splashed trulli on preternaturally quiet, well-lit courtyards seem enchanted as well as enchanting.

It is good, after this, to come back to our modest hotel with its mundane view of a parking lot, its solid functional furniture, its aspidistra, beige walls, television lounge, tea and spinsters.

In fact there is nothing "cute" about trulli, the temptation to think of them as cute—which must arise from our delight in being contained among them coupled with our disbelief that such buildings could exist at all— notwithstanding; they rise from the ground with convincing logic.

Our pleasant hotel is two piazze away from the landmark *rioni.* (We climb past a piazza which seems determined not to borrow from the trullo aes- thetic—Valium over the counter and the latest Parisian perfumes in a phar- macy of conventional architecture.) In the piazza that opens up to the Rione Monti there are shops that sell plates on which trulli are painted; glass "snowballs" with little trulli on which confetti snow drifts (it is not in my heart to find these wonderfully manipulable sealed worlds offensive); grappa with miniature trulli inside the bottles; hot-pink trulli and electric-blue trulli that glow in the dark; trulli overwhelmed by giant mushrooms in colors that never existed, suggesting that the trulli are the habitations of elves or trolls. But (although Lizzie and Anna insist upon chanting, "It's trulli-trulli land, it's trulli-trulli land . . ." Laura: "Is that truly-trulli land or trulli-trulli land? I ask only because I like to know") this is not Munchkinland. (It is estimated that there are five thousand inhabitants in the protected areas alone.)

We are invited into trulli in the Monti quarter. The inside of the cone— into which it would be nice to gaze and to dream—is often sealed off, with an opening for a ladder; this is storage space. Horizontal architectural sup- ports—logs—are used as shelves. In one trullo we enter open space used as living and dining area; the rest of the trullo has been sectioned off by means of curtains for use as bedrooms. There is a tiny kitchen, plumbing, an open hearth. The walls are white inside as well as out. (One would like to see a bright red fire against these pure white walls.) The old woman whose house this is shows us her backyard—a jumble of fig trees, pots and pans, buckets and brooms and freshly laundered clothes—and she shows us pictures of her daughters, who look distant and soignée, one, she says, in Switzerland, the other in Yugoslavia. . . . This is not Munchkinland . . . but it would be hard, we agree, to describe growing up in a trullo to a potential mate without making it sound like a joke.

How could those daughters, how could anyone, have resisted the urge to write graffiti on all those receptive white surfaces?

The old woman accepts our thanks, our lire, and our kisses. Something in her body response to a kiss tells me she has not been touched for a very long time.

I think she invites wanderers into her trullo to show them the pictures of her daughters, though she may think she is governed by other motives.

"I would like to lie down in a trullo with a vault of gold and there dream," D'Annunzio wrote. One can rent a trullo for a holiday, a nice idea. A trullo is a kind of cave.

If one were so to dream, would one's dreaming mind, neatly confined, circle and circle, spiral and spiral, till it came at last to a fine point of rest and equilibrium?

There is a hotel fashioned after a trullo. It is posh, and it has no magic. It would not be nice to stay in this ersatz place. We had a bad meal there. There was no one in the serpentine swimming pool. A small boy climbed over a wall topped with shards of bottle glass to swim in it. A young waiter, to whom we'd given a generous tip, slapped the boy's face and humiliated him—for his entertainment, one supposes—and then stamped with sadistic pleasure on the child's sandal, smiling a twisted smile at us all the while.

At our own hotel the proprietress, who wears silks from Kuala Lumpur, says she is in exile in Alberobello, she is *triste*. Every night she oversees our meals: chicory with fava beans; orecchiette (little ears), pasta made of semolina mixed with durum wheat served with *cime di rape* (a bitter green known to Italian-Americans by its dialect name, broccolirab'); beef and pork stews simmered for hours; spaghetti with goats' livers spiced with red peppers; a spongy bread that is like whole wheat bagels.

The receptionist says the worst thing he ever did was to leave Rome, his wife cries all the time, she does not want to die among trulli, he is *triste*.

One is not used to seeing churches in the Art Nouveau, or Liberty, style. In the pretty Church of Sant'Antonio there is an altar mural in which a cross is transformed into a tree, an Art Nouveau tree; and Peter and Paul appear in flowing Nouveau togas; and Eve's tresses resemble those of a Maxfield

Parrish wood nymph (and this is captivating); and the two cubicle confessionals are Deco-severe; and in white neon is the name of Mary.

Next door to this charming church is a kind of museum, a sad and lifeless place that houses incoherent bits and pieces that remind one of bad poetry, symbols that symbolize nothing: a Victrola, 1930s men's suits, a blue umbrella propped to no effect against a brown wall, a brass bed, a black Madonna, horses' paraphernalia (saddles and spurs), religious kitsch—pictures of a bloody Christ framed in beads and in seashells tortured into the shape of flowers—and cooking implements, and (the sole apparent reason for the museum's existence) a chart detailing amateurishly the stylized symbols *(Primitivi, Magici, Cristiani)* brushed on trulli domes.

In front of Sant'Antonio and this odd little museum, we are startled to see an ugly, clever-looking monkey dressed in overalls and sneakers, its face more intelligent than that of its owner, who sells photographs of the monkey and a little boy in twin poses—crouching, pants split to reveal buttocks and scrotum. Laura thinks this is homosexual pornography. However that may be, there is nothing good-natured or amusing in it; it turns us against the trulli, which we begin to perceive as a joke perpetrated on us.

A plumed horse trots around the main piazza, carrying happy children eating ices in the decorated wagon it pulls. I remember riding, on warm summer evenings, in just such a wagon—a converted ice truck, benches lined up on the sides—on Grandma Rosie's street. The memory of this innocent diversion restores me to good spirits; but Laura is now inclined to file the trulli in her mind as camp—which shows on what fine threads perception hangs.

Laura, Lizzie, Anna, and I have our hair done in a beauty parlor next to a trullo. Lucia, Francesca, and Bianca, three generations of townswomen, come in to gossip and chat. Everything about this ritual—sybaritic, homely, calming—is as familiar to us as bread. It is a kind of comfy communion. I often have my hair done when I am in foreign countries but it is not to have my hair done that I have my hair done.

If there were a contest for the most beautiful town in Italy—a task from which King Solomon might shrink—Locorotondo would surely be a contender, for no corner of the Old City is ugly, as befits a circular town on a round hill. Nine kilometers southeast of Alberobello, Locorotondo rises from the green Murge; dazzlingly white, it seems to rest suspended on a round plate. Its two-story houses are whitewashed twice a year; their steeply pitched limestone gray roofs look as if they might have come from a northern country, the north of England perhaps; the town is flooded with Mediterranean light. This is architecture and town planning that exemplifies the music of geometry, the poetry of shadow and light. A circle is also a maze: The white houses, with their purple, pink, blue, green shutters, their oiled and polished doors, their balconies luxurious with overhanging flowering plants, are set in urban proximity one to another on winding narrow streets, and—as they, like the neighboring trulli, are expressive of individuality within conformity—form unexpected communal courtyards, surprising angles and cutoffs and projections. External staircases provide an additional dimension, another canvas for the play of sunlight and shade. There are no cars in the historical center of Locorotondo; there are pots of plants—not only on balconies but on staircases and grouped on the flat and shiny checkerboard limestone pavement. This is an act of trust, justified; no one will hurt or steal the flowers. Flowers inhabit space and are allies in human habitation. To walk into a maze (for one cannot be in a circular town without trying to find its center or heart) is a gratifying adventure and also an act of trust, but very little faith is required, for the embrace of this town is gentle; one breathes easy.

A child whizzes into a courtyard on a skateboard; he circles around pots of pink flowers.

It is lovely to walk from the street to the stair, or from the street to the door, without the introduction of a curb or fence; it adds to the feeling of communality when one can reach out to touch a beautiful shining doorknob on a house that is without the usual urban defenses. There is nothing barbed or prickly in this town, no apparent demarcation between private and public land.

Perhaps, as some historians and engineers conjecture, the shape and plan of Locorotondo (which a child could trace easily on a map, circles within circles) are analogous to those of a large fortress, surrounded by bulwarks and towers, walls and banks. What was once contained by force is happily contained now, militaristic security having been replaced by emotional security: This is a town in which one feels innocent. The straight, narrow houses with their steep roofs, their central door and symmetrical windows are the kinds of houses a child draws when asked to draw: HOUSE.

There are hanging wrought-iron lamps. There are occasional ocher stone doorposts of Neapolitan Baroque, a satyr's face. (Locorotondo's history is rich; it starts with the Norman Conquest. The town was once under the protection of a Benedictine abbey, later came under the jurisdiction of the Knights of Malta, still later was an outpost of the Republic of Venice.)

For all this, for all its light and charm and uncomplicated beauty, Locorotondo is not a comic-opera town; it has great dignity (it is totally without the boorishness of self-advertisement), and it has a kind of reserve, suitable to a town of houses apparently undefended. The orderliness, which is a form of good manners, of this urban design imposes good manners on those who are privileged to live and to visit here. (Italians have vacation houses here.) The houses leading circularly to the heart of Locorotondo—the heart of Locorotondo is a church, the Church of San Giorgio Martire—speak of the integrity that attaches to following logical, organic rules. Locorotondo is Casbah-inviting, but—though white light is the enemy of secrets—ineffably secretive. It is odd that lives lived in structures so accessible, and unbarricaded, so literally close at hand, should seem more mysterious than lives that are lived behind iron bars. One is tempted to believe that the more proximate a life is, the more mysterious it is. Indeed, Locorotondo is the exception to the rule that in Italy outside is inside: Life is lived behind closed doors here, on roof gardens, or in the protective shadows of archways, discreetly, not boisterously.

A girl sails by on a bicycle and turns a corner into concealing white light.

So far as is known, Geoffrey, Count of Conversano, nephew of Robert Guiscard, the Crusader, founded the Benedictine Abbey of St. Stephen in 1086, giving the monastery, as dowry, the hamlet of San Giorgio, which hamlet, it is believed, occupied the site that is now Locorotondo. The mother church of Locorotondo, San Giorgio Martire, has been rebuilt and expanded several times, most recently in 1828; each time construction materials have been taken from the same piazza, the name of which, changed over the years, cloudily mirrors Italian history: First called the Square of the Holy Spirit or St. Peter's Square, it was then called the Square of the Fascist Revolution, later Piazza Roma; and it is today Piazzo Moro, after Aldo Moro, whose memory is not allowed to die.

St. George, the dragon slayer, suffered martyrdom in Palestine; he was dragged through the streets and beheaded. The beast he killed required daily sacrifices of two sheep. One day, when the supply of sheep had run out, a human victim was sent to appease the foul beast. The victim, chosen by lot, was the daughter of the king. She greeted her fate in the raiments of a bride. St. George subdued the dragon and led it, as if it were a tame dog, by the girdle of the princess, back to the city. After the inhabitants of the city agreed to be baptized—fifteen thousand men were—St. George killed the dragon with his lance.

In the Middle Ages St. George was the patron of knights and of Crusaders; the saint revered as the personification of Christian chivalry continues to be the patron of soldiers and of archers and is also called upon against leprosy, plague—and syphilis. Some irony lies in the fact that the Palestinian soldier-saint is the symbol of English nationalism: His red cross appears on the Union Jack, and the Order of the Garter was founded by Edward III under his patronage. His sculpted image appears in the Church of the Madonna della Greca in Locorotondo; the most famous Renaissance paintings of St. George have found their way out of Italy—Uccello's to London's National Gallery and Raphael's to Washington's National Gallery of Art.

In actual fact, very little is known about St. George, save that he may have been an officer in the army of Diocletian. His popularity, one is bound to assume, owes less to the man than to the dragon. The dragon, or serpent, or crocodile—all creatures lethal, submerged, and ultimately subdued—appears in different forms all over Italy, and has since before the Christian era. The dragon was a metaphor in search of a complement. The dragon as thesis demanded antithesis; it found complement and antithesis in the chivalrous St. George (who, according to late myth, married the princess whose safety and salvation he secured). That St. George pierced the dragon with his lance and tamed it with the princess's girdle is a Freudian flourish on a Jungian fable, a fable in which it is through the offices of a virgin, dressed as a bride, that men are brought to their salvation.

In the deconsecrated Church of the Madonna della Greca just outside the Old City there is a stone Madonna exposing one nipple; the Baby Jesus searches for the other. When cholera struck Locorotondo in 1867, this church was used as a burial place, after which its doors and windows were walled up, not to be reopened till 1893; it was also at that time renovated, as a consequence of which it lost all architectural distinction. Every window in the square in which it stands is covered with a crocheted curtain.

Locorotondo was spared from the pestilence that raged in Puglia in 1690 and 1691 and for this gave thanks to St. Rocco, its patron. In the Church of San Rocco, which has one pitched roof and one trullo roof, St. Rocco, who is black, stands on a palanquin wearing what appears to be a frilly lace garter. St. Rocco, a hermit, miraculously recovered from the plague (he was fed in the forest by a dog) and thereafter cured others. His waning popularity was restored when cholera struck in the nineteenth century—another example of Italian pragmatism. Locorotondo has not one but two saints between it and the plague.

Laura and Lizzie and Anna and I are in the information office in the small square—Piazza Vittorio Emanuele—just inside the Old City gates. The town is very quiet, almost deserted. Laura, who claims at times to have witchy powers (a claim that causes Lizzie no small annoyance, all children, of course, wanting nothing more from their parents than ordinariness), says, "Something is happening. Something is wrong." Moments after she speaks we hear in the distance a dirge, measured, mournful, and sweet. So narrow are the streets emptying into the funnel formed by the piazza that we hear the echo of the music—brass bouncing off white—almost before we hear the music itself. A cry resounds in the piazza: "Shut the door! Shut the door!" Doors are shut, iron gates and shutters rolled down. This is an expression of respect, for the music we hear is that of an approaching funeral procession. I open the door (which is wrong of me, one is meant to stay inside if one is not among the official mourners), to see a twenty-piece brass band wearing royal-blue uniforms and caps and gold buttons and epaulets, preceding a hearse of lacquered black with elaborate silver curlicues; inside the hearse there is an open coffin made of olive wood lined with brass and heaped with flowers. Many hands (Anna's the most persuasive) pull me back before I can see who rests inside. (I peek from a curtain, arousing the ire of Anna, who says one is bound by respect to sit inside in the dark "and feel creepy" and not to look outside "and get excited"; I am shamed but not sufficiently shamed to turn back.) The mourners immediately following the hearse wear black and weep; the marchers at the end of the long snaky line are considerably less solemn; at the very end of the line stragglers giggle and the procession resembles a *passeggiata,* everyone comradely and pleased.

The shutters are rolled up and life goes on as if nothing had happened; people are a little livelier, that is all—it's good to be alive.

On the way back to Alberobello we pass, through an avenue of gothic funereal pines, a cemetery. And I, against the protestations of Laura and Lizzie, who are made nervous by what they perceive to be my deep vein of morbidity, stop. I always find these rows of rectangular "drawers," these stacked marble boxes—in this case a grid four drawers high and twenty-eight across—so pretty. A latter-day version of the pigeonholes or small concave shelves in which the Romans placed the ashes of their dead, they are like a honeycomb for the dead; they please me. I like the eloquent photographs of the dead that adorn them, the receptacles of silver and old glass that hold fresh flowers; I feel kinship here, a necessary transaction between space and death and bodies. But Laura and Lizzie and Anna see the yawning holes into which coffins have not yet been placed and sealed behind marble slabs, and, recalled to the fact that they must someday die—a fact which, as it applies to myself, I find bemusing—they hurry me on.

How much we are—in Puglia it is impossible to forget this—of the earth.

We are in the Grotto of Castellana, below land governed for centuries by Benedictines and for six hundred years by abbesses, making our guided way through a network of subterranean passages a mile long and three hundred feet deep, corridors of alabaster, curtains of peach-and-green stalagmites, rooms of blond crystal, lakes of coral, halls of gold, flower beds of ice and jade—caves known in the Middle Ages but fully explored only in 1940 (every once in a while one comes across evidence that Mussolini was good for something).

In the part of the grotto called the Great Grave there is an opening to the sky, and sunlight together with a light misty rain enters the half-light of the Grave, a shaft of sunlight like that which we see in illuminated Bibles, in a pool of which (this is a memory from childhood) a young David dressed in white, a saint dressed in vermilion, kneels to pray.

Hearty guides lead and follow us, those in the rear ready to succor the weak of heart (of whom I am one); at their signal the chambers before us are eerily illuminated by electricity, the lights in those we have already traversed are doused, and this journey from primeval dark to artificial light causes palpitations not physical in origin. Shadows flicker on dark walls.

Some call these caverns—and in particular the Grotta Bianca (the heart of a world of glowing ice)—the most beautiful in the world; I do not like it here. Perhaps it is the bats. *Pipistrello* is a pretty name for bat; but a bat is a bat by any name, and the sick-sweet smell of bats is here, the tiny flapping of innumerable wings. Perhaps it is the memory of the one fairy tale that in childhood frightened me: the Snow Kingdom, wherein the Snow Queen froze little boys and girls with an icy glare and kept them in her thrall forever. But perhaps it is neither of these; it is the absolute compulsion, among the needles and forests of stalactites and stalagmites (the flora of the unconscious), to use metaphor to light a buried world, to see formations resembling the familiar contents of our lives and conscious minds. The unconscious takes a lantern when it goes to the cellar of the world. Here, says the guide, is the Virgin; here Mussolini—practically the only time one ever hears Mussolini mentioned in Italy is in a watery grotto or a cave, here his face lives on; here is a she-wolf, a crèche, here a camel, a Buddha, a dog (and dental plaque, says Lizzie, whose braces plague her), a cobra (says Anna, who grew up in India in the belief that cobras protected good children), Popsicles, phalluses. As a cave itself is a metaphor, the metaphors heaped upon metaphors place one in the emotional equivalent of a hall of mirrors.

A prudent man, says Jung, does not dare venture into the cellar. This is the cellar of the world; and we prefer gardens. We have seen enough of caves.

In a souvenir shop, eschewing crystal, we buy bangles made of olive wood.

In my dreams of trulli, the cones are made of crystal and I see through them to a shining white city on a hill which is Jerusalem. Ancient women dressed in black come out of the trulli; they wear Coptic crosses and Oriental turbans; they look like my grandmother.

Chapter VIII

CALABRIA:

BETWEEN TWO SEAS

It's easy enough that on a balcony
or in a window frame a woman pauses . . . to be
the one we lose
just by seeing her appear.

And if she lifts her arms
to tie her hair, tender vase:
how much our loss gains
a sudden emphasis,
our sadness brilliance!

> —*Rainer Maria Rilke, "The Roses and the*
> *Windows," translated from the French by*
> *A. Poulin, Jr.*

Is it anything true? Does it grow upon the ground?

> —*Gerard Manley Hopkins,*
> *"Rosa Mystica"*

We are driving through Magna Graecia, that part of Italy colonized by Greece centuries before the birth of Christ, land that was the meeting place of Hellenic, Byzantine, and Roman culture. Hannibal's boots and Hannibal's elephants marched across these mountains, these vast plateaus. These hills, honeycombed with caves, these dark, unexploited forests, were home to brigands, and to anchorites who lived on mortification and on air. But we are not of a scholarly disposition as we make our way between sea and shining sea. The soft breezes from the Ionian on the one hand and the Tyrrhenian on the other cocoon us; the landscape is an envelope for our thoughts, not alien, not confrontational—protective.

We pass stands of sun-dried tomatoes, strings of puckered red peppers, and next to them violet morning glories and creamy garlic in vellum jackets. We drive under immaculate skies on the rim of mountains overlooking blue hills and dark-green forests and high golden pastures into what seems like infinite, seamless space; this land has no horizons our minds and eyes can perceive. Golden eagles soar. We are in this world, so various, so beautiful, and every-morning new, and we are of it, happy and secure, having earned our happiness and security through love: for we have loved the Mezzogiorno and live at psychic high noon.

Driving along the Gulf of Taranto, we are in the area of Metaponto, site of the lost city of Metapontum, where, according to legend, Pythagoras once lived and Cicero later visited (the Greeks introduced wheat, olives, and the vine to Campania, Apulia, Basilicata, and Calabria, though it hurts one's pride to say so). My imagination cannot people these tobacco fields and this coastal land with temples and navies and docks and marketplaces. The sea, the seductive Ionian, calls.

We have rounded the Gulf of Taranto and are now in Basilicata, that narrow region north of Calabria known also as Lucania; in ancient times, if a stranger arrived at sunset and wished to spend the night here, a refusal to oblige him resulted in the imposition of a fine. The mountains meander to the shore.

In this part of God's beautiful world, the marinas are named for parent villages a mile or two away in the hills. So it is with Nova Siri on the shore, where the Pollino mountain chain abruptly and sweetly ends, as conclusively and nicely as stone can meet water, a dignified and happy marriage; and we have found greater hospitality here than we had hoped to expect.

Nothing remains of the cultivated Greek city of Siris (rival to Sybaris, the city of worldly delights), of which Athenaeus wrote: "There is no spot on earth so sweet, so lovely, so to be desired as the banks of that stream upon which Siris stands." In the seventh century it was called the richest and happiest of cities, uniting commerce and art. In 1828, when (at the age of twenty-four) Craufurd Tait Ramage, tutor to the sons of the British consul in Naples, traveled through southern Italy, he found here, on the banks of the river Sinno, a spot "finely wooded, and covered with a profusion of flowers in full blossom . . . a perfect paradise. . . . Numerous flowering creepers hung in graceful festoons from the branches of the poplar; the underwood consisting of the lentiscus, thorn, wild vine, oleander, arbutus, the sweet bay. The dwarf oak abounds everywhere along this coast, and the liquorice plant grows wild and in great luxuriance. . . ." The beauty of the flowers led Ramage to suppose that he was standing in the gardens of Heracleia, the seat of the general council of Greek states, the Hellenic city in which both Stoicism and the idea that mathematics was a way to contemplate God took root.

We found no flowery wilderness (no wild buffalo and "untamed horses . . . galloping through open glades"); we found a playground instead.

Between the world wars it seemed to Gertrude Slaughter as to many observers that all of Calabria, coast and mountains, would become a playground—"and such a one as we have never dreamed of. For there can indeed be few provinces of Europe lovelier or nobler than this, with its great mountain ranges covered with primeval forest, miles of glorious woodland, and an air so soft and yet so exhilarating that no other hills in Europe can boast the like." It was supposed that once the broken rocky coastland of Calabria had been cured of the scourge of malaria, the Ionian—whose name alone was bound to give it a certain allure—would become a new Italian Riviera. These prophecies have in some measure been fulfilled. And yet W. H. Auden and Elizabeth Mayer noted in their Introduction to Goethe's *Italian Journey* that they were "amazed at the similarity between pre–French Revolutionary Italy, which Goethe saw, and post–World War II Italy"; and Edith Clay writes, in her 1986 Note to the First American Edition of *Ramage in South Italy,* that "Ramage could easily find his way were he to start out again on his travels." We traveled through (and high above) woodlands by car, and not by mule; the exuberant loneliness of the landscape was much as Goethe had described it. The Ionian coast—with its stretches of fine white sand and charcoal-gray volcanic sand, its crystal waters, its posturing dramatic rocks, is a merry place (even solemn Milanesi, who drive like demons to get here, lose their inhibitions in Nova Siri), but because of certain physical and man-made anomalies—the train tracks, for example, are inter-posed between the beaches and the road (the silky air rumbles with the sound of passing trains)—it will never be chic and never be pretty; it is accessible, vibrant, gay—a kind of caravansary.

We were not prepared for a playground—a lido, striped umbrellas, discos on rocky promontories and a hotel of white-and-blue tiles, abundant food, and pleasure-seeking Italian guests. We had expected to find lodging in Rocca Imperiale, five kilometers south, across the Basilicata border in Ca-labria, near to which, in mountains high above the blue sea, my father had been born; and Rocca Imperiale had been described to me, rather grimly, by my father's sisters, as consisting of "a kind of hotel, a kind of castle, and a railroad station." From their general and jaundiced description, Rocca Imperiale, 119 kilometers from the provincial capital of Cosenza, seemed to justify Barzini's claim that tracks, in the South, "meandered all over the landscape," and trains stopped at obscure hamlets "only because a powerful person was born or owned a country residence there" or "to lengthen the mileage and enrich the contractor responsible for the construction."

My father's mother, Grandma Rosie, came from the inland village of Canna near Rocca Imperiale; my father's father, Grandpa Fredele, lived at a vertical remove in the nearby hamlet of Oriolo, higher in the high hills. My aunts had returned, thirty years ago, from a visit to Canna and Oriolo like weary combatants from the rubble of a lost war. The greed of their relatives was terrible, they said—nothing was safe from the acquisitive curiosity of their cousins; and the greasy, heavy food lay on their stomachs like fear. Lack of amenities obliged them to relieve themselves along with the animals in the cellar of their cousins' house. Oh! their tortured bowels. Bread indigestible as stone. It happened that while they were there, an edict came from Cosenza that the contents of chamber pots had henceforth not to be flung from the windows of bedchambers but emptied with care from back entries—in retaliation for which invasive command the population of Rocca Imperiale took to using the railroad tracks as a public lavatory, in which communal protest they were joined by the people of Canna and Oriolo—a strange procession of people on foot, people riding on mules and horses and in cars, organized disorder in tribute to the sanctity of the alimentary canal. . . .

Perhaps this story is apocryphal. I remember being told it as clearly as I remember my Aunt Esther's crying on December 7, 1941. . . . But, then, I remember wearing a red dress on that day when Pearl Harbor was bombed; I remember standing underneath the Christmas tree—and surely

we did not have a Christmas tree on December 7. Memory is telescopic.
. . . This story, true in its particulars or not, confirmed what I had always
believed to be true: that my father's family lived in hellish poverty and
ignorance, and that the landscape of poverty was colored brown—like the
halls of tenement buildings, the chocolate-colored painted banisters; and
the water closet, a tall, narrow, spider-haunted place cramped and lit by a
naked bulb, a stingy place, which, for all its narrowness, discouraged privacy. (My mother examined my stools; I do not know what she expected
to find, a beautiful woman in her twenties peering into the toilet for
evidence . . . for evidence of what?)

I had thought of Calabria as a place where bald mountains held you in
a vise, a place of unyielding rock, of bent people who lived in dank caves;
here Grandma Rosie had twelve children, of whom five grew to adulthood—she was a midwife when she was fifteen; here her husband grew to
be the man who became a mercenary, a man who strapped his children to
the fire escapes, in heat and cold, of the dark building on Mulberry Street,
for punishment. Here my father was born—and of those first ten years of
his life, before he came to America, he never spoke.

Daddy and Uncle Lenny married; the girls did not: Aunt Lulu, on whose
deathbed in the room with the view of the Coney Island parachute ride I
played jacks, dead at twenty-three of rheumatic fever; Aunt Lena, who
whistled and made birdcalls and who paid herself the compliment of saying
she had "a terrific 'p' "—a sunny disposition, a happy personality—dead at
sixty-nine of Alzheimer's disease; Aunt Betty, gallantly enduring the sadness
of being the last, all the funerals behind her, one long funeral procession,
stone upon stone piled upon stone, Aunt Lulu, Uncle Lenny, Daddy, Aunt
Lena, Grandma Rosie, Grandpa Fred. . . . What does it mean for an Italian
immigrant family to conquer poverty with a united front? What does it
mean to keep all one's money, and all one's emotional capital, in the family?
. . . I can't subject my family to sociological inquiry, I do not want to go
to Calabria, five kilometers away, I like it here in Nova Siri, where the sun
shines. . . . One of my aunts once told me she never went to Confession—
"And what would I have to confess, missy? I never have anything to
confess." This is one of the most amazing and one of the saddest statements
I have ever heard. . . . Grandpa died of cancer of the throat "and behaved
very well," Betty and Lena said, as if the goodness of one's death were judged
by the amount of trouble one caused one's survivors (whereas in fact it
resides in the disposition of one's soul). . . . Grandma, in her last years, left
her false teeth on the toilet tank every night, to be seen by her protesting

daughters in the morning; and whether this was an act of forgetfulness or of retaliation—and if so, retaliation for what?—is one of those small riddles, essential to understanding, that are unsolvable. She died of having lived. The day her final illness began (it began, of course, at the moment of her birth, but it is not practical to think in these terms), my small children and I were in the country bungalow with her. . . . When I was a child in this house, every night she said to me: "Shut up, make the sign of the Cross, and go to bed," which, in Calabrian dialect, had the power of incantation. Her affection for me was expressed in terms of mild derision: "Pug nose, no can make a bed, no can cook, lazy pug nose." I must once have loved her, because—they say—when I was five years old and Grandma broke her leg, I walked to Dr. Goldberg's office miles away and asked him to teach me how to be a doctor and fix her. I always thought of her as broken. But she cleared land, heaved rocks over her shoulders to level ground around the bungalow when she was to my young eyes already old. She was not broken. Years later, dressed in black, she sat hunched in a corner on her rocker and banged her cane to express disapproval, and smiled. . . . And between these two images— the woman working and the woman-as-crone—I remember little. . . . The day her final illness began, my children and I had just returned from a swim in the lake and we were wearing swimsuits. Suddenly she is in bed, breathing stertorously, her legs splayed, hairpins scattered over the pillow, her gray hair greasy with age fanned out over the pillow, a rosary clutched in her hand. The neighbors, Italian all, are gathered around the bed. I do not know how they got there, how they knew to come. I am waiting for Betty and Lena to arrive. The neighbors say, "You aren't comfortable. Don't you want to change into something comfortable?" They mean: Take your swimsuit off, it isn't decent; but I can't decipher this (it is on account of such lapses that my family considers me not quite right in the head). All I could think of was: What will the children make of this, her womb has fallen, it protrudes from her vagina, what a terrible thing; what picture is being printed in their minds?

It was said that Grandma and Grandpa loved each other very much, but the evidence for this, from my point of view, is sparse. They seldom spoke to each other. Perhaps they spoke when they were alone. Perhaps they were parallelisms that did not or could not meet in speech; perhaps they had no need of speech. . . .

Memory is mockery. The water closet I hated—the one in which I performed in order to satisfy a test the nature of which I did not understand—the brown walls, the narrow stairs of tenements that smelled of fermenting wine belonged, in fact, not to my Calabrian grandparents but to my other set of grandparents, my mother's parents. By the time I'd come along, the houses where Grandma Rosie and Grandpa Fred and Betty and Lena and Lulu lived had pretty wallpaper and dainty cups, and Grandma Rosie embroidered flowers on fine silk bedclothes, and in these houses I received intimations that adults could be kind. Grandma's house smelled of Sunday gravy and of roses, and dirt was rooted out as if it were Original Sin. The country house was ringed about by pear and apple trees, by nature generous, warped into stinginess, pruned to within an inch of their flowery lives. Every Sunday Betty and Lena went out to "tidy up the forest." Memory is sludge. I saw Calabria as enemy. These are tricks of the mind for which there is no accounting. I could write a book about the summer day Aunt Lena and I made grape jelly, and I have perfect recall of the day I judged her to be clever and admirable because of the way she dexterously sliced bananas into the cornflakes (I was fascinated by the intelligence of her hands; I was eight); but I am unenlightened as to why she never married, I do not know the first thing about her inner life.

Perhaps my father followed her as he followed me. I tell it now as if it were a joke—my father following me from Brooklyn, hiding behind lamp-posts in Harlem where I went to hear my jazz musician, my first and very lovely lover, play at Minton's on 128th Street; my father hiding in the mean lobby of our apartment house, waiting, an impotent spy; my father crouched in the areaways of the uptown brownstones that housed the after-hours clubs we went to, a shadow among shadows; my father standing outside the bedroom of the first-floor apartment I'd rented on East Seventh Street when his vigilance began to crush me, standing outside the iron bars of my windows—my windows covered with opaque white soundproofing boards and heavy corduroy drapes which in the candlelight looked like velvet, to protect me from the world and him while I made love.

He fainted when he first saw that apartment. "If you tell me you're leaving home, I'll faint." I did, and he did. He fainted like other people sigh or sneeze; and in this way he terrorized me and my brother. (We tried to laugh our terror away; there was, after all, everything ludicrous about a father who could instruct himself to faint.) "When I have a daughter"—he played that song from *Carousel* and trembled and fainted, for we were not a happy family. "I hope you have lots of locks on your door," he said when my leaving had become a fact; and when he came to my apartment on East Seventh Street, he saw the locks ("Oh, my God! the locks!") and fainted—and fainted again when he saw my double bed. Something bubbled up in him, his eyes glazed over, he trembled, and he crashed. (My strongest fear, on the day I signed my divorce papers, was that my husband, in his unhappiness, would shake to death.)

My father shook, my mother monitored. She sat silently beside my bed and in the morning said: "What terrible things you say in your sleep." She said this the morning after the first night I made love.

And yet my mother's invasions, her tears, her heavy silences had not made me afraid of the Abruzzi, had inspired no dread of that ancestral land. I do not know why this is so.

Aunt Betty says that she and Aunt Lena were never alone with a man. My father was always there.

When we watched TV together, my father seldom took his eyes off my face, he needed to see what emotion I was registering. It was this as much as my taking a lover that caused me to rent the apartment on East Seventh Street. I fled from his love.

My mother's punishing silence would sorrow me forever. And yet it was Calabria I dreaded to see, my father's home.

There have been times in my life when I have thought: This is what it means to be an Italian woman: It means to suffocate.

And there have been times when I have said: Oh, if I had only been born in Calabria and had ten children, I do not want the pain that is peculiar to me.

All the way down the coast I said to Laura: "I'm sorry, I'm sorry. The hotel will be lousy, it'll all be poor, it will be just awful, I'm sorry."

Laura said, "Shut up. If you keep apologizing, you take away my right to get angry"—as if my apologies were a kind of preemptive strike. So we had a fight, while the girls stuck their feet out the windows and sang songs.

In Siri, which is in Basilicata, five kilometers away from Rocca Imperiale in Calabria, the air caresses my skin like satin and the light is liquid gold.

I feel as if a dark-brown curtain will descend when we cross over to Calabria.

"What a twit you are, Ma," Anna says.

"It can rain on one side of the street and not on the other," I say.

"What does that mean?" Anna, rapidly losing interest, asks.

"One day I went for a walk with my father and it was raining on one side of the street and not on the other. So for all we know the sun is not shining in Calabria."

"Lighten up, Anna Magnani," Anna says.

"That's who I should have been," I say gloomily, "Anna Magnani."

"I thought you always wanted to be Audrey Hepburn."

"Both."

"A raving twit," Anna says.

Above Grandma Rosie's bed hangs a picture of the Sacred Heart of Jesus. His heart looks like a radish with green stems. When I look at it my tongue hurts.

My father never spoke of his first ten years in Italy; but toward the end of his life he told me—he told my children—stories of his first years in America. They were always the same stories. I never interrupted the narrative to ask him questions. The stories were designed as much to obscure as to enlighten.

My father never went back to the land of his birth. He never went back to the Little Italy he left when he was sixteen either—not till my brother and I took him there when he was in his early seventies.

He sat in my brother's car, and his head, on its stalk of a neck (he had been ill; his collar was too loose for him), made quick, birdlike movements, side to side: He drank in the world like a child. Mott Street, Hester Street, Mulberry Street. He said that there were tunnels underneath these streets, used by rival Chinese gangs in the old Tong wars, and that he knew them all.

"You're making that up, Pop," my brother said.

"Possibly," my father said.

My father pored over the menu of the restaurant we took him to as Columbus must have pored over navigational charts. Ordering for him was like falling off the edge of the world; it committed him to spending money and, worse, to choice.

"Are you ready to order, Pop?"

"Possibly." My father never said an unequivocal Yes in his life.

(My father had, at some time in his life—probably during the Great

Depression—determined that twenty-five cents was a generous tip, and that was what he tipped, always, no matter what the occasion or the bill. My father, once he got hold of an idea or formed an attachment, never got free of it, particularly when money was involved. My mother bought a new fridge. My father flung his arms around the old one and cried that he loved it, he'd gotten used to it, it was his, no new fridge. He had to be pried off; it was not funny at the time. . . . This, all this, was a form of grief and nostalgia, not of miserliness; he could not bear change or loss.)

We took him to Luna, the day he went back to Little Italy, a restaurant on the block where he once lived. His mother had brought her bread to be baked in Luna's ovens when he was a child, and her holiday roasts. My brother and I were more excited about this closing of the space between the past and the present than he was. Perhaps it was too late for him to make sense of the past. *If the past exists, where is it?* Part of it was here, in this restaurant, but he did not seem to care. He looked mildly bewildered, perhaps because we—my brother and I—were not meant to be here, our presence reshaped the past and the stories of the past. . . .

These are the stories (always the same stories) he told:

He has stolen a bicycle. He is riding down a hill. At the bottom of the hill he crashes into a young man. He appears before a judge, who takes pity on him and awards him a pair of shoes and a suit, his first "American" clothes.

(In a variation on this story he is carrying a knife and has responded to his victim's noisy distress by threatening to slash him. In this version of the story he has not stolen the bike. . . . What never changes is the magnanimity of the judge.)

Every morning, Daddy said, he and Uncle Lenny went to the outdoor produce market, equipped with long, spiked poles, and they spiked and put in the burlap sacks they carried cabbages that rolled off trucks. Simply put, my father and his brother were stealing; it was not in their natures, which responded to necessity, to wait for cabbages to oblige them by rolling off. . . .

It is always cabbages. It is always cabbages that represent unattainable riches and mystery in Calabrian folktales, large cabbages that cover entrances to underground labyrinths in which torment or redemption is found, and monsters who feed upon human flesh, or supernatural spouses, wait. A cabbage is a flower, dense, convoluted, its core hidden and hard. And it is tantalizingly almost white. Anything white was superior, good: white rice, white bread, white eggs, white skin, white stoops, white roses, white soap.

Daddy skipped rope up until the time he had his first heart attack. He was better than I was—and I was a whiz at double Dutch. Daddy'd been a boxer, bantamweight. He'd once fought Eddie Martin, ex–bantamweight champion of the world, in a gym; and he'd won. Eddie Martin was by that time as good as dead, but that was beside the point. The status Daddy'd had as a boxer was never made clear to me—"semi-pro-amateur" he said, he being a master of obfuscation (ask a question and the door slams). One day a neighbor lady showed Grandma Rosie a flier advertising one of Daddy's fights, and Grandma threatened him with a knife (he tells this story very calmly) and forbade him to fight again, and he never did; a pity. He must so much have loved being raised above the crowd; he was five feet two.

He ran away from home, exiting from the fire escape to which he had so often, in every kind of weather, been tied. He signed on as a wiper aboard a freighter bound for California by way of the Panama Canal, on the understanding that this would be an easy job—"wiping rails." In fact it was not; he worked in the boiler room, soot burning into his skin and pitting it. He was arrested for vagrancy the day he arrived in California. After his first night in jail he was recruited by the owner of an apple orchard with whom the sheriff had an arrangement, and he picked apples near Bakersfield. How the boss's son learned that Daddy'd been a boxer does not figure in his story—explanations of any kind bore and irritate him—but soon Daddy was training the boy, running in the morning dew, weaving in and out of trees. He counts this as the happiest time in his life.

It does not matter to me whether these stories are in any or every particular true. What is true is that my father told them, and that is what matters.

We are eating the foods of the South; the buffet table groans with the sunny flavors of Basilicata and Calabria: pasta with eggplant, olives, peppers, tomatoes; potato salad with parsley and mint; potatoes with shredded goat's cheese and sun-dried tomatoes; chicken baked with fresh tomatoes and potatoes and dried oregano; swordfish brushed with lemon and oil and oregano; cabbage and cannellini beans; marinated squid; frittata with cold rice; pasta with tuna and olives and anchovies and red pepper; pasta with broccoli; purple figs. We are drinking wine and San Pellegrino bitters and Italy's wonderful *analcolici* (nonalcoholic drinks)—woodsy Chinotto, orange-flavored Crodino, and a faintly lemony *acqua gassata*.

I keep putting off my trip to Canna.

We spend our days on yellow beach chairs shaded by orange umbrellas and blue umbrellas under a cloudless sky, and the shadows of Frederick's castle fall around us. How wonderful it is to absorb the colors of light with no imperatives to govern us—neither physical beauty nor applied intelligence is required of us here. Birds wheel overhead. Susi, a Roman vacationing alone, has taken us to this beach, her favorite. She is bossy. Italians love to organize others, though they often seem to have trouble organizing themselves. Our limbs are heavy with the sweet ministrations of the sun; our minds drowse. But Susi's choice and even her genial bullying suit us; we are too happy to protest, too somnolent to organize ourselves. We drive through avenues of umbrella pines and cactus with green fruit ripening into orange to the pebbly beach where young boys dive, like swift clean swords, from rocky eminences into the obedient, jade-streaked azure sea. We like our bodies here. All bodies here are sweet and sweet to their owners. Perfection is not required, nor is it the norm (though the young boys are Hellenic gods); the bodies in the buoyant water—undefended because no defense is called for when bodies are not harshly judged, neither worshiped nor scorned—are unashamedly what they are, imperfect flesh. Mothers lounge and loll. Fathers father. As if to tame the presence and the metaphor of the sea, a line of caravans and tents stretches across the beach where the sand meets the railroad tracks; flowered curtains flutter, and the smell of cooking mingles with the smell of salt and pine.

After we sunbathe and swim, our feet are hot on the floor of the car, and then they slap the cool white tiles of the hotel—here it is possible to feel fondness even for one's feet—and we sleep on narrow mattresses of down, Anna's cool sunbrowned hand resting easefully in mine.

In this sunlight one wishes neither for change nor for law. From this place, where Marx and Freud seem irrelevant, from Basilicata in 1906—two years after my father was born ten kilometers away—788,000 emigrants left, in that one year alone, for other lands, the exodus exceeding the birthrate.

On one of the maps we have collected, but only on one, there is this place-name, halfway between Oriolo and Canna: GRIZZUTI. No signpost marks it on the serpentine road; where I reckon it to be, there is only a ravine. But I am immensely moved.

In the Church of the Immaculate Conception in Canna there is this sign: HUNGER KILLS CHILDREN BECAUSE WAR KILLS LOVE. This sentiment, as illogical as it is well intentioned, is all there is to admire in a church that looks like Madame Tussaud's waxworks. In glass cases there are repellent statues, all *dolorose:* a Mary whose suffering has rendered her hideous and hard, a Jesus who seems composed of ashes and ketchup, like a bad stage prop (for the greatest drama ever played).

Poverty and punk: In the winter this town of two thousand people is completely forsaken, forlorn; women as well as the men go to Milan or to Switzerland for work. Now, in the hazy brilliance of a summer afternoon, girls with orange-streaked hair walk, holding pinkies, in the dusty square, wearing brightly colored ponytail holders, their hips swaying gracefully as if they still carried pitchers on their heads. They disappear, giggling, into doorways.

Ocher and gray houses overlook neighboring mountain peaks; flowering vines climb on stone roof terraces like those Grandpa built on all his houses. We have come to Canna with nothing but a name—my Grandma Rosie's maiden name, Catapana—and our wits, now dulled by languid days of sea and sand. No one can tell me if any Catapanas still live.

Our backs prickle. We are being observed by many pairs of eyes peering from behind the slats of shutters. A motorcycle races and roars into the square (which is nothing more than a balcony on a mountaintop . . . with, of all things, a chocolates/gift shop occupying a prim shopfront); the motorcycle circles around us. The cyclist grins, he is friendly, his face leaves nothing to be desired. He is called Mimmo, and he puts himself at our disposal. "How interesting life is!" he says; he is the type of man who creates his own surprises.

Mimmo takes us to the house of Angelina Catapana. Up a flight of crumbling gray steps: Dressed in black, older than God, a woman sits in a doorway of rotting wood. Behind her is the tiled kitchen, a black cavern smelling of dead fires. Her sightless eyes are milky blue. She clutches my hand, my arm; with the utter simplicity of a child she feels my face, my body; her hands are scratchy, they smell like curdled milk. She accepts me as her relative before I am able to frame the question; names pour forth from her toothless mouth—Jimmy, Rosa, Vincenzo Palumbo (but who are they?). Rose, my grandmother, is her sister, she says; but Grandma Rosie never married Johnny Cristino, who is he? Never mind. *Never mind.* She needs to claim me, I am happy to be claimed and pleased to claim her. She has lost her family to America, she is alone, now I am here; this has for a brief moment put the world right. The duration of this moment is impossible to assess; it reaches back into the past and extends into the future, it occupies all of time.

Angelina's accent is very nearly indecipherable. Her hands are eloquent, and so—can this be?—are her blind eyes. Women are now coming out of their houses, pushing past us into the smoke-blackened kitchen. Here is Clara, who, though she claims no relation to my family, looks exactly like Grandma Rosie. Clara pinches my cheek and cries; then she pats and soothes my cheek and cries. "Joy! Joy!" Angelina says. But she is trembling, crying. Here is Patrizia, she is eighteen, and she has a baby; she looks as if she has entered the final stage of her life, as if nothing more will ever happen to her. She cries, too. Mimmo stands by, cool, detached from all emotion, wearing an easy smile that says he was glad to be of service, exercising his prerogative to be skeptical. My Italian has deserted me, it is Anna who speaks; I do not understand what it is I am participating in. A woman the villagers call Angelina's helper comes. She raises Angelina to her feet— Angelina's body is bent double, her ash cane taps—and leads her to a windowless bedroom in which there is a vast bed, a battered chest, a cabinet with one filled cookie jar.

Angelina is exhausted by joy. "I'll come back," I say. "What do you need?" "You," she says. No demand is made of me except never to go away.

"This is *neat,*" Lizzie says.

I say to Anna awkwardly that this meeting has been symbolic, that it has meant just as much as, perhaps more than, if I really were convinced Angelina was my relative. Anna says: "That means you're never going back to see her. That means you lied." She says this without reproach. She says this sadly. What she says is true. What I say is true.

Mimmo offers to drive us in Laura's car to Oriolo. The road is *brutta,* he says. As it is the custom here to soften criticism or negative judgments by circumlocution—*non è bella* (it isn't beautiful) or *non è perfetta* (it isn't perfect) is the usual form—the road must be "ugly" indeed; it is too dangerous, Mimmo says, for a woman who is not native to these mountains to drive; in any case he is on holiday from the navy, he has nothing to do.

Norman Douglas tells us that "to take away the dread of the sea from young boys, [Calabrians] mix into their food small fishes which have been devoured by larger ones and taken from their stomachs—the underlying idea being that these half-digested fry are thoroughly familiar with the storms and perils of the deep and will communicate these virtues to the boys who eat them." I find this not an off-putting but a charming idea, one that seems to have come straight from the womb of myth; but Mimmo dislikes fish, he never eats them.

Now that my mind is stored with images of all these coasts and promontories, gulfs and bays, islands and headlands, rocky cliffs and sandy beaches, wooded hills and gentle pastures, fertile fields, flower gardens, tended trees, festooned vines, mountains wreathed in clouds and the all-encircling sea with its ever-changing colours and moods, for the first time the Odyssey has become a living truth to me.

—*Goethe*, Italian Journey

The road is *brutta,* illogical and twisting, its banks eroded; we hug the mountain on one side, on the other side is a chasm . . . but the plains! the golden plains, the blue hills. Mimmo says, "You can't see the line between sky and land"; and you can't—we feel less than completely tethered to earth in this place of no apparent horizons. But this is not ether; what would happen if a car should approach from the other direction we cannot think (stalemate; improvisation; death). It doesn't seem, so narrow is the road, that a mule could pick his delicate way here; but, "I usually take this at eighty miles an hour," Mimmo says, for which exercise of braggadocio we forgive him, as only a saint (or—it occurs to me as I watch Mimmo watching Anna—a satyr) would volunteer to drive four women on a treacherous road on a visit to people who may or may not exist. We stop to drink sweet mountain water from a stream surrounded by elms, the tree that symbolizes fidelity. I try to imagine Grandma and Grandpa meeting here, but the picture will not hold.

Every time I mention my father the windshield wipers go on and off, swish-swish-stop.

"Anna!"

"Oh, that's been happening since Sorrento," Anna says calmly. "Grandpa's been here all along."

He never stops following me.

* * *

The old city of Oriolo is held in the embrace of a castle; the castle is built into rock, the houses into the castle. There are French lamplights on the very nearly vertical streets; a cherry-red mailbox inscribed with the name Vittorio Emanuele stands across from the sixteenth-century Church of San Giorgio, barred with lock and chain, which a custodian appears from nowhere to open for us. It is very dim; it smells loamy. Above the high altar I make out a stone carving of Christ, a Christ with a very flat aspect standing on a skull, his cross formed by angels' wings. On the altar there are clean white cloths; but we are standing on boards; beneath us the ground is being turned up, the floor of the church is earth and crumbled tiles, and, here and there, there is a gleam of white—skeletons, bones. "It is very strange," the custodian says. "No one knew, when they started to restore this church, that there was a cemetery under here." In this church, on ground no longer hallowed, my grandmother and my grandfather were married almost ninety years ago.

We find no Grizzutis here. I do not look very hard. When an old man waves us higher into the mountain fortress town, I choose wearily not to regard his gesture as definitive. Laura says I am weary from too many family embraces, too many real and too many tenuous connections. It is true that I am very tired. And what would one more meeting—Grandma and Grandpa left here eighty years ago—teach me? Perhaps I might see my father's features in another's face; but what of it? The dead are never far away. Nothing can make my father more real to me than he already is. (I see him in the sun-brown children of the village, dust squirting from between their toes as they run; and this makes me immeasurably sad.) It is a mistake to look for answers here, among imperfect vessels of a cloudy past. What I want to know is: Whom did he love? Did he love me? Was he ever happy (is he happy now)? The answers to these questions are more likely to come to me in dreams.

"Go to the Calabrian Riviera, the Costa Viola," said my friend Jane; so, inspired by her account of a twenty-mile stretch of paradise where the land and sea turned amethyst at sunset, we did. Across the narrow peninsula, from the Ionian, through pine forests, elm, oak, beech, and chestnut trees, we drove east through orchards and lemon groves to ancient olive groves and vineyards, feeling, as from one summit we saw two shining seas, appropriately breathless (this is what space travel must be like); and then choked. For what Jane had neglected to tell us, her memory having spoken to her of perfection, was that many of the sandy beaches of the Costa Viola, interrupted by cliffs and grottoes, could not be reached by car. Jane had had a boat; more important, she had had her Calabrian prince at the rudder, and she would forever after think of this stretch of the Tyrrhenian—of Palmi and Gioia and Bagnara—as the home of true romance.

Those beaches that could be reached by car one wouldn't wish to reach, and herein lay our frustration: Along this coast the sea is liquid turquoise; rocks—including Scylla, where the monster lurked to devour sailors who had escaped the whirlpool of the monster of Charybdis on the coast of Sicily—jut into the sea with beautiful, astonishing impertinence, like mute players gesturing grandiloquently across the waters to Mount Etna and Messina, to Stromboli and the other Aeolian Islands. . . . "The very name of Calabria has no little romance," wrote Edward Lear: the names. But on these beaches trucks and cars are parked. Palmi—whose olive oil was once burned in holy lamps in Russia—and Gioia (names that say magic/romance) have divided souls. For years Italians and passionate travelers alike have fretted that the (ill-named) Calabrian Riviera would become touristed, built up, or industrialized. And indeed these towns, this stretch of land, home once to Roman fortresses and to what is generally supposed to have been the most magnificent monastery in all of Calabria (all, by earthquakes, destroyed), seem to be able to commit themselves neither to factories nor to resorts. (It is for what they regard as failure and vacillation of this kind that northerners laugh at and condescend to southerners; and one does feel a certain irritable impatience here.) So much in Gioia is aborted, abandoned, factories half completed, left to rust, concrete hotels unfinished, deserted—and all the natural charm of buildings resting peacefully in ordained sites is gone. Vineyards cling to rocky terraces descending to the beach below—but the beach is a parking lot. Here, in the Middle Ages, monks provided refuge from the Saracens for men, women, and children of all classes, their simplicity providing them with immunity to marauders; now, in this debilitating squalor, we find no place to rest. At this stage in our journey, comfort is more attractive to us than adventure.

Some people, I am told, have mistaken them for oil platforms: Jane has told me with enthusiasm of the curious fishing boats—the *ontri*—of Bagnara. Swordfish, which come from Arctic waters to spawn in these warm waters, are still harpooned by hand by native fishermen, as they were by Greeks before the birth of Christ. They do so in boats the like of which exists nowhere else in the world: The *ontro* has a steel mast over forty feet tall, on top of which is a tipsy caged platform from which the lookout man—the *guardiano*—spots the fish, steers the boat to it, and, with a harsh cry, alerts the *fiocinatore,* who spears his catch with a ten-foot-long harpoon from a catwalk or extended bowsprit called a *passerella,* which is nearly twice the length of the boat itself. Six men are required to heave one swordfish— usually two swordfish, because they tend to travel in pairs—onto the boat. Landed, the huge fish, which has an element of the ridiculous (imagine five hundred pounds of slippery flesh culminating in a three-foot swordlike bill), is carried on the heads of the women of Bagnara—the *Bagnorote*—to the market.

How these boats and this ritual must have appealed to Jane-in-love: the great fish spawning in warm, hospitable, lapidary waters, traveling in pairs; the boat with its catwalk so closely resembling its prey (a metaphor for lovers, the complementary pursuer and pursued); the women in silent colloquy working in tandem with their men . . . the violet sky, the violet sea.

Armed with this lore, we try to see in Bagnara a seedy charm. It is no use. In the only *pensione* we find, the floor is gritty with sand and sticky with soda pop; video games glare and the television makes loud idiot noises; it is what a hospice for dying Graham Greene characters might look like. Even Anna and Lizzie, full of faith and energy, can't pretend to like it. This is where Despair and Irony might come to die a death inspired by low-cost decadence and acedia.

We have lunch at a roadside trattoria, waiting in the stale heat for a noisy christening celebration to be over before we are served the greasy spaghetti that is the only food the unaccountably angry proprietress offers us. Her fat husband offers us rooms upstairs for the night in a manner both listless and salacious. A man on a motorcycle—helpful? drunk? menacing? (he is certainly bullying; and our judgment has certainly deserted us)—circles and follows us. A child darts in front of the car.

Night finds us in Villa San Giovanni, just outside Reggio, in a barracks-like hotel, musty and smelling of mildew. From my windows near the landing docks I watch ferryboats crisscross the Strait of Messina. These ships, which are called by the names of women—Agata, Igenia, Rosalia—transport people and cars and whole trains to Sicily, to Messina. For me to watch the great *traghetti* sail is sad, it is almost terrible. My journey is ending. The ships' lights startle the inky sky. Once in my life, years ago, I sailed through the strait from Libya, and while no monsters, no rock, and no whirlpool threatened me, it was, in the very old boat I traveled in, a test of viscera and of will (the seasick Italian with whom I shared a cabin woke me up in the night to show me her vomit). I have reached an end. These ships all seem to me to be going *toward;* I am going away. For months I have had the amazed feeling that there was more and more and more to be seen, to be done, to be understood, to be loved. Now I have had from that cornucopia what it is possible for me to have, my path has narrowed to the vanishing point. Now trepidation, perhaps peril, for me consists of going home, entering my old life. In Italy I have felt new. Perhaps I will not like my old life. I am no longer able to speak Italian, it has deserted me. This is not willed disengagement; the world is pouring out through a funnel.

In the National Museum of Archaeology in Reggio, there are two bronze statues dredged from the sea. Noble, colossal, formed in the image of human gods (not, as in the Psalmist's definition of man, somewhere between beasts and angels, but between man and God), they are survivors of a shipwreck five centuries before Christ. Whose hand formed them? Why? Who was transporting them and why, and where were they coming from? What I know about them I know only from pictures: They have full beards, full sensuous lips, long hair. The statue known so coldly as "A" is taller than "B," over whom he seems to exert a benign authority. "A" has brooding ivory eyes. To regard the tenderness in his cheekbones is almost to conclude that anatomy is virtue. The left eye of "B," under his silver eyebrows, is missing. It is an awful wound. If it were possible for statues to feel as well as to express pain, these bronze statues, thought to be of warriors or gods, which seem almost inhabited, almost *spirit*ed, would feel pain. (I am turning into an animist; this is the influence of the South.) Looking at them, one is exhilarated by their beauty, and troubled by paradox—as one is when one regards the body of a loved one who has died: What is empty—this husk—is full of mystery. This shell has secrets; emptied, it is waiting to be revivified. One contemplates the statues not for what they say about death but for what we need to know about life, for what eludes us, for what we do not know but hope someday to understand. We want the secrets their emptiness contains.

At the Cocumella in Sorrento, where we have come to break our journey north to Rome, we climb down the worn Etruscan steps cut out of the cliff to the bathing dock below; we climb down a ladder from the dock to the sea. Standing waist-high in the Mediterranean, we talk in a lazy way about religion with a Neapolitan who praises my daughter for saying she is agnostic, and she calls belief systems *un muro di certezza,* a wall of certitude; she slaps her hands against a gentle wall of waves; the wall breaks and slips through her fingers. "The sea is perfumed," she says, "because it comes from Naples"; Naples is her religion. Sighing, "Naples is beautiful but it doesn't function," the editor of a daily paper says. We are by this time all floating on our backs, talking desultorily, our eyes closed, limbs loose, our bodies occasionally bumping into one another's. "What about death?" I say to the woman who slaps against walls; "isn't it *dolorosa?*" "Not sad," she says, "atrocious." I feel she has gotten the better of the brief exchange. "It's all the fault of the Mafia," the editor says, holding my wrist in the perfumed waters and making lazy circles with his arms; his mind is still on Naples. A wedding dress designer meanwhile describes the gown she will one day make for Anna; they are fast friends, already they have traded jewelry, and the designer has, while lustily eating fried anchovies and chicken salad under a lime tree, told Anna the *triste* story of her life. The editor hooks an ankle over one of mine. "I don't have a twenty-year-old body," I say, half listening to the designer describe the seed pearls she will lavish on Anna's wedding dress, and feeling old. "You have a great face, a good mind, you can't have everything," the editor says reasonably—*"abbastanza,"* enough. Our hips collide and our hands engage. Anna and the designer swim off. The water is crowded with splashing children.

The long corridor of blue-and-cream enfiladed rooms ends with the bar that opens onto the fragrant garden. Tanned bodies, gleaming and scented, retaining their memory of the soft seawater, move languidly. In the opaline light they look, to an equally languid observer, like figures lit behind gauze. As dusk lengthens, personalities take on more definition. The men talk about the rehabilitation and, as the mood grows mellower, the renaissance of Naples. *"Il mare non bagna Napoli* [the sea doesn't bathe Naples]," the editor says, whereupon someone makes the sign to ward off the Evil Eye. A scholar of gesture has determined that there are seventeen meanings to the gesture that signifies the Evil Eye, depending on context and nuance of finger position; the editor makes them all, to the mingled delight and mock or real alarm of all assembled. A vagrant breeze carries the faint sound of faraway music into the lamplit room, and soon voices are raised in song—Neapolitan love songs, subtle (subtlety is not a characteristic usually attributed to Neapolitans; but this is not the Naples of the streets, it is the Naples of the salon), sophisticated, plaintive laments suffused with dark longings and dark humor. . . . As the energy increases, the women play to one another, as if they alone know what it is like to be tormented by the arrows of love; their glances, haughty-warm, hot-cool, slide off the faces of the bemused men, who conduct a dialogue with their hands, as if *they* alone have known betrayal and perfidy. How sweetly man and woman sing to each other of the other's treachery. The play of hands and eyes and voices is elegant; the movements—apparently spontaneous—achieve a stylized eloquence. The wordless hospitality that enfolds us is exquisite.

Aldo, the headwaiter, says, "Will you have nostalgia for us? Sincerely?"

What I would do if I fell seriously ill in Italy I had not stopped to consider. Now there is a storm in my stomach, fire in my bowels; my throat is seared with bile, I am disgusting to myself. This internal rebellion started when I went to the hospital, where, for painfully swollen ankles, I was given a pale-pink powder in a packet (and an otherwise clean bill of health) . . . which didn't prevent an ambulance driver from following me in order to say I had high blood pressure (a lie) and asking me to give him my hotel room number so that he could come early in the morning to "fix me."

I have spent twelve hours in the bathroom. I attribute this illness to the imminence of departure, I think it is an illness of the spirit. Signor Caprio, who before he was an hotel administrator was a chemist, is aggrieved that I have not sought his counsel and his aid. He takes a practical view of my discomfort; he comes to my room bearing a syringe. Laura takes a dim view of Italian medicine and, in particular, of Italians carrying needles aloft. She blocks the bathroom door, her arms outstretched, crying operatically, "No! No! No!," quite as if dear Pino Caprio were a vampire come for his cup of blood. I echo Laura weakly, but only out of some crazy tattered feeling of American chauvinism; in fact I long to be injected with whatever it is Signor Caprio has. Signor Caprio seizes Laura by the waist and tosses her on my bed. Now, feeling like something ridiculous in a pageant, not knowing whether it is Italy or America I choose and represent (Laura, supine, exhorts), I manage to make a circuit of the room to evade Pino Caprio, who gives chase, squirting the plunger of the syringe into the air, leaping over furniture and my discarded clothes, as Laura, upon whom Lizzie is now sitting (and laughing), utters strangled cries. Finally Pino Caprio corners me in the bathroom, grabs a thigh unceremoniously, and plunges a needle in it. Laura shrieks. Lizzie and Anna watch the spectacle with the appreciation of long-frustrated connoisseurs; this is what they had expected of Neapolitans, comic opera. "What was that?" Laura demands in a near swoon. "Vitamin B," Pino Caprio says, and then, grandly, as his eyes say, How could you not trust me?, he says: "I forgive you." Did you sterilize that needle? Laura asks poor Pino. The marble floor of the bathroom feels wonderfully cool to my cheek. I have a hazy impression that I have been disloyal to Laura; I always smile back at people on television who are smiling at me; I am too eager to please. . . . Disloyalty is a ridiculous word in this context; in Italy one doesn't try so hard to please, one is quite naturally pleased and therefore pleasing, I don't want to go home. Imagine smiling back at Miss America.

Pino makes a dignified exit. How could you not trust me? his eyes continue to say. His lips advance beyond this sentence and say again, "I forgive you."

"DID YOU STER*LIZE* THE *NEEEEDLE?*" Lizzie, full of beans, is turning farce into *opera buffa,* composing and singing on the spot. She forces her light soprano down several registers and answers her own question: "MA PERCHÈ YOU DON'T *TRUST* ME" *(basso profundo).*

Pino can be heard in the hallway declaring that even the best of us are mad.

Lizzie improvises on her theme all the way to Rome.

All the way to Rome we see rings of fire in the high parched hills, a bruised sky. Fire has claimed ancient olive trees, hollowing out the great gnarled trunks, whirling like dervishes in their passive shells. The air is sulfurous.

I never went back to Canna. Will Angelina go to her grave believing that America—an American—has abandoned her again? I think my coming was for her a dream and will pass like a dream. I think time has no meaning for her. I leave room for a 10 percent margin of doubt.

We enter Rome when dawn is just a presentiment and make our way through an unfamiliar suburb. On a broad avenue lit only by flares, unsmiling young men are setting up stands to sell fruit and firecrackers and stuffed animals. After many false turns on dark streets, some of which take us by fright, we enter a gate with sudden surprise and we are in the Borgo: safe.

The lights of St. Peter's Square shine steadily against the watery sky. The fountains, like God, self-renewing, returning always to themselves for nourishment (what can we do to make God happy?), splash on cobblestones that pave the way to the basilica like dark and heavy silk. Light strikes Bernini's statues, poised rosily to dance. Peace is gathered here. In this place it does not matter to me that I am leaving; past, present, and future are united here; the rose of memory and the thorn of desire are one. I feel like the good orphan in the folktale, given a single gold coin by the Lord, which coin, however often it is spent, is always mine to spend again. This place, symbol of eternity in which time does not exist, assures me that the world is young. Among the worn coins of sadness and despair is the gold coin of happiness, inexhaustible.

For surely Angelina, her blind eyes, cannot have been the end and meaning of this journey.

SELECTED BIBLIOGRAPHY

Augustine, Saint. *The Confessions of Saint Augustine.* Translated by John K. Ryan. New York: Image Books, 1960.

Bachelard, Gaston. *The Poetics of Space.* Translated by Maria Jolas. Boston: Beacon Press, 1969.

Barzani, Luigi. *The Italians.* New York: Atheneum Publishers, 1977.

Bertarelli, L. V. *Southern Italy.* London: Macmillan and Co., 1925.

Blanchard, Paul. *Southern Italy from Rome to Calabria.* London: Ernest Benn Limited, 1982.

Bloomer, Kent C., and Charles W. Moore. *Body, Memory and Architecture.* New Haven: Yale University Press, 1977.

Blunt, Anthony. *Artistic Theory in Italy, 1450–1600.* Oxford: Oxford University Press, 1962.

Boni, Ada. *The Talisman Italian Cookbook.* New York: Crown Publishers, 1950.

Bugialli, Giuliano. *Giuliano Bugialli's Classic Techniques of Italian Cooking.* New York: Simon & Schuster, 1982.

Calvino, Italo. *Italian Folktales Selected and Retold by Italo Calvino.* New York: Pantheon Books, 1980.

———. *Mr. Palomar.* New York: Harcourt Brace Jovanovich, 1985.

Cellini, Bienvenuto. *Autobiography.* New York: Penguin Books, 1956.

Clark, Eleanor. *Rome and a Villa.* New York: Pantheon Books, 1950.

Clay, Edith, ed. *Ramage in South Italy.* Chicago: Academy Chicago Publishers, 1987.

Cole, J. P. *Italy, an Introductory Geography.* New York: Frederick A. Praeger, 1966.

Cousins, Ewert H. *Bonaventure and the Coincidence of Opposites.* Chicago: Franciscan Herald Press, 1978.

Dante. *The Divine Comedy.* Translated by Allen Mandelbaum. New York: Bantam Books, 1982.

———. *The Divine Comedy.* London: J. M. Dent and Sons, 1941.

D'Aponte, Miriam Gisolfi. "Continuing Ritual Theater: Religious Traditions of the Sorrentine Peninsula and the Coast of Amalfi." Ph.D. diss., City University of New York, 1973.

David, Elizabeth. *Italian Food.* New York: Penguin Books, 1954.

Delaney, John J. *Pocket Dictionary of Saints.* New York: Image Books, 1983.

Dickens, A. G. *The Counter Reformation.* New York: W. W. Norton and Co., 1968.

Douglas, Norman. *Old Calabria.* London: Century Hutchinson, 1988.

Duby, Georges. *The Age of the Cathedrals, Art and Society, 980–1420.* Chicago: The University of Chicago Press, 1981.

Farmer, David Hugh. *The Oxford Dictionary of Saints.* Oxford: Oxford University Press, 1978.

Fasola, Umberto M. *Peter and Paul in Rome.* Rome: Vision Editrice, 1980.

Faure, Gabriel. *The Italian Lakes.* London: The Medici Society, 1923.

Fortis, Umberto. *Jews and Synagogues.* Venice: Edizioni Storti, 1973.

Gardner's Art Through the Ages. New York: Harcourt Brace Jovanovich, 1980.

Goethe, Johann Wolfgang von. *Italian Journey.* San Francisco: North Point Press, 1982.

Guenzi, Carlo. *Le Affinita' Elettive.* Milan: Quaderni della Triennale, Electa, 1985.

Hawthorne, Nathaniel. *The Marble Faun.* New York: Airmont Publishing Co., Inc., N.D.

Hazan, Marcella. *The Classic Italian Cookbook.* New York: Ballantine Books, 1973.

Holler, Anne. *Florencewalks.* New York: Holt, Rinehart and Winston, 1982.

Hutton, Edward. *Naples and Southern Italy.* New York: The Macmillan Company, 1924.

James, Henry. *Henry James on Italy.* New York: Weidenfeld & Nicolson, 1988.

———. *Italian Hours.* New York: The Ecco Press, 1987.

———. *Letters 1843–1875,* vol. 1. Edited by Leon Edel. Cambridge: Harvard University Press, 1974.

McBrien, Richard P. *Catholicism.* Minneapolis: Winston Press, 1980.

McCarthy, Mary. *The Stones of Florence.* New York: Harcourt, Brace and World, 1963.

———. *Venice Observed.* New York: Harcourt, Brace and World, 1963.

McCool, Gerald A., ed. *A Rahner Reader.* New York: Crossroad, 1984.

Machlin, Edda Servi. *The Classic Cuisine of the Italian Jews.* New York: Everest House, 1981.

Mariotti, Mario. *Piazza della Palla.* Florence: Edizioni Alinari, 1981.

Masson, Georgina. *The Companion Guide to Rome.* London: Collins, 1965.

Montaigne. *Montaigne's Travel Journal.* San Francisco: North Point Press, 1983.

Morris, James. *The World of Venice.* New York: Harcourt Brace Jovanovich, 1960.

Morton, H. V. *A Traveller in Italy.* New York: Dodd, Mead and Company, 1964.

———. *A Traveller in Rome.* New York: Dodd, Mead and Company, 1951.

———. *A Traveller in Southern Italy.* New York: Dodd, Mead and Company, 1969.

Muscatine, Doris. *A Cook's Tour of Rome.* New York: Charles Scribner's Sons, 1964.

Origo, Iris. *Images and Shadows, Part of a Life.* London: Century Publishing, 1970.

————. *The World of San Bernardino.* New York: Harcourt, Brace and World, 1962.

Pope-Hennessy, John. *Italian High Renaissance and Baroque Sculpture.* New York: Vintage Books, 1985.

Sartago, Piero. *Italian ReEvolution.* La Jolla: La Jolla Museum of Contemporary Art, 1982.

Scott, Jack Denton. *The Complete Book of Pasta.* New York: Galahad Books, 1968.

Shetterly, Anya M. *Romewalks.* New York: Holt, Rinehart and Winston, 1984.

Singleton, Esther, ed. *Rome as Described by Great Writers.* New York: Dodd, Mead and Company, 1907.

Smith, William J., ed. *Poems from Italy.* New York: Thomas Y. Crowell, 1974.

Stendhal. *A Roman Journal.* New York: Collier Books, 1961.

Tannahill, Reay. *Food in History.* New York: Stein and Day, 1973.

Vasari, Georgio. *Lives of the Artists.* New York: Penguin Books, 1965.

Vico, Giambattista. *The New Science.* Translated by Thomas Goddard Bergin and Max Harold Fisch. Ithaca: Cornell University Press, 1948.

479

About the Author

Barbara Grizzuti Harrison's essays, reports, reviews, and short stories have appeared in such publications as *The New York Times, Harper's Magazine, The New Republic, The Nation, Partisan Review, Commonweal, Ms., Esquire, Traveler, GQ,* and *Vanity Fair.* In 1989 she won an O. Henry Prize for short fiction. She is the author of one novel, *Foreign Bodies,* and three books of nonfiction, *Unlearning the Lie: Sexism in School; Visions of Glory: A History and a Memory of Jehovah's Witnesses;* and *Off Center,* a collection of essays.

Ms. Harrison has lived in Libya, India, and Guatemala and now lives in Brooklyn, where she was born and raised.